U0687565

A Short History of Chinese Philosophy

英汉对照

中国哲学简史

冯友兰 著　赵复三 译

外语教学与研究出版社
FOREIGN LANGUAGE TEACHING AND RESEARCH PRESS
北京 BEIJING

图书在版编目（CIP）数据

中国哲学简史：英汉对照／冯友兰著；赵复三译 . -- 北京：外语教学与研究
出版社，2015.5（2022.6 重印）
　ISBN 978-7-5135-6128-0

Ⅰ . ①中…　Ⅱ . ①冯…　②赵…　Ⅲ . ①哲学史 – 中国 – 英、汉　Ⅳ . ①B2

中国版本图书馆 CIP 数据核字（2015）第 123084 号

出 版 人　王　芳
系列策划　吴　浩
责任编辑　刘　佳
装帧设计　视觉共振设计工作室
出版发行　外语教学与研究出版社
社　　址　北京市西三环北路 19 号（100089）
网　　址　http://www.fltrp.com
印　　刷　中农印务有限公司
开　　本　650×980　1/16
印　　张　42
版　　次　2015 年 6 月第 1 版　2022 年 6 月第 16 次印刷
书　　号　ISBN 978-7-5135-6128-0
定　　价　80.00 元

购书咨询：（010）88819926　电子邮箱：club@fltrp.com
外研书店：https://waiyants.tmall.com
凡印刷、装订质量问题，请联系我社印制部
联系电话：（010）61207896　电子邮箱：zhijian@fltrp.com
凡侵权、盗版书籍线索，请联系我社法律事务部
举报电话：（010）88817519　电子邮箱：banquan@fltrp.com
物料号：261280001

记载人类文明
沟通世界文化
外研社　www.fltrp.com

"博雅双语名家名作"出版说明

　　1840 年鸦片战争以降，在深重的民族危机面前，中华民族精英"放眼看世界"，向世界寻求古老中国走向现代、走向世界的灵丹妙药，涌现出一大批中国主题的经典著述。我们今天阅读这些中文著述的时候，仍然深为字里行间所蕴藏的缜密的考据、深刻的学理、世界的视野和济世的情怀所感动，但往往会忽略：这些著述最初是用英文写就，我们耳熟能详的中文文本是原初英文文本的译本，这些英文作品在海外学术界和文化界同样享有崇高的声誉。

　　比如，林语堂的 *My Country and My People*（《吾国与吾民》）以幽默风趣的笔调和睿智流畅的语言，将中国人的道德精神、生活情趣和中国社会文化的方方面面娓娓道来，在美国引起巨大反响——林语堂也以其中国主题系列作品赢得世界文坛的尊重，并获得诺贝尔文学奖的提名。再比如，梁思成在抗战的烽火中写就的英文版《图像中国建筑史》文稿（*A Pictorial History of Chinese Architecture*），经其挚友费慰梅女士（Wilma C. Fairbank）等人多年的奔走和努力，于 1984 年由麻省理工学院出版社（MIT Press）出版，并获得美国出版联合会颁发的"专业暨学术书籍金奖"。又比如，1939 年，费孝通在伦敦政治经济学院的博士论文以 *Peasant Life in China—A Field Study of Country Life in the Yangtze Valley* 为名在英国劳特利奇书局（Routledge）出版，后以《江村经济》作为中译本书名——《江村经济》使得靠桑蚕为生的"开弦弓村"获得了世界性的声誉，成为国际社会学界研究中国农村的首选之地。

　　此外，一些中国主题的经典人文社科作品经海外汉学家和中国学者的如椽译笔，在英语世界也深受读者喜爱。比如，艾恺（Guy S. Alitto）将他1980 年用中文访问梁漱溟的《这个世界会好吗——梁漱溟晚年口述》一书译成英文（*Has Man a Future? —Dialogues with the Last Confucian*），备受海内外读者关注；

此类作品还有徐中约英译的梁启超著作《清代学术概论》（*Intellectual Trends in the Ch'ing Period*）、狄百瑞（W. T. de Bary）英译的黄宗羲著作《明夷待访录》（*Waiting for the Dawn: A Plan for the Prince*），等等。

有鉴于此，外语教学与研究出版社推出"博雅双语名家名作"系列。

博雅，乃是该系列的出版立意。博雅教育（Liberal Education）早在古希腊时代就得以提倡，旨在培养具有广博知识和优雅气质的人，提高人文素质，培养健康人格，中国儒家六艺"礼、乐、射、御、书、数"亦有此功用。

双语，乃是该系列的出版形式。英汉双语对照的形式，既同时满足了英语学习者和汉语学习者通过阅读中国主题博雅读物提高英语和汉语能力的需求，又以中英双语思维、构架和写作的形式予后世学人以启迪——维特根斯坦有云："语言的边界，乃是世界的边界"，诚哉斯言。

名家，乃是该系列的作者群体。涵盖文学、史学、哲学、政治学、经济学、考古学、人类学、建筑学等领域，皆海内外名家一时之选。

名作，乃是该系列的入选标准。系列中的各部作品都是经过时间的积淀、市场的检验和读者的鉴别而呈现的经典，正如卡尔维诺对"经典"的定义：经典并非你正在读的书，而是你正在重读的书。

胡适在《新思潮的意义》（1919 年 12 月 1 日，《新青年》第 7 卷第 1 号）一文中提出了"研究问题、输入学理、整理国故、再造文明"的范式。秉着"记载人类文明、沟通世界文化"的出版理念，我们推出"博雅双语名家名作"系列，既希望能够在中国人创作的和以中国为主题的博雅英文文献领域"整理国故"，亦希望在和平发展、改革开放的新时代为"再造文明"、为"向世界说明中国"略尽绵薄之力。

外语教学与研究出版社
人文社科出版分社

玖 道家的第二阶段：老子 171

捌 名家 147

柒 儒家的理想主义流派：孟子 125

陆 道家的第一阶段：杨朱 111

伍 墨子：孔子的第一位反对者 91

肆 孔子：第一位教师 71

叁 诸子的由来 57

贰 中国哲学的背景 31

壹 中国哲学的精神 3

作者自序 vii

AUTHOR'S PREFACE *vi*

❶ THE SPIRIT OF CHINESE PHILOSOPHY 2

❷ THE BACKGROUND OF CHINESE PHILOSOPHY 30

❸ THE ORIGIN OF THE SCHOOLS 56

❹ CONFUCIUS, THE FIRST TEACHER 70

❺ MO TZU, THE FIRST OPPONENT OF CONFUCIUS 90

❻ THE FIRST PHASE OF TAOISM: YANG CHU 110

❼ THE IDEALISTIC WING OF CONFUCIANISM: MENCIUS 124

❽ THE SCHOOL OF NAMES 146

❾ THE SECOND PHASE OF TAOISM: LAO TZU 170

拾 道家的第三阶段：庄子 193

拾壹 后期的墨家 219

拾贰 阴阳家和中国早期的宇宙发生论 239

拾叁 儒家的现实主义流派：荀子 265

拾肆 韩非子与法家 287

拾伍 儒家的形而上学 307

拾陆 治国平天下的哲学主张 329

拾柒 汉帝国的理论家：董仲舒 353

拾捌 儒家兴盛和道家再起 375

拾玖 新道家：崇尚理性的玄学 399

贰拾 新道家：豁达率性的风格 425

贰拾壹 中国佛学的基础 443

贰拾贰 禅宗：潜默的哲学 469

贰拾叁 更新的儒家：宇宙论者 489

贰拾肆 更新的儒家：两个学派的开端 517

贰拾伍 更新的儒学：主张柏拉图式理念的理学 541

贰拾陆 更新的儒学中的另一派：宇宙心学 565

贰拾柒 西方哲学的传入 585

贰拾捌 厕身现代世界的中国哲学 609

英文版编者引言 631

注释 644

译后记 655

❿ THE THIRD PHASE OF TAOISM: CHUANG TZU   192

⓫ THE LATER MOHISTS   218

⓬ THE YIN-YANG SCHOOL AND EARLY CHINESE COSMOGONY   238

⓭ THE REALISTIC WING OF CONFUCIANISM: HSÜN TZU   264

⓮ HAN FEI TZU AND THE LEGALIST SCHOOL   286

⓯ CONFUCIANIST METAPHYSICS   306

⓰ WORLD POLITICS AND WORLD PHILOSOPHY   328

⓱ THEORIZER OF THE HAN EMPIRE: TUNG CHUNG-SHU   352

⓲ THE ASCENDANCY OF CONFUCIANISM

AND REVIVAL OF TAOISM   374

⓳ NEO-TAOISM: THE RATIONALISTS   398

⓴ NEO-TAOISM: THE SENTIMENTALISTS   424

㉑ THE FOUNDATION OF CHINESE BUDDHISM   442

㉒ CH'ANISM: THE PHILOSOPHY OF SILENCE   468

㉓ NEO-CONFUCIANISM: THE COSMOLOGISTS   488

㉔ NEO-CONFUCIANISM:

THE BEGINNING OF THE TWO SCHOOLS   516

㉕ NEO-CONFUCIANISM: THE SCHOOL OF PLATONIC IDEAS   540

㉖ NEO-CONFUCIANISM: THE SCHOOL OF UNIVERSAL MIND   564

㉗ THE INTRODUCTION OF WESTERN PHILOSOPHY   584

㉘ CHINESE PHILOSOPHY IN THE MODERN WORLD   608

EDITOR'S INTRODUCTION   630

NOTES   644

BIBLIOGRAPHY COMPILED BY THE EDITOR   647

AUTHOR'S PREFACE

A SHORT history of any subject should not simply be an abridgement of a larger one. It should be a picture complete in itself, rather than a mere inventory of names and "isms." To achieve this, the author should, as a Chinese expression says, "have the whole history in his mind." Only then can he give the reader an adequate and well-rounded account within his chosen limited scope.

According to Chinese historiography, a good historian must have wide scholarship in order to master all his materials, sound judgment to make proper selection of them, and literary talent in order to tell his story in an interesting way. In writing a short history, intended for a general public, the author certainly has less chance to display his scholarship, but he needs more selective judgment and literary talent than he would for writing a longer and strictly scholarly work.

In preparing this work, I have tried to use my best judgment in selecting what I consider the important and relevant from materials which I have mastered. I was very fortunate, however, to have as editor Dr. Derk Bodde, who has used his literary talent to make the style of the book interesting, readable, and comprehensible to the Western reader. He has also made suggestions regarding the selection and arrangement of the material.

Being a short history, this book serves as no more than an introduction to the study of Chinese philosophy. If the reader wishes to know more about the subject, I would refer him to my larger work, *A History of Chinese Philosophy*. The first volume of this has been translated by Dr. Bodde, and he is now translating the second one; also to my more recent work, *The Spirit of Chinese Philosophy*, translated by Mr. E. R. Hughes of Oxford University. Both works are mentioned in the bibliography compiled by Dr. Bodde at the end of the present book. Acknowledgements are due to both Dr. Bodde and Mr. Hughes, from whose books I have borrowed some translations of the Chinese texts appearing herein.

In publishing this book, I welcome the opportunity of expressing my thanks to the Rockefeller Foundation for the grant which made it possible for me to come from China to the University of Pennsylvania as Visiting Professor during the year 1946-47, and which resulted in the writing of this book. Also,

I wish to thank my colleagues and students in the Department of Oriental Studies for their cooperation and encouragement, and especially Dr. Bodde, Associate Professor of Chinese. I am likewise grateful to Dr. A. W. Hummel, Chief of the Asiatic Division, Library of Congress, for his encouragement and help in making arrangements for the publication of the book.

FUNG YU-LAN

June, 1947

University of Pennsylvania

作者自序

小史[1]者，非徒巨著之节略，姓名、学派之清单也。譬犹画图，小景之中，形神自足。非全史在胸，曷克臻此。惟其如是，读其书者，乃觉择焉虽精而语焉犹详也。

历稽载籍，良史必有三长：才，学，识。学者，史料精熟也；识者，选材精当也；才者，文笔精妙也。著小史者，意在通俗，不易展其学，而其识其才，较之学术巨著尤为需要。

余著此书，于史料选材，亦既勉竭绵薄矣，复得借重布德博士（Derk Bodde）之文才，何幸如之。西方读者，倘觉此书易晓，娓娓可读，博士与有力焉；选材编排，博士亦每有建议。

本书小史耳，研究中国哲学，以为导引可也。欲知其详，尚有拙著大《中国哲学史》[2]，亦承布德博士英译；又有近作《新原道》[3]，已承牛津大学休士先生（E. R. Hughes）英译；可供参阅。本书所引中国原籍，每亦借用二君之译文，书此致谢。

一九四六至四七年，余于宾夕法尼亚大学任访问教授，因著此书。此行承洛克斐勒基金会资助，乘此书出版之际，致以谢意。该校东方学系师生诸君之合作、鼓励，亦所感谢；该系中文副教授布德博士，尤所感谢。国会图书馆亚洲部主任恒慕义先生（A. W. Hummel）为此书安排出版，亦致谢意。

冯友兰

一九四七年六月于宾夕法尼亚大学

❶ THE SPIRIT OF CHINESE PHILOSOPHY

The place which philosophy has occupied in Chinese civilization has been comparable to that of religion in other civilizations. In China, philosophy has been every educated person's concern. In the old days, if a man were educated at all, the first education he received was in philosophy. When children went to school, the "Four Books," which consist of the *Confucian Analects*, the *Book of Mencius*, the *Great Learning*, and the *Doctrine of the Mean*, were the first ones they were taught to read. The "Four Books" were the most important texts of Neo-Confucianist philosophy. Sometimes when the children were just beginning to learn the characters, they were given a sort of textbook to read. This was known as the *Three Characters Classic*, and was so called because each sentence in the book consisted of three characters arranged so that when recited they produced a rhythmic effect, and thus helped the children to memorize them more easily. This book was in reality a primer, and the very first statement in it is that "the nature of man is originally good." This is one of the fundamental ideas of Mencius' philosophy.

● Place of Philosophy in Chinese Civilization

To the Westerner, who sees that the life of the Chinese people is permeated with Confucianism, it appears that Confucianism is a religion. As a matter of fact, however, Confucianism is no more a religion than, say, Platonism or Aristotelianism. It is true that the "Four Books" have been the Bible of the Chinese people, but in the "Four Books" there is no story of creation, and no mention of a heaven or hell.

Of course, the terms philosophy and religion are both ambiguous. Philosophy and religion may have entirely different meanings for different people. When men talk about philosophy or religion, they may have quite different ideas in their minds concerning them. For my part, what I call philosophy is systematic, reflective thinking on life. Every man, who has not yet died, is in life. But there are not many who think reflectively on life, and still fewer whose reflective thinking is systematic. A philosopher *must* philosophize; that is to say, he must think reflectively on life, and then express his thoughts systematically.

This kind of thinking is called reflective because it takes life as its object. The theory of life, the theory of the universe, and the theory

壹 中国哲学的精神

哲学在中国文化中的地位，历来被看为可以和宗教在其他文化中的地位相比拟。在中国，哲学是每一个受过教育的人都关切的领域。从前在中国，一个人如果受教育，首先就是受哲学方面的启蒙教育。儿童入学，首先要读的就是《论语》《孟子》《大学》《中庸》。这"四书"也是宋以后道学（在西方被称为"新儒学"）认为最重要的文献。孩子刚学认字，通常所用的课本《三字经》，每三个字为一组，每六个字成一句，偶句押韵，朗读时容易上口，也便于记忆。事实上，这本书乃是中国儿童的识字课本。《三字经》的第一句"人之初，性本善"，便是孟子哲学的基本思想。

● 哲学在中国文化中的地位

在西方人眼里，中国人的生活渗透了儒家思想，儒家俨然成为一种宗教。而事实上，儒家思想并不比柏拉图或亚里士多德思想更像宗教。"四书"在中国人心目中诚然具有《圣经》在西方人心目中的那种地位，但"四书"中没有上帝创世，也没有天堂地狱。

当然，哲学和宗教的含义并不十分明确，不同的人对哲学和宗教的理解可能全然不同。人们谈到哲学或宗教时，心目中所想的可能很不同。就我来说，哲学是对人生的系统的反思。人只要还没有死，他就还是在人生之中，但并不是所有的人都对人生进行反思，至于作系统反思的人就更少。一个哲学家总要进行哲学思考，这就是说，他必须对人生进行反思，并把自己的思想系统地表述出来。

这种思考，我们称之为反思，因为它把人生作为思考的对象。有关人生的学说，有关宇宙的学说以及有关知识的学说，都是由

of knowledge all emerge from this type of thinking. The theory of the universe arises because the universe is the background of life—the stage on which the drama of life takes place. The theory of knowledge emerges because thinking is itself knowledge. According to some philosophers of the West, in order to think, we must first find out what we can think; that is to say, before we start to think about life, we must first "think our thinking."

Such theories are all the products of reflective thinking. The very concept of life, the very concept of the universe, and the very concept of knowledge are also the products of reflective thinking. No matter whether we think about life or whether we talk about it, we are all in the midst of it. And no matter whether we think or speak about the universe, we are all a part of it. Now, what the philosophers call the universe is not the same as what the physicists have in mind when they refer to it. What the philosophers call the universe is *the totality of all that is*. It is equivalent to what the ancient Chinese philosopher, Hui Shih, called "The Great One," which is defined as "that which has nothing beyond." So everyone and everything must be considered part of the universe. When one thinks about the universe, one is thinking reflectively.

When we think about knowledge or speak about knowledge, this thinking and speaking are themselves knowledge. To use an expression of Aristotle, it is "thinking on thinking"; and this is reflective thinking. Here is the vicious circle which those philosophers follow who insist that before we think we must first think about our thinking; just as if we had another faculty with which we could think about thinking! As a matter of fact, the faculty with which we think about thinking is the very same faculty with which we think. If we are skeptical about the capacity of our thinking in regard to life and the universe, we have the same reason to be skeptical about the capacity of our thinking in regard to thinking.

Religion also has something to do with life. In the heart of every great religion there is a philosophy. In fact, every great religion *is* a philosophy with a certain amount of superstructure, which consists of superstitions, dogmas, rituals, and institutions. This is what I call religion.

If one understands the term religion in this sense, which does not really differ very much from common usage, one sees that Confucianism cannot be considered a religion. People have been accustomed to say that there were three religions in China: Confucianism, Taoism, and Buddhism. But Confucianism, as we have seen, is not a religion. As to Taoism, there is a distinction between Taoism as a philosophy, which is

这样的思考中产生的。宇宙是人类生存的背景，是人生戏剧演出的舞台，宇宙论就是这样兴起的。思考本身就是知识，知识论就是由此而兴起的。按照某些西方哲学家的看法，人要思想，首先要弄清楚人能够思考什么，这就是说，在对人生进行思考之前，我们先要对思想进行思考。

这些学说都是反思的产物，甚至"人生"和"生命"的概念、"宇宙"的概念、"知识"的概念也都是反思的产物。人无论是自己思索或与别人谈论，都是在人生之中。我们对宇宙进行思索或与人谈论它，都是在其中进行反思。但哲学家所说的"宇宙"和物理学家心目中的"宇宙"，内涵有所不同。哲学家说到"宇宙"时，所指的是一切存在的整体，相当于中国古代哲学家惠施所说的"大一"，可以给它一个定义，乃是"至大无外"。因此，任何人，任何事物，都在宇宙之中。当一个人对宇宙进行思索时，他就是在反思。

当我们对知识进行思索或谈论时，这种思索和谈论的本身也是知识，用亚里士多德的话来说，它是"关于思索的思索"，这就是"反思"。有的哲学家坚持认为，我们在思索之前，必须先对思索进行思索，仿佛人还有另一套器官，来对思索进行思索，这就陷入了一个恶性循环。其实，我们用来思考的器官只有一个，如果我们怀疑自己对人生和宇宙思考的能力，我们也同样有理由怀疑自己对思索进行思索的能力。

宗教也和人生相关联。任何一种大的宗教，它的核心部分必然有哲学。事实上，每一种大的宗教就是某种哲学加上一定的上层建筑，包括迷信、教义、礼仪和体制。这是我对宗教的认识。

如果从这个意义——也就是人们通常的认识——来看待宗教，就可以看出，儒家不是一种宗教。许多人习惯地认为，儒、道、佛是中国的三种宗教。其实，儒家并不是一种宗教。道家和道教是

called *Tao chia* (the Taoist school), and the Taoist religion (*Tao chiao*). Their teachings are not only different; they are even contradictory. Taoism as a philosophy teaches the doctrine of following nature, while Taoism as a religion teaches the doctrine of working against nature. For instance, according to Lao Tzu and Chuang Tzu, life followed by death is the course of nature, and man should follow this natural course calmly. But the main teaching of the Taoist religion is the principle and technique of how to avoid death, which is expressly working against nature. The Taoist religion has the spirit of science, which is the conquering of nature. If one is interested in the history of Chinese science, the writings of the religious Taoists will supply much information.

As to Buddhism, there is also the distinction between Buddhism as a philosophy, which is called *Fo hsüeh* (the Buddhist learning), and Buddhism as a religion, which is called *Fo chiao* (the Buddhist religion). To the educated Chinese, Buddhist philosophy is much more interesting than the Buddhist religion. It is quite common to see both Buddhist monks and Taoist monks simultaneously participating in Chinese funeral services. The Chinese people take even their religion philosophically.

At present it is known to many Westerners that the Chinese people have been less concerned with religion than other people are. For instance, in one of his articles, "Dominant Ideas in the Formation of Chinese Culture,"[1] Professor Derk Bodde says: "They [the Chinese] are not a people for whom religious ideas and activities constitute an all-important and absorbing part of life.... It is ethics (especially Confucian ethics), and not religion (at least not religion of a formal, organized type), that provided the spiritual basis in Chinese civilization.... All of which, of course, marks a difference of fundamental importance between China and most other major civilizations, in which a church and a priesthood have played a dominant role."

In one sense this is quite true. But one may ask: Why is this so? If the craving for what is beyond the present actual world is not one of the innate desires of mankind, why is it a fact that for most people religious ideas and activities constitute an all-important and absorbing part of life? If that craving is one of the fundamental desires of mankind, why should the Chinese people be an exception? When one says that it is ethics, not religion, that has provided the spiritual basis of Chinese civilization, does it imply that the Chinese are not conscious of those values which are higher than moral ones?

不同的两回事，道家是一种哲学，道教才是宗教。它们的内涵不仅不同，甚至是互相矛盾的：道家哲学教导人顺乎自然，道教却教导人逆乎自然。举例来说，按老庄思想，万物有生必有死，人对于死，顺应自然，完全不必介意，而道教的宗旨却是教导长生术，这不是反乎自然吗？道教含有一种征服自然的科学精神。如果有人对中国科学史有兴趣，《道藏》里许多道士的著作倒是可以提供不少资料。

至于佛教，佛学和佛教也是有区别的。对中国知识分子来说，佛学比佛教有趣得多。在中国传统的丧事仪式中，僧人和道士同时参加，并不令人感到奇怪。中国人对待宗教的态度，也是充满哲学意味的。

今天，许多西方人看到：中国人不像其他民族那样重视宗教。例如，德克·布德教授在《构成中国文化的主要思想》一文中写道："他们（中国人）并不认为宗教思想和宗教活动是生活中的重要部分。……中国文化的精神基础不是宗教（至少不是有组织形式的宗教），而是伦理（特别是儒家伦理）。……这一切使中国和其他主要文明国家把教会和神职人员看为文明的重要组成部分，有基本的不同。"

从某种意义来说，这话一点不错。但是人们会问：这是为什么？如果追求彼岸世界不是人类内心的最深要求之一，为什么对世界许多人来说，宗教信仰和宗教活动成为生活中十分重要的组成部分呢？如果宗教信仰和宗教活动是人类的基本要求之一，何以中国人成为例外呢？有人认为，中国文化的精神基础不是宗教，而是伦理，这是否意味着中国人不曾意识到，在道德伦理之上，还有更高的价值呢？

The values that are higher than the moral ones may be called super-moral values. The love of man is a moral value, while the love of God is a super-moral value. Some people may be inclined to call this kind of value a religious value. But in my opinion, this value is not confined to religion, unless what is meant here by religion differs from its meaning as described above. For instance, the love of God in Christianity is a religious value, while the love of God in the philosophy of Spinoza is not, because what Spinoza called God is really the universe. Strictly speaking, the love of God in Christianity is not really super-moral. This is because God, in Christianity, is a personality, and consequently the love of God by man is comparable to the love of a father by his son, which is a moral value. Therefore, the love of God in Christianity is open to question as a super-moral value. It is a quasi super-moral value, while the love of God in the philosophy of Spinoza is a real super-moral value.

To answer the above questions, I would say that the craving for something beyond the present actual world is one of the innate desires of mankind, and the Chinese people are no exception to this rule. They have not had much concern with religion because they have had so much concern with philosophy. They are not religious because they are philosophical. In philosophy they satisfy their craving for what is beyond the present actual world. In philosophy also they have the super-moral values expressed and appreciated, and in living according to philosophy these super-moral values are experienced.

According to the tradition of Chinese philosophy, its function is not the increase of positive knowledge (by positive knowledge I mean information regarding matters of fact), but the elevation of the mind—a reaching out for what is beyond the present actual world, and for the values that are higher than the moral ones. It was said by the *Lao-tzu*: "To work on learning is to increase day by day; to work on *Tao* (the Way, the Truth) is to decrease day by day." (See ch. 48.) I am not concerned with the difference between increasing and decreasing, nor do I quite agree with this saying of Lao Tzu. I quote it only to show that in the tradition of Chinese philosophy there is a distinction between working on learning and working on *Tao* (the Way). The purpose of the former is what I call the increase of positive knowledge, that of the latter is the elevation of the mind. Philosophy belongs in the latter category.

比伦理道德更高的价值可以称之为超伦理道德的价值。爱人是一个道德价值，爱神是一个超越道德的价值，有的人或许喜欢称之为宗教价值。但是如果有人征求我的意见，我会说，这个价值不仅限于宗教，除非宗教在这里的含义和我在上面所说的不同。举例来说，基督徒看爱神是一个宗教价值；而在斯宾诺莎的哲学思想里，神的含义就是宇宙。严格说来，基督徒所说的爱神，也并不是超越道德伦理的，基督教所信仰的神是具有位格的，因此，基督徒爱神可以比拟为儿子爱父亲，而儿子爱父亲便是一个伦理价值。因此，基督教所讲的爱神是否超越道德，便成了问题。它只是类似超道德，而斯宾诺莎哲学中的"爱神"才是真正超越道德的价值。

现在来回答上面的问题。人不满足于现实世界而追求超越现实世界，这是人类内心深处的一种渴望，在这一点上，中国人和其他民族的人并无二致。但是中国人不那么关切宗教，是因为他们太关切哲学了；他们的宗教意识不浓，是因为他们的哲学意识太浓了。他们在哲学里找到了超越现实世界的那个存在，也在哲学里表达和欣赏那个超越伦理道德的价值；在哲学生活中，他们体验了这些超越伦理道德的价值。

根据中国哲学的传统，哲学的功能不是为了增进正面的知识（我所说的正面知识是指对客观事物的信息），而是为了提高人的心灵，超越现实世界，体验高于道德的价值。《道德经》第四十八章说："为学日益，为道日损。"这里不谈"损"和"益"的区别，我对老子这句话也并不完全同意。援引这句话是为了借此表明：中国哲学传统对于"学"和"道"是有所区别的。"学"就是我在前面所说的增长正面知识，"道"则是心灵的提高。哲学是在后一个范畴之中的。

The view that the function of philosophy, especially metaphysics, is not the increase of positive knowledge, is expounded by the Viennese school in contemporary Western philosophy, though from a different angle and for a different purpose. I do not agree with this school that the function of philosophy is only the clarification of ideas, and that the nature of metaphysics is only a lyric of concepts. Nevertheless, in their arguments one can see quite clearly that philosophy, especially metaphysics, would become nonsense if it did attempt to give information regarding matters of fact.

Religion does give information in regard to matters of fact. But the information given by religion is not in harmony with that given by science. So in the West there has been the conflict between religion and science. Where science advances, religion retreats; and the authority of religion recedes before the advancement of science. The traditionalists regretted this fact and pitied the people who had become irreligious, considering them as having degenerated. They ought indeed to be pitied, if, besides religion, they had no other access to the higher values. When people get rid of religion and have no substitute, they also lose the higher values. They have to confine themselves to mundane affairs and have nothing to do with the spiritual ones. Fortunately, however, besides religion there is philosophy, which provides man with an access to the higher values—an access which is more direct than that provided by religion, because in philosophy, in order to be acquainted with the higher values, man need not take the roundabout way provided by prayers and rituals. The higher values with which man has become acquainted through philosophy are even purer than those acquired through religion, because they are not mixed with imagination and superstition. In the world of the future, man will have philosophy in the place of religion. This is consistent with Chinese tradition. It is not necessary that man should be religious, but it *is* necessary that he should be philosophical. When he is philosophical, he has the very best of the blessings of religion.

● Problem and Spirit of Chinese Philosophy

The above is a general discussion of the nature and function of philosophy. In the following remarks I shall speak more specifically about Chinese philosophy. There is a main current in the history of Chinese philosophy, which may be called the spirit of Chinese philosophy. In order to understand this spirit, we must first make clear the problem that most Chinese philosophers have tried to solve.

哲学，特别是形而上学，其功能不是要增长正面知识，这一点在当代西方哲学中，已有维也纳学派加以阐述。但是，维也纳学派是从另一个角度，为了另一个目的。我不同意这一学派认为哲学的功能只是为了澄清概念，把形而上学的性质看成只是概念的抒情诗；但是，从他们的论辩中可以清楚看到，如果哲学果真去谋求提供正面知识，它将陷于荒谬。

宗教倒是提供有关实际的正面信息，但是，它所提供的信息与科学提供的不同。因此，在西方出现宗教与科学的冲突。科学每前进一步，宗教便后退一步；它的权威在科学前进的历程中不断被削弱。维护传统的人们对这个事实感到遗憾，惋惜大众离开宗教，结果是自身的衰退。如果除宗教外，没有什么办法可以达到更高的价值，则今日人们的宗教意识日益淡薄，的确应当为之惋惜，因为大众抛弃了宗教，也就抛弃了更高的价值。他们只得被囿于现实世界之中，而与精神世界隔绝。幸好除宗教外，还有哲学能够达到更高的价值。而且，这条通道比宗教更直接，因为通过哲学达到更高价值，人不需要绕圈子，经由祈祷和仪式。人经过哲学达到的更高价值比经由宗教达到的更高价值，内容更纯，因为其中不掺杂想象和迷信。将来的世界里，哲学将取代宗教的地位，这是合乎中国哲学传统的。人不需要宗教化，但是人必须哲学化。当人哲学化了，他也就得到了宗教所提供的最高福分。

● 中国哲学的精神和问题

上面对哲学的性质和功能，作了一般性的论述，下面将具体地谈中国哲学。在中国哲学的历史进程中，有一个主流，可以称之为中国哲学的精神。为了解它，我们需要首先看一下，中国大多数哲学家力求解决的是些什么问题。

There are all kinds and conditions of men. With regard to any one of these kinds, there is the highest form of achievement of which any one kind of man is capable. For instance, there are the men engaged in practical politics. The highest form of achievement in that class of men is that of the great statesman. So also in the field of art, the highest form of achievement of which artists are capable is that of the great artist. Although there are these different classes of men, yet all of them are men. What is the highest form of achievement of which a man *as a man* is capable? According to the Chinese philosophers, it is nothing less than being a sage, and the highest achievement of a sage is the identification of the individual with the universe. The problem is, if men want to achieve this identification, do they necessarily have to abandon society or even to negate life?

According to some philosophers, this is necessary. The Buddha said that life itself is the root and fountainhead of the misery of life. Likewise, Plato said that the body is the prison of the soul. And some of the Taoists said that life is an excrescence, a tumor, and death is to be taken as the breaking of the tumor. All these ideas represent a view which entails separation from what may be called the entangling net of the matter-corrupted world; and therefore, if the highest achievement of a sage is to be realized, the sage has to abandon society and even life itself. Only thus can the final liberation be attained. This kind of philosophy is what is generally known as "other-worldly philosophy."

There is another kind of philosophy which emphasizes what is in society, such as human relations and human affairs. This kind of philosophy speaks only about moral values, and is unable to or does not wish to speak of the super-moral ones. This kind of philosophy is generally described as "this-worldly." From the point of view of a this-worldly philosophy, an other-worldly philosophy is too idealistic, is of no practical use and is negative. From the point of view of an other-worldly philosophy, a this-worldly philosophy is too realistic, too superficial. It may be positive, but it is like the quick walking of a man who has taken the wrong road: the more quickly he walks the further he goes astray.

There are many people who say that Chinese philosophy is a this-worldly philosophy. It is difficult to state that these people are entirely right or entirely wrong. Taking a merely superficial view, people who hold this opinion cannot be said to be wrong, because according to their view, Chinese philosophy, regardless of its different schools of thought, is directly or indirectly concerned with government and ethics. On the surface, therefore, it is concerned chiefly with society, and not with

　　人是各式各样的。每一种人,都可以取得最高的成就。例如,有的人从政,在这个领域里,最高成就便是成为一个伟大的政治家。同样,在艺术领域里,最高成就便是成为一个伟大的艺术家。人可能被分为不同等级,但他们都是人。就做人来说,最高成就是什么呢?按中国哲学说,就是成圣,成圣的最高成就是:个人和宇宙合而为一。问题在于,如果人追求天人合一,是否需要抛弃社会,甚至否定人生呢?

　　有的哲学家认为,必须如此。释迦牟尼认为,人生就是苦难的根源;柏拉图认为,身体是灵魂的监狱。有的道家认为,生命是个赘疣,是个瘤,死亡是除掉那个瘤。所有这些看法都主张人应该从被物质败坏了的世界中解脱出来。一个圣人要想取得最高的成就,必须抛弃社会,甚至抛弃生命。唯有这样,才能得到最后的解脱。这种哲学通常被称为"出世"的哲学。

　　还有一种哲学,强调社会中的人际关系和人事。这种哲学只谈道德价值,因此对于超越道德的价值觉得无从谈起,也不愿去探讨。这种哲学通常被称为"入世"的哲学。站在入世哲学的立场上,出世的哲学过于理想化,不切实际,因而是消极的。从出世哲学的立场看,入世哲学过于实际,也因而过于肤浅;它诚然积极,但是像一个走错了路的人,走得越快,在歧途上就走得越远。

　　许多人认为,中国哲学是一种入世的哲学,很难说这样的看法完全对或完全错。从表面看,这种看法不能认为就是错的,因为持这种见解的人认为,中国无论哪一派哲学,都直接或间接关切政治和伦理道德。因此,它主要关心的是社会,而不关心宇宙;关心的

the universe; with the daily functions of human relations, not hell and heaven; with man's present life, but not his life in a world to come. When he was once asked by a disciple about the meaning of death, Confucius replied: "Not yet understanding life, how can you understand death?" (*Analects*, XI, 11.) And Mencius said: "The sage is the acme of human relations" (*Mencius*, IVa, 2), which, taken literally, means that the sage is the morally perfect man in society. From a surface point of view, with the ideal man being of this world, it seems that what Chinese philosophy calls a sage is a person of a very different order from the Buddha of Buddhism and the saints of the Christian religion. Superficially, this would seem to be especially true of the Confucian sage. That is why, in ancient times, Confucius and the Confucianists were so greatly ridiculed by the Taoists.

This, however, is only a surface view of the matter. Chinese philosophy cannot be understood by oversimplification of this kind. So far as the main tenet of its tradition is concerned, if we understand it aright, it cannot be said to be wholly this-worldly, just as, of course, it cannot be said to be wholly other-worldly. It is both of this world *and* of the other world. Speaking about the Neo-Confucianism of the Sung dynasty, one philosopher described it this way: "It is not divorced from daily ordinary activities, yet it goes straight to what antedated Heaven." This is what Chinese philosophy has striven for. Having this kind of spirit, it is at one and the same time both extremely idealistic and extremely realistic, and very practical, though not in a superficial way.

This-worldliness and other-worldliness stand in contrast to each other as do realism and idealism. The task of Chinese philosophy is to accomplish a synthesis out of these antitheses. That does not mean that they are to be abolished. They are still there, but they have been made into a synthetic whole. How can this be done? This is the problem which Chinese philosophy attempts to solve.

According to Chinese philosophy, the man who accomplishes this synthesis, not only in theory but also in deed, is the sage. He is both this-worldly and other-worldly. The spiritual achievement of the Chinese sage corresponds to the saint's achievement in Buddhism, and in Western religion. But the Chinese sage is not one who does not concern himself with the business of the world. His character is described as one of "sageliness within and kingliness without." That is to say, in his inner sageliness, he accomplishes spiritual cultivation; in his kingliness without, he functions in society. It is not necessary that the sage should be the

是人际关系的日常功能，而不关心地狱或天堂；关心人的今生，而不关心他的来生。《论语》第十一章十一节记载，有一次，孔子的学生子路问孔子："敢问死？"孔子回答说："未知生，焉知死？"孟子曾说："圣人，人伦之至也。"（《孟子·离娄章句上》）这无异于说，圣人是道德完美的人。就表面看，中国哲学所说的圣人是现世中的人，这和佛家所描述的释迦牟尼或基督教所讲的圣徒，迥然异趣，特别是儒家所说的圣人，更是如此。这便是引起中国古代道家嘲笑孔子和儒家的原因。

不过，这只是从表面上看问题。用这种过分简单的办法是无从了解中国哲学的。中国传统哲学的主要精神，如果正确理解的话，不能把它称作完全是入世的，也不能把它称作完全是出世的。它既是入世的，又是出世的。有一位哲学家在谈到宋朝道学时说它："不离日用常行内，直到先天未画前。"这是中国哲学努力的方向。由于有这样的一种精神，中国哲学既是理想主义的，又是现实主义的；既讲求实际，又不肤浅。

入世和出世是对立的，正如现实主义和理想主义是对立的一样。中国哲学的使命正是要在这种两极对立中寻求它们的综合。这是否要取消这种对立？但它们依然在那里，只是两极被综合起来了。怎么做到这一点呢？这正是中国哲学力图解决的问题。

按中国哲学的看法，能够不仅在理论上，而且在行动中实现这种综合的，就是圣人。他既入世，又出世；中国圣人的这个成就相当于佛教中的佛和西方宗教里的圣徒。但是，中国的圣人不是不食人间烟火、漫游山林、独善其身。他的品格可以用"内圣外王"四个字来刻画：内圣，是说他的内心致力于心灵的修养；外王，是说他在社会活动中好似君王。这不是说他必须是一国的政府首脑，

actual head of the government in his society. From the standpoint of practical politics, for the most part, the sage certainly has no chance of being the head of the state. The saying "sageliness within and kingliness without" means only that he who has the noblest spirit should, theoretically, be king. As to whether he actually has or has not the chance of being king, that is immaterial.

Since the character of the sage is, according to Chinese tradition, one of sageliness within and kingliness without, the task of philosophy is to enable man to develop this kind of character. Therefore, what philosophy discusses is what the Chinese philosophers describe as the *Tao* (Way, or basic principles) of sageliness within and kingliness without.

This sounds like the Platonic theory of the philosopher-king. According to Plato, in an ideal state, the philosopher should be the king or the king should be a philosopher; and in order to become a philosopher, a man must undergo a long period of philosophical training before his mind can be "converted" from the world of changing things to the world of eternal ideas. Thus according to Plato, as according to the Chinese philosophers, the task of philosophy is to enable man to have the character of sageliness within and kingliness without. But according to Plato, when a philosopher becomes a king, he does so against his will—in other words, it is something forced on him, and entails a great sacrifice on his part. This is what was also held by the ancient Taoists. There is the story of a sage who, being asked by the people of a certain state to become their king, escaped and hid himself in a mountain cave. But the people found the cave, smoked him out and compelled him to assume the difficult task. (*Lü-shih Ch'un-ch'iu*, I, 2.) This is one similarity between Plato and the ancient Taoists, and it also shows the character of other-worldliness in Taoist philosophy. Following the main tradition of Chinese philosophy, the Neo-Taoist, Kuo Hsiang of the third century A.D., revised this point.

According to Confucianism, the daily task of dealing with social affairs in human relations is not something alien to the sage. Carrying on this task is the very essence of the development of the perfection of his personality. He performs it not only as a citizen of society, but also as a "citizen of the universe," *t'ien min* as Mencius called it. He must be conscious of his being a citizen of the universe, otherwise his deeds would not have super-moral value. If he had the chance to become a king he would gladly serve the people, thus performing his duty both as a citizen of society, and as a citizen of the universe.

从实际看，圣人往往不可能成为政治首脑。"内圣外王"是说，政治领袖应当具有高尚的心灵。至于有这样的心灵的人是否就成为政治领袖，那无关紧要。

按照中国传统，圣人应具有内圣外王的品格，中国哲学的使命就是使人得以发展这样的品格。因此，中国哲学讨论的问题就是内圣外王之道；这里的"道"是指道路，或基本原理。

听起来，这有点像柏拉图所主张的"哲学家—国王"理论。柏拉图认为，在一个理想国里，哲学家应当成为国王，或国王应当成为哲学家。一个人怎样能成为哲学家呢？柏拉图认为，这个人必须先经过长期的哲学训练，使他在瞬息万变的世界事物中长成的头脑得以转到永恒理念的世界中去。由此看来，柏拉图和中国哲学家持有同样的主张，认为哲学的使命是使人树立起内圣外王的品格。但是按照柏拉图的说法，哲学家成为国王是违反了自己的意志，担任国王是强加给他的职务，对他是一种自我牺牲。中国古代的道家也持这样的观点。《吕氏春秋·贵生》篇里载有一个故事讲，古代一个圣人被国人拥戴为君，圣人逃上山去，藏在一个山洞里，国人跟踪而去，用烟把圣人从山洞里熏出来，强迫他当国君。这是柏拉图思想和中国古代道家相近的一点，从中也可看出道家哲学中的出世思想。到公元三世纪，新道家郭象根据中国主流哲学的传统，修改了道家思想中的这一点。

按照儒家思想，圣人并不以处理日常事务为苦，相反地，正是在这些世俗事务之中陶冶性情，使人培养自己以求得圣人的品格。他把处世为人看作不仅是国民的职责，而且如孟子所说，把它看为是"天民"的职责。人而成为"天民"，必须是自觉的，否则，他的所作所为，就不可能具有超越道德的价值。如果他因缘际会，成为国君，他会诚意正心去做，因为这不仅是事人，也是事天。

Since what is discussed in philosophy is the *Tao* (Way) of sageliness within and kingliness without, it follows that philosophy must be inseparable from political thought. Regardless of the differences between the schools of Chinese philosophy, the philosophy of every school represents, at the same time, its political thought. This does not mean that in the various schools of philosophy there are no metaphysics, no ethics, no logic. It means only that all these factors are connected with political thought in one way or another, just as Plato's *Republic* represents his whole philosophy and at the same time is his political thought.

For instance, the School of Names was known to indulge in such arguments as "a white horse is not a horse," which seems to have very little connection with politics. Yet the leader of this school, Kung-sun Lung, "wished to extend this kind of argument to rectify the relationship between names and facts in order to transform the world." We have seen in our world today how every statesman says his country wants only peace, but in fact, when he is talking about peace, he is often preparing for war. Here, then, there is a wrong relationship between names and facts. According to Kung-sun Lung, this kind of wrong relationship should be rectified. This is really the first step towards the transformation of the world.

Since the subject matter of philosophy is the *Tao* of sageliness within and kingliness without, the study of philosophy is not simply an attempt to acquire this kind of knowledge, but is also an attempt to develop this kind of character. Philosophy is not simply something to be *known*, but is also something to be *experienced*. It is not simply a sort of intellectual game, but something far more serious. As my colleague, Professor Y. L. Chin, has pointed out in an unpublished manuscript: "Chinese philosophers were all of them different grades of Socrates. This was so because ethics, politics, reflective thinking, and knowledge were unified in the philosopher; in him, knowledge and virtue were one and inseparable. His philosophy required that he live it; he was himself its vehicle. To live in accordance with his philosophical convictions was part of his philosophy. It was his business to school himself continually and persistently to that pure experience in which selfishness and egocentricity were transcended, so that he would be one with the universe. Obviously this process of schooling could not be stopped, for stopping it would mean the emergence of his ego and the loss of his universe. Hence cognitively he was eternally groping, and conatively he was eternally behaving or trying to behave. Since these could not be separated, in him

　　既然哲学所探讨的是内圣外王之道，它自然难以脱离政治。在中国哲学里，无论哪派哲学，其哲学思想必然也就是它的政治思想。这不是说，中国各派哲学里没有形而上学、伦理学或逻辑，而是说，它们都以不同形式与政治思想联系在一起，正如柏拉图的《理想国》既代表了柏拉图的全部哲学，又同时就是他的政治思想。

　　举例来说，名家所辩论的"白马非马"，似乎与政治毫不相干，但名家代表人物公孙龙"欲推是辩，以正名实，而化天下焉"（《公孙龙子·迹府》）。在今日世界，政治家们个个都标榜他的国家一心追求和平，事实上，我们不难看到，有的一面侈谈和平，一面就在准备战争。这就是名实不符。按公孙龙的意见，这种名实不符应当纠正。的确，要改变世界，这就是需要加以改变的第一步。

　　既然哲学以内圣外王之道为主题，研究哲学就不是仅仅为了寻求哲学的知识，还要培养这样的品德。哲学不仅是知识，更重要的，它是生命的体验。它不是一种智力游戏，而是十分严肃的事情。金岳霖教授在一篇未发表的论文中说："中国哲学家，在不同程度上，都是苏格拉底，因为他把伦理、哲学、反思和知识都融合在一起了。就哲学家来说，知识和品德是不可分的，哲学要求信奉它的人以生命去实践这个哲学，哲学家只是载道的人而已，按照所信奉的哲学信念去生活，乃是他的哲学的一部分。哲学家终身持久不懈地操练自己，生活在哲学体验之中，超越了自私和自我中心，以求与天合一。十分清楚，这种心灵的操练一刻也不能停止，因为一旦停止，自我就会抬头，内心的宇宙意识就将丧失。因此，从认识角度说，哲学家永远处于追求之中；从实践角度说，他永远在行动或将要行动。这些都是不可分割的。在哲学家身上就体现着'哲学家'

there was the synthesis of the philosopher in the original sense of that term. Like Socrates, he did not keep office hours with his philosophy. Neither was he a dusty, musty philosopher, closeted in his study, sitting in a chair on the periphery of life. With him, philosophy was hardly ever merely a pattern of ideas exhibited for human understanding, but was a system of precepts internal to the conduct of the philosopher; and in extreme cases his philosophy might even be said to be his biography."

- **The Way in which Chinese Philosophers Expressed Themselves**

A Western student beginning the study of Chinese philosophy is instantly confronted with two obstacles. One, of course, is the language barrier; the other is the peculiar way in which the Chinese philosophers have expressed themselves. I will speak about the latter first.

When one begins to read Chinese philosophical works, the first impression one gets is perhaps the briefness and disconnectedness of the sayings and writings of their authors. Open the *Confucian Analects* and you will see that each paragraph consists of only a few words, and there is hardly any connection between one paragraph and the next. Open a book containing the philosophy of Lao Tzu, and you will find that the whole book consists of about five thousand words—no longer than a magazine article; yet in it one will find the whole of his philosophy. A student accustomed to elaborate reasoning and detailed argument would be at a loss to understand what these Chinese philosophers were saying. He would be inclined to think that there was disconnectedness in the thought itself. If this were so, there would be no Chinese philosophy. For disconnected thought is hardly worthy of the name of philosophy.

It may be said that the apparent disconnectedness of the sayings and writings of the Chinese philosophers is due to the fact that these sayings and writings are not formal philosophical works. According to Chinese tradition, the study of philosophy is not a profession. Everyone should study philosophy just as in the West everyone should go to church. The purpose of the study of philosophy is to enable a man, *as a man*, to be a man, not some particular kind of man. Other studies—not the study of philosophy—enable a man to be some special kind of man. So there were no professional philosophers; and non-professional philosophers did

这个字本来含有的智慧和爱的综合。他像苏格拉底一样，不是按上下班时间来考虑哲学问题的；他也不是尘封的、陈腐的哲学家，把自己关在书斋里、坐在椅中，而置身于人生的边缘。对他来说，哲学不是仅供人们去认识的一套思想模式，而是哲学家自己据以行动的内在规范，甚至可以说，一个哲学家的生平，只要看他的哲学思想便可以了然了。"

● 中国哲学家表达自己思想的方式

一个开始学习中国哲学的西方学生，首先遇到的困难是语言的障碍，其次是中国哲学家表达自己思想的方式。这里，先从后一个问题说起。

一个西方人开始阅读中国哲学著作时，第一个印象也许是，这些作者的言论和著述往往十分简短，甚至互不连贯。打开《论语》，每一小段只包含几个字，各段之间往往也没有联系。打开《老子》，全书只有约五千字，只相当于一般杂志上一篇文章的篇幅，但是老子的全部哲学都在其中了。习惯于长篇大论地进行理性论辩的学生，遇到这种情况，会感到摸不着头脑，不知这些中国哲学家在说什么，由此不免会认为，这是中国哲学家的思想不够连贯。假若果真是这样，中国哲学就不存在了。不相连贯的思想，怎能称得上是哲学呢？

可以说，中国哲学家的言论著述，表面看来似乎不相连贯，乃是由于它们本不是专门的哲学著作。按照中国传统，学习哲学不是一个专门的行业。人人都应当读经书，正如在西方传统看来，人人都应当去教堂。读哲学是为了使人得以成为人，而不是为了成为某种特殊的人。因此，中国没有专业的哲学家，非专业的哲学家不认为

not have to produce formal philosophical writings. In China, there were far more philosophers who produced no formal philosophical writings than those who did. If one wishes to study the philosophy of these men, one has to go to the records of their sayings or the letters they wrote to disciples and friends. These letters did not belong to just one period in the life of the person who wrote them, nor were the records written only by a single person. Disconnectedness or even inconsistency between them is, therefore, to be expected.

The foregoing may explain why the writings and sayings of some philosophers are disconnected; but it does not explain why they are brief. In some philosophic writings, such as those of Mencius and Hsün Tzu, one does find systematic reasoning and arguments. But in comparison with the philosophic writings of the West, they are still not articulate enough. The fact is that Chinese philosophers were accustomed to express themselves in the form of aphorisms, apothegms, or allusions, and illustrations. The whole book of the *Lao-tzu* consists of aphorisms, and most of the chapters of the *Chuang-tzu* are full of allusions and illustrations. This is very obvious. But even in writings such as those of Mencius and Hsün Tzu, mentioned above, when compared with the philosophical writings of the West, there are still too many aphorisms, allusions, and illustrations. Aphorisms must be very brief; allusions and illustrations must be disconnected.

Aphorisms, allusions, and illustrations are thus not articulate enough. Their insufficiency in articulateness is compensated for, however, by their suggestiveness. Articulateness and suggestiveness are, of course, incompatible. The more an expression is articulate, the less it is suggestive—just as the more an expression is prosaic, the less it is poetic. The sayings and writings of the Chinese philosophers are so inarticulate that their suggestiveness is almost boundless.

Suggestiveness, not articulateness, is the ideal of all Chinese art, whether it be poetry, painting, or anything else. In poetry, what the poet intends to communicate is often not what is directly said in the poetry, but what is not said in it. According to Chinese literary tradition, in good poetry "the number of words is limited, but the ideas it suggests are limitless." So an intelligent reader of poetry reads what is outside the poem; and a good reader of books reads "what is between the lines." Such is the ideal of Chinese art, and this ideal is reflected in the way in which Chinese philosophers have expressed themselves.

自己要写专门的哲学著作。在中国历史上，没有专门哲学著作的哲学家比有专门著作的哲学家，为数多得多。如果要想读这些人的著作，就需要从他们对友人和学生的言论集和书信中去辑录，这些书信的写作时间不一，记录作者言论的人也不是同一个人，因此，其中不免有不相连贯，甚至互相矛盾的地方，这是不足为怪的。

以上所述可以说明，何以有些中国哲学家的著述中，内容不相连贯，但还没有说明，何以有些中国哲学家的著述十分简短。在有些哲学家如孟子、荀子的著作里，的确也有长篇大论的文章。但是，如果和西方哲学家的著作相较，它们仍然显得篇幅短小，未曾把道理讲透。这是因为中国哲学家惯于用格言、警句、比喻、事例等形式表述思想。《老子》全书都是以格言形式写成，《庄子》书中充满寓言和故事。即便在中国哲学家中以说理见长的孟子和荀子，把他们的著作和西方哲学家的著作相较，其中的格言、比喻和事例也比西方哲学著作中要多。格言总是简短的，而比喻和事例则总是自成段落，与前后文字不相衔接的。

用格言、比喻和事例来说理，难免有不够透彻的地方，只能靠其中的暗示补足。明述和暗示正好相反，一句话越明晰，其中就越少暗示的成分，正如一种表达，越是采取散文的形式，就越不像是诗。中国哲学家的语言如此不明晰，而其中所含的暗示则几乎是无限的。

富于暗示而不是一泻无余，这是中国诗歌、绘画等各种艺术所追求的目标。在诗歌中，诗人往往意在言外。在中国文学传统中，一首好诗往往是"言有尽而意无穷"。因此，一个慧心的读者，读诗时能从诗句之外去会意，读书时能从字里行间去会意。这是中国艺术所追求的情趣，它也同样成为中国哲学家表述思想时的风格。

The ideal of Chinese art is not without its philosophical background. In the twenty-sixth chapter of the *Chuang-tzu* it is said: "A basket-trap is for catching fish, but when one has got the fish, one need think no more about the basket. A foot-trap is for catching hares; but when one has got the hare, one need think no more about the trap. Words are for holding ideas, but when one has got the idea, one need no longer think about the words. If only I could find someone who had stopped thinking about words and could have him with me to talk to!" To talk with someone who has stopped thinking about words is not to talk with words. In the *Chuang-tzu* the statement is made that two sages met without speaking a single word, because "when their eyes met, the *Tao* was there." According to Taoism, the *Tao* (the Way) cannot be told, but only suggested. So when words are used, it is the suggestiveness of the words, and not their fixed denotations or connotations, that reveals the *Tao*. Words are something that should be forgotten when they have achieved their purpose. Why should we trouble ourselves with them any more than is necessary? This is true of the words and rhymes in poetry, and the lines and colors in painting.

During the third and fourth centuries A.D., the most influential philosophy was the Neo-Taoist School, which was known in Chinese history as the *hsüan hsüeh* (the dark or mystic learning). At that time there was a book entitled *Shih-shuo Hsin-yü*, which is a record of the clever sayings and romantic activities of the famous men of the age. Most of the sayings are very brief, some consisting of only a few words. It is stated in that book (ch. 4) that a very high official once asked a philosopher (the high official was himself a philosopher), what was the difference and similarity between Lao-Chuang (i.e., Lao Tzu and Chuang Tzu) and Confucius. The philosopher answered: "Are they not the same?" The high official was very much pleased with this answer, and instantly appointed the philosopher as his secretary. Since the answer consists of only three words in the Chinese language, this philosopher has been known as the three-word secretary. He could not say that Lao-Chuang and Confucius had nothing in common, nor could he say that they had everything in common. So he put his answer in the form of a question, which was really a good answer.

The brief sayings in the *Confucian Analects* and in the philosophy of the *Lao-tzu* are not simply conclusions from certain premises which have been lost. They are aphorisms full of suggestiveness. It is the suggestiveness that is attractive. One may gather together all the ideas

中国艺术的这种风格是有其哲学背景的。《庄子》第二十六章《外物》篇最后说："荃者所以在鱼，得鱼而忘荃；蹄者所以在兔，得兔而忘蹄；言者所以在意，得意而忘言。吾安得夫忘言之人而与之言哉！"得忘言之人而与之言，这时两人不是用语言来交谈，《庄子》书中说到的两位圣人，相遇而不言，因为"目击而道存矣"（《庄子·田子方》）。按照道家的思想，道不可道，只能暗示。语言的作用不在于它的固定含义，而在于它的暗示，引发人去领悟道。一旦语言已经完成它的暗示的作用，就应把它忘掉，为什么还要让自己被并非必要的语言所拖累呢？诗的文字和音韵是如此，绘画的线条和颜色也是如此。

在公元三、四世纪期间，玄学（在西方称之为"新道家"）是在中国思想界影响最大的哲学流派。当时有一部书，名为《世说新语》，其中记载当时名士们的隽语韵事，所记载的名士言论，往往十分简短，有的甚至只有几个字。这部书的《文学》篇里记载，一位高官（本人也是一个哲学家）问一位哲学家，老、庄和孔子思想上的异同何在。哲学家回答道："将无同？"这位高官对哲学家的回答很满意，立即委派他做自己的秘书。这位哲学家的回答只有三个字，因此他被称为"三字掾"（"掾"是古代官署属员的通称）。他回答高官的问题，既无法说老、庄与孔子毫无共同之处，又无法说他们之间毫无区别。于是，他用回问的方式作为答复，实在是一个聪明的回答。

《论语》和《老子》两书中的简短词句，并不是本来根据某种讨论前提作出的结论，现在由于前半遗失而使它们显得无头无脑。它们是充满提示的箴言。正由于富于提示，才使它们具有巨大的吸引力。

one finds in the *Lao-tzu* and write them out in a new book consisting of fifty thousand or even five hundred thousand words. No matter how well this is done, however, it is just a new book. It may be read side by side with the original *Lao-tzu*, and may help people a great deal to understand the original, but it can never be a substitute for the original.

Kuo Hsiang, to whom I have already referred, was one of the great commentators on Chuang Tzu. His commentary was itself a classic of Taoist literature. He turned the allusions and metaphors of Chuang Tzu into a form of reasoning and argument, and translated his poems into prose of his own. His writing is much more articulate than that of Chuang Tzu. But between the suggestiveness of Chuang Tzu's original and the articulateness of Kuo Hsiang's commentary, people may still ask: Which is better? A monk of the Buddhist Ch'an or Zen school of a later period once said: "Everyone says that it was Kuo Hsiang who wrote a commentary on Chuang Tzu; I would say it was Chuang Tzu who wrote a commentary on Kuo Hsiang."

- **The Language Barrier**

It is true of all philosophical writings that it is difficult for one to have a complete understanding and full appreciation of them if one cannot read them in the original. This is due to the language barrier. Because of the suggestive character of Chinese philosophical writings, the language barrier becomes even more formidable. The suggestiveness of the sayings and writings of the Chinese philosophers is something that can hardly be translated. When one reads them in translation, one misses the suggestiveness; and this means that one misses a great deal.

A translation, after all, is only an interpretation. When one translates a sentence from, say, the *Lao-tzu*, one gives one's own interpretation of its meaning. But the translation may convey only one idea, while as a matter of fact, the original may contain many other ideas besides the one given by the translator. The original is suggestive, but the translation is not, and cannot be. So it loses much of the richness inherent in the original.

There have been many translations of the *Lao-tzu* and the *Confucian Analects*. Each translator has considered the translations of others unsatisfactory. But no matter how well a translation is done, it is bound to be poorer than the original. It needs a combination of all the translations already made and many others not yet made, to reveal the richness of the *Lao-tzu* and the *Confucian Analects* in their original form.

　　我们如果把《老子》书中提到的概念列举出来，重述一遍，可能用上五万字或五十万字，它可能帮助读者了解《老子》一书的含义，但它本身将成为另一本书，而永不可能代替《老子》的原著。

　　在前面，我曾经提到过的郭象是《庄子》一书的著名注释家。他的注释本身就是道家的一本重要古典文献。他把庄子使用的寓言和隐喻，用理性论辩的方式加以阐述，又把《庄子》书中的诗句用散文予以重述，他的论述比《庄子》一书清晰得多。但是，《庄子》原书富于提示，郭象的注释则明晰具体。人们会问，两者之中，哪个更好呢？后来一位禅宗僧人曾说："曾见郭象注庄子，识者云：却是庄子注郭象。"（《大慧普觉禅师语录》卷二十二）

● 语言障碍

　　任何人如果不能用原文阅读某种哲学著作，要想完全理解原著，的确会有困难，这是由于语言的障碍。中国哲学著作由于它们的提示性质，语言的困难就更大。中国哲学家的言论和著述中的种种提示，很难翻译。当它被翻译成外文时，它由提示变成一种明确的陈述。失去了提示的性质，就失去了原著的味道。

　　任何翻译的文字，说到底，只是一种解释。当我们把《老子》书中的一句话译成英文时，我们是在按照自己的理解来阐述它的含义。译文通常只能表达一种含义，而原文却可能还有其他层次的含义。原文是提示性质的，译文则不可能做到这一点。于是，原文中的丰富含义，在翻译过程中大部分丢失了。

　　《老子》和《论语》都有许多种译本。每个译者都不免认为其他译本不够满意。但是，无论一个译本如何力求完美，它总不及原著。只有把《老子》和《论语》的所有译本，加上将来的各种新译本，才可能显示《老子》和《论语》原书的风貌。

Kumarajiva, of the fifth century A.D., one of the greatest translators of the Buddhist texts into Chinese, said that the work of translation is just like chewing food that is to be fed to others. If one cannot chew the food oneself, one has to be given food that has already been chewed. After such an operation, however, the food is bound to be poorer in taste and flavor than the original.

五世纪时的佛教高僧鸠摩罗什是把佛教经典译成中文的一位翻译大家。他曾说，翻译工作恰如嚼饭喂人。如果一个人自己不能吃饭，要吃别人的唾余，所吃到嘴里的当然没有原来那饭的香味和鲜味。

❷ THE BACKGROUND OF CHINESE PHILOSOPHY

In the last chapter I said that philosophy is systematic reflective thinking on life. In thinking, the thinker is usually conditioned by the surroundings in which he lives. Being in certain surroundings, he feels life in a certain way, and there are therefore in his philosophy certain emphases or omissions, which constitute the characteristics of that philosophy.

This is true of an individual, as it is also true of a people. In this chapter I shall try to say something about the geographic and economic background of the Chinese people in order to show how and why Chinese civilization in general, and Chinese philosophy in particular, are what they are.

● Geographic Background of the Chinese People

In the *Confucian Analects* Confucius said: "The wise man delights in water; the good man delights in mountains. The wise move; the good stay still. The wise are happy; the good endure." (VI, 21.) In reading this saying, I feel there is in it something which suggests a difference between the people of ancient China and those of ancient Greece.

China is a continental country. To the ancient Chinese their land was the world. There are two expressions in the Chinese language which can both be translated as the world. One is "all beneath the sky" and the other is "all within the four seas." To the people of a maritime country such as the Greeks, it would be inconceivable that expressions such as these could be synonymous. But that is what happens in the Chinese language, and it is not without reason.

From the time of Confucius until the end of the last century, no Chinese thinkers had the experience of venturing out upon the high seas. Confucius and Mencius lived not far from the sea, if we think in modern terms of distance, yet in the *Analects*, Confucius mentions the sea only once. He is recorded as saying: "If my way is not to prevail, I shall get upon a raft and float out to the sea. He who will go with me will be [Chung] Yu." (V, 6.) Chung Yu was a disciple of Confucius known for his courage and bravery. It is said in the same work that when Chung Yu heard this statement, he was much pleased. Confucius, however, was not so pleased by Chung Yu's overenthusiasm, and remarked: "Yu is more brave than

贰 中国哲学的背景

在前一章里我曾说，哲学是对人生的系统反思。人在思想时，总不免受到生活环境的制约，处于某种环境之中，他对生活就有某种感受，在他的哲学思想里就不免有些地方予以强调，而另一些地方又受到忽略，这些就构成了他的哲学思想特色。

这种情况就个人来说是如此，就一个民族来说，也是如此。在这一章里，我将对中国的地理环境和经济环境略作分析，可以帮助我们对中国文化何以有某些特点，有一个一般的了解，具体到中国哲学何以有某些特点，也是一样。

● 中华民族的地理环境

在《论语》里，孔子说："知者乐水，仁者乐山。知者动，仁者静。知者乐，仁者寿。"(《雍也》第二十一节）读孔子的这段话，使我想到古代中国人和古代希腊人思想不同的由来。

中国是一个大陆国家。在古代中国人心目中，世界就是他们生活的这片土地。在中文里，有两个词语常常被用来表达"世界"，一个是"普天之下"，一个是"四海之内"。住在海洋国家的人民，如希腊人，会不明白，居住在"四海之内"（比如说，住在克里特岛上），怎么就是住在"普天之下"。而在中文里，它就是如此，而且是有理由的。

从孔子的时代直到十九世纪末，中国的思想家们从来没有到海上冒险的经历。在现代人看来，孔子和孟子所住的地方都离海不远。但是在《论语》里，孔子只有一次提到海："道不行，乘桴浮于海。从我者，其由与？"(《公冶长》第六节）仲由即子路，在孔子的学生中，以勇敢著名。据说，仲由听到孔子的这句话，非常高兴。孔子却并没有因仲由的过分热心而高兴，他说："由也，

myself. I do not know what to do with him." (*Ibid.*)

Mencius's reference to the sea is likewise brief. "He who has seen the sea," he says, "finds it difficult to think anything about other waters; and he who has wandered to the gate of the sage, finds it difficult to think anything about the words of others." (VIIa, 24.) Mencius is no better than Confucius, who thought only of "floating out to sea." How different were Socrates, Plato, and Aristotle, who lived in a maritime country and wandered from island to island!

● Economic Background of the Chinese People

The ancient Chinese and Greek philosophers not only lived under different geographic conditions, but different economic ones as well. Since China is a continental country, the Chinese people have to make their living by agriculture. Even today the portion of the Chinese population engaged in farming is estimated at 75 to 80 percent. In an agrarian country, land is the primary basis of wealth. Hence, throughout Chinese history, social and economic thinking and policy have centered around the utilization and distribution of land.

Agriculture in such an economy is equally important not only in peacetime but in wartime as well. During the period of the Warring States (480-222 B.C.), a period in many ways similar to our own, in which China was divided into many feudal kingdoms, every state devoted its greater attention to what were then called "the arts of agriculture and war." Finally the state of Ch'in, one of the seven leading states of the time, gained supremacy both in agriculture and war, and as a result succeeded in conquering the other states and thus bringing a unification to China for the first time in her history.

In the social and economic thinking of Chinese philosophers, there is a distinction between what they call "the root" and "the branch." "The root" refers to agriculture and "the branch" to commerce. The reason for this is that agriculture is concerned with production, while commerce is merely concerned with exchange. One must have production before one can have exchange. In an agrarian country, agriculture is the major form of production, and therefore throughout Chinese history, social and economic theories and policies have all attempted "to emphasize the root and slight the branch."

好勇过我，无所取材。"（意思说，仲由虽然勇敢，可惜不能裁度事理。同上）

孟子提到海的话也同样简短。他说："观于海者难为水，游于圣人之门者难为言。"（《孟子·尽心章句上》）孔子只想，泛舟浮于海，孟子也只是望海惊叹，并不比孔子好多少。对比之下，苏格拉底、柏拉图和亚里士多德，出生在海洋国家，漫游列岛，又是多么不同啊！

● 中华民族的经济背景

古代中国和古代希腊的哲学家们不仅生活在不同的地理环境之中，还生活在不同的经济环境之中。中国是个大陆国家，中华民族历来依靠农业来维持生存。直到今日，中国的农业人口还在全体人口中占百分之七十五至八十。在一个农业国家里，财富的首要基础是土地。因此，在中国历史上，一切社会、经济思想以至政府的政策措施都以土地的分配和利用为中心。

在一个农业国家里，无论和平时期或战争时期，农业都同样重要。中国历史上，公元前四八〇至前二二二年是战国时期——和今日世界在很多方面都颇为相似。当时中国分裂为许多封建的小王国。每个小国都把"耕战之术"作为国家的要务。最后，"七雄"中的秦国，在经济和军事上都占优势，得以战胜其他六国，从而使中国在历史上第一次实现了政治统一。

中国哲学家们的社会经济思想都强调要区别"本"和"末"，农业生产被认为是立国之本，而商业则被看为是立国之末端，因为经济生产主要靠农业，而商业只关系到产品的交换。商品的交换终究要以生产为前提，在一个以农业为基础的国家里，农产品是主要的产品，因此在中国历史上，各种社会、经济的理论和政策都重农轻商。

The people who deal with the "branch," that is, the merchants, were therefore looked down upon. They were the last and lowest of the four traditional classes of society, the other three being scholars, farmers, and artisans. The scholars were usually landlords, and the farmers were the peasants who actually cultivated the land. These were the two honorable professions in China. A family having "a tradition of studying and farming" was something of which to be proud.

Although the "scholars" did not actually cultivate the land themselves, yet since they were usually landlords, their fortunes were tied up with agriculture. A good or bad harvest meant their good or bad fortune, and therefore their reaction to the universe and their outlook on life were essentially those of the farmer. In addition their education gave them the power to express what an actual farmer felt but was incapable of expressing himself. This expression took the form of Chinese philosophy, literature, and art.

- **Value of Agriculture**

In the *Lü-shih Ch'un-ch'iu*, a compendium of various schools of philosophy written in the third century B.C., there is a chapter titled "The Value of Agriculture." In this chapter a contrast is made between the mode of life of people who are engaged in the "root" occupation—the farmers, and that of those who are engaged in the "branch" occupation— the merchants. The farmers are primitive and simple and therefore always ready to accept commands. They are childlike and innocent and therefore unselfish. Their material properties are complex and difficult to move, and therefore they do not abandon their country when it is in danger. Merchants, on the other hand, are corrupt and therefore not obedient. They are treacherous and therefore selfish. They have simple properties which are easy to transport, and therefore they usually abandon their country when it is in danger. Hence this chapter asserts that not only is agriculture economically more important than commerce, but the mode of life of the farmers is also superior to that of the merchants. Herein lies "the value of agriculture." (XXVI, 3.) The author of this chapter found that the mode of life of people is conditioned by their economic background, and his evaluation of agriculture again shows that he was himself conditioned by the economic background of his time.

In this observation of the *Lü-shih Ch'un-ch'iu*, we find the root and source of the two main trends of Chinese thought, Taoism and

在一个重农轻商的国家里，商人自不免受到轻视。在中国的传统社会里，把民众按行业分为士、农、工、商四等，士通常是来自地主阶级，农就是从事农业生产的农民，这两种行业受到社会的尊重，任何人出身于"耕读世家"，往往引以为傲。

读书人通常并不亲自耕地，但他们一般出身于地主家庭，家庭的兴衰和农业生产的好坏直接联系在一起：农业收成好，他们受益；农业收成坏，他们也受连累。因此，他们的宇宙观和人生观都主要反映了农民的思想。再加上他们受过教育，使他们得以表达农民自己没法表达的思想，这种表达在中国就采取了哲学、文学和艺术的形式。

● 《上农》——农业的价值

著于公元前三世纪的《吕氏春秋》书中，辑有各家哲学撮要，有一章名为《上农》，其中比较农民的生活方式和商人的生活方式，认为农民像婴儿那样单纯朴实，惯于顺服长上，比较不自私，他们的物质财产复杂多样、难于移动，因此，国家遭难时，农民不会弃置不顾；商人则自私奸诈，计谋多、不顺服，他们的财产简单、易于转移，因此国家有难时，商人往往自己逃跑，不顾国家。这一章认为，把农业和商业相比，不仅农业对国家更重要，而且农民的生活方式也比商人的生活方式高尚。这就是为什么要以农业为上。（见《吕氏春秋》第二十六篇第三节）这一章的作者看出：人的生活方式受经济背景的制约，而他以农业为上的思想又显示那个时代的经济背景对他的思想制约。

从《吕氏春秋》的观察中，反映出中国哲学里道家和儒家关于社会、经济两派思想的根源。这两派思想主张如同两极那样

Confucianism. They are poles apart from one another, yet they are also the two poles of one and the same axis. They both express, in one way or another, the aspirations and inspirations of the farmer.

- **"Reversal Is the Movement of *Tao*"**

Before considering the difference between these two schools, let us first take up a theory which both of them maintained. This is that both in the sphere of nature and in that of man, when the development of anything brings it to one extreme, a reversal to the other extreme takes place; that is, to borrow an expression from Hegel, everything involves its own negation. This is one of the main theses of Lao Tzu's philosophy and also that of the *Book of Changes* as interpreted by the Confucianists. It was no doubt inspired by the movements of the sun and moon and the succession of the four seasons, to which farmers must pay particular heed in order to carry on their own work. In the Appendices of the *Book of Changes*, it is said: "When the cold goes, the warmth comes, and when the warmth comes, the cold goes." (Appendix III.) And again: "When the sun has reached its meridian, it declines, and when the moon has become full, it wanes." (Appendix I.) Such movements are referred to in the Appendices as "returning." Thus Appendix I says: "In returning we see the mind of Heaven and Earth." Similarly in the *Lao-tzu* we find the words: "Reversal is the movement of the *Tao*." (Ch. 40.)

This theory has had a great effect upon the Chinese people and has contributed much to their success in overcoming the many difficulties which they have encountered in their long history. Convinced of this theory, they remain cautious even in time of prosperity, and hopeful even in time of extreme danger. In the late war, the concept provided the Chinese people with a sort of psychological weapon, so that even in its darkest period, most people lived on the hope which was expressed in the phrase: "The dawn will soon come." It was this "will to believe" that helped the Chinese people to go through the war.

This theory has also provided the principal argument for the doctrine of the golden mean, favored by Confucianist and Taoist alike. "Never too much" has been the maxim of both. For according to it, it is better for one to be wrong by having too little, than to be wrong by having too much, and to be wrong by leaving things undone, than to be wrong by overdoing them. For by having too much and overdoing, one runs the risk of getting the opposite of what one wants.

背反，但它们又像同一个轴的两极，两个方面都同样反映了农民的思想。

● "反者道之动"

在比较儒道两家的不同思想之前，让我们先看一下两家共同的一种理论思想，就是都注意到，无论在自然和人生的领域里，任何事物发展到极端，就有一种趋向，朝反方向的另一极端移动。借用黑格尔的哲学术语，任何事物都包含了对它自己的否定。这是老子哲学思想的一个主题，也是儒家阐发《易经》时的一个主题。它无疑受到太阳、月亮运行和四季嬗替的启发。对农民来说，注意这些自然变化是农业生产的必需。在"易传"中说："寒往则暑来，暑往则寒来。"（《系辞下》）又说："日中则昃，月盈则食。"（《丰卦·彖辞》）"易传"中称这样的运动为"复"，《复卦·彖辞》说："复，其见天地之心乎？"在《道德经》第四十章，我们也读到类似的话，说："反者道之动。"

这个理论对中华民族有巨大的影响，帮助中华民族在漫长的历史中克服了无数的困难。中国人深信这个理论，因此经常提醒自己要"居安思危"；另一方面，即使处于极端困难之中，也不失望。在刚结束不久的抗日战争中，这种希望成为中国民众的心理武器，即使处于最黑暗的时期，还深信："黎明即将到来。"正是由这种信仰形成的意志帮助中国人民度过了这场战争。

这个理论还对儒家和道家都主张的中庸之道提供了主要论据。"不为已甚"、"毋太过"成为儒道两家共同的格言。"过犹不及"，但处事宁愿不及，也不要过甚，因为行事过分，就将适得其反。

- **Idealization of Nature**

Taoism and Confucianism differ because they are the rationalization or theoretical expression of different aspects of the life of the farmers. The farmers are simple in their living and innocent in their thought. Seeing things from their point of view, the Taoists idealized the simplicity of primitive society and condemned civilization. They also idealized the innocence of children and despised knowledge. In the *Lao-tzu* it is said: "Let us have a small country with few inhabitants.... Let the people return to the use of knotted cords [for keeping records]. Let them obtain their food sweet, their clothing beautiful, their homes comfortable, their rustic tasks pleasurable. The neighbouring state might be so near at hand that one could hear the cocks crowing in it and dogs barking. But the people would grow old and die without ever having been there." (Ch. 80.) Is this not an idyllic picture of a farmer's country?

The farmers are always in contact with nature, so they admire and love nature. This admiration and love were developed by the Taoists to the fullest extent. They made a sharp distinction between what is of nature and what is of man, the natural and the artificial. According to them, what is of nature is the source of human happiness and what is of man is the root of all human suffering. They were, as the Confucianist Hsün Tzu puts it, "blinded by nature and had no knowledge of man." (*Hsün-tzu*, ch. 21.) As the final development of this trend of thinking, the Taoists maintained that the highest achievement in the spiritual cultivation of a sage lies in the identification of himself with the whole of nature, i.e., the universe.

- **Family System**

The farmers have to live on their land, which is immovable, and the same is true of the scholar landlords. Unless one has special talent, or is especially lucky, one has to live where one's father or grandfather lived, and where one's children will continue to live. That is to say, the family in the wider sense must live together for economic reasons. Thus there developed the Chinese family system, which was no doubt one of the most complex and well-organized in the world. A great deal of Confucianism is the rational justification or theoretical expression of this social system.

The family system was the social system of China. Out of the five traditional social relationships, which are those between sovereign and subject, father and son, elder and younger brother, husband and wife,

● 对自然的理想化

道家和儒家不同，因为他们是对农民生活中的不同方面加以理论化。农民生活简单，思想纯真。道家从这一点出发，谴责文明，鼓吹返朴归真；把儿童的天真烂漫理想化，鄙视知识。《道德经》第八十章说："小国寡民，……使民复结绳而用之。甘其食，美其服，安其居，乐其俗。邻国相望，鸡犬之声相闻，民至老死不相往来。"这不是对农民社会的田园诗式颂歌吗？

农民时刻和自然打交道，他们爱自然。道家把这种爱慕发挥到淋漓尽致，同时把属于自然和属于人的东西严格区分：一个是自然的，另一个是人为的。自然令人快乐，人为给人痛苦。战国时期的儒家思想家荀子评论道家"蔽于天而不知人"（《荀子·解蔽》）。道家这种思想最后发展到主张"天人合一"，即人与自然、与宇宙合一。

● 家族制度

农民靠土地生活，而土地是无法挪动的。地主阶级出身的读书人也无法离开土地。一个人若没有特殊的才能，他无法离开祖辈生活的这片土地，他的子孙也只有世世代代生活在这片土地上。这就是说，同一个家庭的后代，由于经济的原因，不得不生活在一起。由此发展起中国的家族制度，它的复杂性和组织性是世界少有的。儒家思想在很大程度上便是这种家族制度的理性化。

中国的社会制度便是家族制度。传统中国把社会关系归纳成五种，即君臣、父子、兄弟、夫妇、朋友。在这五种社会关系中，

and friend and friend, three are family relationships. The remaining two, though not family relationships, can be conceived of in terms of the family. Thus the relationship between sovereign and subject can be conceived of in terms of that between father and son, and that between friend and friend in terms of the one between elder and younger brother. So, indeed, was the way in which they were usually conceived. But these are only the major family relationships, and there were many more. In the *Erh Ya*, which is the oldest dictionary of the Chinese language, dating from before the Christian era, there are more than one hundred terms for various family relationships, most of which have no equivalent in the English language.

For the same reason ancestor worship developed. In a family living in a particular place, the ancestor worshiped was usually the first of the family who had established himself and his descendants there on the land. He thus became the symbol of the unity of the family, and such a symbol was indispensable for a large and complex organization.

A great part of Confucianism is the rational justification of this social system, or its theoretical expression. Economic conditions prepared its basis, and Confucianism expressed its ethical significance. Since this social system was the outgrowth of certain economic conditions, and these conditions were again the product of their geographical surroundings, to the Chinese people both the system and its theoretical expression were very natural. Because of this, Confucianism naturally became the orthodox philosophy and remained so until the invasion of industrialization from modern Europe and America changed the economic basis of Chinese life.

• This-worldliness and Other-worldliness

Confucianism is the philosophy of social organization, and is also the philosophy of daily life. Confucianism emphasizes the social responsibilities of man, while Taoism emphasizes what is natural and spontaneous in him. In the *Chuang-tzu,* it is said that the Confucianists roam within the bounds of society, while the Taoists roam beyond it. In the third and fourth centuries A.D., when Taoism again became influential, people used to say that Confucius valued *ming chiao* (the teaching of names denoting the social relationships), while Lao Tzu and Chuang Tzu valued *tzu jan* (spontaneity or naturalness). These two trends of Chinese philosophy correspond roughly to the traditions of classicism and romanticism in Western thought. Read the poems of Tu

三种是家庭关系，另两种虽不是家庭关系，却也可以看作是家庭关系的延伸。譬如君臣关系，被看成是父子关系；朋友则被看作是兄弟关系。这还只是主要的家庭关系，此外还有许多。在中国最古老的辞书——著于公元前的《尔雅》一书中，有关家庭各种关系的名称有一百多种，其中多数在英语中没有与之相当的词语。

中国的祖先崇拜也是这样发展起来的。世代居住在一个地方的一族人，他们追溯首先在这地方定居的祖先，敬拜他。祖先成为家族的共同象征，作为一个巨大复杂的组织，这样一个象征是必不可少的。

儒家思想中的一大部分是这种社会制度的理性论证，也就是它的理论表现。经济环境成为这种社会制度的基础，儒家思想反映了它的伦理价值。由于这种社会制度是一定经济条件的产物，这些经济条件又是地理环境的产物。因此，对中华民族来说，这个社会制度和它的理论表现都是自然而然的。正是因此，儒家思想成为中国正统的哲学，一直保持到近代欧洲和北美工业化的潮流侵入中国，改变了中国社会的经济基础为止。

● **入世和出世**

儒家思想不仅是中国的社会哲学，也是中国人的人生哲学。儒家思想强调个人的社会责任，道家则强调人内心自然自动的秉性。《庄子》书中说：儒家游方之内，道家游方之外。方，就是指社会。公元三、四世纪（魏晋）间，道家思想再次兴起。当时人认为，孔子重"名教"（把各种社会关系规范化），老庄贵"自然"（顺应事物和人的本性）。中国哲学中的这两种思潮，大体类似于西方思想中的古典主义和浪漫主义两种思潮。试读杜甫和李白两人的诗，

Fu and Li Po, and one sees in them the difference between Confucianism and Taoism. These two great poets lived during the same period (eighth century A.D.), and concurrently expressed in their poems the two main traditions of Chinese thought.

Because it "roams within the bounds of society," Confucianism appears more this-worldly than Taoism, and because it "roams beyond the bounds of society," Taoism appears more other-worldly than Confucianism. These two trends of thought rivaled one another, but also complemented each other. They exercised a sort of balance of power. This gave the Chinese people a better sense of balance in regard to this-worldliness and other-worldliness.

There were Taoists in the third and fourth centuries who attempted to make Taoism closer to Confucianism, and there were also Confucianists in the eleventh and twelfth centuries who attempted to make Confucianism closer to Taoism. We call these Taoists the Neo-Taoists and these Confucianists the Neo-Confucianists. It was these movements that made Chinese philosophy both of this world and of the other world, as I pointed out in the last chapter.

● Chinese Art and Poetry

The Confucianists took art as an instrument for moral education. The Taoists had no formal treatises on art, but their admiration of the free movement of the spirit and their idealization of nature gave profound inspiration to the great artists of China. This being the case, it is no wonder that most of the great artists of China took nature as their subject. Most of the masterpieces of Chinese painting are paintings of landscapes, animals and flowers, trees and bamboos. In a landscape painting, at the foot of a mountain or the bank of a stream, one always finds a man sitting, appreciating the beauty of nature and contemplating the *Tao* or Way that transcends both nature and man.

Likewise in Chinese poetry we find such poems as that by T'ao Ch'ien (A.D. 372-427):

I built my hut in a zone of human habitation,

Yet near me there sounds no noise of horse or coach,

Would you know how that is possible?

A heart that is distant creates a wilderness round it.

I pluck chrysanthemums under the eastern hedge,

Then gaze long at the distant summer hills.

这两位伟大的诗人都生活于八世纪，从他们的诗里却不难分辨出中国思想两大流派——儒家和道家——对两人的不同思想影响。

儒家"游方之内"，显得比道家入世；道家"游方之外"，显得比儒家出世。这两种思想看来相反，其实却是相反相成，使中国人在入世和出世之间，得以较好地取得平衡。

在三、四世纪间，有一批道家试图使道家思想靠近儒家思想，后世称他们为"新道家"；在十一、十二世纪间（宋朝），也有一批儒家试图使儒家思想靠近道家思想，后世称他们为"新儒家"。这些运动使中国哲学既是入世的，又是出世的。在本书第一章里，我已经指出了这一点。

● **中国艺术与诗歌**

儒家把艺术看作是道德教育的工具。道家对艺术没有正面提出系统的见解，但是他们追求心灵的自由流动，把自然看为最高理想，这给了中国的伟大艺术家无穷的灵感。由于这一点，许多中国艺术家把自然作为艺术的对象，就不足为怪了。中国美术作品中的许多杰作都是写山水、花鸟、树木、竹枝。在许多山水画里，山脚下、溪水边，往往能看见一个人，静坐沉醉在天地的大美之中，从中领会超越于自然和人生之上的妙道。

在中国的诗歌里，让我们读陶渊明（公元三七二至四二七年）的诗《饮酒·其五》：

结庐在人境，而无车马喧。

问君何能尔？心远地自偏。

采菊东篱下，悠然见南山。

The mountain air is fresh at the dusk of day;

The flying birds two by two return.

In these things there lies a deep meaning;

Yet when we would express it, words suddenly fail us.[1]

Here we have Taoism at its best.

● The Methodology of Chinese Philosophy

In Chinese philosophy, the farmer's outlook not only conditioned its content, such as that reversal is the movement of the *Tao*, but, what is more important, it also conditioned its methodology. Professor Northrop has said that there are two major types of concepts, that achieved by intuition and that by postulation. "A concept by intuition," he says, "is one which denotes, and the complete meaning of which is given by, something which is immediately apprehended. 'Blue' in the sense of the sensed color is a concept by intuition.... A concept by postulation is one the complete meaning of which is designated by the postulates of the deductive theory in which it occurs.... 'Blue' in the sense of the number of a wave-length in electro-magnetic theory is a concept by postulation."[2]

Northrop also says that there are three possible types of concepts by intuition: "The concept of the differentiated aesthetic continuum. The concept of the indefinite or undifferentiated aesthetic continuum. The concept of the differentiation." (*Ibid.*, p. 187.) According to him, "Confucianism may be defined as the state of mind in which the concept of the indeterminate intuited manifold moves into the background of thought and the concrete differentiations in their relativistic, humanistic, transitory comings and goings form the content of philosophy." (*Ibid.*, p. 205.) But in Taoism, it is the concept of the indefinite or undifferentiated aesthetic continuum that forms the content of philosophy. (*Ibid.*)

I do not quite agree with all Northrop has said in this essay, but I think he has here grasped the fundamental difference between Chinese and Western philosophy. When a student of Chinese philosophy begins to study Western philosophy, he is glad to see that the Greek philosophers also made the distinction between Being and Non-being, the limited and the unlimited. But he feels rather surprised to find that the Greek philosophers held that Non-being and the unlimited are inferior to Being and the limited. In Chinese philosophy the case is just the reverse.

山气日夕佳，飞鸟相与还。
此中有真意，欲辨已忘言。

这正是道家所追求的最高精神境界。

● 中国哲学的方法论

农民的眼界不仅制约着中国哲学的内容，如前举的"反者道之动"，更重要的是它还制约着中国哲学的方法论。诺斯洛普教授（Prof. S. C. Northrop）曾提出：概念可分两种，一种来自直觉，一种来自假定。"来自直觉的概念指向某个事物，它的完整的意义可以立即从某个事物领会到。例如，蓝色是人对某种颜色的感觉，它是由直觉得到的概念。……至于由假设得出的概念，它的完整的意义是根据一个假设，用演绎法推演出来，从而认定的。……例如，'蓝色'用来描述电磁波的波长数字时，它是一个假定的概念。"

诺斯洛普教授还进一步说到，来自直觉的概念又可以分为三种："在连续审视中已予区分的概念；连续审视而还未予区分或称不确定的概念；以及区分的概念。"（同上）按照他的意见，"儒家的思想可以界定为一种精神状态，其中不明确的概念以直觉、多重的运动构成思想的背景；而具体的区分的概念则以相对的、人文主义的、过渡性的往复形成哲学的内容。"（同上书，第二○五页）至于道家思想，"则是以连续审视而不确定或未区分的概念构成哲学的内容。"（同上）

对诺斯洛普教授这篇文章中的观点，我并不完全同意。但是，在这些话里，他的确抓住了中西哲学的基本不同点。一个读哲学的中国学生开始学习西方哲学时，他会高兴地看到希腊哲学家也区别"有"和"无"，有限和无限。但是，希腊哲学家认为"无"和无限低于"有"和有限，这又使中国学生惊异不解，因为按中国哲学的看法，应该倒过来才对。之所以会产生这种不同的见解，是因为

The reason for this difference is that Being and the limited are the distinct, while Non-being and the unlimited are the indistinct. Those philosophers who start with concepts by postulation have a liking for the distinct, while those who start with intuition value the indistinct.

If we link what Northrop has pointed out here with what I mentioned at the beginning of this chapter, we see that the concept of the differentiated aesthetic continuum, from which come both the concept of the undifferentiated aesthetic continuum and that of differentiation (*Ibid.*, p. 187), is basically the concept of the farmers. What the farmers have to deal with, such as the farm and crops, are all things which they immediately apprehend. And in their primitivity and innocence, they value what they thus immediately apprehend. It is no wonder then, that their philosophers likewise take the immediate apprehension of things as the starting point of their philosophy.

This also explains why epistemology has never developed in Chinese philosophy. Whether the table that I see before me is real or illusory, and whether it is only an idea in my mind or is occupying objective space, was never seriously considered by Chinese philosophers. No such epistemological problems are to be found in Chinese philosophy (save in Buddhism, which came from India), since epistemological problems arise only when a demarcation between the subject and the object is emphasized. And in the aesthetic continuum, there is no such demarcation. In it the knower and the known is one whole.

This also explains why the language used by Chinese philosophy is suggestive but not articulate. It is not articulate, because it does not represent concepts in any deductive reasoning. The philosopher only tells us what he sees. And because of this, what he tells is rich in content, though terse in words. This is the reason why his words are suggestive rather than precise.

The Greeks lived in a maritime country and maintained their prosperity through commerce. They were primarily merchants. And what merchants have to deal with first are the abstract numbers used in their commercial accounts, and only then with concrete things that may be immediately apprehended through these numbers. Such numbers are what Northrop

"有"和有限都是明确的,而"无"和无限则是不明确的。由假设观念出发的哲学家喜欢明确的东西,而由直觉出发,则需要重视不明确的东西。

如果我们把诺斯洛普在这里所说的和我在本章开始时所说的结合起来,就会看见:在连续审视中已予区分的概念,由它衍生出还未区分的概念和分辨的概念(同上书,第一八七页),都在基本上是农民的概念。农民日常与之打交道的,诸如田地和庄稼,都是他们一看就认识的东西。他们处于原始和纯真的心态之中,把直接认知的东西看为宝贵的东西,这就无怪反映他们思想的哲学家们也同样把直接认知的东西看为哲学思维的出发点。

这也足以解释何以认识论在中国哲学里从未得到发展的原因。中国哲学家们对于自己眼前的这张桌子究竟是真实的,抑或只是幻觉的存在,从不认真对待(唯有佛家是对它认真对待的,而佛学来自印度)。认识论的问题之所以产生,是由于主观和客观已经有了明确的界限。而在一个连续审视过程之中,还没有明确区分主观与客观之间的界限,认识的主体和认识的客体还是浑然一体的。

这也有助于说明,中国哲学的语言何以是提示性的而并不明晰。它不明晰,因为它不代表用理性演绎得出的概念。哲学家只是告诉人们,他看见了什么。因此,他所述说的内容非常丰富,而使用的语言却很简短。这就是何以中国哲学家的语言往往只作提示而并不明确的原因。

● 海洋国家和大陆国家

希腊人生活在海洋国家里,靠贸易维持繁荣,他们首先是商人。商人就要与账目的抽象数字打交道,然后,他们才和数字所代表的具体事物打交道。这些数字是诺斯洛普所说的来自假设的

called concepts by postulation. Hence Greek philosophers likewise took the concept by postulation as their starting point. They developed mathematics and mathematical reasoning. That is why they had epistemological problems and why their language was so articulate.

But merchants are also townsmen. Their activities demand that they live together in towns. Hence they have a form of social organization not based on the common interest of the family so much as on that of the town. This is the reason why the Greeks organized their society around the *city* state, in contrast with the Chinese social system, which may be called that of the *family* state, because under it the state is conceived of in terms of the family. In a city state the social organization is not autocratic, because among the same class of townsmen, there is no moral reason why one should be more important than, or superior to, another. But in a family state the social organization is autocratic and hierarchic, because in a family the authority of the father is naturally superior to that of the son.

The fact that the Chinese were farmers also explains why China failed to have an industrial revolution, which is instrumental for the introduction of the modern world. In the *Lieh-tzu* there is a story which says that the Prince of the State of Sung once asked a clever artisan to carve a piece of jade into the leaf of a tree. After three years the artisan completed it, and when the artificial leaf was put upon the tree, it was made so wonderfully that no one could distinguish it from the real leaves. Thereupon the Prince was much pleased. But when Lieh Tzu heard it, he said: "If nature took three years to produce one leaf, there would be few trees with leaves on them! (*Lieh-tzu*, ch. 8.) This is the view of one who admires the natural and condemns the artificial. The way of life of the farmers is to follow nature. They admire nature and condemn the artificial, and in their primitivity and innocence, they are easily made content. They desire no change, nor can they conceive of any change. In China there have been not a few notable inventions or discoveries, but we often find that these were discouraged rather than encouraged.

With the merchants of a maritime country conditions are otherwise. They have greater opportunity to see different people with different customs and different languages; they are accustomed to change and are not afraid of novelty. Nay, in order to have a good sale for their goods, they have to encourage novelty in the manufacture of what they are going to sell. It is no accident that in the West, the industrial revolution was

概念，因此，希腊哲学家也以从假设得到的概念作为思维的出发点。他们发展了数学和数学的思维。这就解释了为什么认识论成为他们的问题，而且使用的语言如此明晰。

商人同时又是居住在城镇中的人。他们的活动要求他们在城镇聚居，因此他们的社会组织不是根据家族的共同利益，而更多是反映城镇的共同利益。这是何以希腊人以城邦为中心来组成社会，而中国的社会制度则或许可以称之为"家邦"，因为在中国的社会制度下，是通过家族来理解国家的。在一个城邦里，社会组织难以形成专制独裁统治，因为在同一等级的城镇居民中，难以找出理由来论证张三比李四更重要，应当享有更高的社会地位；但是在一个"家邦"里，社会组织是按人生来的地位，等级式地形成的，在一个家庭里，父亲的权威天然地高于儿子的权威。

中国人大多数是农民，这也可以用来说明，何以中国未能兴起一个工业革命，把中国带入现代世界。在《列子》一书里，有一个故事说，宋国国君有一次叫一个巧匠按照树叶雕刻一瓣玉叶。巧匠用三年时间刻出了一瓣玉叶，它如此逼真，以至无人能把它与真的树叶区别出来。国君感到十分得意。列子听说这事后评论说："使天地之生物，三年而成一叶，则物之有叶者寡矣。"（《列子·说符》）这是崇尚自然、谴责人为的人的见解。农民的生活方式容易倾向于顺乎自然。他们爱慕自然，谴责人为，在原始的纯真中，也很容易满足。他们不喜欢变革，也无法想象事物会变化。在中国历史上，曾有不少发明和发现，但它们不曾受到鼓励，却相反受到了打击。

处身在海洋国家的商人们，情况迥然不同。他们有更多的机会见到语言、风俗都不同的他族人民。他们习惯于变化，对新奇事物并不惧怕。而且为了货物得以销售，他们必须对所制造的货物不断

first started in England, which is also a maritime country maintaining her prosperity through commerce.

What was quoted earlier in this chapter from the *Lü-shih Ch'un-ch'iu* about merchants can also be said of the people of maritime countries, provided that, instead of saying that they are corrupt and treacherous, we say that they are refined and intelligent. We can also paraphrase Confucius by saying that the people of maritime countries are the wise, while those of continental countries are the good. And so we repeat what Confucius said: "The wise delight in water; the good delight in mountains. The wise move; the good stay still. The wise are happy; the good endure."

It is beyond the scope of this chapter to enumerate evidences to prove the relationship between the geographic and economic conditions of Greece and England on the one hand, and the development of Western scientific thought and democratic institutions on the other. But the fact that the geographic and economic conditions of Greece and England are quite different from those of China suffices to constitute a negative proof for my thesis in regard to Chinese history as mentioned in this chapter.

- ### The Permanent and the Changeable in Chinese Philosophy

The advancement of science has conquered geography, and China is no longer isolated "within the four seas." She is having her industrialization too, and though much later than the Western world, it is better late than never. It is not correct to say that the East has been invaded by the West. Rather it is a case in which the medieval has been invaded by the modern. In order to live in a modern world, China has to be modern.

One question remains to be asked: If Chinese philosophy has been so linked with the economic conditions of the Chinese people, does what has been expressed in Chinese philosophy possess validity only for people living under those conditions?

The answer is yes and no. In the philosophy of any people or any time, there is always a part that possesses value only in relation to the economic conditions of that people or of that time, but there is always another part that is more than this. That which is not relative has lasting value. I hesitate to say that it is absolute truth, because to determine what is absolute truth is too great a task for any human being, and is reserved for God alone, if there be one.

Let us take an instance in Greek philosophy. The rational justification

创新。西方的工业革命首先发生在英国这样一个靠贸易维持繁荣的海洋国家，不是偶然的。

在本章前面援引的《吕氏春秋》中对商人的评论，也可以用来形容海洋国家的人民，只是要作一点修正，把抨击商人奸诈、不讲道德，改为赞许他们聪明精巧。我们还可以仿效孔子的话说：海洋国家的人聪明，大陆国家的人善良。然后照孔子的话说："知者乐水，仁者乐山。知者动，仁者静。知者乐，仁者寿。"

由于篇幅所限，这里不能详细论证希腊和英国在地理、经济条件上的相似之处，以及科学思想与民主政治之何以在西方兴起。但希腊和英国的地理、经济条件与中国迥然不同，就足以从反面论证我在本章对中国历史的论点。

● **中国哲学中的"常"与"变"**

科学的发展已经战胜了地理的限制，今日中国已不再是封闭在"四海之内"。中国也走上了工业化的道路，虽然还落后于西方，但来得迟比不来好。说东方被西方侵略，并不确切，不如说是现代化侵入了中世纪世界。中国要在现代世界生存，就必须现代化。

人们会问一个问题：既然中国哲学产生于过去中国的经济环境之中，它的内容是否只对过去的中国才有意义？

这个看法，也对，也不对。任何民族在任何时代的哲学里，总有一些内容只对处于当时经济条件下的大众有用，但是，除此之外，还会有一部分哲学思想具有持久的价值。我不敢说那是绝对真理，任何人都不可能担当起判定绝对真理的任务，只有神——如果有神的话——才能决定什么是绝对真理。

让我们从希腊哲学中取一个实例：亚里士多德曾论证奴隶制度

of the slave system by Aristotle must be considered as a theory that is relative to the economic conditions of Greek life. But to say this is not to say that there is nothing that is not relative in the social philosophy of Aristotle. The same holds true for Chinese thought. When China is industrialized, the old family system must go, and with it will go its Confucianistic rational justification. But to say this is not to say that there is nothing that is not relative in the social philosophy of Confucianism.

The reason for this is that the society of ancient Greece and ancient China, though different, both belong to the general category which we call society. Theories which are the theoretical expression of Greek or Chinese society, are thus also in part expressions of society in general. Though there is in them something that pertains only to Greek or Chinese societies *per se*, there must also be something more universal that pertains to society in general. It is this latter something that is not relative and possesses lasting value.

The same is true of Taoism. The Taoist theory is certainly wrong which says that the utopia of mankind is the primitivity of a bygone age. With the idea of progress, we moderns think that the ideal state of human existence is something to be created in the future, not something that was lost in the past. But what some moderns think of as the ideal state of human existence, such as anarchism, is not wholly dissimilar from that thought of by the Taoists.

Philosophy also gives us an ideal of life. A part of that ideal, as given by the philosophy of a certain people or a certain time, must pertain only to the kind of life resulting from the social conditions of that people or that time. But there must also be a part that pertains to life in general, and so is not relative but has lasting value. This seems to be illustrated in the case of the Confucianist theory of an ideal life. According to this theory, the ideal life is one which, though having a very high understanding of the universe, yet remains within the bounds of the five basic human relationships. The nature of these human relationships may change according to circumstances. But the ideal itself does not change.

One is wrong, then, when one insists that since some of the five human relationships have to go, therefore the Confucianist ideal of life must go as well. And one is also wrong when one insists that since this ideal of life is desirable, therefore all the five human relationships must likewise be retained. One must make a logical analysis in order to distinguish between what is permanent and what is changeable in the history of

的合理性，这是古代希腊人的经济生活对他的思想制约。指出这一点，并不是说亚里士多德的全部社会哲学都只具有一时的意义。这个道理同样适用于中国思想。中国实现工业化后，旧的家族制度势必衰颓，儒家对家族制度所作理性论证的话也将随之而去。指出这一点，并不是说，儒家的社会哲学中就都是相对的东西了。

　　这是因为，古代希腊和中国的社会虽然不同，却都是属于我们称之为"社会"的这个大概念。有关希腊社会和中国社会的理论，其中有一部分是只对希腊或中国有效的理论，但同时，也都有一部分是有关人类社会的一般性理论。正是这后一部分，具有持久的而不是一时的价值。

　　这个道理也同样可以应用于道家思想。道家认为人类的理想国在于回到原始，这显然是错的。现代人相信历史是进步的，认为人类生活的理想国在于人类未来的创造，而不是在已经过去的古代。但是，有些现代人把无政府主义看作人类的理想国，这与道家的思想不无相似之处。

　　哲学还提供一种人生的理想。这种理想中有一部分是提出这种人生哲学的哲学家所处时代、地区和经济条件的产物，但也还有一部分是对于人生的一般见解，因此，不是只有一时的意义，而还有持久的意义。儒家的人生哲学大概可以属于这一类。按照儒家的理论，理想的人生虽然包含对宇宙的高度认识，但还是处在三纲五常的范围之内。这些人际关系的内容性质虽然随环境而变化，但是理想本身不会改变。如果认为，五种伦常关系的某些内容已经失去时效，因此儒家的人生理想应当全部抛弃，这显然是错的。反过来，如果因为儒家的人生理想应当保持，从而认为五种社会关系也不应改变，这显然也是错的。我们在学习哲学史时，应当对其中哪些是有永久价值的，哪些是可以改变的，进行合乎逻辑的分析。每一种

philosophy. Every philosophy has that which is permanent, and all philosophies have something in common. This is why philosophies, though different, can yet be compared with one another and translated one in terms of the other.

Will the methodology of Chinese philosophy change? That is to say, will the new Chinese philosophy cease to confine itself to "concept by intuition"? Certainly it will, and there is no reason why it should not. In fact, it is already changing. In regard to this change, I shall have more to say in the last chapter of this book.

哲学中，都有永久性的东西，各种哲学也总有其共同性的东西，正因此，不同的哲学才能互相比较，并进行翻译诠释。

中国哲学的方法论将来是否会改变？也就是说，新的中国哲学是否会不再把哲学思想局限于"由直觉得到的概念"之内？这是当然的，它没有理由不这样做。事实上，它已经在变化。本书末章将对这种变化作进一步探讨。

❸ THE ORIGIN OF THE SCHOOLS

In the last chapter I said that Confucianism and Taoism are the two main streams of Chinese thought. They became so only after a long evolution, however, and from the fifth through the third centuries B.C. they were only two among many other rival schools of thought. During that period the number of schools was so great that the Chinese referred to them as the "hundred schools."

● Ssu-ma T'an and the Six Schools

Later historians have attempted to make a classification of these "hundred schools." The first to do so was Ssu-ma T'an (died 110 B.C.), father of Ssu-ma Ch'ien (145-ca. 86 B.C.), and the author with him of China's first great dynastic history, the *Shih Chi* or *Historical Records*. In the last chapter of this work Ssu-ma Ch'ien quotes an essay by his father, titled "On the Essential Ideas of the Six Schools." In this essay Ssu-ma T'an classifies the philosophers of the preceding several centuries into six major schools, as follows:

The first is the *Yin-Yang chia* or *Yin-Yang* school, which is one of cosmologists. It derives its name from the *Yin* and *Yang* principles, which in Chinese thought are regarded as the two major principles of Chinese cosmology, *Yin* being the female principle, and *Yang* the male principle, the combination and interaction of which is believed by the Chinese to result in all universal phenomena.

The second school is the *Ju chia* or School of Literati. This school is known in Western literature as the Confucianist school, but the word *ju* literally means "literatus" or scholar. Thus the Western title is somewhat misleading, because it misses the implication that the followers of this school were scholars as well as thinkers; they, above all others, were the teachers of the ancient classics and thus the inheritors of the ancient cultural legacy. Confucius, to be sure, is the leading figure of this school and may rightly be considered as its founder. Nevertheless the term *ju* not only denotes "Confucian" or "Confucianist," but has a wider implication as well.

The third school is that of the *Mo chia* or Mohist school. This school had a close-knit organization and strict discipline under the leadership of Mo Tzu. Its followers actually called themselves the Mohists. Thus the title of this school is not an invention of Ssu-ma T'an, as were some of the other schools.

叁 诸子的由来

在上一章里，我说到，儒家和道家是中国思想中的两个主要流派，这是经过长期演化的结果。从公元前五世纪到前三世纪末，儒道两家只是许多互相竞争的学派中的两派。在这时期中，思想流派多到如此程度，以至在中国历史上称之为"诸子百家"。

● 司马谈和六家

后代史家试图对"百家"进行分类。首先进行这种尝试的是司马谈（卒于公元前一一〇年），他是司马迁（公元前一四五至前八六？年）的父亲，父子二人著述了中国第一部通史性质的《史记》。在《史记》最后一章，司马迁援引了他的父亲司马谈的一篇文章《论六家要旨》，其中，司马谈把在他之前几个世纪中的哲学家分为六家。

首先是阴阳家。它是讲宇宙论的一派，由于它把宇宙的原理归结为阴阳两个主要原则，因此被称为阴阳家。阴是代表女性的原则，阳是代表男性的原则，两者相生相克，相反相成，由此产生了中国人心目中所见的宇宙一切现象。

第二个学派是儒家。儒字的本义是读书人（儒生）或思想者。在西方称之为"孔子学派"，这个名字没有指出，它的队伍主要是由学者和思想家所组成。他们讲授古代的经书，因此是古代文化的传承者。孔子无疑是这一学派的领袖人物，也是这一学派的创始人。但这一学派之称为"儒"，还有更广的含义。

第三个学派是墨家。这一学派在墨子领导下，内部有严格的纪律和组织。这一派已经自称是"墨者"，所以，它的名称不像其他某些学派的名称，是司马谈的发明；"墨者"的名称是原来就有的。

The fourth school is the *Ming chia* or School of Names. The followers of this school were interested in the distinction between, and relation of, what they called "names" and "actualities."

The fifth school is the *Fa chia* or Legalist school. The Chinese word *fa* means pattern or law. The school derived from a group of statesmen who maintained that good government must be one based on a fixed code of law instead of on the moral institutions which the literati stressed for government.

The sixth school is the *Tao-Te chia* or School of the Way and its Power. The followers of this school centered their metaphysics and social philosophy around the concept of Non-being, which is the *Tao* or Way, and its concentration in the individual as the natural virtue of man, which is *Te*, translated as "virtue" but better rendered as the "power" that inheres in any individual thing. This group, called by Ssu-ma T'an the *Tao-Te* school, was later known simply as the *Tao chia*, and is referred to in Western literature as the Taoist school. As pointed out in the first chapter, it should be kept carefully distinct from the Taoist religion.

● Liu Hsin and His Theory of the Beginning of the Schools

The second historian who attempted to classify the "hundred schools" was Liu Hsin (ca. 46 B.C.-A.D. 23). He was one of the greatest scholars of his day, and, with his father Liu Hsiang, made a collation of the books in the Imperial Library. The resulting descriptive catalogue of the Imperial Library, known as the "Seven Summaries," was taken by Pan Ku (A.D. 32-92) as the basis for the chapter, *Yi Wen Chih* or "Treatise on Literature," contained in his dynastic history, the *History of the Former Han Dynasty*. In this "Treatise" we see that Liu Hsin classifies the "hundred schools" into ten main groups. Out of these, six are the same as those listed by Ssu-ma T'an. The other four are the *Tsung-Heng chia* or School of Diplomatists, *Tsa chia* or School of Eclectics, *Nung chia* or School of Agrarians, and *Hsiao-shuo chia* or School of Story Tellers. In conclusion, Liu Hsin writes:

"The various philosophers consist of ten schools, but there are only nine that need be noticed." By this statement he means to say that the School of Story Tellers lacks the importance of the other schools.

In this classification itself, Liu Hsin did not go very much further than Ssu-ma T'an had done. What was new, however, was his attempt for the first time in Chinese history to trace systematically the historical origins of the different schools.

第四个学派是名家。这一派的兴趣是分辨名实，究明它们之间的关系。

第五个学派是法家。在中文里，"法"的含义是规范或法律。这一学派源自一些政治家不赞成当时一些儒生强调政府要以德治国，他们认为，一个好的政府必须建立在一个成文法典的基础之上。

第六个学派是道德家或称道家。这一派人的形而上学和社会思想都"尚无"，"无"也就是"道"，并认为它是人天生的本性，也就是"德"。"德"是"道"在任何事物内的具体化，成为事物内含的能力，如果把它译成英文，或许译作"能力"较妥。司马谈把这一派称为道德家，后来简称为道家。在第一章里，我曾指出，道家和道教必须加以区别。

● **刘歆和他关于各家缘起的理论**

试图对"百家"进行分类的第二位历史家是刘歆（约公元前四六至公元二三年）。他是当时最著名的学者之一。他和他的父亲刘向一起，对宫廷所藏图书进行整理，分类编目。这个附有说明的分类编目名为《七略》。后来，另一位汉代历史家班固（公元三二至九二年）便用《七略》作为《汉书·艺文志》的基础。从《艺文志》中可以看出，刘歆把诸子百家分为十类，其中六家同于司马谈所列出的六家。另四家为：纵横家，这是当时的外交家；以及杂家，这是当时不拘于一家之言的折中派；还有农家和小说家。刘歆在结论中说："诸子十家，其可观者，九家而已。"意思是说，小说家不如其他九家重要。

在这个分类中，刘歆并没有比司马谈深入多少，但他系统追溯了各家的起源，这在中国历史上是第一次。

Liu Hsin's theory has been greatly elaborated by later scholars, especially by Chang Hsüeh-ch'eng (1738-1801) and the late Chang Ping-lin. In essence, it maintains that in the early Chou dynasty (1122?-256 B.C.), before the social institutions of that age disintegrated, there was "no separation between officers and teachers." In other words the officers of a certain department of the government were at the same time the transmitters of the branch of learning pertaining to that department. These officers, like the feudal lords of the day, held their posts on a hereditary basis. Hence there was then only "official learning" but no "private teaching." That is to say, nobody taught any branch of learning as a private individual. Any such teaching was carried on only by officers in their capacity as members of one or another department of the government.

According to this theory, however, when the Chou ruling house lost its power during the later centuries of the Chou dynasty, the officers of the governmental departments lost their former positions and scattered throughout the country. They then turned to the teaching of their special branches of knowledge in a private capacity. Thus they were then no longer "officers," but only private "teachers." And it was out of this separation between teachers and officers that the different schools arose.

Liu Hsin's whole analysis reads as follows: "The members of the *Ju* school had their origin in the Ministry of Education.... This school delighted in the study of the *Liu Yi* [the Six Classics or six liberal arts] and paid attention to matters concerning human-heartedness and righteousness. They regarded Yao and Shun [two ancient sage emperors supposed to have lived in the twenty-fourth and twenty-third centuries B.C.] as the ancestors of their school, and King Wen [1120?-1108? B.C. of the Chou dynasty] and King Wu [son of King Wen] as brilliant exemplars. To give authority to their teaching, they honored Chung-ni [Confucius] as an exalted teacher. Their teaching is the highest truth. 'That which is admired must be tested.' The glory of Yao and Shun, the prosperity of the dynasties of Yin and Chou, and the achievements of Chung-ni are the results discovered by testing their teaching.

"Those of the Taoist school had their origin in the official historians. By studying the historical examples of success and failure, preservation and destruction, and calamity and prosperity, from ancient to recent times, they learned how to hold what is essential and to grasp the fundamental. They guarded themselves with purity and emptiness, and with humbleness and meekness maintained themselves.... Herein lies the strong point of this school.

"Those of the *Yin-Yang* school had their origin in the official astronomers. They respectfully followed luminous heaven, and the

刘歆的理论经后来的学者，特别是章学诚（公元一七三八至一八〇一年）、章炳麟（公元一八六九至一九三六年）予以发展。刘歆的理论主要是说，在周朝（公元前一一二二〔一〇四六〕[1]至前二五六年）礼崩乐坏（即社会动乱、政制解体）之前，即周朝前期，吏与师不分。换句话说，政府各个部门的官员便负责把有关这一部门的知识传下去。这些官吏和贵族诸侯一样，是世袭的。因此，当时只有"官学"，没有"私学"。这就是说，当时没有任何私人教师，担任教师的都是政府的官吏。

按照这个理论，当后来周朝皇室失去权力时，官吏们也失去了原来的优裕地位，而散落民间，他们便以私人身份招收学生，传授他们的知识。这时，他们已经不是"官"，而成为"师"。就在教师与官吏分化的过程中，兴起了诸子百家。

刘歆这段分析的原文是：

"儒家者流，盖出于司徒之官，……游文于六经之中，留意于仁义之际，祖述尧舜，宪章文武，宗师仲尼，以重其言，于道最为高。孔子曰：'如有所誉，其有所试。'唐虞之隆，殷周之盛，仲尼之业，已试之效者也。

"道家者流，盖出于史官，历记成败存亡祸福古今之道，然后知秉要执本，清虚以自守，卑弱以自持，……此其所长也。

"阴阳家者流，盖出于羲和之官，敬顺昊天，历象日月星辰，

successive symbols of the sun and moon, the stars and constellations, and the divisions of times and seasons. Herein lies the strong point of this school.

"Those of the Legalist school had their origin in the Ministry of Justice. They emphasized strictness in rewarding and punishing, in order to support a system of correct conduct. Herein lies the strong point of this school.

"Those of the School of Names had their origin in the Ministry of Ceremonies. For the ancients, where titles and positions differed, the ceremonies accorded to them were also different. Confucius has said: 'If names be incorrect, speech will not follow its natural sequence. If speech does not follow its natural sequence, nothing can be established.' Herein lies the strong point of this school.

"Those of the Mohist school had their origin in the Guardians of the Temple. The temple was built with plain wooden rafters and thatched roofs; hence their teaching emphasized frugality. The temple was the place where the Three Elders and Five Experienced Men were honored; hence their teaching emphasized universal love. The ceremony of selecting civil officials and that of military exercises were also held in the temple; hence their teaching emphasized the preferment of virtue and ability. The temple was the place for sacrifice to ancestors and reverence to fathers; hence their teaching was to honor the spirits. They accepted the traditional teaching of following the four seasons in one's conduct; hence their teaching was against fatalism. They accepted the traditional teaching of exhibiting filial piety throughout the world; hence they taught the doctrine of 'agreeing with the superior.' Herein lies the strong point of this school.

"Those of the Diplomatist school had their origin in the Ministry of Embassies... [They taught the art of] following general orders [in diplomacy], instead of following literal instructions. Herein lies the strength of their teaching.

"Those of the Eclectic school had their origin in the Councillors. They drew both from the Confucianists and the Mohists, and harmonized the School of Names and the Legalists. They knew that the nation had need of each of these, and saw that kingly government should not fail to unite all. Herein lies the strong point of this school.

"Those of the Agricultural school had their origin in the Ministry of Soil and Grain. They taught the art of sowing the various kinds of grain and urged people to plow and to cultivate the mulberry so that the clothing and food of the people would be sufficient.... Herein lies the strong point of this school.

"Those of the School of Story Tellers had their origin in the Petty Offices. This school was created by those who picked up the talk of streets and alleys and repeated what they heard wherever they went.... Even if in their teaching but a single word can be chosen, still there is some contribution." ("Treatise on Literature" in the *History of the Former Han Dynasty*.)

敬授民时，此其所长也。

　　"法家者流，盖出于理官，信赏必罚，以辅礼制。……此其所长也。

　　"名家者流，盖出于礼官。古者名位不同，礼亦异数。孔子曰：'必也正名乎！名不正则言不顺，言不顺则事不成。'此其所长也。

　　"墨家者流，盖出于清庙之守。茅屋采椽，是以贵俭；养三老五更，是以兼爱；选士大射，是以上贤；宗祀严父，是以右鬼；顺四时而行，是以非命；以孝视天下，是以尚同：此其所长也。

　　"纵横家者流，盖出于行人之官。孔子曰：'诵《诗》三百，使于四方，不能专对，虽多亦奚以为？'又曰：'使乎，使乎！'言其当权事制宜，受命而不受辞，此其所长也。

　　"杂家者流，盖出于议官。兼儒、墨，合名、法，知国体之有此，见王治之无不贯，此其所长也。

　　"农家者流，盖出于农稷之官。播百谷，劝耕桑，以足衣食，……此其所长也。

　　"小说家者流，盖出于稗官。街谈巷语，道听涂说者之所造也。……如或一言可采，此亦刍荛狂夫之议也。"（《汉书·艺文志》）

This is what Liu Hsin says about the historical origin of the ten schools. His interpretation of the significance of the schools is inadequate, and his attribution of certain of them to certain "Ministries" is in some cases arbitrary. For instance, in describing the teaching of the Taoists, he touches only on the ideas of Lao Tzu, and omits those of Chuang Tzu altogether. Moreover, there appears to be no similarity between the teaching of the School of Names and the functions of the Ministry of Ceremonies, save that both emphasized the making of distinctions.

- **A Revision of Liu Hsin's Theory**

Yet though the details of Liu Hsin's theory may be wrong, his attempt to trace the origin of the schools to certain political and social circumstances certainly represents a right point of view. I have quoted him at length because his description of the various schools is itself a classic in Chinese historiography.

The study of Chinese history has made great progress in China in recent times, especially during the few years just before the Japanese invasion of 1937. In the light of recent research, therefore, I have formed a theory of my own in regard to the origin of the philosophic schools. In spirit this theory agrees with that of Liu Hsin, but it must be expressed in a different way. This means that things have to be seen from a new angle.

Let us imagine what China looked like politically and socially in, say, the tenth century B.C. At the top of the political and social structure, there was the King of the Chou royal house, who was the "common lord" of all the different states. Under him were hundreds of states, each owned and governed by its Princes. Some of them were established by the founders of the Chou dynasty, who had allotted the newly conquered territory as feudal fiefs to their relatives. Others were ruled by the former rivals of the Chou house, who now, however, acknowledged the King of Chou as their "common lord."

Within each state, under the Prince, the land was again divided into many fiefs, each with its own feudal lord, who were relatives of the Prince. At that time, political power and economic control were one and the same. Those who had the land were the political and economic masters of it, and of the people who lived on it. They were the *chün tzu*, a term which literally means "sons of the Princes," but which was used as a common designation of the class of the feudal lords.

以上是刘歆关于十家来源的陈述。他对于各家意义的阐述并不充分，对有些流派所由来的官职，也有任意牵强之处，例如：关于道家，他只说到老子的思想，对庄子竟全未涉及。尤其是说到名家时，没有注意到它的主张与礼官职司并无相近之处，只不过他们都注意各种名分的区别。

● 对刘歆理论的修正

刘歆理论的某些细节虽可能有错误，但他从政治和社会环境去探求各家的由来，无疑是一种正确的观点。上面较多地引述了他的见解，因为他对各家的描述已成为中国史料学在这方面的一种经典式见解。

当代以来，尤其是一九三七年抗日战争前几年，中国史学的研究有了长足的进步。根据这些研究成果，我对诸子百家的起源形成了自己的见解。我的理论在精神上和刘歆是一致的，但需要换一种方式来说明，这就是说，对这问题要用一个新的角度来考察。

让我们来想象一下，公元前十世纪中国的政治和社会是什么样子。在政治社会结构顶端的是国君和周王室，后者是列国的"共主"。在周王室下面是数以百计的小国，分别由这些小国的国君统治。其中有些是周王朝开国时所封给皇族贵胄的，还有一些是由原与周王室争霸的诸侯所统治，这些诸侯后来尊周为"共主"，因而受册封的。

在每一个小国里，国君又把国土分为若干采邑，封给他的家族成员，使这些家族成员成为诸侯。当时的政治权力和经济权力是不分的。拥有采邑的诸侯，既是土地的领主，成为经济的主人，又是采邑百姓的主人。他们被称为"君子"，意思是"国君之子"，这也成为封建诸侯的共同名称。

The other social class was that of the *hsiao jen*, meaning small men, or *shu min*, meaning common people or the mass. These were the serfs of the feudal lords, who cultivated the land for the *chün tzu* in time of peace, and fought for them in time of war.

The aristocrats were not only the political rulers and landlords, but also the only persons who had a chance to receive an education. Thus the houses of the feudal lords were not only centers of political and economic power, but also centers of learning. Attached to them were officers who possessed specialized knowledge along various lines. But the common people, for their part, had no chance to become educated, so that among them there were no men of learning. This is the fact behind Liu Hsin's theory that in the early Chou dynasty "there was no separation between officers and teachers."

This feudal system was formally abolished by the First Emperor of the Ch'in dynasty in 221 B.C. But hundreds of years before that, the system had already begun to disintegrate, whereas thousands of years later, economic remnants of feudalism still remained in the form of the power of the landlord class.

Historians of modern time are still not agreed as to what were the causes of the disintegration of the feudal system. Nor is it within the scope of this chapter to discuss these causes. For the present purpose, it is sufficient to say that in Chinese history the period between the seventh and third centuries B.C. was one of great social and political transformation and change.

We are not sure just when the disintegration of the feudal system began. Already as early as the seventh century B.C. there were aristocrats who through the wars of the time, or for other reasons, lost their lands and titles, and thus fell to the level of the common people. There were also common people who through skill or favoritism became high officials of the state. This illustrates the real significance of the disintegration of the Chou dynasty. It was not only the disintegration of the political power of a particular royal house, but—and this is more important—

of an entire social system.

With this disintegration, the former official representatives of the various branches of learning became scattered among the common people. They had either been actual nobles themselves, or had been specialists holding hereditary offices in the service of the aristocratic ruling families. This is the significance of a quotation made by Liu Hsin from Confucius in the course of the same "Treatise" partially quoted from

另一个社会阶级是"小人"或"庶民"，意思是普通百姓。他们是封建诸侯的农奴，平时为君子（诸侯）种田服劳役，战时为君子作战服兵役。

贵族不仅是政治统治者、地主，而且是唯一有机会受教育的阶级。因此，诸侯的家宅不仅是政治和经济权力的中心，还是文化的中心：各种各样有专长、有某项知识的人，都要投靠诸侯，指望为诸侯所用。至于普通百姓，既没有受教育的机会，自然也没有文化知识，因此在他们中间也没有出现什么学者。这就是刘歆所说西周时期"吏师不分"的历史背景。

中国的这种封建制度到公元前二二一年秦朝建立后被废除。在它被正式废除前几百年间，这种制度已经逐渐瓦解，而两千年后，这种封建制度的残余，还保留在地主阶级的权势之中。

现代的历史学家对于中国封建制度何以瓦解的原因，迄今没有一致意见。这里由于篇幅所限，也不可能探讨这些原因，但我们只要记住一点就够了，即公元前七世纪到前三世纪——春秋战国时期——是中国社会政治大转变的时期。

中国早期的政治封建制度，究竟几时开始瓦解，现在还难以断定。但可以说，公元前七世纪时，已经有贵族由于战争或其他原因，失去了土地和封号，降为庶民。另一方面，也有庶民，由于技有专长或其他原因，获得诸侯的宠信，成为高官。这是周朝礼崩乐坏的真正意义，不仅周室的政治权力瓦解了，更重要的是，整个社会制度瓦解了。

在社会政治瓦解过程之中，各种知识的官方代表散落民间。这些人可能自己就是贵族，或者是以一技之长服侍君王诸侯、获得世袭官职的官吏。在上面援引的刘歆的《艺文志》中，他还援引了孔子

above: "When ceremonies become lost [at the court], it is necessary to search for them in the countryside."

Thus when these former nobles or officials scattered throughout the country, they maintained a livelihood by carrying on, in a private capacity, their specialized abilities or skills. Those of them who expressed their ideas to other private individuals became professional "teachers," and thus there arose the separation between the teacher and the officer.

The word "school" in this chapter is a translation of the Chinese word *chia*, which at the same time is used to denote a family or home. Hence it suggests something personal or private. There could be no *chia* of thought before there were persons who taught their own ideas in a private capacity.

Likewise there were different kinds of *chia* because these teachers were specialists in varying branches of learning and of the arts. Thus there were some who were specialists in the teaching of the classics and the practicing of ceremonies and music. These were known as the *ju* or literati. There were also specialists in the art of war. These were the *hsieh* or knights. There were specialists in the art of speaking, who were known as the *pien-che* or debaters. There were specialists in magic, divination, astrology, and numerology, who were known as the *fang-shih*, or practitioners of occult arts. There were also the practical politicians who could act as private advisers to the feudal rulers, and who were known as *fa-shu chih shih* or "men of methods." And finally, there were some men who possessed learning and talent, but who were so embittered by the political disorders of their time that they retired from human society into the world of nature. These were known as the *yin-che* or hermits or recluses.

According to my theory, it is from these six different kinds of people that the six schools of thought as listed by Ssu-ma T'an originated. Paraphrasing Liu Hsin, therefore, I would say:

Members of the *Ju* school had their origin in the literati.

Members of the Mohist school had their origin in the knights.

Members of the Taoist school had their origin in the hermits.

Members of the School of Names had their origin in the debaters.

Members of the *Yin-Yang* school had their origin in the practitioners of occult arts.

Members of the Legalist school had their origin in the "men of methods."

The explanations of these statements will be found in the chapters that follow.

在《论语》中所说的一句话：“礼失而求诸野”，也就是这个意思。

就是这样，先前的贵族官吏，散落民间后，凭他们的专门知识或技能，开馆招收生徒，以维持生计。这些传授知识、发挥议论的私人教师，就成为“师”。这是“师”与“吏”分离的开始。

在中文里，“家”首先是指家庭或住家，它表明是个人的或私人的事情。在有教师以私人身份讲学、发表个人的意见之前，谈不到有思想家。

既然这些教师各有自己的专长，又是各人发挥自己的思想见解，于是有些教师以讲授经书、礼乐见长，他们被称为“儒”或“士”；还有些教师精通兵法或武艺，他们被称为“侠”；还有些教师擅长辩论，被称为“辩者”；另有一些人以巫医、星相、占卜、术数见长，他们的知识被称为“方术”，这些人被称为“方士”；还有一些人凭对政治的实际知识，献纵横捭阖之策，成为诸侯王公的顾问或官员，被称为“法术之士”；最后，还有些人，具有学识才干，而对当时的现实政治失望，遁入山林，被称为“隐者”。

按照我的理论，从这六种人里面，形成了司马谈所称的六家。套用刘歆的说法，我们可以说：

儒家者流，盖出于文士；

墨家者流，盖出于游侠之士；

道家者流，盖出于隐者；

名家者流，盖出于辩者；

阴阳家者流，盖出于方士；

法家者流，盖出于法术之士。

以下各章将对上述见解逐一进行解释。

❹ CONFUCIUS, THE FIRST TEACHER

Confucius is the latinized name of the person who has been known in China as K'ung Tzu or Master K'ung.[1] His family name was K'ung and his personal name Ch'iu. He was born in 551 B.C. in the state of Lu, in the southern part of the present Shantung province in eastern China. His ancestors had been members of the ducal house of the state of Sung, which was descended from the royal house of Shang, the dynasty that had preceded the Chou. Because of political troubles, the family, before the birth of Confucius, had lost its noble position and migrated to Lu.

The most detailed account of Confucius' life is the biography which comprises the forty-seventh chapter of the *Shih Chi* or *Historical Records* (China's first dynastic history, completed ca. 86 B.C.). From this we learn that Confucius was poor in his youth, but entered the government of Lu and by the time he was fifty had reached high official rank. As a result of political intrigue, however, he was soon forced to resign his post and go into exile. For the next thirteen years he traveled from one state to another, always hoping to find an opportunity to realize his ideal of political and social reform. Nowhere, however, did he succeed, and finally as an old man he returned to Lu, where he died three years later in 479 B.C.

• Confucius and the Six Classics

In the last chapter I said that the rise of the philosophic schools began with the practice of private teaching. So far as modern scholarship can determine, Confucius was the first person in Chinese history thus to teach large numbers of students in a private capacity, by whom he was accompanied during his travels in different states. According to tradition, he had several thousand students, of whom several tens became famous thinkers and scholars. The former number is undoubtedly a gross exaggeration, but there is no question that he was a very influential teacher, and what is more important and unique, China's first private teacher. His ideas are best known through the *Lun Yü* or *Confucian Analects*, a collection of his scattered sayings which was compiled by some of his disciples.

Confucius was a *ju* and the founder of the *Ju* school, which has been known in the West as the Confucian school. In the last chapter we saw how Liu Hsin wrote regarding this school that it "delighted in the study of the *Liu Yi* and emphasized matters concerning human-heartedness and righteousness." The term *Liu Yi* means the "six arts," i.e., the six liberal arts, but it is more commonly translated as the "Six Classics." These are

肆 孔子：第一位教师

孔子姓孔名丘，出生于公元前五五一年的鲁国，在今山东省南部，祖先是周朝之前的商朝后裔，商朝被周朝取代后，后裔被封宋国。由于政治动乱，孔氏家族在孔子出生前已经失去贵族身份，迁居鲁国。

孔子生平详见中国最早的史籍《史记》（约完成于公元前八六年）第四十七章《孔子世家》。从中可以知道，孔子家世贫寒，在鲁国政府任职，到五十岁时已经升到高位。由于政局混乱，被迫退职出走。此后十三年间，他周游列国，指望有机会实现他的政治、社会改革理想，却到处碰壁；晚年回到鲁国故乡，三年后逝世，时为公元前四七九年。

● 孔子与六经

在上一章里我说，中国古代的各派哲学家由于有了私学而兴起。其中，孔子是中国历史上大量招收私人学生的第一人，有些学生还陪伴他周游列国。传统的说法里，孔子有三千弟子，其中七十人成为大贤。"三千弟子"的说法显然夸大，但他无疑是一位有影响的教师，而且，更重要的是，他是创立私学的第一人。他的思想见于他的言论集《论语》，这是由他的几个学生搜集编纂而成的。

孔子是一个"儒生"，是儒家学派的创始人。上一章曾经提到，刘歆论到儒家时说："游文于六经之中，留意于仁义之际。"孔子时代的私学，讲授"六艺"，是指儒生应当学习的《诗》《书》《礼》

the *Yi* or *Book of Changes*, the *Shih* or *Book of Odes* (or *Poetry*), the *Shu* or *Book of History*, the *Li* or *Rituals* or *Rites*, the *Yüeh* or *Music* (no longer preserved as a separate work), and the *Ch'un Ch'iu* or *Spring and Autumn Annals*, a chronicle history of Confucius' state of Lu extending from 722 to 479 B.C., the year of Confucius' death. The nature of these classics is clear from their titles, with the exception of the *Book of Changes*. This work was in later times interpreted by the Confucianists as a treatise on metaphysics, but originally it was a book of divination.

Concerning the relation of Confucius with the Six Classics, there are two schools of traditional scholarship. One maintains that Confucius was the author of all these works, while the other maintains that Confucius was the author of the *Spring and Autumn Annals*, the commentator of the *Book of Changes*, the reformer of the *Rituals* and *Music*, and the editor of the *Book of History* and *Book of Odes*.

As a matter of fact, however, Confucius was neither the author, commentator, nor even editor of any of the classics. In some respects, to be sure, he was a conservative who upheld tradition. Thus in the rites and music he did try to rectify any deviations from the traditional practices or standards, and instances of so doing are reported in the *Lun Yü* or *Analects*. Judging from what is said of him in the *Analects*, however, Confucius never had any intention of writing anything himself for future generations. The writing of books in a private rather than official capacity was an as yet unheard of practice which developed only after the time of Confucius. He was China's first private teacher, but not its first private writer.

The Six Classics had existed before the time of Confucius, and they constituted the cultural legacy of the past. They had been the basis of education for the aristocrats during the early centuries of feudalism of the Chou dynasty. As feudalism began to disintegrate, however, roughly from the seventh century B.C. onward, the tutors of the aristocrats, or even some of the aristocrats themselves—men who had lost their positions and titles but were well versed in the Classics—began to scatter among the people. They made their living, as we have seen in the last chapter, by teaching the Classics or by acting as skilled "assistants," well versed in the rituals, on the occasion of funeral, sacrifice, wedding, and other ceremonies. This class of men was known as the *ju* or literati.

● Confucius as an Educator

Confucius, however, was more than a *ju* in the common sense of the word. It is true that in the *Analects* we find him, from one point of view, being portrayed merely as an educator. He wanted his disciples to be

《乐》以及《易》《春秋》这六门功课，它们就构成六经。其中的《诗经》《书经》《礼记》，从书名就可以知道它们的内容。另一本《乐经》现已佚失，《春秋》是鲁国编年史，记载了鲁国从公元前七二二年至前四七九年（即孔子卒年）的历史。《易经》原来是一本卜筮之书，后来儒家把它作为形而上学来看待。

关于孔子和六经的关系，学术界历来有两种意见，一派认为六经是孔子所著；另一派认为，孔子著《春秋》，编《诗经》和《书经》，评注《易经》，修订《礼记》和《乐经》。

其实，六经之中，没有一卷是孔子所著、所编、所评注或编纂。孔子在有些方面是维护传统的保守派。在礼和乐两方面，他对于背离传统的做法的确进行了纠正，在《论语》中不乏这样的记载。从《论语》中有关孔子的论述看，孔子并不是有意识地写书给后人阅读。当时，私人著述还未兴起。孔子是中国的第一位私人教师，但他并不是中国的第一位私人著述家。私人著述是在孔子之后才兴起的。

早在孔子之前，六经便已经存在了。它们是孔子所继承的文化遗产。周朝最初的几个世纪里，便以六经中的材料作为教育皇族子弟的教材。大约从公元前七世纪起，周朝的封建统治开始没落，皇族子弟的教师，以及有些皇族成员本人都散落民间，以教授经书为生，有的因谙习礼仪而成为人家婚丧嫁娶、祭祀或其他礼仪的襄礼（司仪）。这些人被称为"儒"。

● 作为教育家的孔子

孔子并不仅仅是通常意义的"儒生"。在《论语》中，我们所见的孔子的确只是一位教师。他希望经他教导的学生成为国家和

"rounded men" who would be useful to state and society, and therefore he taught them various branches of knowledge based upon the different classics. His primary function as a teacher, he felt, was to interpret to his disciples the ancient cultural heritage. That is why, in his own words as recorded in the *Analects*, he was "a transmitter and not an originator." (*Analects*, VII, 1.) But this is only one aspect of Confucius, and there is another one as well. This is that, while transmitting the traditional institutions and ideas, Confucius gave them interpretations derived from his own moral concepts. This is exemplified in his interpretation of the old custom that on the death of a parent, a son should mourn three years. Confucius commented on this: "The child cannot leave the arms of its parents until it is three years old. This is why the three years' mourning is universally observed throughout the world." (*Analects*, XVII, 21.) In other words, the son was utterly dependent upon his parents for at least the first three years of his life; hence upon their death he should mourn them for an equal length of time in order to express his gratitude. Likewise when teaching the Classics, Confucius gave them new interpretations. Thus in speaking of the *Book of Poetry*, he stressed its moral value by saying: "In the *Book of Poetry* there are three hundred poems. But the essence of them can be covered in one sentence: 'Have no depraved thoughts.'" (*Analects*, II, 2.) In this way Confucius was more than a mere transmitter, for in transmitting, he originated something new.

This spirit of originating through transmitting was perpetuated by the followers of Confucius, by whom, as the classical texts were handed down from generation to generation, countless commentaries and interpretations were written. A great portion of what in later times came to be known as the Thirteen Classics developed as commentaries in this way on the original texts.

This is what set Confucius apart from the ordinary literati of his time, and made him the founder of a new school. Because the followers of this school were at the same time scholars and specialists on the Six Classics, the school became known as the School of the Literati.

● The Rectification of Names

Besides the new interpretations which Confucius gave to the classics, he had his own ideas about the individual and society, heaven and man.

In regard to society, he held that in order to have a well-ordered one, the most important thing is to carry out what he called the rectification of names. That is, things in actual fact should be made to accord with

社会的栋梁之材，即所谓"成人"，因此，他以经书包含的各种知识教诲学生。作为教师，他认为自己的首要任务是向青年学生解释古代的文化遗产。因此，在《论语》中，孔子说他自己"述而不作"。但是，这只是孔子的一个方面；他还有另一方面，在解释古代的典制、思想时，孔子是以自己对道德的理解去诠释古代的经书。例如古礼规定，父母死，儿子要为父母服"三年之丧"，孔子解释这一点时说："子生三年，然后免于父母之怀。夫三年之丧，天下之通丧也。"（《论语·阳货》）这是说，孩子出生后，前三年离不开父母的怀抱。因此，儿子为父母守丧，也应有三年，以感父母之恩。再如讲授《诗经》的时候，他强调其中的伦理价值，说："《诗》三百，一言以蔽之，曰'思无邪'。"（《论语·为政》）这些实例都说明，孔子在讲授经书时，注入了新的东西。

孔子的弟子也仿效老师，在传授经书时注入了自己的思想见解。这样，在历代传授经书的过程中，形成了无数注解和诠释，后来形成的《十三经注疏》，其中大部分便是对六经的注疏。

这是孔子和与他同时的其他儒生不同的地方，使他成为一个学派的创始人。由于这派学者都是谙习六经的专家，因此他们被称为"儒家"。

● 正名

孔子不仅对经书予以新的解释，他对个人与社会、人与天、与其他人的关系也都有自己的见解。

关于社会，他认为，一个社会要想能够走上轨道、井然有序，首要的是"正名"。这就是说，客观存在的种种事物应当与它们名字

the implication attached to them by names. Once a disciple asked him what he would do first if he were to rule a state, whereupon Confucius replied: "The one thing needed first is the rectification of names." (*Analects*, XIII, 3.) On another occasion one of the dukes of the time asked Confucius the right principle of government, to which he answered: "Let the ruler be ruler, the minister minister, the father father, and the son son." (*Analects*, XII, 11.) In other words, every name contains certain implications which constitute the essence of that class of things to which this name applies. Such things, therefore, should agree with this ideal essence. The essence of a ruler is what the ruler ideally ought to be, or what, in Chinese, is called "the way of the ruler." If a ruler acts according to this way of the ruler, he is then truly a ruler, in fact as well as in name. There is an agreement between name and actuality. But if he does not, he is no ruler, even though he may popularly be regarded as such. Every name in the social relationships implies certain responsibilities and duties. Ruler, minister, father, and son are all the names of such social relationships, and the individuals bearing these names must fulfill their responsibilities and duties accordingly. Such is the implication of Confucius' theory of the rectification of names.

● Human-heartedness and Righteousness

With regard to the virtues of the individual, Confucius emphasized human-heartedness and righteousness, especially the former. Righteousness (*yi*) means the "oughtness" of a situation. It is a categorical imperative. Every one in society has certain things which he ought to do, and which must be done for their own sake, because they are the morally right things to do. If, however, he does them only because of other non-moral considerations, then even though he does what he ought to do, his action is no longer a righteous one. To use a word often disparaged by Confucius and later Confucianists, he is then acting for "profit." *Yi* (righteousness) and *li* (profit) are in Confucianism diametrically opposed terms. Confucius himself says: "The superior man comprehends *yi*; the small man comprehends *li*." (*Analects*, IV, 16.) Herein lies what the later Confucianists called the "distinction between *yi* and *li*," a distinction which they considered to be of the utmost importance in moral teaching.

The idea of *yi* is rather formal, but that of *jen* (human-heartedness) is

的本来含义一致起来。《论语·子路》篇记载，孔子的弟子子路问老师："卫国国君期待您去施政治国，您准备首先做什么？"孔子回答说："必也正名乎！"（一定要先正名分。）《论语·颜渊》篇还记载，一次，齐景公问政于孔子，孔子对曰："君君，臣臣，父父，子子。"（君要像君，臣要像臣，父要像父，子要像子。）换句话说，每类事物有一个共同的名字，这个名字含有一定的含义。这类事物应该做到与它们名字的含义，也就是其理想的本质相一致。一个国君的本质就是一个理想的国君应有的品质，即"为君之道"。如果一个君王按照为君之道行事，他就不仅有君的"名"（名分），也有君的"实"（实质），成为名实一致。如果一个君王空有其名，而没有君王应具的品质，即便在大众面前他是君王，其实他配不上"君"的名字。在社会关系中，每一个名字包含有一定的社会责任和义务。君、臣、父、子，在社会里，各有责任和义务，任何人有其名，就应当完成其责任和义务。这便是孔子主张"正名"的意义。

● 仁义

对于个人的品德，孔子强调仁和义，尤其是仁。义者宜也，即一个事物应有的样子。它是一种绝对的道德律。社会的每个成员必须做某些事情，这些事情本身就是目的，而不是达到其他目的的手段。如果一个人遵行某些道德，是为了不属于道德的其他考虑，即便他所做的客观上符合道德的要求，也仍然是不义。用孔子和后来的儒家常用的一个贬词来形容，这是图"利"。儒家认为"义"和"利"是截然相反的。孔子说："君子喻于义，小人喻于利。"（《论语·里仁》）后来的儒家常常强调"义利之辨"，认为这是道德学说中最重要的一点。

"义"是一种观念形式的规范，"仁"的观念则具体得多。一个人

much more concrete. The formal essence of the duties of man in society is their "oughtness," because all these duties are what he ought to do. But the material essence of these duties is "loving others," i.e., *jen* or human-heartedness. The father acts according to the way a father should act who loves his son; the son acts according to the way a son should act who loves his father. Confucius says: "Human-heartedness consists in loving others." (*Analects*, XII, 22.) The man who really loves others is one able to perform his duties in society. Hence in the *Analects* we see that Confucius sometimes uses the word *jen* not only to denote a special kind of virtue, but also to denote all the virtues combined, so that the term "man of *jen*" becomes synonymous with the man of all-round virtue. In such contexts, *jen* can be translated as "perfect virtue."

● *Chung* and *Shu*

In the *Analects* we find the passage: "When Chung Kung asked the meaning of *jen*, the master said: '... Do not do to others what you do not wish yourself....'" (XII, 2.) Again, Confucius is reported in the *Analects* as saying: "The man of *jen* is one who, desiring to sustain himself, sustains others, and desiring to develop himself, develops others. To be able from one's own self to draw a parallel for the treatment of others; that may be called the way to practise *jen*." (VI, 28.)

Thus the practice of *jen* consists in consideration for others. "Desiring to sustain oneself, one sustains others; desiring to develop oneself, one develops others." In other words: "Do to others what you wish yourself." This is the positive aspect of the practice, which was called by Confucius *chung* or "conscientiousness to others." And the negative aspect, which was called by Confucius *shu* or "altruism," is: "Do not do to others what you do not wish yourself." The practice as a whole is called the principle of *chung* and *shu*, which is "the way to practice *jen*."

This principle was known by some of the later Confucianists as the "principle of applying a measuring square." That is to say, it is a principle by which one uses oneself as a standard to regulate one's conduct. In the *Ta Hsüeh* or *Great Learning*, which is a chapter of the *Li Chi* (*Book of Rites*), a collection of treatises written by the Confucianists in the third and second centuries B.C., it is said: "Do not use what you dislike in your superiors in the employment of your inferiors. Do not use what you dislike in your inferiors in the service of your superiors. Do not use what you dislike in those who are before, to precede those who are behind. Do not use what you dislike in those who are behind, to follow those who are

在社会里行事为人，有他应循的义务，那是他应该做的。但是这些义务的本质应当是"爱人"，即"仁"。为父之道就是由爱子之心出发去对待儿子，为子之道就是由爱父之心出发去对待父亲。《论语·颜渊》篇中记载：樊迟问仁，孔子回答说："爱人。"一个人必须对别人存有仁爱之心，才能完成他的社会责任。因此，在《论语》里，孔子用"仁"这个字时，有时不是仅指一种特定的品德，而是泛指人的所有德性，这便是"仁人"一词的含义。在这场合下，"仁"的含义是"品德完美"。

● **忠恕**

《论语·颜渊》篇里记载，仲弓问仁，孔子回答说："……己所不欲，勿施于人。……"《论语·雍也》篇里还记载，孔子说："夫仁者，己欲立而立人，己欲达而达人。能近取譬，可谓仁之方也已。"

因此，仁的实践包含了为人着想。"己欲立而立人，己欲达而达人。"换句话说，"己之所欲，亦施于人。"这是"仁"的积极方面，尽己为人谓之忠。"仁"的含义并不仅是"己之所欲，亦施于人"，还有另一方面"恕"，就是"己所不欲，勿施于人"。这两方面合起来，称作"忠恕之道"，孔子认为，这就是把仁付诸实践的途径，也就是孔子所说的"仁之方"。

后来，有的儒家把忠恕之道称为"絜矩之道"，意思是说，以自己作为尺度来规范自己的行为。《礼记》中有一章《大学》，汇集了公元前三世纪到前二世纪，儒家的一些著述，其中说："所恶于上毋以使下，所恶于下毋以事上，所恶于前毋以先后，所恶于后毋以从前，

before. Do not use what you dislike on the right, to display toward the left. Do not use what you dislike on the left, to display toward the right. This is called the principle of applying a measuring square."

In the *Chung Yung* or *Doctrine of the Mean*, which is another chapter of the *Li Chi*, attributed to Tzu-ssu, the grandson of Confucius, it is said: "*Chung* and *shu* are not far from the Way. What you do not like done to yourself, do not do to others.... Serve your father as you would require your son to serve you.... Serve your ruler as you would require your subordinate to serve you.... Serve your elder brother as you would require your younger brother to serve you.... Set the example in behaving to your friends as you would require them to behave to you...."

The illustration given in the *Great Learning* emphasizes the negative aspect of the principle of *chung* and *shu*; that in the *Doctrine of the Mean* emphasizes its positive aspect. In each case the "measuring square" for determining conduct is in one's self and not in other things.

The principle of *chung* and *shu* is at the same time the principle of *jen*, so that the practice of *chung* and *shu* means the practice of *jen*. And this practice leads to the carrying out of one's responsibilities and duties in society, in which is comprised the quality of *yi* or righteousness. Hence the principle of *chung* and *shu* becomes the alpha and omega of one's moral life. In the *Analects* we find the passage: "The master said: 'Shen [the personal name of Tseng Tzu, one of his disciples], all my teachings are linked together by one principle.' 'Quite so,' replied Tseng Tzu. When the master had left the room, the disciples asked: 'What did he mean?' Tseng Tzu replied: 'Our master's teaching consists of the principle of *chung* and *shu*, and that is all.'" (IV, 15.)

Everyone has within himself the "measuring square" for conduct, and can use it at any time. So simple as this is the method of practising *jen*, so that Confucius said: "Is *jen* indeed far off? I crave for *jen*, and lo! *jen* is at hand!" (*Analects*, VII, 29.)

Knowing *Ming*

From the idea of righteousness, the Confucianists derived the idea of "doing for nothing." One does what one ought to do, simply because it is morally right to do it, and not for any consideration external to this moral compulsion. In the *Analects*, we are told that Confucius was ridiculed by a certain recluse as "one who knows that he cannot succeed, yet keeps on

所恶于右毋以交于左，所恶于左毋以交于右，此之谓絜矩之道。"

《礼记》中还有一章《中庸》，传说是孔子的孙子子思所作。其中第十三节说："忠恕违道不远，施诸己而不愿，亦勿施于人。……所求乎子，以事父……所求乎臣，以事君……所求乎弟，以事兄……所求乎朋友，先施之……"

上述《大学》的段落着重讲的是一个人本着"忠"和"恕"的原则做人时，怎样由人及己，懂得所不当做的方面；引自《中庸》的段落着重讲的则是一个人本着"忠"和"恕"的原则做人时，推己及人，怎样主动去做。无论是哪种情况，用以衡量自己行为的准则，都出乎自己，而不在于别人。

"忠"和"恕"的做人原则也就是"仁"的原则。因此，一个人按"忠""恕"行事为人，也就是"仁"的实践。这种实践引导人去完成对社会的责任和义务，其中就包含了"义"这种为人的品质。因此，"忠"和"恕"乃是人的道德生活的开头，也是它的完成。《论语》中，孔子说："'参乎！吾道一以贯之。'曾子曰：'唯。'子出。门人问曰：'何谓也？'曾子曰：'夫子之道，忠恕而已矣。'"（《论语·里仁》）

每人内心都有衡量行为的一把尺（絜矩），随时都在使用它来衡量别人和自己。实践"仁"的方法就是这样简单。因此孔子说："仁远乎哉？我欲仁，斯仁至矣。"（《论语·述而》）

知命

儒家从"义"又发展出"为而无所求"的思想。人做自己所当做的，因为这是道德本身的要求，而不是由于道德要求之外的任何考虑。在《论语·宪问》篇里，一位隐士讥讽孔子说他是"知其不可

trying to do it." (XIV, 41.) We also read that another recluse was told by a disciple of Confucius: "The reason why the superior man tries to go into politics, is because he holds this to be right, even though he is well aware that his principle cannot prevail." (XVIII, 7)

As we shall see, the Taoists taught the theory of "*doing* nothing," whereas the Confucianists taught that of "doing *for* nothing." A man cannot do nothing, according to Confucianism, because for every man there is something which he ought to do. Nevertheless, what he does is "for nothing," because the value of doing what he ought to do lies in the doing itself, and not in the external result.

Confucius' own life is certainly a good example of this teaching. Living in an age of great social and political disorder, he tried his best to reform the world. He traveled everywhere and, like Socrates, talked to everybody. Although his efforts were in vain, he was never disappointed. He knew that he could not succeed, but kept on trying.

About himself Confucius said: "If my principles are to prevail in the world, it is *Ming*. If they are to fall to the ground, it is also *Ming*." (*Analects*, XIV, 38.) He tried his best, but the issue he left to *Ming*. *Ming* is often translated as Fate, Destiny or Decree. To Confucius, it meant the Decree of Heaven or Will of Heaven; in other words, it was conceived of as a purposeful force. In later Confucianism, however, *Ming* simply means the total existent conditions and forces of the whole universe. For the external success of our activity, the cooperation of these conditions is always needed. But this cooperation is wholly beyond our control. Hence the best thing for us to do is simply to try to carry out what we know we ought to carry out, without caring whether in the process we succeed or fail. To act in this way is "to know *Ming*." To know *Ming* is an important requirement for being a superior man in the Confucian sense of the term, so that Confucius said: "He who does not know *Ming* cannot be a superior man." (*Analects*, XX, 2.)

Thus to know *Ming* means to acknowledge the inevitability of the world as it exists, and so to disregard one's external success or failure. If we can act in this way, we can, in a sense, never fail. For if we do our duty, that duty through our very act is morally done, regardless of the external success or failure of our action.

而为之者"。《论语·微子》篇中，子路告诉另一位隐士老人说："君子之仕也，行其义也。道之不行，已知之矣。"

后面将会说到，道家主张"无为"，儒家则教导"为而无所求"。在儒家看来，一个人不可能什么事都不做，因为每人都有应当去做的事情。但他做这些事情时，并不是为了其他的什么目的，一个人做所当做的事情，其价值就在"做"之中，而不在于达到什么外在的结果。

孔子自己的一生就是这种主张的例证。他处身在一个社会政治动乱的时代，竭尽己力去改造世界，像苏格拉底那样周游列国，与各种各样的人交谈；虽然一切努力都没有效果，他从不气馁，明知不可能成功，却仍然坚持不懈。

《论语·宪问》篇里记载孔子论到自己时说："道之将行也与，命也；道之将废也与，命也。"他尽了己力之所及，而把事情的成败交付给命。"命"字通常译作"命数"或"命运"或"天意"，就孔子来说，这个字的含义是"天命"或"天意"。换句话说，这是朝着一定目标前去的一股力量。到了后期儒家，"命"的含义是宇宙间一切存在的条件和一切在运动的力量。我们从事各种活动，其外表成功，都有赖于各种外部条件的配合。但是，外部条件是否配合，完全不是人力所能控制的。因此，人所能做的只是竭尽己力，成败在所不计。这种人生态度就是"知命"。按照孔子的看法，"知命"是作为君子的一个重要条件，因此他说："不知命，无以为君子也。"（《论语·尧曰》）

这就是说，要认识世界存在的必然性，这就是"知命"，就是个人对外在的成败利钝在所不计。如果这样行为为人，在某种意义上说，我们就永不失败。这是说，如果我们做所当做的，遵行了自己的义务，这义务在道德上便已完成，而不在于从外表看，它是否得到了成功，或遭到了失败。

As a result, we always shall be free from anxiety as to success or fear as to failure, and so shall be happy. This is why Confucius said: "The wise are free from doubts; the virtuous from anxiety; the brave from fear." (*Analects*, IX, 28.) Or again: "The superior man is always happy; the small man sad." (VII, 36.)

● Confucius' Spiritual Development

In the Taoist work, the *Chuang-tzu*, we see that the Taoists often ridiculed Confucius as one who confined himself to the morality of human-heartedness and righteousness, thus being conscious only of moral values, and not super-moral value. Superficially they were right, but actually they were wrong. Thus speaking about his own spiritual development, Confucius said: "At fifteen I set my heart on learning. At thirty I could stand. At forty I had no doubts. At fifty I knew the Decree of Heaven. At sixty I was already obedient [to this Decree]. At seventy I could follow the desires of my mind without overstepping the boundaries [of what is right]." (*Analects*, II, 4)

The "learning" which Confucius here refers to is not what we now would call learning. In the *Analects*, Confucius said: "Set your heart on the *Tao*." (VII, 6.) And again: "To hear the *Tao* in the morning and then die at night, that would be all right." (IV, 9.) Here *Tao* means the Way or Truth. It was this *Tao* which Confucius at fifteen set his heart upon learning. What we now call learning means the increase of our knowledge, but the *Tao* is that whereby we can elevate our mind.

Confucius also said: "Take your stand in the *li* [rituals, ceremonies, proper conduct]." (*Analects*, VIII, 8.) Again he said: "Not to know the *li* is to have no means of standing." (XX, 3.) Thus when Confucius says that at thirty he could "stand," he means that he then understood the *li* and so could practice proper conduct.

His statement that at forty he had no doubts means that he had then become a wise man. For, as quoted before, "The wise are free from doubts."

Up to this time of his life Confucius was perhaps conscious only of moral values. But at the age of fifty and sixty, he knew the Decree of Heaven and was obedient to it. In other words, he was then also conscious of super-moral values. Confucius in this respect was like Socrates. Socrates thought that he had been appointed by a divine order to awaken the Greeks, and Confucius had a similar consciousness of

能够这样做，人就不必拳拳于个人得失，也不怕失败，就能保持快乐。这就是孔子何以说："知者不惑，仁者不忧，勇者不惧。"（《论语·子罕》）也是因此，他又说："君子坦荡荡，小人长戚戚。"（《论语·述而》）

● 孔子的心灵修养

在道家著作《庄子》一书中，我们看到道家往往嘲笑孔子的眼光只限于仁义道德，只知道德价值，却不知道还有超越道德的价值。从表面看，他们所说是对的，而从深一层看，他们其实是错的。孔子对自己的灵性修养曾说："吾十有五而志于学，三十而立，四十而不惑，五十而知天命，六十而耳顺，七十而从心所欲，不逾矩。"（《论语·为政》）

孔子所说的"学"，不是我们今天所说的"学"。在《论语·述而》篇中，孔子说："志于道。"在《论语·里仁》篇中，孔子又说："朝闻道，夕死可矣。"这里所说的"道"，含义是"道路"或"真理"。孔子说他自己"十有五而志于学"，是说懂得了立志学道。现在人们所说的"学"，是指"增长知识"，而"道"则是指悟性的提高。

孔子还说："立于礼。"（包括礼仪和举止得当。）（《论语·泰伯》）他又说："不知礼无以立也。"（《论语·尧曰》）这就是孔子所说"三十而立"的含义，意思是他到三十岁时，懂得了行事为人的准则。

他说四十而不惑，从前引《论语·子罕》篇"知者不惑"可以知道，他回顾自己，到四十岁时，懂得了人生的智慧。

直到这时候，孔子所认识到的大概只是道德价值。但是自此以后，到五十、六十岁，他懂得了天命和顺命。换句话说，这时他进一步懂得了在道德以上的价值。在这方面，孔子和苏格拉底有点相像。苏格拉底觉得自己是承受了天命来唤醒希腊人，孔子也觉得自己

a divine mission. For example, when he was threatened with physical violence at a place called K'uang, he said: "If Heaven had wished to let civilization perish, later generations (like myself) would not have been permitted to participate in it. But since Heaven has not wished to let civilization perish, what can the people of K'uang do to me?" (*Analects*, IX, 5.) One of his contemporaries also said: "The world for long has been without order. But now Heaven is going to use the Master as an arousing tocsin." (*Analects*, III, 24.) Thus Confucius in doing what he did, was convinced that he was following the Decree of Heaven and was supported by Heaven; he was conscious of values higher than moral ones.

The super-moral value experienced by Confucius, however, was, as we shall see, not quite the same as that experienced by the Taoists. For the latter abandoned entirely the idea of an intelligent and purposeful Heaven, and sought instead for mystical union with an undifferentiated whole. The super-moral value which they knew and experienced, therefore, was freer from the ordinary concepts of the human relationships.

At seventy, as has been told above, Confucius allowed his mind to follow whatever it desired, yet everything he did was naturally right of itself. His actions no longer needed a conscious guide. He was acting without effort. This represents the last stage in the development of the sage.

● Confucius' Position in Chinese History

Confucius is probably better known in the West than any other single Chinese. Yet in China itself, though always famous, his place in history has changed considerably from one period to another. Historically speaking he was primarily *a* teacher, that is, only one teacher among many. But after his death, he gradually came to be considered as *the* teacher, superior to all others. And in the second century B.C. he was elevated to an even higher plane. According to many Confucianists of that time, Confucius had actually been appointed by Heaven to begin a new dynasty that would follow that of Chou. Though in actual fact without a crown or a government, he had ideally speaking become a king who ruled the whole empire. How this apparent contradiction had happened, these Confucianists said, could be found out by studying the esoteric meaning supposedly contained in the *Spring and Autumn Annals*. This

承受了一种神圣的呼召。例如在《论语·子罕》篇里记载，孔子及随从弟子曾在匡这个地方遭到拘禁。孔子说："天之将丧斯文也，后死者不得与于斯文也；天之未丧斯文也，匡人其如予何！"（意思是：如果天意是要让文明灭亡，后人如我者流就不会有参与文明的机会，既然上天没有要让文明毁灭的意思，匡人就阻挡不住我的工作。）《论语·八佾》篇还记载孔子率弟子过仪这个地方，会晤了当地小官，这位官员见到孔子之后说："天下之无道也久矣，天将以夫子为木铎。"（意思是：天下无道已久，上天是要把夫子当作唤醒大众的警钟吧。）由此我们可以看到，孔子在做他的工作时，意识到他是在遵行天命，受到上天的呵护，换句话说，他意识到那比道德更高的价值。

孔子所意识到的比道德更高的价值，和道家所意识到的有所不同。道家并不承认一个有智慧、有目标的上天，他们所寻求的是与浑元真体的神秘结合。因此，道家所主张和经验的超道德价值比通常所说人际关系中的价值观念更为超脱世俗。

如我们在上面所谈到的，孔子到七十岁时，可以从心所欲，而所做的都合于规范，他的行为不再需要意识去引导，可以顺乎自然。这表明了圣人在心灵修养上最后阶段的造诣。

● 孔子在中国历史上的地位

在西方，人们最熟悉的一个中国人大概就是孔子。在中国，孔子虽然家喻户晓，但是他在历史上的地位却经历了巨大的变化。就历史说，他生前主要是一位教师，是许多教师中的一位；但在去世之后，渐渐被尊为"唯一"的夫子，地位凌驾于所有其他教师之上。到公元前二世纪（西汉）时，司马迁尊孔子为"至圣"，他的地位又被提高了。当时有些儒家甚至认为，孔子受命于天，继承周朝之后，开辟了一个新朝代，这个朝代没有皇朝，也没有帝王，但孔子成为无冕的"素王"。这个说法如何能与历史相适应呢？按照这批

was supposed by them not to be a chronicle of Confucius' native state (as it actually was), but an important political work written by Confucius to express his ethical and political ideas. Then in the first century B.C., Confucius came to be regarded as even more than a king. According to many people of that time, he was a living god among men—a divine being who knew that after his time there would someday come the Han dynasty (206 B.C.-A.D. 220), and who therefore, in the *Spring and Autumn Annals,* set forth a political ideal which would be complete enough for the men of Han to realize. This apotheosis was the climax of Confucius' glory, and in the middle of the Han dynasty Confucianism could properly be called a religion.

The time of glorification, however, did not last very long. Already beginning in the first century A.D., Confucianists of a more rationalistic type began to get the upper hand. Hence in later times Confucius was no longer regarded as a divine being, though his position as that of *the* Teacher remained high. At the very end of the nineteenth century, to be sure, there was a brief revival of the theory that Confucius had been divinely appointed to be a king. Soon afterward, however, with the coming of the Chinese Republic, his reputation fell until he came to be regarded as something less than *the* Teacher, and at present most Chinese would say that he was primarily *a* teacher, and certainly a great one, but far from being the only teacher.

Confucius, however, was already recognized in his own day as a man of very extensive learning. For example, one of his contemporaries said: "Great indeed is the Master K'ung! His learning is so extensive that he cannot be called by a single name." (*Analects,* IX, 2.) From the quotations given earlier, we may see that he considered himself the inheritor and perpetuator of ancient civilization, and was considered by some of his contemporaries as such. By his work of originating through transmitting, he caused his school to reinterpret the civilization of the age before him. He upheld what he considered to be best in the old, and created a powerful tradition that was followed until very recent years, when, as in Confucius' own time, China again came face to face with tremendous economic and social change. In addition, he was China's first teacher. Hence, though historically speaking he was only *a* teacher, it is perhaps not unreasonable that in later ages he was regarded as *the* teacher.

儒家学者的意见，早在《春秋》中便已预示了这一点。他们认为，孔子修《春秋》的本意并不是为鲁国修史，而是代王者立法，有王者之道，而无王者之位，故称素王。到公元前一世纪时，孔子被推崇到比君王更高的地位。当时不少人认为，孔子是一位人间的神祇，他预知在他以后会有一个汉朝，而预先悬示一个政治理念，使汉朝有所遵循，把它付诸实现。这种说法盛行于西汉末年，这时的孔子位极尊荣，儒家俨然成了一种宗教。

这个时期并不太长。东汉初年（公元一世纪初），儒家中崇尚理性的一派渐占上风。自此以后，孔子在人们心目中，不再是一位神祇，但他还是人们心目中最崇高的"夫子"。直到十九世纪末，认为孔子受命于天，应当成为帝王的理论又曾盛行一时。此后不久，清朝被推翻，民国成立。孔子在人们心目中的地位下降到人师之下。现在，多数中国人还是承认孔子是一位伟大的教师，但不再是唯一的夫子了。

孔子生前已是人们公认的渊博学者。《论语·子罕》篇记载，达巷党人曰："大哉孔子！博学而无所成名。"（意思是说，达巷党这地方有人说，孔子是个伟大人物，学问广博，以至很难用某一方面的专长来概括他的成就。）从前面引述中可以看到，孔子认为自己继承了古代文明，极力加以复兴，当时人们也是这样看他。他自称对古代文明"述而不作"，其实他的学派对古代文明重新诠释，取古代文明的精华，创立了一个文明传统，一直延续到晚近的时代。现在，中国又面临一个经济、社会巨大变革的时代。孔子在历史上虽然只是许多教师中的一位，但明中叶后尊崇他为"至圣先师"，可以说是不无道理的。

❺ MO TZU, THE FIRST OPPONENT OF CONFUCIUS

The next major philosopher after Confucius was Mo Tzu. His family name was Mo and his personal name was Ti. As the *Shih Chi* or *Historical Records* does not say where he came from, and in fact tells us almost nothing about his life, there has been a difference of opinion regarding his native state. Some scholars hold that he was a native of Sung (in what is today eastern Honan and western Shantung), and others that he came from Lu, the same state as Confucius. His exact dates are also uncertain, but probably he lived sometime within the years 479-381 B.C. The main source for the study of his thought is the book bearing his name, the *Mo-tzu*, which contains 53 chapters and is a collection of writings by his followers as well as by himself.

Mo Tzu was the founder of a school known after his name as the Mohist school. In ancient times his fame was as great as that of Confucius, and his teaching was no less influential. The contrast between the two men is interesting. Confucius felt a sympathetic understanding for the traditional institutions, rituals, music, and literature of the early Chou dynasty, and tried to rationalize and justify them in ethical terms; Mo Tzu, on the contrary, questioned their validity and usefulness, and tried to replace them with something that was simpler but, in his view, more useful. In short, Confucius was the rationalizer and justifier of the ancient civilization, while Mo Tzu was its critic. Confucius was a refined gentleman, while Mo Tzu was a militant preacher. A major aim of his preaching was to oppose both the traditional institutions and practices, and the theories of Confucius and the Confucianists.

● Social Background of the Mohist School

During the feudal age of the Chou dynasty, kings, princes, and feudal lords all had their military specialists. These were the hereditary warriors who constituted the backbone of the armies of that time. With the disintegration of feudalism that took place in the latter part of the Chou dynasty, however, these warrior specialists lost their positions and titles, scattered throughout the country, and made a living by offering their services to anyone who could afford to employ them. This class of people was known as the *hsieh* or *yu hsieh*, terms which can both be translated as "knights-errant." Concerning such knights-errant, the *Shih Chi* says: "Their words were always sincere and trustworthy, and their actions always quick and decisive. They were always true to what they promised,

伍 墨子：孔子的第一位反对者

　　孔子之后的一个主要哲学家是墨子。他姓墨名翟。《史记》中没有记述墨翟的身世，对他的生平几乎没有涉及。关于墨子是哪国人，历来有不同的看法。有的学者认为，墨翟是宋国（今河南东部、山东西部）人，有的学者认为，墨翟和孔子一样，同是鲁国人。他的生卒年代也同样不可考，大概生活在公元前四七九至前三八一年之间。研究墨翟思想的主要资料是《墨子》一书，其中有五十三章，是墨翟及其后学的著作汇编。

　　墨子创立了以他的姓氏命名的学派。在古代，墨子的名声和他的思想影响与孔子几乎不相上下。比较两人之间南辕北辙的不同主张十分有趣。孔子对周代早期的传统典制、礼仪、音乐、文学都抱同情理解的态度，并从伦理上予以解释，论证它们的意义。墨子则恰恰相反，质疑它们的合理性和实用性，并力求使之简化，而且照他看来更为适用。简言之，孔子对古代文明的态度是加以理性化、合理化，墨子则对古代文明持批判态度；孔子是一位文雅有修养的君子，墨子则是一位充满战斗精神的布道家。他的说教的宗旨是反对传统的典章制度及其实践，反对孔子和儒家的各种理论。

● 墨家的社会背景

　　在周代，帝王公侯都拥有自己的军事专家，这些人是世袭的武士，是当时军队中的骨干。周朝后期统治权力解体，这些军事家丧失了权力和爵位，散落全国，只求有人雇佣，得以维持生计。他们被称为"侠"或"游侠"。《史记》中称他们："其言必信，其行必果，

and without regard to their own persons, they would rush into dangers threatening others." (Ch. 124.) Such was their professional ethics. A large part of Mo Tzu's teaching was an extension of this ethics.

In Chinese history both the *ju* or literati and the *hsieh* or knights-errant originated as specialists attached to the houses of the aristocrats, and were themselves members of the upper classes. In later times the *ju* continued to come mainly from the upper or middle classes, but the *hsieh*, on the contrary, more frequently were recruited from the lower classes. In ancient times, such social amenities as rituals and music were all exclusively for the aristocrats; from the point of view of the common man, therefore, they were luxuries that had no practical utility. It was from this point of view that Mo Tzu and the Mohists criticised the traditional institutions and their rationalizers, Confucius and the Confucianists. This criticism, together with the elaboration and rationalization of the professional ethics of their own social class, that of the *hsieh*, constituted the central core of the Mohist philosophy.

There is plenty of evidence for the inference that Mo Tzu and his followers came from the *hsieh*. From the *Mo-tzu*, as well as from other contemporary sources, we know that the Mohists constituted a strictly disciplined organization capable of military action. The leader of the Mohist organization was called the *Chü Tzu*, "Great Master," and had the authority of life or death over the members of the group. We are also told that Mo Tzu was the first "Great Master" of his group, and that at least once he actually led his followers to prepare for the military defense of Sung, when that state was threatened with invasion from the neighboring state of Ch'u.

The story of this episode is interesting. It is said in the *Mo-tzu* that a noted mechanical inventor, Kung-shu Pan, then employed by the state of Ch'u, had completed the construction of a new weapon for attacking city walls. Ch'u was preparing to attack Sung with this new weapon. Hearing of this, Mo Tzu went to Ch'u to persuade its king to desist. There he and

Kung-shu Pan made a demonstration before the king of their weapons of attack and defense. Mo Tzu first untied his belt and laid out a city with it, using a small stick as a weapon. Kung-shu Pan thereupon set up nine different miniature machines of attack, but Mo Tzu nine times repulsed him. Finally, Kung-shu Pan had used up all his machines of attack, while Mo Tzu was far from being exhausted in the defense. Then Kung-shu Pan said: "I know how to defeat you, but I will not say it." To which Mo Tzu replied: "I know what it is, but I too will not say it."

已诺必诚，不爱其躯，赴士之厄困。"（《游侠列传》）这是他们的武士道德。墨学中，有一大部分便是这种武士道德的延伸。

在中国历史上，"儒"和"侠"都是依附于贵族的专门人才，他们自己也属于社会的上层。后来，儒生继续来自上层或中层阶级，侠则更多来自下层阶级。在古代，各种典章制度和礼乐都是贵族专用的，在普通百姓眼中，这些典制礼乐都是奢侈的繁文缛节，没有丝毫用处。墨子和墨家正是以此为出发点，批判传统典制和对它加以粉饰的孔子与儒家。墨家哲学的内容，主要便是这种批判和对游侠道德的辩护。

关于墨子和他的追随者来自游侠，有许多凭证。从《墨子》一书和当时的其他许多著述中都可以看到，墨家有一个严密的组织，足以进行军事行动。墨家的这种组织的首领称为"钜子"（"大师"），对本团体成员，操有生杀大权。墨子就是他的团体的第一位"钜子"。他至少曾有一次，为宋国遭受楚国入侵的威胁而组织防御。

这段故事的情节很有趣。《墨子·公输》篇里记载，当时楚国雇用了一个机械发明家公输般，发明了一种攻城的武器。楚国将使用这种武器进攻宋国。墨子得讯后，前往楚国，劝阻楚王出兵。在楚王面前，公输般演习他准备用以进攻宋国的新式武器，墨子则表演他准备用以防御楚国进攻的防御武器。墨子首先解下腰带，用以划出一座城，用小木棍标志武器。公输般采用了九种攻城机械来进攻，都被墨子的防御武器挡住了。最后，公输般的进攻武器都已用尽，而墨子的防御武器却还有余。公输般不肯认输，说："我知道怎样击败你，但是我不说。"墨子回答："我知道你想用的那个办法，我也不说！"

On being asked by the king what was meant, Mo Tzu continued: "Kung-shu Pan is thinking of murdering me. But my disciples Ch'in Ku-li and others, numbering three hundred men, are already armed with my implements of defense, waiting on the city wall of Sung for the invaders from Ch'u. Though I be murdered, you cannot exterminate them." To which the king exclaimed: "Very well! Let us not attack Sung." (Ch. 50.)

If this story is true, it would give a good example for our present world in settling disputes between two countries. A war would not need to be fought in the field. All that would be necessary would be for the scientists and engineers of the two countries to demonstrate their laboratory weapons of attacking and defense, and the war would be decided without fighting!

Regardless of whether the story is true or not, it illustrates the nature of the Mohist organization, which is also confirmed from other sources. Thus in the *Huai-nan-tzu*, a work of the second century B.C., it is stated that "the disciples of Mo Tzu were one hundred and eighty in number, all of whom he could order to enter fire or tread on sword blades, and whom even death would not cause to turn on their heels." (Ch. 20.) And in the *Mo-tzu* itself, no less than nine chapters deal with the tactics of fighting a defensive war and the techniques of building instruments for defending city walls. All of this shows that the Mohists, as originally constituted, were a group of warriors.

Mo Tzu and his followers, however, differed from the ordinary knights-errant in two respects. In the first place, the latter were men ready to engage in any fighting whatever, only provided that they were paid for their efforts or favored by the feudal lords. Mo Tzu and his followers, on the contrary, were strongly opposed to aggressive war; hence they agreed to fight only in wars that were strictly for self-defense. Secondly, the ordinary *hsieh* confined themselves wholly to their code of professional ethics. Mo Tzu, however, elaborated this professional ethics and gave it a rationalistic justification. Thus though Mo Tzu's background was that of a *hsieh*, he at the same time became the founder of a new philosophic school.

● Mo Tzu's Criticism of Confucianism

According to Mo Tzu, "the principles of the Confucianists ruin the whole world in four ways": (1) The Confucianists do not believe in the existence of God or of spirits, "with the result that God and the spirits are displeased." (2) The Confucianists insist on elaborate funerals and

楚王问他们，到底是什么意思？墨子回答说："公输般想谋害我。但是，我的弟子禽滑厘等三百人，已经用我设计的武器武装起来，在宋国城墙上等候着楚国军队的进攻。我可以被谋杀，但是楚军无法杀尽他们。"楚王听后说："如此说来，我们就放弃对宋国的进攻。"

如果这段故事属实，它对今日世界倒是一个好榜样，两个敌对国家不必在战场上厮杀，只要双方的科学家、工程师来到一起，把各自实验室里的攻击防御武器都展示出来，不需要走上战场，便可以决定胜负了。

无论这段故事是否属实，它足以说明墨家的军事性质。还可以再看其他史料如《淮南子》，这是公元前二世纪的著作，其中《泰族训》篇说："墨子服役者百八十人，皆可使赴汤蹈刃，死不旋踵。"在《墨子》书中，至少有九处论到防御战争的战术和武器。这都足以说明，墨家原来是一个武士的组织。

墨子及其追随者与当时的其他游侠有两点不同：首先，其他游侠只是雇佣兵，谁雇用，便为谁卖命；墨子和他的追随者们则反对任何侵略战争，他们只为防御性战争效劳。其次，通常的"侠"只是墨守武士的职业道德；墨子和他的追随者则对武士的职业道德进行理性化的解释。因此，他创立了一个新的哲学流派。

● 墨子对儒家的批判

墨子认为，"儒之道足以丧天下者，四政焉"：第一，儒者不相信天或鬼，结果是"天鬼不悦"；第二，儒家坚持厚葬，特别是父母

the practice of three years of mourning on the death of a parent, so that the wealth and energy of the people are thereby wasted. (3) The Confucianists lay stress on the practice of music, leading to an identical result. (4) The Confucianists believe in a predetermined fate, causing the people to be lazy and to resign themselves to this fate. (The *Mo-tzu*, ch. 48.) In another chapter entitled "Anti-Confucianism," the *Mo-tzu* also says: "Even those with long life cannot exhaust the learning required for their [Confucianist] studies. Even people with the vigor of youth cannot perform all the ceremonial duties. And even those who have amassed wealth cannot afford music. They [the Confucianists] enhance the beauty of wicked arts and lead their sovereign astray. Their doctrine cannot meet the needs of the age, nor can their learning educate the people." (Ch. 39.)

These criticisms reveal the differing social backgrounds of the Confucianists and Mohists. Already before Confucius, persons who were better educated and more sophisticated had been abandoning the belief in the existence of a personal God and of divine spirits. People of the lower classes, however, had, as always in such matters, lagged behind in this rise of skepticism, and Mo Tzu held the point of view of the lower classes. This is the significance of his first point of criticism against the Confucianists. The second and third points, too, were made from the same basis. The fourth point, however, was really irrelevant, because, though the Confucianists often spoke about *Ming* (Fate, Decree), what they meant by it was not the predetermined fate attacked by Mo Tzu. This has been pointed out in the last chapter, where we have seen that *Ming*, for the Confucianists, signified something that is beyond human control. But there are other things that remain within man's power to control if he will exert himself. Only after man has done everything he can himself, therefore, should he accept with calm and resignation what comes thereafter as inevitable. Such is what the Confucianists meant when they spoke of "knowing *Ming*."

● All-embracing Love

Mo Tzu makes no criticism of the Confucianists' central idea of *jen* (human-heartedness) and *yi* (righteousness); in the *Mo-tzu*, indeed, he speaks often of these two qualities and of the man of *jen* and man of *yi*. What he means by these terms, however, differs somewhat from the concept of them held by the Confucianists. For Mo Tzu, *jen* and *yi* signify an all-embracing love, and the man of *jen* and man of *yi* are persons who practice this all-embracing love. This concept is a central one in Mo Tzu's

去世，子女要守三年之丧，浪费了民众的财富精力；第三，儒家"盛为声乐以淫遇民"，结果只是少数贵族奢侈享受；第四，儒家主张宿命论，造成民众怠惰顺命。（见《墨子·公孟》）在《非儒》篇里，墨子还说："累寿不能尽其学，当年不能行其礼，积财不能赡其乐，繁饰邪术以营世君，盛为声乐以淫遇民，其道不可以期世，其学不可以导众。"

　　这些批评显示出儒家和墨家的不同社会背景。早在孔子之前，一些有学识、有思想的人已经开始放弃对天帝鬼神的信仰。这时，开始兴起一种怀疑主义思潮。处于社会底层的大众，通常总是落后于社会新思潮，墨子所反映的正是当时社会下层民众的观点。上面墨子批判儒家的第一点，其意义就在于此。墨子批判儒家的第二、三点，也是由这个思想基础出发的。墨子批判儒家的第四点其实并没有击中要害，因为儒家虽然经常谈到命，其含义却并不是墨子所攻击的宿命论。在上一章里已经指出了这一点，儒家所说的命，是指人力所无法控制的某种力量。而除此以外，还有一些方面是人只要努力就能控制的。因此，人对外部世界首先应当尽力而为，只有在竭尽所能之后，才沉静接受人力所无法改变的部分。这是儒家所讲的"知命"。

● 兼爱

　　墨子对孔子的中心思想——仁义——并没有提出异议。在《墨子》一书中，墨子经常提到仁义和仁人、义人，但是其含义和儒家略有不同。墨子认为，仁义都是"兼爱"的表现。"兼爱"是墨子

philosophy, and represents a logical extension of the professional ethics of the class of *hsieh* (knights-errant) from which Mo Tzu sprang. This ethics was, namely, that within their group the *hsieh* "enjoy equally and suffer equally." (This was a common saying of the *hsieh* of later times.) Taking this group concept as a basis, Mo Tzu tried to broaden it by preaching the doctrine that everyone in the world should love everyone else equally and without discrimination.

In the *Mo-tzu*, there are three chapters devoted to the subject of all-embracing love. In them, Mo Tzu first makes a distinction between what he calls the principles of "discrimination" and "all-embracingness." The man who holds to the principle of discrimination says: It is absurd for me to care for friends as much as I would for myself, and to look after their parents as I would my own. As a result, such a man does not do very much for his friends. But the man who holds to the principle of all-embracingness says, on the contrary: I must care for my friends as much as I do for myself, and for their parents as I would my own. As a result, he does everything he can for his friends. Having made this distinction, Mo Tzu then asks the question: Which of these two principles is the right one?

Mo Tzu thereupon uses his "tests of judgment" to determine the right and wrong of these principles. According to him, every principle must be examined by three tests, namely: "Its basis, its verifiability, and its applicability." A sound and right principle "should be based on the Will of Heaven and of the spirits and on the deeds of the ancient sage-kings." Then "it is to be verified by the senses of hearing and sight of the common people." And finally, "it is to be applied by adopting it in government and observing whether it is beneficial to the country and the people." (*Mo-tzu*, ch. 35.) Of these three tests, the last is the most important. "Being beneficial to the country and the people" is the standard by which Mo Tzu determines all values.

This same standard is the chief one used by Mo Tzu to prove the desirability of all-embracing love. In the third of three chapters, all of which are titled "All-embracing Love," he argues:

"The task of the human-hearted man is to procure benefits for the world and to eliminate its calamities. Now among all the current calamities of the world, which are the greatest? I say that attacks on small states by large ones, disturbances of small houses by large ones, oppression of the weak by the strong, misuse of the few by the many, deception of the simple by the cunning, and disdain toward the humble by the honored: these are the misfortunes of the world.... When we come

哲学的中心思想，它是墨子所由出身的游侠们的职业道德的自然延伸。他们的职业道德是，游侠之间，"有福同享，有祸同当"（这是后来侠客们常说的话）。墨子以这种思想为基础，把它扩大推广，主张天下所有的人都应当不分高低，彼此相爱。

在《墨子》书中，有三章都以兼爱为主旨。其中，墨子首先区分他所说的"兼"与"别"。坚持爱有"区分"的人认为，要我把朋友看成如同自己一样，把朋友的父母看成如同自己的父母一样，是荒谬的。结果，这样的人对朋友十分冷漠。主张兼爱的人则恰恰相反，认为我应当像关心自己那样关心朋友和朋友的父母。结果是，他为朋友竭尽己力。墨子在例举上述两种情况后问道，这两种原则，谁是谁非？

为了衡量"兼"与"别"以及各种原则孰是孰非，墨子提出了衡量是非的"三表"，即三项准则：第一，人做事是否根据天和神灵的意志，与古代圣王的事业一致，这是事物之本；其次，所做的事应当是百姓能够耳闻目睹、加以验证的事，这是事物之原（验证）；第三，由政府付诸实施，看是否对国家、百姓有利，即所谓事物之用。（见《墨子·非命》上篇、中篇）三表之中，衡量价值的标准是"对国家和民众有利"。

这也是墨子据以论证"兼爱"的主要原则。在《兼爱》下篇里，墨子论证说：

"仁人之事者，必务求兴天下之利，除天下之害。然当今之时，天下之害孰为大？曰：若大国之攻小国也，大家之乱小家也，强之劫弱，众之暴寡，诈之谋愚，贵之傲贱，此天下之害也。……姑尝

to think about the causes of all these calamities, how have they arisen? Have they arisen out of love of others and benefiting others? We must reply that it is not so. Rather we should say that they have arisen out of hate of others and injuring others. If we classify those in the world who hate others and injure others, shall we call them 'discriminating' or 'all-embracing'? We must say that they are 'discriminating'. So, then, is not 'mutual discrimination' the cause of the major calamities of the world? Therefore the principle of 'discrimination' is wrong.

"Whoever criticizes others must have something to substitute for what he criticizes. Therefore I say: 'Substitute all-embracingness for discrimination.' What is the reason why all-embracingness can be substituted for discrimination? The answer is that when everyone regards the states of others as he regards his own, who will attack these other states? Others will be regarded like the self. When everyone regards the cities of others as he regards his own, who will seize these other cities? Others will be regarded like the self. When everyone regards the houses of others as he regards his own, who will disturb these other houses? Others will be regarded like the self.

"Now, when states and cities do not attack and seize one another, and when clans and individuals do not disturb and harm one another, is this a calamity or a benefit to the world? We must say it is a benefit. When we come to consider the origin of the various benefits, how have they arisen? Have they arisen out of hate of others and injuring others? We must say not so. We should say that they have arisen out of love of others and benefiting others. If we classify those in the world who love others and benefit others, shall we call them 'discriminating' or 'all-embracing'? We must say that they are 'all-embracing'. Then is it not the case that 'mutual all-embracingness' is the cause of the major benefit of the world? Therefore I say that the principle of 'all-embracingness' is right." (*Mo-tzu*, ch. 16.)

Thus, using a utilitarianistic argument, Mo Tzu proves the principle of all-embracing love to be absolutely right. The human-hearted man whose task it is to procure benefits for the world and eliminate its calamities, must establish all-embracing love as the standard of action both for himself and for all others in the world. When everyone in the world acts according to this standard, "then attentive ears and keen eyes will respond to serve one another, limbs will be strengthened to work for one another, and those who know the proper principle will untiringly instruct others. Thus the aged and widowers will have support and nourishment with which to round out their old age, and the young and weak and orphans will have a place of support in which to grow up. When all-embracing love is adopted as the standard, such are the consequent benefits."(*Ibid.*) This, then, is Mo Tzu's ideal world, which can be created only through the practice of all-embracing love.

　　本原若众害之所自生，此胡自生？此自爱人、利人生与？即必曰非然也，必曰从恶人、贼人生。分名乎天下恶人而贼人者，兼与？别与？即必曰别也。然即之交别者，果生天下之大害者与？是故别非也。

　　"非人者，必有以易之。……是故子墨子曰：兼以易别。然即兼之可以易别之故何也？曰：藉为人之国若为其国，夫谁独举其国以攻人之国者哉？为彼者犹为己也。为人之都若为其都，夫谁独举其都以伐人之都者哉？为彼犹为己也。为人之家若为其家，夫谁独举其家以乱人之家者哉？为彼犹为己也。

　　"然即国都不相攻伐，人家不相乱贼，此天下之害与？天下之利与？即必曰天下之利也。姑尝本原若众利之所自生，此胡自生？此自恶人、贼人生与？即必曰非然也，必曰从爱人、利人生。分名乎天下爱人而利人者，别与？兼与？即必曰兼也。然即之交兼者，果生天下之大利者与？是故子墨子曰：兼是也。"

　　这样，墨子以功利主义的论辩证明"兼爱"的原则是完全正确的，仁人以利世除害为宗旨，就必须以"兼爱"作为处世为人的标准。如果天下人都能这样做，"以兼为正。是以聪耳明目相为视听乎，是以股肱毕强相为动宰乎，而有道肆相教诲。是以老而无妻子者，有所侍养以终其寿；幼弱孤童之无父母者，有所放依以长其身。今唯毋以兼为正，即若其利也。"（同上）这是墨子的理想世界。他认为，唯有实行兼爱，才能创造出这个理想世界。

● **The Will of God and Existence of Spirits**

There remains, however, a basic question: How to persuade people thus to love one another? One may tell them, as was said above, that the practice of all-embracing love is the only way to benefit the world and that every human-hearted man is one who practices all-embracing love. Yet people may still ask: Why should I personally act to benefit the world and why should I be a human-hearted man? One may then argue further that if the world as a whole is benefited, this means benefit for every individual in the world as well. Or as Mo Tzu says: "He who loves others, must also be loved by others. He who benefits others, must also be benefited by others. He who hates others, must also be hated by others. He who injures others, must also be injured by others." (*Mo-tzu*, ch. 17.) Thus, then, the love of others is a sort of personal insurance or investment, which "pays," as Americans would say. Most people, however, are too shortsighted to see the value of a long term investment of this sort, and there are a few instances in which such an investment does, indeed, fail to pay.

In order, therefore, to induce people to practice the principle of all-embracing love, Mo Tzu, in addition to the foregoing arguments, introduces a number of religious and political sanctions. Thus in the *Mo-tzu* there are chapters on "The Will of Heaven," and also ones titled "Proof of the Existence of Spirits." In these we read that God exists; that He loves mankind; and that His Will is that all men should love one another. He constantly supervises the activities of men, especially those of the rulers of men. He punishes with calamities persons who disobey His Will, and rewards with good fortune those who obey. Besides God, there are also numerous lesser spirits who likewise reward men who practice all-embracing love, and punish those who practice "discrimination."

In this connection there is an interesting story about Mo Tzu: "When Mo Tzu was once ill, Tieh Pi came to him and inquired: 'Sir, you hold that the spirits are intelligent and control calamities and blessings. They reward the good and punish the evil. Now you are a sage. How then can you be ill? Is it that your teaching is not entirely correct or that the spirits are after all not intelligent?' Mo Tzu replied: 'Though I am ill, why should the spirits be unintelligent? There are many ways by which a man can contract diseases. Some are contracted from cold or heat, some from fatigue. If there are a hundred doors and only one be closed, will there not be ways by which robbers can enter?'" (*Mo-tzu*, ch. 48.) In modern

● 天志和明鬼

这里还有一个基本问题，如何能劝说世人实行彼此相爱？如上所述，墨子认为，实行兼爱是济世利人的唯一道路，人唯有实行兼爱才是一个仁人。但是，人们还会问："为什么我作为个人，要为世界的利益献身呢？为什么我要追求做一个仁人呢？"墨家会说，世界的利益就包括了其中每一个人的利益，为世界谋利益就是为自己谋利益。墨子便说过："夫爱人者，人必从而爱之；利人者，人必从而利之。恶人者，人必从而恶之；害人者，人必从而害之。"（《兼爱中》）这样说来，爱人成了一种投资、一种为自己的社会保险，自己可以从中得益，或像美国人的口头语所说："赚了！"（"It pays."）多数人往往目光短小，看不到长期投资的利益，但这种长期"投资"也可能并不带来回报。

为使人们实行兼爱，墨子除了上述的论辩以外，还采用一些宗教和政治的教诲。在《墨子》书中有《天志》篇、《明鬼》篇，其中讲有神，神爱世人，神的心意就是要世人彼此相爱。神经常监察世人的言行，特别是君主的言行。凡不遵行神意的人，就会受到神的降灾惩罚；凡遵行神意的人，神就报以好运。在神之下，还有无数神灵，也同样奖赏实行兼爱之人，惩罚实行交相别的人。

《墨子·公孟》篇里有一个与此相关的墨子的故事很有趣。其中说："子墨子有疾，跌鼻进而问曰：'先生以鬼神为明，能为祸福，为善者赏之，为不善者罚之。今先生圣人也，何故有疾？意者，先生之言有不善乎？鬼神不明知乎？'子墨子曰：'虽使我有病，何遽不明？人之所得于病者多方，有得之寒暑，有得之劳苦，百门而闭一门焉，则盗何遽无从入哉？'"如果使用现代逻辑学的语言，

logical terminology, Mo Tzu would say that punishment by the spirits is a sufficient cause for the disease of a man, but not its necessary cause.

● A Seeming Inconsistency

Here it is timely to point out that both the Mohists and the Confucianists seem to be inconsistent in their attitude toward the existence of spirits and the performance of rituals connected with the spirits. Certainly it seems inconsistent for the Mohists to have believed in the existence of the spirits, yet at the same time to have opposed the elaborate rituals that were conducted on the occasion of funerals and of the making of sacrifices to the ancestors. Likewise, it seems inconsistent that the Confucianists stressed those funeral and sacrificial rituals, yet did not believe in the existence of the spirits. The Mohists, for their part, were quite ready to point out this seeming inconsistency as regards the Confucianists. Thus we read in the *Mo-tzu*: "Kung-meng Tzu [a Confucianist] said: 'There are no spirits.' Again he said: 'The superior man should learn the rituals of sacrifice.' Mo Tzu said: 'To hold that there are no spirits, and yet to learn sacrificial ceremonies, is like learning the ceremonies of hospitality when there are no guests, or throwing fish nets when there are no fish.'" (Ch. 48.)

Yet the seeming inconsistencies of the Confucianists and Mohists are both unreal. According to the former, the reason for performing the sacrificial rituals is no longer a belief that the spirits actually exist, though no doubt this was the original reason. Rather, the performance springs from the sentiment of respect toward his departed forebears held by the man who offers the sacrifice. Hence the meaning of the ceremonies is poetic, not religious. This theory was later developed by Hsün Tzu and his school of Confucianism in detail, as we shall see in chapter thirteen of this book. Hence there is no real inconsistency at all.

Likewise there is no actual inconsistency in the Mohist point of view, for Mo Tzu's proof of the existence of spirits is done primarily in order that he may introduce a religious sanction for his doctrine of all-embracing love, rather than because of any real interest in supernatural matters. Thus in his chapter on "Proof of the Existence of Spirits," he attributes the existing confusion of the world to "a doubt (among men) as to the existence of spirits and a failure to understand that they can reward the good and punish the bad." He then asks: "If now all the people of the world could be made to believe that the spirits can reward the good and punish the bad, would the world then be in chaos?" (Ch. 31.) Thus his

墨子将会说：人之所以得病，由于神灵惩罚，是一个充分原因，但不是一个必然原因。

● 一个看似表里不一的问题

在这里需要指出一点：墨家和儒家对待神灵以及敬拜神灵的态度似乎都有自相矛盾的地方。墨家既信奉鬼神，却反对丧葬和祭祀祖先时要献大量祭牲的繁文缛节；儒家强调祭祀的重要性，却不信有鬼神。墨家对儒家在这方面的自相矛盾，毫不客气地予以指出。《墨子·公孟》篇里所记的公孟子是个儒家人士。他说："‘无鬼神。’又曰：‘君子必学祭礼。’"子墨子曰："执无鬼而学祭礼，是犹无客而学客礼也，是犹无鱼而为鱼罟也。"

其实，儒家和墨家这种似乎自相矛盾的地方只是表面上的不一致。丧葬祭祀在古代受到重视，起初是源于对鬼神的信仰，但儒家重视丧葬礼仪，不是由于信奉鬼神，而是由于重视去世的祖先。可以说，儒家重视仪礼，是一种诗情，而不是出自宗教。儒家的这个理论后来经荀子而进一步发展，在本书第十三章将会说到这个问题。因此，对儒家来说，这种表面上自相矛盾的地方，实际上并不存在。

墨子的观点其实也没有自相矛盾。他论证鬼神的存在，是为他的兼爱理论作张本，而不是对超自然有什么特别的兴趣。在《明鬼》下篇里，墨子认为，世上之所以混乱，源于"疑惑鬼神之有与无之别，不明乎鬼神之能赏贤而罚暴也"。接下去，他问道："今若使天下之人偕若信鬼神之能赏贤而罚暴也，则夫天下岂乱哉！"所以，

doctrine of the Will of God and the existence of spirits is only to induce people to believe that they will be rewarded if they practice all-embracing love, and punished if they do not. Such a belief among the people was something useful; hence Mo Tzu wanted it. "Economy of expenditure" in the funeral and sacrificial services was also useful; hence Mo Tzu wanted it too. From his ultra-utilitarian point of view, there was no inconsistency in wanting both things, since both were useful.

● **Origin of the State**

Besides religious sanctions, political ones are also needed if people are to practice all-embracing love. In the *Mo-tzu*, there are three chapters titled "Agreement with the Superior," in which Mo Tzu expounds his theory of the origin of the state. According to this theory, the authority of the ruler of a state comes from two sources: the will of the people and the Will of God. Furthermore, the main task of the ruler is to supervise the activities of the people, rewarding those who practice all-embracing love and punishing those who do not. In order to do this effectively, his authority must be absolute. At this point we may ask: Why should people voluntarily choose to have such an absolute authority over them?

The answer, for Mo Tzu, is that the people accept such an authority, not because they prefer it, but because they have no alternative. According to him, before the creation of an organized state, people lived in what Thomas Hobbes has called "the state of nature." At this early time, "everyone had his own standard of right and wrong. When there was one man, there was one standard. When there were two men, there were two standards. When there were ten men, there were ten standards. The more people there were, the more were there standards. Every man considered himself as right and others as wrong." "The world was in great disorder and men were like birds and beasts. They understood that all the disorders of the world were due to the fact that there was no political ruler. Therefore, they selected the most virtuous and most able man of

the world, and established him as the Son of Heaven." (*Mo-tzu*, ch. 11.)
Thus the ruler of the state was first established by the will of the people,
in order to save themselves from anarchy.

In another chapter bearing the same title, Mo Tzu says: "Of
old when God and the spirits established the state and cities and
installed rulers, it was not to make their rank high or their emolument

他关于"天志"和"明鬼"的理论只是为了教人相信，实行兼爱，
将得上天奖赏；如不实行兼爱，则将受上天惩罚。大众持这样的信
仰，将有利于在人间建立理想世界，因此墨子采取这样的主张。在
丧葬和祭祀中"节用"，也有利于大众，因此墨子也主张这样的方
针。墨子的思想从极端功利主义出发，崇奉鬼神，而主张薄葬节
礼，两者之间并不矛盾，因为都有利于大众实行兼爱。

● **国家的起源**

照墨子看来，为使民众实行兼爱，不仅要有宗教的规范，还要
有政治的规范。《墨子》书中有《尚同》篇，分上中下三章，其中
阐述了墨子关于国家起源的理论。墨子认为，国家的权威有两个来
源：其一来自民众，另一来自天志。国君的任务应当是监察民众，
对实行兼爱的予以奖赏，不实行的则予以惩罚。为有效实行这种监
察，国君要有绝对的权威。说到这里，人们会问，人民大众为什么
自愿选择这样一个绝对威权来君临统治大众呢？

墨子的回答是，人民大众接受这个权威，不是出于自愿，而是
出于无奈，因为除此以外，别无选择。照他看来，在国家兴起之
前，社会大众生活在汤马斯·霍布斯描绘的"自然状态"之中。《墨
子·尚同》上篇中说：在初民社会中，"盖其语，人异义。是以一
人则一义，二人则二义，十人则十义，其人兹众，其所谓义者亦兹
众。是以人是其义，以非人之义，故交相非也。……天下之乱，至
若禽兽然。夫明乎天下之所以乱者，生于无政长。是故选天下之贤
可者，立以为天子"。据墨子的看法，国君最初是顺应民众的意愿
而产生，以免民众陷于无政府状态。

在《尚同》中篇里，墨子又说："古者上帝鬼神之建设国都、立正
长也，非高其爵、厚其禄、富贵佚而错之也，将以为万民兴利除害、

substantial.... It was to procure benefits for the people and eliminate their adversities; to enrich the poor and increase the few; and to bring safety out of danger and order out of confusion." (Ch. 12.)According to this statement, therefore, the state and its ruler were established through the Will of God.

No matter what was the way in which the ruler gained his power, once he was established, he, according to Mo Tzu, issued a mandate to the people of the world, saying: "Upon hearing good or evil, one shall report it to one's superior. What the superior thinks to be right, all shall think to be right. What the superior thinks to be wrong, all shall think to be wrong." (Ch. 11.) This leads Mo Tzu to the following dictum: "Always agree with the superior; never follow the inferior." (*Ibid.*)

Thus, Mo Tzu argues, the state must be totalitarian and the authority of its ruler absolute. This is an inevitable conclusion to his theory of the origin of the state. For the state was created precisely in order to end the disorder which had existed owing to the confused standards of right and wrong. The state's primary function, therefore, is, quoting Mo Tzu, "to unify the standards." Within the state only one standard can exist, and it must be one which is fixed by the state itself. No other standards can be tolerated, because if there were such, people would speedily return to "the state of nature" in which there could be nothing but disorder and chaos. In this political theory we may see Mo Tzu's development of the professional ethics of the *hsieh*, with its emphasis upon group obedience and discipline. No doubt it also reflects the troubled political conditions of Mo Tzu's day, which caused many people to look with favor on a centralized authority, even if it were to be an autocratic one.

So, then, there can be only one standard of right and wrong. Right, for Mo Tzu, is the practice of "mutual all-embracingness," and wrong is the practice of "mutual discrimination." Through appeal to this political sanction, together with his religious one, Mo Tzu hoped to bring all people of the world to practice his principle of all-embracing love.

Such was Mo Tzu's teaching, and it is the unanimous report of all sources of his time that in his own activities he was a true example of it.

富贫众寡、安危治乱也。"照这里所说，则国家和君主乃是按照神的意志而设立的。

无论国君的权力是从哪里产生的，按墨子的看法，君主一旦建立起来，就向民众发出号令："发政于天下之百姓，言曰：闻善而不善，皆以告其上。上之所是必皆是之，上之所非必皆非之。"（《墨子·尚同上》）由此引出墨子的名言："上同而不下比"（同上），意思是：对最高领导，要事事同意，而不要跟随下面的人。

按照墨子的理论，国家的性质必然是极权主义的，国君的权力必定是绝对化的。这是从他的国家起源理论所导致的必然结论。因为国家之所以产生就是为了制止人们由各行其是而产生的混乱。因此，依墨子的说法，国家的职责就是"一同国之义"（同上）。在一国之内，只能有一个是非标准（"义"），这个"义"只能由国家制定。一国之内，不能容忍多重标准，那将导致混乱，使民众又回到"自然状态"中去，结果除混乱外，一无所成。从这种政治理论中可以看到，墨子把"侠"的职业道德发展到政治理论，强调集体纪律和集体的顺服。它也反映了墨子时代的政治混乱局面，使许多人倾向中央集权，认为即便专制，也比混乱要好。

这样，墨子主张，必须划一是非的标准（一义）。照墨子的主张，"是"就是"交相兼"，"非"就是"交相别"。墨子指望通过这样的政治规范，再加上宗教的规范，可以使天下之人都实行兼爱。

这便是墨子学说的梗概。从当时各种文献记载看来，墨子自己便是奉行这些原则的范例。

❻ THE FIRST PHASE OF TAOISM: YANG CHU

In the *Confucian Analects*, we are told that Confucius, while traveling from state to state, met many men whom he called *yin che*, "those who obscure themselves," and described as persons who had "escaped from the world." (XIV, 39.) These recluses ridiculed Confucius for what they regarded as his vain efforts to save the world. By one of them he was described as "the one who knows he cannot succeed, yet keeps on trying to do so." (XIV, 41.) To these attacks, Tzu Lu, a disciple of Confucius, once replied: "It is unrighteous to refuse to serve in office. If the regulations between old and young in family life are not to be set aside, how is it then that you set aside the duty that exists between sovereign and subject? In your desire to maintain your personal purity, you subvert the great relationship of society [the relationship between sovereign and subject]." (*Ibid.*, XVIII, 7.)

● **The Early Taoists and the Recluses**

The recluses were thus individualists who "desired to maintain their personal purity." They were also, in a sense, defeatists who thought that the world was so bad that nothing could be done for it. One of them is reported in the *Analects* to have said: "The world is a swelling torrent, and is there anyone to change it?" (XVIII, 6.) It was from men of this sort, most of them living far away from other men in the world of nature, that the Taoists were probably originally drawn.

The Taoists, however, were not ordinary recluses who "escaped the world," desiring to "maintain their personal purity," and who, once in retirement, made no attempt ideologically to justify their conduct. On the contrary, they were men who, having gone into seclusion, attempted to work out a system of thought that would give meaning to their action. Among them, Yang Chu seems to have been the earliest prominent exponent.

Yang Chu's dates are not clear, but he must have lived between the time of Mo Tzu (c. 479-c. 381 B.C.) and Mencius (c. 371-c. 289 B.C.).

This is indicated by the fact that though unmentioned by Mo Tzu, he, by the time of Mencius, had become as influential as were the Mohists. To quote Mencius himself: "The words of Yang Chu and Mo Ti fill the world." (*Mencius*, IIIb, 9.) In the Taoist work known as the *Lieh-tzu*, there is one chapter entitled "Yang Chu," which, according to the traditional view, represents Yang Chu's philosophy.[1] But the authenticity of the

陆 道家的第一阶段：杨朱

在《论语·宪问》篇里记载，孔子周游列国时，曾遇到许多"避世"的"隐者"。这些隐士嘲笑孔子一心济世，都归于徒然。其中一个名为晨门的隐士称孔子是"知其不可而为之者"（《论语·宪问》第四十一节）。孔子的弟子子路为老师辩护说："不仕无义。长幼之节，不可废也；君臣之义，如之何其废之？欲洁其身，而乱大伦。"（《论语·微子》第七节）

● 早期道家与隐者

这些隐者是"欲洁其身"的个人主义者。从某种意义上说，他们又是认为世界败坏、无可救药的失败主义者。按《论语·微子》篇第六节所载，其中有一个隐者对孔子的门徒说："滔滔者天下皆是也，而谁以易之？"（意思是，天下像滔滔洪水泛滥那样，有谁能改变它呢？）这些人远离世俗，遁迹山林，早期道家大概便是从他们中间产生的。

但是，一般隐者既已"远离世俗""欲洁其身"，也就不再介意社会对他们的评论，不去为自己做什么辩护。早期道家则在遁世之后，还为他们的生活方式说出一套道理，杨朱便是其中最突出的一个。

杨朱的生卒年月已不可考，但大致可以知道，他生活于墨子（约公元前四七九至前三八一年）和孟子（约公元前三七一至前二八九年）的年代之间，因为在《墨子》一书中，未曾提到过杨朱，而在《孟子》书中，杨朱已经是一位著名人物，像墨子一样。《孟子·滕文公章句下》第九节说道："杨朱、墨翟之言盈天下。天下之言不归杨，则归墨。"在道家著作《列子》一书中，有一章《杨朱》篇，

Lieh-tzu has been much questioned by modern scholarship, and the view expressed in most of the "Yang Chu" chapter is not consistent with Yang Chu's ideas as reported in other early reliable sources. Its tenets are those of extreme hedonism (hence Forke's title, *Yang Chu's Garden of Pleasure*), whereas in no other early writings do we find Yang Chu being accused as a hedonist. Yang Chu's actual ideas, unfortunately, are nowhere described very consecutively, but must be deduced from scattered references in a number of works by other writers.

- **Yang Chu's Fundamental Ideas**

The *Mencius* says: "The principle of Yang Chu is: 'Each one for himself.' Though he might have profited the whole world by plucking out a single hair, he would not have done it." (VIIa, 26.) The *Lü-shih Ch'un-ch'iu* (third century B.C.) says: "Yang Sheng valued self." (XVII, 7.) The *Han-fei-tzu* (also third century) says: "There is a man whose policy it is not to enter a city which is in danger, nor to remain in the army. Even for the great profit of the whole world, he would not exchange one hair of his shank…. He is one who despises things and values life." (Ch. 50.) And the *Huai-nan-tzu* (second century B.C.) says: "Preserving life and maintaining what is genuine in it, not allowing things to entangle one's person: this is what Yang Chu established." (Ch. 13.)

In the above quotations, the Yang Sheng of the *Lü-shih Ch'un-ch'iu* has been proved by recent scholars to be Yang Chu, while the man who "for the great profit of the whole world, would not exchange one hair of his shank" must also be Yang Chu or one of his followers, because no other man of that time is known to have held such a principle. Putting these sources together, we can deduce that Yang Chu's two fundamental ideas were: "Each one for himself," and "the despising of things and valuing of life." Such ideas are precisely the opposite of those of Mo Tzu, who held the principle of an all-embracing love.

The statement of Han Fei Tzu that Yang Chu would not give up a hair from his shank even to *gain* the entire world, differs somewhat from what Mencius says, which is that Yang Chu would not sacrifice a single hair even in order to *profit* the whole world. Both statements, however, are consistent with Yang Chu's fundamental ideas. The latter harmonizes with his doctrine of "each one for himself"; the former with that of "despising things and valuing life." Both may be said to be but two aspects of a single theory.

历来认为其中反映了杨朱的哲学，但当代学者多半认为《列子》是伪书，《列子》书中杨朱的思想与更早的著作记载的杨朱思想往往不一致，它的论点主要是一种极端享乐主义。（因此，佛克教授关于杨朱的著作命名为《杨朱的乐园》。）而在更早的著作中，我们未曾见到有任何地方称杨朱是享乐主义者。不幸的是，我们只能从其他著述中辑录杨朱的思想言论，却无法把它们贯穿成篇。

● 杨朱的基本思想

《孟子·尽心章句上》第二十六节说："孟子曰：'杨子取为我，拔一毛而利天下，不为也。'"公元前三世纪的《吕氏春秋》中《审分览·不二》篇说："杨生贵己。"公元前三世纪的另一部书《韩非子》中《显学》篇说："今有人于此，义不入危城，不处军旅，不以天下大利易其胫一毛，……轻物重生之士也。"公元前二世纪《淮南子·氾论训》篇中说："全性保真，不以物累形，杨子之所立也。"

上面援引《吕氏春秋》，其中所说"杨生"，据当代学者的考证，就是杨朱。"不以天下大利易其胫一毛"应也是指杨朱或他的追随者，因为我们不知道，当时除杨朱一派外，还有什么人持这样的主张。把这些资料放在一起，可以看出，杨朱有两个基本思想：其一是"人人为自己"，其二是"轻物重生"。这和墨子的"兼爱"思想正好相反。

《韩非子》书中说杨朱"不以天下大利易其胫一毛"，和《孟子》书中说杨朱"拔一毛以利天下，而不为也"，两者含义还有所不同，后者正是杨朱"人人为自己"的思想，而前者则是杨朱"轻物重生"的思想，但两者和杨朱的基本思想是一致的，它们是同一个理论的两个方面。

● **Illustrations of Yang Chu's Ideas**

In Taoist literature, illustrations may be found for both the above mentioned aspects of Yang Chu's ideology. In the first chapter of the *Chuang-tzu*, there is a story about a meeting between the legendary sage-ruler Yao and a hermit named Hsü Yu. Yao was anxious to hand over his rule of the world to Hsü Yu, but the latter rejected it, saying: "You govern the world and it is already at peace. Suppose I were to take your place, would I do it for the name? Name is but the shadow of real gain. Would I do it for real gain? The tit, building its nest in the mighty forest, occupies but a single twig. The tapir, slaking its thirst from the river, drinks only enough to fill its belly. You return and be quiet. I have no need of the world." Here was a hermit who would not take the world, even were it given to him for nothing. Certainly, then, he would not exchange it for even a single hair from his shank. This illustrates Han Fei Tzu's account of Yang Chu.

In the above mentioned chapter titled "Yang Chu" in the *Lieh-tzu*, there is another story which reads: "Ch'in Tzu asked Yang Chu: 'If by plucking out a single hair of your body you could save the whole world, would you do it?' Yang Chu answered: 'The whole world is surely not to be saved by a single hair.' Ch'in Tzu said: 'But supposing it possible, would you do it?' Yang Chu made no answer. Ch'in Tzu then went out and told Meng-sun Yang. The latter replied: 'You do not understand the mind of the Master. I will explain it for you. Supposing by tearing off a piece of your skin, you were to get ten thousand pieces of gold, would you do it?' Ch'in Tzu said: 'I would.' Meng-sun Yang continued: 'Supposing by cutting off one of your limbs, you were to get a whole kingdom, would you do it?' For a while Ch'in Tzu was silent. Then Meng-sun Yang said: 'A hair is unimportant compared with the skin. A piece of skin is unimportant compared with a limb. But many hairs put together are as important as a piece of skin. Many pieces of skin put together are as important as a limb. A single hair is one of the ten thousand parts of the body. How can you disregard it?'" This is an illustration of the other aspect of Yang Chu's theory.

In the same chapter of the *Lieh-tzu*, Yang Chu is reported to have said: "The men of antiquity, if by injuring a single hair they could have profited the world, would not have done it. Had the world been offered to them as their exclusive possession, they would not have taken it. If everybody would refuse to pluck out even a single hair, and everybody would refuse to take the world as a gain, then the world would be in perfect order." We cannot be sure that this is really a saying of Yang Chu, but it sums up very well the two aspects of his theory, and the political philosophy of the early Taoists.

● 杨朱思想举例

从道家文献资料中可以找出杨朱上述两方面思想的实例。《庄子》第一章里有一个故事，叙述传说中的圣王尧，想把王位传给一位名为许由的隐士。许由拒不接受，说："子治天下，天下既已治也。而我犹代子，吾将为名乎？名者，实之宾也。吾将为宾乎？鹪鹩巢于深林，不过一枝；偃鼠饮河，不过满腹。归休乎君，予无所用天下为！"尧愿把天下白白赠送给许由，许由也不要。当然，如果要许由拔小腿上的一根毛来换天下，他更不情愿。这正是韩非子笔下的杨朱的形象。

《列子》书中以杨朱为题的一篇还有另一个故事，其中说，"禽子问杨朱曰：'去子体之一毛以济一世，汝为之乎？'杨子曰：'世固非一毛之所济'。禽子曰：'假济，为之乎？'杨子弗应。禽子出，语孟孙阳。孟孙阳曰：'子不达夫子之心，吾请言之，有侵若肌肤获万金者，若为之乎？'曰：'为之。'孟孙阳曰：'有断若一节得一国，子为之乎？'禽子默然有间。孟孙阳曰：'一毛微于肌肤，肌肤微于一节，省矣。然则积一毛以成肌肤，积肌肤以成一节。一毛固一体万分中之一物，奈何轻之乎？'"这是杨朱思想中另一方面的一个例证。

在《列子·杨朱》篇中，还记述了据说是杨朱的话说："古之人，损一毫利天下不与也，悉天下奉一身不取也。人人不损一毫，人人不利天下，天下治矣。"我们无法断定这话是否确实出自杨朱，但它很好地总结了上述理论的两方面和早期道家的政治哲学。

● **Yang Chu's Ideas as Expressed in the *Lao-tzu* and *Chuang-tzu***

Reflections of Yang Chu's main ideas can be found in portions of the *Lao-tzu* and some chapters of the *Chuang-tzu* and the *Lü-shih Ch'un-ch'iu*. In the latter work there is a chapter titled "The Importance of Self," in which it is said: "Our life is our own possession, and its benefit to us is very great. Regarding its dignity, even the honor of being Emperor could not compare with it. Regarding its importance, even the wealth of possessing the world would not be exchanged for it. Regarding its safety, were we to lose it for one morning, we could never again bring it back. These three are points on which those who have understanding are careful." (I, 3.) This passage explains why one should despise things and value life. Even an empire, once lost, may some day be regained, but once dead, one can never live again.

The *Lao-tzu* contains passages expressing the same idea. For example: "He who in his conduct values his body more than he does the world, may be given the world. He who in his conduct loves himself more than he does the world, may be entrusted with the world." (Ch. 13.) Or: "Name or person, which is more dear? Person or fortune, which is more important?" (Ch. 44.) Here again appears the idea of despising things and valuing life.

In the third chapter of the *Chuang-tzu*, titled "Fundamentals for the Cultivation of Life," we read: "When you do something good, beware of reputation; when you do something evil, beware of punishment. Follow the middle way and take this to be your constant principle. Then you can guard your person, nourish your parents, and complete your natural term of years." This again follows Yang Chu's line of thought, and, according to the earlier Taoists, is the best way to preserve one's life against the harms that come from the human world. If a man's conduct is so bad that society punishes him, this is obviously not the way to preserve his life. But if a man is so good in his conduct that he obtains a fine reputation, this too is not the way to preserve his life. Another chapter of the *Chuang-tzu* tells us: "Mountain trees are their own enemies, and the leaping fire is the cause of its own quenching. Cinnamon is edible, therefore the cinnamon tree is cut down. *Ch'i* oil is useful, therefore the *ch'i* tree is gashed." (Ch. 4.) A man having a reputation of ability and usefulness will suffer a fate just like that of the cinnamon and *ch'i* trees.

Thus in the *Chuang-tzu* we find passages that admire the usefulness of the useless. In the chapter just quoted, there is the description of a

● 老庄著作中的杨朱思想

从《老子》一书和《庄子》中的若干章，以及《吕氏春秋》中，都可以看到对杨朱思想的评论反思。在《吕氏春秋》书中，有一篇《孟春纪·重己》，其中说："今吾生之为我有，而利我亦大矣。论其贵贱，爵为天子，不足以比焉；论其轻重，富有天下，不可以易之；论其安危，一曙失之，终身不复得。此三者，有道者之所慎也。"这段话解释了人何以应当轻物重生。失去一个帝国，还有机会可以复得，但人若死去，就不可能复活。

在《老子》书中，也有这个思想。例如《道德经》第十三章中说："贵以身为天下，若可寄天下；爱以身为天下，若可托天下。"这是说，一个人如果把自己的行事为人看成比得天下更贵重，这样的人，就可以把天下托付给他；一个人如果珍惜自己甚于贪爱天下，就可以把天下托付给他。又如《道德经》第四十四章说："名与身，孰亲？身与货，孰多？"这些都是轻物重生思想的表现。

《庄子》第三章《养生主》篇中说："为善无近名，为恶无近刑。缘督以为经，可以保身，可以全生，可以养亲，可以尽年。"这也是依循杨朱的思想，按早期道家看来，这是全生避害的最佳方法。如果一个人的行为败坏到遭受社会的惩罚，当然无法全生。但是，如果一个人的社会声誉太好，也不利于全生。《庄子》第四章《人间世》篇中说："山木自寇也，膏火自煎也。桂可食，故伐之；漆可用，故割之。"人如果有才能、有用处，则他的命运将和桂树、漆树的命运一样。

因此，在《庄子》书中，我们看到其中称颂"无用之用"。《人间世》里，讲到一棵高大的栎社树，因为木质疏松，没有用处，

sacred oak, which, because its wood was good for nothing, had been spared the ax, and which said to someone in a dream: "For a long time I have been learning to be useless. There were several occasions on which I was nearly destroyed, but now I have succeeded in being useless, which is of the greatest use to me. If I were useful, could I have become so great?" Again it is said that "the world knows only the usefulness of the useful, but does not know the usefulness of the useless." (Ch. 4.) To be useless is the way to preserve one's life. The man who is skillful in preserving life must not do much evil, but neither must he do much good. He must live midway between good and evil. He tries to be useless, which in the end proves of greatest usefulness to him.

● Development of Taoism

In this chapter we have been seeing the first phase in the development of early Taoist philosophy. Altogether there have been three main phases. The ideas attributed to Yang Chu represent the first. Those expressed in the greater part of the *Lao-tzu* represent the second. And those expressed in the greater part of the *Chuang-tzu* represent the third and last phase. I say the greater part of the *Lao-tzu* and *Chuang-tzu*, because in the *Lao-tzu* there are also to be found ideas representing the first and third phases and in the *Chuang-tzu* ideas of the first and second phases. These two books, like many others of ancient China, are really collections of Taoist writings and sayings, made by differing persons in different times, rather than the single work of any one person.

The starting point of Taoist philosophy is the preservation of life and avoiding of injury. Yang Chu's method for so doing is "to escape." This is the method of the ordinary recluse who flees from society and hides himself in the mountains and forests. By doing this he thinks he can avoid the evils of the human world. Things in the human world, however, are so complicated that no matter how well one hides oneself, there are always evils that cannot be avoided. There are times, therefore, when the method of "escaping" does not work.

The ideas expressed in the greater part of the *Lao-tzu* represent an attempt to reveal the laws underlying the changes of things in the universe. Things change, but the laws underlying the changes remain unchanging. If one understands these laws and regulates one's actions in conformity with them, one can then turn everything to one's advantage. This is the second phase in the development of Taoism.

所以匠人不去砍伐。大树托梦对人说："长期以来，我致力于只求无用。曾有几次，我都几乎死去，现在才成功达到无用的目的，对我来说，这就是最大的用处。"《人间世》篇末说："人皆知有用之用，而莫知无用之用也。" 无用乃是全生之道。懂得全生之道的人，不仅不能作恶多端，为善也不能过分，他只能处于善恶之间、有用和无用之间，正是无用，最终证明他的大用。

● 道家思想的发展

在这一章里，我们所见到的是先秦道家思想的第一阶段。先秦道家思想总共有三个阶段。以杨朱为代表的是第一阶段。《老子》书中大部分所代表的是第二阶段。《庄子》书中大部分则是第三，也就是最后的阶段。在这里说"《老子》书中大部分"、"《庄子》书中大部分"，是因为《老子》书中也杂有道家第一阶段和第三阶段的思想；《庄子》书中也杂有道家第一和第二阶段思想。这两部著作，也和中国古代的许多其他著作一样，是这一派学说的言论著作的汇编，而不是任何个人的作品。

道家哲学的出发点是保全生命、避免损害生命。为达到这个目的，杨朱的做法是"逃避"。这是隐士们通常的做法：逃离社会、遁迹山林，指望这样就可以不致沾染人世的罪恶污秽。但是，人间如此复杂，无论个人怎样逃避，也难以完全逃避其中的罪恶污秽，因此，"逃避"并不能达到目的。

《老子》书中大部分论述是试图显示宇宙万物变化的法则。在这些道家看来，事物虽然千变万化，但在各种变化的底层，事物演变的法则并不改变。人如果懂得这些法则，按照这些法则来安排自己的行动，就可以使事物的演变对于自己有利。这是先秦道家思想发展的第二阶段。

Even so, however, there is no absolute guarantee. In the changes of things, both in the world of nature and of man, there are always unseen elements. So despite every care, the possibility remains that one will suffer injury. This is why the *Lao-tzu* says with still deeper insight: "The reason that I have great disaster is that I have a body. If there were no body, what disaster could there be?" (Ch. 13.) These words of greater understanding are developed in much of the *Chuang-tzu*, in which occur the concepts of the equalization of life with death, and the identity of self with others. This means to see life and death, self and others, from a higher point of view. By seeing things from this higher point of view, one can transcend the existing world. This is also a form of "escape"; not one, however, from society to mountains and forests, but rather from this world to another world. Here is the third and last phase of development in the Taoism of ancient times.

All these developments are illustrated by a story which we find in the twentieth chapter of the *Chuang-tzu*, titled "The Mountain Tree." The story runs:

"Chuang Tzu was traveling through the mountains, when he saw a great tree well covered with foliage. A tree-cutter was standing beside it, but he did not cut it down. Chuang Tzu asked him the reason and he replied: 'It is of no use.' Chuang Tzu then said: 'By virtue of having no exceptional qualities, this tree succeeds in completing its natural span.'

"When the Master (Chuang Tzu) left the mountains, he stopped at the home of a friend. The friend was glad and ordered the servant to kill a goose and cook it. The servant asked: 'One of the geese can cackle. The other cannot. Which shall I kill?' The Master said: 'Kill the one that cannot cackle.' Next day, a disciple asked Chuang Tzu the question: 'Yesterday the tree in the mountains, because it had no exceptional quality, succeeded in completing its natural span. But now the goose of our host, because it had no exceptional quality, had to die. What will be your position?'

"Chuang Tzu laughed and said: 'My position will lie between having exceptional qualities and not having them. Yet this position only seems to be right, but really is not so. Therefore those who practice this method are not able to be completely free from troubles. If one wanders about with *Tao* and *Te* (the Way and its spiritual power), it will be otherwise.'"

Then Chuang Tzu went on to say that he who links himself with *Tao* and *Te* is with the "ancestor of things, using things as things, but not being used by things as things. When that is so, what is there that can trouble him?"

即便如此，人还是感到生命岌岌可危。无论自然或人类社会的变化中，总有难以预见的因素。因此，无论人怎样保护自己，还是难免受到伤害，这是《老子》书中第十三章喟叹"吾所以有大患者，为吾有身；及吾无身，吾有何患"的由来。这个思想在《庄子》书中加以进一步发挥，成为"齐万物，一死生"的思想。它意味着，从一个更高的观点来看一己与外界、生与死。从这个更高的观点看事物，就可以超越自己以外的世界。这是另一种形式的"逃避"，它不是从世俗社会逃往山林，而是从这个世界逃往另一个世界。这是古代道家思想的第三阶段。

在《庄子》书中《山木》篇里有一个故事，很好地说明了这几种思想。

"庄子行于山中，见大木，枝叶盛茂，伐木者止其旁而不取也。问其故，曰：'无所可用。'庄子曰：'此木以不材得终其天年。'

"夫子出于山，舍于故人之家。故人喜，命竖子杀雁而烹之。竖子请曰：'其一能鸣，其一不能鸣，请奚杀？'主人曰：'杀不能鸣者。'

"明日，弟子问于庄子曰：'昨日山中之木，以不材得终其天年；今主人之雁，以不材死。先生将何处？'

"庄子笑曰：'周将处乎材与不材之间。材与不材之间，似之而非也，故未免乎累。若夫乘道德而浮游则不然。'"

接下去，庄子讲，人浮游于道德，就是浮游于万物的初始状态，役使万物，而不为万物所役，那样，还有什么能拖累他呢？

In this story, the first part illustrates the theory of preserving life as practiced by Yang Chu, while the second part gives that of Chuang Tzu. "Having exceptional quality" corresponds to the doing of good things, mentioned in the earlier quotation from the third chapter of the *Chuang-tzu.* "Having no exceptional quality" corresponds to the doing of bad things in that same quotation. And a position between these two extremes corresponds to the middle way indicated in that quotation. Yet if a man cannot see things from a higher point of view, none of these methods can absolutely guarantee him from danger and harm. To see things from a higher point of view, however, means to abolish the self. We may say that the early Taoists were selfish. Yet in their later development this selfishness became reversed and destroyed itself.

这个故事的第一部分是讲杨朱保全生命的理论，第二部分是讲庄子的理论，"材"是《养生主》篇中所说的"为善"，"不材"是《养生主》篇中所说的"为恶"，"处于材与不材之间"就是《养生主》篇中所说的"缘督以为经"，就是遵循中道。但是，人若不能从一个更高的观点看世上事物，则这些方法都不能使他免于灾难。为从一个更高的观点看世上事物，就要无我。我们可以说，早期道家的思想是从私——即有我——出发的，在后来的发展中，"私"被倒过来，被否定了。

❼ THE IDEALISTIC WING OF CONFUCIANISM: MENCIUS

According to the *Historical Records* (ch. 74), Mencius (371?-289? B.C.) was a native of the state of Tsou, in the present southern part of Shantung province in East China. He was linked with Confucius through his study under a disciple of Tzu-ssu, who in turn was Confucius' grandson. At that time, the Kings of Ch'i, a larger state also in present Shantung, were great admirers of learning. Near the west gate of their capital, a gate known as Chi, they had established a center of learning which they called Chi-hsia, that is, "below Chi." All the scholars living there "were ranked as great officers and were honored and courted by having large houses built for them on the main road. This was to show to all the pensioned guests of the feudal lords that it was the state of Ch'i that could attract the most eminent scholars in the world." (*Ibid.*)

Mencius for a while was one of these eminent scholars, but he also traveled to other states, vainly trying to get a hearing for his ideas among their rulers. Finally, so the *Historical Records* tell us, he retired and with his disciples composed the *Mencius* in seven books. This work records the conversations between Mencius and the feudal lords of his time, and between him and his disciples, and in later times it was honored by being made one of the famous "Four Books," which for the past one thousand years have formed the basis of Confucian education.

Mencius represents the idealistic wing of Confucianism, and the somewhat later Hsün Tzu the realistic wing. The meaning of this will become clear as we go on.

● The Goodness of Human Nature

We have seen that Confucius spoke very much about *jen* (human-heartedness), and made a sharp distinction between *yi* (righteousness) and *li* (profit). Every man should, without thought of personal advantage, unconditionally do what he ought to do, and be what he ought to be. In other words, he should "extend himself so as to include others," which, in essence, is the practice of *jen*. But though Confucius held these doctrines, he failed to explain *why* it is that a man should act in this way. Mencius, however, attempted to give an answer to this question, and in so doing developed the theory for which he is most famed: that of the original goodness of human nature.

Whether human nature is good or bad—that is, what, precisely, is the nature of human nature—has been one of the most controversial

柒 儒家的理想主义流派：孟子

按照《史记》所载，孟子（约公元前三七一至前二八九年）出生于战国时代的邹国，在今山东南部。他从孔子的孙子子思的学生学习儒家思想理论。当时，在山东半岛东部的齐国，国君热心学术，网罗学者，把他们安顿在首都西门附近的稷下学宫。按《史记》记载，学者们"皆命曰列大夫，为开第康庄之衢，高门大屋，尊宠之。览天下诸侯宾客，言齐能致天下贤士也"。

孟子曾是稷下的著名学者，也曾周游列国，试图以自己的思想影响当时列国王侯，但都遭到冷遇。按《史记》记载，他最后返回故里，与弟子著《孟子》七卷，其中记载了孟子与当时王侯的谈话，与弟子们的对话。《孟子》一书被后代儒家尊为"四书"之一，成为儒家经书之一。

在儒家思想中，孟子代表了其中理想主义的一派，稍后的荀子则是儒家的现实主义一派，他们的历史作用将在本书中逐步显现出来。

● 性善说

我们已经看到孔子十分重视"仁"，并且严格区分"义"和"利"。人之所以为人，就是要行义而不谋利。换句话说，就是要"推己及人"。这就是"仁"的实践。孔子虽然十分强调这一点，但并未充分阐述人何以应当这样做。孟子试图回答这个问题，在这样做之中，他发展出使他垂名后世的"人性本善说"。

人性本善或人性本恶——究竟怎样认识人性——这是中国哲学里

problems in Chinese philosophy. According to Mencius, there were, in his time, three other theories besides his own on this subject. The first was that human nature is neither good nor bad. The second was that human nature can be either good or bad (which seems to mean that in the nature of man there are both good and bad elements), and the third was that the nature of some men is good, and that of others is bad. (*Mencius*, VIa, 3-6.) The first of these theories was held by Kao Tzu, a philosopher who was contemporary with Mencius. We know more about it than the other theories through the long discussions between him and Mencius which are preserved for us in the *Mencius*.

When Mencius holds that human nature is good, he does not mean that every man is born a Confucius, that is, a sage. His theory has some similarity with one side of the second theory mentioned above, that is, that in the nature of man there are good elements. He admits, to be sure, that there are also other elements, which are neither good nor bad in themselves, but which, if not duly controlled, can lead to evil. According to Mencius, however, these are elements which man shares in common with other living creatures. They represent the "animal" aspect of man's life, and therefore, strictly speaking, should not be considered as part of the "human" nature.

To support his theory, Mencius presents numerous arguments, among them the following: "All men have a mind which cannot bear [to see the suffering of] others.... If now men suddenly see a child about to fall into a well, they will without exception experience a feeling of alarm and distress.... From this case we may perceive that he who lacks the feeling of commiseration is not a man; that he who lacks a feeling of shame and dislike is not a man; that he who lacks a feeling of modesty and yielding is not a man; and that he who lacks a sense of right and wrong is not a man. The feeling of commiseration is the beginning of human-heartedness. The feeling of shame and dislike is the beginning of righteousness. The feeling of modesty and yielding is the beginning of propriety. The sense of right and wrong is the beginning of wisdom. Man has these four beginnings, just as he has four limbs…. Since all men have these four beginnings in themselves, let them know how to give them full development and completion. The result will be like fire that begins to burn, or a spring which has begun to find vent. Let them have their complete development, and they will suffice to protect all within the four seas. If they are denied that development, they will not suffice even to serve one's parents." (*Mencius*, IIa, 6.)

All men in their original nature possess these "four beginnings," which, if fully developed, become the four "constant virtues," so greatly

争论最多的问题之一。孟子在《告子章句上》第三节到第六节里，曾列举当时除他以外还有另外三种不同的理论。第一种是认为，人性无所谓善恶；第二种是认为，人性可以从善，也可以从恶（这种意见似乎意味着认为人性之中有善因，也有恶因）；还有第三种意见认为，有的人性善，有的人性恶。在这三种意见中，持第一种意见的代表人物是告子，他是与孟子同时的一位哲学家。《孟子》书中记载，他和孟子曾进行很长的讨论，因此我们得以较多了解讨论的具体内容。

孟子主张人性善，并不是认为，人人生下来便是一位孔圣人。他的理论与上述第二种意见的一方面有点相近，承认人的本性中有些因素，本身无所谓善或恶，但如人不加以节制，它就将导致恶。孟子认为，这是人与野兽共同的地方，它们反映了人里面有野兽的本能方面。但严格说来，这不是"人性"。

孟子从多方面论辩以支持他的理论。在《孟子·公孙丑章句上》记载孟子说：

"人皆有不忍人之心。……今人乍见孺子将入于井，皆有怵惕恻隐之心。……由是观之，无恻隐之心，非人也；无羞恶之心，非人也；无辞让之心，非人也；无是非之心，非人也。恻隐之心，仁之端也；羞恶之心，义之端也；辞让之心，礼之端也；是非之心，智之端也。人之有是四端也，犹其有四体也。……凡有四端于我者，知皆扩而充之矣，若火之使然，泉之始达。苟能充之，足以保四海；苟不充之，不足以事父母。"

人的本性，都有上述"四端"，如果加以充分发展，它们便成长为孔子所强调的"四德"。这些品德，如果不受外力阻碍，会在

emphasized in Confucianism. These virtues, if not hindered by external conditions, develop naturally from within, just as a tree grows by itself from the seed, or a flower from the bud. This is the basis of Mencius' controversy with Kao Tzu, according to whom human nature is in itself neither good nor bad, and for whom morality is therefore something that is artificially added from without.

There remains another question, which is: Why should man allow free development to his "four beginnings," instead of to what we may call his lower instincts? Mencius answers that it is these four beginnings that differentiate man from the beasts. They should be developed, therefore, because it is only through their development that man is truly a "man." Mencius says: "That whereby man differs from birds and beasts is but slight. The mass of the people cast it away, whereas the superior man preserves it." (*Mencius*, IVb, 19.) Thus he answers a question which had not occurred to Confucius.

● Fundamental Difference between Confucianism and Mohism

Here we find the fundamental difference between Confucianism and Mohism. One of Mencius' self-appointed tasks was to "oppose Yang Chu and Mo Ti." He says: "Yang's principle of 'each one for himself' amounts to making one's sovereign of no account. Mo's principle of 'all-embracing love' amounts to making one's father of no account. To have no father and no sovereign is to be like the birds and beasts…. These pernicious opinions mislead the people and block the way of human-heartedness and righteousness." (*Mencius*, IIIb, 9.) It is very clear that Yang Chu's theory opposes human-heartedness and righteousness, since the essence of these two virtues is to benefit others, while Yang Chu's principle is to benefit oneself. But Mo Tzu's principle of all-embracing love also aimed to benefit others, and he was even more outspoken in this respect than the Confucianists. Why, then, does Mencius lump him together with Yang Chu in his criticism?

The traditional answer is that according to Mohist doctrine, love should have in it no gradations of greater or lesser love, whereas according to Confucianism, the reverse is true. In other words, the Mohists emphasized equality in loving others, while the Confucianists emphasized gradation. This difference is brought out in a passage in the *Mo-tzu* in which a certain Wu-ma Tzu is reported as saying to Mo Tzu: "I cannot practice all-embracing love. I love the men of Tsou [a nearby state] better than I love those of *Yüeh* [a distant state]. I love the men of Lu [his own state] better than I love those of Tsou. I love the men of my

人内心自然生长，如同树由树种成长为大树，如同花由花苞开放为花一样。告子则认为，人性无所谓善恶，道德意识只是后来外界施加给人的。这是孟子与告子看法不同的地方。

还有一个问题是，人为什么要去发展德之四端，而不去发展低下的野兽本能呢？《孟子·离娄章句下》第十九节记载，孟子说："人之所以异于禽兽者几希，庶民去之，君子存之。"这是说，德之四端乃是人区别于野兽之所在，人只有发展德之四端，才能真正成为人。在这里，孟子回答了孔子未曾遇到的一个问题。

● 论儒家与墨家的基本不同点

正是在这里，我们可以看出儒家与墨家的不同之处。孟子担当起的一个任务是在《滕文公章句下》第九节所说的"言距杨墨"。他认为："杨氏为我，是无君也；墨氏兼爱，是无父也。无父无君，是禽兽也。……杨墨之道不息，孔子之道不著，是邪说诬民，充塞仁义也。"十分明显的一点是，主张仁义的都强调利人，而杨朱所讲的是利己，主张利己，就是反对仁义。问题是墨子讲兼爱，这也是利人，墨子在这方面甚至比孔子讲得更为明确，然则孟子为什么把墨子和杨朱归在一起加以反对呢？

历来对这问题的回答是：按照墨子的学说，爱是没有等级、差别的；而按照儒家的学说，爱是有等级、差别的。在《墨子》书中已指出了两家的差异。有一位巫马，对墨子说：我无法实行兼爱。我爱邹（邻国）人胜于越（远邻国家）人，爱鲁（本国）人胜于邹人，

own district better than I love those of Lu. I love the members of my own clan better than I love those of my district. I love my parents better than I love the men of my clan. And I love myself better than I love my parents." (*Mo-tzu*, ch. 46.)

Wu-ma Tzu was a Confucianist, and the representation of him as saying, "I love myself better than I love my parents," comes from a Mohist source and is probably an exaggeration. Certainly it is not consistent with the Confucianist emphasis on filial piety. With this exception, however, Wu-ma Tzu's statement is in general agreement with the Confucianist spirit. For according to the Confucianists, there should be degrees in love.

Speaking about these degrees, Mencius says: "The superior man, in his relation to things, loves them but has no feeling of human-heartedness. In his relation to people, he has human-heartedness, but no deep feeling of family affection. One should have feelings of family affection for the members of one's family, but human-heartedness for people; human-heartedness for people, but love for things." (*Mencius*, VIIa, 45.) In a discussion with a Mohist by the name of Yi Chih, Mencius asked him whether he really believed that men love their neighbors' children in the same way as they love their brothers' children; the love for a brother's child is naturally greater. (*Mencius*, IIIa, 5.) This, according to Mencius, is quite proper; what should be done is to extend such love until it includes the more distant members of society. "Treat the aged in your family as they should be treated, and extend this treatment to the aged of other people's families. Treat the young in your family as they should be treated, and extend this treatment to the young of other people's families." (*Mencius*, Ia, 7.) Such is what Mencius calls "extending one's scope of activity to include others." (*Ibid.*) It is an extension based on the principle of graded love.

To extend the love for one's family so as to include persons outside it as well, is to practice that "principle of *chung* [conscientiousness to others] and *shu* [altruism]" advocated by Confucius, which in turn is equivalent to the practice of human-heartedness. There is nothing forced in any of these practices, because the original natures of all men have in them a feeling of commiseration, which makes it impossible for them to bear to see the suffering of others. The development of this "beginning" of goodness causes men naturally to love others, but it is equally natural that they should love their parents to a greater degree than they love men in general.

Such is the Confucianist point of view. The Mohists, on the contrary, insist that the love for others should be on a par with the love for parents. Regardless of whether this means that one should love one's parents less,

爱我乡人胜于鲁人，爱我家人胜于乡人，爱我亲胜于家人，爱我身胜于爱我亲。

巫马子是儒家，《墨子》书中记他说："吾爱吾身，胜于爱吾亲。"这有点蹊跷，不符合儒家主张的孝道，大概是墨家对儒家的夸张之词。除这一点之外，巫马子所讲的爱有等级差别是符合儒家主张的。

孟子在《尽心章句上》第四十五节谈到爱有等级时说："君子之于物也，爱之而弗仁；于民也，仁之而弗亲。亲亲而仁民，仁民而爱物。"这也是说，爱是有等级差别的。《滕文公章句上》第五节记载，有一位墨家人士夷之与孟子交往的故事。孟子问夷之是否真的相信，人爱邻居的孩子可以和爱自己弟兄的孩子一样，因为人爱自己弟兄的孩子总是自然要比爱邻居的孩子多些。在孟子看来，这是完全正常的。由此前进一步，人应当把这种爱推广到邻居和社会其他成员。《孟子·梁惠王章句上》第七节记载孟子的主张："老吾老，以及人之老；幼吾幼，以及人之幼。"这就是孟子在同一节里所说的"善推其所为"。这是在"爱有等级"的原则下发展出来的。

从爱家人推广到爱其他人，就是实践孔子所说的"忠恕之道"，也就是"仁"的实践。在这些实践中，没有任何勉强的成分，因为人的本性就有恻隐之心，不忍看到别人受苦。由这一点善端推而广之，就使人自然地爱别人，而且也同样自然地爱父母多于爱众人。

这是儒家的观点。墨子则坚持爱众人与爱父母应当没有差别。不管这在实际上意味着少爱一点父母，或多爱一点众人，总之，

or love others more, the fact remains that the Confucianist type of graded love should be avoided at all costs. It is with this in mind that Mencius attacks the Mohist principle of all-embracing love as meaning that a man treats his father as of no account.

The above difference between the Confucianist and the Mohist theory of love has been pointed out very clearly by Mencius and by many others after him. Besides this, however, there is another difference of a more fundamental nature. This is, that the Confucianists considered human-heartedness as a quality that develops naturally from within the human nature, whereas the Mohists considered all-embracing love as something artificially added to man from without.

Mo Tzu may also be said to have answered a question that did not occur to Confucius, namely: Why should man practice human-heartedness and righteousness? His answer, however, is based on utilitarianism, and his emphasis on supernatural and political sanctions to compel and induce people to practice all-embracing love is not consistent with the Confucianist principle that virtue should be done for its own sake. If we compare the *Mo-tzu's* chapter on "All-Embracing Love," as quoted above in the fifth chapter, with the quotations here from the *Mencius* on the four moral beginnings in man's nature, we see very clearly the fundamental difference between the two schools.

- **Political Philosophy**

We have seen earlier that the Mohist theory of the origin of state is likewise a utilitarianistic one. Here again the Confucianist theory differs. Mencius says: "If men have satisfied their hunger, have clothes to wear, and live at ease but lack good teaching, they are close to the birds and beasts. The sage [Shun, a legendary sage-ruler] was distressed about this and appointed Hsieh as an official instructor to teach men the basic relationships of life. Father and son should love each other. Ruler and subject should be just to each other. Husband and wife should distinguish their respective spheres. Elder and younger brothers should have a sense of mutual precedence. And between friends there should be good faith." (*Mencius*, IIIa, 4.) The existence of the human relationships and the moral principles based on them is what differentiates man from birds and beasts. The state and society have their origin in the existence of these human relationships. Therefore, according to the Mohists, the state exists because it is useful. But according to the Confucianists, it exists because it ought to exist.

是要消弭儒家主张的有差别之爱。孟子正是有鉴于这一点而责难"墨氏兼爱，是无父也"。

孟子和在他之后的其他许多思想家都曾清楚指出儒墨两家在爱的理论上的上述分歧。不仅如此，儒墨两家还有一个更根本性的分歧：儒家认为，人顺其本性，就自然发展出仁的品德；而墨家则认为，兼爱是要靠外力加之于人的。

对儒家来说，人为什么要行仁义，是不需要提出的问题，因为这是人的本性。墨家则回答了人何以需要行仁义这个问题。墨子的回答是为了功利的缘故，为此他求助于超自然和政治的强制力量，这与儒家主张道德必须出于人的自愿，又是互相矛盾的。如果把《墨子》书中关于兼爱的三章与《孟子》书中论人性中"德之四端"相比较，这种根本分歧是十分明显的。

● **政治哲学**

前面曾指出，墨子关于国家起源的理论也是以功利为基础的，这和儒家的理论也是不同的。在《孟子·滕文公章句上》第四节中，孟子说："人之有道也，饱食、暖衣、逸居而无教，则近于禽兽。圣人有忧，使契为司徒，教以人伦：父子有亲，君臣有义，夫妇有别，长幼有序，朋友有信。"人伦关系和基于人伦的道德是人之所以区别于禽兽的地方。社会和国家的起源要追溯到社会中人伦关系的存在。墨家认为，国家之所以存在是因为它有用；儒家则认为，国家之所以存在是因为它应当存在。

Men have their full realization and development only in human relationships. Like Aristotle, Mencius maintains that "man is a political animal" and can fully develop these relationships only within state and society. The state is a moral institution and the head of the state should be a moral leader. Therefore in Confucianist political philosophy only a sage can be a real king. Mencius pictures this ideal as having existed in an idealized past. According to him, there was a time when the sage Yao (supposed to have lived in the twenty-fourth century B.C.) was Emperor. When he was old, he selected a younger sage, Shun, whom he had taught how to be a ruler, so that at Yao's death, Shun became Emperor. Similarly, when Shun was old, he again selected a younger sage, Yü, to be his successor. Thus the throne was handed from sage to sage, which, according to Mencius, is as it ought to be.

If a ruler lacks the ethical qualities that make a good leader, the people have the moral right of revolution. In that case, even the killing of the ruler is no longer a crime of regicide. This is because, according to Mencius, if a sovereign does not act as he ideally ought to do, he morally ceases to be a sovereign and, following Confucius' theory of the rectification of names, is a "mere fellow," as Mencius says. (*Mencius*, IIb, 8.) Mencius also says: "The people are the most important element [in a state]; the spirits of the land and the grain are secondary; and the sovereign is the least." (*Mencius*, VIIb, 14.) These ideas of Mencius have exercised a tremendous influence in Chinese history, even as late as the revolution of 1911, which led to the establishment of the Chinese Republic. It is true that modern democratic ideas from the West played their role too in this event, but the ancient native concept of the "right of revolution" had a greater influence on the mass of the people.

If a sage becomes king, his government is called one of kingly government. According to Mencius and later Confucianists, there are two kinds of government. One is that of the *wang* or (sage) king; the other is that of the *pa* or military lord. These are completely different in kind.

The government of a sage-king is carried on through moral instruction and education; that of a military lord is conducted through force and compulsion. The power of the *wang* government is moral, that of the *pa* government, physical. Mencius says in this connection: "He who uses force in the place of virtue is a *pa*. He who is virtuous and practices human-heartedness is a *wang*. When one subdues men by force, they do not submit to him in their hearts but only outwardly, because they have

　　人只有在人际关系中才能够充分发展。孟子和亚里士多德一样，认为"人是一种政治动物"。人的各种人伦关系只有在国家和社会之中才能发展。国家是一种道德体制，国家的领袖也应当是社会的道德领袖。因此，在儒家的政治哲学中，只有圣人才能成为真正的君主。孟子进一步，把这种理想描绘成古代曾经有过的事实。他说，在远古时代，圣人尧（传说生活于公元前二十四世纪）是国君。尧年老，选择一位年轻的圣人舜，授以圣王之道，把王位禅让给舜。舜年老时，同样选择了禹，最后把王位禅让给禹。这样，王位由老一代圣人传给年轻一代圣人。孟子认为，这是王位嬗替之道。

　　如果国君缺少领袖的道德品质，据孟子看法，百姓有一种道德权利，进行革命。这时候，如果把国君杀掉，只是杀一个不义之人，不算"弑君"。在《孟子·公孙丑章句下》第八节，孟子认为，国君如果言行举止不配做一个国君，按孔子"正名"的主张，他在道德上就已不再是国君，而变成了一个"独夫"。在《尽心章句下》第十四节，孟子说："民为贵，社稷次之，君为轻。"孟子的这些思想在中国历史上有巨大的影响，直到一九一一年，推翻帝制，建立民国，其中虽然有近代西方民主思想的影响，但中国自古以来主张的"革命权利"在民众中间拥有更大的影响。

　　如果一个圣人成为国君，他的统治便称为"王道"。按照孟子和后来儒家的看法，政治统治有两种，一种是"王道"，一种是"霸道"。王道是"圣王之道"，霸道则是依靠暴力实行统治，它们是性质完全不同的两种统治。圣王之道是靠道德教诲和教育来贯彻的，霸道则是以强制手段来推行的。王道的力量来自道德教化，而霸道的力量则来自武力。在《公孙丑章句上》第三节里，孟子说："以力假仁者霸，霸必有大国；以德行仁者王，王不待大。汤以七十里，

insufficient strength to resist. But when one gains followers by virtue, they are pleased in their hearts and will submit of themselves as did the seventy disciples to Confucius." (*Mencius*, IIa, 3.)

This distinction between *wang* and *pa* has always been maintained by later Chinese political philosophers. In terms of contemporary politics, we may say that a democratic government is a *wang* government, because it represents a free association of people, while a Fascist government is that of a *pa*, because it reigns through terror and physical force.

The sage-king in his kingly government does all he can for the welfare and benefit of the people, which means that his state must be built on a sound economic basis. Since China has always been overwhelmingly agrarian, it is natural that, according to Mencius, the most important economic basis of kingly government lies in the equal distribution of land. His ideal land system is what has been known as the "well-field system." According to this system, each square *li* (about one third of a mile) of land is to be divided into nine squares, each consisting of one hundred Chinese acres. The central square is known as the "public field," while the eight surrounding squares are the private land of eight farmers with their families, each family having one square. These farmers cultivate the public field collectively and their own fields individually. The produce of the public field goes to the government, while each family keeps for itself what it raises from its own field. The arrangement of the nine squares resembles in form the Chinese character for "well" 井, which is why it is called the "well-field system." (*Mencius* IIIa, 3.)

Describing this system further, Mencius states that each family should plant mulberry trees around its five-acre homestead in its own field so that its aged members may be clothed with silk. Each family should also raise fowls and pigs, so that its aged members may be nourished with meat. If this is done, everyone under the kingly government can "nourish the living and bury the dead without the least dissatisfaction, which marks the beginning of the kingly way." (*Mencius*, Ia, 3.)

It marks, however, only the "beginning," because it is an exclusively economic basis for the higher culture of the people. Only when everyone has received some education and come to an understanding of the human relationships, does the kingly way become complete.

The practice of this kingly way is not something alien to human nature, but is rather the direct outcome of the development by the

文王以百里。以力服人者，非心服也，力不赡也；以德服人者，中心悦而诚服也，如七十子之服孔子也。"

孟子以后的中国政治哲学家都持守这种"王"和"霸"的区别。如果以当代政治学的原理来对照，我们可以说，民主政治便是王道，因为它是人民大众的自由结合；法西斯统治则是霸道，因为它以恐怖和暴力来推行统治。

圣王遵行王道，自然竭尽所能来促进人民大众的福利，这就意味着，国家必定要建立在一个健全的经济基础之上。中国从来都是农业国家，照孟子看来，遵行王道，最重要的健全经济基础就是在农民中间实行土地的平均分配。他在《滕文公章句上》第三节描述他理想中的土地制度是实行"井田制"。中国历来衡量距离以"里"为单位（约相当于三分之一英里），如果把每一平方里划为九个方块，每一方块面积包含一百亩（中国传统的土地丈量单位）。孟子主张把九块方田的中央一块作为"公田"，周围八块田地分给八家农户。他们各自耕种自己的一块田地，又共同耕种中间的"公田"；公田的出产归皇家，私田的出产归农民自己。这个安排的形式，很像中文的"井"字，因此，它被称为"井田制"。

孟子进一步描绘在他理想中的农村，每户人家以五亩土地作为居住的房屋，房屋周围种植桑树，桑叶可以养蚕，这样，每户人家的老人可以穿上丝绸的锦衣。每户人家还要饲养生猪、家禽，这样，老人可以有肉吃。如果实行这个理想，按《孟子·梁惠王章句上》第三节记载："是使民养生丧死无憾也。养生丧死无憾，王道之始也。"

这还只是"王道之始"，因为照孟子的看法，经济只是更高文化的起步。只有当人人都受到适当教育、懂得人伦之道，这时，王道才能完全实现。

照孟子看来，王道不离人的本性。它是圣王循其"怜悯之心"

sage-king of his own "feeling of commiseration." As Mencius says: "All men have a mind which cannot bear [to see the suffering of] others. The early kings, having this unbearing mind, thereby had likewise an unbearing government." (*Mencius*, IIa, 6.) The "unbearing mind" and feeling of commiseration are one in Mencius' thought. As we have seen, the virtue of human-heartedness, according to the Confucianists, is nothing but the development of this feeling of commiseration; this feeling in its turn cannot be developed save through the practice of love; and the practice of love is nothing more than the "extension of one's scope of activity to include others," which is the way of *chung* and *shu*. The kingly way or kingly government is nothing but the result of the king's practice of love, and his practice of *chung* and *shu*.

According to Mencius, there is nothing esoteric or difficult in the kingly way. The *Mencius* (Ib, 9) records that on one occasion, when an ox was being led to sacrifice, King Hsüan of Ch'i saw it and could not endure "its frightened appearance, as if it were an innocent person going to the place of death." He therefore ordered that it be replaced by a sheep. Mencius then told the King that this was an example of his "unbearing mind," and if he could only extend it to include human affairs, he could then govern in the kingly way. The King replied that he could not do this because he had the defect of loving wealth and feminine beauty. Whereupon Mencius told the King that these are things loved by all men. If the King, by understanding his own desires, would also come to understand the desires of all his people, and would take measures whereby the people might satisfy these desires, this would result in the kingly way and nothing else.

What Mencius told King Hsüan is nothing more than the "extension of one's own scope of activity to include others," which is precisely the practice of *chung* and *shu*. Here we see how Mencius developed the ideas of Confucius. In his exposition of this principle, Confucius had limited himself to its application to the self-cultivation of the individual, while by Mencius its application was extended to government and politics. For Confucius, it was a principle only for "sageliness within," but by Mencius it was expanded to become also a principle for "kingliness without."

Even in the former sense of "sageliness within," Mencius expresses his concept of this principle more clearly than did Confucius. He says: "He who has completely developed his mind, knows his nature. He who

加以发展的结果。这就是《孟子·公孙丑章句上》第六节所说："人皆有不忍人之心。先王有不忍人之心，斯有不忍人之政矣。"这里所说"不忍人之心"和怜悯之心，在孟子思想中是一回事。在儒家看来，"仁"乃是怜悯之心的发展结果，怜悯之心要靠实行仁爱才能发展，实行仁爱，就是"推己及人"，而这就是"忠恕之道"。王道乃是君王实行仁爱的结果，也是君王实行"忠恕之道"的结果。

在孟子看来，实行王道并没有什么奥秘或困难之处。《孟子·梁惠王章句上》第七节里记载，有一次齐宣王坐在堂上，有人牵牛经过堂下，齐宣王问：把牛牵到哪里去？仆人回答说：把牛牵去献祭。宣王说：把牛放了吧，我实在不忍看它颤栗害怕的样子，像是无罪而被处死。仆人问：那么，还要不要献祭呢？宣王说：祭祀怎么可以废除？换上一只羊去献祭吧。孟子听说此事，问齐宣王，是否确有其事。宣王回答，确有其事。孟子说，凭这种善心，推而广之，就可以实行王道了。在《梁惠王章句下》第五节记载，齐宣王向往王道，只是未能实行。孟子问："王如善之，则何为不行？"齐宣王承认，因为自己太爱财货、女色。孟子告诉宣王，这是天下人的通好。如果国君从自己所爱好而想到天下人都有同好，设法去满足天下人，这就是实行王道了。

孟子对齐宣王所说，无非是"善推其所为"，这正是实行"忠恕之道"。从这里可以看到，孟子怎样发展孔子的原理，使它更加清楚。孔子对他的原理的解释限于个人品德修养的范围，孟子则把它推广到政治和治理国家的范围。孔子解释他的原理时，只讲到"内圣"，孟子则把它推广到"外王"的范围。

即便在"内圣"的范围之内，孟子也比孔子讲得更清楚。在《尽心章句上》第一节，孟子说："尽其心者，知其性也。知其性，

knows his nature, knows Heaven." (*Mencius*, VIIa, 1.) The mind here referred to is the "unbearing mind" or the "feeling of commiseration." It is the essence of our nature. Hence when we fully develop this mind, we know our nature. And according to Mencius, our nature is "what Heaven has given to us." (*Mencius*, VIa, 15.) Therefore, when we know our nature, we also know Heaven.

- **Mysticism**

According to Mencius and his school of Confucianism, the universe is essentially a moral universe. The moral principles of man are also metaphysical principles of the universe, and the nature of man is an exemplification of these principles. It is this moral universe that Mencius and his school mean when they speak of Heaven, and an understanding of this moral universe is what Mencius calls "knowing Heaven." If a man knows Heaven, he is not only a citizen of society, but also a "citizen of Heaven," *t'ien min*, as Mencius says. (*Mencius*, VIIa, 19.) Mencius further makes a distinction between "human honors" and "heavenly honors." He says: "There are heavenly honors and human honors. Human-heartedness, righteousness, loyalty, good faith, and the untiring practice of the good: these are the honors of Heaven. Princes, ministers, and officials: these are the honors of man." (*Mencius*, VIa, 16.) In other words, heavenly honors are those to which a man can attain in the world of values, while human honors are purely material concepts in the human world. The citizen of Heaven, just because he is the citizen of Heaven, cares only for the honors of Heaven, but not those of man.

Mencius also remarks: "All things are complete within us. There is no greater delight than to realize this through self-cultivation. And there is no better way to human-heartedness than the practice of the principle of *shu*." (*Mencius*, VIIa, 1.) In other words, through the full development of his nature, a man cannot only know Heaven, but can also become one with Heaven. Also when a man fully develops his unbearing mind, he has within him the virtue of human-heartedness, and the best way to human-heartedness is the practice of *chung* and *shu*. Through this practice, one's egoism and selfishness are gradually reduced. And when they are reduced, one comes to feel that there is no longer a distinction between oneself and others, and so of distinction between the individual and the universe. That is to say, one becomes identified with the universe as a whole. This leads to a realization that "all things are complete within us." In this phrase we see the mystical element of Mencius' philosophy.

则知天矣。"这里所讲的"心",便是"不忍人之心",也就是"恻隐之心"。这是人的本性,因此,发展人的本心便是知晓人的本性。在《告子章句上》第十五节里,孟子讲到人的本性,说:"此天之所与我者。"所以,知道人的本性,也就知道了天道。

● 神秘主义

孟子和儒家之中他的这一流派认为,宇宙从根本来说,是一个道德的宇宙。人间的道德原则也是流行于宇宙之中的形而上学原理,人性便是这些原理的实证。孟子和他的学派说到"天"时,就是指这个由道德主宰的宇宙,懂得了这个由道德主宰的宇宙,就是孟子所说的"知天"。一个人如果知道了天道,他便不仅是一个国民,还是孟子在《尽心章句上》第十九节所说的一个"天民"。在《告子章句上》第十六节,孟子还进一步区别所谓"天爵"和"人爵"说:"有天爵者,有人爵者。仁义忠信,乐善不倦,此天爵也;公卿大夫,此人爵也。"照他看来,天爵是指人在精神价值领域中的成就,而人爵则是人间纯物质领域的观念,天民所关心的是天爵,而不是人爵。

在《尽心章句上》第四节,孟子还说:"万物皆备于我矣。反身而诚,乐莫大焉。强恕而行,求仁莫近焉。"换句话说,人如果充分发展人的本性,不仅可以知天,而且可以与天合一。在生活中,一个人如果充分发展不忍人之心,就得到了仁,实行忠恕之道便是到达仁的最佳道路。在这样的生活实践之中,人的自我中心和自私将会逐渐减少,使人觉得"人"和"己"之间不再有别,"人"和"天"之间的差别也不复存在。这时,个人和宇宙便融合一体,实现孟子所说"万物皆备于我"。这句话使我们看到孟子哲学中的神秘主义成分。

We will understand this mysticism better, if we turn to Mencius' discussion on what he calls the *Hao Jan Chih Ch'i*, a term which I translate as the "Great Morale." In this discussion Mencius describes the development of his own spiritual cultivation.

The *Mencius* (IIa, 2) tells us that a disciple asked Mencius of what he was a specialist. Mencius replied: "I know the right and wrong in speech, and am proficient in cultivating my *Hao Jan Chih Ch'i*." The questioner then asked what this was, and Mencius replied: "It is the *Ch'i*, supremely great, supremely strong. If it be directly cultivated without handicap, then it pervades all between Heaven and Earth. It is the *Ch'i* which is achieved by the combination of righteousness and *Tao* [the way, the truth], and without these it will be weakened."

Hao Jan Chih Ch'i is a special term of Mencius. In later times, under his increasing influence, it came to be used not infrequently, but in ancient times it appears only in this one chapter. As to what it signifies, even Mencius admits that "it is hard to say." (*Ibid.*) The context of this discussion, however, includes a preliminary discussion about two warriors and their method of cultivating their valor. From this I infer that Mencius' *Ch'i* (a word which literally means vapor, gas, spiritual force) is the same *ch'i* as occurs in such terms as *yung ch'i* (courage, valor) and *shih ch'i* (morale of an army). That is why I translate *Hao Jan Chih Ch'i* as the "Great Morale." It is of the same nature as the morale of the warriors. The difference between the two, however, is that this *Ch'i* is further described as *hao jan*, which means "great to a supreme degree." The morale which warriors cultivate is a matter concerning man and man, and so is a moral value only. But the Great Morale is a matter concerning man and the universe, and therefore is a super-moral value. It is the morale of the man who identifies himself with the universe, so that Mencius says of it that "it pervades all between Heaven and Earth."

The method of cultivating the Great Morale has two aspects. One may be called the "understanding of *Tao*"; that is, of the way or principle that leads to the elevation of the mind. The other aspect is what Mencius calls the "accumulation of righteousness"; that is, the constant doing of what one ought to do in the universe as a "citizen of the universe." The combination of these two aspects is called by Mencius "the combination of righteousness and *Tao*."

After one has reached an understanding of *Tao* and the long accumulation of righteousness, the Great Morale will appear naturally of itself. The least bit of forcing will lead to failure. As Mencius says: "We

在这里让我们看一下孟子所讲的"浩然之气"，可以帮助我们进一步了解孟子哲学中的神秘主义成分。孟子谈"浩然之气"，和他的精神修养是联系在一起的。

在《公孙丑章句上》第二节记载，孟子和他的学生公孙丑有一段对话，学生问："敢问夫子何所长？"曰："我知言，我善养吾浩然之气。""敢问何谓浩然之气？"曰："难言也。其为气也，至大至刚，以直养而无害，则塞于天地之间。其为气也，配义与道；无是，馁也。"

"浩然之气"是孟子的一个专有用语。后世，孟子的思想影响逐渐上升，使用这个术语的思想家逐渐增多，在先秦，"浩然之气"只见于《孟子·公孙丑章句上》。至于它的含义，连孟子也说："难言也。"这段对话的上下文是讲两个武士培养勇敢精神的不同方法。从这里，我的推论是：孟子所讲的"气"是由人的"勇气""士气"而来。这和武士的气概是一回事，但两者之间有一点差别，"浩然之气"的"浩然"比武士的勇气更广泛、也更超乎世俗。武士们的气概是指人与人的关系，因此，它仅仅是道德范围的事情；浩然之气则是人和宇宙之间的关系，因此，它是超越道德的价值。它是人和宇宙融为一体的气概，因此孟子说它是"塞于天地之间"。

培养浩然之气的办法分两方面：一个方面是"明道"，提高人对"道"的领悟；另一方面是孟子所称的"积义"，即坚持不懈地做"天民"所当做的事情。这两方面结合起来就是孟子所说的"配义与道"。

一个人如果从体验中懂得了道，又长期行义，在他身上自然就有浩然之气，但如果有一点勉强，浩然之气就消逝了。在《公孙丑

should not be like the man of Sung. There was a man of Sung who was grieved that his grain did not grow fast enough. So he pulled it up. Then he returned to his home with great innocence, and said to his people: 'I am tired today, for I have been helping the grain to grow.' His son ran out to look at it, and found all the grain withered." (*Ibid.*)

When one grows something, one must on the one hand do something for it, but on the other never "help it to grow." The cultivation of the Great Morale is just like the growing of the grain. One must do something, which is the practice of virtue. Though Mencius here speaks of righteousness rather than human-heartedness, there is no practical difference, since human-heartedness is the inner content, of which righteousness is the outer expression. If one constantly practices righteousness, the Great Morale will naturally emerge from the very center of one's being.

Although this *Hao Jan Chih Ch'i* sounds rather mysterious, it can nevertheless, according to Mencius, be achieved by every man. This is because it is nothing more than the fullest development of the nature of man, and every man has fundamentally the same nature. His nature is the same, just as every man's bodily form is the same. As an example, Mencius remarks that when a shoemaker makes shoes, even though he does not know the exact length of the feet of his customers, he always makes shoes, but not baskets. (*Mencius*, VIa, 7.) This is so because the similarity between the feet of all men is much greater than their difference. And likewise the sage, in his original nature, is similar to everyone else. Hence every man can become a sage, if only he gives full development to his original nature. As Mencius affirms: "All men can become Yao or Shun [the two legendary sage-rulers previously mentioned]." (*Mencius*, VIb, 2.) Here is Mencius' theory of education, which has been held by all Confucianists.

章句上》的同一段对话中，孟子用宋人"揠苗助长"的故事来告诫人们"无若宋人然"。

人们种植庄稼时，要为庄稼生长做许多事情，但有一样事情万万不能做，就是去拔苗助长。人"养其浩然之气"也像种庄稼一样，最需要做的事情便是积累善德。孟子在这里虽然说得更多的是"积义"，而不是"积仁"，其实它们的实际内容是一样的，仁是指内涵，义是指外面的表现。一个人如果经常行义，浩然之气便会从他内心自然地涌现出来。

听起来，"浩然之气"似乎有点神妙莫测，但是，孟子认为，每个人都能在自己身上培养浩然之气，因为这无非就是发挥人的自然本性，而这种自然本性是人人都有的。人的本性相同，正如人人都有一个身体，都有五官四肢。在《告子章句上》第七节里，孟子以比喻说："不知足而为屦，我知其不为蒉（草篮）也。屦之相似，天下之足同也。"制鞋匠不必知道天下人人的脚的尺寸，因为人们的脚，共同之处比相异之处要多。依同样的道理，圣人顺其本性，与世上万人都相接近。因此，世人只要充分发展本性，人人都可以成圣人。《告子章句下》第二节记载孟子认为，"人皆可以为尧舜"。这是孟子的教育思想，此后的儒家都继承了孟子的这个思想。

❽ THE SCHOOL OF NAMES

The term *Ming chia* has sometimes been translated as "sophists," and sometimes as "logicians" or "dialecticians." It is true that there is some similarity between the *Ming chia* and the sophists, logicians, and dialecticians, but it is also true that they are not quite the same. To avoid confusion, it is better to translate *Ming chia* literally as the School of Names. This translation also helps to bring to the attention of Westerners one of the important problems discussed by Chinese philosophy, namely that of the relation between *ming* (the name) and *shih* (the actuality).

- **The School of Names and the "Debaters"**

Logically speaking, the contrast between *ming* and *shih* in ancient Chinese philosophy is something like that between subject and predicate in the West. For instance, when we say: "This is a table," or "Socrates is a man," "this" and "Socrates" are *shih* or actualities, while "table" and "man" are *ming* or names. This is obvious enough. Let us, however, try to analyze more exactly just what the *shih* or *ming* are, and what their relationship is. We are then apt to be led into some rather paradoxical problems, the solution of which brings us to the very heart of philosophy.

The members of the School of Names were known in ancient times as *pien che* (debaters, disputers, arguers). In the chapter of the *Chuang-tzu* titled "The Autumn Flood," Kung-sun Lung, one of the leaders of the School of Names, is represented as saying: "I have unified similarity and difference, and separated hardness and whiteness. I have proved the impossible as possible and affirmed what others deny. I have controverted the knowledge of all the philosophers, and refuted all the arguments brought against me." (*Chuang-tzu*, ch. 17.) These words are really applicable to the School of Names as a whole. Its members were known as persons who made paradoxical statements, who were ready to dispute with others, and who purposely affirmed what others denied and denied what others affirmed. Ssu-ma T'an (died 110 B.C.), for example, in his essay, "On the Essential Ideas of the Six Schools," wrote: "The School of Names conducted minute examinations of trifling points in complicated and elaborate statements, which made it impossible for others to refute their ideas." (*Historical Records*, ch. 120.)

Hsün Tzu, a Confucianist of the third century B.C., describes Teng Hsi (died 501 B.C.) and Hui Shih as philosophers who "liked to deal with

捌 名家

名家这个学派，在英文里有时被译作"智者学派"（sophists），有时被译作"逻辑家"（logicians）或"辩证法家"（dialecticians）。名家与西方传统哲学中的智者学派、逻辑家、辩证法家确有某些相似之处，但并不完全相同。为避免混乱，还是称它"名家"较妥，为西方人由此而注意到中国哲学里"名"和"实"的关系这个重要问题，也是有好处的。

● 名家和"辩者"

就逻辑说，先秦中国哲学所讲的"名"与"实"的对立，有点像西方语言中主词和宾词的关系。例如，当我们说"这是一张桌子"或"苏格拉底是一个男人"，"这"和"苏格拉底"是"实"，"桌子"和"男人"则是"名"。让我们进一步具体分析一下，名和实的实质是什么，它们的关系是什么。这不免把我们带入一些似非而是的矛盾问题，实际上正是进入了哲学的中心问题。

先秦称"名家"为"辩者"。《庄子·秋水》篇里记载，名家的代表性人物公孙龙曾以下面这段话介绍自己："龙少学先王之道，长而明仁义之行；合同异，离坚白，然不然，可不可，困百家之知，穷众口之辩。"这些话对名家都是适用的。名家往往说一些似非而是的话，在与人辩论中，往往对别人否定的加以肯定，而对别人肯定的又加以否定，以此而著名。司马谈在《论六家要旨》文中便说："名家苛察缴绕，使人不得反其意。"（《史记·太史公自序》）

公元前三世纪的儒家思想家荀子描述邓析（死于公元前五〇一年）和惠施"好治怪说，玩琦辞"（《荀子·非十二子》）。《吕氏春秋

strange theories and indulge in curious propositions." (*Hsün-tzu*, ch. 6.) Likewise, the *Lü-shih Ch'un-ch'iu* mentions Teng Hsi and Kung-sun Lung as among those known for their paradoxical arguments. (XVIII, 4 and 5.) And the chapter titled "The World" in the *Chuang-tzu*, after listing the paradoxical arguments famous at that time, mentions the names of Hui Shih, Huan T'uan, and Kung-sun Lung. These men, therefore, would seem to have been the most important leaders of this school.

About Huan T'uan we know nothing further, but about Teng Hsi, we know that he was a famous lawyer of his time; his writings, however, no longer are preserved, and the book today bearing the title of *Teng-hsi-tzu* is not genuine. The *Lü-shih Ch'un-ch'iu* says that when Tzu-ch'an, a famous statesman, was minister of the state of Cheng, Teng Hsi, who was a native of that state, was his major opponent. He used to help the people in their lawsuits, for which services he would demand a coat as a fee for a major case, and a pair of trousers for a minor one. So skilful was he that he was patronized by numerous people; as their lawyer, he succeeded in changing right into wrong and wrong into right, until no standards of right and wrong remained, so that what was regarded as possible and impossible fluctuated from day to day. (XVIII, 4.)

Another story in the same work describes how, during a flood of the Wei River, a certain rich man of the state of Cheng was drowned. His body was picked up by a boatman, but when the family of the rich man went to ask for the body, the man who had found it demanded a huge reward. Thereupon the members of the family went to Teng Hsi for advice. He told them: "Merely wait. There is nobody else besides yourselves who wants the body." The family took his advice and waited, until the man who had found the body became much troubled and also went to Teng Hsi. To him Teng Hsi said: "Merely wait. There is nobody else but you from whom they can get the body." (*Ibid.*) We are not told what was the final end of this episode!

It would thus seem that Teng Hsi's trick was to interpret the formal letter of the law in such a way as to give varying interpretations in different cases at will. This was how he was able to "conduct minute examinations of trifling points in complicated and elaborate statements, which made it impossible for others to refute his ideas." He thus devoted himself to interpreting and analyzing the letter of the law, while disregarding its spirit and its connection with actuality. In other words, his attention was directed to "names," instead of to "actualities." Such was the spirit of the School of Names.

From this we may see that the *pien che* were originally lawyers, among whom Teng Hsi was evidently one of the first. He was, however,

提到邓析和公孙龙时，也说他们是"言意相离"、"言心相离"（《审应览·离渭·淫辞》)。《庄子·天下》篇列举当时著名的哲学反论（或"悖论"）之后，还举出惠施、桓团、公孙龙的名字。由此可见，这些人是名家最主要的人物。

对于桓团，我们别无所知。对于邓析，我们知道，他是当时一位著名的诉讼专家，他的著述已经佚失，现在流传的《邓析子》乃是伪书。《吕氏春秋·审应览·离渭》篇中说："子产治郑，邓析务难之。与民之有狱者约，大狱一衣，小狱襦袴。民之献衣、襦袴而学讼者，不可胜数。以非为是，以是为非，是非无度，而可与不可日变。"

《吕氏春秋》同一篇里还记述了一个故事，洧河水灾，郑国一富人溺死。尸体被一舟子捞起，向死者家属索要巨款，方肯归还尸体。死者家属向邓析求计，邓析说："不妨等待，因为没有别人会要那具死尸。"死者家属按邓析之策拖延等候。捞起尸体的舟子也去向邓析求计，邓析教他说："不妨等待，因为死者家属只有来你这里，才能买回死者尸体。"《吕氏春秋》没有记载这个故事的结局。

看来，邓析的手法是利用法律条款的文字，在不同情况下作不同的解释。这是他得以"苟察缴绕，使人不得反其意"的办法。他撇开法律条文要联系实际情况这个基本原则，专在法律条款上做文字游戏。换句话说，他只讲"名"，而切断"名"与"实"的联系。这便是名家思想主张的实质。

从这里可以看到，"辩者"源自诉讼专家，邓析便是其中最早的人物。但他只是分析"名""实"问题的一个先驱，在哲学上的

only a beginner in the analysis of names, and made no real contribution to philosophy as such. Hence the real founders of the School of Names were the later Hui Shih and Kung-sun Lung.

Concerning these two men the *Lü-shih Ch'un-ch'iu* tells us: "Hui Tzu [Hui Shih] prepared the law for King Hui of Wei (370-319 B.C.). When it was completed and was made known to the people, the people considered it to be good." (XVIII, 5.) And again: "The states of Chao and Ch'in entered into an agreement which said: 'From this time onward, in whatever Ch'in desires to do, she is to be assisted by Chao, and in whatever Chao desires to do, she is to be assisted by Ch'in.' But soon afterward Ch'in attacked the state of Wei, and Chao made ready to go to Wei's assistance. The King of Ch'in protested to Chao that this was an infringement of the pact, and the King of Chao reported this to the Lord of P'ing-yüan, who again told it to Kung-sun Lung. Kung-sun Lung said: 'We too can send an envoy to protest to the King of Ch'in, saying: "According to the pact, each side guarantees to help the other in whatever either desires to do. Now it is our desire to save Wei, and if you do not help us to do so, we shall charge you with infringement of the pact."'" (*Ibid.*)

Again we are told in the *Han-fei-tzu*: "When discussions on 'hardness and whiteness' and 'having no thickness' appear, the governmental laws lose their effect." (Ch. 41.) We shall see below that the doctrine of "hardness and whiteness" is one of Kung-sun Lung, while that of "having no thickness" is one of Hui Shih.

From these stories we may see that Hui Shih and Kung-sun Lung were, to some extent, connected with the legal activities of their time. Indeed, Kung-sun Lung's interpretation of the pact between Chao and Ch'in is truly in the spirit of Teng Hsi. Han Fei Tzu considered the effect of the "speeches" of these two gentlemen on law to be as bad as that of the practice of Teng Hsi. It may seem strange that Han Fei Tzu, himself a Legalist, should oppose, as destructive to law, the "discussions" of a school which had originated with lawyers. But, as we shall see in chapter

14, Han Fei Tzu and the other Legalists were really politicians, not jurists.

Hui Shih and Kung-sun Lung represented two tendencies in the School of Names, the one emphasizing the relativity of actual things, and the other the absoluteness of names. This distinction becomes evident when one comes to analyze names in their relationship to actualities. Let us take the simple statement, "This is a table." Here the word "this" refers to the concrete actuality, which is impermanent and may come and go.

贡献不大，真正创立名家哲学的是惠施和公孙龙。

《吕氏春秋》对这两个人物作了以下的简介："惠子为魏惠王（公元前三七〇至前三一九年在位）为法，为法已成，以示诸民人，民人皆善之。"（《审应览·淫辞》）在同篇里又说："秦赵相与约，约曰：'自今以来，秦之所欲为，赵助之；赵之所欲为，秦助之。'居无几何，秦兴兵攻魏，赵欲救之。秦王不悦，使之让赵王曰：'约曰，秦之所欲为，赵助之；赵之所欲为，秦助之。今秦欲攻魏，而赵因欲救之，此非约也。'赵王以告平原君，平原君以告公孙龙。公孙龙曰：亦可以发使而让秦王曰，'赵欲救之，今秦王独不助赵，此非约也。'"

《韩非子·问辩》篇中又说："坚白、无厚之词章，而宪令之法息。"我们在本章下面将会知道，"坚白"是公孙龙的学说，"无厚"是惠施的学说。韩非子认为公孙龙和惠施的一套论辩时兴起来是破坏了法律。

从上引各书可以知道，惠施和公孙龙与战国时期的法律活动是有联系的。公孙龙对秦、赵两国盟约的解释和邓析的思想是一致的。韩非认为，惠施和公孙龙关于法律的言论和邓析对法律条款玩弄文字游戏，其与破坏法律并无二致。韩非子自己是一位法家，却对由诉讼专家出身的法家探讨问题持反对态度，岂不令人感到奇怪？在本书第十四章里，我们将会看到，韩非子和其他法家其实是政客，并不是法学家。

惠施和公孙龙代表了名家的两种不同倾向，惠施强调现实的相对性，公孙龙则强调名的绝对性。当我们分析"名"与"实"的关系时，便可看出两人的不同倾向了。试举一个简单的例子来说明。当我们说"这是一张桌子"时，"这"是指具体的事物，它是在

The word "table," however, refers to an abstract category or name which is unchanging and always remains as it is. The "name" is absolute, but the "actuality" is relative. Thus "beauty" is the name of what is absolutely beautiful, but "a beautiful thing" can only be relatively so. Hui Shih emphasized the fact that actual things are changeable and relative, while Kung-sun Lung emphasized the fact that names are permanent and absolute.

● Hui Shih's Theory of Relativity

Hui Shih (fl. 350-260 B.C.) was a native of the state of Sung, in the present province of Honan. We know that he once became premier of King Hui of Wei (370-319 B.C.), and that he was known for his great learning. His writings, unfortunately, are lost, and what we know of his ideas may be deduced only from a series of "ten points" preserved in the chapter titled "The World" in the *Chuang-tzu*.

The first of these points is: "The greatest has nothing beyond itself, and is called the Great One. The smallest has nothing within itself, and is called the Small One." These two statements constitute what are called analytical propositions. They make no assertions in regard to the actual, for they say nothing about what, in the actual world, is the greatest thing and the smallest thing. They only touch upon the abstract concepts or names: "greatest" and "smallest." In order to understand these two propositions fully, we should compare them with a story in the chapter titled "The Autumn Flood" in the *Chuang-tzu*. From this it will become apparent that in one respect Hui Shih and Chuang Tzu had very much in common.

This story describes how in autumn, when the Yellow River was in flood, the Spirit of the River, who was very proud of his greatness, moved down the river to the sea. There he met the Spirit of the Sea, and realized for the first time that his river, great as it was, was small indeed in comparison with the sea. Yet when, full of admiration, he talked with the Spirit of the Sea, the latter replied that he himself, in his relationship to Heaven and Earth, was nothing more than a single grain lying within a great warehouse. Hence he could only be said to be "small," but not to be "great." At this the River Spirit asked the Sea Spirit: "Are we right then in saying that Heaven and Earth are supremely great and the tip of a hair is supremely small?" The Sea Spirit answered: "What men know is less than what they do not know. The time when they are alive is less than the time when they are not alive.... How can we know that the tip of a hair

变动中的，随时可能出现，也随时可以消逝。"桌子"则是一个抽象概念，它是固定不变的一个"名"。据此，可以说"美"是一切美丽的东西的共同名字，但如果说"一个美丽的东西"，它只能是相对的存在。惠施强调现实事物的不断变化和相对性；公孙龙则强调"名"是不变的、绝对的。

- ● 惠施关于事物相对性的理论

　　惠施（约生活于公元前三五〇至前二六〇年间），战国时宋国（在今河南）人，曾在魏惠王时任宰相，以学识渊博著名。他的著作不幸已经佚失，其中思想只能见于《庄子·天下》篇中列举的十点。

　　第一点是："至大无外，谓之大一；至小无内，谓之小一。"这两句话都是现在所称的"分析命题"。它们并未指认任何现实事物，说哪个就是"至大"，哪个就是"至小"。它只是说到"至大"和"至小"这两个抽象概念。为充分了解这两个命题，需要把它和《庄子·秋水》篇中的一个故事进行比较，从中我们将发现，惠施和庄子的思想在一个方面是十分一致的。

　　这个故事说，秋天来到，黄河河水上涨，河伯（河神的名字）为自己的伟大十分得意。及至随河水入海，才在汪洋大海中发现自己微不足道。河伯对海神北海若说，本来以为自己多么浩瀚，现在和大海相比，才认识到自己多么渺小。北海若回答说，若和天地相比，北海也无非是大谷仓里一颗细小的米粒。因此，只能称自己为"小"，而不能称自己为"大"。河伯又问北海若，如此说来，天地是否可以称作"至大"，而一根头发的毫末则是"至小"？北海若回答说，人所知道的要比他所不知道的少得多，人的生命比他没有存在的时间要短得多，人如何敢说，头发的毫末就是"至小"，

is the extreme of smallness, and Heaven and Earth are the extreme of greatness?" And he then went on to define the smallest as that which has no form, and the greatest as that which cannot be enclosed (by anything else). This definition of the supremely great and supremely small is similar to that given by Hui Shih. (*Chuang-tzu*, ch. 17.)

To say that Heaven and Earth are the greatest of things and that the tip of a hair is the smallest is to make assertions about the actual, the *shih*. It makes no analysis of the names of the actualities, the *ming*. These two propositions are what are called synthetic propositions and both may be false. They have their basis in experience; therefore their truth is only contingent, but not necessary. In experience, things that are great and things that are small are all relatively so. To quote the *Chuang-tzu* again: "If we call a thing great, because it is greater than something else, then there is nothing in the world that is not great. If we call a thing small because it is smaller than something else, then there is nothing in the world that is not small."

We cannot through actual experience decide what is the greatest and what is the smallest of actual things. But we can say independently of experience that that which has nothing beyond itself is the greatest, and that which has nothing within itself is the smallest. "Greatest" and "smallest," defined in this way, are absolute and unchanging concepts. Thus by analyzing the names, "Great One" and "Small One," Hui Shih reached the concept of what is absolute and unchanging. From the point of view of this concept, he realized that the qualities and differences of actual concrete things are all relative and liable to change.

Once we understand this position of Hui Shih, we can see that his series of "points," as reported by the *Chuang-tzu*, though usually regarded as paradoxes, are really not paradoxical at all. With the exception of the first, they are all illustrations of the relativity of things, and expressions of what may be called a theory of relativity. Let us study them one by one.

"That which has no thickness cannot be increased [in thickness], yet it is so great that it may cover one thousand miles." This states that the great and the small are so only relatively. It is impossible for that which has no thickness to be thick. In this sense it may be called small. Nevertheless, the ideal plane of geometry, though without thickness, may at the same time be very long and wide. In this sense it may be called great.

天地就是"至大"呢？然后，北海若说，大和小，都因有形，而后才有大小；其实，至小就无形可言，至大就不可能有任何范围。这个故事里关于"至大"和"至小"的解说和惠施的解说十分相似。

说天地是最大的事物，秋毫之末是最小的事物，都是就现实而言，因此所论的是"实"，它还未分析到"名"。关于"至大"和"至小"的这两个命题都属于所谓"综合命题"，它们都以现实为基础，它们的真实性都不是必然，而只是或然。在现实经验中，大的东西和小的东西都只是相对而言。正如《庄子·秋水》篇里所说，如果以事物相互比较，"因其所大而大之，则万物莫不大；因其所小而小之，则万物莫不小"。

人不可能通过现实的经验来决定现实事物之中，哪个是最大，哪个是最小。但如脱出经验的范围，我们可以说，无外的乃是"至大"，无内的乃是"至小"。以这样的方式来界定"至大"和"至小"，它们的定义就成为绝对的、不可更改的概念了。惠施通过对"大一"和"小一"的分析，得出了绝对的、不会改变的概念。从这两个概念出发，他认识到现实事物中的"质"和"区别"都是相对的，都是会改变的。

我们只要懂得惠施的这个基本观点，就能理解《庄子·天下》篇中举出惠施的十点主张（"惠施十事"），看似矛盾，在实质上并不然。除去上述的第一点，其他九点都是论证事物的相对性，可以说，这是一种对事物相对性的学说。下面让我们逐一考察一下。

"无厚，不可积也，其大千里。"这是说，"大"和"小"都只是相对而言。一个没有厚度的东西不可能使它厚起来，就这一点说，它可以被称为"小"。然而，几何学中的平面，它没有任何厚度，却可以很长很宽，就这一点说，它又可以被称为"大"。

"The heavens are as low as the earth; mountains are on the same level as marshes." This, too, states that the high and the low are so only relatively. "The sun at noon is the sun declining; the creature born is the creature dying." This states that everything in the actual world is changeable and changing.

"Great similarity differs from little similarity. This is called little-similarity-and-difference. All things are in one way all similar, in another way all different. This is called great-similarity-and-difference." When we say that all men are animals, we thereby recognize that all human beings are similar in the fact that they are human beings, and are also similar in the fact that they are animals. Their similarity in being human beings, however, is greater than that in being animals, because being a human being implies being an animal, but being an animal does not necessarily imply being a human being. For there are other kinds of animals as well, which are different from human beings. It is this kind of similarity and difference, therefore, that Hui Shih calls little-similarity-and-difference. However, if we take "beings" as a universal class, we thereby recognize that all things are similar in the fact that they are beings. But if we take each thing as an individual, we thereby recognize that each individual has its own individuality and so is different from other things. This kind of similarity and difference is what Hui Shih calls great-similarity-and-difference. Thus since we can say that all things are similar to each other, and yet can also say that all things are different from each other, this shows that their similarity and difference are both relative. This argument of the School of Names was a famous one in ancient China, and was known as the "argument for the unity of similarity and difference."

"The South has no limit and yet has a limit." "The South has no limit" was a common saying of the day. At that time, the South was a little known land very much like the West of America two hundred years ago. For the early Chinese, the South was not limited by sea as was the East, nor by barren desert as were the North and West. Hence it was popularly regarded as having no limit. Hui Shih's statement may thus perhaps be merely an expression of his superior geographical knowledge, that the South is, eventually, also limited by the sea. Most probably, however, it means to say that the limited and the unlimited are both only relatively so.

"I go to the state of Yüeh today and arrived there yesterday." This states that "today" and "yesterday" are relative terms. The yesterday of today

"天与地卑，山与泽平。"这是说，高和低也都只有相对的意义。"日方中方睨，物方生方死。"这是说，现实中的一切事物都是可变的，都是在变的。

"大同而与小同异，此之谓小同异；万物毕同毕异，此之谓大同异。"我们说，人都是动物，这是指他们都是人，因此有相似的方面。同时，他们都是动物，因此有动物之间相似的方面。他们作为人的相似性比他们作为动物的共同性大，这是因为，作为人，就意味着是动物，但动物并不一定就是人，除人之外，还有与人不同的其他许多种动物。惠施所说的"小同异"就是指这里的相似性和不同性，每类事物有共同点，这是大同；每类事物中不同种属间又有它们的共同性，这是小同。但是，如果我们把"万有"作为一个普遍的类，就由此认识到，万物都相似，因为它们都是存在物。但是，如果我们把每个个体事物看作一个个体，每个个体都有它自身的特性，使它和其他存在物分别开。这种相似性和不同性乃是惠施所说的"大同异"。因此，我们可以说，万物都彼此相似，也可以说，万物各不相同。由此可见，它们的相似性和不同性都是相对的。名家的这个论辩在古代中国十分著名，被称为"合同异之辩"。

"南方无穷而有穷"。当时人们惯说"南方无垠"。当时中国中原地带的人对南方十分无知，有点像二百年前来到北美的欧洲移民心目中的"西部"。在古代中国人的心目中，南方并不像东方，被海所限，也不像西方和北方，被沙漠所限，南方是无限的。惠施所说，南方无穷而有穷，可能因为他对南方有更多的知识，知道南方也有山海，更可能是他认为，"无穷"和"有穷"也只是相对的一对概念。

"今日适越而昔来"。"今"和"昔"都只是相对的。今天所说

was the today of yesterday, and the today of today will be the yesterday of tomorrow. Herein lies the relativity of the present and the past.

"Connected rings can be separated." Connected rings cannot be separated unless they are destroyed. But destruction may, from another point of view, be construction. If one makes a wooden table, from the point of view of the wood, it is destruction, but from the point of view of the table, it is construction. Since destruction and construction are relative, therefore "connected rings can be separated" without destroying them.

"I know the center of the world. It is north of Yen and south of Yüeh." Among the states of the time, Yen was in the extreme north and Yüeh in the extreme south. The Chinese regarded China as being the world. Hence it was a matter of common sense that the center of the world should be south of Yen and north of Yüeh. Hui Shih's contrary assertion here is well interpreted by a commentator of the third century A.D., Ssu-ma Piao, who says: "The world has no limit, and therefore anywhere is the center, just as in drawing a circle, any point on the line can be the starting point."

"Love all things equally; Heaven and Earth are one body." In the preceding propositions, Hui Shih argues that all things are relative and in a state of flux. There is no absolute difference, or absolute separation among them. Everything is constantly changing into something else. It is a logical conclusion, therefore, that all things are one, and hence that we should love all things equally without discrimination. In the *Chuang-tzu* it is also said: "If we see things from the point of view of their difference, even my liver and gall are as far from each other as are the states of Ch'u and Yüeh. If we see things from the point of view of their similarity, all things are one." (Ch. 5.)

● Kung-sun Lung's Theory of Universals

The other main leader of the School of Names was Kung-sun Lung (fl. 284-259 B.C.), who was widely known in his day for his sophistic arguments. It is said that once when he was passing a frontier, the frontier guards said: "Horses are not allowed to pass." Kung-sun Lung replied: "My horse is white, and a white horse is not a horse." And so saying, he passed with his horse.

Instead of emphasizing, as did Hui Shih, that actual things are relative and changeable, Kung-sun Lung emphasized that names are absolute and permanent. In this way he arrived at the same concept of Platonic ideas or universals that has been so conspicuous in Western philosophy.

的昨天，就是昨天所说的今天；今天所说的"今天"，到明天便成为"昨天"了。这便是时间观念中的"现在"和"过去"的相对性。

"连环可解也。"连环除非被毁，是无法分解的。但是，如果以木匠制作一张桌子来说，从树木看，这是破坏；从桌子看，这是建设。所以，破坏和建设也是相对的，又是相衔接的。因此可以说，连环可以分解而不必毁坏它们。

"我知天下之中央，燕之北越之南是也。"当时燕国在极北，而越国在极南，居于中原的华夏族认为自己就是在天下的中央，它理所当然是在燕国之南，越国之北。惠施在这里所作的反论，后来公元三世纪的司马彪曾经作了很好的诠释说："天下无方，故所在为中；循环无端，故所在为始也。"

"泛爱万物，天地一体也。"在此之前，惠施论证了万物相对存在于流动不居之中。事物之间没有绝对的不同，也没有绝对的隔离。事物都在不停地转化为别的东西。因此，就逻辑来说，万物为一。因此，人应当同样地爱万物。《庄子·德充符》中也说："自其异者视之，肝胆楚越也；自其同者视之，万物皆一也。"因此，人应当泛爱万物，不加区别才是。

● 公孙龙关于共相的学说

名家的另一位重要人物是公孙龙（活动于公元前二八四至前二五九年间），他以善辩在当时著名。据说，有一次，他经过一个关隘，守兵说："马不能在此经过。"公孙龙回答说："我的马是白马，白马非马。"守兵无言以对，于是，公孙龙牵马过关了。

惠施强调现实中存在的事物都是相对的、可变的，公孙龙则强调"名"是绝对的、恒久不变的。这使他达到与柏拉图一样的"理念"或"共相"观念。这种"理念论"在西方哲学中具有非常突出的地位。

In his work titled the *Kung-sun Lung-tzu*, there is a chapter called "Discourse on the White Horse." Its main proposition is the assertion that "a white horse is not a horse." This proposition Kung-sun Lung tries to prove through three arguments. The first is: "The word 'horse' denotes a shape; the word 'white' denotes a color. That which denotes color is not that which denotes shape. Therefore I say that a white horse is not a horse." In terms of Western logic, we may say that this argument emphasizes the difference in the intension of the terms "horse," "white," and "white horse." The intension of the first term is one kind of animal, that of the second is one kind of color, and that of the third is one kind of animal plus one kind of color. Since the intension of each of the three terms is different, therefore a white horse is not a horse.

The second argument is: "When a horse is required, a yellow horse or a black one may be brought forward, but when one requires a white horse, a yellow or a black horse cannot be brought forward... Therefore a yellow horse and a black horse are both horses. They can only respond to a call for a horse but cannot respond to a call for a white horse. It is clear that a white horse is not a horse." And again: "The term 'horse' neither excludes nor includes any color; therefore yellow and black ones may respond to it. But the term 'white horse' both excludes and includes color. Yellow and black horses are all excluded because of their color. Therefore only a white horse can fit the requirements. That which is not excluded is not the same as that which is excluded. Therefore I say that a white horse is not a horse." In terms of Western logic, we may say that this argument emphasizes the difference in the extension of the terms "horse" and "white horse." The extension of the term "horse" includes all horses, with no discrimination as to their color. The extension of the term "white horse," however, includes only white horses, with a corresponding discrimination of color. Since the extension of the term "horse" and "white horse" is different, therefore a white horse is not a horse.

The third argument is: "Horses certainly have color. Therefore there are white horses. Suppose there is a horse without color, then there is only the horse as such. But how then, do we get a white horse? Therefore a white horse is not a horse. A white horse is 'horse' together with 'white.' 'Horse' with 'white' is not horse." In this argument, Kung-sun Lung seems to emphasize the distinction between the universal, "horseness," and the

公孙龙的著作《公孙龙子》中有一章题为《白马论》，其中主要命题是"白马非马"。对此，公孙龙从三方面来加以论证。第一，"马"这个字是表明一种形状，"白"是表明一种颜色。表明一种颜色并不表明一个形象，因此，白马非马。如果用西方逻辑的语言，可以说，这个论辩强调的是"马"、"白"和"白马"三个词的内涵不同。"马"的内涵是一种动物；"白"的内涵是一种颜色；"白马"的内涵是一种动物而且还具有一种颜色。由于这三个词的内涵不同，因此白马非马。

第二个论证是：如果有人要一匹马，这时马夫牵过来的可以是一匹黄马或一匹黑马；但如果要的是白马，就不能把黄马或黑马牵出来。……如果有人要马，马夫如有黄马或黑马，都可以应声说有；但如果要的是白马，他就不能应声说有。这岂不是白马非马？再者，"马"这个词并不包括、也不排除任何颜色。因此，有人要马时，黄马、白马都可以应命。而"白马"这个词，既包括颜色，又排除颜色，黄马和黑马都因其颜色而被排除，只有一匹白马才能应命，那未被排除的和被排除的当然不一样。因此，"一匹白马不是一匹马"。如用西方逻辑学的语言来说，这个论辩强调的是"马"与"白马"的外延不同。"马"的外延包括一切马，不管它们是什么颜色。"白马"这个词的外延却只是指"白颜色的马"，其中排斥了其他颜色的马。既然"马"与"白马"的外延不同，因此，白马非马。

第三个论证是：马当然有颜色，因此而有白马。假设有无色的马，那样的话，"马"就只有本质，没有形体。然则，白马又由何而来呢？因此，"白"不是"马"；"白马"的含义是"马"加上"白"，它和"马"已经不是一样的含义，因此，白马非马。在这个论证中，公孙龙似乎强调"马"的共相和"白马"的共相不同。所有的马都

universal, "white-horseness." The universal, horseness, is the essential attribute of all horses. It implies no color and is just "horse as such." Such "horseness" is distinct from "white-horseness." That is to say, the horse as such is distinct from the white horse as such. Therefore a white horse is not a horse.

Besides horse as such, there is also white as such, that is, whiteness. In the same chapter it is said: "White [as such] does not specify what is white. But 'white horse' specifies what is white. Specified white is not white." Specified white is the concrete white color which is seen in this or that particular white object. The word here translated as "specified" is *ting*, which also has the meaning of "determined." The white color which is seen in this or that white object is determined by this or that object. The universal, "whiteness," however, is not determined by any one particular white object. It is the whiteness unspecified.

The *Kung-sun Lung-tzu* contains another chapter entitled "Discourse on Hardness and Whiteness." The main proposition in this chapter is that "hardness and whiteness are separate." Kung-sun Lung tries to prove this in two ways. The first is expressed in the following dialogue: "[Supposing there is a hard and white stone], is it possible to say hard, white, and stone are three? No. Can they be two? Yes. How? When without hardness one finds what is white, this gives two. When without whiteness one finds what is hard, this gives two. Seeing does not give us what is hard but only what is white, and there is nothing hard in this. Touching does not give us what is white but only what is hard, and there is nothing white in this." This dialogue uses epistemological proof to show that hardness and whiteness are separated from each other. Here we have a hard and white stone. If we use our eyes to see it, we only get what is white, i.e., a white stone. But if we use our hands to touch it, we only get what is hard, i.e., a hard stone. While we are sensing that the stone is white, we cannot sense that it is hard, and while we are sensing that it is hard, we cannot sense that it is white. Epistemologically speaking, therefore, there is only a *white stone* or a *hard stone* here, but not a *hard and white stone*. This is the meaning of the saying: "When without hardness one finds what is white, this gives two. When without whiteness one finds what is hard, this gives two."

Kung-sun Lung's second argument is a metaphysical one. Its general idea is that both hardness and whiteness, as universals, are unspecified in regard to what particular object it is that is hard or that is white. They can be manifested in any or all white or hard objects. Indeed, even if in the physical world there were no hard or white objects at all, none the less, the universal, hardness, would of necessity remain hardness, and the universal, whiteness, would remain whiteness. Such hardness and

具有马的共相，但其中不包含颜色，马的共相与白马的共相不同，因此，白马非马。

除"马"的共相外，还有"白"的共相，那就是"白色"这个概念。在同一篇里说，白的共相并未说明什么是白。"白马"一词则把"白"界定了，经过界定的"白"和"白"的共相又不是一回事，特定的白是在特定的物体之中显现出来、"定"了下来的。而白的共相是未经任何特定物体加以界定的，它是未经界定的"白"。

《公孙龙子》书中还包括一篇《坚白论》，其主要命题是"离坚白"（坚硬与白色是分离的）。公孙龙从两方面来论证这个命题。其一在下面的对话中表现出来。设想有一块坚硬的白石。是否可以说，"坚白石，三，可乎？曰：不可。曰：二，可乎？曰：可。曰：何哉？曰：无坚得白，其举也二；无白得坚，其举也二。……视不得其所坚而得其所白者，无坚也。拊不得其所白而得其所坚，得其坚也，无白也。"这段对话从认识论方面论证，坚和白是彼此分离的。用手摸，可以得出"坚硬"的结论；用眼看，可以得出"白"的结论，但没有"坚白石"。这就是"无坚得白，其举也二；无白得坚，其举也二"的意思。

公孙龙的第二个论证是形而上学性质的。它的意思说，"坚"和"白"作为共相，并未指明，哪个具体事物是坚，哪个具体事物是白。它可以在任何坚硬或纯白的东西中表现出来。即使在物质世界里没有坚硬或白的东西，"坚硬"和"白"的概念还存在着，

whiteness are quite independent of the existence of physical stones or other objects that are hard and white. The fact that they are independent universals is shown by the fact that in the physical world there are some objects that are hard but not white, and other objects that are white but not hard. Thus it is evident that hardness and whiteness are separate from each other.

With these epistemological and metaphysical arguments Kung-sun Lung established his proposition that hardness and whiteness are separate. This was a famous proposition in ancient China, and was known as the argument for "the separateness of hardness and whiteness."

In the *Kung-sun Lung-tzu* there is yet another chapter entitled "Discourse on *Chih* and *Wu*." By *wu* Kung-sun Lung means concrete particular things, while by *chih* he means abstract universals. The literal meaning of *chih* is, as a noun, "finger" or "pointer," or, as a verb, "to indicate." Two explanations may be given as to why Kung-sun Lung uses the word *chih* to denote universals. A common term, that is, a name, to use the terminology of the School of Names, denotes a class of particular things and connotes the common attributes of that class. An abstract term, on the contrary, denotes the attribute or universal. Since the Chinese language has no inflection, there is no distinction in form between a common term and an abstract one. Thus, in Chinese, what Westerners would call a common term may also denote a universal. Likewise, the Chinese language has no articles. Hence, in Chinese, such terms as "horse," "the horse," and "a horse" are all designated by the one word *ma* or "horse." It would seem, therefore, that fundamentally the word *ma* denotes the universal concept, "horse," while the other terms, "a horse," "the horse," etc., are simply particularized applications of this universal concept. From this it may be said that, in the Chinese language, a universal is what a name points out, i.e., denotes. This is why Kung-sun Lung refers to universals as *chih* or "pointers."

Another explanation of why Kung-sun Lung uses *chih* to denote the universal, is that *chih* (finger, pointer, etc.) is a close equivalent of another word, also pronounced *chih* and written almost the same, which means "idea" or "concept." According to this explanation, then, when Kung-sun Lung speaks of *chih* (pointer), he really means by it "idea" or "concept." As can be seen from his arguments above, however, this "idea" is for him not

这些概念是不依赖于物质而独立存在的。"坚白"这个概念可以离开物质而存在,只要看现实世界中,有的东西硬而不白,有的东西白而不硬。这足以证明,坚与白并非必然联系在一起,它们是彼此分离的。

公孙龙用这些认识论和形而上学的论辩证明"坚"与"白"是分离的。这是中国古代哲学中著名的"离坚白"论。

在《公孙龙子》书中还有一篇《指物论》。公孙龙用"物"来表示具体事物,用"指"来表示抽象的"共相"。"指"字作为名词时,它的本意是"手指"或"指示器";作为动词时,它的含义是"指示"。为什么公孙龙用"指"来代表"共相"?有两种解释。在名家的哲学词汇中,一个名词是一类具体事物,它们具有那一类事物的共同特性。而一个抽象的语词则指一种属性或共相。由于中国语言和欧洲语言不同,方块字不像拼音文字,没有因格(主动或被动)、性(阴性或阳性)、身(第一身、第三身等)、时(过去、现在、未来)、数(单数或复数),而在词尾做出变化,因此,一个名词(如"指")和一个抽象语词(如"指")没有形式上的区别。结果,在西方语词中的一个共同语词,也可以用来指一种共相。中国语言中还没有冠词,因此,"马"、"一匹马"、"这匹马",都以一个"马"字来表示。于是,"马"字基本是用以表示一个共相,而其他语词如"一匹马"、"这匹马"则是共相的具体应用。因此可以说,在中国语言中,一个共相是由一个名词来表达的,这是公孙龙何以用"指"来表达共相这个意思。

关于公孙龙用"指"来表达共相的含义,还有另一种解释,就是"指"字与"旨"字相通。"旨"字常用作"要旨",含有"观念"和"概念"的意思。按照这种解释,公孙龙用"指"字时,他的意思是指"观念"或"概念"。公孙龙的上述论辩表明,他使用"概念"

the subjective idea spoken of in the philosophy of Berkeley and Hume, but rather the objective idea as found in the philosophy of Plato. It is the universal.

In the final chapter of the *Chuang-tzu* we find a series of twenty-one arguments attributed without specification to the followers of the School of Names. Among them, however, it is evident that some are based upon the ideas of Hui Shih, and others upon those of Kung-sun Lung, and they can be explained accordingly. They used to be considered as paradoxes, but they cease to be such once we understand the fundamental ideas of their authors.

- **Significance of the Theories of Hui Shih and Kung-sun Lung**

Thus by analyzing names, and their relation with, or their distinction from, actualities, the philosophers of the School of Names discovered what in Chinese philosophy is called "that which lies beyond shapes and features." In Chinese philosophy a distinction is made between "being that lies within shapes and features," and "being that lies beyond shapes and features." "Being that lies within shapes and features" is the actual, the *shih*. For instance, the big and the small, the square and the round, the long and the short, the white and the black, are each one class of shapes and features. Anything that is the object or possible object of experience has shape and feature, and lies within the actual world. Conversely, any object in the actual world that has shape and feature is the object or possible object of experience.

When Hui Shih enunciated the first and last of his series of "points," he was talking about what lies beyond shapes and features. "The greatest," he said, "has nothing beyond itself. This is called the Great One." This defines in what manner the greatest is as it is. "Love all things equally; Heaven and Earth are one." This defines of what the greatest consists. This last statement conveys the idea that all is one and one is all. Since all is one, there can be nothing beyond the all. The all is itself the greatest one, and since there can be nothing beyond the all, the all cannot be the object of experience. This is because an object of experience always stands in apposition to the one who experiences. Hence if we say that the all can be an object of experience, we must also say that there is something that stands in apposition to the all and is its experiencer. In other words, we must say that that which has nothing beyond itself at the same time has

并不是像柏克莱或休谟哲学中所指的反映主观的概念，而是如柏拉图哲学中的"理念"，乃是反映客观的一个概念。

在《庄子》一书最末的《天下》篇里，列举了名家的二十一种论辩，并没有说，它们出自名家的何人。其中，明显的是，有些显然以惠施的思想为基础，有些则由公孙龙而来，用惠施的思想或公孙龙的思想，就可以加以解释。过去，这些观点都被看作"反论"，但我们一旦知道了惠施和公孙龙的基本思想，就可以懂得，这些其实并非"反论"。

● 惠施和公孙龙学说的意义

名家的哲学解析名实，在中国哲学思想中揭示出一个形象之外的世界。中国哲学里，对"形象之内"和"形象之外"是加以区别的。"形象之内"是"实"，例如大与小、方与圆、长与短、白与黑，它们都是指一类形象和属性。人们经验中的任何对象或可能成为经验对象的东西，都有形象和属性，都是在现实世界之中。反过来也可以认为，现实世界中的任何形象与属性都是经验的对象，或可能成为经验的对象。

惠施在他的"十事"中，开头和结尾是谈形象之外的世界。他说"至大无外，谓之大一"，是说处于有限之中的人所能指认的"至大"是怎样一回事。"泛爱万物，天地一体也"，这是说明至大包含什么。"天地一体"意味着，万有即是一，一即是万有。由于万有即是一，因此，在万有之外，更无他物。既然如此，万有不可能成为人的经验的对象。这是因为一个经验对象必然要处于经验着的人的对面。如果我们说，万有可以成为经验的对象，我们就必须说，在万有对面，必定有一个能经验万有的经验者。这就变成了，在至大

something beyond itself, which is a manifest contradiction.

Kung-sun Lung, too, discovered what lies beyond shapes and features, because the universals he discussed can likewise not be objects of experience. One can see a white something, but one cannot see the universal whiteness as such. All universals that are indicated by names lie in a world beyond shapes and features, though not all universals in that world have names to indicate them. In that world, hardness is hardness and whiteness is whiteness, or as Kung-sun Lung said: "Each is alone and true." (*Kung-sun Lung-tzu*, ch. 5.)

Hui Shih spoke of "loving all things equally," and Kung-sun Lung also "wished to extend his argument in order to correct the relations between names and actualities, so as thus to transform the whole world." (*Ibid.*, ch. 1.) Both men thus apparently considered their philosophy as comprising the "*Tao* of sageliness within and kingliness without." But it was left to the Taoists fully to apply the discovery made by the School of Names of what lies beyond shapes and features. The Taoists were the opponents of this school, but they were also its true inheritors. This is illustrated by the fact that Hui Shih was a great friend of Chuang Tzu.

无外的大一之外，还有一个东西。这是显然自相矛盾的。

公孙龙也揭示了在形象和属性之外的共相。他讨论到，共相不可能成为经验的对象。人可以看见一件白的什么东西，但是无法看见作为共相的"白"。凡名词指向的共相都在另一个世界里，那里没有形象和属性，其中有些共相甚至没有名字。在那个世界里，"坚硬"就是"坚硬"，"白"就是"白"，如公孙龙所说"独而正"，每个共相都是独立而又真实的。

惠施说："泛爱万物。"公孙龙也说："欲推是辩，以正名实，而化天下焉。"两人都显然认为，他们的哲学是内圣外王之道。但是，真正把名家所揭示的形象之外的世界的意义充分发挥出来的乃是道家。道家反对名家，然而真正继承名家的却是道家。惠施和庄子两人是好朋友，正好说明了这一点。

❾ THE SECOND PHASE OF TAOISM: LAO TZU

According to tradition, Lao Tzu (a name which literally means the "Old Master") was a native of the state of Ch'u in the southern part of the present Honan province, and was an older contemporary of Confucius, whom he is reputed to have instructed in ceremonies. The book bearing his name, the *Lao-tzu*, and in later times also known as the *Tao Te Ching* (*Classic of the Way and Power*), has therefore been traditionally regarded as the first philosophical work in Chinese history. Modern scholarship, however, has forced us drastically to change this view and to date it to a time considerably after Confucius.

● **Lao Tzu the Man and *Lao-tzu* the Book**

Two questions arise in this connection. One is about the date of the man, Lao Tzu (whose family name is said to have been Li, and personal name, Tan), and another about the date of the book itself. There is no necessary connection between the two, for it is quite possible that there actually lived a man known as Lao Tan who was senior to Confucius, but that the book titled the *Lao-tzu* is a later production. This is the view I take, and it does not necessarily contradict the traditional accounts of Lao Tzu the man, because in these accounts there is no statement that the man, Lao Tzu, actually wrote the book by that name. Hence I am willing to accept the traditional stories about Lao Tzu the man, while at the same time placing the book, *Lao-tzu*, in a later period. In fact, I now believe the date of the book to be later than I assumed when I wrote my *History of Chinese Philosophy*. I now believe it was written or composed after Hui Shih and Kung-sun Lung, and not before, as I there indicated. This is because the *Lao-tzu* contains considerable discussion about the Nameless, and in order to do this it would seem that men should first have become conscious of the existence of names themselves.

My position does not require me to insist that there is absolutely no connection between Lao Tzu the man and *Lao-tzu* the book, for the book may indeed contain a few sayings of the original Lao Tzu. What I maintain, however, is that the system of thought in the book as a whole cannot be the product of a time either before or contemporary with that of Confucius. In the pages following, however, to avoid pedantry, I shall refer to Lao Tzu as having said so and so, instead of stating that the book *Lao-tzu* says so and so, just as we today still speak of sunrise and sunset, even though we know very well that the sun itself actually neither rises nor sets.

玖 道家的第二阶段：老子

历来以老子为楚国人（今河南省南部），与孔子同时而比孔子年长，传说孔子曾问礼于老子；《老子》一书被认为是中国第一部哲学著作。经近代学者考证，上述看法有很大改变，有的学者认为老子出生时代晚于孔子。

● 老子其人和《老子》其书

传说老子姓李，名聃。对读中国哲学的人来说，重要的问题有二：老子是什么时代的人，《老子》这部书是什么时代的书。这两个问题之间并没有必然联系。很可能，老子出生在孔子之前，而《老子》这部书是后人依托之作。这也正是我的看法。这样，历来对老子生平的说法不必全都否定，历来的说法中并没有提老子著有《老子》其书。因此，我倾向于接受传统关于老子生平的说法，而同时把《老子》一书的著作年代放到后来。在我写《中国哲学史》（两卷本）时，曾提出《老子》一书的著作年代大概在惠施和公孙龙之前，现在我认为《老子》一书的著作年代比我以前所设想的更晚，应在惠施和公孙龙之后。这是因为《老子》书中有不少关于"无名"的讨论，这只能是在人们对"名"的观念有了发展之后。

我所持的这种观点并不要求我认定老子其人和《老子》其书毫无关系。《老子》书中也可能有若干段落是来自老子。我的看法是，《老子》一书的思想体系不可能产生于孔子之前，或与孔子同时。在下面，为避免卖弄之嫌，在援引《老子》时，我还是援旧例称老子如何如何说，如同我们今天仍旧用"日出"、"日落"这些词语，虽然我们知道，太阳在太空中并没有出，也没有入。

● *Tao*, the Unnamable

In the last chapter, we have seen that the philosophers of the School of Names, through the study of names, succeeded in discovering "that which lies beyond shapes and features." Most people, however, think only in terms of "what lies within shapes and features," that is, the actual world. Seeing the actual, they have no difficulty in expressing it, and though they use names for it, they are not conscious that they are names. So when the philosophers of the School of Names started to think about the names themselves, this thought represented a great advance. To think about names is to think about thinking. It is thought about thought and therefore is thought on a higher level.

All things that "lie within shapes and features" have names, or, at least, possess the possibility of having names. They are namable. But in contrast with what is namable, Lao Tzu speaks about the unnamable. Not everything that lies beyond shapes and features is unnamable. Universals, for instance, lie beyond shapes and features, yet they are not unnamable. But on the other hand, what is unnamable most certainly does lie beyond shapes and features. The *Tao* or Way of the Taoists is a concept of this sort.

In the first chapter of the *Lao-tzu* we find the statement: "The *Tao* that can be comprised in words is not the eternal *Tao*; the name that can be named is not the abiding name. The Unnamable is the beginning of Heaven and Earth; the namable is the mother of all things." And in chapter thirty-two: "The *Tao* is eternal, nameless, the Uncarved Block.... Once the block is carved, there are names." Or in chapter forty-one: "The *Tao*, lying hid, is nameless." In the Taoist system, there is a distinction between *yu* (being) and *wu* (non-being), and between *yu-ming* (having-name, namable) and *wu-ming* (having-no-name, unnamable). These two distinctions are in reality only one, for *yu* and *wu* are actually simply abbreviated terms for *yu-ming* and *wu-ming*. Heaven and Earth and all things are namables. Thus Heaven has the name of Heaven, Earth the name Earth, and each kind of thing has the name of that kind. There being Heaven, Earth and all things, it follows that there are the names of Heaven, Earth, and all things. Or as Lao Tzu says: "Once the Block is carved, there are names." The *Tao*, however, is unnamable; at the same time it is that by which all namables come to be. This is why Lao Tzu says: "The Unnamable is the beginning of Heaven and Earth; the namable is the mother of all things."

● 道，无名

在上一章里，我们看到，名家的思想家们揭示出"超乎形象之外"或说"形而上"的存在。大多数人只思考"形而下"的存在，即现实世界。他们觉得，现实世界是可见的，因此，表达它时并无困难；在表达时，虽然使用名字，也不觉得那仅仅是"名"。名家的思想家开始对"名"进行讨论，在思维上乃是一大进步，对"名"的思考乃是对"思考"进行思考，它是在一个更高层次上的思维。

一切"形而下"的事物都有名字，或至少有命名的可能，它们是可以命名的。老子却指出，除了"可以命名的"之外，还有"无法命名的"。形而上的事物也并非都无法命名，例如共相，它们是形而上的，却不是"无法命名的"。但从另一方面看，凡"无以命名的"必定是形而上的。道家所说的"道"和"德"便是属于这一类的概念。

在《老子》第一章里，开头便说："道可道，非常道；名可名，非常名。无名，天地之始；有名，万物之母。"在第三十二章里又说："道常无名，朴。虽小，天下莫能臣。……始制有名。"再看第四十一章："道隐无名。"在道家思想中，区别"有"和"无"、"有名"和"无名"；其实，这两个区别只是一个区别，只是"有名"和"无名"的区别，"有"和"无"只是"有名"和"无名"的缩称。天地万物都是可以赋予名字的，故此，称天为天，称地为地，万物各从其类，各有其名。有天地万物，就有天地万物之名。因此老子说："始制有名。""道"是无从命名的，而万物之名又都是由道而来，这便是老子所说："无名，天地之始；有名，万物之母。"

Since the *Tao* is unnamable, it therefore cannot be comprised in words. But since we wish to speak about it, we are forced to give it some kind of designation. We therefore call it *Tao*, which is really not a name at all. That is to say, to call the *Tao Tao*, is not the same as to call a table table. When we call a table table, we mean that it has some attributes by which it can be named. But when we call the *Tao Tao*, we do not mean that it has any such namable attributes. It is simply a designation, or to use an expression common in Chinese philosophy, *Tao* is a name which is not a name. In Chapter twenty-one of the *Lao-tzu* it is said: "From the past to the present, its [*Tao's*] name has not ceased to be, and has seen the beginning [of all things]." The *Tao* is that by which anything and everything comes to be. Since there are always things, *Tao* never ceases to be and the name of *Tao* also never ceases to be. It is the beginning of all beginnings, and therefore it has seen the beginning of all things. A name that never ceases to be is an abiding name, and such a name is in reality not a name at all. Therefore it is said: "The name that can be named is not the abiding name."

"The Unnamable is the beginning of Heaven and Earth." This proposition is only a formal and not a positive one. That is to say, it fails to give any information about matters of fact. The Taoists thought that since there are things, there must be that by which all these things come to be. This "that" is designated by them as *Tao*, which, however, is really not a name. The concept of *Tao*, too, is a formal and not a positive one. That is to say, it does not describe anything about what it is through which all things come to be. All we can say is that *Tao*, since it is that through which all things come to be, is necessarily not a mere thing among these other things. For if it were such a thing, it could not at the same time be that through which *all* things whatsoever come to be. Every kind of thing has a name, but *Tao* is not itself a thing. Therefore it is "nameless, the Uncarved Block."

Anything that comes to be is a being, and there are many beings. The coming to be of beings implies that first of all there is Being. These words, "first of all," here do not mean first in point of time, but first in a logical sense. For instance, if we say there was first a certain kind of animal, then man, the word "first" in this case means first in point of time. But if we say that first there must be animals before there are men, the word "first" in this case means first in a logical sense. The statement about "the origin

道作为万物本原，无从命名，所以无法用语言表达它。但我们又想要表达它，便不得不用语言来加以形容。称它为"道"，"道"其实不是一个名字。这就是说，我们称道为道，和我们称一张桌子为桌子是不同的。当我们称呼一张桌子为桌子时，它有某些属性，使我们可以称它为"桌子"。但是我们称"道"为"道"时，不是因为它有某些可以名状的属性，这个名字只是一个指称，或用中国哲学惯用的词语，称它是"无名之名"。《老子》第二十一章说："自古及今，其名不去，以阅众甫。"道是万物之所由来。既然物从来自在，道就从来自在，道这个指称也就从来自在。它是一切起源的起源，因此它见到了一切的起源。"道"这个名字既然从来自在，因此它长存，而这在现实之中根本不是一个名字。因此《老子》第一章里说："名可名，非常名。"

"无名，天地之始"。这只是一个形式的命题，而不是一个积极的命题。这就是说，它并没有对话题提供任何信息。道家认为，既然有万物，万物必定有它们的由来，于是便把这个"由来"称作"道"。它其实不是一个名字。"道"这个概念也只是一个形式命题，并不是一个积极命题。这就是说，它对万物所由来的这个"由来"，并没有作任何描述。我们所能说的是，"道"既是万物之所由来，它就不是万物之一；如果它是万物之一，它就不是万物之所由来。每一个事物都有一个名字，道不是一个事物，因此，它没有名字，因此，"道常无名，朴"。

任何事物，自一开始出现就是一个存在物，万有便是由此而来，万有意味着首先必须有存在。这里所用的"首先"，并不是指时间中的某一点，而是指逻辑上的先后。举例来说，我们说，世上必须首先有某种动物，然后才有人。这句话里的"首先有某种动物"，是指时间上的先后。但是如果我们说，有人类之前，先要有动物，这里的"先"，是指逻辑上的先后。达尔文的"物种起源论"

of the species" makes an assertion about matters of fact, and required many years' observation and study by Charles Darwin before it could be made. But the second of our sayings makes no assertion about matters of fact. It simply says that the existence of men logically implies the existence of animals. In the same way, the being of all things implies the being of Being. This is the meaning of Lao Tzu's saying: "All things in the world come into being from Being (*Yu*); and Being comes into being from Non-being (*Wu*)." (Ch. 40.)

This saying of Lao Tzu does not mean that there was a time when there was only Non-being, and that then there came a time when Being came into being from Non-being. It simply means that if we analyze the existence of things, we see there must first be Being before there can be any things. *Tao* is the unnamable, is Non-being, and is that by which all things come to be. Therefore, before the being of Being, there must be Non-being, from which Being comes into being. What is here said belongs to ontology, not to cosmology. It has nothing to do with time and actuality. For in time and actuality, there is no Being; there are only beings.

There are many beings, but there is only one Being. In the *Lao-tzu* it is said: "From *Tao* there comes one. From one there comes two. From two there comes three. From three there comes all things." (Ch. 42.) The "one" here spoken of refers to Being. To say that "from *Tao* comes one," is the same as that from Non-being comes Being. As for "two" and "three," there are many interpretations. But this saying, that "from one there comes two. From two there comes three. From three there comes all things," may simply be the same as saying that from Being come all things. Being is one, and two and three are the beginning of the many.

● The Invariable Law of Nature

In the final chapter of the *Chuang-tzu*, "The World," it is said that the leading ideas of Lao Tzu are those of the *T'ai Yi* or "Super One," and of Being, Non-being, and the invariable. The "Super One" is the *Tao*.

From the *Tao* comes one, and therefore *Tao* itself is the "Super One." The "invariable" is a translation of the Chinese word *ch'ang*, which may also be translated as eternal or abiding. Though things are ever changeable and changing, the laws that govern this change of things are not themselves changeable. Hence in the *Lao-tzu* the word *ch'ang* is used to show what is always so, or in other words, what can be considered as a rule. For

是对历史事实做了多年观察之后作出的论断。但是，上述"有人类之前，先要有动物"这句话并没有对事实作出任何论断。它只是在逻辑上指出，有人类之前，必先有动物。依同样的道理，万有必须首先有"有"，这就是老子在《道德经》第四十章所说"天下万物生于有，有生于无"的含义。

老子的这句话并不意味着，从前曾有一个"无"的时期，后来从"无"之中跳出"有"。它只是说，如果我们分析事物的存在，就会看见，首先需要有"有"，而后才能出现事物。"道"是不可名状的，是"非有"，正由于"非有"的存在，才能出现"有"和"万有"。因此，在出现"有"之前，需要有"非有"，或称"无"，从逻辑说，若没有"无"，便没有"有"和"万有"。这里所说的是本体论，不是宇宙论，它与时间和现实没有关系。在时间和现实之中，没有"有"，有的只是具体的万物。

存在着的事物有千千万万，但只是一个"有"。《道德经》第四十二章说："道生一，一生二，二生三，三生万物。"这里所说的"一"，即"有"。说"道生一"，也就是说"有"生于"无"。关于"二"和"三"，有许多不同的解释，《道德经》在这里所说"一生二，二生三，三生万物"，意思就是从"有"产生出万物。有是一，二和三则是"多"的开始。

● **自然的不变规律**

《庄子·天下》篇里说，老子"建之以常无有，主之以太一"。这是说，老子的学说以"太一"和"无有为常"作为主旨。太一即道，道生一，因此，道称为"太一"。"常"的含义是永久、永在。万物都是变动不居的，但决定万物变动的法则却是不变的。因此，《老子》书中的"常"字，既是"恒常"，又是"常则"。如《老子》

instance, Lao Tzu tells us: "The conquest of the world comes invariably from doing nothing." (Ch. 48.) Or again: "The way of Heaven has no favorites, it is invariably on the side of the good man." (Ch. 79.)

Among the laws that govern the changes of things, the most fundamental is that "when a thing reaches one extreme, it reverts from it." These are not the actual words of Lao Tzu, but a common Chinese saying, the idea of which no doubt comes from Lao Tzu. Lao Tzu's actual words are: "Reversing is the movement of the *Tao*" (Ch. 40), and: "To go further and further means to revert again." (Ch. 25.) The idea is that if anything develops certain extreme qualities, those qualities invariably revert to become their opposites.

This constitutes a law of nature. Therefore: "It is upon calamity that blessing leans, upon blessing that calamity rests." (Ch. 58.) "Those with little will acquire, those with much will be led astray." (Ch. 22.) "A hurricane never lasts the whole morning, nor a rainstorm the whole day." (Ch. 23.) "The most yielding things in the world master the most unyielding." (Ch. 43.) "Diminish a thing and it will increase. Increase a thing and it will diminish." (Ch. 42.) All these paradoxical theories are no longer paradoxical, if one understands the fundamental law of nature. But to the ordinary people who have no idea of this law, they seem paradoxical indeed. Therefore Lao Tzu says: "The gentleman of the low type, on hearing the Truth, laughs loudly at it. If he had not laughed, it would not suffice to be the Truth." (Ch. 41.)

It may be asked: Granted that a thing, on reaching an extreme, then reverts, what is meant by the word "extreme"? Is there any absolute limit for the development of anything, going beyond which would mean going to the extreme? In the *Lao-tzu* no such question is asked and therefore no answer is given. But if there had been such a question, I think Lao Tzu would have answered that no absolute limit can be prescribed for all things under all circumstances. So far as human activities are concerned, the limit for the advancement of a man remains relative to his subjective feelings and objective circumstances. Isaac Newton, for example, felt that compared with the total universe, his knowledge of it was no more than the knowledge of the sea possessed by a boy who is playing at the seashore. With such a feeling as this, Newton, despite his already great achievements in physics, was still far from reaching the limits of advancement in his learning. If, however, a student, having just finished his textbook on physics, thinks that he then knows all there is to know

第四十八章说："取天下常以无事。"又如第七十九章说："天道无亲，常与善人。"

在主宰事物变化的法则中，最根本的一条是中国人常说的一句话："物极必反。"这四个字源自老子的思想，但不是老子的原话。老子的原话见《道德经》第四十章"反者道之动"和第二十五章所说："有物混成，先天地生。……吾不知其名，字之曰'道'，强为之名曰'大'。大曰逝，逝曰远，远曰反。"

这是老子归纳的自然法则。因此，《道德经》第五十八章说："祸兮，福之所倚；福兮，祸之所伏。"又如第二十二章所说："少则得，多则惑。"第二十三章又说："飘风不终朝，骤雨不终日。"第四十三章说："天下之至柔，驰骋天下之至坚。"又如第四十二章所说："故物或损之而益，或益之而损。"所有这些看似反论的话，只要人懂得了自然的根本法则，便知道它们不是反论。只是常人不懂得自然法则，便觉得它们真是难解。因此，老子在第四十一章说："下士闻道，大笑之。不笑不足以为道。"

人们会问，如果物极必反，那么"极"在哪里呢？任何事物的发展超过了人们认为的极限，那又将如何呢？是否还有一个绝对的限度呢？在《道德经》里，没有提出这个问题，因此也没有对它的明确答案。但是，如果当时有人对老子提出这个问题，我估计，老子的回答将是，万物在任何情况下，都没有预先划出的绝对限度。就人类的活动来说，人的进化到哪里为止，全在于人的主观感觉和客观情况。以牛顿为例，他自认对宇宙的知识只相当于一个在海滩上玩耍的孩子对大海的了解。牛顿尽管在物理学方面已经取得巨大的成就，他的自我感觉是在知识领域里，还远远没有走到极限。但是，如果有一个高中学生，读完了高中物理学教科书，就此认为自己

about science, he certainly cannot make further advancement in his learning, and will as certainly "revert back." Lao Tzu tells us: "If people of wealth and exalted position are arrogant, they abandon themselves to unavoidable ruin." (Ch. 9.) Arrogance is the sign that one's advancement has reached its extreme limit. It is the first thing that one should avoid.

The limit of advancement for a given activity is also relative to objective circumstances. When a man eats too much, he suffers. In overeating, what is ordinarily good for the body becomes something harmful. One should eat only the right amount of food. But this right amount depends on one's age, health, and the quality of food one eats.

These are the laws that govern the changes of things. By Lao Tzu they are called the invariables. He says: "To know the invariables is called enlightenment." (Ch. 16.) Again: "He who knows the invariable is liberal. Being liberal, he is without prejudice. Being without prejudice, he is comprehensive. Being comprehensive, he is vast. Being vast, he is with the Truth. Being with the Truth, he lasts forever and will not fail throughout his lifetime." (*Ibid.*)

● Human Conduct

Lao Tzu warns us: "Not to know the invariable and to act blindly is to go to disaster." (*Ibid.*) One should know the laws of nature and conduct one's activities in accordance with them. This, by Lao Tzu, is called "practicing enlightenment." The general rule for the man "practicing enlightenment" is that if he wants to achieve anything, he starts with its opposite, and if he wants to retain anything, he admits in it something of its opposite. If one wants to be strong, one must start with a feeling that one is weak, and if one wants to preserve capitalism, one must admit in it some elements of socialism.

Therefore Lao Tzu tells us: "The sage, putting himself in the background, is always to the fore. Remaining outside, he is always there.

Is it not just because he does not strive for any personal end, that all his personal ends are fulfilled?" (Ch. 7.) Again: "He does not show himself; therefore he is seen everywhere. He does not define himself; therefore he is distinct. He does not assert himself; therefore he succeeds. He does not boast of his work; therefore he endures. He does not contend, and

已经掌握了物理学的全部知识，也就不可能在科学知识上再有所进步，而且将会"倒退"。老子在《道德经》第九章告诉人们："金玉满堂，莫之能守。富贵而骄，自遗其咎。"骄傲就是一个人的进步已到达极限的标志，它是任何人首先要力戒的事情。

任何一种活动的前进极限还要看客观的情况。人如果吃得太多，就会噎食。吃得太多时，本来对人身体有益的食物会倒转来成为对人有害。人在饮食上应当适度，至于多少是"适度"，则要看各人的年龄、健康和食品的质量而定。

这些是左右事物变化的法则，老子称之为"常"。《道德经》第十六章说："知常曰明。"接下去说："知常容，容乃公，公乃王，王乃天，天乃道，道乃久，没身不殆。"这是说，知道事物变化的常理，人的思想就明智，明智的人就得以避免偏见；没有偏见，人的思想才能全面；思想全面才能胸怀广阔；胸怀广阔的人得见真理；得见真理的人将持续不败，终身也不会跌倒。

● 为人处世

在《道德经》第十六章里，老子告诫人们："不知常，妄作，凶。"人应当懂得天地间万事万物流动变化、相反相成的常理，为人处世要合乎自然的常理，这便是老子所说的"知常曰明"。具体如何实践呢？老子以为，一个人如果想要成就某件事，他就要把自己放在成就事情的对面；如果他想保持任何事情，就要承认在事情之中已经有了它自身的对立面。如果一个人想要强大，他就首先要看到自己处在一个软弱的地位。如果人们想要保持资本主义，就要首先看到其中已有某种社会主义成分。

因此，在《道德经》第七章里，老子向人们说："圣人后其身而身先，外其身而身存。非以其无私邪？故能成其私。"在第二十二章里，他又说："不自见，故明；不自是，故彰。不自伐，故有功；

for that very reason no one in the world can contend with him." (Ch. 22.) These sayings illustrate the first point of the general rule.

In the *Lao-tzu* we also find: "What is most perfect seems to have something missing, yet its use is unimpaired. What is most full seems empty, yet its use is inexhaustible. What is most straight seems like crookedness. The greatest skill seems like clumsiness. The greatest eloquence seems like stuttering." (Ch. 45.) Again: "Be twisted and one shall be whole. Be crooked and one shall be straight. Be hollow and one shall be filled. Be tattered and one shall be renewed. Have little and one shall obtain. But have much and one shall be perplexed." (Ch. 22.) This illustrates the second point of the general rule.

Such is the way in which a prudent man can live safely in the world and achieve his aims. This is Lao Tzu's answer and solution to the original problem of the Taoists, which was, how to preserve life and avoid harm and danger in the human world. (See end of Ch. 6 above.) The man who lives prudently must be meek, humble, and easily content. To be meek is the way to preserve your strength and so be strong. Humility is the direct opposite of arrogance, so that if arrogance is a sign that a man's advancement has reached its extreme limit, humility is a contrary sign that that limit is far from reached. And to be content safeguards one from going too far, and therefore from reaching the extreme. Lao Tzu says: "To know how to be content is to avoid humiliation; to know where to stop is to avoid injury." (Ch. 45.) Again: "The sage, therefore, discards the excessive, the extravagant, the extreme." (Ch. 29.)

All these theories are deducible from the general theory that "reversing is the movement of the *Tao*." The well-known Taoist theory of *wu-wei* is also deducible from this general theory. *Wu-wei* can be translated literally as "having-no-activity" or "non-action." But using this translation, one should remember that the term does not actually mean complete absence of activity, or doing nothing. What it does mean is lesser activity or doing less. It also means acting without artificiality and arbitrariness.

Activities are like many other things. If one has too much of them, they become harmful rather than good. Furthermore, the purpose of doing something is to have something done. But if there is over-doing, this results in something being over-done, which may be worse than not having the thing done at all. A well-known Chinese story describes how two men were once competing in drawing a snake; the one who would finish his drawing first would win. One of them, having indeed finished his drawing, saw that the other man was still far behind, so decided to improve it by adding feet to his snake. Thereupon the other man said: "You have lost the competition, for a snake has no feet." This is an illustration

不自矜，故长。夫唯不争，故天下莫能与之争。"不自是、不自伐，这是老子所强调的首要之点。

在《道德经》第四十五章里，老子还说："大成若缺，其用不弊。大盈若冲，其用不穷。大直若屈，大巧若拙，大辩若讷。"第二十二章又说："曲则全，枉则直，洼则盈，敝则新，少则得，多则惑。"不求全，这是老子所强调的第二点。

道家最关心的问题是：人生在世，怎样才能全生？怎样才能避祸？（请参阅本书第六章末）这里便是老子的回答。他认为，一个谨慎的人应当温和、谦虚、知足。温和就能保持自己的力量强大。谦虚就能使人不断进步。凡事知足，使人处任何事情，不致过分。如第三十二章告诫人们："知止所以不殆。"又如第二十九章所说："是以圣人去甚，去奢，去泰（过分）。"

所有这些都可以从"反者道之动"的原理中引申出来。道家的"无为"，也同样可以从这个总原理中引申出来。道家主张无为，并不是叫人完全不动，或不做任何事情。它的用意是叫人不要以多为胜，"少"就是抓住要害；也意味着，行事为人不要矫揉造作，不要恣肆放荡。

人的活动也如其他东西一样，过多就反而有害。人做一桩事，是想完成那一桩事。如果做得过分，结果可能比不做更糟。中国有"画蛇添足"的故事，叙述两个人比赛画蛇，先完成者获胜。而那个先完成者看另一个人落在后面，就利用自己占先的富余时间，为所画的蛇再添上四只脚。这样一来，他所画的就不是蛇，结果转胜

of over-doing which defeats its own purpose. In the *Lao-tzu* we read: "Conquering the world is invariably due to doing nothing; by doing something one cannot conquer the world." (Ch. 48.) The term "doing nothing" here really means "not over-doing."

Artificiality and arbitrariness are the opposite of naturalness and spontaneity. According to Lao Tzu, *Tao* is that by which all things come to be. In this process of coming to be, each individual thing obtains something from the universal *Tao*, and this something is called *Te*. *Te* is a word that means "power" or "virtue," both in the moral and non-moral sense of the latter term. The *Te* of a thing is what it naturally is. Lao Tzu says: "All things respect *Tao* and value *Te*." (Ch. 51.) This is because *Tao* is that by which they come to be, and *Te* is that by which they are what they are.

According to the theory of "having-no-activity," a man should restrict his activities to what is necessary and what is natural. "Necessary" means necessary to the achievement of a certain purpose, and never over-doing. "Natural" means following one's *Te* with no arbitrary effort. In doing this one should take simplicity as the guiding principle of life. Simplicity (*p'u*) is an important idea of Lao Tzu and the Taoists. *Tao* is the "Uncarved Block" (*p'u*), which is simplicity itself. There is nothing that can be simpler than the unnamable *Tao*. *Te* is the next simplest, and the man who follows *Te* must lead as simple a life as possible.

The life that follows *Te* lies beyond the distinctions of good and evil. Lao Tzu tells us: "If all people of the world know that beauty is beauty, there is then already ugliness. If all people of the world know that good is good, there is then already evil." (Ch. 2.) Lao Tzu, therefore, despised such Confucian virtues as human-heartedness and righteousness, for according to him these virtues represent a degeneration from *Tao* and *Te*. Therefore he says: "When the *Tao* is lost, there is the *Te*. When the *Te* is lost, there is [the virtue of] human-heartedness. When human-heartedness is lost, there is [the virtue of] righteousness. When righteousness is lost, there are the ceremonials. Ceremonials are the degeneration of loyalty and good faith, and are the beginning of disorder in the world." (Ch. 38.) Here we find the direct conflict between Taoism and Confucianism.

People have lost their original *Te* because they have too many desires and too much knowledge. In satisfying their desires, people are seeking for happiness. But when they try to satisfy too many desires, they obtain

为败。这是告诫人：行事过分，将招来失败。老子在《道德经》第四十八章里说："取天下常以无事，及其有事，不足以取天下。"意思也是说，行事不要过分，并不是叫人不要做事。

矫揉造作和轻率放肆是顺其自然的对立面。老子认为，道就是万物之所由来。万物在生成过程之中，都有"道"在其中。在万物之中的"道"就是"德"，"德"的含义是"能力"或"品德"，它可以解释为万物本有的品质，也可以解释为在人伦关系中的德行。因此，"德"就是事物的本性。这就是《道德经》第五十一章所说的"万物莫不尊道而贵德"，"道"是万物的由来，"德"则是万物本性的依据。

按照"无为"的理论，人的活动应限于"必要和顺乎自然"的范围。"必要"是指达到某个具体有限的目标；"顺乎自然"是指按照时势和事物的本性，不强行要求。人行事为人，要力求平易朴实。"朴"是老子和道家的一个重要思想。道就是"朴"之最，因为它连名字也没有（《道德经》第三十七章称道是"无名之朴"）。其次是"德"，它就是事物天生的本性。人要循德求道，道和德就要求人简朴。

人顺德，就是顺事物的本性行事，这时人的生活就超越了世俗的是非善恶。老子在《道德经》第二章告诉人们："天下皆知美之为美，斯恶已；皆知善之为善，斯不善已。"因此，老子蔑视儒家道德所主张的仁义，认为那是由于人对万物的由来和万物的本性疏离而产生的。《道德经》第三十八章说："失道而后德，失德而后仁，失仁而后义，失义而后礼。夫礼者，忠信之薄而乱之首。"这是道家和儒家思想冲突的一个事例。

照道家的看法，人失去了原有的德，乃是因为欲望太多，知识太多。人竭力满足欲望，以求快乐。但是，欲壑难填，当人力求满足

an opposite result. Lao Tzu says: "The five colors blind the eye. The five notes dull the ear. The five tastes fatigue the mouth. Riding and hunting madden the mind. Rare treasures hinder right conduct." (Ch. 12.) Therefore, "there is no disaster greater than not knowing contentment with what one has; no greater sin than having desire for acquisition." (Ch. 46.) This is why Lao Tzu emphasizes that people should have few desires.

Likewise Lao Tzu emphasizes that people should have little knowledge. Knowledge is itself an object of desire. It also enables people to know more about the objects of desire and serves as a means to gain these objects. It is both the master and servant of desire. With increasing knowledge people are no longer in a position to know how to be content and where to stop. Therefore, it is said in the *Lao-Tzu*: "When knowledge and intelligence appeared, Gross Artifice began." (Ch. 18.)

- **Political Theory**

From these theories Lao Tzu deduces his political theory. The Taoists agree with the Confucianists that the ideal state is one which has a sage as its head. It is only the sage who can and should rule. The difference between the two schools, however, is that according to the Confucianists, when a sage becomes the ruler, he should do many things for the people, whereas according to the Taoists, the duty of the sage ruler is not to do things, but rather to undo or not to do at all. The reason for this, according to Lao Tzu, is that the troubles of the world come, not because there are many things not yet done, but because too many things are done. In the *Lao-tzu* we read: "The more restrictions and prohibitions there are in the world, the poorer the people will be. The more sharp weapons the people have, the more troubled will be the country. The more cunning craftsmen there are, the more pernicious contrivances will appear. The more laws are promulgated, the more thieves and bandits there will be." (Ch. 57.)

The first act of a sage ruler, then, is to undo all these. Lao Tzu says:

"Banish wisdom, discard knowledge, and the people will be benefited a hundredfold. Banish human-heartedness, discard righteousness, and the people will be dutiful and compassionate. Banish skill, discard profit, and thieves and robbers will disappear." (Ch. 19.) Again: "Do not exalt the worthies, and the people will no longer be contentious. Do not value treasures that are hard to get, and there will be no more thieves. If the people never see such things as excite desire, their mind will not be confused. Therefore the sage rules the people by emptying their minds,

无穷的欲望时，所达到的适得其反。老子在《道德经》第十二章说："五色令人目盲，五音令人耳聋，五味令人口爽；驰骋畋猎令人心发狂，难得之货令人行妨。"因此，《道德经》第四十六章说："祸莫大于不知足，咎莫大于欲得。"这是老子强调清心寡欲的由来。

和强调寡欲相联，老子还强调，人要弃智。老子看到，知识本身就是欲望的一个对象；它又引起人的更多欲望，成为人满足欲望、达到目的的帮手。知识既是欲望的主人，又是欲望的仆人。人的知识越多，就越不知足，不知止。因此，《道德经》第十八章说："智慧出，有大伪。"

● **政治理论**

从上述思想中，老子发展出他的政治理论。道家和儒家相同的一点是：认为在理想国里，国家首脑应当是一个圣人，唯有圣人才能担当起治国的重任，圣人也应该成为理想国的统治者。道家和儒家不同的地方在于：儒家认为，圣人治国，应当为大众多做事情；而道家认为，圣人治国，不是要忙于做事，而是要裁撤废除过去本不应做的事情，以至"无为"。老子认为，世事纷繁，种种烦恼，不是因为事情做得太少，而是因为事情做得过多。《道德经》第五十七章里写道："天下多忌讳，而民弥贫；民多利器，国家滋昏；人多伎巧，奇物滋起；法令滋彰，盗贼多有。"

老子认为，圣人治国的第一桩事乃是废除这些事情。如《道德经》第十九章所说："绝圣弃智，民利百倍；绝仁弃义，民复孝慈；绝巧弃利，盗贼无有。"又如《道德经》第三章所说："不尚贤，使民不争；不贵难得之货，使民不为盗；不见可欲，使民心不乱。

filling their bellies, weakening their wills, and toughening their sinews, ever making the people without knowledge and without desire." (Ch. 3.)

The sage ruler would undo all the causes of trouble in the world. After that, he would govern with non-action. With non-action, he does nothing, yet everything is accomplished. The *Lao-tzu* says: "I act not and the people of themselves are transformed. I love quiescence and the people of themselves go straight. I concern myself with nothing, and the people of themselves are prosperous. I am without desire, and the people of themselves are simple." (Ch. 57.)

"Do nothing, and there is nothing that is not done." This is another of the seemingly paradoxical ideas of the Taoists. In the *Lao-tzu* we read: "*Tao* invariably does nothing and yet there is nothing that is not done." (Ch. 37.) *Tao* is that by which all things come to be. It is not itself a thing and therefore it cannot act as do such things. Yet all things come to be. Thus *Tao* does nothing, yet there is nothing that is not done. It allows each thing to do what it itself can do. According to the Taoists, the ruler of a state should model himself on *Tao*. He, too, should do nothing and should let the people do what they can do themselves. Here is another meaning of *wu-wei* (non-action), which later, with certain modifications, becomes one of the important theories of the Legalists (*Fa chia*).

Children have limited knowledge and few desires. They are not far away from the original *Te*. Their simplicity and innocence are characteristics that every man should if possible retain. Lao Tzu says: "Not to part from the invariable *Te* is to return to the state of infancy." (Ch. 28.) Again: "He who holds the *Te* in all its solidity may be likened to an infant." (Ch. 55.) Since the life of the child is nearer to the ideal life, the sage ruler would like all of his people to be like small children. Lao Tzu says: "The sage treats all as children." (Ch. 49.) He "does not make them enlightened, but keeps them ignorant." (Ch. 65.)

"Ignorant" here is a translation of the Chinese *yu*, which means ignorance in the sense of simplicity and innocence. The sage not only wants his people to be *yu*, but wants himself to be so too. Lao Tzu says: "Mine is the mind of the very ignorant." (Ch. 20.) In Taoism *yu* is not a vice, but a great virtue.

But is the *yu* of the sage really the same as the *yu* of the child and the common people? Certainly not. The *yu* of the sage is the result of a conscious process of cultivation. It is something higher than knowledge,

是以圣人之治，虚其心，实其腹，弱其志，强其骨，常使民无知无欲。"

圣人治国，要除掉世上祸害的根源。继此之后，圣人将实行无为而治。无为而无不为，世事将自然取得成就。这便是《道德经》第五十七章所说："我无为，而民自化；我好静，而民自正；我无事，而民自富；我无欲，而民自朴。"

道家的另一个看似矛盾的主张是"无为而无不为"。《道德经》第三十七章说："道常无为，而无不为。"道是万物之所由来。它不是万物中之一，因此它也不像万物那样不断流动，但万物自然从中生发出来，万物流动不居就是道。因此，道常无为，而无不为。道家认为，国君就应当以道为法，自己无为，而让大众各尽其能。这是"无为"的另一层意思。它经过若干演化，后来成为法家的一个重要主张。

儿童的知识和欲望都比成人少。他们离德不远。因此，《道德经》第二十八章说："常德不离，复归于婴儿。"第五十五章说："含德之厚，比于赤子。"婴儿的率性纯真是人人都应当极力保持的。正因为儿童的生活最接近人的原初状态，所以圣君期望他的民众都像婴儿。如《道德经》第四十九章所说："百姓皆注其耳目，圣人皆孩之。"又如《道德经》第六十五章所说："古之善为道者，非以明民，将以愚之。"

这里的"愚"是指质朴纯真。圣人不仅希望他的子民"愚"，也希望自己愚，如《道德经》第二十章所说："我愚人之心也哉！"在道家思想中，愚并不是一件坏事，倒是一项巨大的美德。

但是，圣人的"愚"和常人、和儿童的"愚"是否一样呢？当然不一样。圣人的"愚"是修养得来的。它高于知识，比知识是

something more, not less. There is a common Chinese saying: "Great wisdom is like ignorance." The *yu* of the sage is great wisdom, and not the *yu* of the child or of ordinary people. The latter kind of *yu* is a gift of nature, while that of the sage is an achievement of the spirit. There is a great difference between the two. But in many cases the Taoists seemed to have confused them. We shall see this point more clearly when we discuss the philosophy of Chuang Tzu.

多一些东西，而不是少了一些东西。中国人有一句谚语："大智若愚。"圣人的愚是大智，而不是常人和儿童的"愚"。常人和儿童的"愚"是自然决定的，圣人的"愚"是心灵经过努力而达到的成就，两者之间是截然不同的。后来的道家往往对两者不加区别，在下面讨论庄子的哲学思想时，我们对这一点会看得更清楚。

⑩ THE THIRD PHASE OF TAOISM: CHUANG TZU

Chuang Chou, better known as Chuang Tzu (c. 369-c. 286), is perhaps the greatest of the early Taoists. We know little of his life save that he was a native of the little state of Meng on the border between the present Shantung and Honan provinces, where he lived a hermit's life, but was nevertheless famous for his ideas and writings. It is said that King Wei of Ch'u, having heard his name, once sent messengers with gifts to invite him to his state, promising to make him chief minister. Chuang Tzu, however, merely laughed and said to them: "... Go away, do not defile me.... I prefer the enjoyment of my own free will." (*Historical Records*, ch. 63.)

● **Chuang Tzu the Man and *Chuang-tzu* the Book**

Though Chuang Tzu was a contemporary of Mencius and a friend of Hui Shih, the book titled the *Chuang-tzu*, as we know it today, was probably compiled by Kuo Hsiang, Chuang Tzu's great commentator of the third century A.D. We are thus not sure which of the chapters of *Chuang-tzu* the book were really written by Chuang Tzu himself. It is, in fact, a collection of various Taoist writings, some of which represent Taoism in its first phase of development, some in its second, and some in its third. It is only those chapters representing the thought of this third climactic phase that can properly be called Chuang Tzu's own philosophy, yet even they may not all have been written by Chuang Tzu himself. For though the name of Chuang Tzu can be taken as representative of the last phase of early Taoism, it is probable that his system of thought was brought to full completion only by his followers. Certain chapters of the *Chuang-tzu*, for example, contain statements about Kung-sun Lung, who certainly lived later than Chuang Tzu.

● **Way of Achieving Relative Happiness**

The first chapter of the *Chuang-tzu*, titled "The Happy Excursion," is a simple text, full of amusing stories. Their underlying idea is that there are varying degrees in the achievement of happiness. A free development of our natures may lead us to a relative kind of happiness; absolute happiness is achieved through higher understanding of the nature of things.

拾 道家的第三阶段：庄子

　　庄周（约公元前三六九至前二八六年），通称庄子，在早期道家中大概是最伟大的一个思想家。后人对他的生平所知很少，只知道他是蒙国（今山东、河南两省边境的小国）人，毕生过着隐士式的生活，但思想和著述已驰名当时。据《史记·老子韩非列传》所记，楚威王曾慕庄周名，遣使者携带礼物往谒庄周，聘请他出任楚国宰相。庄周笑答说："子亟去，无污我。……我宁游戏污渎之中自快，无为有国者所羁，终身不仕，以快吾志焉。"

● 庄子其人和《庄子》其书

　　庄子与孟子同时，和名家的惠施是好朋友，但我们现在所知的《庄子》一书很可能是公元三世纪注释《庄子》的思想家郭象所编著。现在我们很难断定《庄子》书中，哪些篇章是庄周本人所著。事实上，《庄子》是一部道家思想汇编。其中，有些篇反映了道家第一阶段的思想，有些反映了道家第二阶段的思想，有些则反映了道家第三阶段的思想。这些反映道家第三阶段思想的篇章才称得上是庄子自己的著作，即便这一部分，也难以断定其中哪些篇确是庄周本人的手笔，因为虽说庄子的思想代表了道家的第三阶段，但庄子思想体系可能是到他的弟子的时代才完成。例如《庄子》书中包含了对公孙龙思想的评论，而公孙龙活动的时代是在庄子之后。

● 得到相对快乐的途径

　　《庄子》第一章《逍遥游》文字简单，却充满了有趣的故事。这些故事蕴含的思想是说，人们所说的快乐，其实其中有不同的层次。自由发展人的本性，可以带来相对的快乐，但要达到"至乐"，必须对事物本性有更高的了解。

To carry out the first of these requirements, the free development of our nature, we should have a full and free exercise of our natural ability. That ability is our *Te*, which comes directly from the *Tao*. Regarding the *Tao* and *Te*, Chuang Tzu has the same idea as Lao Tzu. For example, he says: "At the great beginning there was Non-being. It had neither being nor name and was that from which came the One. When the One came into existence, there was the One but still no form. When things obtained that by which they came into existence, it was called the *Te*." (Ch. 12.) Thus our *Te* is what makes us what we are. We are happy when this *Te* or natural ability of ours is fully and freely exercised, that is, when our nature is fully and freely developed.

In connection with this idea of free development, Chuang Tzu makes a contrast between what is of nature and what is of man. "What is of nature," he says, "is internal. What is of man is external.... That oxen and horses should have four feet is what is of nature. That a halter should be put on a horse's head, or a string through an ox's nose, is what is of man." (Ch. 17.) Following what is of nature, he maintains, is the source of all happiness and goodness, while following what is of man is the source of all pain and evil.

Things are different in their nature and their natural ability is also not the same. What they share in common, however, is that they are all equally happy when they have a full and free exercise of their natural ability. In "The Happy Excursion" a story is told of a very large and a small bird. The abilities of the two are entirely different. The one can fly thousands of miles, while the other can hardly reach from one tree to the next. Yet they are both happy when they each do what they are able and like to do. Thus there is no absolute uniformity in the natures of things, nor is there any need for such uniformity. Another chapter of the *Chuang-tzu* tells us: "The duck's legs are short, but if we try to lengthen them, the duck will feel pain. The crane's legs are long, but if we try to shorten them, the crane will feel grief. Therefore we are not to amputate what is by nature long, nor to lengthen what is by nature short." (Ch. 8.)

Such, however, is just what artificiality tries to do. The purpose of all laws, morals, institutions, and governments, is to establish uniformity and suppress difference. The motivation of the people who try to enforce this uniformity may be wholly admirable. When they find something that

　　为达到快乐，第一步便是充分发展人的本性，为此人要能自由发挥天赋的才能。人的天赋才能便是他的"德"，而"德"则是直接来自"道"。庄子对"道"和"德"的看法和老子相同，例如《庄子·天地》篇中说："泰初有无，无有无名；一之所起，有一而未形。物得以生，谓之德。"从中可以看到庄子认为，德是人之所以成为人，或说，"德"是人的本质。当人得以充分并自由地发挥他的天赋才能时，他就感到快乐。

　　和自由发展自己这个思想相联，庄子把天然和人为做了一个对比。在《庄子·秋水》篇里河神河伯与海神北海若有一段对话，北海若说："天在内，人在外，……牛马四足，是谓天；络马首，穿牛鼻，是谓人。"顺乎天然，乃是一切快乐和善良之所由来，而服从于人为则是痛苦和邪恶的由来。

　　万物的本性和天赋的能力各有不同。它们之间的共同点是：当它们充分并自由发挥天赋才能时，便同样感到快乐。《庄子·逍遥游》篇里叙述大鹏和小鸟的故事。大鹏和小鸟的飞翔能力全然不同。大鹏能够扶摇直上九万里，小鸟甚至从一棵树飞到另一棵树都感到勉强。但是大鹏和小鸟各尽所能地飞翔时，都感到自己非常快乐。这说明，万物本性不是生来一致的，强求一致也并无必要。《庄子·骈拇》篇里还有一处说："凫胫（脚骨）虽短，续之则忧；鹤胫虽长，断之则悲。故性长非所断，性短非所续，无所去忧也。"人要想戕贼万物本性，强求一致，是徒劳无益的。

● **政治与社会哲学**

　　上面举出天然和人为的异趣。一切体制、政府、法律、道德，所求达到的便是强求一律和压制差异。这样强求一律的人，其动机或许是可敬的，但是，把自己认为好的东西强加给别人，其结果是

is good for them, they may be anxious to see that others have it also. This good intention of theirs, however, only makes the situation more tragic. In the *Chuang-tzu* there is a story which says: "Of old, when a seabird alighted outside the capital of Lu, the Marquis went out to receive it, gave it wine in the temple, and had the *Chiu-shao* music played to amuse it, and a bullock slaughtered to feed it. But the bird was dazed and too timid to eat or drink anything. In three days it was dead. This was treating the bird as one would treat oneself, not the bird as a bird.... Water is life to fish but is death to man. Being differently constituted, their likes and dislikes must necessarily differ. Therefore the early sages did not make abilities and occupations uniform." (Ch. 18.) When the Marquis treated the bird in a way which he considered the most honorable, he certainly had good intentions. Yet the result was just opposite to what he expected. This is what happens when uniform codes of laws and morals are enforced by government and society upon the individual.

This is why Chuang Tzu violently opposes the idea of governing through the formal machinery of government, and maintains instead that the best way of governing is through non-government. He says: "I have heard of letting mankind alone, but not of governing mankind. Letting alone springs from the fear that people will pollute their innate nature and set aside their *Te*. When people do not pollute their innate nature and set aside their *Te*, then is there need for the government of mankind?" (Ch. 11.)

If one fails to leave people alone, and tries instead to rule them with laws and institutions, the process is like putting a halter around a horse's neck or a string through an ox's nose. It is also like lengthening the legs of the duck or shortening those of the crane. What is natural and spontaneous is changed into something artificial, which is called by Chuang Tzu "overcoming what is of nature by what is of man." (Ch. 17.) Its result can only be misery and unhappiness.

Thus Chuang Tzu and Lao Tzu both advocate government through non-government, but for somewhat different reasons. Lao Tzu emphasizes his general principle that "reversing is the movement of the *Tao*." The more one governs, he argues, the less one achieves the desired result. And Chuang Tzu emphasizes the distinction between what is of nature and what is of man. The more the former is overcome by the latter, the more there will be misery and unhappiness.

Thus far we have only seen Chuang Tzu's way of achieving relative happiness. Such relative happiness is achieved when one simply follows what is natural in oneself. This every man can do. The political and social

适得其反。《庄子·至乐》篇讲了一个寓言，从前有一只海鸟飞到内陆，栖息在鲁国京城郊外。"鲁侯御而觞之于庙，奏九韶以为乐，具太牢以为膳。鸟乃眩视忧悲，不敢食一脔，不敢饮一杯，三日而死，此以己养养鸟也，非以鸟养养鸟也。……鱼处水而生，人处水而死，彼必相与异，其好恶故异也。故先圣不一其能，不同其事。"鲁侯以上宾之礼待鸟，他的动机诚然是好的，而结果却适得其反。政府和社会在法律和道德上强求一律，其结果也就像鲁侯待海鸟一样。

这是庄子何以强烈反对政府运用其机构实行统治的原因。他认为，最好的治理办法就是无为而治。《庄子·在宥》篇说："闻在宥（在，自在；宥，宽容）天下，不闻治天下也。在之也者，恐天下之淫其性也；宥之也者，恐天下之迁其德也。天下不淫其性，不迁其德，有治天下者哉！"

如果不让大众享受自由，而以政治、法律统治大众，那就如同络马首、穿牛鼻，又如同续鸭胫、断鹤胫一样。本来率性自然的，变成人为的，那就如同《庄子·秋水》篇所说的"以人灭天"，其结果只能是悲惨不幸。

庄子和老子都主张"无为而治"，但是所持的理由却不完全相同。老子着眼在"反者道之动"，认为统治者如果一心加强统治，就越是达不到所想达到的结果。庄子则强调天然和人为之不同，统治者越是靠人为的手段来统治，悲惨和不幸就越多。

说到这里，我们所谈的还只是庄子所说的"相对快乐"。达到相对快乐的途径是让人顺他的天性去生活，这是每个人都能做到的。

philosophy of Chuang Tzu aimes at achieving precisely such relative happiness for every man. This and nothing more is the most that any political and social philosophy can hope to do.

- **Emotion and Reason**

Relative happiness is relative because it has to depend upon something. It is true that one is happy when one has a full and free exercise of one's natural ability. But there are many ways in which this exercise is obstructed. For instance, there is death which is the end of all human activities. There are diseases which handicap human activities. There is old age which gives man the same trouble. So it is not without reason that the Buddhists consider these as three of the four human miseries, the fourth, according to them, being life itself. Hence, happiness which depends upon the full and free exercise of one's natural ability is a limited and therefore relative happiness.

In the *Chuang-tzu* there are many discussions about the greatest of all disasters that can befall man, death. Fear of death and anxiety about its coming are among the principal sources of human unhappiness. Such fear and anxiety, however, may be diminished if we have a proper understanding of the nature of things. In the *Chuang-tzu* there is a story about the death of Lao Tzu. When Lao Tzu died, his friend Chin Shih, who had come after the death, criticized the violent lamentations of the other mourners, saying: "This is to violate the principle of nature and to increase the emotion of man, forgetting what we have received [from nature]. These were called by the ancients the penalty of violating the principle of nature. When the Master came, it was because he had the occasion to be born. When he went, he simply followed the natural course. Those who are quiet at the proper occasion and follow the natural course, cannot be affected by sorrow or joy. They were considered by the ancients as the men of the gods, who were released from bondage." (Ch. 3.)

To the extent that the other mourners felt sorrow, to that extent they suffered. Their suffering was the "penalty of violating the principle of nature." The mental torture inflicted upon man by his emotions is sometimes just as severe as any physical punishment. But by the use of understanding, man can reduce his emotions. For example, a man of understanding will not be angry when rain prevents him from going

庄子的政治社会哲学正是要为大众谋求这种相对的快乐。政治和社会哲学所能做到的也只止于此。

● **感情和理性**

相对快乐之所以相对，是因为它需要依靠别的东西。一个人能够自由充分地发挥天赋的才能，便感觉到快乐，这是事实。但是，人这样做时，总要遇到许多阻力。举例来说，死亡使得人不再能够活动，还有各种疾病和老年来临，都使人无法充分活动。难怪佛家认为人的老、病、死是"众生皆苦"的三项，另一项"苦"是生命本身。因此，人要自由充分发挥天赋才能却又不得不受到限制，由此所得的快乐也只能是相对的快乐。

在《庄子》书中有不少地方讨论到人生最大的苦难——死亡。人们不快乐的一个重要原因，便是惧怕死的来临和由此而来的忧虑。这种恐惧和忧虑是可以消除的，关键在于人对事物的本性有一个正确的洞察。《庄子·养生主》篇里有一个关于老子之死的故事说，老子死后，他的朋友秦失前来吊唁，看到其他前来吊唁的人过分悲痛，就加以批评说："是遁天倍情，忘其所受，古者谓之遁天之刑。适来，夫子时也；适去，夫子顺也。安时而处顺，哀乐不能入也。古者谓是帝之悬解。"这是说，人违反了自然的法则，去增多人的感情，而忘记了从自然已经得到的教诲。这就是违反自然法则所受的惩罚。夫子之来，有他出生的时机，夫子之去，是顺从自然的必由之路。懂得夫子的来去，都是适时、顺势，就不致为悲伤或欢乐所扰。古人把这样的人看为神人，他们已经得到了解脱。

吊唁死者而悲痛时，人在精神上受苦，是由于自己的感情，感情悲痛越深，受苦也越深。苦楚的根源是期望人不死，违反了自然的法则，即所谓"遁天之刑"。人对万事万物增加理解，就可以减少由感情造成的痛苦。例如，天下雨，使人不能外出，成人不会对天

out, but a child often will. The reason is that the man possesses greater understanding, with the result that he suffers less disappointment or exasperation than the child who does get angry. As Spinoza has said: "In so far as the mind understands all things are necessary, so far has it greater power over the effects, or suffers less from them." (*Ethics*, Pt. 5, Prop. VI.) Such, in the words of the Taoists, is "to disperse emotion with reason."

A story about Chuang Tzu himself well illustrates this point. It is said that when Chuang Tzu's wife died, his friend Hui Shih went to condole. To his amazement he found Chuang Tzu sitting on the ground, singing, and on asking him how he could be so unkind to his wife, was told by Chuang Tzu: "When she had just died, I could not help being affected. Soon, however, I examined the matter from the very beginning. At the very beginning, she was not living, having no form, nor even substance. But somehow or other there was then her substance, then her form, and then her life. Now by a further change, she has died. The whole process is like the sequence of the four seasons, spring, summer, autumn, and winter. While she is thus lying in the great mansion of the universe, for me to go about weeping and wailing would be to proclaim myself ignorant of the natural laws. Therefore I stop." (*Chuang-tzu*, ch. 18.) On this passage the great commentator Kuo Hsiang comments: "When ignorant, he felt sorry. When he understood, he was no longer affected. This teaches man to disperse emotion with reason." Emotion can be counteracted with reason and understanding. Such was the view of Spinoza and also of the Taoists.

The Taoists maintained that the sage who has a complete understanding of the nature of things, thereby has no emotions. This, however, does not mean that he lacks sensibility. Rather it means that he is not disturbed by the emotions, and enjoys what may be called "the peace of the soul." As Spinoza says: "The ignorant man is not only agitated by external causes in many ways, and never enjoys true peace in the soul, but lives also ignorant, as it were, both of God and of things, and as soon as he ceases to suffer, ceases also to be. On the other hand, the wise man, in so far as he is considered as such, is scarcely moved in his mind, but, being conscious by a certain eternal necessity of himself, of God, and things, never ceases to be, and always enjoys the peace of the soul." (*Ethics*, Pt. 5, Prop. XLII.)

发怒，儿童却忍不住会发脾气。其原因是成人比儿童多了解事理，所受到的挫折失望感也就比儿童要少得多。斯宾诺莎曾说过："人越多了解事物的因果由来，他就能越多地掌握事件的后果，并减少由此而来的苦楚。"用道家的话来说，这就是"以理化情"。

《庄子·至乐》篇里有一个关于庄子的故事，最足以说明这一点。"庄子妻死，惠子吊之，庄子则方箕踞鼓盆而歌。惠子曰：'与人居，长子老身，死不哭亦足矣，又鼓盆而歌，不亦甚乎！'庄子曰：'不然。是其始死也，我独何能无概然！察其始而本无生，非徒无生也而本无形，非徒无形也而本无气。杂乎芒芴之间，变而有气，气变而有形，形变而有生，今又变而之死，是相与为春秋冬夏四时行也。人且偃然寝于巨室，而我嗷嗷然随而哭之，自以为不通乎命，故止也。'"注释《庄子》的西晋大思想家郭象就这个故事评论说：庄子在懵懂无知时，他是悲恸的；及至醒悟以后，他就不再悲恸。讲这个故事，是为了启发重情的人，使他明理而得以排遣感情上的沉重负担（"斯所以诲有情者，将令推至理以遣累也"）。感情可以通过理性和理解去化解，这是斯宾诺莎的观点，道家的观点也正是如此。

道家认为，圣人洞察事物本性，因此没有感情的冲动，这并不是说圣人便没有对事物的感觉。毋宁说，他不为感情所扰以至失去"心灵的宁静"。斯宾诺莎曾说："懵懂无知的人不仅由于外界的各种因素而焦躁不安，以至永不得享受心灵的宁静，他还对神和万事都懵懂无知，若不痛苦，便无法生活，真正不痛苦时，也就不存在了。有智慧的人，在他被认为有智慧的范围内，心神泰然，还由于意识到神、万物和自我，因具有某种永远的必然性而时刻存在，由此得以安享心灵的宁静。"（《伦理学》第五部分，命题第四十二）

Thus by his understanding of the nature of things, the sage is no longer affected by the changes of the world. In this way he is not dependent upon external things, and hence his happiness is not limited by them. He may be said to have achieved absolute happiness. Such is one line of Taoist thought, in which there is not a little atmosphere of pessimism and resignation. It is a line which emphasizes the inevitability of natural processes and the fatalistic acquiescence in them by man.

• Way of Achieving Absolute Happiness

There is another line of Taoist thought, however, which emphasizes the relativity of the nature of things and the identification of man with the universe. To achieve this identification, man needs knowledge and understanding of still a higher level, and the happiness resulting from this identification is really absolute happiness, as expounded in Chuang Tzu's chapter on "The Happy Excursion."

In this chapter, after describing the happiness of large and small birds, Chuang Tzu adds that among human beings there was a man named Lieh Tzu who could even ride on the wind. "Among those who have attained happiness," he says, "such a man is rare. Yet although he was able to dispense with walking, he still had to depend upon something." This something was the wind, and since he had to depend upon the wind, his happiness was to that extent relative. Then Chuang Tzu asks: "But suppose there is one who chariots on the normality of the universe, rides on the transformation of the six elements, and thus makes excursion into the infinite, what has he to depend upon? Therefore it is said that the perfect man has no self; the spiritual man has no achievement; and the true sage has no name." (Ch. 1.)

What is here said by Chuang Tzu describes the man who has achieved absolute happiness. He is the perfect man, the spiritual man, and the true sage. He is absolutely happy, because he transcends the ordinary distinctions of things. He also transcends the distinction between the self and the world, the "me" and the "non-me." Therefore he has no self. He is one with the *Tao*. The *Tao* does nothing and yet there is nothing that is not done. The *Tao* does nothing, and therefore has no achievements. The sage is one with the *Tao* and therefore also has no achievements. He may rule the whole world, but his rule consists of just leaving mankind alone, and letting everyone exercise his own natural ability fully and freely. The *Tao* is nameless and so the sage who is one with the *Tao* is also nameless.

　　圣人洞察事物的本性，因此不会由于世上的各种变化而心中波涛汹涌。他的生命独立于外界事物，因此他的心灵快乐也不受外界所左右。他可以说是达到了"至乐"。这是道家思想中的一派，这一派强调事物有其自身的进程，人只能对它顺服，其中自然不免含有悲观认命的色彩。

● 达到至乐的途径

　　道家中还有另一派思想，强调事物的本性便是不停地变动，因而是相对的，人的努力目标是"天人合一"。为做到这一点，人需要对事物有更高一层的理解，由此得到的快乐才是"至乐"，这是庄子在《逍遥游》篇中所发挥的观点。

　　在《逍遥游》篇中，描述大鹏和小鸟各自都感到快乐之后，庄子说，战国时期郑国的一位思想家列子，能够御风而行。顺应自然而能如此，在世间已不多见。但列子虽不必徒步行路，还要靠风，因此，他的快乐还是相对的。如果有人凭藉自然的本性，顺应六气（阴、阳、风、雨、晦、明）的变化，而游于无穷之中，他还需要依赖什么东西呢？在庄子看来，这样的人是至人、神人、圣人，"至人无己，神人无功，圣人无名"。

　　庄子在这里描述了在他理想中达到至乐的人，这是完美的人、心灵自由的人、真正的圣人。他能够纯然快乐，因为他超越了普通事物的界限，还超越了我与世界、我与非我、主观与客观的界限。这就是说，他超越了"我"，达到"无我"的境界，与道合一。道无为而无不为，因为"无为"，所以"无功"；圣人与道合而为一，因此也"无功"。圣人治天下，就是让世人自由自在，自由充分地发挥所有的才能。道"无名"，圣人与道合一，因此也"无名"。

● **The Finite Point of View**

The question that remains is this: How can a person become such a perfect man? To answer it, we must make an analysis of the second chapter of the *Chuang-tzu*, the *Ch'i Wu Lun*, or "On the Equality of Things." In the "Happy Excursion" Chuang Tzu discusses two levels of happiness, and in "On the Equality of Things" he discusses two levels of knowledge. Let us start our analysis with the first or lower level. In our chapter on the School of Names, we have said that there is some similarity between Hui Shih and Chuang Tzu. Thus in the *Ch'i Wu Lun*, Chuang Tzu discusses knowledge of a lower level which is similar to that found in Hui Shih's ten so-called paradoxes.

The chapter *Ch'i Wu Lun* begins with a description of the wind. When the wind blows, there are different kinds of sound, each with its own peculiarity. These this chapter calls "the sounds of earth." But in addition there are other sounds that are known as "the sounds of man." The sounds of earth and the sounds of man together constitute "the sounds of Heaven."

The sounds of man consist of the words (*yen*) that are spoken in the human world. They differ from such "sounds of earth" as those caused by the wind, inasmuch as when words are said, they represent human ideas. They represent affirmations and denials, and the opinions that are made by each individual from his own particular finite point of view. Being thus finite, these opinions are necessarily one-sided. Yet most men, not knowing that their opinions are based on finite points of view, invariably consider their own opinions as right and those of others as wrong. "The result," as the *Ch'i Wu Lun* says, "is the affirmations and denials of the Confucianists and Mohists, the one regarding as right what the other regards as wrong, and regarding as wrong what the other regards as right."

When people thus argue each according to his own one-sided view, there is no way either to reach a final conclusion, or to determine which side is really right or really wrong. The *Ch'i Wu Lun* says "Suppose that you argue with me. If you beat me, instead of my beating you, are you necessarily right and am I necessarily wrong? Or, if I beat you, and not you me, am I necessarily right and are you necessarily wrong? Is one of us right and the other wrong? Or are both of us right or both of us wrong? Neither you nor I can know, and others are all the more in the dark. Whom shall we ask to produce the right decision? We may ask someone who agrees with you; but since he agrees with you, how can he make the decision? We may ask someone who agrees with me; but since he agrees with me, how can he make the decision? We may ask someone who

● 有限的观点

到这里，还剩下的问题是：一般人怎样能够成为完美的人？为回答这个问题，我们必须读《庄子》的第二篇《齐物论》。在第一篇《逍遥游》里，庄子分析了快乐的两个层次；在《齐物论》里，他又分析了知识的两个层次。让我们先从最初步的层次说起。在讨论名家的一章里，曾说到庄子和惠施之间有某些相似之点。在《齐物论》里，庄子讨论低层次的知识，和"惠施十事"中的反论相比较，可以看出它们的相似之处。

《齐物论》的第一节里描述风吹的时候，发出各种声音，每种声音都有它的特点，这些被称为"地籁"。此外还有"人籁"。"地籁"和"人籁"一起，又组成"天籁"。

"人籁"就是人世间的"言语"。它与"地籁"不同之处就在于言语反映人的思想，其中包含肯定与否定，还有人们从各自的局限性出发的观点和主张。这些意见既然有局限性，因此就有片面性。但是大多数人并不意识到自己的局限性，往往认为自己正确，而别人则是错误的。结果是："有儒墨之是非，以是其所非而非其所是。"

人们各按自己的片面观点争论是非，在这种情况下，不可能达到一个一致的结论，也不可能认定某一方就是完全正确或完全错误。《齐物论》中说："既使我与若辩矣，若胜我，我不若胜，若果是也，我果非也邪？我胜若，若不吾胜，我果是也，而果非也邪？其或是也，其或非也邪？其俱是也，其俱非也邪？我与若不能相知也，则人固受其黮暗，吾谁使正之？使同乎若者正之？既与若同矣，恶能正之！使同乎我者正之？既同乎我矣，恶能正之！使异乎

agrees with both you and me; but since he agrees with both you and me, how can he make the decision? We may ask some one who differs from both you and me; but since he differs from both you and me, how can he make the decision?"

This passage is reminiscent of the manner of argument followed by the School of Names. But whereas the members of that school argue thus in order to contradict the common sense of ordinary people, the *Ch'i Wu Lun's* purpose is to contradict the followers of the School of Names. For this school did actually believe that argument could decide what is really right and really wrong.

Chuang Tzu, on the other hand, maintains that concepts of right and wrong are built up by each man on the basis of his own finite point of view. All these views are relative. As the *Ch'i Wu Lun* says: "When there is life, there is death, and when there is death, there is life. When there is possibility, there is impossibility, and when there is impossibility, there is possibility. Because there is right, there is wrong. Because there is wrong, there is right." Things are ever subject to change and have many aspects. Therefore many views can be held about one and the same thing. Once we say this, we assume that a higher standpoint exists. If we accept this assumption, there is no need to make a decision ourselves about what is right and what is wrong. The argument explains itself.

- **The Higher Point of View**

To accept this premise is to see things from a higher point of view, or, as the *Ch'i Wu Lun* calls it, to see things "in the light of Heaven." "To see things in the light of Heaven" means to see things from the point of view of that which transcends the finite, which is the *Tao*. It is said in the *Ch'i Wu Lun*: "The 'this' is also 'that.' The 'that' is also 'this.' The 'that' has a system of right and wrong. The 'this' also has a system of right and wrong. Is there really a distinction between 'that' and 'this'? Or is there really no distinction between 'that' and 'this'? That the 'that' and the 'this' cease to be opposites is the very essence of *Tao*. Only the essence, an axis as it were, is the center of the circle responding to the endless changes. The right is an endless change. The wrong is also an endless change. Therefore it is said that there is nothing better than to use the 'light.'" In other words, the 'that' and the 'this,' in their mutual opposition of right and wrong, are like an endlessly revolving circle. But the man who sees things from the point of view of the *Tao* stands, as it were, at the center of the circle. He understands all that is going on in the movements of the circle, but

我与若者正之？既异乎我与若矣，恶能正之！使同乎我与若者正之？既同乎我与若矣，恶能正之！"

这一段论辩使我们想起名家论辩的风格。但名家的论辩是为了驳倒一般人凭常识而来的观点，《齐物论》的论辩的目的则在于驳倒名家的论点，因为名家认为，事情的是非，就看哪一方能够驳倒对方。

庄子则认为，人们的是非观念是根据他们的局限性观点建立起来的。所有这样的观点都是相对的，《齐物论》说："方生方死，方死方生；方可方不可，方不可方可；因是因非，因非因是。"事物总是在不断变化之中，自然有许多方面。于是对同一个事物，可以有各种不同的观点。当我们这样说时，我们便已经假定，还有更高一层的看法。如果接受这个假定，我们就不必再论断事情双方的孰是孰非。论辩双方既然都有限、都片面，便已经说明了问题。

● **更高层次的观点**

接受这个前提，就意味着从一个更高的出发点看事物，有如《齐物论》所说"照之于天"，就是超越任何有局限性的观点，比照事物的本能，也就是照之于道。《齐物论》中说："是亦彼也，彼亦是也。彼亦一是非，此亦一是非。果且有彼是乎哉？果且无彼是乎哉？彼是莫得其偶，谓之道枢。枢始得其环中，以应无穷。是亦一无穷，非亦一无穷也。故曰莫若以明。"换句话说，有"此"就有"彼"，它们之间孰是孰非，往复循环，如同一个圆圈。人若站在道的观点来看问题，就如同站在圆圈的中心，他看得到圆圈上每一点的运动，而他自己则站在运动以外。这并不是由于他

does not himself take part in these movements. This is not owing to his inactivity or resignation, but because he has transcended the finite and sees things from a higher point of view. In the *Chuang-tzu*, the finite point of view is compared with the view of the well-frog. The frog in the well can see only a little sky, and so thinks that the sky is only so big.

From the point of view of the *Tao*, everything is just what it is. It is said in the *Ch'i Wu Lun*: "The possible is possible. The impossible is impossible. The *Tao* makes things and they are what they are. What are they? They are what they are. What are they not? They are not what they are not. Everything is something and is good for something. There is nothing which is not something or is not good for something. Thus it is that there are roof-slats and pillars, ugliness and beauty, the peculiar and the extraordinary. All these by means of the *Tao* are united and become one." Although all things differ, they are alike in that they all constitute something and are good for something. They all equally come from the *Tao*. Therefore from the viewpoint of the *Tao*, things, though different, yet are united and become one.

The *Ch'i Wu Lun* says again: "To make a distinction is to make some construction. But construction is the same as destruction. For things as a whole there is neither construction nor destruction, but they turn to unity and become one." For example, when a table is made out of wood, from the viewpoint of that table, this is an act of construction. But from the viewpoint of the wood or the tree, it is one of destruction. Such construction or destruction are so, however, only from a finite point of view. From the viewpoint of the *Tao*, there is neither construction nor destruction. These distinctions are all relative.

The distinction between the "me" and the "non-me" is also relative. From the viewpoint of the *Tao*, the "me" and the "non-me" are also united and become one. The *Ch'i Wu Lun* says: "There is nothing larger in the world than the point of a hair, yet Mount T'ai is small. There is nothing older than a dead child, yet Peng Tsu [a legendary Chinese Methuselah] had an untimely death. Heaven and Earth and I came into existence together, and all things with me are one." Here we again have Hui Shih's dictum: "Love all things equally, Heaven and Earth are one body."

　　无所作为、逡巡不前，乃是因为他超越了有限，从一个更高的观点看事物。庄子把囿于有限的观点比作"井底之蛙"，只看到天的一角，便以为那就是天的全体。

　　从道的观点看事物，每个事物只有那么一点大，如同《齐物论》中所说："可乎可，不可乎不可。道行之而成，物谓之而然。恶乎然？然于然；恶乎不然？不然于不然。物固有所然，物固有所可。无物不然，无物不可。故为是举莛与楹，厉与西施，恢诡谲怪，道通为一。"意思是说，由道而生成万物，事物的名称是人把它叫出来的。"可"有它可的原因，"不可"有它不可的原因；"是"有它是的原因，"不是"有它不是的原因。为什么是？自有它是的道理；为什么不是？自有它不是的道理。为什么"可"？自有它可的道理；为什么"不可"？自有它不可的道理。万物本来都有它们的道理，万物也本来都有它们得以存在的根据。没有什么东西毫无存在的价值，没有什么东西不可以存在。所以小草茎和大厅柱、丑陋的女人和美丽的西施，以及一切千奇百怪的东西，从道的观点看，它们都是可以相通为一的。

　　接下去，《齐物论》又说："其分也，成也；其成也，毁也。凡物无成与毁，复通为一。"以制造一张桌子为例，从桌子的角度看，这是建造；从树的角度看，这是破坏。叫它建造也好，叫它破坏也好，这都是从有限的角度看它；如果从道的角度看，则建造和破坏都是相对的，都没有绝对的意义，因此无成也无毁。

　　再如"我"与"非我"，这也是相对的。从道的观点看，"我"与"非我"也是相通的，因此也通而为一。这就是《齐物论》中所说："天下莫大于秋毫之末，而大山为小；莫寿于殇子，而彭祖为夭。天地与我并生，而万物与我为一。"这又使我们想到惠施所说的："泛爱万物，天地一体也。"

● Knowledge of the Higher Level

This passage in the *Ch'i Wu Lun*, however, is immediately followed by another statement: "Since all things are one, what room is there for speech? But since I have already spoken of the one, is this not already speech? One plus speech make two. Two plus one make three. Going on from this, even the most skillful reckoner will not be able to reach the end, and how much less able to do so are ordinary people! If proceeding from nothing to something we can reach three, how much further shall we reach, if we proceed from something to something! Let us not proceed. Let us stop here." It is in this statement that the *Ch'i Wu Lun* goes a step further than Hui Shih, and begins to discuss a higher kind of knowledge. This higher knowledge is "knowledge which is not knowledge."

What is really "one" can neither be discussed nor even conceived. For as soon as it is thought of and discussed, it becomes something that exists externally to the person who is doing the thinking and speaking. So since its all-embracing unity is thus lost, it is actually not the real "one" at all. Hui Shih said: "The greatest has nothing beyond itself and is called the Great One." By these words he described the Great One very well indeed, yet he remained unaware of the fact that since the Great One has nothing beyond itself, it is impossible either to think or speak of it. For anything that can be thought or spoken of has something beyond itself, namely, the thought and the speaking. The Taoists, on the contrary, realized that the "one" is unthinkable and inexpressible. Thereby, they had a true understanding of the "one" and advanced a step further than did the School of Names.

In the *Ch'i Wu Lun* it is also said: "Referring to the right and the wrong, the 'being so' and 'not being so': if the right is really right, we need not dispute about how it is different from the wrong; if the 'being so' is really being so, we need not dispute about how it is different from 'not being so.' ... Let us forget life. Let us forget the distinction between right and wrong. Let us take our joy in the realm of the infinite and remain there." The realm of the infinite is the realm wherein lives the man who has attained to the *Tao*. Such a man not only has knowledge of the "one," but also has actually experienced it. This experience is the experience of living in the realm of the infinite. He has forgotten all the distinctions

● 更高层次的知识

上引《齐物论》中的段落，接下去又说："既已为一矣，且得有言乎？既已谓之一矣，且得无言乎？一与言为二，二与一为三。自此以往，巧历不能得，而况其凡乎！故自无适有以至于三，而况自有适有乎！无适焉，因是已。"这是说，既然万物都通为一，具有同一性，那还需要说什么呢？但是，既已说了一，这不是已经有言了吗？"一"加上"言"，便成了"二"；"二"再加上一，便成了三。即便有一个最善于计数的人，也无法把数目数算到尽头，何况凡人呢？由无到有，已经出现了三，如果是从有到有，还能数到尽头吗？不必再数，就此停住吧。这里，《齐物论》比惠施的思想前进一步，开始讨论更高层次的知识。这更高层次的知识便是"不知之知"。

"一"究竟是什么？这不仅无法讨论，而且不可思议。任何人只要开始对"一"进行思想或议论，它立刻变成在这个人之外、已经存在的某种事物。这样，"一"不再是本来包含万物的"一"，它已经变成了另外的一个什么。惠施说："至大无外，谓之大一。"惠施这样形容"大一"，可以说，已经尽其所能。但是，惠施没有意识到，大一既是"至大无外"，因此难以设想，无可名状。任何可以设想、可以名状的东西，都必须有在它之外的一个思想或形状。道家则认识到，"一"是不可思议、不可言说的，这比名家的认识显然前进了一步。

《齐物论》中又说："是不是，然不然。是若果是也，则是之异乎不是也亦无辩；然若果然也，则然之异乎不然也，亦无辩。忘年忘义，振于无竟，故寓诸无竟。"这是说，任何东西，有"是"，便有"不是"；有"然"，便有"不然"。"是"果真是"是"，就和"不是"有区别，这样就不须辩论；"然"果真是"然"，就和"不然"有区别，也不须辩论。忘掉年龄生死，忘掉是非仁义，遨游于无穷的

of things, even those involved in his own life. In his experience there remains only the undifferentiable one, in the midst of which he lives.

Described in poetical language, such a man is he "who chariots on the normality of the universe, rides on the transformations of the six elements, and thus makes excursion into the infinite." He is really the independent man, so his happiness is absolute.

Here we see how Chuang Tzu reached a final resolution of the original problem of the early Taoists. That problem is how to preserve life and avoid harm and danger. But, to the real sage, it ceases to be a problem. As is said in the *Chuang-tzu*: "The universe is the unity of all things. If we attain this unity and identify ourselves with it, then the members of our body are but so much dust and dirt, while life and death, end and beginning, are but as the succession of day and night, which cannot disturb our inner peace. How much less shall we be troubled by worldly gain and loss, good-luck and bad-luck!" (Ch. 20.) Thus Chuang Tzu solved the original problem of the early Taoists simply by abolishing it. This is really the philosophical way of solving problems. Philosophy gives no information about matters of fact, and so cannot solve any problem in a concrete and physical way. It cannot, for example, help man either to gain longevity or defy death, nor can it help him to gain riches and avoid poverty. What it can do, however, is to give man a point of view, from which he can see that life is no more than death and loss is equal to gain. From the "practical" point of view, philosophy is useless, yet it can give us a point of view which is very useful. To use an expression of the *Chuang-tzu*, this is the "usefulness of the useless." (Ch. 4.)

Spinoza has said that in a certain sense, the wise man "never ceases to be." This is also what Chuang Tzu means. The sage or perfect man is one with the Great One, that is, the universe. Since the universe never ceases to be, therefore the sage also never ceases to be. In the sixth chapter of the *Chuang-tzu*, we read: "A boat may be stored in a creek; a net may be stored in a lake; these may be said to be safe enough. But at midnight a strong man may come and carry them away on his back. The ignorant do not see that no matter how well you store things, smaller ones in larger ones, there will always be a chance for them to be lost. But if you store the universe in the universe, there will be no room left for it to be lost. This is the great truth of things. Therefore the sage makes excursions into

境域，也就是生活在无限的境界之中。

用诗的语言来说，这样的人就是"乘天地之正，而御六气之辨，以游无穷者"。这样的人独立于化外，因此，他的快乐是绝对的快乐。

由此可以看到，庄子怎样解决早期道家最初提出的问题，即：怎样全生？怎样避祸？对于真正的圣人来说，这已经不成其为问题了。如《庄子·田子方》篇所说："夫天下也者，万物之所一也。得其所一而同焉，则四肢百体将为尘垢，而死生终始将为昼夜而莫之能滑，而况得丧祸福之所介乎！"这是说，宇宙中万物本是一体。如果人达到与万物一体，这时，人的肢体无非是尘埃；生死终始，无非是日夜的继续，不足以干扰人内心的宁静；至于世俗的得失、时运好坏，更不足挂齿。这样，庄子解决早期道家根本问题的办法是一笔勾销了这个问题，这正是在哲学上解决了这个问题。哲学对客观事实并不提供任何信息，因此，哲学对现实问题并不试图去具体地解决。举例来说，哲学不能帮助人长生不老，也不能帮助人发财致富。它所能做的是：给人一种观点，使人看到生比死所胜无几，人所失去的也就是他所得到的。从"实际"的观点看，哲学无用，但哲学可以给我们一种有用的观点。在《庄子·外物》篇中，把它称作"无用之用"。

斯宾诺莎曾说，在某种意义上，智慧人是长生不老的。这也是庄子的观点，他认为圣人或称"至人"，与"大一"（即宇宙）是一体，宇宙永在，因此圣人也长生不老。《庄子·大宗师》篇里说："夫藏舟于壑，藏山于泽，谓之固矣。然而夜半有力者负之而走，昧者不知也。藏小大有宜，犹有所遁。若夫藏天下于天下而不得所遁，是恒物之大情也。……故圣人将游于物之所不得遁而皆存。"人无论把他珍贵的东西藏在什么地方，都可能被偷，如果他把宇宙藏在宇宙之中，如有想偷的人，即便偷了宇宙，也没有收藏的地方，这是关乎万有的至大真理。因此，圣人在那不可能被偷的东西——

that which cannot be lost, and together with it he remains." It is in this sense that the sage never ceases to be.

• Methodology of Mysticism

In order to be one with the Great One, the sage has to transcend and forget the distinctions between things. The way to do this is to discard knowledge, and is the method used by the Taoists for achieving "sageliness within." The task of knowledge in the ordinary sense is to make distinctions; to know a thing is to know the difference between it and other things. Therefore to discard knowledge means to forget these distinctions. Once all distinctions are forgotten, there remains only the undifferentiable one, which is the great whole. By achieving this condition, the sage may be said to have knowledge of another and higher level, which is called by the Taoists "knowledge which is not knowledge."

In the *Chuang-tzu* there are many passages about the method of forgetting distinctions. In the sixth chapter, for example, a report is given of an imaginary conversation between Confucius and his favorite disciple, Yen Hui. The story reads: "Yen Hui said: 'I have made some progress.' 'What do you mean?' asked Confucius. 'I have forgotten human-heartedness and righteousness,' replied Yen Hui. 'Very well, but that is not enough,' said Confucius. Another day Yen Hui again saw Confucius and said: 'I have made some progress.' 'What do you mean?' asked Confucius. 'I have forgotten rituals and music,' replied Yen Hui. 'Very well, but that is not enough,' said Confucius. Another day Yen Hui again saw Confucius and said: 'I have made some progress.' 'What do you mean?' asked Confucius. 'I sit in forgetfulness,' replied Yen Hui.

"At this Confucius changed countenance and asked: 'What do you mean by sitting in forgetfulness?' To which Yen Hui replied: 'My limbs are nerveless and my intelligence is dimmed. I have abandoned my body and discarded my knowledge. Thus I become one with the Infinite. This is what I mean by sitting in forgetfulness.' Then Confucius said: 'If you have become one with the Infinite, you have no personal likes and dislikes. If you have become one with the Great Evolution [of the universe], you are one who merely follow its changes. If you really have achieved this, I should like to follow your steps.'"

Thus Yen Hui achieved "sageliness within" by discarding knowledge. The result of discarding knowledge is to have no knowledge. But there is a difference between "*having-no* knowledge" and "having *no-knowledge*." The state of "*having-no* knowledge" is one of original ignorance, whereas that of "having *no-knowledge*" comes only after one has passed through a

宇宙——中遨游，也和宇宙并存。正是在这个意义上，庄子认为，圣人是长生不老的。

● **神秘主义的方法论**

　　圣人为与"大一"一体，就需要超越并忘记事物之间的界限。怎样做到这一点呢？这就是"弃智"，这正是道家为达到"内圣"所取的途径。在一般人看来，知识的使命便是区别万物。人要知道一项事物，便要能区别它与其他东西的不同之处。因此，弃绝知识便是弃绝这些区别。人把万物间的区别统统忘记时，剩下的只有万物还未生成的状况。可以说，圣人拥有的知识是另一个更高层次的知识，是"无知之知"。

　　《庄子》书中，有很多地方说到忘却万物区别的方法。《大宗师》篇中写孔子与他心爱的弟子颜回的一段对话："颜回曰：'回益矣。'仲尼曰：'何谓也？'曰：'回忘仁义矣。'曰：'可矣，犹未也。'他日，复见，曰：'回益矣。'曰：'何谓也？'曰：'回忘礼乐矣。'曰：'可矣，犹未也。'他日，复见，曰：'回益矣。'曰：'何谓也？'曰：'回坐忘矣。'仲尼蹴然曰：'何谓坐忘？'颜回曰：'隳肢体，黜聪明，离形去知，同于大通，此谓坐忘。'仲尼曰：'同则无好也，化则无常也，而果其贤乎？丘也请从而后也。'"

　　这段对话表明颜回追求"内圣外王"之道，在庄子看来，成圣之道需要摒弃知识。摒弃知识的结果，自然便没有知识。但是，"无知之知"和"无知"是两回事。"无知"是人的原初状态，而"无知之知"则是人经过"有知"而后达到的"无知"阶段。人的

prior stage of having knowledge. The former is a gift of nature, while the latter is an achievement of the spirit.

Some of the Taoists saw this distinction very clearly. It is significant that they used the word "forget" to express the essential idea of their method. Sages are not persons who remain in a state of original ignorance. They at one time possessed ordinary knowledge and made the usual distinctions, but they since forgot them. The difference between them and the man of original ignorance is as great as that between the courageous man and the man who does not fear simply because he is insensible to fear.

But there were also Taoists, such as the authors of some chapters of the *Chuang-tzu*, who failed to see this difference. They admired the primitive state of society and mind, and compared sages with children and the ignorant. Children and the ignorant have no knowledge and do not make distinctions, so that they both seem to belong to the undifferentiable one. Their belonging to it, however, is entirely unconsciousness. They remain in the undifferentiable one, but they are not conscious of the fact. They are ones who *have-no* knowledge, but not who have *no-knowledge*. It is the latter acquired state of *no-knowledge* that the Taoists call that of the "knowledge which is not knowledge."

原初状态的无知是自然的恩赐，而人达到"无知之知"则是心灵（亦即灵性）的成就。

道家中有一派人对这一点有很清楚的体会。他们用"忘"字来概括自己心灵修养的方法和体会，是很有意思的一点。圣人并不是天真无邪到老未变，圣人也曾追求通常的知识，努力分辨事物和事情人物的是非得失，但后来把这些都"忘"了。圣人和孩童的区别就如同明知艰险而前进和不知艰险而前行，两者之间有巨大的差别。

但是，在道家之中，包括《庄子》书中有几篇的作者，也有一些人看不到这两者之间的差别。他们爱慕社会和个人的原始状况，把圣人和孩提及愚钝的无知相比。孩提和愚人没有知识，无从分辨不同事物和事情的是非善恶，他们似乎也像"道通为一"所说的那样，但他们不是自觉的。他们是"无知"，而不是"无知之知"。唯有从世俗知识的衡量判断中超脱出来，这才是道家所说的"无知之知"。

⦾ THE LATER MOHISTS

In the *Mo-tzu*, there are six chapters (Chs. 40-45) which differ in character from the other chapters and possess a special logical interest. Of these, chapters forty to forty-one are titled "Canons" and consist of definitions of logical, moral, mathematical, and scientific ideas. Chapters forty-two to forty-three are titled "Expositions of the Canons," and consist of explanations of the definitions contained in the preceding two chapters. And chapters forty-four and forty-five are titled "Major Illustrations" and "Minor Illustrations" respectively. In them, several topics of logical interest are discussed. The general purpose of all six chapters is to uphold the Mohist point of view and refute, in a logical way, the arguments of the School of Names. The chapters as a whole are usually known as the "Mohist Canons."

In the last chapter we have seen that in the *Ch'i Wu Lun*, Chuang Tzu discussed two levels of knowledge. On the first level, he proved the relativity of things and reached the same conclusion as that of Hui Shih. But on the second level, he went beyond him. On the first level, he agreed with the School of Names and criticized common sense from a higher point of view. On the second level, however, he in turn criticized the School of Names from a still higher point of view. Thus the Taoists refuted the arguments of the School of Names as well, but the arguments they used are, logically speaking, on a higher level than those of the School of Names. Both their arguments and those of the School of Names require an effort of reflective thinking to be understood. Both run counter to the ordinary canons of common sense.

The Mohists as well as some of the Confucianists, on the other hand, were philosophers of common sense. Though the two groups differed in many ways, they agreed with one another in being practical. In opposition to the arguments of the School of Names, they developed, almost along similar lines of thought, epistemological and logical theories to defend common sense. These theories appear in the "Mohist Canons" and in the chapter titled "On the Rectification of Names" in the *Hsün-tzu*, the author of which, as we shall see in chapter thirteen, was one of the greatest Confucianists of the early period.

拾壹 后期的墨家

在《墨子》书中，有六篇（第四十到第四十五篇）与全书的其他部分不同，它们在逻辑学上有特殊的价值。这六篇中，第四十到第四十一篇标题《经上》《经下》，内容包含有逻辑、伦理、数学和科学思想的定义；第四十二到第四十三篇标题《经说上》《经说下》，对前两章中的定义加以解释；第四十四到第四十五篇标题《大取》《小取》，就字义说是"举例"，其中讨论了几个有逻辑意义的题目。这六篇的中心是以逻辑的方式树立墨子的主张，批判名家的思想，六篇合在一起，就是通常所称的"墨经"。

在前一章里，我们分析了庄子所论述的两个层次的知识。在第一个层次上，他论述了事物的相对性，达到了与惠施一致的结论。在这层次上，庄子同意名家，而从更高的角度批判了常识的观点。在第二个层次上，庄子超越了惠施，并从更高的观点批判了名家的论辩，这样，道家便也批判了名家；而道家的论证，从逻辑观点看，比名家的论证处于更高的层次。道家和名家的论证都否定人们的常识观点。为了解它们，需要对它们进行认真的反思。

在另一方面，墨家和儒家中的一部分都站在常识观点的一方。他们两家虽然有许多不同，但是都主张要从实际出发，这是两家的共同之处。为反对名家的论辩，他们几乎是沿着相似的思想路线，从认识论和逻辑的理论来维护常识的观点。这些理论便构成"墨经"的内容，儒家在这方面的思想见于《荀子》的《正名》篇。荀子是先秦时期重要的儒家思想家之一，在后面第十三章里，将对他进行讨论。

- **Discussions on Knowledge and Names**

The epistemological theory set forth in the "Mohist Canons" is a kind of naïve realism. There is, it maintains, a knowing faculty which "is that by means of which one knows, but which itself does not necessarily know." (Ch. 42.) The reason for this is that, in order to have knowledge, the knowing faculty must be confronted with an object of knowledge. "Knowledge is that in which the knowing [faculty] meets the object and is able to apprehend its form and shape." (Ch. 42.) Besides the sensory organs for knowing, such as those of seeing and hearing, there also exists the mind, which is "that by means of which one understands the object of knowledge." (*Ibid.*) In other words, the mind interprets the impressions of external objects which are brought to it by the senses.

The "Mohist Canons" also provide various logical classifications of knowledge. From the point of view of its source, knowledge is to be classified into three types: that derived through the personal experience of the knower; that transmitted to him by authority (i.e., obtained by him either through hearsay or written records); and knowledge by inference (i.e., obtained through making deductions on the basis of what is known about what is unknown). Also from the point of view of the various objects of knowledge, it is to be classified into four kinds: knowledge of names, that of actualities, that of correspondence, and that of action. (Ch. 40.)

It will be remembered that names, actualities, and their relationships to one another, were the particular interest of the School of Names. According to the "Mohist Canons," "a name is that with which one speaks about a thing," while "an actuality is that about which one speaks." (Ch. 42.) When one says: "This is a table," "table" is a name, and is that with which one speaks about "this," while "this" is the actuality about which one is speaking. Expressed in terms of Western logic, a name is the predicate of a proposition, and an actuality is the subject of it.

In the "Mohist Canons," names are classified into three kinds: general, classifying, and private. "'Thing' is a general name. All actualities must bear this name. 'Horse' is a classifying name. All actualities of that sort must have that name. 'Tsang' [the name of a person] is a private name. This name is restricted to this actuality." (Ch. 42.)

● 关于知识和名的讨论

"墨经"中的认识论理论是一种朴素的实在论。它认为，人具有认识事物的能力，它是"所以知也，而不必知"（《经说上》），就是说，人依赖认知能力才得以取得知识，但并不因有认知能力就必定有知识。其原因是，人的认知能力必须与一个知识对象打交道。"知也者，以其知过物而能貌之。"（同上）这是说，人以其认知能力和对象接触，得以辨它的形相，由此构成知识。除去视觉、听觉这些感觉器官，人还需要有一个思维的器官，在中国古代把它称作心。"心也者，以其知论物。"（同上）就是说，人能理解对象要靠心之所知。也就是说，人以其感官把外界事物的印象传达到心，心则对这些印象进行分析综合，加以解释。

"墨经"也从逻辑上对知识加以分类。以不同的来源而论，把知识分为三类：从个人直接经验而来的知识，从权威而来的知识（即听来的，或从文字中读来的），从推论而来的知识（从已知推到未知）。以知识的不同对象而论，分为四类：对"名"的知识，对"实"的知识，"对应"的知识，以及行动的知识。（见《经上》）

我们都记得，名家特别注意"名""实"和两者之间的关系。"墨经"里《经说上》对"名""实"的解释是："所以谓，名也；所谓，实也。"就是说，"名"是人用以指事物的代号，"实"是人所指的事物。当一个人说"这是一张桌子"时，"桌子"是名，人又藉以指物，这"物"就是"实"。用西方逻辑学的术语来说，"名"是一个命题的宾语，而"实"则是一个命题的主语。

"墨经"把"名"分为三类：达名、类名、私名。《经说上》称："名：物，达也；有实，必待文名也命之。马，类也；若实也者，必以是名也命之。臧（个人的名字），私也；是名也，止于是实也。"这是说，"物"是一般名词，一切"实"（实体）都要归入"物"之中。马是类名，凡马这类实体都必须冠以马的名称。臧是私人的名字，只限用于臧一个人这个"实"。

The knowledge of correspondence is that which knows which name corresponds to which actuality. Such kind of knowledge is required for the statement of such a proposition as: "This is a table." When one has this kind of knowledge, one knows that "names and actualities pair with each other." (Ch. 42.)

The knowledge of action is the knowledge of how to do a certain thing. This is what Americans call "know-how."

● Discussions on Dialectic

Of the chapter titled "Minor Illustrations," a large part is devoted to the discussions of dialectic. This chapter says: "Dialectic serves to make clear the distinction between right and wrong, to discriminate between order and disorder, to make evident points of similarity and difference, to examine the principles of names and actualities, to differentiate what is beneficial and what is harmful, and to remove doubts and uncertainties. It observes the happenings of all things, and investigates the order and relation between the various judgments. It uses names to designate actualities, propositions to express ideas, statements to set forth causes, and taking and giving according to classes." (Ch.45.)

The first part of this passage deals with the purpose and function of dialectic; the second part with its methodology. In another part of the same chapter, it is said that there are seven methods of dialectic: "A particular judgment indicates what is not all so. A hypothetical judgment indicates what is at present not so. Imitation consists in taking a model. What is imitated is what is taken as a model. If the cause is in agreement with the imitation, it is correct. If it is not in agreement with the imitation, it is not correct. This is the method of imitation. The method of comparison consists in using one thing to explain another. The method of parallel consists in comparing two series of propositions consistently throughout. The method of analogy says: 'You are so. Why should I alone not be so?' The method of extension consists in attributing the same to what is not known as to what is known. When the other is said to be the same [as this], how can I say that it is different?" (Ch. 45.)

The method of imitation in this passage is the same as that of "using statements to set forth causes" of the preceding quotation. And the

对应的知识是指：知道哪个"名"与哪个"实"对应。例如，当人说"这是一张桌子"时，他就必须有对应的知识。有这种知识就是《经说上》所说的"名实耦"。

行动的知识是指怎样做一桩具体事情的知识，它相当于美国人常说的"怎么干"的知识（know how）。

● 关于"辩"的讨论

《小取》篇中的大部分都是关于"辩"的讨论。其中说："夫辩者，将以明是非之分，审治乱之纪，明同异之处，察名实之理，处利害，决嫌疑焉。摹略万物之然，论求群言之比。以名举实，以辞抒意，以说出故。以类取，以类予。"这里所说的是：为分清是非，区别治乱，辨明各种事物之间的相似相异之处，考察名实的原理，分析利害，排除疑虑，明辨是十分必要的。它考察一切发生的事情、对各种事情的论断以及它们之间的关系。它循名求实，指陈命题，以表达思想、论述，提出事物由来之"故"，决定取舍原则。

这段话的前半部分是讲"辩"的目的与作用，后半部分则是讲"辩"的方法。《小取》篇中的另一处说：辩有七种方法，"或也者，不尽也。假也者，今不然也。效者，为之法也；所效者，所为之法也。故中效，则是也；不中效，则非也。此效也。辟也者，举也物而以明之也。侔也者，比辞而俱行也。援也者，曰：子然，我奚独不可以然也？推也者，以其所不取之，同于其所取者，予之也。是犹谓也者同也，吾岂谓也者异也。"在这一段话里，"或"是指特称论断，不能尽然。"假"是假设，它还未成为现实。"效"是摹拟，它意味着摹拟一个模型：如果仿效出来的与模型相同，它就是正确的；如果仿效出来的与模型不合，它就是错误的。这便是摹拟法。"辟"是比较法，用一物来解释另一物。"侔"是把两组命题平行地比较下来。"援"是类推法，"如果你是这样，我何以不能这样？""推"，是从已知求未知、延伸而论的方法。

这一段内"效"的方法，也就是前一段内的"以说出故"。这一

method of extension is the same as the "taking and giving according to classes" of the preceding passage. These are the two most important of the methods, and correspond roughly to the deductive and inductive methods of Western logic.

Before giving further explanation of these two methods, something may be said regarding what in the "Mohist Canons" is called a cause. A cause is defined as "that with which something becomes," and is also classified into two kinds, the major and minor. (Ch. 40.) "A minor cause is one with which something may not necessarily be so, but without which it will never be so." "A major cause is one with which something will necessarily be so, and without which it will never be so." (Ch. 42.) It is evident that what the "Mohist Canons" call a minor cause is what in modern logic would be called a necessary cause, while what the "Mohist Canons" call a major cause is what modern logic would describe as a necessary and sufficient cause. In modern logic there is the distinction of yet another kind of cause, the sufficient cause, which is one with which something will necessarily be so, but without which it may or may not be so. This distinction the Mohists failed to make.

In modern logical reasoning, if we want to know whether a general proposition is true or not, we verify it with facts or experiment. If, for example, we want to make sure that certain bacteria are the cause of a certain disease, the way to verify the matter is to take as a formula the general proposition that the bacteria A are the cause of the disease B, and then make an experiment to see whether the supposed cause really produces the expected result or not. If it does, it really is the cause; if not, it is not. This is deductive reasoning and is also what the "Mohist Canons" call the method of imitation. For to take a general proposition as a formula is to take it as a model, and to make an experiment with it is to make an imitation of it. That the supposed cause produces the expected result, means that "the cause is in agreement with the imitation." And that it does not, means that "the cause is not in agreement with the imitation."

It is in this way that we can distinguish a true from a false cause, and determine whether a cause is a major or minor one.

As regards the other form of reasoning through extension, it may be illustrated through the dictum that all men are mortal. We are able to make this dictum, because we know that all men of the past were mortal, and that men of today and of the future are the same in kind as those of the past. Hence we draw the general conclusion that all men are mortal. In this inductive reasoning, we use "the method of extension." That men

段内"推"的方法，也就是前一段内的"以类取，以类予"。这是两种极其重要的方法，大致相当于西方逻辑学的演绎法和归纳法。

在进一步阐述这两种方法之前，需要懂得"墨经"中所说的"故"。《经上》说："故，所得而后成也。"还把"故"分成"大故"和"小故"两种。在《经说上》中解释说："小故，有之不必然，无之必不然。""大故，有之必然，无之必不然。"如果用现代逻辑的术语来说，"小故"就是事物的必要原因，"大故"就是事物的必要而且充分原因。在现代逻辑中，还有一种情况是：事物中的充分原因，有它，事物就必然，如果没有它，事物或然或不然。墨家的逻辑还未曾指出这一种可能情况。

在现代逻辑思维中，如果要判断一个一般命题是否正确，可以把它与事实印证，或用实验结果来印证。举例来说，如果我们要判断，细菌 A 是导致疾病 B 的原因，我们就把它作为一个公式来做实验，如果细菌 A 的确导致疾病 B，这命题便是正确的，否则，这便是错误的。这是演绎推理，也就是"墨经"中所说的"效"的方法。把一个一般命题作成公式，就是把它作为一个模型（模式），根据这个公式进行实验，就是模拟。如果假设的原因产生预期的结果，那么，这原因和它所模拟的结果是一致的；否则，这原因和它所模拟的模型证明了不一致。我们使用这办法可以辨明，假定的原因是否真实，以及它是否是必要原因，或充分原因。

关于推论思维，可以举一句人所共知的话为例："人不免一死。"我们能够这样说，因为过去的一切人都难逃死亡。现在和将来的人，和过去的人在种类上是一样的，因此，我们得出一个一般性的结论，人不免一死。在这个归纳思维中，我们用的是"推论思维"。

of the past were mortal is what is known. And that men of today and of the future are and will be mortal is what is not known. To say that all men are mortal, therefore, is "to attribute the same to what is not known as to what is known." We can do this because "the other is said to be the same [as this]." We are "taking and giving according to class."

- ● **Clarification of All-embracing Love**

Versed in the method of dialectic, the later Mohists did much in clarifying and defending the philosophical position of their school.

Following the tradition of Mo Tzu's utilitarianistic philosophy, the later Mohists maintain that all human activities aim at obtaining benefit and avoiding harm. Thus in the "Major Illustrations" we are told: "When one cuts a finger in order to preserve a hand, this is to choose the greater benefit and the lesser harm. To choose the lesser harm is not to choose harm, but to choose benefit.... If on meeting a robber one loses a finger so as to save one's life, this is benefit. The meeting with the robber is harm. Choice of the greater benefit is not a thing done under compulsion. Choice of the lesser harm is a thing done under compulsion. The former means choosing from what has not yet been obtained. The latter means discarding from what one has already been burdened with." (Ch. 44.) Thus for all human activities the rule is: "Of the benefits, choose the greatest; of the harms, choose the slightest." (*Ibid.*)

Both Mo Tzu and the later Mohists identified the good with the beneficial. Beneficialness is the essence of the good. But what is the essence of beneficialness? Mo Tzu did not raise this question, but the later Mohists did and gave an answer. In the first "Canon," it is said: "The beneficial is that with the obtaining of which one is pleased. The harmful is that with the obtaining of which one is displeased." (Ch. 40.) Thus the later Mohists provided a hedonistic justification for the utilitarianistic philosophy of the Mohist school.

This position reminds us of the "principle of utility" of Jeremy

Bentham. In his *Introduction to the Principles of Morals and Legislation*, Bentham says: "Nature has placed mankind under the governance of two sovereign masters, pain and pleasure. It is for them alone to point out what we ought to do.... The principle of utility recognizes this subjection, and assumes it for the foundation of that system, the object of which is

过去的人都最终死去，是一个众所周知的事实。但今日和将来的人都不免要死，这还未实现，因此是未知的。因此，说"人不免一死"是把已经知道的事实延伸到未死的人身上。我们这样做是因为，现在和未来的人与过去的人在种类上是一样的。这就是"墨经"所说的"以类取，以类予"。

● 澄清兼爱说

后期墨家运用"辩"的方法，得以极大地澄清了墨家的哲学思想和立场。

后期墨家继承了墨子功利主义思想的传统，主张人类的一切活动都是为了趋利避害。正是因此，在《大取》中说："断指以存腕，利之中取大，害之中取小也。害之中取小，子非取害也，取利也。……遇盗人，而断指以免身，利也；其遇盗人，害也。……利之中取大，非不得已也；害之中取小，不得已也。所未有而取焉，是利之中取大也；于所既有而弃焉，是害之中取小也。"由此得出的人类活动准则是："利之中取大，害之中取小。"

墨子和后期墨家都认为"义，利也"。利是义的本质。那么，利的本质又是什么呢？墨子未曾提出这个问题。后期墨家则提出了这个问题，也作出了回答。《经上》说："利，所得而喜也。""害，所得而恶也。"这样，后期墨家为墨家的功利主义哲学提出了一个享乐主义的解释。

后期墨家的这种观点 使我们想起十八、十九世纪间英国哲学家杰利米·边沁（Jeremy Bentham，一七四八至一八三二年）的"功利原理"。他在《道德和立法原理导论》第一章开宗明义说："自然把人类置于两个主人的统治之下，这两个主人就是：痛苦和快乐。正是这两位主人指示我们应该做些什么。""功利原理承认这种统治关系，并把它作为全部思想体系的基础，目的在于通过理性和法律

to rear the fabric of felicity by the hands of reason and law." (P. 1.) Thus Bentham reduces good and bad to a question of pleasure and pain. According to him the aim of morality is "the greatest happiness of the greatest number." (*Ibid.*)

This is also what the later Mohists do. Having defined "the beneficial," they go on to define the virtues in the light of this concept. Thus in the first "Canon" we find: "Righteousness consists in doing the beneficial." "Loyalty consists in benefiting one's ruler." "Filial piety consists in benefiting one's parents." "Meritorious accomplishment consists in benefiting the people." (Ch. 40.) "Benefiting the people" means "the greatest happiness of the greatest number."

Regarding the theory of all-embracing love, the later Mohists maintain that its major attribute is its all-embracing character. In the "Minor Illustrations" we read: "In loving men one needs to love *all* men before one can regard oneself as loving men. In not loving men one does not need not to love any man [before one can regard oneself as not loving men]. Not to have all-embracing love is not to love men. When riding horses, one need not ride all horses in order to regard oneself as riding a horse. For if one rides only a few horses, one is still riding horses. But when not riding horses, one must ride no horse at all in order to regard oneself as not riding horses. This is the difference between all-inclusiveness [in the case of loving men] and the absence of all-inclusiveness [in the case of riding horses]." (Ch. 44.)

Every man, as a matter of fact, has someone whom he loves. Every man, for example, loves his own children. Hence the mere fact that a man loves someone does not mean that he loves men in general. But on the negative side, the fact that he does wrong to someone, even his own children, does mean that he does not love men. Such is the reasoning of the Mohists.

● Defense of All-embracing Love

Against this view of the later Mohists, there were at that time two main objections. The first was that the number of men in the world is infinite; how, then, is it possible for one to love them all? This objection was referred to under the title: "Infinity is incompatible with all-embracing love." And the second objection was that if failure to love a

来织造幸福。" 这样，边沁把善恶归结为快乐和痛苦的问题。在他看来，道德的目标是 "谋求最大多数人的最大快乐"。

后期墨家所做的也正是如此。他们首先确立 "有利" 的定义，然后在这个基础之上确立品德的含义，在于对人有利。因此，在《经上》篇里说："义，利也。""忠，以为利而强低也。""孝，利亲也。""功，利民也。""利民" 也就是 "谋求最大多数人的最大快乐"。

关于墨子的兼爱学说，后期墨家认为，它的最大特色在于 "兼"，也就是广泛包容。《小取》篇说："爱人，待（有待于）周（周全包容）爱人，而后为爱人。不爱人，不待周不爱人，不失周爱，因为不爱人矣。乘马，不待周乘马；而后为乘马也。有乘于马，因为乘马矣。逮至不乘马，待周不乘马（要等到所有的马都不骑），而后为不乘马。此一周而一不周者也。" 这是说，人要爱一切人，才算爱人；而不爱人，则不需要不爱一切人。这与骑马不同，人不需要骑遍所有的马才算骑马，只要骑过几匹马，就是会骑马了。至于不骑马的人，则必须不曾骑过任何马才算数。这是爱人与骑马不同的地方。爱人待 "周" 爱世人，乘马则不必待周乘万马。

事实上，每个人都有少数心爱的人。举例来说，人都爱自己的儿女。因此，一个人仅仅爱几个人，不能算是泛爱众人。而从反面来看，一个人如果对某个人加以伤害，那就足以说明他不爱人。这是墨家的观点。

● 为 "兼爱" 辩

当时，反对后期墨家这种观点的，主要有两派意见：其一认为，天下之人无数，一个人怎能做到爱天下人？这种反对意见被概括称作 "无穷害兼"；第二种反对意见认为，如果未曾爱某个人，就是

single man means failure to love men in general, there should then be no such punishment as "killing a robber." This objection was known under the title: "To kill a robber is to kill a man." The later Mohists used their dialectic to try to refute these objections.

In the second "Canon" there is the statement: "Infinity is not incompatible with all-embracingness. The reason is given under 'full or not.'" (Ch. 40.) The second "Exposition of the Canons" develops this statement as follows: "Infinity: (Objection:) 'If the South has a limit, it can be included *in toto*. [There was a common belief in ancient China that the South had no limit] If it has no limit, it cannot be included *in toto*. It is impossible to know whether it has a limit or not and hence it is impossible to know whether it can all be included or not. It is impossible to know whether people fill this [space] or not, and hence it is impossible to know whether they can be included *in toto* or not. This being so, it is perverse to hold that all people can be included in our love.' (Answer:) 'If people do not fill what is unlimited, then [the number of] people has a limit, and there is no difficulty in including anything that is limited [in number]. But if people do fill what is unlimited, then what is [supposed to be] unlimited is limited, and then there is no difficulty in including what is limited.'" (Ch. 43.)

"To kill a robber is to kill a man" is the other major objection to the Mohists, because killing a man is not consistent with loving all men equally and universally. To this objection the "Minor Illustrations" answers as follows:

"A white horse is a horse. To ride a white horse is to ride a horse. A black horse is a horse. To ride a black horse is to ride a horse. Huo [name of a person] is a man. To love Huo is to love a man. Tsang [name of a person] is a man. To love Tsang is to love a man. This is to affirm what is right.

"But Huo's parents are men. Yet when Huo serves his parents, he is not serving men. His younger brother is a handsome man. Yet when he loves his younger brother, he is not loving handsome men. A cart is wood, but to ride a cart is not to ride wood. A boat is wood, but to ride a boat is not to ride wood. A robber is a man, but that there are many robbers does not mean that there are many men; and that there are no robbers does not mean that there are no men.

"How is this explained? To hate the existence of many robbers is not to hate the existence of many men. To wish that there were no robbers is not to wish that there were no men. The world generally agrees on

未曾爱天下人，那么，杀一个强盗就违反兼爱的宗旨了，这种反对意见称作"杀盗，杀人也"。后期墨家就运用他们的"辩"来驳倒这些反对意见。

《经下》中说："无穷不害兼，说在盈否。"意思是说，"无穷"与"兼"可以相容，全看"盈与否"。《经说下》对此解释说："无（反对一方）：'南方有穷则可尽（古代中国认为南方无垠），无穷则不可尽。有穷无穷未可智，则可尽不可尽未可智。人之盈之否未可智，人之可尽不可尽亦未可智。而必人之可尽爱也，悖。'（答）：'人若不盈无穷，则人有穷也，尽有穷无难。盈无穷，则无穷尽也，尽有穷无难。'"反对一方的立论是：历来认为南方辽阔无垠，那里的人有多少，也说不清，却说统统都爱，岂非荒谬！"墨经"回答说，如果南方辽阔无垠，人填补不满南方，那么人的数目就是有限的。要一一数尽南方的人，也就不难了。如果无垠的南方能被人填满，那么，南方就不是无垠，因此，把南方的人都包括在内，也就可以做到了。

"杀盗，杀人也"，这是反对墨家的另一个论点，如果杀一个强盗，就说明兼爱一切人是不可能的。《小取》篇对此回答说：

"白马，马也；乘白马，乘马也。骊马，马也；乘骊马，乘马也。获（有人名获），人也；爱获，爱人也。臧（有人名臧），人也；爱臧，爱人也。此乃是而然者也。

"获之亲，人也；获事其亲，非事人也。其弟，美人也；爱弟，非爱美人也。车，木也；乘车，非乘木也。船，木也；乘船，非乘木也。盗人，人也；多盗，非多人也；无盗，非无人也。

"奚以明之？恶多盗，非恶多人也；欲无盗，非欲无人也。

this. And this being the case, although a robber-man is a man, yet to love robbers is not to love men, and not to love robbers is not to love men. Likewise to kill a robber-man is not to kill a man. There is no difficulty in this proposition." (Ch. 45.)

With such dialectic as this the later Mohists refuted the objection that the killing of a robber is inconsistent with their principle of all-embracing love.

- **Criticism of Other Schools**

Using their dialectic, the later Mohists not only refute the objections of other schools against them, but also make criticisms of their own against these schools. For example, the "Mohist Canons" contain a number of objections against the arguments of the School of Names. Hui Shih, it will be remembered, had argued for the "unity of similarity and difference." In his ten paradoxes he passed from the premise that "all things are similar to each other," to the conclusion: "Love all things equally. Heaven and Earth are one body." This, for the later Mohists, is a fallacy arising from the ambiguity of the Chinese word *t'ung*. *T'ung* may be variously used to mean "identity," "agreement," or "similarity." In the first "Canon" there is a statement which reads: "*T'ung*: There is that of identity, that of part-and-whole relationship, that of co-existence, and that of generic relation." (Ch. 40.) And the "Exposition" explains further: "*T'ung*: That there are two names for one actuality is identity. Inclusion in one whole is part-and-whole relationship. Both being in the same room is co-existence. Having some points of similarity is generic relation." (Ch. 42.)The same "Canon" and "Exposition" also have a discussion on "difference," which is just the reverse of *t'ung*.

The "Mohist Canons" fail actually to mention Hui Shih by name. As a matter of fact, no name is ever mentioned in these chapters. But from this analysis of the word *t'ung*, Hui Shih's fallacy becomes clear. That all things are similar to each other means that they have generic relationship, that they are of the same class, the class of "things." But that Heaven and Earth are one body means that they have a part-and-whole relationship. The truth of the one proposition as applied to a particular situation cannot be inferred from the truth of the other, even though the same word, *t'ung*, is used in both cases.

As regards Kung-sun Lung's argument for "the separation of hardness and whiteness," the later Mohists thought only in terms of concrete

世相与共是之。若若是，则虽盗人人也，爱盗非爱人也，不爱盗非不爱人也，杀盗人非杀人也。无难矣。"

后期墨家便是使用这样的"辩"来驳倒"杀盗违反兼爱"的论点。

● 对其他学派的批判

后期墨家使用"辩"术，不仅反驳名家对墨家的批评，还运用"辩"术批判名家。例如"墨经"包含有一些批判名家的论辩。我们记得，惠施曾有"合同异"的论点。他在"十事"中，由"万物毕同"的前提引申到"泛爱万物，天地一体也"的结论。在后期墨家看来，这种引申是谬误的，原因在于"同"字的含义模糊。《经上》说："同，重、体、合、类。"这是说，同有四种，一是雷同；二是局部与整体的质同；三是同存；四是同源。《经说上》又就此解释说："同：二名一实，重同也。不外于兼，体同也。俱处于室，合同也。有以同，类同也。"《经上》和《经说上》还讨论了"异"，它的含义与"同"正好相反。

"墨经"没有点惠施的名字（不仅没有点惠施的名字，而且没有点任何人的名字）。但从对"同"的剖析中，惠施的错误是十分明显的。"万物毕同"，只表明它们同属于"物"，因此是"类同"。至于说"天地一体"，这是说，天地之间有一种局部和整体的"体同"关系。一个表明"类同"的命题，尽管它是真实的，并不能由此推论出另一个"体同"的命题也是真实的，虽然它们都用了"同"这个词。

关于公孙龙的"离坚白"论点，在《经上》和《经说下》里也涉及了。后期墨家从现实自然世界里，石头的坚硬性和它的白色

hard and white stones as they actually exist in the physical universe. Hence they maintained that the qualities of hardness and whiteness both simultaneously inhere in the stone. As a result, they "are not mutually exclusive," but "must pervade each other." (Chaps. 40, 42.)

The later Mohists also criticized the Taoists. In the second "Canon" we read: "Learning is useful. The reason is given by those who oppose it." (Ch. 41.) The second "Exposition" comments on this: "Learning: By maintaining that people do not know that learning is useless, one is thereby informing them of this fact. This informing that learning is useless, is itself a teaching. Thus by holding that learning is useless, one teaches. This is perverse." (Ch. 43.)

This is a criticism of a statement in the *Lao-tzu*: "Banish learning and there will be no grieving." (Ch. 20.) According to the later Mohists, learning and teaching are related terms. If learning is to be banished, so is teaching. For once there is teaching, there is also learning, and if teaching is useful, learning cannot be useless. The very teaching that learning is useless proves in itself that it is useful.

In the second "Canon" we read: "To say that in argument there is no winner is necessarily incorrect. The reason is given under 'argument.'" The second "Exposition" comments on this: "In speaking, what people say either agrees or disagrees. There is agreement when one person says something is a puppy, and another says it is a dog. There is disagreement when one says it is an ox, and another says it is a horse. [That is to say, when there is disagreement, there is argument] When neither of them wins, there is no argument. Argument is that in which one person says the thing is so, and another says it is not so. The one who is right will win." (Ch. 43.)

In the second "Canon" we also read: "To hold that all speech is perverse is perverse. The reason is given under 'speech.'" (Ch. 41.) The second "Exposition" comments on this: "[To hold that all speech] is perverse, is not permissible. If the speech of this man [who holds this doctrine] is permissible, then at least this speech is not perverse, and there is some speech that is permissible. If the speech of this man is not permissible, then it is wrong to take it as being correct." (Ch. 43.)

The second "Canon" also says: "That knowing it and not knowing it are the same, is perverse. The reason is given under 'no means.'" (Ch. 41.)

并不是互相排斥，而是可以并存在一块石头之中的事实，得出"坚白，不相外也"（《经上》），"必相盈也"（《经说下》）。

后期墨家还批评了道家。《经下》中说："学之益也，说在诽者。"《经说下》篇解释说："学：也以为不知学之无益也，故告之也。是使智学之无益也，是教也，以尝为无益也，教，悖。"

这个批评是针对《老子》书中第二十章的一句话："绝学无忧。"后期墨家认为，学与教是相关联的。如果"学"可以弃绝，那么"教"也同样将予弃绝了。有教就有学，"教"如果有用，"学"就不是无用。"绝学无忧"如果是真理，就证明"学"之为用。

《经下》说："谓辩无胜，必不当，说（事理）在辩。"《经说下》篇解释说："谓：所谓非同也，则异也。同则或谓之狗，其或谓之犬也。异则或谓之牛，或谓之马也。俱无胜，是不辩也。辩也者，或谓之是，或谓之非，当者（说得对的）胜也。"这是说，两人指物言事时，彼此若看法不一，则必然不同意。一人指物说，这是狗，另一人称它为犬，这还是同；若一人指称，那是牛，另一人指称，那是马，这便是异。有异便有辩论，若无人称胜，那不是辩论。"辩"是指：一人说，此物如此，另一人说，不是这样。两人之中，谁说得符合实际，谁就得胜。

《经下》又说："以言为尽悖，悖。说在其言。"《经说下》篇解释说："以：悖，不可也。之人之言可，是不悖，则是有可也。之人之言不可，以当，必不审。"这是说，认为"一切话语都无是处"，这在事实上是不可能的。因如果这句话是对的，那就证明，并非所有的话都是错的，至少，这句话还是对的。如果确认这人的话不能成立，那么，以这句话为得当的人就错了。

《经下》篇又说："知知之否之足用也，悖，说在无以也。"这里指出，把知与不知看为一样，这是荒谬的，就在于这种说法没有根据。

And the second "Exposition" comments: "When there is knowledge, there is discussion about it. Unless there is knowledge, there is no means [of discussion]." (Ch. 43.)

Yet again the second "Canon" states: "To condemn criticism is perverse. The reason is given under 'not to condemn.'" (Ch. 41.) On which the second "Exposition" comments: "To condemn criticism is to condemn one's own condemnation. If one does not condemn it, there is nothing to be condemned. When one cannot condemn it, this means not to condemn criticism." (Ch. 43.)

These are all criticisms against Chuang Tzu. Chuang Tzu maintained that nothing can be decided in argument. Even if someone wins, he said, the winner is not necessarily right or the loser necessarily wrong. But according to the later Mohists, Chuang Tzu, by expressing this very doctrine, showed himself in disagreement with others and was himself arguing. If he won the argument, did not this very fact prove him to be wrong? Chuang Tzu also said: "Great argument does not require words." And again: "Speech that argues falls short of its aim." (*Chuang-tzu*, ch. 2.) Hence "all speech is perverse." Furthermore, he held that everything is right in its own way and in its own opinion, and one should not criticize the other. (*Ibid.*) But according to the later Mohists, what Chuang Tzu said itself consists of speech and itself constitutes a criticism against others. So if all speech is perverse, is not this saying of Chuang Tzu also perverse? And if all criticism against others is to be condemned, then Chuang Tzu's criticism should be condemned first of all. Chuang Tzu also talked much about the importance of having no knowledge. But such discussion is itself a form of knowledge. When there is no knowledge, there can be no discussion about it.

In criticizing the Taoists, the later Mohists pointed out certain logical paradoxes that have also appeared in Western philosophy. It is only with the development of a new logic in recent times that these paradoxes have been solved. Thus in contemporary logic, the criticisms made by the later Mohists are no longer valid. Yet it is interesting to note that the later Mohists were so logically minded. More than any other school of ancient China, they attempted to create a pure system of epistemology and logic.

《经说下》解释说："智，论之，非智无以也。"这是说，只要有知识，就有对它的议论，除非没有知识，就没有了议论的根据。

　　《经下》篇还说："非诽者悖，说在弗非。"这是说，谴责批评是错误的，理由见"莫怪他人"释。《经说下》解释说："诽非，己之诽也不非，诽非可非也。不可非也，是不非诽也。"这是说，谁谴责批评，这话首先就谴责了他自己。如果不能用这句话谴责自己，则意味着不能谴责批评。

　　这些都是针对庄子的批评。庄子认为争论是非毫无意义。即便一个人在争论中赢了，也不表明就是对了，输了的一方也并不意味着就是错了。而在后期墨家看来，庄子提出这样的主张就是在与人辩论。如果他赢了，岂不正好证明他的主张是错的吗？《庄子·齐物论》中说"大辩不言"，又说"辩也者，有不见也"（凡争论者，总有见识不到之处），所以"言未始有常（定论）"，各人是其所是，非其所非，各种说法都有自己的道理。这都是庄子对其他各家的批评，而如果一切言论都是荒谬的，庄子自己的言论岂不也是荒谬？庄子还主张"弃智"，而庄子自己的言论就形成一种知识，如果真正抛弃一切知识，那么对庄子的主张也就不必讨论。

　　后期墨家在批评道家时所指出的反论，在西方哲学中也曾出现过。西方近年发展的新逻辑解决了这个问题。按照现代西方逻辑，后期墨家的这种逻辑不再能够成立。虽然如此，后期墨家的缜密思想、富于逻辑头脑，还是令人惊叹的。他们在建立知识论和逻辑方面的努力，可以说超过了古代中国的任何其他学派。

⑫ THE YIN-YANG SCHOOL AND EARLY CHINESE COSMOGONY

In the second chapter of this book I said that the *Yin-Yang* School had its origin in the occultists. These occultists were anciently known as the *fang shih*, that is, practitioner of occult arts. In the "Treatise on Literature" (ch. 30) in the *History of the Former Han Dynasty*, which is based on the *Seven Summaries* by Liu Hsin, these occult arts are grouped into six classes.

- ● **The Six Classes of Occult Arts**

The first is astrology. "Astrology," says this chapter in the *Han History*, "serves to arrange in order the twenty-eight constellations, and note the progressions of the five planets and of the sun and the moon, so as to record thereby the manifestations of fortune and misfortune."

The second deals with almanacs. "Almanacs," says the same treatise, "serve to arrange the four seasons in proper order, to adjust the times of the equinoxes and solstices, and to note the concordance of the periods of the sun, moon, and five planets, so as thereby to examine into the actualities of cold and heat, life and death.... Through this art, the miseries of calamities and the happiness of prosperity all appear manifest."

The third is connected with the Five Elements. "This art," says the "Treatise on Literature," "arises from the revolutions of the Five Powers [Five Elements], and if it is extended to its farthest limits, there is nothing to which it will not reach."

The fourth is divination by means of the stalks of the milfoil plant and that done with the tortoise shell or shoulder bones of the ox. These were the two main methods of divination in ancient China. In the latter method, the diviner bored a hole in a tortoise shell or a flat piece of bone, and then applied heat to it by a metal rod in such a way as to cause cracks to radiate from the hole. These cracks were interpreted by the diviner according to their configuration as an answer to the question asked. In the former method, the diviner manipulated the stalks of the milfoil in such a way as to produce certain numerical combinations which could be interpreted by means of the *Book of Changes*. Such interpretation was the primary purpose of the original corpus of this work.

The fifth group is that of miscellaneous divinations and the sixth is the system of forms. The latter included physiognomy together with what in later times has been known as *feng-shui*, literally, "wind and water." *Feng-shui* is based on the concept that man is the product of the universe. Hence his house or burial place must be so arranged as to be in harmony with the natural forces, i.e., with "wind and water."

拾贰 阴阳家和中国早期的宇宙发生论

本书第二章曾说到，先秦的阴阳家源自古代的方术，行方术的即是术士。《汉书·艺文志》根据刘歆《七略·术数略》，把方术分为六类。

● 六种术数

第一种是天文。《汉书·艺文志》中说："天文者，序二十八宿，步五星日月，以纪吉凶之象。"

第二种是历谱。《艺文志》中说："历谱者，序四时之位，正分至之节，会日月五星之辰，以考寒暑杀生之实。……凶厄之患，吉隆之喜，其术皆出焉。"

第三种是五行。《艺文志》中说："其法亦起五德（金木水火土，谓之五德）终始，推其极则无不至。"

第四种是蓍龟，这是中国古代的两种占卜方法。后一种方法是在龟甲或平骨上钻一洞，放在火上烤，小洞四周受热后出现裂纹。管占卜的巫史据以判断所问事项吉凶，称作"卜"。前一种方法是由巫史取蓍草，每两株为一份，最后所剩，非奇数即偶数。如是六次，得出每三个一组的组合，再查《易经》卦象、爻象，据以判断所问事项吉凶，称为"筮"。

第五种是杂占，第六种是形法。后者包括相面术和后来所称的"风水"。"风水"所依据的理论是，以人为宇宙的产物，又是宇宙的组成部分，因此，人的住处和死后"阴宅"（墓地）必须与自然环境（风水）谐调。

In the days when feudalism was in its prime during the early centuries of the Chou dynasty, every aristocratic house had attached to it hereditary experts in these various occult arts, who had to be consulted when any act of importance was contemplated. But with the gradual disintegration of feudalism, many of these experts lost their hereditary positions and scattered throughout the country, where they continued to practice their arts among the people. They then came to be known as the *fang shih* or practitioners of occult arts.

Occultism or magic is itself, of course, based on superstition, but it has often been the origin of science. The occult arts share with science the desire to interpret nature in a positive manner, and to acquire the services of nature through its conquest by man. Occultism becomes science when it gives up its belief in supernatural forces, and tries to interpret the universe solely in terms of forces that are natural. The concepts of what these natural forces are may in themselves initially look rather simple and crude, yet in them we find the beginnings of science.

Such has been the contribution of the *Yin-Yang* school to Chinese thought. This school represents a scientific tendency in the sense that it tried to give a positive interpretation to natural events in terms solely of natural forces. By the word positive I mean that which has to do with matters of fact.

In ancient China there were two lines of thought that thus tried to interpret the structure and origin of the universe. One is found in the writings of the *Yin-Yang* school, while the other is found in some of the "Appendices" added by anonymous Confucianists to the original text of the *Book of Changes*. These two lines of thought seem to have developed independently. In the "Grand Norm" and "Monthly Commands," which we will examine below, there is stress on the Five Elements but no mention of the *Yin* and *Yang*; in the "Appendices" of the *Book of Changes*, on the contrary, much is said about the *Yin* and *Yang*, but nothing about the Five Elements. Later, however, these two lines of thought became intermingled. This was already the case by the time of Ssu-ma T'an (died 110 B.C.), so that in the *Historical Records* he lumps them together as the *Yin-Yang* school.

● The Five Elements as Described in the "Grand Norm"

The term *Wu Hsing* is usually translated as the Five Elements. We should not think of them as static, however, but rather as five dynamic and interacting forces. The Chinese word *hsing* means "to act" or "to

周朝初年封建制全盛时期，每个贵族都有世袭的术士。贵族有任何重要行动之前，必先问卜。随封建制的逐渐没落，这些贵族世家的术士渐渐失去地位，散落社会，但继续以方术为生。这是"方士"的由来。

术数或法术本是来自迷信，但它们往往是古代科学的萌芽。方术和科学都试图以积极态度解释自然现象，使人得以征服自然，使自然为人所用。方术对超自然力量不再迷信后，它便开始试图解释自然现象，而向科学转变。人类最初对自然力量的观念尽管十分原始简单，但它终究是科学的开始。

这是阴阳家对中国思想的贡献。阴阳家试图以自然力量来解释自然现象，代表了一种科学探索的倾向。它总是和事实打交道，就这一点来说，它具有积极的意义。

由此我们看到，在古代中国，人们为理解宇宙的由来和宇宙的结构，有两种不同的思想路线。其一是以阴阳家为代表的思想路线。另一是由一些佚名的儒家，以"易传"（注释）的方式，写在《易经》正文的后面。这两种思想似乎各自独立地发展。下面要讲的《洪范》和《月令》，注重五行，而不曾提及阴阳。在"易传"里则相反，谈及阴阳的地方很多，而不提五行。后来，这两条思想路线渐渐融会一起，在司马谈的时候已经如此，以致《史记》中，把它们放在一起，统称阴阳家了。

●《洪范》所描述的五行

五行在英文里通常译作"Five Elements"，意思是"五种元素"。但如果把它们看作内容固定的五种元素就错了；它们是五种能动的、

do," so that the term *Wu Hsing*, literally translated, would mean the Five Activities, or Five Agents. They are also known as the *Wu Te*, which means Five Powers.

The term *Wu Hsing* appears in a text traditionally said to antedate the twentieth century B.C. (See the *Book of History*, Part III, Book II, ch. I, 3.) The authenticity of this text cannot be proved, however, and even if it were proved, we cannot be sure whether the term *Wu Hsing* means the same thing in it as it does in other texts whose date is better fixed. The first really authentic account of the *Wu Hsing*, therefore, is to be found in another section of the *Book of History* (Part V, Book 4), known as the *Hung Fan* or "Great Plan" or "Grand Norm." Traditionally, the "Grand Norm" is said to be the record of a speech delivered to King Wu of the Chou dynasty by the Viscount of Chi, a prince of the Shang dynasty which King Wu conquered at the end of the twelfth century B.C. In this speech, the Viscount of Chi in turn attributes his ideas to Yü, traditional founder of the Hsia dynasty who is said to have lived in the twenty-second century B.C. These traditions are mentioned as examples of the way the writer of this treatise tried to give importance to the *Wu Hsing* theory. As to the actual date of the "Grand Norm," modern scholarship inclines to place it within the fourth or third centuries B.C.

In the "Grand Norm" we are given a list of "Nine Categories." "First [among the categories]," we read, "is that of the *Wu Hsing*. The first [of these] is named Water; the second, Fire; the third, Wood; the fourth, Metal; the fifth, Soil. [The nature of] Water is to moisten and descend; of Fire, to flame and ascend; of Wood, to be crooked and straighten; of Metal, to yield and to be modified; of Soil, to provide for sowing and reaping."

Next comes the category of the Five Functions. "Second," we read, "is that of the Five Functions. The first [of these] is personal appearance; the second, speech; the third, vision; the fourth, hearing; the fifth, thought. Personal appearance should be decorous; speech should follow order; vision should be clear; hearing, distinct; thought, profound. Decorum produces solemnity; following order, regularity; clearness, intelligence; distinctness, deliberation; profundity, wisdom."

Skipping now to the eighth of the Nine Categories, we come to what the "Grand Norm" calls the various indications: "The eighth is that of various indications. These are rain, sunshine, heat, cold, wind, and seasonableness. When these five come fully and in their regular order, the various plants will be rich and luxuriant. If there is extreme excess in any of them, disaster follows. The following are the favorable indications: the solemnity of the sovereign will be followed by seasonable rain; his

相互作用的力量。在中文里，"行"的意思是"行动"或"作为"，因此，它的本义应当是五种动因、五种活动。在中国古籍里，也称"五德"，意思是"五种能力"。

"五行"这个名词曾出现于《书经》中《夏书·甘誓》，传统的说法，它是公元前二十一世纪的文献。但《夏书·甘誓》的真实性无法证明；即便此篇不是伪书，也无法证明《甘誓》篇中的"五行"与其他问世年代确实可考的典籍中所说"五行"内容是一致的。关于"五行"的可靠记载，见于《书经》中的《洪范》篇。按传统的说法，公元前十二世纪末，周武王克商之后，商朝贵族箕子对周武王陈述来自夏朝大禹的治国大法，这是《洪范》篇的来历。传说夏禹生活于公元前二十二世纪。《洪范》篇的作者引述传说的古代历史，意在表明"五行"说的重要来历。至于写作《洪范》篇的真实年代，据现代学者考订，应是公元前四世纪至前三世纪。

《洪范》篇中举出"九畴"："一、五行：一曰水，二曰火，三曰木，四曰金，五曰土。水曰润下，火曰炎上，木曰曲直，金曰从革，土爰稼穑。"然后是"五事"："一曰貌，二曰言，三曰视，四曰听，五曰思。貌曰恭，言曰从，视曰明，听曰聪，思曰睿。恭作肃，从作乂，明作哲，聪作谋，睿作圣。"

下面跳到"九畴"中的第八："庶征（各种象征）：曰雨，曰旸（日晒），曰燠（热），曰寒，曰风。曰时（各有其时）五者来备，各以其叙（顺序来临），庶草蕃庑（作物茂盛）。一极备，凶（五者任一过多，将成灾难）；一极无（五者缺一），凶。曰休征（吉兆）：曰肃，时雨若（国君肃穆，随之有雨）；曰乂，时旸若（国君顺时，阳光

regularity, by seasonable sunshine; his intelligence, by seasonable heat; his deliberation, by seasonable cold; his wisdom, by seasonable wind. The following are the unfavorable indications: the madness of the sovereign will be followed by steady rain; his insolence, by steady sunshine; his idleness, by steady heat; his haste, by steady cold; his ignorance, by steady wind."

In the "Grand Norm" we find that the idea of the *Wu Hsing* is still crude. In speaking of them, its author is still thinking in terms of the actual substances, water, fire, etc., instead of abstract forces bearing these names, as the *Wu Hsing* came to be regarded later on. The author also tells us that the human and natural worlds are interlinked; bad conduct on the part of the sovereign results in the appearance of abnormal phenomena in the world of nature. This theory, which was greatly developed by the *Yin-Yang* school in later times, is known as that of "the mutual influence between nature and man."

Two theories have been advanced to explain the reasons for this interaction. One is teleological. It maintains that wrong conduct on the part of the sovereign causes Heaven to become angry. That anger results in abnormal natural phenomena, which represent warnings given by Heaven to the sovereign. The other theory is mechanistic. It maintains that the sovereign's bad conduct automatically results in a disturbance of nature and thus mechanically produces abnormal phenomena. The whole universe is a mechanism. When one part of it becomes out of order, the other part must be mechanically affected. This theory represents the scientific spirit of the *Yin-Yang* school, while the other reflects its occult origin.

- **The "Monthly Commands"**

The next important document of the *Yin-Yang* school is the *Yüeh Ling* or "Monthly Commands," which is first found in the *Lü-shih Ch'un-ch'iu*, a work of the late third century B.C., and later was also embodied in the *Li Chi* (*Book of Rites*). The "Monthly Commands" gains its name from the fact that it is a small almanac which tells the ruler and men generally what they should do month by month in order to retain harmony with the forces of nature. In it, the structure of the universe is described in terms of the *Yin-Yang* school. This structure is spacio-temporal, that is, it relates both to space and to time. The ancient Chinese, being situated in the northern hemisphere, quite naturally regarded the south as the

适度）；曰哲，时燠若（国君明哲，气温适当）；曰谋，时寒若（国君深思熟虑，寒冷适度）；曰圣，时风若（国君明智，和风适时）。曰咎征（国君过失，伴有征象）：曰狂，恒雨若（国君暴狂，伴有大雨）；曰僭，恒旸若（国君粗野，伴有骄阳）；曰豫，恒燠若（国君怠惰，伴有酷热）；曰急，恒寒若（国君急躁，伴有冬寒）；曰蒙，恒风若（国君无知，伴有风灾）。"

在《洪范》中，五行观念还处于粗糙阶段。作者在谈到五行时，所想的还是具体的水、火等，还没有如后来那样，以水、火等代表抽象的力量。作者还让读者看到，人类社会和自然世界是联结在一起的，国君的恶行伴随有自然界的不正常现象。这个理论在后代发展成为"天人感应"学说。

对天人感应，有两种解释。其一是基于目的论的解释，认为国君恶行使天地震怒，天地震怒便造成自然界的不正常现象，以给国君警告。另一种理论则是比较机械式的解释，认为整个宇宙乃是一个机械的整体，其中任何一部分失去平衡，其他部分势必受到牵连。国君的过失必然造成宇宙天地失去平衡，于是就产生不正常的自然现象。这种学说反映了阴阳家中的科学精神，而前面一种学说则更多反映了它来自方术的社会根源。

● 《月令》

阴阳家的另一部重要文献是《月令》，首见于《吕氏春秋》。这是公元前三世纪末的著述，后来又载入《礼记》。《月令》这部著作的名称是由于它告诉国君和大众，每个月当做什么，不当做什么，以求得与天地万物的和谐。在《月令》书中，以阴阳家的观念构筑起宇宙的架构。这个宇宙结构是一个时空架构，就是说，它与空间、时间都有关系。古代中国由于位在北半球，自然热在南方，

direction of heat and the north as that of cold. Hence the *Yin-Yang* school correlated the four seasons with the four compass points. Summer was correlated with the south; winter with the north; spring with the east, because it is the direction of sunrise; and autumn with the west, because this is the direction of sunset. The school also regarded the changes of day and night as representing, on a miniature scale, the changes of the four seasons of the year. Thus morning is a miniature representation of spring; noon, of summer; evening, of autumn; and night, of winter.

South and summer are hot, because south is the direction and summer the time in which the Power or Element of Fire is dominant. North and winter are cold, because north is the direction and winter the time in which the Power of Water is dominant, and water is associated with ice and snow, which are cold. Likewise, the Power of Wood is dominant in the east and in spring, because spring is the time when plants (symbolized by "wood") begin to grow and the east is correlated with spring. The Power of Metal is dominant in the west and in autumn, because metal was regarded as something hard and harsh, and autumn is the bleak time when growing plants reach their end, while the west is correlated with autumn. Thus four of the five Powers are accounted for, leaving only the Power of Soil without a fixed place and season. According to the "Monthly Commands," however, Soil is the central of the Five Powers, and so occupies a place at the center of the four compass points. Its time of domination is said to be a brief interim period coming between summer and autumn.

With such a cosmological theory, the *Yin-Yang* school tried to explain natural phenomena both in terms of time and space, and furthermore maintained that these phenomena are closely interrelated with human conduct. Hence, as stated above, the "Monthly Commands" sets forth regulations as to what the sovereign should do month by month, which is the reason for its name.

Thus we are told: "In the first month of spring the east wind resolves the cold. Creatures that have been torpid during the winter begin to move.... It is in this month that the vapors of heaven descend and those of earth ascend. Heaven and earth are in harmonious co-operation. All plants bud and grow." (*Book of Rites*, ch. 4.)

Because man's conduct should be in harmony with the way of nature, we are told that in this month, "He [the sovereign] charges his assistants to disseminate [lessons of] virtue and harmonize governmental orders, so as to give effect to the expressions of his satisfaction and to bestow his favors to the millions of the people.... Prohibitions are issued against

冷在北方。因此，阴阳家把一年四季和地理上的四个方向组合在一起：夏季和南方结合；冬季和北方结合；春季和东方结合，这是太阳升起的地方；秋季和西方结合，那是太阳落下的地方。阴阳家还把一天中的日夜比作一年四季的缩影：早晨代表春季，中午代表夏季，傍晚代表秋季，午夜则代表冬季。这样就把时间和空间完全联结起来了。

南方和夏天之所以热，因为热在南方，就时间说，夏季是炎热季节，火德盛。北方和冬天则冷，因为冷在北方，就时间说，冬季是严寒季节，水德盛，水和冰雪是连在一起的。按照同样的推理，东方是春季，木德为主，因为春天万木茂盛，故此，东方总是和春天联结在一起。金德则代表西方，又和秋季相连，因为金属代表坚硬、严酷，秋季又是肃杀之气盛，万木萧条，走向衰亡。这样，"五德"中的四德和南北东西四个方向已经结合，只剩下土德未曾与一个方位和季节相连。按照《月令》书，土德在五德里是居中的，因此，在地理上，土德代表中央，它统治的时间，据说是夏秋之间的一段短暂时间。

阴阳家以这样的一个宇宙论的理论解释了四季的自然现象，还把它和四方连为一体，而且更进一步，把自然现象和人文现象联结起来。正是在这样的理论基础上，《月令》书规定君王每月应当做什么，不应当做什么，这也就是《月令》书名的由来。

因此，我们从《礼记·月令》书中读到："孟春之月，……东风解冻，蛰虫始振，……是月也，天气下降，地气上腾，天地和同，草木萌动。"人的行为应当与自然相应一致，因此，书中又说：在此月，君主"命相布德和令，行庆施惠，下及兆民。……禁止伐木。

cutting down trees. Nests should not be thrown down.... In this month no warlike operations should be undertaken; the undertaking of such is sure to be followed by calamities from Heaven. This avoidance of warlike operations means that they are not to be commenced on our side."

If, in each month, the sovereign fails to act in the manner befitting that month, but instead follows the conduct appropriate to another month, abnormal natural phenomena will result. "If in the first month of spring, the governmental proceedings proper to summer are carried out, rain will fall unseasonably, plants and trees will decay prematurely, and the state will be kept in continual fear. If the proceedings proper to autumn are carried out, there will be great pestilence among the people, boisterous winds will work their violence, and rain will descend in torrents.... If the proceedings proper to winter are carried out, pools of water will produce destructive effects, and snow and frost will prove very injurious...."

- **Tsou Yen**

A major figure of the *Yin-Yang* school in the third century B.C. was Tsou Yen. According to Ssu-ma Ch'ien's *Shih Chi* or *Historical Records*, Tsou Yen was a native of the State of Ch'i in the central part of present Shantung province, and lived shortly after Mencius. He "wrote essays totaling more than a hundred thousand words," but all have since been lost. In the *Historical Records* itself, however, Ssu-ma Ch'ien gives a fairly detailed account of Tsou Yen's theories.

According to this work (Ch. 74), Tsou Yen's method was "first to examine small objects, and to extend this to large ones until he reached what was without limit." His interests seem to have been centered on geography and history.

As regards geography, Ssu-ma Ch'ien writes: "He began by classifying China's notable mountains, great rivers and connecting valleys; its birds and beasts; the productions of its waters and soils, and its rare products;

and from this he extended his survey to what is beyond the seas, and which men are unable to see.... He maintained that what scholars call the Middle Kingdom [i.e., China] holds a place in the whole world of but one part in eighty-one. He named China the Spiritual Continent of the Red Region.... Besides China [there are other continents] similar to the Spiritual Continent of the Red Region, making [with China] a total of nine continents.... Around each of these is a small encircling sea, so that men and beasts cannot pass from one to another. These [nine continents] form one division. There are nine divisions like this. Around their outer edge is a vast ocean which encompasses them at the point where heaven and earth meet."

毋覆巢，……是月也，不可以称兵，称兵必天殃。兵戎不起，不可从我始。"

如果君王行事违反了《月令》书的规定，就会造成不正常的自然现象，例如："孟春行夏令，则雨水不时，草木早落，国时有恐；行秋令，则其民大疫，飙（暴）风暴雨总至，藜莠蓬蒿并兴；行冬令，则水潦为败，雪霜大挚，首种不入。"

● 邹衍

邹衍是公元前三世纪阴阳家的一个主要人物。按《史记》所载，邹衍是齐国（今山东省中部）人，在孟子之后不久。他"著书十余万言"，均已佚失。幸亏司马迁在《史记》中还保存有关邹衍学说的详尽说明。

按照《史记·孟子荀卿列传》所载，邹衍的方法是："必先验小物，推而大之，至于无垠。"他的兴趣似乎主要在于地理和历史。

关于地理，司马迁写道，邹衍"先列中国名山大川，通谷禽兽，水土所殖，物类所珍，因而推之，及海外人之所不能睹。……以为儒者所谓中国者，于天下乃八十一分居其一分耳。中国名曰赤县神州。……中国外如赤县神州者九，乃所谓九州也。于是有稗海环之，人民禽兽莫能相通者，如一区中者，乃为一州。如此者九，乃有大瀛海环其外，天地之际焉。"

As regards Tsou Yen's historical concepts, Ssu-ma Ch'ien writes: "He first spoke about modern times, and from this went back to the time of Huang Ti [the legendary Yellow Emperor], all of which has been recorded by scholars. Moreover, he followed the great events in the rise and fall of ages, recorded their omens and institutions, and extended his survey backward to the time when heaven and earth had not yet been born, to what was profound and abstruse and not to be examined.... Starting from the time of the separation of heaven and earth and coming down, he made citations of the revolutions and transformations of the Five Powers, and the [different ways of] government and different omens appropriate to each of the Powers."

● A Philosophy of History

The last few lines of the quotation show that Tsou Yen developed a new philosophy of history, according to which historical changes are interpreted in accordance with the revolutions and transformations of the Five Powers. The details of this theory are not reported by Ssu-ma Ch'ien, but it is treated in one section of the *Lü-shih Ch'un-ch'iu*, even though in this section Tsou Yen's name is not explicitly mentioned. Thus this work states (XIII, 2):

"Whenever an Emperor or King is about to arise, Heaven must first manifest some favorable omen to the common people. In the time of the Yellow Emperor, Heaven first made huge earthworms and mole crickets appear. The Yellow Emperor said: 'The force of Soil is in ascendancy.' Therefore he assumed yellow as his color, and took Soil as the pattern for his affairs.

"In the time of Yü [founder of the Hsia dynasty] Heaven first made grass and trees appear which did not die in the autumn and winter. Yü said: 'The force of Wood is in ascendancy.' Therefore he assumed green as his color and took Wood as the pattern for his affairs.

"In the time of T'ang [founder of the Shang dynasty] Heaven made some knife blades appear in the water. T'ang said: 'The force of Metal is in ascendancy.' He therefore assumed white as his color and took Metal as the pattern for his affairs.

"In the time of King Wen [founder of the Chou dynasty] Heaven made a flame appear, while a red bird, holding a red book in its mouth, alighted on the altar of soil of the House of Chou. King Wen said: 'The force of Fire is in ascendancy.' Therefore he assumed red as his color, and took Fire as the pattern of his affairs."

至于邹衍的历史观点，司马迁写道：邹衍"先序今以上至黄帝，学者所共术，大并世盛衰，因载其机祥度制，推而远之，至天地未生，窈冥不可考而原也"。"称引天地剖判以来，五德转移，治各有宜，而符应若兹"。这是说，由近及远，上溯黄帝，这是学者已共述。他又按历史大事，时代盛衰，记其征兆、体制，一直上溯到远古洪荒，天地未生之时。然后自开天辟地起，历数五德连转，治法虽殊，均与五德相应。

● **历史哲学**

上面引文的末段表明：邹衍发展出一个新的历史哲学，用五德的转移来解释历史，它既是变化的，又是有规律的。司马迁在《史记》中并没有详述邹衍这种学说的内容，但是，《吕氏春秋》书中介绍了这种学说，尽管其中并未提及邹衍的名字。原文如下：

"凡帝王者之将兴也，天必先见祥乎下民。黄帝之时，天先见大螾大蝼。黄帝曰：土气胜。土气胜，故其色尚黄，其事则土。

"及禹之时，天先见草木秋冬不杀。禹曰：木气胜。木气胜，故其色尚青，其事则木。

"及汤之时，天先见金刃生于水。汤曰：金气胜。金气胜，故其色尚白，其事则金。

"及文王之时，天先见火。赤乌衔丹书集于周社。文王曰：火气胜。火气胜，故其色尚赤，其事则火。

"Water will inevitably be the next force that will succeed Fire. Heaven will first make the ascendancy of Water manifest. The force of Water being in ascendancy, black will be assumed as its color, and Water will be taken as the pattern for affairs.... When the cycle is complete, the operation will revert once more to Soil."

The *Yin-Yang* school maintained that the Five Elements produce one another and also overcome one another in a fixed sequence. It also maintained that the sequence of the four seasons accords with this process of the mutual production of the Elements. Thus Wood, which dominates spring, produces Fire, which dominates summer. Fire in its turn produces Soil, which dominates the "center"; Soil again produces Metal, which dominates autumn; Metal produces Water, which dominates winter; and Water again produces Wood, which dominates spring.

According to the above quotation, the succession of dynasties likewise accords with the natural succession of the Elements. Thus Earth, under whose Power the Yellow Emperor ruled, was overcome by the Wood of the Hsia dynasty. The Wood of this dynasty was overcome by the Metal of the Shang dynasty, Metal was overcome by the Fire of the Chou dynasty, and Fire would in its turn be overcome by the Water of whatever dynasty was to follow the Chou. The Water of this dynasty would then again be overcome by the Soil of the dynasty following, thus completing the cycle.

As described in the *Lü-shih Ch'un-ch'iu*, this is but a theory, but soon afterward it had its effect in practical politics. Thus in the year 221 B.C., the First Emperor of the Ch'in dynasty, known as Ch'in Shih-Huang-Ti (246-210 B.C.), conquered all the rival feudal states and thus created a unified Chinese empire under the Ch'in. As the successor to the Chou dynasty, he actually believed that "the force of Water is in ascendancy," and so, according to Ssu-ma Ch'ien's *Historical Records*, "assumed black as his color" and "took Water as the pattern for affairs." "The name of the Yellow River," says the *Historical Records*, "was changed to that of Power Water, because it was supposed to mark the beginning of the Power of

Water. With harshness and violence, and an extreme severity, everything was decided by the law. For by punishing and oppressing, by having neither human-heartedness nor kindness, but only conforming to strict justice, there would come an accord with [the transformations of] the Five Powers." (Ch. 6.)

Because of its very harshness, the Ch'in dynasty did not last long, and was soon succeeded by that of Han (206 B.C.-A.D. 220). The Han Emperors also believed that they had become Emperors "by virtue of" one of the Five Powers, but there was considerable dispute as to which of the Powers it was. This was because some people maintained that the

"代火者必将水，天且先见水气胜。水气胜，故其色尚黑，其事则水。水气至而不知，数备，将徙于土。"（《有始览·应同》）

阴阳家认为，五行按照一定顺序，相生相克；还认为，一年四季也按五行相生的顺序嬗替。木盛于春，木生火；火盛于夏，火生土；土盛于中央，土生金；金盛于秋，金生水；水盛于冬，水又生木，木盛于春。

按以上引文看来，朝代的更替也是遵循五行相生的顺序。黄帝以土德王，被以木德王的夏朝所取代；以木德王的夏朝又被以金德王的商朝所取代；以金德王的商朝又被以火德王的周朝所取代。周朝将被以水德王的王朝所取代；以水德王的朝代又将被以土德王的朝代所取代。这样，历朝历代按五行顺序周而复始。

按照《吕氏春秋》的陈述，这只不过是一种历史哲学理论。然而，不久之后它便对现实政治产生作用。公元前二二一年，秦始皇帝（公元前二五九至前二一〇年）征服六国，建立起统一中国古代列国的秦帝国。秦继承周朝，始皇帝确信，秦是以水德王。按司马迁《史记·秦始皇本纪》所载，秦始皇"推终始五德之传，以为周得火德，秦代周德，从所不胜。方今水德之始"，其色尚黑，其事则水，将黄河改名"德水"，"以为水德之始。刚毅戾深，事皆决于法，刻削毋仁恩和义，然后合五德之数"。

由于严酷寡恩，秦朝不久就被汉朝（公元前二〇六至公元二二〇年）所取代。汉代历朝皇帝相信自己也是本五德而王；至于汉朝究竟靠什么"德"而王，仍有不少争论。当时有些人认为，汉朝

Han was the successor of the Ch'in, and therefore ruled through Soil, whereas others maintained that the Ch'in had been too harsh and short to be counted as a legitimate dynasty, so that the Han dynasty was actually the successor of the Chou. Support for both sides was found from many omens which were subject to varying interpretations. Finally, in 104 B.C., the Emperor Wu decided and formally announced that Soil was the Power for the Han. Even afterward, however, there were still differences of opinion.

Following the Han dynasty, people no longer paid very much attention to this question. Yet as late as 1911, when the last dynasty was brought to an end by the Chinese Republic, the official title of the Emperor was still "Emperor through [the Mandate of] Heaven and in accordance with the Movements [of the Five Powers]."

- ### The *Yin* and *Yang* Principles as Described in the "Appendices" of the *Book of Changes*

The theory of the Five Elements interpreted the structure of the universe, but did not explain the origin of the world. This was provided by the theory of the *Yin* and *Yang*.

The word *yang* originally meant sunshine, or what pertains to sunshine and light; that of *yin* meant the absence of sunshine, i.e., shadow or darkness. In later development, the *Yang* and *Yin* came to be regarded as two cosmic principles or forces, respectively representing masculinity, activity, heat, brightness, dryness, hardness, etc., for the *Yang*, and femininity, passivity, cold, darkness, wetness, softness, etc., for the *Yin*. Through the interaction of these two primary principles, all phenomena of the universe are produced. This concept has remained dominant in Chinese cosmological speculation down to recent times. An early reference to it appears already in the *Kuo Yü* or *Discussions of the States* (which was itself compiled, however, probably only in the fourth or third century B.C.). This historical work records that when an earthquake occurred in the year 780 B.C., a savant of the time explained: "When the *Yang* is concealed and cannot come forth, and when the *Yin* is repressed and cannot issue forth, then there are earthquakes." (*Chou Yü*, I, 10.)

Later, the theory of the *Yin* and *Yang* came to be connected primarily with the *Book of Changes*. The original corpus of this book consists of what are known as the eight trigrams, each made up of combinations of three divided or undivided lines, as follows: ☰, ☷, ☲, ☵, ☳, ☴, ☶, ☱. By

既然是继承秦朝，应当以土德王；也有人认为，秦朝严酷少恩，不能算作一个正式的朝代，应当认为汉朝是继承周朝。持不同意见的双方都举出支持自己的祥兆，以示自己一方的主张符合天意。最后，公元前一〇四年，汉武帝决定，汉朝是以土德王。但此后，争论并未结果。

汉以后各朝对这个问题，不像汉朝那样激烈争论。但直到一九一一年清朝覆灭之前的历代皇帝，都称自己是"奉天承运"，所指就是承受"五德"转移的时运。

● "易传"中描述的阴阳原则

五行学说的意义在于解说宇宙的结构，但并没有解释世界的来源。阴阳的学说则填补了这个需要。

"阳"这个字的本义是阳光，或任何与阳光相连的事物。"阴"的本义则是指没有阳光的阴影和黑暗。后来，它们的含义逐渐发展成为宇宙中的两种相反相成的力量，阳代表男性、主动、热、光明、干燥、坚硬等；阴则代表女性、被动、冷、阴暗、柔软等。宇宙一切现象都是由阴阳两个原则、两种力量的相互作用而产生。这样一种宇宙观念，在公元前八世纪初已经产生。记载中国古代事迹的《国语》一书（成书于公元前四世纪到前三世纪之间），其中《周语上》记载公元前七八〇年（幽王二年），西周地震，三川壅塞，当时博学的史官伯阳父评论说："阳伏而不能出，阴迫而不能烝，于是有地震。"

后来，阴阳的理论主要是和《易经》联系在一起。《易经》原书是为解释"八卦"（正式名称是"八经卦"）。每"卦"包含三个完整或分成两截的直线，如：☰, ☷, ☲, ☵, ☳, ☴, ☶, ☱。

combining any two of these trigrams with one another into diagrams of six lines each, ☰, ☷, ☳, etc., a total of sixty-four combinations is obtained which are known as the sixty-four hexagrams. The original text of the *Book of Changes* consists of these hexagrams, and of descriptions of their supposed symbolic meaning.

According to tradition, the eight trigrams were invented by Fu Hsi, China's first legendary ruler, antedating even the Yellow Emperor. According to some scholars, Fu Hsi himself combined the eight trigrams so as to obtain the sixty-four hexagrams; according to others, this was done by King Wen of the twelfth century B.C. The textual comments on the hexagrams as a whole and on their *hsiao* (the individual lines in each hexagram) were, according to some scholars, written by King Wen; according to others, the comments on the hexagrams were written by King Wen, while those on the *hsiao* were by the Duke of Chou, the illustrious son of King Wen. Whether right or wrong, these attributions attest the importance which the Chinese attached to the eight trigrams and sixty-four hexagrams.

Modern scholarship has advanced the theory that the trigrams and hexagrams were invented early in the Chou dynasty as imitations of the cracks formed on a piece of tortoise shell or bone through the method of divination that was practiced under the Shang dynasty (1766?-1123? B.C.), the dynasty that preceded the Chou. This method has already been mentioned at the beginning of this chapter. It consisted of applying heat to a shell or bone, and then, according to the cracks that resulted, determining the answer to the subject of divination. Such cracks, however, might assume an indefinite number of varying configurations, and so it was difficult to interpret them according to any fixed formula. Hence during the early part of the Chou dynasty this kind of divination seems to have been supplemented by another method, in which the stalks of a certain plant, known as the milfoil, were shuffled together so as to get varying combinations yielding odd and even numbers. These combinations were limited in number and so could be interpreted according to fixed formulas. It is now believed that the undivided and divided (i.e., odd and even) lines of the trigrams and hexagrams were graphic representations of these combinations. Thus the diviners, by shuffling the stalks of the milfoil, could obtain a given line or set of lines, and then, by reading the comments on it contained in the *Book of Changes*, could give an answer to the question on which divination was made.

This, then, was the probable origin of the *Book of Changes*, and explains its title, which refers to the changing combinations of lines. Later,

如果把任何两"卦"组合在一起，可以发展出六十四个排列组合样式，称为六十四卦（正式名称是"六十四别卦"），即䷀，䷁，䷂，等等。《易经》本文就包含这六十四卦，以及对每一种卦象含义作出的解释。

中国传统认为，八卦是黄帝之前、传说中的中国第一个君王伏羲氏所创立，有的古代学者说，伏羲亲自从八卦演出六十四卦；另一些学者则说，这是公元前十二世纪时，周文王演化出来的。六十四卦的每一卦象都有解释，称"卦辞"；每卦之中的每一横划也有解释，称"爻辞"。有的古代学者认为，所有卦辞、爻辞，都出自文王；另一些古代学者则认为，卦辞出于文王，爻辞出自其子周公。无论这些学说孰是孰非，它们总的说来都表明，八卦和六十四卦在中国人心目中的极大重要性。

现代学者的看法认为：八卦的前身是商朝（约公元前一七六六〔一六〇〇〕至前一一二二〔一〇四六〕年）盛行的以甲骨受火龟裂的纹路占卜。这种裂纹千变万化，如按固定图像以论天象人事的吉凶自然十分困难。周初渐渐改用蓍草占卜，巫人在一束蓍草中，以两株为一份，分置一旁；最后所剩，或为单数，或为双数，便以乾（一横）或坤（一横分成两短横）为记。现代学者认为，八卦或六十四卦便是这种蓍草占卜的结果，然后对照《易经》，以解读卦象所示的吉凶。

这大概是《易经》的起源。这部书被称为《易》（意为"变易"），

however, many supplementary interpretations were added to the *Book of Changes,* some moral, some metaphysical, and some cosmological. These were not composed until the latter part of the Chou dynasty, or even the earlier portion of the following Han dynasty, and are contained in a series of appendices known as the "Ten Wings." In this chapter we shall discuss only the cosmological interpretations, leaving the remainder for chapter fifteen.

Besides the concept of *Yin* and *Yang,* another important idea in the "Appendices" is that of number. Since divination was usually regarded by the ancients as a method for revealing the mystery of the universe, and since divination through the use of stalks of the milfoil plant was based on the combination of varying numbers, it is not surprising that the anonymous writers of the "Appendices" tended to believe that the mystery of the universe is to be found in numbers. According to them, therefore, the numbers of the *Yang* are always odd, and those of the *Yin* are always even. Thus in "Appendix III" we read: "The number for Heaven [i.e., *Yang*] is one; that for Earth [i.e. *Yin*] is two; that for Heaven is three; that for Earth is four; that for Heaven is five; that for Earth is six; that for Heaven is seven; that for Earth is eight; that for Heaven is nine; that for Earth is ten. The numbers for Heaven and the numbers for Earth correspond with and complement one another. The numbers of Heaven [put together] are twenty-five; the numbers of Earth [put together] are thirty; the numbers of both Heaven and Earth [put together] are fifty-five. It is by these numbers that the evolutions and mystery of the universe are performed."

Later the *Yin-Yang* school tried to connect the Five Elements with the *Yin* and *Yang* by means of numbers. Thus it maintained that one, the number for Heaven, produces Water, and six, the number for Earth, completes it. Two, the number for Earth, produces Fire, and seven, the number for Heaven, completes it. Three, the number for Heaven, produces Wood, and eight, the number for Earth, completes it. Four, the number for Earth, produces Metal, and nine, the number for Heaven, completes it. Five, the number for Heaven, produces Soil, and ten, the number for Earth, completes it. Thus one, two, three, four and five are the numbers that produce the Five Elements; six, seven, eight, nine and ten are the numbers that complete them.[1] This is the theory, therefore, that was used to explain the statement just quoted above: "The numbers for Heaven and the numbers for Earth correspond with and complement one another." It is remarkably similar to the theory of the Pythagoreans in ancient Greece, as reported by Diogenes Laertius, according to which the

大概也是由此而来。后来，对《易》的补充解释渐渐增多，有些是关于道德方面的箴言，有些是形而上领域的看法，有些则是对宇宙的看法。这些补充解释直到周朝末期甚至汉朝初年才以"附录"形式写入《易经》后面，称作"十翼"。本章将只限于讨论其中有关宇宙论的部分，其他部分将留待第十五章再讨论。

在"易传"中，除阴阳的观念外，另一个重要的概念是"数"。古代人以占卜来探求宇宙的奥秘，用著草占卜又离不开数目的变化。因此，"易传"的无名作者们相信宇宙的奥秘在数字之中，是毫不足怪的。首先，他们把"阳"看为单数，把"阴"看为偶数。因此，"易传"《系辞上》说："天一地二，天三地四，天五地六，天七地八，天九地十。天数五，地数五，五位相得而各有合。天数二十有五，地数三十，凡天地之数，五十有五，此所以成变化而行鬼神也。"

后来的阴阳家试图用数字把五行与阴阳联系起来，于是称："天之数，一，生水；地之数，六，成之。地之数，二，生火；天之数，七，成之。天之数，三，生木；地之数，八，成之。地之数，四，生金；天之数，九，成之。天之数，五，生土；地之数，十，成之。"这样，一、二、三、四、五，都是产生五行的数字，六、七、八、九、十，则是完成之数（见《礼记·月令》，孟春之月"其数八"，郑玄注，孔颖达疏）。这个理论正好用于解释前面《系辞上》的引文："天数五，地数五，五位相得则各有合。"这与古希腊哲学中毕达哥拉斯学派的思想惊人地相似。据古希腊学者戴奥吉尼·莱修斯

four elements of Greek philosophy, namely Fire, Water, Earth and Air, are derived, though indirectly, from numbers.[2]

This, however, is in China a comparatively late theory, and in "Appendices" themselves there is no mention of the Five Elements. In these "Appendices" each of the eight trigrams is regarded as symbolizing certain things in the universe. Thus we read in "Appendix V": "(The trigram) *Ch'ien* ☰ is Heaven, round, and is the father.... (The trigram) *K'un* ☷ is Earth and is the mother.... (The trigram) *Chen* ☳ is thunder.... (The trigram) *Sun* ☴ is wood and wind.... (The trigram) *K'an* ☵ is water... and is the moon.... (The trigram) *Li* ☲ is fire and the sun.... (The trigram) *Ken* ☶ is mountain.... (The trigram) *Tui* ☱ is marsh."

In the trigrams, the undivided lines symbolize the *Yang* principle, and the divided lines the *Yin* principle. The trigrams *Ch'ien* and *K'un*, being made up entirely of undivided and divided lines respectively, are the symbols *par excellence* of the *Yang* and *Yin*, while the remaining six trigrams are supposedly produced through the intercourse of these primary two. Thus *Ch'ien* and *K'un* are father and mother, while the other trigrams are usually spoken of in the "Appendices" as their "sons and daughters."

Thus the first line (from the bottom) of *Ch'ien* ☰, combined with the second and third lines of *K'un* ☷, results in *Chen* ☳, which is called the eldest son. The first line of *K'un*, similarly combined with *Ch'ien*, results in *Sun* ☴, which is called the eldest daughter. The second line of *Ch'ien*, combined with the first and third lines of *K'un*, results in *K'an* ☵, which is called the second son. The second line of *K'un*, similarly combined with *Ch'ien*, results in *Li* ☲, which is called the second daughter. The third line of *Ch'ien*, combined with the first and second lines of *K'un*, results in *Ken* ☶, which is called the youngest son. And the third line of *K'un*, similarly combined with *Ch'ien*, results in *Tui* ☱, which is called the youngest daughter.

This process of combination or intercourse between *Ch'ien* and

K'un, which results in the production of the remaining six trigrams, is a graphic symbolization of the process of intercourse between the *Yin* and the *Yang*, whereby all things in the world are produced. That the world

（Diogenes Laertius）所述，毕达哥拉斯认为，世上万物全由火、水、土、风（空气）四个元素构成，它们又都是由数字演化而来。

用数字把五行和阴阳联系起来，在中国是一个较晚出的学说，在"易传"中，并没有提五行。在"易传"中，每一卦都象征宇宙中的某个事物。《说卦传》中的解释是：

乾，☰，为天，为圜，为君，为父。

坤，☷，为地，为母。

震，☳，为雷。

巽，☴，为木，为风。

坎，☵，为水，为月。

离，☲，为火，为日。

艮，☶，为山。

兑，☱，为泽。

在每一卦中，没有中断的一横代表阳，有中断的一横代表阴。乾卦由三个没有中断的三横组成，代表纯阳。坤卦由三个中断的三横组成，代表纯阴。其他六卦则都是乾坤相交而成，因此，乾和坤被认为是父母，其他六卦是子女：

以乾☰的第一爻（由下端数起），与坤☷的第二、三爻结合，成为震☳，称为"长男"。

以坤的第一爻，与乾的第二、三爻结合，成为巽☴，称为"长女"。

以乾的第二爻，与坤的第一、三爻结合，成为坎☵，称为"中男"。

以坤的第二爻，与乾的第一、三爻结合，成为离☲，称为"中女"。

以乾的第三爻，与坤的第一、二爻结合，成为艮☶，称为"少男"。

以坤的第三爻，与乾的第一、二爻结合，成为兑☱，称为"少女"。

乾和坤的相交、结合，产生其他六卦，这象征着天地万物都由

of things is produced through such intercourse of the *Yin* and *Yang*, is similar to the fact that living beings are produced through the intercourse of the male and female. It will be remembered that the *Yang* is the male principle, and the *Yin*, the female principle.

In "Appendix III" of the *Book of Changes* we read: "There is an intermingling of the genial influences of heaven and earth, and the transformation of all things proceeds abundantly. There is a communication of seed between male and female, and all things are produced." Heaven and earth are the physical representations of the *Yin* and *Yang*, while *Ch'ien* and *K'un* are their symbolic representations. The *Yang* is the principle that "gives beginning" to things; the *Yin* is that which "completes" them. Thus the process of the production of things by the *Yang* and *Yin* is completely analogous to that of the production of living beings by the male and female.

In the religion of the primitive Chinese, it was possible to conceive of a father god and mother goddess who actually gave birth to the world of things. In the *Yin-Yang* philosophy, however, such anthropomorphic concepts were replaced by, or interpreted in terms of, the *Yin* and *Yang* principles, which, though analogous to the female and male of living beings, were nevertheless conceived of as completely impersonal natural forces.

阴阳相交而成；亦如所有生物都由雌雄两性结合而产生一样，而阴则象征雌性，阳则象征雄性。

《系辞下》说："天地氤氲，万物化醇；男女媾精，万物化生。"天和地是阴阳两气的物质表现；"乾""坤"则是阴阳两气的象征。《系辞上》说："乾知大始，坤作成物。"生命的起源来自雄性，而生命的完成则在于雌性。天地万物的生成就如同生物界的两性结合一样。

考察中国的原始宗教，可以设想，最初有男性的神和女性的神，他们结合，由此产生世界万物。这种拟人的原始宗教发展到后来，两性由阴阳两个力量代表，由此导致了论述阴阳两气相生相克、相反相成的宇宙论哲学，这时，雌雄两性转化成为没有人格的自然力量了。

⓭ THE REALISTIC WING OF CONFUCIANISM: HSÜN TZU

The three greatest figures of the School of Literati in the Chou dynasty were Confucius (551-479 B.C.), Mencius (371?-289? B.C.) and Hsün Tzu. The latter's dates are not definitely known, but probably lay within the years 298 and 238 B.C.

Hsün Tzu's personal name is K'uang, but he was also known under the alternative name of Hsün Ch'ing. He was a native of the state of Chao in the southern part of the present Hopei and Shansi provinces. The *Shih Chi* or *Historical Records* says in its biography of him (ch. 74) that when he was fifty he went to the state of Ch'i, where he was probably the last great thinker of the academy of Chi-hsia, the great center of learning of that time. The book bearing his name contains thirty-two chapters, many of them detailed and logically developed essays which probably come directly from his pen.

Among the literati, Hsün Tzu's thought is the antithesis of that of Mencius. Some people say that Mencius represents the left wing of the school, while Hsün Tzu represents its right wing. This saying, while suggestive, is too much of a simplified generalization. Mencius was left in that he emphasized individual freedom, but he was right in that he valued super-moral values and therefore was nearer to religion. Hsün Tzu was right in that he emphasized social control, but left in that he expounded naturalism and therefore was in direct opposition to any religious ideas.

• Position of Man

Hsün Tzu is best known because of his theory that human nature is originally evil. This is directly opposed to that of Mencius according to which human nature is originally good. Superficially, it may seem that Hsün Tzu had a very low opinion of man, yet the truth is quite the contrary. Hsün Tzu's philosophy may be called a philosophy of culture. His general thesis is that everything that is good and valuable is the product of human effort. Value comes from culture and culture is the achievement of man. It is in this that man has the same importance in the universe as Heaven and Earth. As Hsün Tzu says: "Heaven has its seasons, Earth has its resources, man has his culture. This is what is meant [when it is said that man] is able to form a trinity [with Heaven and Earth]." (*Hsün-tzu*, ch. 17.)

拾叁 儒家的现实主义流派：荀子

先秦儒家中三个最重要的人物是孔子、孟子和荀子。荀子的生卒年代已无从查考，大概是在公元前二九八至前二三八年之间。

荀子本名况，又号荀卿，赵国（今河北、山西南部）人。《史记·孟子荀卿列传》中说，荀子五十岁到齐国。当时齐国国君为广揽学人，修建稷下学宫。荀子大概是稷下学宫的最后一位大思想家。《荀子》一书共三十二章，其中许多篇论述详赅，逻辑周密，大概出自他自己笔下。

在儒家中间，荀子的思想与孟子的思想正好针锋相对。有人认为，孟子代表儒家的左翼，荀子则代表儒家的右翼。这种说法虽能令人一新耳目，但不免过于简单化。孟子强调个人自由，就这一点说，他可以被看为是"左"的，但孟子重视超越道德的价值，与宗教比较接近。荀子强调社会对个人的控制，就这一点说，他可以说是"右"的；但他重视自然主义，与任何宗教思想都不相容，就这一点说，又可以说是"左"的。

● 人的地位

荀子以主张"人性恶"而著名。这与孟子所主张的"人性本善"正好相反。表面看来，荀子对人性的评价很低，而事实上，恰恰相反，荀子的理论可以称之为一种文化哲学。他的理论主旨是认为，一切良善和有价值的事物都是人所创造的。价值来自文化，而文化则是人的创造性成就。因此，在宇宙中，人和天地同等重要。荀子在著名的《天论》中说："天有其时，地有其财，人有其治，夫是谓之能参。"

Mencius said that by developing one's mind to the utmost, one knows one's nature, and by knowing one's nature, one knows Heaven. (*Mencius*, VIIa, 1.) Thus, according to Mencius, a sage, in order to become a sage, must "know Heaven." But Hsün Tzu maintains, on the contrary: "It is only the sage who does not seek to know Heaven." (*Hsün-tzu*, ch. 17.)

According to Hsün Tzu, the three powers of the universe, Heaven, Earth and man, each has its own particular vocation: "The stars make their rounds; the sun and moon alternately shine; the four seasons succeed one another; the *Yin* and *Yang* go through their great mutations; wind and rain are widely distributed; all things acquire their harmony and have their lives." (*Ibid.*) Such is the vocation of Heaven and Earth. But the vocation of man is to utilize what is offered by Heaven and Earth and thus create his own culture. Hsün Tzu asks: "Is it not much better to heap up wealth and use it advantageously than to exalt Heaven and think about it?" (*Ibid.*) And then he continues: "If we neglect what man can do and think about Heaven, we fail to understand the nature of things." (*Ibid.*) For in so doing, according to Hsün Tzu, man forgets his own vocation; by daring to "think" about Heaven, he arrogates the vocation of Heaven. This is "to give up that wherewith man can form a trinity with Heaven and Earth, and yet still desire such a trinity. This is a great illusion." (*Ibid.*)

● Theory of Human Nature

Human nature, too, should be cultured, for, from Hsün Tzu's view, the very fact that it is uncultured means that it cannot be good. Hsün Tzu's thesis is that "the nature of man is evil; his goodness is acquired training." (*Hsün-tzu*, ch. 23.) According to him, "nature is the unwrought material of the original; what are acquired are the accomplishments and refinements brought about by culture. Without nature there would be nothing upon which to add the acquired. Without the acquired, nature could not become beautiful of itself." (*Ibid.*)

Although Hsün Tzu's view of human nature is the exact opposite of that of Mencius, he agrees with him that it is possible for every man to become a sage, if he choose. Mencius had said that any man can become a Yao or Shun (two traditional sages). And Hsün Tzu says likewise that "any man in the street can become a Yü [another traditional sage]." (*Ibid.*) This agreement has led some people to say that there is no real difference between the two Confucians after all. Yet as a matter of fact, despite this seeming agreement, the difference is very real.

孟子说:"尽其心者,知其性也。知其性,则知天矣。"(《孟子·尽心章句上》)因此,在孟子看来,人要成圣,必须"知天"。荀子正相反,认为:"惟圣人为不求知天。"(《天论》)

荀子在《天论》中提出,天、地、人构成宇宙的三个力量,它们又各有自己的作用:"列星随旋,日月递照,四时代御,阴阳大化,风雨博施,万物各得其和以生。"这是天和地的作用。至于人的作用,则是运用天时地利,以创造自身的文化。《天论》中问道:"大天而思之,孰与物蓄而制之?"这是说,与其颂赞苍天,何若积聚财富、运用得当?他又接着说:"故错〔措〕人而思天,则失万物之情。"就是说,如果忽略人所当做的而去"思天",就不可能懂得万物的性情。人忘记自己的职责去"思天",就是干犯天的职责。荀子称,这是"舍其所以参,而愿其所参,则惑矣"。人与天地合参,就应该恪尽职责,如果人不尽自己的职责,而想与天地合参,那只是空想。

● **关于人性的学说**

按照荀子的看法,人性也应当受到教养,没有教养就不可能成善。在《性恶》篇中,荀子说:"人之性,恶;其善者,伪〔人为〕也。"在《礼论》中,探讨了人的先天和后天的关系,他说:人"性者,本始材朴也;伪者,文理隆盛也。无性则伪之无所加,无伪则性不能自美。"这是说,先天和后天同等重要,在其中实际是强调了人的主观能动性。

荀子的人性论虽然与孟子正相反,但是他同意孟子所说,人皆可以为尧舜。他自己也说过:"涂之人可以为禹。"(《性恶》)有的人由于看到孟子、荀子两人的相同之点,于是认为这两位儒家并无根本的不同,其实,他们之间的不同是不容抹杀的。

According to Mencius, man is born with the "four beginnings" of the four constant virtues. By fully developing these beginnings, he becomes a sage. But according to Hsün Tzu, man is not only born without any beginnings of goodness, but, on the contrary, has actual "beginnings" of evilness. In the chapter titled "On the Evilness of Human Nature," Hsün Tzu tries to prove that man is born with inherent desire for profit and sensual pleasure. But, despite these beginnings of evilness, he asserts that man at the same time possesses intelligence, and that this intelligence makes it possible for him to become good. In his own words: "Every man on the street has the capacity of knowing human-heartedness, righteousness, obedience to law and uprightness, and the means to carry out these principles. Thus it is evident that he can become a Yü." (*Ibid.*) Thus whereas Mencius says that any man can become a Yao or Shun, because he is originally good, Hsün Tzu argues that any man can become a Yü, because he is originally intelligent.

● **Origin of Morality**

This leads to the question: How, then, can man become morally good? For if every man is born evil, what is the origin of good? To answer this question, Hsün Tzu offers two lines of argument.

In the first place, Hsün Tzu maintains that men cannot live without some kind of a social organization. The reason for this is that, in order to enjoy better living, men have need of co-operation and mutual support. Hsün Tzu says: "A single individual needs the support of the accomplishments of hundreds of workmen. Yet an able man cannot be skilled in more than one line, and one man cannot hold two offices simultaneously. If people all live alone and do not serve one another, there will be poverty." (Ch. 10.) Likewise, men need to be united in order to conquer other creatures: "Man's strength is not equal to that of the ox; his running is not equal to that of the horse; and yet ox and horse are used by him. How is this? I say that it is because men are able to form social organizations, whereas the others are unable.... When united, men have greater strength; having greater strength, they become powerful; being powerful, they can overcome other creatures." (*Ibid.*)

For these two reasons, men must have a social organization. And in order to have a social organization, they need rules of conduct. These are the *li* (rites, ceremonies, customary rules of living) which hold an important place in Confucianism generally, and are especially emphasized by Hsün Tzu. Speaking about the origin of the *li*, he says: "Whence do the

按孟子的看法，人生来就有仁、义、礼、智"四善端"，人只要充分发展这四善端，就可以成圣。而荀子的看法是，人生来不仅没有善端，倒相反，生来就有恶端。在《性恶》篇中，荀子试图证明，人生来就有贪图利益和感官享受的欲望；但是人又生来就有智性，使人可以成善。在《性恶》篇中，荀子说："涂之人也，皆有可以知仁、义、法、正之质，皆有可以能仁、义、法、正之具，然则其可以为禹，明矣。"孟子认为人皆可以为尧舜，因为人的本性是善的；荀子认为涂人皆可以为大禹，是因为人有智性。

● 道德的根源

由此势必引导到下面的问题：人怎样能够在道德上达到善？如果按荀子所说，人生来就有恶端，那么，善又是从何而来呢？在回答这个问题时，荀子提出两个论据。

首先，荀子指出，人的生存离不开社会组织。若没有在社会组织中的合作和互相支持，人不可能改善自己的生活。在《富国》篇中，他说："百技所成，所以养一人也。而人不能兼技，人不能兼官，离居不相待则穷。"这是从个人求生存的角度来说的。荀子还从人需要在竞争中求生存指出，人"力不若牛，走不若马，而牛马为用，何也？曰：人能群，彼不能群也。……一则多力，多力则强，强则胜物"（《荀子·王制》）。

为这两项理由，人需要社会组织。为使社会组织起来，人们需要有共同的行为准则。因此而需要有礼（用礼来规范人和人之间的关系，如何相待，制定日常生活的共同准则）。儒家一般说来，都重视仪礼，荀子对此更加强调。"礼"是由何而来的呢？荀子在

li arise? The answer is that man is born with desires. When these desires are not satisfied, he cannot remain without seeking their satisfaction. When this seeking for satisfaction is without measure or limit, there can only be contention. When there is contention, there will be disorder. When there is disorder, everything will be finished. The early kings hated this disorder, and so they established the *li* [rules of conduct] and *yi* [righteousness, morality], to set an end to this confusion." (Ch. 19.)

In another chapter, Hsün Tzu writes: "People desire and hate the same things. Their desires are many, but things are few. Since they are few there will inevitably be strife." (Ch. 10.) Hsün Tzu here points to one of the fundamental troubles in human life. If people did not all desire and hate the same things—for instance, if one liked to conquer and the other enjoyed being conquered—there would be no trouble between them and they would live together quite harmoniously. Or, if all the things that everyone desired were very plentiful, like the free air, then too there would be no trouble. Or yet again if people could live quite apart from one another, the problem would be much simpler. But the world is not so ideal. People must live together, and in order to do so without contention, a limit must be imposed on everyone in the satisfaction of his desires. The function of the *li* is to set this limit. When there are the *li*, there is morality. He who acts according to the *li* acts morally. He who acts against them acts immorally.

This is one line of Hsün Tzu's argument to explain the origin of moral goodness. It is quite utilitarianistic, and resembles that of Mo Tzu.

Hsün Tzu also employs another line of argument. He writes: "Man is not truly man in the fact that he, uniquely, has two feet and no hair [over his body], but rather in the fact that he makes social distinctions. Birds and beasts have fathers and offspring, but not the affection between father and son. They are male and female, but do not have the proper separation between males and females. Hence in the Way of Humanity there must be distinctions. No distinctions are greater than those of society. No social distinctions are greater than the *li*." (Ch. 5.)

Here Hsün Tzu points out the difference between what is of nature and what is of culture, or, as Chuang Tzu puts it, what is of nature and what is of man. The fact that birds and beasts have fathers and offspring and that they are either male or female, is a fact of nature. The social relationships between father and son, husband and wife, on the contrary, are products of culture and civilization. They are not gifts of nature,

《礼论》中说："礼起于何也？曰：人生而有欲，欲而不得，则不能无求，求而无度量分界，则不能不争；争则乱，乱则穷。先王恶其乱也，故制礼义以分之，以养人之欲，给人之求，使欲必不穷乎物，物必不屈于欲，两者相持而长，是礼之所起也。"这是说，人生而有欲，有欲就有求，求满足欲望而无节制，必定引起竞争，有争就有乱，乱则一事无成。先王制定礼（个人行为准则）义（道德），就是为了杜绝社会和思想的混乱。

在《富国》篇中，荀子还说："欲恶同物，欲多而物寡，寡则必争矣。"这里，荀子提出人类社会种种问题的根源，就在于人们所爱和所恨的都是同样的东西。举例来说，如果有一个人喜欢征服别人，而另一个人则喜欢被征服，这两个和睦共处便不成问题。再假如人们所喜爱的东西十分丰富，如同空气那么多，那也就不成问题。或者，人们在生活中隔得很远，互不相干，彼此之间的问题也会简单得多。但是，世间不是那样理想的地方，人们必须住在一起，又无法避免竞争，于是对每个人的欲望都不能不加以节制。"礼"的作用就是规定应有的节制。凡建立起"礼"的地方，就形成"道德"；按"礼"而行的人就是有道德的人，违反"礼"的人就是没有道德的人。

这是荀子论述道德和善的起源的一个论点，它的思想基础是功利主义，和墨子的思想很相近。

荀子还使用另一个论据。他在《非相》篇中说："人之所以为人者，非特以其二足而无毛也，以其有辨也。夫禽兽有父子而无父子之亲，有牝牡而无男女之别，故人道莫不有辨。辨莫大于分，分莫大于礼。"

这里，荀子指出了自然和文化的区别，或用庄子的词汇说，何为天，何为人。禽兽有父子、有雌雄，这是自然。在人类社会里，有父子关系、夫妻关系，这是文化和文明的产物。这不是自然的恩赐，

but achievements of spirit. Man should have social relations and the *li*, because it is these that distinguish him from birds and beasts. According to this line of argument, man must have morality, not because he cannot help it, but because he ought to have it. This line of argument is more akin to that of Mencius.

In Confucianism, *li* is a very comprehensive idea. It can be translated as ceremonies, rituals, or rules of social conduct. It is all these, but in the above arguments, it is taken more or less in the third sense. In this sense, the function of the *li* is to regulate. The *li* provide regulation for the satisfaction of man's desires. But in the sense of ceremonies and rituals, the *li* have another function, that of refining. In this sense, the *li* give refinement and purification to man's emotions. In this latter interpretation, Hsün Tzu also made a great contribution.

- **Theory of Rites and Music**

For the Confucianists, the most important of the ceremonies are those of mourning and sacrifice (especially to the ancestors). These ceremonies were universal at that time, and as popularly practiced they contained not a little of superstition and mythology. In justifying them, however, the Confucianists gave them new interpretations and read into them new ideas. These we find in the *Hsün-tzu* and the *Li Chi* or *Book of Rites*.

Among the Confucian classics, there are two devoted to the rites. One is the *Yi Li* or *Book of Etiquette and Ceremonial*, which is a factual record of the procedures of ceremonies as practiced at that time. The other is the *Li Chi*, which consists of the interpretations on the ceremonies given by the Confucianists. I believe that most of the chapters of the *Li Chi* were written by the followers of Hsün Tzu.

Our mind has two aspects, the intellectual and the emotional. When our loved ones die, we know, through our intellect, that the dead are dead and that there is no rational ground for believing in the immortality of the soul. If we were to act solely under the direction of our intellect, therefore, we would need no mourning rites. But since our mind also has its emotional aspect, this causes us, when our loved ones die, to hope that the dead may live again and that there may be a soul that will continue existing in the other world. When we thus give way to our fancy, we take superstition as truth, and deny the judgment of our intellect.

而是人类的精神成就。人应当有社会关系和"礼"，这是区别人与禽兽的标志。按照这个论据，人的道德不是自然产生，而是由于人的需要，这个论点和孟子的论点比较接近。

在儒家思想中，"礼"的含义十分广泛。它可以意味着仪式、礼节或社会行为准则。"礼"可用以指所有这些内容，但在上面的论述中，"礼"的含义更多是指社会行为的准则。这时，礼所起的是规范作用。"礼"在人满足欲望时，加以规范。但是在用于礼节、礼仪时，礼有另一种作用，就是文化教养。在这个意义上，礼净化人的感情，使它纯洁、典雅。在这方面，荀子也做出了巨大的贡献。

● 关于礼乐的学说

在儒家的仪礼中，最重要的是祭（祭神）祀（祀祖先）。在古代，这些仪礼十分普遍，其中自然搀杂有不少迷信和神话的色彩。在《荀子》和《礼记》中可以看到，儒家对祭祀提出了新的解释，赋予它们新的意义。在儒家经典之中，有两部书专谈仪礼。一部是《仪礼》，叙述举行祭祀时的仪式细节。另一部书是《礼记》，内容是对仪礼的解释。据我看，《礼记》中的大部分是荀子门人所作。

人的头脑有两个方面的作用，一方面是智性的作用，另一方面是感情的作用。当我们的亲人去世时，从智性上我们知道，人死不能复生，而且也没有任何凭证表明灵魂永生不灭。如果纯粹按理性来说，为死者举行葬礼，并无需要。但是，人的头脑还有感情的作用。这使我们在亲人去世时，希望他再生，希望死者有一个灵魂，在另一个世界中继续活下去。当我们让这样的幻想在脑中驰骋时，我们把迷信看作真理，而否定了理性的判断。

Thus there is a difference between what we know and what we hope. Knowledge is important, but we cannot live with knowledge only. We need emotional satisfaction as well. In determining our attitude towards the dead, we have to take both aspects into consideration. As interpreted by the Confucianists, the mourning and sacrificial rites did precisely this. I have said that these rites were originally not without superstition and mythology. But with the interpretations of the Confucianists, these aspects were purged. The religious elements in them were transformed into poetry, so that they were no longer religious, but simply poetic.

Religion and poetry are both expressions of the fancy of man. They both mingle imagination with reality. The difference between them is that religion takes what it itself says as true, while poetry takes what it itself says as false. What poetry presents is not reality, and it knows that it is not. Therefore it deceives itself, yet it is a conscious self-deception. It is very unscientific, yet it does not contradict science. In poetry we obtain emotional satisfaction without obstructing the progress of the intellect.

According to the Confucianist, when we perform the mourning and sacrificial rites, we are deceiving ourselves without being really deceived. In the *Li Chi*, Confucius is reported to have said: "In dealing with the dead, if we treat them as if they were really dead, that would mean a want of affection, and should not be done. If we treat them as if they were really alive, that would mean a want of wisdom, and should not be done." (Ch. 2.) That is to say, we cannot treat the dead simply as we know, or hope, them to be. The middle way is to treat them both as we know and as we hope them to be. This way consists in treating the dead as if they were living.

In his "Treatise on Rites," Hsün Tzu says: "The rites are careful about the treatment of man's life and death. Life is the beginning of man, death is his end. If the beginning and end of man are both well treated, the Way of Humanity is complete.... If we render adequate service to our parents when they are living but not when they are dead, that means that we respect our parents when they have knowledge, but neglect them when they do not. One's death means that one is gone forever. That is the last chance for a subject to serve his sovereign, and a son his parents.... The mourning rites serve to decorate the dead by the living, to send off the dead as if they were still living, and to render the same service to the dead as that to the living, a service uniform from the beginning to the end....

这样，人的知识和人的追求便分离了。知识是重要的，但人不是只靠知识活着。我们还有感情上的需要，要求满足。在对待死者的态度上，我们需要同时顾及两个方面。儒家所讲的葬礼和祭祀便是为此而设的。前面讲到，这些葬仪、祭礼，最初都不免带有迷信和神话的色彩，经儒家的重新诠释，剔除了那些迷信和神话色彩，宗教的因素转变成为诗了。它们不再是宗教意味的行动，而成为诗意的了。

宗教和诗都是人在幻想的表现，它们都把想象和现实混合在一起。两者的区别在于：宗教把它所说的看为真的，而诗歌知道它所说是虚幻的。诗歌所提供的不是现实，这是诗人自己知道的，因此，诗人在诗的想象中所做的只是欺骗自己。在这样做时，诗人是自觉的，它不符合科学，但并不反对科学。在诗歌中，人们得到了感情的满足，却并不阻碍智性的发展和追求。

按照儒家的说法，当我们举行丧葬和祀祖的仪式时，我们是在欺骗自己，却又并未真正被欺骗。据《礼记·檀弓》篇所载，孔子曾说："之死而致死之，不仁，而不可为也；之死而致生之，不智，而不可为也。"这就是说，对待死者，既不能完全照着所知道的去做，又不能完全照着所希望的去做。中道则是：既要照着所知道的去做，又要照着所希望的去做，对待已经去世的人就如同对待他们生时那样。

荀子在《礼论》中说："礼者，谨于治生死者也。生，人之始也；死，人之终也；终始俱善，人道毕矣。……夫厚其生而薄其死，是敬其有知而慢其无知也，是奸人之道而背叛之心也。……故死之为道也，一而不可得再复也，臣之所以致重其君，子之所以致重其亲，于是尽矣。""丧礼者，以生者饰死者也，大象其生以送其死也。故如死如生，如亡如存，终始一也。……故丧礼者，无它焉，

Therefore the function of the mourning rites is to make clear the meaning of life and death, to send off the dead with sorrow and respect, and thus to complete the end of man." (Ch. 19.)

In the same chapter, Hsün Tzu says: "The sacrificial rites are the expression of man's affectionate longing. They represent the height of piety and faithfulness, of love and respect. They represent also the completion of propriety and refinement. Their meaning cannot be fully understood except by the sages. The sages understand their meaning. Superior men enjoy their practice. They become the routine of the officer. They become the custom of the people. Superior men consider them to be the activity of man, while ordinary people consider them as something that has to do with spirits and ghosts.... They exist to render the same service to the dead as to the living, to render the same service to the lost as to the existing. What they serve has neither shape nor even a shadow, yet they are the completion of culture and refinement." With this interpretation, the meaning of the mourning and sacrificial rites becomes completely poetic, not religious.

There are other kinds of sacrifice besides those offered to ancestors. These Hsün Tzu interprets from the same point of view. In his chapter titled "Treatise on Nature," one passage reads: "Why is it that it rains after people have offered sacrifice for rain? Hsün Tzu said: 'There is no reason for that. It is the same as if there had been rain without praying for it. When there is an eclipse of the sun and the moon, we make demonstrations to save them. When rain is deficient, we pray for it. And when there are important affairs, we divine before we reach any decision. We do these things not because we can thereby get what we want. They are simply a sort of decorum. The superior man considers them as a sort of decorum, while ordinary people consider them as having supernatural force. One will be happy if one considers them as a sort of decorum; one will not, if one considers them as having supernatural force.'" (Ch. 17.)

We pray for rain, and divine before we make any important decision, because we want to express our anxiety. That is all. If we were to take prayer as really being able to move the gods, or divination as really being able to make predictions about the future, this would result in superstition with all its consequences.

Hsün Tzu is also the author of a "Treatise on Music," in which he writes: "Man cannot be without joy, and when there is joy, it must have a physical embodiment. When this embodiment does not conform to the right principle, there will be disorder. The early kings hated this disorder, and so they established the music of the *Ya* and *Sung* [two of the divisions of the *Book of Odes*] to guide it. They caused its music to be joyful and not degenerate, and its beauty to be distinct and not limited. They caused it in its indirect and direct appeals, its complexity and simplicity, its

明死生之义，送以哀敬而终周藏也。" 这是说，葬礼的作用是向生者表明人生和死亡的意义，以悲痛和尊敬来送别死者，是隆重表示人的一生的完成。

荀子在《礼论》中又说："祭者，志意思慕之情也，忠信爱敬之至矣，礼节文貌之盛矣，苟非圣人，莫之能知也。圣人明知之，士君子安行之，官人以为守，百姓以成俗。其在君子，以为人道也；其在百姓，以为鬼事也。……事死如事生，事亡如事存，状乎无形影，然而成文。" 在这样的解释之中，葬仪和祭礼已不再有宗教的意味，而完全成为诗意的表现了。

除了祀祖之外，还有其他的祭仪。荀子对它们的解释也出自与此相同的观点。《天论》中有一段话说："云而雩，何也？曰：无何也，犹不雩而雨也。日月食而救之，天旱而雩，卜筮然后决大事，非以为得求也，以文之也。故君子以为文，而百姓以为神。以为文则吉，以为神则凶也。"

从这里看荀子的思想，为降雨而祈祷，为做重大决定而占卜，是为了表示重视，不是为了求以得之。如果认为向神祈祷，便能感动神明，或卜筮便能知未来，那将成为迷信，造成迷信的后果。

荀子还曾著有《乐论》，其中说："人不能不乐，乐则不能无形。形而不为道，则不能无乱。先王恶其乱也，故制《雅》《颂》之声以道之，使其声足以乐而不流，使其文足以辨而不谌，使其曲直、

frugality and richness, its rests and notes, to stir up the goodness in men's minds and to prevent evil feelings from gaining any foothold. This is the manner in which the early kings established music." (Ch. 20.) Thus music, for Hsün Tzu, functions as an instrument for moral education. This has been the prevailing Confucianist view of music.

● Logical Theories

In the *Hsün-tzu* there is a chapter titled "On the Rectification of Names." This subject is an old one in Confucianism. The term itself was originated by Confucius, as we have seen in chapter four. He said: "Let the ruler be ruler, the subject be subject; let the father be father and the son be son." (*Analects*, XII, 11.) Likewise Mencius said: "To be without the relationship of ruler and of father is to be like the beasts." (*Mencius*, IVb, 9.) Because the interests of these two thinkers were purely ethical, their application of the rectification of names was likewise confined primarily to the sphere of ethics. Hsün Tzu, however, lived in an age when the School of Names was flourishing. Hence his theory of the rectification of names possesses logical as well as ethical interest.

In his chapter, "On the Rectification of Names," Hsün Tzu first describes his epistemological theory, which is similar to that of the later Mohists. He writes: "That in man by which he knows is [called the faculty of] knowing. That in [the faculty of] knowing which corresponds [to external things] is called knowledge." (Ch. 22.) The faculty of knowing consists of two parts. One is what he calls "the natural senses," such as those of the ears and eyes. The other is the mind itself. The natural senses receive impressions, and the mind interprets and gives meaning to them. Hsün Tzu writes: "The mind gives meaning to impressions. It gives meaning to impressions, and only then, by means of the ear, can sound be known; by means of the eye, can forms be known.... When the five senses note something but cannot classify it, and the mind tries to identify it but fails to give it meaning, then one can only say that there is no knowledge." (*Ibid.*)

As to the origin and use of names, Hsün Tzu says: "Names were made in order to denote actualities, on the one hand so as to make evident the distinctions between superior and inferior [in society], and on the other hand to distinguish similarities and differences." (*Ibid.*) That is to say, names were originated partly for ethical and partly for logical reasons.

繁省、廉肉、节奏足以感动人之善心，使夫邪污之气无由得接焉，是先王立乐之方也。"由此看来，荀子是把音乐作为道德教育的工具，这是儒家对音乐的一般看法。

● 关于逻辑的理论

《荀子》书中有《正名》篇，这是儒家哲学的一个老题目，原本是孔子提出来的（本书第四章已经说到），《论语·颜渊》篇中说："君君，臣臣，父父，子子。"孟子也说："无父无君，是禽兽也。"孔子和孟子两位都关注伦理问题，因此，他们对正名的解释也是就其伦理意义来立论的。荀子所生活的时代是名家十分活跃的时代，因此，他关于正名的理论不仅着眼在伦理，还反映了对逻辑的关注。

在《正名》篇里，荀子首先阐述他对于知识的理论看法，与后期墨家的观点比较接近。他说："所以知之在人者谓之知，知有所合谓之智。"这是说，人所赖以认知的功能称作"知"，人所赖以判断自身的认知与外部世界是否相合的功能称作"智"。人所赖以认知的功能，又分成两部分，一部分是荀子所称的"天官"，如耳目；另一部分是心，即头脑。天官接收印象，头脑则对感官的印象作出解释，说明它们的意义。在《正名》篇里，荀子又说："心有征知。征知，则缘耳而知声可也，缘目而知形可也。……五官簿之而不知，心征之而无说，则人莫不然谓之不知。"这是说，五官可以注意到某些感官收到的印象，但如果一个人不能对它们加以分类，如果头脑不能辨认它们，并赋予意义，则只能说，这个人无知。

关于"名"的由来及其运用，《正名》篇里说："制名以指实，上以明贵贱，下以辨同异。"这是说，"名"的由来，一部分是伦理（即社会）的需要，一部分是由于逻辑思辨的需要。

As to the logical use of names, he says: "Names are given to things. When things are alike, they are named alike; when different, they are named differently.... The one who knows that different actualities have different names, and who therefore never refers to different actualities otherwise than by different names, will not experience any confusion. Likewise he who refers to the same actualities should never use any other but the same names." (*Ibid.*)

Regarding the logical classification of names, he writes further: "Although things are innumerable, there are times when we wish to speak of them all in general, so we call them 'things.' 'Things' is the most general term. We press on and generalize; we generalize and generalize still more, until there is nothing more general. Then only we stop. There are times when we wish to speak of one aspect, so we say 'birds and beasts.' 'Birds and beasts' is the great classifying term. We press on and classify. We classify and classify still more, until there is no more classification to be made, and then we stop."(*Ibid.*) Thus Hsün Tzu distinguishes two kinds of names, the general and the classifying. The general name is the product of the synthetic process of our reasoning, while the classifying name is that of its analytic process.

All names are man-made. When they were in the process of invention, there was no reason why an actuality should be designated by one particular name rather than another. The animal that came to be known as "dog," for example, might equally well have been called "cat" instead. Once, however, certain names came through convention to be applied to certain actualities, they could be attached to these and none other. As Hsün Tzu explains: "There are no names necessarily appropriate themselves. Names were named by convention. But when the convention having been established, it has become customary, this is called an appropriate name." (*Ibid.*)

He also writes: "Should a true King arise, he must certainly follow the ancient terms and make the new ones." (*Ibid.*) Thus the invention of new names and determination of their meanings is a function of the ruler and his government. Hsün Tzu says: "When the kings had regulated names, the names were fixed and actualities distinguished. Their principles were thus able to be carried out, and their will could be known. They thus

关于"名"的逻辑功用，荀子在《正名》篇中说：给事物命名，"同则同之，异则异之……知异实者之异名也，故使异实者莫不异名也，不可乱也，犹使异实者莫不同名也"。这是说，万物各有赋予它们的名字。凡相近的事物，名称也相近；不同的事物，则名称也不同。这样可以使人知道，不同的现实有不同的名字，不致引起混淆。

关于"名"的逻辑分类，荀子说："万物虽众，时而欲遍举之，故谓之物。物也者，大共名也。推而共之，共则有共，至于无共然后止。有时而欲遍举之，故谓之鸟兽。鸟兽也者，大别名也。推而别之，别则有别，至于无别然后止。"这是说，万物虽多不胜数，有时我们想泛指它们的整体，就称之谓"物"。"物"是最最一般性的词语。如果继续泛指外物，势必陷于穷尽。有时，我们想说的是局部，例如，鸟兽。它是分类名词。如果继续这样分类下去，又将陷于穷尽，不得不停止下来。这样，荀子把"名"分为两类：共名、别名。共名是人进行综合思考的产物，别名则是人进行分析思考的产物。

所有的名称都是人的创造。在为万物命名时，何以这样命名，其实都是强加给它们的。称之为"狗"的动物，本来也可以称之为"猫"。但等到一个名字被大众所接受之后，这个"名"和这个"实"的关系便约定俗成了。这便是荀子在《正名》篇所说："名无固宜，约之以命。约定俗成谓之宜。"

荀子还说："若有王者起，必将有循于旧名，有作于新名。"（《正名》）这是说，当一个新的王朝兴起，新的君王和他的政府的职责，首先就是制订一套新的名字。荀子说："故王者之制名，名定而实辨，道行而志通，则慎率民而一焉。故析辞擅作名以乱正名，使民疑惑，人多辩讼，则谓之大奸，其罪犹为符节、度量之罪也。"这是说，新的君王借制订事物名称，推行他的意志；先为大众所知，

carefully led the people to unity. Therefore, the making of unauthorized distinctions between words, and the making of new words, so as thus to confuse the correct nomenclature, cause the people to be in doubt, and bring much litigation, was called great wickedness. It was a crime like that of using false credentials or false measures." (*Ibid.*)

- **Fallacies of Other Schools**

Hsün Tzu considered most of the arguments of the School of Names and the later Mohists to be based upon logical sophistries and so fallacious. He grouped them into three classes of fallacies.

The first is what he calls "the fallacy of corrupting names with names." (*Ibid.*) In this class, he includes the Mohist argument that "to kill a robber is not to kill a man." This is because, according to Hsün Tzu, the very fact of being a robber implies being a man, since by extension the category which bears the name "man" includes the category which has the name "robber." When one speaks of a robber, therefore, one means by this a being who is at the same time a man.

The second class Hsün Tzu calls "the fallacy of corrupting names with actualities." (*Ibid.*) In this group he includes the argument that "mountains and abysses are on the same level," which is a rephrasing by Hsün Tzu of Hui Shih's argument that "mountains and marshes are on the same level." Actualities, being concrete, are individual cases, while names, being abstract, represent general categories or rules. When one tries to disprove general rules by individual exceptions, the result is a corruption of the name by the actuality. Thus a particular abyss that happens to be located on a high mountain may indeed be on the same level as a particular mountain that happens to be on low land. But one cannot infer from this exceptional instance that all abysses are on the same level with all mountains.

The third class is what Hsün Tzu calls "the fallacy of corrupting actualities with names." (*Ibid.*) Here he includes the Mohist argument that "ox-and-horse are not horse," an argument which is the same in kind as Kung-sun Lung's statement that "a white horse is not a horse." If one examines the name of ox-and-horse, one sees that it is indeed not equivalent to that of the name horse. Yet as a matter of fact some of the creatures belonging to the group known as "ox-and-horse" are, as actualities, indeed horses.

Hsün Tzu then concludes that the rise of all these fallacies is due to the fact that no sage-king exists. Were there to be such a sage-king, he

然后领导大众达到统一。如果另立新名，惑乱人心，就是大奸，其罪如同伪造文件、使用假量器一样。

● 论其他学派的谬误

荀子认为，名家和后期墨家的思辨大部分建立在逻辑诡辩上，因而是谬误的。他就运用逻辑上"名"与"实"的关系，把这些谬误分为三类。

第一类谬误是他所称的"惑于用名以乱名"。在这类谬误中，包括后期墨家所称："杀盗非杀人也。"荀子认为，盗意味着他首先是人，"人"的概念，其外延大于"盗"的概念，而且包括"盗"的概念；因此，称"盗"时，同时就指是一个人，杀盗也就是杀其人。

第二类谬误是荀子所称的"惑于用实以乱名"。在这类谬误中包括"山渊平"的论点，这是根据惠施所说"山与泽平"而来。荀子认为，现实是个别的具体化，名则是抽象的一般范畴。用个别去否定一般，势必以实乱名。如果一座高山上有湖泽，这湖泽实际可能和低地的山处在同一平面上。但是，不能以这个例外的个案而推论说，所有的高山和所有的湖泽都一般高。

第三类谬误是荀子所称的"惑于用名以乱实"。公孙龙曾说"白马非马"。墨辩的"牛马非马"和公孙龙的论辩实质上是一样的。如果考察牛马这个名，它确实不能相等于马，但如果实际考察被称为"牛马"的动物，就会发现它们其实是马。这就是荀子所称的"以名乱实"。

荀子总结这三类谬误所以兴起，乃是由于没有圣王。如果

would use his political authority to unify the minds of the people, and lead them to the true way of life in which there is no place or need for disputation and argument.

Hsün Tzu here reflects the spirit of the troubled age of his time. It was an age in which men longed desperately for a political unification which would bring these troubles to an end. Such a unification, though in actual fact one of China only, was regarded, by these people, as equivalent to a unification of the whole world.

Among Hsün Tzu's disciples, the two most famous were Li Ssu and Han Fei Tzu, both of whom were to have a great influence on Chinese history. Li Ssu later became Prime Minister of the First Emperor of the Ch'in dynasty, the man who finally forcibly unified China in 221 B.C. Together with his master, he labored not only for a political but an ideological unification as well, a movement which culminated in the Burning of the Books in 213 B.C. The other disciple, Han Fei Tzu, became a leading figure in the Legalist school which supplied the theoretical justification for this political and ideological unification. The ideas of this school will be described in the next chapter.

有圣王统治，圣王将会运用他的权威以统一大众的思想，引导大众走上人生的正道，那时就不再需要争论和论辩。

荀子的思想反映了他所处的动乱时代。当时，人们渴望政治统一，结束动乱。这种统一在当时称之为"统一天下"，实际上所指的就是统一中国。

在荀子的门生中，最著名的是李斯和韩非子两人，他们两人在中国历史上都有巨大的影响。李斯后来成为秦朝始皇帝手下的宰相。秦始皇在公元前二二一年以武力统一了中国。李斯辅佐秦始皇，不仅在政治上统一中国，而且企图在政治思想上也实行统一。这项方针的具体贯彻最后导致了公元前二一三年的焚书坑儒。荀子的另一个著名学生韩非子，是法家的领袖，他的理论为秦始皇在政治和思想上统一中国的政策提供了理论根据。下一章就介绍这一学派的思想。

⑭ HAN FEI TZU AND THE LEGALIST SCHOOL

The feudalistic society of the early Chou dynasty operated according to two principles: one was that of the *li* (rituals, ceremonies, rules of conduct, mores); the other was that of the *hsing* (penalties, punishments). The *li* formed the unwritten code of honor governing the conduct of the aristocrats, who were known as *chün tzu* (a term literally meaning son of a prince, princely man, or gentleman); the *hsing*, on the contrary, applied only to the people of ordinary birth who were known as *shu jen* (common men) or *hsiao jen* (small men). This is the meaning of the saying in the *Li Chi (Book of Rites)*: "The *li* do not go down to the common people; the *hsing* do not go up to the ministers." (Ch. 10.)

- ● **Social Background of the Legalists**

This was possible because the structure of Chinese feudalistic society was comparatively simple. Kings, princes, and feudal lords were all related to each other either by blood or by marriage. In theory the princes of each state were subordinate to the king, and the feudal lords within these states were in turn subordinate to their prince. But in actual fact, these nobles, having long inherited their rights from their ancestors, came in the course of time to regard these rights as existing independently of their theoretical allegiance to their superiors. Thus the many states that belonged to the hegemony theoretically controlled by the central Chou King were in actual fact semi-independent, and within each of these states there were likewise many semi-independent "houses" of lesser nobles. Being relatives, these various feudatories maintained social and diplomatic contacts, and transacted business, if any, according to their unwritten code of "gentleman's agreements." That is to say, their conduct was governed by *li*.

The kings and princes at the top had no direct dealings with the common people. They left such matters to the lesser feudal lords, each of whom ruled the common people living within his own fief. Since such fiefs were usually not large, their populations were limited. Hence the nobles were able in considerable measure to rule the people under them on a personal basis. Punishments were applied to keep their subjects obedient. Thus we find that in early Chinese feudalistic society, relationships, both high and low, were maintained on a basis of personal influence and personal contact.

拾肆 韩非子与法家

西周封建社会的运转，所依靠的是两项权力原则：礼和刑。礼包括仪文、礼节、举止行为的规定，以及社会习俗所构成的不成文法。它的应用范围只限贵族，称为"君子"（它的字面含义是君王之子，像君王那样举止的人，有文化教养的人）。刑即惩罚，它的应用范围是普通百姓，即"庶人"，或称"小人"（琐小的人）。《礼记》称："礼不下庶人，刑不上大夫。"这说明了这两项原则的不同应用范围。

● 法家的社会背景

中国封建社会得以靠这两条原则而运转，因为西周封建社会的结构相对简单。天子、诸侯、大夫之间，有血缘关系和联姻关系把他们联结在一起。理论上，每一个侯国都从属于周天子，在侯国里，小贵族又从属于王侯大贵族。但实际上，大小诸侯从祖先那里继承领土和贵族特权，年代已久，并不觉得周天子和他们有什么关系。因此，周天子只有名义，并无实权，各侯国事实上处于半独立状态；在这些侯国里的大夫（统率的范围称"家"）也是处于半独立状态。这些王侯彼此都是亲戚，按照大家的不成文法，保持着私人关系、外交关系，以至商业往来。这种"君子协定"式的关系便是"礼"。

天子、诸侯都生活在社会金字塔的顶尖上，和庶民大众没有直接的交道，如果需要打交道，也是由下级诸侯、小贵族去做。王公贵族各有自己的封地，由于这些封地都不大、人口也不多，因此，贵族通常可以实行个人统治，靠刑罚来迫使庶民服从。可以看出，在西周封建社会里，各种社会关系主要是靠个人接触和个人关系来维持的。

The disintegration of this type of society in the later centuries of the Chou dynasty brought with it far-reaching social and political changes. The social distinctions between the class of princely men on the one hand and small men on the other were no longer so absolutely demarcated. Already in the time of Confucius, we see how aristocrats sometimes lost their land and titles, and how members of the common people, either by talent or good luck, succeeded in becoming socially and politically prominent. The old fixity of social classes was breaking down. Likewise, as time wore on, the territories of the larger states became ever larger through aggression and conquest. In order to carry on warfare or prepare for war, these states needed a strong government, that is, a government with a high concentration of power. As a consequence, the structure as well as the functions of government became ever more complex than formerly.

New situations brought with them new problems. Such were the conditions faced by all the rulers of the feudal states of the time, and it was the common endeavor of all the schools of thought since Confucius to solve these problems. Most of their proposed solutions, however, were not realistic enough to be practical. What the rulers needed were not idealistic programs for doing good to their people, but realistic methods for dealing with the new situations faced by their government.

There were certain men who had a keen understanding of real and practical politics. The rulers of the time used to seek the advice of these men, and if their suggestions proved effective, they often became trusted advisers of the rulers, and in some cases became Prime Ministers. Such advisers were known as *fang shu chih shih* or "men of method."

They were so called because they developed methods for governing large areas; methods which left a high concentration of power in the person of the ruler, and which they boasted were foolproof. According to them, it was quite unnecessary that a ruler be a sage or superman. By faithfully applying their methods, a person of even merely average intelligence could govern, and govern well. There were also some "men of method" who went further and supplied a rational justification or theoretical expression for their techniques. It was this that constituted the thought of the Legalist school.

Thus it is wrong to associate the thought of the Legalist school with jurisprudence. In modern terms, what this school taught was the theory and method of organization and leadership. If one wants to organize people and be their leader, one will find that the Legalist theory and practice are still instructive and useful, but only if one is willing to follow totalitarian lines.

这种关系在此后若干世纪里逐渐削弱，西周封建社会制度的瓦解带来了影响深远的社会、政治变化。公侯君子和庶民小人的社会分野逐渐模糊。孔子的时代已经可以看到，有的贵族失去封地和称号，有才能或运气好的庶民百姓，也有的上升到显贵的地位。社会各阶层原有的僵硬界限逐渐被打破。与此同时，大国用侵略、兼并的手法，扩大统治的领土。在这形势下，各国为准备战争或防御入侵，都需要强化国家的统治，就是说，需要集中权力。这就使政府的结构和行使职权都日益复杂化了。

新的形势带来了新的问题，对各国都一样。面对这样的形势，从孔子起的各派思想家都力求解决君王的各种问题。他们建议的解决办法往往并不切合实际，各国君王所爱听的不是劝他们怎样谋求民众的福祉，而是要能应付眼前难题的灵计妙策。

在谋士中也有少数是懂得现实政治的，各国君王通常也愿听听他们有什么看法。如果他们的建议行之有效，国王就待如上宾，甚至委以高位。这些谋士就是被称为"方术之士"的一班人。

他们以此得名，是因为他们为君王公侯出谋划策，告诉统治者怎样统治广大的封地、怎样把权力集中到自己的手里。他们鼓吹：君王不需要是圣人或超人，只要实行他们提出的一套方略，一个仅具中人之资的人就可以把国家治理得井井有条。还有一些方术之士，为他们鼓吹的统治方略提出理论根据，这便构成了法家的思想主张。

因此，如果对"法家"望文生义，以为法家便是主张法学，这便错了。法家的主张，用现代语言来说，乃是一套组织领导的理论和方法。一个人如果想走极权主义道路，组织大众，充当领袖，就会认为法家的理论和方法颇有一点道理。

- Han Fei Tzu, the Synthesizer of the Legalist School

In this chapter, I take Han Fei Tzu as the culminating representative of the Legalist school. He was a descendant of the royal house of the state of Han, in present Western Honan province. The *Shih Chi* or *Historical Records* says of him: "Together with Li Ssu, he studied under Hsün Tzu. Li Ssu considered himself not equal to Han Fei." (Ch. 63.) He was an able writer and composed a lengthy work bearing his name in fifty-five chapters. Ironically enough, it was in Ch'in, the state which more than any other applied his principles and thus conquered the other states, that he died in prison in 233 B.C. The cause was a political intrigue on the part of his former fellow student, Li Ssu, who was an official in Ch'in, and who may have been jealous of the growing favor accorded to Han Fei Tzu.

Before Han Fei Tzu, who was the last and greatest theorizer of the Legalist school, there had been three groups, each with its own line of thought. One was headed by Shen Tao, a contemporary of Mencius, who held that *shih* was the most important factor in politics and government. Another was headed by Shen Pu-hai (died 337 B.C.), who stressed that *shu* was the most important factor. Still another was headed by Shang Yang, also known as Lord Shang (died 338 B.C.), who, for his part, emphasized *fa*. *Shih* means power or authority; *fa* means law or regulation; *shu* means the method or art of conducting affairs and handling men, i.e., "statecraft."

Han Fei Tzu considered all three alike as indispensable. He said: "The intelligent ruler carries out his regulations as would Heaven, and handles men as if he were a divine being. Being like Heaven, he commits no wrong, and being like a divine being, he falls into no difficulties. His *shih* [power] enforces his strict orders, and nothing that he encounters resists him.... Only when this is so can his laws [*fa*] be carried out in concert." (*Han-fei-tzu*, ch. 48.) The intelligent ruler is like Heaven because he acts in accordance with law fairly and impartially. This is the function of *fa*. He is like a divine being, because he has the art of handling men, so that men are handled without knowing how they are handled. This is the function of the *shu*. And he has the authority or power to enforce his orders. This is the function of *shih*. These three together are "the implements of emperors and kings" (ch. 43), no one of which can be neglected.

● **Legalist Philosophy of History**

Perhaps the Chinese traditional respect for past experience stems from the ways of thought of their overwhelmingly agrarian population. Farmers are rooted to the soil and travel but rarely. They cultivate their

● **韩非子，法家的集大成者**

在本章里，便以韩非子作为法家的思想代表。他是韩国（今河南西部）皇室后裔，《史记·老子韩非列传》称他"与李斯俱事荀卿，斯自以为不如非"。韩非子以著书立说见长，著有《韩非子》五十五篇。具有历史讽刺意味的是，战争时代，秦国采用了韩非子的主张，得以兼并六国，成就霸业；韩非子因而声望日隆，由此遭到秦国宰相、他的旧日同窗李斯嫉妒，被陷害下狱，最终死于秦国狱中，时在公元前二三三年。

韩非子是法家的集大成者。在他之前，法家分三派。一派以慎到为首，慎到和孟子是同时代人，他主张在政治和治国方术中，"势"，即权力与威势，最为重要。第二派以申不害（死于公元前三三七年）为首，强调"术"，即政治权术。第三派以商鞅（又称商君，死于公元前三三八年）为首，强调"法"，即法律和规章制度。

韩非子认为这三者都必不可少。他在《韩非子·八经》篇中说："明主之行制也天，其用人也鬼。天则不非，鬼则不困。势行教严，逆而不违，……然后一行其法。"明君如天，执法公正，这是"法"的作用。他驾驭人时，神出鬼没，令人无从捉摸，这是"术"。他拥有威严，令出如山，这是"势"。三者"不可一无，皆帝王之具也"（《韩非子·定法》）。

● **法家的历史哲学**

中国人办事往往依循过去惯例，这可能与大多数民众都是农民有关。农民为所耕种的土地所束缚，很少旅行。他们年复一年，

land in accordance with seasonal changes which repeat themselves year after year. Past experience is a sufficient guide for their work, so that whenever they want to try something new, they first look back to past experience for precedent.

This mentality has influenced Chinese philosophy a great deal, so that since the time of Confucius, most philosophers have appealed to ancient authority as justification for their own teaching. Thus Confucius' ancient authorities were King Wen and the Duke of Chou, of the beginning of the Chou dynasty. In order to improve upon Confucius, Mo Tzu appealed to the authority of the legendary Yü, who supposedly lived a thousand years earlier than King Wen and the Duke of Chou. Mencius, to get the better of the Mohists, went still further back to Yao and Shun, who were supposed to have antedated Yü. And finally the Taoists, in order to gain a hearing for their ideas against those of both the Confucianists and Mohists, appealed to the authority of Fu Hsi and Shen Nung, who were reputed to have lived several centuries earlier than either Yao or Shun.

By thus looking to the past, these philosophers created a regressive view of history. Although belonging to different schools, they all agreed that the golden age of man lies in the past rather than the future. The movement of history since then has been one of progressive degeneration. Hence man's salvation consists not in the creation of something new, but in a return to what has already existed.

To this view of history the Legalists, the last major school of the Chou period, took sharp exception. They fully understood the changing needs of the time and viewed them realistically. Although admitting that the people of ancient times were more innocent and in this sense perhaps more virtuous, they maintained that this was due to material circumstances rather than to any inherent superior goodness. Thus according to Han Fei Tzu, anciently "there were few people but plenty of supplies, and therefore the people did not quarrel. But nowadays people do not consider a family of five children as large, and each child having again five children, before the death of the grandfather there may be twenty-five grandchildren. The result is that there are many people but few supplies, and that one has to work hard for a meager return. So the people fall to quarreling." (*Han-fei-tzu*, ch. 49.)

Because of these completely new circumstances, according to Han Fei Tzu, new problems can only be solved by new measures. Only a fool can fail to realize this obvious fact. Han Fei Tzu illustrates this kind of folly with a story: "There was once a man of Sung who tilled his field. In the midst of the field stood a stem of a tree, and one day a hare in full course

按季节变化耕耘作物，凭过去的经验就够用了。因此，如果遇到新事，首先就想过去有什么经验可以遵循。

这个传统思维方式对中国哲学有巨大的影响。从孔子的时代起，多数哲学家都要找古代的权威来支持自己的学说。孔子喜欢援引的古代权威是西周的文王、周公。墨子与儒家辩论时，援引比文王、周公更古老的夏禹。孟子为能凌驾墨家之上，往往援引尧舜，因为他们是传说中比夏禹更早的圣王。最后，道家为胜过儒家和墨家，又请出伏羲、神农，据说他们比尧舜还要早几百年。

这些哲学家在这样做的时候，事实上是建立了一种历史退化观。这些哲学家，思想主张虽然各有不同，但是，他们的历史观却有一个共同点：人类社会的黄金时代在过去，而不在将来。自古代的"黄金时代"以来，历史是在日渐退化。因此，人的拯救不在于创立新的，而要靠退回到古代去。

先秦时期各主要思想流派中最后出现的法家，在这方面是一个鲜明的例外。法家深深懂得，每个时代的变化，都有它不得不变的原因，因此只能现实地对待世界。古代的人们比较纯朴，就此而言，或许值得称颂，但那是当时的物质条件造成的，并不是说，古代人们的品德就普遍比后代人高尚。韩非子认为，古者，"人民少而财有余，故民不争。……今人有五子不为多，子又有五子，大父未死而有二十五孙。是以人民众而货财寡，事力劳而供养薄，故民争"（《韩非子·五蠹》）。

韩非子认为，由于这些全新的情况产生的新问题，只能用新的方法解决，只有蠢人才看不到事实的变化，而这类蠢人是的确存在的的。韩非子曾说了一个关于蠢人的故事："宋人有耕者，田中有株，

rushed against that stem, broke its neck, and died. Thereupon the man left his plough and stood waiting at that tree in the hope that he would catch another hare. But he never caught another hare and was ridiculed by the people of Sung. If, however, you wish to rule the people of today by the methods of government of the early kings, you do exactly the same thing as the man who waited by the tree.... Therefore affairs go according to their time, and preparations are made in accordance with affairs." (*Ibid.*)

Before Han Fei Tzu, Lord Shang already said similarly: "When the guiding principles of the people become unsuited to the circumstances, their standards of value must change. As conditions in the world change, different principles are practised." (*Book of Lord Shang*, II, 7.)

This conception of history as a process of change is a commonplace to our modern mind, but it was revolutionary viewed against the prevailing theories of the other schools of ancient China.

- **Way of Government**

To meet new political circumstances, the Legalists proposed new ways of government, which, as stated above, they claimed to be infallible. The first necessary step, according to them, was to set up laws. Han Fei Tzu writes: "A law is that which is recorded on the registers, set up in the government offices, and promulgated among the people." (*Han-fei-tzu*, ch. 38.) Through these laws the people are told what they should and should not do. Once the laws are promulgated, the ruler must keep a sharp watch on the conduct of the people. Because he possesses *shih* or authority, he can punish those who violate his laws, and reward those who obey them. By so doing he can successfully rule the people, no matter how numerous they may be.

Han Fei Tzu writes on this point: "In his rule of a state, the sage does not depend upon men doing good themselves, but brings it about that they can do no wrong. Within the frontiers of a state, there are no more than ten people who will do good of themselves; nevertheless, if one brings it about that the people can do no wrong, the entire state can be kept peaceful. He who rules a country makes use of the majority and neglects the few, and so does not concern himself with virtue but with law." (Ch. 50.)

Thus with law and authority, the ruler rules his people. He need

兔走触株，折颈而死；因释其耒而守株，冀复得兔。兔不可复得，而身为宋国笑。今欲以先王之政，治当世之民，皆守株之类也。""是以圣人不期修古，不法常可，论世之事，因为之备。"（同上）

早在韩非子之前，商君便已说过类似的话："民道弊而所重易也，世事变而行道异也。"（《商君书·开塞》）

在现代人看来，历史不断变化，这几乎是众所周知的。但在古代中国，和当时各派思想家的见解相较，这种看法实在是一种革命的观点。

● 治国之道

法家为了适应新的政治情况，建议采用新的方法治理国家。照法家看来，这些是颠扑不破的治国方法，首先是制定法律。韩非子写道："法者，编著之图籍，设之于官府，而布之于百姓者也。"（《韩非子·难三》）法的作用是告诉百姓，什么应该去做，什么不应该做。法律颁布之后，君王必须监察百姓的行为。君王拥有权势，可以惩罚违犯王法的人，也可以奖赏顺服王法的人。君王这样做，就可顺利统治百姓，无论百姓如何为数众多，都可以统治。

关于这一点，韩非子写道："夫圣人之治国，不恃人之为吾善也，而用其不得为非也。恃人之为吾善也，境内不什数；用人不得为非，一国可使齐。为治者用众而舍寡，故不务德而务法。"（《韩非子·显学》）这是说，圣人治国，不是要使人人都自觉行善，而着眼于使大众不能作恶。在一国之中，能自觉行善的，不会超过十个人。但只要民众不作恶，国家就可以保持太平。君王治国，着眼在大多数，至于其他少数，无关宏旨。因此，要着力的是执法，而不是立德。

按照这个理论，君王统治百姓，靠的是法律和威势，他不需要

have no special ability or high virtue, nor need he, as the Confucianists maintained, set a personal example of good conduct, or rule through personal influence.

It may be argued that this procedure is not really foolproof, because the ruler needs ability and knowledge to make laws and keep a watch on the conduct of the people, who may be large in number. The Legalists answer this objection by saying that the ruler need not do all these things himself. If he merely possesses *shu*, the art of handling men, he can then get the right men to do everything for him.

The concept of *shu* is of philosophical interest. It is also one aspect of the old doctrine of the rectification of names. The term used by the Legalists for this doctrine is "holding the actualities responsible for their names." (*Han-fei-tzu*, ch. 43.)

By "actualities," the Legalists mean the individuals who hold government office, while by "names," they mean the titles of the offices thus held. These titles are indicative of what the individuals who hold the office in question should ideally accomplish. Hence "holding the actualities responsible for their names," means holding the individuals who occupy certain offices responsible for carrying out what should be ideally accomplished in these offices. The ruler's duty is to attach a particular name to a particular individual, that is to say, confer a given office upon a given person. The functions pertaining to this office have already been defined by law and are indicated by the name given to it. Hence the ruler need not, and should not, bother about the methods used to carry out his work, so long as the work itself is done and well done. If it is well done, the ruler rewards him; if not, he punishes him. That is all.

It may yet be asked how the ruler is to know which man is the best for a certain office. The Legalists answer that this too can be known by the same *shu* or method of statecraft. Han Fei Tzu says: "When a minister makes claims, the ruler gives him work according to what he has claimed, but holds him wholly responsible for accomplishment corresponding to this work. When the accomplishment corresponds to this work, and the work corresponds to what the man has claimed he could do, he is rewarded. If the accomplishment does not correspond to the work, nor the work correspond to what the man has claimed for himself, he is punished." (Ch. 7.) After this procedure has been followed in several instances, if the ruler is strict in his rewards and punishments, incompetent people will no longer dare to take office even if it is offered to them. Thus all incompetents are eliminated, leaving government positions only to those who can successfully fill them.

有特殊的才能或品德，也不需要像儒家所说，"为政以德，譬如北辰，而众星拱之"，靠君王的品德和人格影响去感召百姓。

有人可以说，君王采取这样的办法治国，需要有能力制定法律，还要监察为数众多的百姓是否违犯了法律，决不是轻而易举的事情。法家对此的回答是：君王不用事必躬亲，只要他有驾驭人的权术，就可以物色到适当的人去为统治者办事。

"术"这个概念有什么哲学意义呢？它也是"正名"这个古老学说中的一方面。法家对"正名"的解说是："循名而责实。"（《韩非子·定法》）

这里的"实"，按法家的学说是指在政府任职的官吏个人；"名"是指政府职务的名称，是任职官吏应当完成的职责。因此，"循名而责实"意味着担任一定职务的官吏有责任完成他的职务所要求的各项工作。君王的职责是把某项名义的职务授给某个人。这项职务所要求的工作已经在法律中明确规定，因此，君王只关心某个官吏是否恪尽职守，至于怎样完成工作要求，这是官吏的事情，不需要君主具体指导。君主所要过问的只是：完成任务有赏，完不成任务受罚，仅此而已。

这样，人们还会问：君王怎样知道哪个人适合哪项工作呢？对此，法家的回答是：只要靠"术"，就可以知道。在《韩非子·二柄》中说："为人臣者陈而言，君以其言授之事，专以其事责其功。功当其事，事当其言，则赏；功不当其事，事不当其言，则罚。"这样认真实行，赏罚分明，经过几次，无能之辈就不敢承担他们力不能胜的职务，即便给他们，他们也不敢接受。这样，没有能力的人就被淘汰下去，只有能胜任的人在政府职务上任职了。

Yet the problem still remains: How is the ruler to know whether an "actuality" does in fact correspond to its "name"? The Legalist reply is that it is up to the ruler himself, if he is uncertain, to test the result. If he is not sure that his cook is really a good cook, he can settle the matter simply by tasting his cooking. He need not always judge results for himself, however. He can appoint others to judge for him, and these judges will then, in their turn, be held strictly responsible for their names.

Thus, according to the Legalists, their way of government is really foolproof. The ruler need only retain the authority of rewards and punishments in his own hands. He will then rule by "doing nothing, yet there is nothing that is not done."

Such rewards and punishments are what Han Fei Tzu calls "the two handles of the ruler." (Ch. 7.) Their effectiveness derives from the fact that it is the nature of man to seek profit and to avoid harm. Han Fei Tzu says: "In ruling the world, one must act in accordance with human nature. In human nature there are the feelings of liking and disliking, and hence rewards and punishments are effective. When rewards and punishments are effective, interdicts and commands can be established, and the way of government is complete." (Ch. 48.)

Han Fei Tzu, as a student of Hsün Tzu, was convinced that human nature is evil. But he differed from Hsün Tzu in that he was not interested in the latter's stress on culture as a means of changing human nature so as to make it something good. According to him and the other Legalists, it is precisely because human nature is what it is, that the Legalist way of government is practical. The Legalists proposed this way of government on the assumption that man is what he is, i.e., naturally evil, and not on the assumption that he is to be converted into what he ought to be.

● Legalism and Taoism

"Doing nothing, yet there is nothing that is not done." This is the Taoist idea of *wu wei*, having-no-activity or non-action, but it is also a

Legalist idea. According to Han Fei Tzu and the Legalists, the one great virtue required of a ruler is that he follow the course of non-action. He should do nothing himself but should merely let others do everything for him. Han Fei Tzu says: "Just as the sun and moon shine forth, the four seasons progress, the clouds spread, and the wind blows, so does the ruler not encumber his mind with knowledge, or himself with selfishness. He relies for good government or disorder upon laws and

但是，还有问题：君王怎样能够知道，某个官吏这个"实"和他所担负的"名"是否相称呢？法家的回答是：这在于君王，如果他没有把握，他就去考察结果，如同君王不知道他的厨子是否胜任，就去品尝厨子烧出的菜肴。在监督官员方面，君王也可以委派别人去做。这些监察官员的人，自己也在君王监察之下。

按照法家的说法，治理国家并不是必须选贤任能，君王只需要把赏罚大权掌握在自己手里就可以了，这样，他就可以"无为而无不为"。

掌握赏罚两项大权，就是韩非子所说的治国"二柄"。它们之所以有效，是因为人性趋利而避害。韩非子说："凡治天下，必因人情。人情者，有好恶，故赏罚可用。赏罚可用，则禁令可立，而治道具矣。"这是说，君王治天下，行事要循人性。人性之中，有所爱，也有所憎，因此，赏罚便能发挥作用。赏罚能起作用，便能做到令行禁止，于是治世之道便已具备了。

韩非子是荀子的学生，深信人性恶。他与荀子不同的地方在于，他对通过文化教育使人向善，不感兴趣。韩非子和其他法家认为，正因为人性恶，所以法家的治国方针，全从实际出发，并不寄希望于把大众改造成新人。

- **法家与道家**

"无为而无不为"。这是道家的思想，它也是法家的思想。在韩非子和法家看来，君王应当具备的一项品质便是"为无为"，自己表现出"无为而治"：君王不应当亲自动手做任何事情，一切需要办的事情都应假手别人去做。韩非子说，君王应如"日月所照，四时所行，云布风动；不以智累心，不以私累己；寄治乱于法术，

methods [*shu*]; leaves right and wrong to be dealt with through rewards and punishments; and refers lightness and heaviness to the balance of the scale." (Ch. 29.) In other words, the ruler possesses the implements and mechanism through which government is conducted, and having these, does nothing, yet there is nothing that is not done.

Taoism and Legalism represent the two extremes of Chinese thought. The Taoists maintained that man originally is completely innocent; the Legalists, on the other hand, that he is completely evil. The Taoists stood for absolute individual freedom; the Legalists for absolute social control. Yet in the idea of non-action, the two extremes meet. That is to say, they had here some common ground.

Under somewhat different wording, the Legalist way of government was also maintained by the later Taoists. In the *Chuang-tzu* we find a passage that speaks about "the way of employing human society." In this passage distinctions are made between having activity and having-no-activity, and between "being employed by the world" and "employing the world." Having-no-activity is the way of employing the world; having-activity is the way of being employed by the world. The ruler's reason for existence is to rule the whole world. Hence his function and duty is not to do things himself, but to tell others to do them for him. In other words, his method of rule is to employ the world by having-no-activity. The duty and function of subordinates, on the other hand, is to take orders and do things accordingly. In other words, the function of the subordinate is to be employed by the world by having activity. The same passage says: "The superior must have no activity, so as thus to employ the world; but the subordinates must have activity, so as thus to be employed by the world. This is the invariable way." (*Chuang-tzu*, ch. 13.)

The *Chuang-tzu* continues: "Therefore, the rulers of old, although their knowledge spread throughout the whole universe, did not themselves think. Although their eloquence beautified all things, they did not themselves speak. Although their abilities exhausted all things within the four seas, they did not themselves act." (*Ibid.*) A ruler should be so, because if he once thinks about something, this means that there is something else about which he does not think; yet his whole duty and function is to think about *all* things under his rule. The solution, therefore, is for him not to try to think, speak, and act himself, but merely to tell others to think, speak, and act in his place. In this way he does nothing, and yet there is nothing that is not done.

托是非于赏罚，属轻重于权衡"（《韩非子·大体》）。换句话说，君王拥有政府运作的机制和工具，他自己不必做任何事情，而执政掌权所要办的事情却都办了。

道家和法家代表中国思想传统的两个极端：道家认为，人本来是天真无邪的，法家则认为人生来性恶；道家鼓吹个人绝对自由，法家主张社会控制一切。但是在"无为"这一点上，两个极端倒会合了，就是说，它们两个极端之间具有同一性。

后期道家对法家所主张的治国之道，也持同样的看法，只是说法略有不同。《庄子·天道》篇中称帝王之德在于"乘天地，驰万物，而用人群"。在这一段里讲"无为也，则用天下而有余；有为也，则为天下用而不足"。在区别"无为"和"有为"之后，又说："上必无为而用天下，下必有为为天下用，此不易之道也。"君主的存在就是为统治天下。因此，他的作用和职责不在于做任何事情，而在于发号施令，让别人为他做事。换句话说，他的统治方法就是：以无为而用天下。另一方面，属下的职责和作用则是接受命令，按令行事。换句话说，属下的作用便是被使用去做事。这就是同一段末后所说："上必无为而用天下，下必有为为天下用，此不易之道也。"

《庄子·天道》篇接下去又说："故古之王天下者，知虽落天地，不自虑也；辨虽雕万物，不自说也；能虽穷海内，不自为也。"统治者就应该如此，因为如果他一旦去思想任何事情，就表明还有他未曾想的事情，而他的职责本应该想到在他统治下的一切事情。因此，君王就应该不想、不说、不做；只命令别人替他去想、去说、去做。这样，他便可以无为，而凡事都由别人办好了。

As to the detailed procedure by which the ruler is thus to "employ the world," the same passage says: "Those of old who made manifest the great *Tao*, first made manifest Heaven, and *Tao* and *Te* came next. *Tao* and *Te* being manifested, the virtues of human-heartedness and righteousness came next. These being manifested, the division of offices came next. These being manifested, actualities and names came next. These being manifested, employment without interference came next. This being manifested, examinations and discriminations came next. These being manifested, judgment of right and wrong came next. This being manifested, rewards and punishments came next. With the manifestation of rewards and punishments, the foolish and the wise assumed their proper positions, the noble and the humble occupied their proper places, and the virtuous and the worthless were employed according to their nature.... This is perfect peace, the acme of good government." (*Ibid.*)

It is clear that the latter part of this program is the same as that of the Legalists. Yet the passage goes on by saying: "Those of antiquity who spoke about the great *Tao*, mentioned actualities and names only at the fifth step, and rewards and punishments only at the ninth step. He who speaks immediately about actualities and names, does not know the fundamentals [that underlie them]. He who speaks immediately about rewards and punishments, does not know their beginning.... Such a one knows the implements of government, but not its principles. He can be employed by the world, but is not sufficient to employ the world. He is a one-sided man and only knows how to talk." (*Ibid.*)

Here we have the criticism of the Taoists against the Legalists. The Legalist way of government requires unselfishness and impartiality on the part of the ruler. He must punish those who ought to be punished, even though they be his friends and relatives, and he must reward those who ought to be rewarded, even though they be his enemies. If he fails only a few times to do this, the whole mechanism breaks down. Such requirements are too much for a man of only average intelligence. He who can really fulfill them is nothing less than a sage.

The Confucianists maintained that the people should be governed by *li* and morality, not by law and punishment. They upheld the traditional way of government, but did not realize that the circumstances that had once rendered this way practical had already changed. In this respect, they were conservative. In another respect, however, they were at the same time revolutionary, and reflected in their ideas the changes of the

至于君王用天下的具体步骤，《天道》篇中说："是故古之明大道者，先明天而道德次之，道德已明而仁义次之，仁义已明而分守次之，分守已明而形名次之，形名已明而因任次之，因任已明而原省次之，原省已明而是非次之，是非已明而赏罚次之，赏罚已明而愚知处宜，贵贱履位；仁贤不肖袭情，必分其能，必由其名。以此事上，以此畜下，以此治物，以此修身，知谋不用，必归其天，此之谓太平，治之至也。"

这些具体步骤的后半，显然和法家的主张是一样的。但是，《天道》篇接下去说："古之语大道者，五变而形名可举，九变而赏罚可言也。骤而语形名，不知其本也；骤而语赏罚，不知其始也。倒道而言，忤道而说者，人之所治也，安能治人！骤而语形名赏罚，此有知治之具，非知治之道；可用于天下，不足以用天下，此之谓辩士，一曲之人也。"

这是道家对法家的批判。法家的治国之道要求君王公正无私。他应当赏罚严明，即便当罚的是亲人朋友，也不徇私；即便当赏的人是仇人，也不歧视。如果君王不能公正无私，哪怕只失误几次，整个机制便将崩溃。法家宣称只要具有中人之资，便能治国，而实际上，只有圣人，才能具备君王的资质。

● **法家与儒家**

儒家认为，要靠礼和道德，而不是靠法律与刑罚来治理百姓。他们主张沿用西周初期的体制，而没有觉察到，社会情况已经变化，先前推行礼治的社会条件已经不复存在了。这时，他们还指望靠老办法治国，就成为保守派了。但在另一方面，他们又是革命派，因为在他们的思想里，反映了时代的变化，他们不再坚持以

time. Thus they no longer upheld the traditional class distinctions that were based merely on the accident of birth or fortune. Confucius and Mencius, to be sure, continued to speak about the difference between the princely man and the small man. Yet for them, this distinction depended upon the moral worth of the individual, and was not necessarily based upon inherited class differences.

I pointed out at the beginning of this chapter that in early Chinese feudalistic society, the nobles were governed according to the *li*, but the common people only according to the punishments. Hence the Confucian insistence that not only the nobles, but the mass of the people as well, should be governed by *li* rather than by punishment, was in fact a demand for a higher standard of conduct to be applied to the people. In this sense the Confucianists were revolutionary.

In Legalist thought, too, there were no class distinctions. Everyone was equal before law and the ruler. Instead of elevating the common people to a higher standard of conduct, however, the Legalists lowered the nobles to a lower standard by discarding *li* and putting sole reliance on rewards and punishments for all alike.

The Confucianist ideas are idealistic, while those of the Legalists are realistic. That is the reason why, in Chinese history, the Confucianists have always accused the Legalists of being mean and vulgar, while the Legalists have accused the Confucianists of being bookish and impractical.

出身贵贱和财产多少来划分社会阶级。孔子和孟子还继续强调君子和小人的分野，但这个分野，现在变成以道德来划分，而不是以家世来划分了。

本章开始时，我曾指出，先秦中国封建社会里，"礼"是君王统治贵族的准绳，"刑"是君王统治百姓的工具。儒家坚持以礼治国，这样，"礼"不仅是统治贵族的准绳，也成为统治庶民百姓的准绳，这是对庶民百姓提出了更高的要求。就这一点说，儒家是革命的。

法家的思想也和儒家一样，没有社会阶级高下的区别。人人在法律和统治者面前，地位都一样。但是，法家所做的不是把庶民的地位提高，而是把贵族的地位降低，靠奖惩来统治一切人，这就把"礼"抛到一边去了。

儒家的主张是理想主义的，法家的主张是现实主义的。在中国历史上，儒家一向指责法家卑鄙、粗野，而法家则总是指责儒家书生气、不切实际。

ⓖ CONFUCIANIST METAPHYSICS

In chapter twelve we have seen that the *Yi Ching* or *Book of Changes* (also known simply as the *Yi*) was originally a book of divination. Later the Confucianists gave it cosmological, metaphysical, and ethical interpretations, which constitute the "Appendices" now found in the *Book of Changes.*

The cosmological theory contained in the "Appendices" has already been considered in chapter twelve, and we shall revert to it again in chapter twenty-three. In the present chapter we shall confine ourselves to the metaphysical and ethical theories found in the "Appendices" and in the *Chung Yung.*

The *Chung Yung* or *Doctrine of the Mean* is one of the chapters in the *Li Chi* (*Book of Rites*). According to tradition, it was written by Tzu-ssu, the grandson of Confucius, but in actual fact a large part of it seems to have been written at a somewhat later date. The "Appendices" and the *Chung Yung* represent the last phase in the metaphysical development of ancient Confucianism. So great is their metaphysical interest, indeed, that the Neo-Taoists of the third and fourth centuries A.D. considered the *Yi* as one of the three major classics of speculative philosophy, the others being the *Lao-tzu* and *Chuang-tzu*. Similarly, Emperor Wu (502-549) of the Liang dynasty, himself a Buddhist, wrote commentaries on the *Chung Yung*, and in the tenth and eleventh centuries, monks of the Ch'an sect of Buddhism also wrote such commentaries, which marked the beginning of Neo-Confucianism.

• The Principles of Things

The most important metaphysical idea in the "Appendices," as in Taoism, is that of *Tao*. Yet it is quite different from the concept of *Tao* of the Taoists. For the latter, *Tao* is nameless, unnamable. But for the authors of the "Appendices," not only is *Tao* namable, but, strictly speaking, it is *Tao* and *Tao* only that is thus namable.

We may distinguish between the two concepts by referring to the *Tao* of Taoism as the *Tao*, and to that of the "Appendices" as *tao*. The *Tao* of Taoism is the unitary "that" from which springs the production and change of all things in the universe. The *tao* of the "Appendices," on the contrary, are multiple, and are the principles which govern each separate category of things in the universe. As such, they are somewhat analogous

拾伍 儒家的形而上学

　　在第十二章里，我们看到，《易经》本来是一部占卜的书。后来，儒家赋予它以宇宙论、形而上学的意义，并且从宇宙论联系到伦理，进行阐释，这便是现在附于《易经》之后的"易传"。

　　在第十二章里，已经讨论了"易传"的宇宙论解释。本书第二十三章还将回到儒家赋予《易经》的宇宙论意义这个问题上来，本章的探讨则将限于"易传"和《中庸》的形而上学的伦理学说方面。

　　《中庸》是《礼记》中的一章，按照传统的说法，它是孔子的孙子子思所作。事实上，其中大部分是后来的著作。"易传"和《中庸》代表了先秦儒家形而上学发展的最后阶段。这一时期儒家对形而上学的兴趣如此浓厚，以至公元三、四世纪的新道家把《易经》和《道德经》、《庄子》三部书列为"三玄"。公元六世纪上半叶，笃信佛教的梁武帝（公元五〇二至五四九年在位）亲自为《中庸》写注释。公元十到十一世纪（宋朝）佛教禅宗的僧人也写作这样的注释，由此开启了"新儒家"的时代。

● 事物之"理"

　　道是"易传"，也是道家认为最重要的形而上学概念。但是，"易传"中的"道"的观念和道家的"道"的观念是不同的。道家的"道"的观念是无名、不可名状的，而在"易传"的作者们心目中，"道"是可以名状的，而且严格说来，也只有"道"是可以名状的。

　　我们需要把道家所说的"道"和"易传"所说的道加以区别。道家所说的"道"是宇宙万物及其变化所由产生的那个"一"。"易传"中的道则是"多"，是统辖宇宙万物中每类事物的个别的"理"。

to the concept of the "universal" in Western philosophy. Kung-sun Lung, as we have seen, regarded hardness as a universal of this kind, since it is this hardness that enables concrete objects in our physical universe to be hard. Likewise, in the terminology of the "Appendices," that by which hard things are hard would be called the *tao* of hardness. This *tao* of hardness is separable from the hardness of individual physical objects, and constitutes a namable metaphysical principle.

There are many such *tao*, such as the *tao* of sovereignship and of ministership, or of fatherhood and sonhood. They are what a sovereign, a minister, a father, and a son *ought* to be. Each of them is represented by a name, and an individual should ideally act according to these various names. Here we find the old theory of the rectification of names of Confucius. In him, however, this was only an ethical theory, whereas in the "Appendices" it becomes metaphysical as well.

The *Yi*, as we have seen, was originally a book of divination. By the manipulation of the stalks of the milfoil plant, one is led to a certain line of a certain hexagram, the comments on which in the *Yi* are supposed to provide the information one is seeking. Hence these comments are to be applied to the various specific cases in actual life. This procedure led the authors of the "Appendices" to the concept of the formula. Seeing the *Yi* from this point of view, they considered the comments on the hexagrams and the individual lines of these hexagrams as formulas, each representing one or more *tao* or universal principles. The comments on the entire sixty-four hexagrams and their 384 individual lines are thus supposed to represent all the *tao* in the universe.

The hexagrams and their individual lines are looked upon as graphic symbols of these universal *tao*. "Appendix III" says: "The *Yi* consists of symbols." Such symbols are similar to what in symbolic logic are called variables. A variable functions as a substitute for a class or a number of classes of concrete objects. An object belonging to a certain class and satisfying certain conditions can fit into a certain formula with a certain variable; that is, it can fit into the comment made on a certain hexagram or a certain line within a hexagram, these hexagrams or lines being taken as symbols. This formula represents the *tao* which the objects of this class ought to obey. From the point of view of divination, if they obey it, they

就这一点来说，它有点像西方哲学中的"共相"。我们曾经看到，公孙龙认为"坚"就是使得宇宙间事物坚硬的那个"理"。"易传"的作者们也同样认为，使得物质坚硬的乃是坚硬之道。这个"坚硬之道"可以和个别物质的坚硬性分离出来，成为可以名状的形而上学原理。

像这样的"道"——形而上学原理——可以举出很多，如君王之道、大臣之道、为父之道、为子之道，等等。这是作为君主、大臣、父亲、儿子的规范。它们各有其名，每个人由于社会地位也就此有了自己的称谓名字，而且应当按这种社会地位规定的名字去圆满完成它的内容。这令人想起孔子关于"正名"的古老学说。就孔子来说，这只是他的伦理学说，而在"易传"里，它还构成了形而上学的一部分。

如前所述，《易经》本是一部占卜之书。巫者取一把蓍草，每两根一次，取出放在一旁，最后剩下的或是单数，或是双数，记录下来，这样连续六次，所得结果就构成一卦。《易经》中对这一卦的卦辞就应是神对卜者所求问事项的指示。这些卦辞、爻辞要准备回答各种世俗事务、各种情况下的问题。"易传"的作者们根据这种情况，需要制定各种标准答案，这些卦辞、爻辞就是回答求问事项的各种公式。每一卦都代表一种或几种"道"，也就是事物的普遍性原理。对六十四卦和三百八十四爻的释辞就被认为其中包括了宇宙所有的"道"。

这些卦和爻被看作是宇宙之道的图像。这就是"易传"中《系辞下》所说："易者，象也。"这些象征和现代符号逻辑（symbolic logic）所称的"变数"很相近。在这里，变数的作用是作为某类或某些类具体事物的替代物。属于某一类别，并且满足某些条件的一个具体事物，可以纳入某个公式和某个变数，因此也可以纳入某个卦辞和爻辞所说的内容。在这里，卦和爻就是这事物的符号或象征。这个公式便代表着某种道，成为某类对象所应当遵循的指示。

will enjoy good luck, but if not, they will suffer bad fortune. From the point of view of moral teaching, if they obey it, they are right, but if not, they are wrong.

The first of the sixty-four hexagrams, *Ch'ien*, for example, is supposed to be the symbol of virility, while the second hexagram, *K'un*, is that of docility. Everything that satisfies the condition of being virile can fit into a formula in which the symbol of *Ch'ien* occurs, and everything that satisfies the condition of being docile can fit into one in which the symbol of *K'un* occurs. Hence the comments on the hexagram *Ch'ien* and its individual lines are supposed to represent the *tao* for all things in the universe that are virile; those on the hexagram *K'un* and its individual lines represent the *tao* for all things that are docile.

Thus in "Appendix I," the section dealing with the hexagram *K'un* says: "If it takes the initiative, it will become confused and lose the way. If it follows, it will docilely gain the regular [way]." And in "Appendix IV": "Although the *Yin* has its beauties, it keeps them under restraint in its service of the king, and does not dare to claim success for itself. This is the *tao* of Earth, of a wife, of a subject. The *tao* of Earth is, not to claim the merit of achievement, but on another's behalf to bring things to their proper issue."

Quite the opposite is the hexagram of *Ch'ien*, the symbol of Heaven, of a husband, of a sovereign. The judgments made on this hexagram and its individual lines represent the *tao* of Heaven, of a husband, of a sovereign.

Hence if one wants to know how to be a ruler or a husband, one should look up what is said in the *Yi* under the hexagram *Ch'ien*, but if one wants to know how to be a subject or a wife, one should look under the hexagram *K'un*. Thus in "Appendix III" it is said: "With the expansion of the use of the hexagrams, and the application of them to new classes, everything that man can do in the world is there." Again: "What does the *Yi* accomplish? The *Yi* opens the door to the myriad things in nature and brings man's task to completion. It embraces all the governing principles of the world. This, and no more or less, is what the *Yi* accomplishes."

It is said that the name of the *Yi* has three meanings: (1) easiness and simpleness, (2) transformation and change, and (3) invariability.[1] Transformation and change refers to the individual things of the universe. Simpleness and invariability refers to their *tao* or underlying principles.

从占卜的观点说，如果遵从卦辞、爻辞的指示，卜者就会得到好运，否则就将遭到厄运。从伦理的观点看，遵从这些卦辞和爻辞，就是"对"的，否则就是"错"的。

以六十四卦的第一卦"乾"来说，它是雄性的代表，也是雄浑、雄劲；以第二卦"坤"来说，它是雌性、温良、驯顺的代表。因此，任何能满足"雄浑"条件的事物，都可以纳入"乾"象；任何能满足雌性、温良条件的事物，都可以纳入"坤"象。乾的卦辞和爻辞都可以认为是代表了宇宙万物中雄性事物的"道"；坤的卦辞和爻辞则可以认为是代表了宇宙万物中雌性事物的"道"。

因此，"易传"《象辞》论到坤卦说："先，迷失道；后，顺得常。"这是说，如果居先，将迷失道路；如果居后，则将顺利而得常道。"易传"《坤文言》说："阴虽有美，含之以从王事，弗敢成也。地道也，妻道也，臣道也。地道无成而代有终也。"这是说，阴虽美，却含蓄以事君，不敢居功。这是大地之道，为妻、为臣之道，大地从不居功，只代万物以成其事。

乾卦则正相反。它是天的象征，君王的象征，夫婿的象征。乾的卦辞、爻辞代表天道、君主之道、为夫之道。

因此，如果一个人要想知道为君之道、为夫之道，就应当读"易传"《乾文言》。如果一个人要想知道为臣之道、为妻之道，就应该读坤卦的卦辞、爻辞。这就是"易传"《系辞上》所说：把卦辞"引而申之，触类而长之，天下之能事毕矣"。又说："夫易，何为者也？夫易：开物成务（开启物性，助人成就事务），冒（覆盖）天下之道，如斯而已者也。"

《易纬·乾凿度》说："易，一名而含三义：所谓易也，变易也，不易也。"这是说，"易"既意味简易，又意味着变化，又意味着不变。变化是指万物而言，简易不变是指其中之"道"而言。事物

Things ever change, but *tao* are invariable. Things are complex, but *tao* are easy and simple.

● **The *Tao* of the Production of Things**

Besides the *tao* of every class of things, there is another *Tao* for all things as a whole. In other words, besides the specific multiple *tao*, there is a general unitary *Tao* which governs the production and transformation of all things. "Appendix III" says: "One *Yang* and one *Yin*: this is called the *Tao*. That which ensues from this is goodness, and that which is completed thereby is the nature [of man and things]." This is the *Tao* of the production of things, and such production is the major achievement of the universe. In "Appendix III" it is said: "The supreme virtue of Heaven is to produce."

When a thing is produced, there must be that which is able to produce it, and there must also be that which constitutes the material from which this production is made. The former is the active element and the latter the passive one. The active element is virile and is the *Yang*; the passive element is docile and is the *Yin*. The production of things needs the cooperation of these two elements. Hence the words: "One *Yang* and one *Yin*: this is the *Tao*."

Everything can in one sense be *Yang* and in another sense *Yin*, according to its relation with other things. For instance, a man is *Yang* in relation to his wife, but *Yin* in relation to his father. The metaphysical *Yang* which produces all things, however, can only be *Yang*, and the metaphysical *Yin* out of which everything is produced can only be *Yin*. Hence in the metaphysical statement: "One *Yang* and one *Yin*: this is called the *Tao*," the *Yin* and *Yang* thus spoken of are *Yin* and *Yang* in the absolute sense.

It is to be noticed that two kinds of statement occur in the "Appendices." The first consists of statements about the universe and the concrete things in it; the other consists of statements about the system of abstract symbols of the *Yi* itself. In "Appendix III" it is said: "In the *Yi* there is the Supreme Ultimate which produces the Two Forms. The Two Forms produce the Four Emblems, and these Four Emblems produce the eight trigrams." Although this saying later became the foundation of the metaphysics and cosmology of the Neo-Confucianists, it does not refer to the actual universe, but rather to the system of symbols in the *Yi*. According to the "Appendices," however, these symbols and formulas

常变，但其中的道是不变的。万物是复杂的，但道是简单易明的。

● 万物生成之"道"

各类事物各有自身的"道"以外，万物又有其共同的"道"。换句话说，除了物各有殊的"道"之外，还有统摄万物生成变化的一个总的"道"。《系辞上》说："一阴一阳之谓道。继之者善也，成之者性也。"这是生成万物的"道"。宇宙便以生成万物作为它的最大成就，所以《系辞下》说："天地之大德曰生。"

世上有一物生成，必定有生成该物的物质，还有该物生成的依据。前者可以说是一物生成的被动因素，后者可以说是一物生成的主动因素。被动因素是阴，主动因素是阳。万物生成需要阴、阳两个因素的互相作用。因此，"一阴一阳之谓道"。

每一样事物都可以从一个意义说是阴，从另一个意义说则是阳，这取决于它和其他事物的关系。例如，一个男子，对妻子说，他是阳；而作为父亲的儿子，他是阴。但生成万物的阳，就其形而上的意义说，只能是阳；万物所由生的阴，就其形而上的意义说，只能是阴。因此，《系辞上》所说的"一阴一阳之谓道"，其中的"阴"和"阳"都是就其绝对意义而说的。

需要注意到，在"易传"中有两类不同的陈述句：一类是关于宇宙和其中包含的万物，另一类则是关于《易经》本身抽象符号的体系。《系辞上》说："易有太极，是生两仪，两仪生四象，四象生八卦。"虽然后来新的儒家把这几句话作形而上学和宇宙论的基础，这几句话并不是指宇宙的生成，而是指《易经》中的符号系统。但是"易传"中认为：《易》与天地准。"这是说，在宇宙之中有这些

have their exact counterparts in the universe itself. Hence the two kinds of statement are really interchangeable. Thus the saying, "one *Yang* and one *Yin*: this is called *Tao*," is a statement about the universe. Yet it is interchangeable with the other saying that "in the *Yi* there is the Supreme Ultimate which produces the Two Forms." The *Tao* is equivalent to the Supreme Ultimate, while the *Yin* and *Yang* correspond to the Two Forms.

"Appendix III" also states: "The supreme virtue of Heaven is to produce." Again: "To produce and to reproduce is the function of the *Yi*." Here again are two kinds of statement. The former relates to the universe, and the latter to the *Yi*. Yet they are at the same time interchangeable.

- ### The *Tao* of the Transformation of Things

One meaning of the name *Yi*, as we have seen, is transformation and change. The "Appendices" emphasize that all things in the universe are ever in a process of change. The comment on the third line of the eleventh hexagram states: "There is no level place without a bank, and no departure without a return." This saying is considered by the "Appendices" as the formula according to which things undergo change. This is the *Tao* of the transformation of all things.

If a thing is to reach its completion and the state of completion is to be maintained, its operation must occur at the right place, in the right way, and at the right time. In the comments of the *Yi*, this rightness is usually indicated by the words *cheng* (correct, proper) and *chung* (the mean, center, middle). As to *cheng* "Appendix I" states: "The woman has her correct place within, and the man has his correct place without. The correctness of position of man and woman is the great principle of Heaven and Earth.... When the father is father, and the son son; when the elder brother is elder brother, and the younger brother younger brother; when husband is husband, and wife wife: then the way of the family is correct. When it is correct, all under Heaven will be established."

Chung means neither too much nor too little. The natural inclination of man is to take too much. Hence both the "Appendices" and the *Lao-tzu* consider excess a great evil. The *Lao-tzu* speaks about *fan* (reversal, ch. 40) and *fu* (returning, ch. 16), and the "Appendices" also speak about *fu*. Among the hexagrams, indeed, there is one titled *Fu* (the 24th hexagram). "Appendix I" says about this hexagram: "In *Fu* we see the mind of Heaven and Earth."

Using this concept of *fu*, "Appendix VI" interprets the order of

符号和公式的确切对应物。因此，这两类陈述又能够互相对换。以"一阴一阳之谓道"这句话来说，这是指宇宙而言，但它和《系辞上》所说"易有太极，是生两仪"又是可以互换的。"道"和"太极"是相当的，而阴和阳则是它的两种形式，即"两仪"。

《系辞下》又说"天地之大德曰生"，它与《系辞上》所说"生生之谓易"是两种不同性质的陈述句。前者联系到宇宙，后者则联系到《易经》，但它们又是可以相互替换的。

● **万物变易之"道"**

"易"这个字的三重含义中有一重含义是"变化、变易"。"易传"强调的一点是：宇宙万物都处于不断变化之中。泰卦九三爻辞说："无平不陂，无往不复。"在"易传"中，把这句爻辞看作是万物变化的公式，是万物变易之"道"。

如果一个事物要达到生长的顶点，并且保持在生长的顶点上，它的运行就必须在所发生的地点、时间和发生的方式上都恰到好处。在《易经》的卦辞、爻辞中，把这种"恰到好处"称作"正""中"。关于"正"，《易·家人卦》的《象辞》说："女正位乎内，男正位乎外；男女正，天地之大义也。……父父，子子，兄兄，弟弟，夫夫，妇妇，而家道正；正家而天下定矣。"

"中"的含义是既不过多，又不过少。人的天性倾向于过分。因此，"易传"和《老子》都把过分看作大恶。《老子》书第四十章讲"反"，第十六章讲"复"；"易传"也讲"复"。在《易经》中，第二十四卦便是"复"。它的《象辞》说："复，其见天地之心乎！"这是说，复卦的卦象，体现了天地运行的规律。

"易传"的《序卦》运用"复"的概念来解说六十四卦的排列

arrangement of the sixty-four hexagrams. The *Yi* was originally divided into two books. This "Appendix" considers the first of these as dealing with the world of nature, and the second as dealing with that of man. Concerning the first book, it says: "Following the existence of Heaven and Earth, there is the production of all things. The space between Heaven and Earth is full of all these things. Hence [the hexagram] *Ch'ien* [Heaven] and [the hexagram] *K'un* [Earth] are followed by the hexagram *Tun*, which means fullness." Then the "Appendix" tries to show how each hexagram is usually followed by another which is opposite in character.

About the second book, this same "Appendix" says: "Following the existence of Heaven and Earth, there is the existence of all things. Following the existence of all things, there is the distinction of male and female. Following this distinction, there is the distinction between husband and wife. Following this distinction, there is the distinction between father and son. Following this distinction, there is the distinction between sovereign and subject. Following this distinction, there is the distinction between superiority and inferiority. Following this distinction, there are social order and justice." Then, as in the case of the first part of the *Yi*, the "Appendix" tries to show how one hexagram is usually followed by another which is opposite in character.

The sixty-third hexagram is *Chi-chi*, which means something accomplished. At this point this "Appendix" says: "But there can never be an end of things. Hence *Chi-chi* is followed by *Wei-chi* [the sixty-fourth hexagram, meaning something not yet accomplished]. With this hexagram, [the *Yi*] comes to a close."

According to this interpretation, the arrangement of the hexagrams implies at least three ideas: (1) that all that happens in the universe, natural and human alike, forms a continuous chain of natural sequence; (2) that in the process of evolution, everything involves its own negation; and (3) that in the process of evolution, "there can never be an end of things."

The "Appendices" agree with the *Lao-tzu* that in order to do something with success, one must be careful not to be too successful; and that in order to avoid losing something, one must complement it with something of its opposite. Thus "Appendix III" says: "The man who keeps danger in mind is one who retains his position. The man who keeps ruin in mind is one who survives. The man who has disorder in mind is one who has peace. Therefore, the superior man, when all is peaceful, does not forget danger. When he is acting, he does not forget about ruin. When he has society under control, he does not forget disorder. Hence it is possible, with his own person secure, for him to protect the state."

顺序。《易经》本来分《上经》《下经》两部分。《序卦》认为：上经是讲自然世界，下经则是讲人间世界。关于上经，在《序卦》中说："有天地，然后万物生焉。盈天地之间者，唯万物，故受之以屯。屯者，盈也。"因此，在《易经》中，继乾（天）卦坤（地）卦之后，第三卦便随之以屯卦，屯的含义是满足。《序卦》接下去指出，每一卦之后，往往随之以性质相反的卦象，相反相成而相满足。

关于下经，《序卦》中说："有天地，然后有万物；有万物，然后有男女；有男女，然后有夫妇；有夫妇，然后有父子；有父子，然后有君臣；有君臣，然后有上下；有上下，然后礼义有所错。"然后，如同上经说明一样，《序卦》继以说明，每卦之后，通常总是与它性质相反的一卦。

第六十三卦是"既济"，含义是"事成"。《序卦》就此说道："物不可穷也，故受之以未济，终焉。"这是说，在"既济"之后，继以"未济"，表明事虽成，而犹有未成。《易》到此结束。

这样来解释《易》六十四卦的排列，其中至少包含有三点意义：第一，宇宙中发生的一切，包括自然和人生，构成一种连绵不断的自然顺序锁链。第二，在这样的演化过程中，每一事物都处于向自我否定的运动之中。第三，在这样的演化过程中，事物永无穷尽。

"易传"和《老子》持守一样的看法：人若想做成一点事情，就不要指望一帆风顺，马到成功；若想不失去已有的东西，就要从事物的反面多着想一点。这就是《系辞下》所说："危者，安其位者也；亡者，保其存者也；乱者，在其治者也。是故，君子安而不忘危，存而不忘亡，治而不忘乱，是以身安而国家可保也。"

The "Appendices" also agree with the *Lao-tzu* that modesty and humbleness are the great virtues. "Appendix I" remarks: "It is the way of Heaven to diminish the swollen and augment the modest. It is the way of Earth to subvert the swollen and give free course to the modest.... It is the way of man to hate the swollen and love the modest. Modesty, in a high position, sheds luster on it; in a low position it cannot be passed by unobserved. This is the final goal of the superior man."

● The Mean and Harmony

The idea of *chung* is fully developed in the *Chung Yung* or *Doctrine of the Mean*. *Chung* is like the Aristotelian idea of the "golden mean." Some would understand it as simply doing things no more than halfway, but this is quite wrong. The real meaning of *chung* is neither too much nor too little, that is, just right. Suppose that one is going from Washington to New York. It will then be just right to stop at New York, but to go right through to Boston, will be to do too much, and to stop at Philadelphia, will be to do too little. In a prose poem by Sung Yü of the third century B.C., he describes a beautiful girl with the words: "If she were one inch taller, she would be too tall. If she were one inch shorter, she would be too short. If she used powder, her face would be too white. If she used rouge, her face would be too red." (*Wen Hsüan, chüan* 19) The description means that her figure and complexion were just right. "Just right" is what the Confucianists call *chung*.

Time is an important factor in the idea of being just right. It is just right to wear a fur coat in winter, but it is not just right to wear it in summer. Hence the Confucianists often use the word *shih* (time or timely) in conjunction with the word *chung*, as in the term *shih chung* or "timely mean." Mencius, for example, says of Confucius: "When it was proper to go into office, then to go into it; when it was proper to remain out of office, then to remain out of it; when it was proper to continue in it long, then to continue in it long; when it was proper to withdraw from it quickly, then to withdraw from it quickly: such was Confucius." (*Mencius*, IIa, 22.) Hence "among the sages, Confucius was the timely one." (*Ibid.*, Vb, 1.)

The *Chung Yung* says: "To have no emotions of pleasure or anger, sorrow or joy, welling up: this is to be described as the state of *chung*. To have these emotions welling up but in due proportion: this is to be described as the state of *ho* [harmony]. *Chung* is the chief foundation of the world. *Ho* is the great highway for the world. Once *chung* and *ho* are

"易传"和《老子》持同样看法的另一点是：谦虚、自居于下是重要的品德。《易·谦卦》的《象辞》说："天道亏盈而益谦，地道变盈而流谦，鬼道害盈而福谦，人道恶盈而好谦。谦，尊而光，卑而不可逾，君子之终也。"上天之道，凡自高的必降为卑，自卑的必升为高。为人之道，也是一样：君子所求，便以自谦为终极的宗旨。

●"中"与"和"

《中庸》对于"中"的意义作了充分发挥。"中"和古希腊亚里士多德所主张的"中道为贵"（the golden mean）颇为相近。有的人错以为，主张中道就是凡事只应求其半，行其半。其实，"中"的真正含义是"恰如其分"、"恰到好处"。如果一个人要从华盛顿到纽约，结果穿越纽约而到了波士顿，那就是过分；如果只到费城，那就是不及。公元前三世纪中国诗人宋玉曾经在《登徒子好色赋》中描绘一位美人说："增之一分则太长，减之一分则太短；著粉则太白，施朱则太赤。"（《文选》卷十九）这里描绘的一位美女，身体和容貌都恰到好处。这就是儒家所谓的"中"。

在"中"这个概念里，时间是个重要的组成部分。冬天穿皮大衣是"正好"，但如果在夏天，就成为可笑的了。因此，儒家往往把"时"与"中"联系起来，如"时中"，含义是懂得"适当其时"又"恰如其分"地行事。孟子称孔子："可以仕则仕，可以止则止，可以久则久，可以速则速。"（《孟子·公孙丑章句上》）正是因此，所以孟子称颂说："孔子，圣之时者也。"（《孟子·万章章句下》）

《中庸》第一章上写道："喜怒哀乐之未发，谓之中；发而皆中节，谓之和。中也者，天下之大本也；和也者，天下之达道也。

established, Heaven and Earth maintain their proper position, and all creatures are nourished." (Ch. 1.) When the emotions do not come forth at all, the mind neither goes too far nor falls short. It is just right. This is an illustration of the state of *chung*. And when the emotions do come forth, but in due proportion, this is also the state of *chung* for harmony results from *chung*, and *chung* serves to harmonize what might otherwise be discordant.

What is said about the emotions also applies to the desires. In personal conduct as well as in social relations, there are medium points which serve as right limits for the satisfaction of the desires and the expression of the emotions. When all desires and emotions of a person are satisfied and expressed to the right degree, the person achieves a harmony within his person which results in good mental health. Likewise, when all the desires and feelings of the various types of people who comprise a society are satisfied and expressed to the right degree, the society achieves harmony within itself which results in peace and order.

Harmony is the reconciling of differences into a harmonious unity. The *Tso Chuan* reports a speech by the statesman Yen Tzu (died 493 B.C.), in which he makes a distinction between harmony and uniformity or identity. Harmony, he says, may be illustrated by cooking. Water, vinegar, pickles, salt, and plums are used to cook fish. From these ingredients there results a new taste which is neither that of the vinegar nor of the pickles. Uniformity or identity, on the other hand, may be likened to the attempt to flavor water with water, or to confine a piece of music to one note. In both cases there is nothing new.[2] Herein lies the distinction between the Chinese words *t'ung* and *ho*. T'ung means uniformity or identity, which is incompatible with difference. *Ho* means harmony, which is not incompatible with difference; on the contrary, it results when differences are brought together to form a unity. But in order to achieve harmony, the differences must each be present in precisely their proper proportion, which is *chung*. Thus the function of *chung* is to achieve harmony.

A well-organized society is a harmonious unity in which people of differing talents and professions occupy their proper places, perform their proper functions, and are all equally satisfied and not in conflict with one another. An ideal world is also a harmonious unity. The *Chung Yung* says: "All things are nurtured together without injuring one another. All courses are pursued without collision. This is what makes Heaven and Earth great." (Ch. 30.)

致中和，天地位焉，万物育焉。"人的感情还未迸发出来时，内心里无所谓"过分"或"不及"，这时称为"中"。当人的感情倾泻出来，而保持恰如其分，这时也仍然是"中"。"和"来自"中"，"中"又是调和各种心情所必需。

这个思想适用于人的感情，也同样适用于人的欲望。个人的行为或人的社会关系中，都有一个中点，使人在表达感情和满足欲望时，知乎所止。当人的感情和欲望都表现得合乎分寸，他内心便达到一种平衡，这是精神健康所必需的。对整个社会来说，也是如此。如果在一个社会里，各种人都懂得对自己的欲望和感情适度地满足，这时，社会便达到和谐、安定、秩序井然。

"和"便是协调分歧，达成和睦一致。《左传》中曾经记载，昭公二十年（公元前五二二年），齐国大夫晏婴（？至前五〇〇年）有一段话，分析"和"与"同"的区别说："和如羹焉，水、火、醯（音希，醋）、醢（音海，肉和鱼制成的酱）、盐、梅以烹鱼肉。"这些调料合在一起，产生一种新的味道，既不是醋又不是酱的味道。"同"则如同以开水作调料，或一个乐曲只准用一个声音，并不引进任何新的味道。在中文里，"同"意味着单调一律，不容许有任何不同；"和"则意味着和谐，它承认不同，而把不同联合起来成为和谐一致。这种和谐需要一个条件，就是：各种不同成分之间，要有适当的比例，这就是"中"，"中"的作用则是达成"和"。

一个有组织的社会里，有各种不同才能、不同行业的人，各有自己的地位，完成不同的作用，各得其所，彼此没有冲突。一个理想的社会，也是这样和谐的一体。如《中庸》第三十章所说："万物并育而不相害，道并行而不相悖，……此天地之所以为大也。"

Harmony of this sort, which includes not only human society, but permeates the entire universe, is called the Supreme Harmony. In "Appendix I" of the *Yi*, it is said: "How vast is the originating power of [the hexagram] *Ch'ien*.... Unitedly to protect the Supreme Harmony: this is indeed profitable and auspicious."

- **The Common and the Ordinary**

The *Chung Yung* says: "What Heaven confers is called the nature. The following of this nature is called the Way [*Tao*]. The cultivation of this Way is called spiritual culture. The Way is that which no man for a moment can do without. What a man can do without is not the Way." (Ch. 1.) Here we touch upon the idea of the importance of the common and the ordinary, which is another important concept in the *Chung Yung*. This concept is expressed by the word *yung*, in the title of this work, which means common or ordinary.

Everyone finds it necessary to eat and drink every day. Hence eating and drinking are the common and ordinary activities of mankind. They are common and ordinary just because they are so important that no man can possibly do without them. The same is true of human relations and moral virtues. They appear to some people as so common and ordinary as to be of little value. Yet they are so simply because they are so important that no man can do without them. To eat and drink, and to maintain human relations and moral virtues, is to follow the nature of man. It is nothing else but the Way or *Tao*. What is called spiritual culture or moral instruction is nothing more than the cultivation of this Way.

Since the Way is that which no man in actual fact can do without, what is the need of spiritual culture? The answer is that although all men are, to some extent, really following the Way, not all men are sufficiently enlightened to be conscious of this fact. The *Chung Yung* says: "Amongst men there are none who do not eat and drink, but there are few who really appreciate the taste." (Ch. 4.) The function of spiritual culture is to give people an understanding that they are all, more or less, actually following the Way, so as to cause them to be conscious of what they are doing.

Furthermore, although all men are, as a matter of necessity, compelled to follow the Way to some extent, not all can follow it to perfection. Thus no one can live in a society utterly devoid of human relationships;

这种和谐，不仅是指人类社会，它也渗透全宇宙，构成所谓"太和"。《易·乾卦》的《彖辞》说："大哉乾元，……保合太和，乃利贞。"这是说，乾的生发能力多么浩瀚，……联成一气，保有至高的和谐，这就是大吉大利。

● "庸"与"常"

《中庸》第一章说："天命之谓性，率性之谓道，修道之谓教。道也者，不可须臾离也，可离非道也。"这里提出了看似"普通"和"寻常"事物的重要性，这是《中庸》的另一个重要思想，它以"庸"来表示，意思就是"普通"和"寻常"。

人们每天都需要吃饭喝水，因此，吃饭喝水成为人类的日常活动。它们如此重要，又如此寻常，成为人人不能离开的事物。在人们的日常生活里，人际关系和道德也同样是不能须臾离开的。有的人觉得，人际关系和道德是十分寻常的事情，因此并不觉得它们有什么价值。其实，任何人离开了它们便无法生活。吃饭，喝水，人际关系，道德价值，都无非是顺乎人性，这便是"率性之谓道"。所谓精神文化、道德教育，其实就是培养"道"的意识。

既然"道"是人人每天生活所不能离开的，那么，何必再讲精神文化呢？对这问题的回答是：虽然所有的人都在不同程度上遵循"道"来生活，并不是所有的人都充分认识这个事实。《中庸》第四章里说："人莫不饮食也，鲜能知味也。"精神文化的作用就在于使人懂得他们其实是在循"道"而行，使人们懂得自己生活的意义，这和懵懂的生活，是大不一样的。

进一步说，虽然人人都不得不遵循"道"来生活，并不是所有的人都能做得完美。人既然生活在社会里，便不免有种种人际关系，

at the same time there are few who can meet with perfection all the requirements made by these human relationships. The function of spiritual culture is to perfect what man is, as a matter of fact, already doing to a greater or lesser degree.

Thus the *Chung Yung* says: "The Way of the superior man is obvious and yet obscure. The ordinary man and ordinary woman in all their ignorance can yet have knowledge of it, yet in its perfection even a sage finds in it something which he does not know. The ordinary man and ordinary woman with all their stupidity can yet practice it, yet in its perfection even a sage finds in it something which he cannot practice.... Thus the Way of the superior man begins with the relationship between husband and wife, but in its fullest extent reaches to all that is in Heaven and Earth." (Ch. 12.) Thus though all men, even in their ignorance and stupidity, are following the Way to some extent, spiritual cultivation is nevertheless required to bring them to enlightenment and perfection.

● Enlightenment and Perfection

In the *Chung Yung*, this perfection is described as *ch'eng* (sincerity, realness) and goes together with enlightenment. The *Chung Yung* says: "Progress from perfection to enlightenment is called the nature. From enlightenment to perfection it is called spiritual culture. When there is perfection, there is enlightenment. When there is enlightenment, there is perfection." (Ch. 21.) That is to say, once one understands all the significance of the ordinary and common acts of daily life, such as eating, drinking, and the human relationships, one is already a sage. The same is true when one practices to perfection what one understands. One cannot fully understand the significance of these things unless one practices them. Nor can one practice them to perfection, unless one fully understands their significance.

The *Chung Yung* says again: "The quality of *ch'eng* does not simply consist in perfecting oneself. It is that whereby one perfects all other things. The perfection of the self lies in the quality of *jen* [human-heartedness]. The perfection of other things lies in wisdom. In this is the virtue of the nature. It is the way through which comes the union between inner and outer." (Ch. 25.) The meaning of this passage seems clear, yet I wonder whether the words, human-heartedness and wisdom, should not be interchanged.

The *Chung Yung* says also: "It is only he who has the most *ch'eng* who can develop his nature to the utmost. Able to do this, he is able to do the

在处理这些人际关系时，很少人能做得完美。精神文化的作用便是使人能够成为一个高尚，以至完美的人。

这便是《中庸》第十二章所说："君子之道费而隐。夫妇之愚，可以与知焉，及其至也，虽圣人亦有所不知焉；夫妇之不肖，可以能行焉，及其至也，虽圣人亦有所不能焉。……君子之道，造端乎夫妇；及其至也，察乎天地。"因此，虽然所有的人，包括愚和不肖，都多少是在循道而行。为提高他们的觉悟，以"至善"作为自己的人生目标，精神文化是十分必要的。

● 从启蒙到止于至善：明与诚

在《中庸》里，至善被称为"诚"（真诚、纯真），和"明"是连在一起的。《中庸》第二十一章说："自诚明，谓之性；自明诚，谓之教。诚则明矣，明则诚矣。"这是说，人如果真正懂得了普通、寻常生活中吃喝、人际关系的重要意义，他就已经是一个圣人了。一个人如果把他所领会的都付诸实践，他也就是圣人了。人只有在自己的实践中，才能懂得这些普通、寻常事的真正意义；也只有真正懂得了它们的意义，才能做得完美。

《中庸》第二十五章还说："诚者非自成己而已也，所以成物也。成己，仁也；成物，知也。性之德也，合内外之道也。"这是说，诚不是仅仅为了成全自己，它还是成全万物的途径。成全自己，这是仁德；成全万物，这是智慧。诚是人天性中的品德，人内心和外部世界的道理都在其中结合起来了。这段话的意思应该是清楚的，但我设想，"仁"和"知"两个字的位置或许应该调换一下。

《中庸》第二十二章还说："唯天下至诚，为能尽其性；能尽其性，

same to the nature of other men. Able to do this, he is able to do the same to the nature of things. Able to do this, he can assist the transforming and nourishing operations of Heaven and Earth. Being able to do this, he can form a trinity with Heaven and Earth." (Ch. 22.)

While perfecting oneself, one must also see that others are likewise perfected. One cannot perfect oneself while disregarding the perfection of others. The reason is that one can develop one's nature to the utmost only through the human relationships, that is, within the sphere of society. This goes back to the tradition of Confucius and Mencius, that for self-perfection one must practice *chung, shu*, and human-heartedness; that is, it consists in helping others. To perfect oneself is to develop to the utmost what one has received from Heaven. And to help others is to assist the transforming and nourishing operations of Heaven and Earth. By fully understanding the significance of these things, one is enabled to form a trinity with Heaven and Earth. Such understanding is what the *Chung Yung* calls enlightenment, and forming a trinity in this way is what it calls perfection.

Is anything extraordinary needed in order to achieve this trinity? No, nothing more is needed than to do the common and ordinary things and to do them "just right," with understanding of their full significance. By so doing, one can gain the union of inner and outer, which is not only a trinity of Heaven, Earth, and man, but means a unity of man *with* Heaven and Earth. In this way one can achieve other-worldliness, yet at the same time not lose this-worldliness. It is with the development of this idea that the later Neo-Confucianists attacked the other-worldly philosophy of Buddhism.

Such is the Confucianist way of elevating the mind to a state in which the individual becomes one with the universe. It differs from the Taoist method, which is, through the negation of knowledge, to elevate the mind above the mundane distinctions between the "this" and the "other." The Confucianist method, on the other hand, is, through the extension of love, to elevate the mind above the usual distinctions between the self and other things.

则能尽人之性；能尽人之性，则能尽物之性；能尽物之性，则可以赞天地之化育；可以赞天地之化育，则可以与天地参矣。"这是说，唯有天下至诚之人，才能充分发挥人的天性；能充分发挥自己天性的人，才能充分发挥别人的天性；而后才能充分发挥万物的本性，而后才能帮助天地化育万物；而后才能与天地合为一体。

一个人如果力求完善自己，他就会看到，为此也必须同时完善他人。一个人如果不关心别人的完善，自己便不可能完善。这是因为，人要充分发展自己的天性，必须充分发展他的人际关系，也就是在社会之中。这就回到了孔子、孟子的传统，人要想完善自己，必须实行忠恕、仁义，这就包含了帮助别人。人要想完善自己，就必须充分发展受自上苍的天性，帮助别人就是参与天地化育万物的工作。一个人如果真正懂得了这一切，他就与天地合参，成为一体了。《中庸》所讲的"明"，便是这个意思：人做到与天地合参，便是完美。

为做到与天地合参，人是否需要做什么特别的事情呢？并不需要，所需要的只是做那些普通、寻常的事情，完全懂得它们的意义，并把它们做得"恰到好处"。在这样做时，人的内心和外部世界连接起来了，这不仅是人与天地合参，而是天人合一。这时，人虽在世界之中，却又超越了世界。后来新的儒家便是以发展这个思想来批判佛家的出世哲学。

这便是儒家把人心提高到天人境界的途径。它与道家所主张的弃绝知识、齐万物、一死生的做法不同，儒家的途径是通过爱的延伸，使人心得以超越我与他人的界限，也超越我与物的界限。

⑯ WORLD POLITICS AND WORLD PHILOSOPHY

It is said that "history never repeats itself," yet also that "there is nothing new under the sun." Perhaps the whole truth lies in a combination of these two sayings. From a Chinese point of view, so far as international politics is concerned, the history of our world in the present and immediately preceding centuries looks like a repetition of the Chinese history of the Ch'un Ch'iu and Chan Kuo periods.

● **Political Conditions Preceding the Unification by Ch'in**

The Ch'un Ch'iu period (722-481 B.C.) is so named because it is the period covered by the *Ch'un Ch'iu* or *Spring and Autumn Annals*. And the Chan Kuo period (480-222 B.C.) derives its name, which means Warring States, from the fact that it was a period of intensified warfare between the feudal states. As we have seen, men's conduct during the feudal age was governed by *li* (ceremonies, rituals, rules of proper conduct). Not only were there *li* governing the conduct of the individual, but also those for the state as well. Some of these were to be practiced in time of peace, but others were designed for use in war. These peacetime and wartime *li*, as observed by one state in its relations to another, were equivalent to what we now would call international law.

We see that in recent times international law has become more and more ineffective. In late years there have been many instances in which one nation has attacked another without first sending an ultimatum and declaring war, or the airplanes of one nation have bombed the hospitals of another, while pretending that they did not see the red cross. And in the periods of Chinese history mentioned above, we see a similar decline in the effectiveness of the *li*.

In the Ch'un Ch'iu period, there were still people who respected the international *li*. The *Tso Chuan* reports a famous battle of Hung that took place in 638 B.C. between the states of Ch'u and Sung. The old-fashioned

Duke Hsiang of Sung personally directed the Sung forces. At a certain moment, the Ch'u army was crossing a river to form its lines, whereupon the commander under Duke Hsiang immediately asked for permission to attack the army during its crossing. To this the Duke replied, however, that he would not attack an army before it had formed its lines. The result was a disastrous defeat of the Sung army, in which the Duke himself was wounded. In spite of this, however, he defended his original decision,

拾陆 治国平天下的哲学主张

人们常说，"历史不会重演。"人们又说，"阳光之下并无新事。"真理或者在于把两者结合起来。在中国人看来，从近代到现代直到今天的世界政治历史，很像是中国古代春秋战国时代的重演。

● 秦朝统一中国前的中国政治情况

中国古代的春秋时期（公元前七二二至前四八一年），得名于这一时期的历史载入称为《春秋》的史书之中。继春秋之后的战国时期（公元前四八○至前二二二年），得名于这一时期列国之间战争加剧。前面说到，中国封建时期人们的行为受"礼"（仪式、礼制、行为规范等）的制约。不仅个人行为要受"礼"的制约，国家的行动也同样受到"礼"的制约，其中有些是为和平时期的国际交往，有些则是对国际战争时期各国行动的约束。为和平时期国际交往和战争时期对交战双方的约束，就相当于今天的所谓"国际法"。

我们看到，在当今世界里，国际法已经日益失去作用，一国不提出最后通牒而突然袭击另一国，或一国的空军轰炸敌对国家的医院，推托说未曾看见医院房顶的红十字标志，已经屡见不鲜。在中国古代的春秋战国时期，不受国际关系中的"礼法"制约，也同样可见。

本来，春秋时期还有人遵守国际关系中的礼法。《左传》中记载公元前六三八年，楚、宋两国的泓水之战。宋国国君宋襄公亲自指挥军队进行这场战争。当楚国军队渡河进击时，宋襄公部将要求趁楚军渡河时出击。宋襄公回答说，敌军未组成阵势，不能进击。结果，宋军大败，宋襄公本人也受伤。在这种情况下，宋襄公还是

saying: "A superior man does not inflict a second wound on one who has already been wounded, nor does he take prisoner any one who has gray hair." This infuriated one of his commanders, who told the Duke: "If it is good to refrain from inflicting a second wound, why not refrain from inflicting any wound at all? If it is good to refrain from taking prisoner any one who has gray hair, why not surrender to your enemy?" (*Tso Chuan*, twenty-second year of Duke Hsi.) What the Duke said accorded with the traditional *li*, which represented the chivalrous spirit of the feudal knights. What the commander said represented the practice of a changing age.

It is interesting though discouraging to note that all the known methods which statesmen of today use in an effort to keep peace among nations are much the same as those which the statesmen of these early periods of Chinese history attempted without success. For example, a conference for the limitation of armaments was held in 551 B.C. (*Tso Chuan*, twenty-seventh year of Duke Hsiang.) Some time later a proposal was made to divide the "world" of that time into two "spheres of influence"; one in the east, to be controlled by the King of Ch'i with the title of Eastern Emperor; the other in the west, to be controlled by the King of Ch'in with the title of Western Emperor. (*Historical Records*, ch. 46.) There were also various alliances of states with one another. During the Chan Kuo period these fell into two general patterns: the "vertical," which ran from north to south, and the "horizontal," which ran from west to east. At that time there were seven major states, of which Ch'in was the most aggressive. The vertical type of alliance was one directed against Ch'in by the other six states, and was so called because Ch'in lay in the extreme west, while the other six states were scattered to the east of it, ranging from north to south. The horizontal type of alliance, on the other hand, was one in which Ch'in combined with one or more of the other six states in order to attack the remainder, and therefore was extended from the west toward the east.

Ch'in's policy was "to make alliance with distant states, but attack the ones that were near." In this way it always eventually succeeded in breaking up the vertical alliances that opposed it. By its superiority in "agriculture and war" and extensive use of "fifth column" techniques among the other states, Ch'in, after a series of bloody campaigns, succeeded in conquering the other six states one by one, and finally unified the whole of China in 221 B.C. Thereupon the King of Ch'in gave to himself the grandiose title of First Emperor of Ch'in (Ch'in Shih-huang-ti) by which he is known to history. At the same time he abolished feudalism and thus for the first time in history created a centralized Chinese empire under the Ch'in dynasty.

坚持自己的守则说："君子不重伤（伤敌人两次），不擒二毛（头发灰白之人）。"襄公手下武将怒问襄公："若爱重伤，则如勿伤；爱其二毛，则如服焉。"（对受伤之敌不再加害，何若根本不去伤害敌人？不擒有灰白头发的敌兵，何不索性对敌投降！）宋襄公所奉行的战争时期礼法，体现的是封建武士的风度，而他的部将所说则是反映了时代的变化。

有趣却又令人沮丧的是，现代政治家争取国际和平的办法都是中国古代政治家曾经使用过而都遭到失败的办法。例如，公元前五五一年（《左传》襄公二十七年）曾举行过一次国际会议，试图限制各国的军事扩张。后来，将当时的"天下"（即中国）划分为东、西两大势力范围，分由当时最强大的齐国、秦国控制。齐王称"东帝"，秦王称"西帝"（见《史记·田敬仲完世家》）。战国时期，列国之间组织联盟，一称"合纵"，一称"连横"。当时中国有七个比较强大的国家，称为"七霸"，其中处于西端的秦国最为野心勃勃，"合纵"是六国联合对秦的联盟；秦国则采取联合六国中的任何其他国家，攻击与秦对抗的国家，这是由西向东的联盟，称为"连横"。

秦国以"远交近攻"的策略击破东方诸国"合纵"的联盟。它依靠"耕战"的优势，还在六国内广泛使用专事政治阴谋活动的"第五纵队"，终于得以逐一战败六国，在公元前二二一年统一全中国。秦王自封"秦始皇帝"，在中国历史上以此得名。他还废除以领地分封皇室、诸侯的旧法，改在全国设郡县，把政治权力集中，在中国创立了中央集权的庞大帝国。

● The Unification of China

Though the First Emperor was thus the first to achieve actual unity, the desire for such unity had been cherished by all people for a long time previous. In the *Mencius* we are told that King Hui of Liang asked: "How may the world be at peace?" To which Mencius replied: "When there is unity, there will be peace." "But who can unify the world?" asked the King. "He who does not delight in killing men can unify it," answered Mencius. (Ia, 6.) This statement clearly expresses the aspiration of the time.

The word "world" used here is a translation of the Chinese term *t'ien-hsia,* which literally means "all beneath the sky." Some translators render it as "empire," because, so they maintain, what the Chinese in ancient times called the *t'ien-hsia* was confined to the limits of the Chinese feudal states. This is quite true. But we should not confuse the intension of a term with its extension as it was understood by the people of a particular time. The latter usage is limited by the knowledge of facts possessed by these people, but the former is a matter of definition. For instance, we cannot say that the word *jen* (persons) should be translated as "Chinese," simply because in ancient times what the Chinese meant by the word was confined to people of Chinese blood. When the ancient Chinese spoke about *jen,* what they meant was really human beings, even though at that time their knowledge of human beings was limited to those of China. In the same way, when they spoke about the *t'ien-hsia,* they meant the world, even though in early times their knowledge of the world did not extend beyond the Chinese states.

From the age of Confucius onward, the Chinese people in general and their political thinkers in particular began to think about political matters in terms of the world. Hence the unification of China by Ch'in seemed, to the people of that time, very much as the unification of the whole world would seem to us today. Since the unification of 221 B.C., for more than two thousand years, with the exception of certain periods which the Chinese have considered as abnormal, they have lived under one government in one world. They have thus been accustomed to a centralized organization that would operate for world peace. But in recent times they have been plunged into a world with international political conditions similar to those of the remote periods of the Ch'un Ch'iu and Chan Kuo. In the process they have been compelled to change their

● 中国的统一

始皇帝第一次真正实现了中国的统一，但是在他之前很久，中国人便久已期盼出现一个"天下"一统的中国。《孟子·梁惠王章句上》记载，梁惠王问孟子："天下恶乎定？"孟子回答："定于一。"梁惠王又问："孰能一之？"孟子回答："不嗜杀人者能一之。"孟子的话清楚反映了时代的愿望。

本章使用的"世界"是译自中文的"天下"一词，它的字面意义是"普天之下"。有的英文译著把"天下"译成"帝国"，因为当时的所谓"天下"，实际上只是指周天子和诸侯的领地总和。这确是当时的现实情况，但是我们在使用一个词语时，不能把它的内涵和外延混为一谈。"天下"的定义应当是它内涵的意义，当时人们对它的理解和它本身应有的定义不是一回事。举例来说，在中国古代，称"人"时，所指的就是"中国人"，但我们不能把中国古文中的"人"这个词语翻译解释为"中国人"。中国古代文献中的"人"，所指的乃是生物学意义的"人"，虽然当时人们对"人"的知识只限于对"中国人"的知识。同样的道理，古代中国人说"天下"时，他们所指的是"世界"，不过他们当时所知道的"天下"只限于"中国"范围。

从孔子的时代起，中国人虽然只生活在中国的地域之中，但他们的精神世界，特别是思想家的精神世界，却自认是生活在世界之中，所考虑的政治问题也是从世界范围来着眼。因此，秦统一的虽然只是中国全境，在当时人们看来，这就如同今日人们心目中的统一全世界了。从公元前二二一年起，此后两千多年，除去其中很短的、被中国人认为不正常的时期之外，中国人始终认为是生活在"普天之下"的世界里，受一个中央政府管辖。因此，中国人惯以为，要有一个中央机构来实现世界和平。但是，现代世界的格局，很像中国古代的春秋战国时代。在今日世界里，中国人不得不被迫

habits of thinking and acting. In this respect, in the eyes of the Chinese, there has been a repetition of history, which has contributed much to their present suffering. (See note at the end of the chapter.)

- ## The Great Learning

To illustrate the internationalistic character of Chinese philosophy, let us turn now to some of the ideas of the *Ta Hsüeh*, or *Great Learning*. The *Ta Hsüeh*, like the *Chung Yung*, is a chapter in the *Li Chi* (*Book of Rites*), and like the *Chung Yung*, it was, during the Sung dynasty (960-1279), grouped by the Neo-Confucianists with the *Confucian Analects* and the *Mencius*, to form the "Four Books" which comprised the primary texts for Neo-Confucian philosophy.

The *Great Learning* was attributed by the Neo-Confucianists, though with no real proof, to Tseng Tzu, one of the chief disciples of Confucius. It was considered by them to be an important manual for the learning of *Tao*. Its opening section reads:

"The teaching of the *Great Learning* is to manifest one's illustrious virtue, love the people, and rest in the highest good.... The ancients who wished to manifest illustrious virtue throughout the world, first ordered well their own states. Wishing to order well their own states, they first regulated their own families. Wishing to regulate their own families, they first cultivated their own selves. Wishing to cultivate their own selves, they first rectified their own minds. Wishing to rectify their own minds, they first sought for absolute sincerity in their thoughts. Wishing for absolute sincerity in their thoughts, they first extended their knowledge. This extension of knowledge consists in the investigation of things.

"Things being investigated, only then did their knowledge become extended. Their knowledge being extended, only then did their thought become sincere. Their thought being sincere, only then did their mind become rectified. Their mind being rectified, only then did their selves become cultivated. Their selves being cultivated, only then did their families become regulated. Their families being regulated, only then did their states become rightly governed. Their states being rightly governed, only then could the world be at peace."

These statements have been known as the three "main cords" and eight "minor wires" of the *Ta Hsüeh*. According to later Confucianists, the three cords really comprise only one cord, which is "to manifest one's illustrious virtue." "To love the people" is the way "to manifest one's illustrious virtue," while "to rest in the highest good" is "to manifest one's illustrious virtue" in the highest perfection.

改变自己的传统思维方式和行为方式，但在精神状态上，却觉得今日世界很像中国古代的春秋战国时期，因此就容易有"历史重演"的感觉。这种重演的历史为中国人民带来了现在的种种苦难。（请参阅本章末的注释）

● 《大学》

为说明中国哲学的世界性质，在这里可以略举《大学》中的一些思想，从中可见一斑。《大学》和《中庸》一样，都是《礼记》中的一章。宋代（公元九六〇至一二七九年）的道学家把《论语》、《孟子》和《大学》、《中庸》并列为"四书"，成为道学（西方称为"新儒家"）的基本文献。

道学家认为，《大学》是孔子的门生曾参所作（但还没有文献足以证明这一点），是学习"道学"的重要资料。它的第一章是这样开头的：

"大学之道，在明明德，在亲民，在止于至善。……古之欲明明德于天下者，先治其国；欲治其国者，先齐其家；欲齐其家者，先修其身；欲修其身者，先正其心；欲正其心者，先诚其意；欲诚其意者，先致其知；致知在格物。

"物格而后知至，知至而后意诚，意诚而后心正，心正而后身修，身修而后家齐，家齐而后国治，国治而后天下平。"

这段话被称为《大学》的"三纲领"、"八条目"。按照后来儒家的说法，"三纲领"其实归结到一点，或称它为一条纲领，就是"在明明德"。"仁者爱人"便是"明明德"的途径；而"明明德"的终极完成便是"止于至善"。

The "eight wires" are likewise really only one wire, which is the cultivation of one's own self. In the above quotation, the steps preceding the cultivation of the self, such as the investigation of things, extension of knowledge, etc., are the ways and means for cultivating the self. And the steps following the cultivation of the self, such as the regulation of the family, etc., are the ways and means for cultivating the self to its highest perfection, or as the text says, for "resting in the highest good." Man cannot develop his nature to perfection unless he tries his best to do his duties in society. He cannot perfect himself without at the same time perfecting others.

"To manifest one's illustrious virtue" is the same as "to cultivate one's self." The former is merely the content of the latter. Thus several ideas are reduced to a single idea, which is central in Confucianism.

It is unnecessary that one should be head of a state or of some world organization, before one can do something to bring good order to the state and peace to the world. One should merely do one's best to do good for the state as a member of the state, and do good for the world as a member of the world. One is then doing one's full share of bringing good order to the state and peace to the world. By thus sincerely trying to do one's best, one is resting in the highest good.

For the purpose of the present chapter, it is enough to point out that the author of the *Ta Hsüeh* was thinking in terms of world politics and world peace. He was not the first to think in this way, but it is significant that he did it so systematically. For him, the good order of one's own state is neither the final goal in terms of politics nor in terms of the spiritual cultivation of the self.

Here we need not discuss the problem of how the investigation of things can be the ways and means for the spiritual cultivation of the self. This problem will return to us when we take up Neo-Confucianism later.

● Eclectic Tendency in the *Hsün-tzu*

In the world of Chinese philosophy, the latter part of the third century B.C. saw a strong tendency towards syncretism and eclecticism. The major work of the School of Eclectics, the *Lü-shih Ch'un-ch'iu*, was composed at that time. But, although this work devoted chapters to most

"八条目"也同样可以归结为一条，便是"修身"。在上面所引的《大学》这段话中，"修身"之前的"格物"、"致知"等，是修身的方式和途径。继"修身"之后的"齐家"、"治国"、"平天下"，是"修身"以至于"止善"的方式和途径，目的是"止于至善"。人若不尽其所能去完成对社会的责任，便不能充分发挥自己的天赋才性，"自欲立而立人，自欲达而达人"，人若不帮助别人达到完美，自己也就不可能达到完美。

"明明德"和"修身"是一回事，"修身"的内容就是在"明明德"。由这里可以看出：这几个思想最后归结为一个中心，这便是儒家的中心思想。

一个人不需要谋求担当国家或世界的领导，才能对国家福祉、世界和平做出贡献。作为国家一分子，尽责尽力，同样可以对国家的福祉做出贡献；作为世界一分子，尽责尽力，也一样可以对世界做出贡献。这样真诚地竭尽己力，就是"止于至善"。

就本章来说，重要的是指出，《大学》的作者是着眼于世界的治理与和平来考虑问题的，只要指出这一点就够了。《大学》的作者并不是这样考虑问题的第一人，但值得注意的是，他如此系统地思考了这个问题，在他看来，无论是个人的"修身"，或本国的"修明之治"，都不是为政的最终目的。

这里不准备讨论格物致知怎样成为心灵修养的方式和途径；在后面讨论道学的时候，这个问题还会再度出现的。

●《荀子》中的折中倾向

在中国古代哲学史上，公元前三世纪下半叶（秦汉之际）出现一种调和、折中的趋势。折中学派的主要著作《吕氏春秋》便是这个历史时期的作品。在《吕氏春秋》一书中，对当时各种思想流派

of the schools of its time, it failed to give a theoretical justification for the idea of eclecticism as such. Both Confucianist and Taoist writers, however, did present such a theory, which shows how, despite their other differences, they both reflected the eclectic spirit of the time.

These writers agreed that there is a single absolute Truth which they called the *Tao*. Most of the different schools have seen some one particular aspect of the *Tao*, and in this sense have made some contribution to its manifestation. The Confucianist writers, however, maintained that it was Confucius who had seen the whole Truth, and so the other schools were subordinate to the Confucian school, though in a sense complementary to it. The Taoist writers, on the contrary, maintained that it was Lao Tzu and Chuang Tzu who had seen the whole Truth, and therefore that Taoism was superior to all other schools.

In the *Hsün-tzu* there is a chapter titled "On Freedom from Blindness," in which we read:

"In the past, the traveling scholars were blinded, so they had different schools of thought. Mo Tzu was blinded by utility and did not know the value of culture. Sung Tzu [a contemporary of Mencius, who maintained that the desires of men are really very few] was blinded by desire, but did not know [that men seek for] gain. Shen Tzu [Shen Tao, a member of the Legalist school] was blinded by law but did not know [the value of] talent. Shen Tzu [Shen Puhai, another member of the Legalist school] was blinded by authority but did not know wisdom. Hui Tzu [Hui Shih of the shool of Names] was blinded by words but did not know facts. Chuang Tzu was blinded by what is of nature but did not know what is of man.

"From the point of view of utility, the *Tao* is nothing more than seeking for profit. From the point of view of [fewness of] desires, the *Tao* is nothing more than satisfaction. From the point of view of law, the *Tao* is nothing more than regulations. From the point of view of authority, the *Tao* is nothing more than caprice. From the point of view of what is of nature, the *Tao* is nothing more than *laissez-faire*. From the point of view of words, the *Tao* is nothing more than argumentation.

"These different views are single aspects of the *Tao*. The essence of the *Tao* is constant and includes all changes. It cannot be grasped by a single corner. Those with perverted knowledge who see only a single aspect of the *Tao* will not be able to comprehend its totality.... Confucius was human-hearted and wise and was not blinded. Therefore he comprehended the *Tao* and was sufficient to be ranked with the early rulers." (Ch. 21.)

In another chapter Hsün Tzu says: "Lao Tzu had vision regarding acquiescence, but did not see exertion. Mo Tzu had vision regarding uniformity, but did not see individuality. Sung Tzu had vision regarding

都有所论述，但并没有对折中主义思想的兴起，从理论上来解释清楚。这一时期的儒家和道家却都流露出折中主义的倾向，表明它们尽管有各种不同的见解，但都反映了时代的折中主义精神。

这些思想家都承认有一个绝对真理，就是它们所称的"道"。各种不同的思想流派，着重"道"的不同方面，对"道"的认识，都做出了贡献。儒家认为，其他学派虽也有所贡献，但只有孔子领会了全部真理，因此其他学派都只是儒家的支流。道家则认为，老子和庄子才是全面领会了"道"所包含的全部真理，因此，道家应当凌驾于其他学派之上。

在《荀子·解蔽》篇中，有一段话说：

"昔宾孟之蔽者，乱家（周游列国的学人）是也。墨子蔽于用而不知文，宋子蔽于欲而不知得，慎子蔽于法而不知贤，申子蔽于执而不知知，惠子蔽于辞而不知实，庄子蔽于天而不知人。

"故由用谓之道，尽利矣；由俗谓之道，尽嗛（疑惑）矣；由法谓之道，尽数矣；由执谓之道，尽便矣；由辞谓之道，尽论矣；由天谓之道，尽因矣。此数具者，皆道之一隅也。

"夫道者，体常而尽变，一隅不足以举之。曲知之人，观于道之一隅而未之能识也。……孔子仁知且不蔽，故学乱术（深明道术）足以为先王者也。"

荀子在《天论》中又说："老子有见于诎（屈），无见于信（伸）；墨子有见于齐（共性），无见于畸（个性）；宋子有见于少（欲望

[the fact that the desires of some men are] few, but did not see [the fact that those of other men are] many." (Ch. 17.) According to Hsün Tzu, the vision and blindness of a philosopher go together. He has vision, yet usually at the same time is blinded by his vision. Hence the excellence of his philosophy is at the same time its shortcoming.

● Eclectic Tendency in the *Chuang-tzu*

The author of the last chapter of the *Chuang-tzu, T'ien Hsia* or "The World," gives the Taoist view of syncretism. This chapter is really a summarized account of ancient Chinese philosophy. We are not sure who the author was, but he was certainly one of the best historians and critics of early Chinese philosophy.

This chapter first makes a distinction between the whole Truth and partial truth. The whole Truth is the *Tao* of "sageliness within and kingliness without," the study of which is called "the *Tao* method." Partial truth is a particular aspect of the whole Truth, the study of which is called "the art method." This chapter says: "In the world there are many who use the art method. Each one considers his own [thought] as perfect without need of any addition. Where is there then what the ancients called the *Tao* method?... There is that by which the sage flourishes; there is that through which the king completes his achievement. Both originate in the One."

The One is the "*Tao* of sageliness within and kingliness without." The chapter goes on to make a distinction between the fundamental and the branch, the fine and the coarse, in the *Tao*. It says: "How perfect were the men of old.... They understood the fundamental principles and connected them with minute regulations reaching to all points of the compass, embracing the great and the small, the fine and the coarse; their influence was everywhere.

"Some of their teachings which were correctly embodied in measures and institutions are still preserved in ancient laws and the records of historians. Those teachings that were recorded in the books of *Poetry*,

History, Rites, and *Music* were known to most of the gentlemen and teachers of [the states of] Tsou and Lu [i.e., the Confucianists]. The *Book of Poetry* describes aims; the *Book of History* describes events; the *Rites* direct conduct; *Music* secures harmony. The *Yi* [*Book of Changes*] shows the principles of the *Yin* and *Yang.* The *Ch'un Ch'iu* [*Spring and Autumn Annals*] shows names and duties."

Thus the *T'ien Hsia* chapter maintains that the Confucianists had some connection with the *Tao.* But what they knew is confined to "measures and institutions." They knew nothing about the underlying

不多的少数人），无见于多（欲望无穷的多数人）。" 荀子以为，哲学家们的洞见和他们的短处常常纠结在一起，哲学家往往有自己的洞察力，而往往因此又自恃太甚，结果洞见之处又恰好成为他的盲点，他的哲学的长处又同时成为他的哲学中的短处。

● 《庄子》哲学中的折中倾向

《庄子》书中最后的一篇《天下》篇陈述了道家的调和观点。《天下》篇其实是对中国古代哲学各流派的评述。我们不知道它的作者姓名，但这位作者实在是中国古代哲学史上一位杰出的哲学史家和评论家。

《天下》篇里首先区别真理的总体和局部。真理的总体是内圣外王之"道"，对"道"的研究成为"道术"。局部真理是真理总体中的某一部分，对局部真理的研究称为"方术"。《天下》篇中说："天下之治方术者多矣，皆以其有为不可加矣。古之所谓道术者，果恶乎在？……圣有所生，王有所成，皆原于一。"

这个"一"就是"内圣外王之道"。《天下》篇接下去又区别道有本末、精粗之分。它说："古之人其备乎！……明于本数，系于末度，六通四辟，小大精粗，其运无乎不在。其明而在数度者，旧法世传之史尚多有之。其在于《诗》《书》《礼》《乐》者，邹鲁之士（儒家）缙绅先生多能明之。《诗》以道志，《书》以道事，《礼》以道行，《乐》以道和，《易》以道阴阳，《春秋》以道名分。"

《天下》篇里认为，儒家对道的阐述不无道理，但儒家所见只是"数"和"度"，对更根本的原理并无所知。这就是说，儒家

principle. That is to say, they knew only the coarser aspects and lesser branches of the *Tao*, but not what is fine and fundamental in it.

The *T'ien Hsia* chapter continues by saying: "Now the world is in great disorder. The virtuous and the sage are obscured. *Tao* and virtue lose their unity and many in the world get hold of some one aspect of the whole to enjoy for themselves. The case is like the senses of hearing, sight, smell, and taste, which have specific functions, but cannot be interchanged. Or like the skill of the various artisans, which are each excellent in its kind and useful in its turn, yet are not comprehensive. Each is a student of some one aspect.... Thus the *Tao* of sageliness within and kingliness without becomes obscured and loses its clearness; it becomes repressed and loses its development."

Then the same treatise makes a classification of the different schools, granting to each that it has "heard" of some one aspect of the *Tao*, but at the same time making sharp criticisms of the school's shortcomings. Lao Tzu and Chuang Tzu are greatly admired. Yet, remarkably enough, these two leaders of Taoism, like the other schools, are by implication criticized by the remark that they, too, have merely "heard some one aspect of the *Tao*."

It thus seems to be the implication of the *T'ien Hsia* chapter that the Confucianists knew the concrete "measures and institutions" but not their underlying principle, whereas the Taoists knew the principle but not the measures and institutions. In other words, the Confucianists knew the "branches" of the *Tao*, but not its fundamental aspect, while the Taoists knew its fundamental aspect, but not its branches. Only a combination of the two constitutes the whole Truth.

● Eclecticism of Ssu-Ma T'an and Liu Hsin

This eclectic tendency was continued in the Han dynasty. The *Huai-nan-tzu* or *Book of the Prince of Huai-nan* is a book of the same nature as the *Lü-shih Ch'un-ch'iu*, though with a stronger tendency towards

Taoism. In addition to this book, the two historians, Ssu-ma T'an (died 110 B.C.) and Liu Hsin (ca. 46 B.C-A.D. 23), who have been quoted in chapter three, also display eclectic tendencies. Of them, Ssu-ma T'an was a Taoist. In the essay quoted in chapter three, "On the Essentials of the Six Schools," he says: "In the 'Great Appendix' ['Appendix III'] of the *Yi*, there is the statement: 'In the world there is one purpose, but there are a hundred ideas about it; there is a single goal, but the paths toward it differ.' This is just the case with the different schools of thought.... all of

所见只是"道"的"末端"和粗的方面，还不是"道"的根本和精微之处。

接下去，《天下》篇说："天下大乱，贤圣不明（不得彰明），道德不一，天下多得一察焉以自好。譬如耳目鼻口，皆有所明，不能相通。犹百家众技也，皆有所长，时有所用。虽然，不该不遍，一曲之士也。……是故内圣外王之道，暗而不明，郁（受压）而不发。"

接下去，《天下》篇区分了学术思想的不同流派，各派虽也有所"闻"于道，但都不能免于偏蔽。老子和庄子虽受到称颂，但这两位道家的代表人物，也同被列为"古之道术有在于是者"，这是含蓄地批评他们所见也只是道术的一方面。

由上所述，《天下》篇似乎认为，儒家看到具体的器物、度数，而不知它们所依据的基本原理；道家看到了基本原理，却不懂得器物和度数。换句话说，儒家知道"道"的枝干，而不懂得它的根本；道家懂得"道"的根本，却不知道它的枝干。只有把两者结合起来，才能构成真理的全部。

● 司马谈和刘歆的折中主义思想

这种折中主义的思想倾向一直继续到汉朝。《淮南子》和《吕氏春秋》的根本性质是一样的，只是更倾向于道家。除《淮南子》一书外，还有两位历史家——司马谈和刘歆也同样表现出折中的思想倾向。其中的司马谈本人便是一位道家。在本书第三章曾加以援引的司马谈所著《论六家要旨》中曾说："《易大传》：'天下一致而百虑，同归而殊涂。'夫阴阳、儒、墨、名、法、道德，此务为

which seek social order but follow widely different paths in their words of explanation, some of which are clear and others not." (*Historical Records*, ch. 130.) He then goes on to mention the excellencies and shortcomings of the six philosophic schools, but concludes by considering Taoism as combining all the best points of the other schools, and therefore as being superior to all.

Liu Hsin, on the other hand, was a Confucianist. In his *Seven Summaries*, as quoted in the chapter on literature contained in the *History of the Former Han Dynasty*, he lists ten schools of thought, and quotes the same passage from "Appendix III" of the *Book of Changes* as does Ssu-ma T'an. Then he concludes: "Each of the schools developed its strong points; and each developed knowledge and investigation to the utmost in order to set forth clearly its main purposes. Although they had prejudices and shortcomings, still a summary of their teachings shows that they were branches and descendants of the *Liu Yi* (Six Classics).... If one were able to cultivate the *Liu Yi* and observe the sayings of the nine schools [omitting that of the Story Tellers as of no philosophical importance], discarding their errors and gathering their good points, it would be possible to master the manifold aspects of thought." (*History of the Former Han Dynasty*, ch. 30.)

All these statements reflect the strong desire for unity that existed even in the world of thought. The people of the third century B.C., discouraged by centuries of inter-state warfare, longed for a political unification; their philosophers, consequently, also tried to bring about a unification in thought. Electicism was the first attempt. Eclecticism in itself, however, cannot build a unified system. The eclectics believed in the whole Truth, and hoped by selecting from the various schools their "strong points," to attain to this Truth or *Tao*. What they called the *Tao*, however, was, it is to be feared, simply a patch-work of many disparate elements, unconnected by any underlying organic principle, and hence unworthy of the high title they attached to it.

Dr. Derk Bodde writes: "I would question this statement. The Six Dynasties (third through sixth century), Yüan (1280-1367) and Ch'ing (1644-1911) periods, for example, were in actual fact of so long duration as to accustom the Chinese to the idea of disunity or foreign domination, even though such a situation was in theory regarded as 'abnormal.' Moreover, even in the 'normal' periods of unity, there was often extensive political maneuvering and military action against a succession

治者也，直所从言之异路，有省不省耳。"（《史记·太史公自序》）他接着指出六家之所长和所短。结束时认为，道家得各家之长，因此在其他五家之上。

刘歆和司马谈不同，他是一位儒家。在《汉书·艺文志》的《七略》里，他列举了十个思想流派。他也援引了司马谈所引的《易大传》所说："天下一致而百虑，同归而殊涂。"然后总结说："今异家者各推所长，穷知究虑，以明其指，虽有蔽短，合其要归，亦'六经'之支与流裔。……若能修六艺之术，而观此九家（十家之中最后列入的小说家，在哲学上无关宏旨）之言，舍短取长，则可以通万方之略矣。"

所有这些看法反映了当时思想界寻求共同点的强烈愿望。公元前三世纪的人们疲于列国之间几百年的战争，渴望政治上统一，哲学家们也一样谋求思想上的一致。折中主义便是这样的一个尝试。但是，折中主义并不能构成一个自身的思想体系。折中主义者相信真理的总体，指望从各家思想中取其所长，而达到真理，也就是"道"。然而他们所称的"道"，恐怕只是把许多不同的思想缀合在一起，并没有一个有机统一的基本道理，因此，很难称作真理。

〔注〕对中国民族主义的一点说明（参阅本章"中国的统一"一节）

布德博士对于"中国的统一"一节最后的论断提出质疑。他说："中国从三世纪到六世纪的'六朝'、元朝（公元一二八〇〔一二〇六〕至一三六七〔一三六八〕年）和清朝（公元一六四四〔一六一六〕至一九一一年）的统治时间都很长，使中国人已经适应了国家的分裂或被外族统治，尽管从理论上说，这种局面还被认为是'不正常'。再者，即使在'正常'的、国家统一的历史时期中，也不断出现政治动乱或针对

of outside peoples, such as the Hsiung-nu, as well as against occasional rebels within the empire. I would hardly regard the present conditions as presenting an unfamiliar situation to the Chinese, therefore, even though their effects are accentuated by the fact that they operate on a truly worldwide scale."

The historical facts which Dr. Bodde mentions are no doubt correct, but what concerns me in this paragraph is not these historical facts themselves, but what the Chinese people up to the end of the last century, or even the beginning of this century, have felt about them. The emphasis upon the foreign domination of the Yüan and Ch'ing dynasties is one made from the point of view of modern nationalism. It is true that from early times the Chinese have made a sharp distinction between *Chung Kuo* or *hua hsia* (Chinese) and *yi ti* (barbarian), but the emphasis of this distinction is more cultural than racial. The Chinese have traditionally considered that there are three kinds of living beings: Chinese, barbarians, and beasts. Of these, the Chinese are most cultured, the barbarians come next, and the beasts are completely uncultured.

When the Mongols and Manchus conquered China, they had already to a considerable extent adopted the culture of the Chinese. They dominated the Chinese politically, but the Chinese dominated them culturally. They therefore did not create a marked break or change in the continuity and unity of Chinese culture and civilization, with which the Chinese were most concerned. Hence traditionally the Chinese have considered the Yüan and Ch'ing as simply two of the many dynasties that have followed each other in Chinese history. This can be seen from the official arrangement of the dynastic histories. The Ming dynasty, for instance, in one sense represented a nationalistic revolution against the Yüan; nevertheless, the official *History of the Yüan Dynasty*, compiled under the Ming, treated the Yüan as the normal successor of the purely Chinese Sung dynasty. Likewise Huang Tsung-hsi (1610-1695), one of the nationalistic scholars who opposed the Manchus, in his *Sung Yüan Hsüeh-an* or *Biographical History of Confucianist Philosophers of the*

Sung and Yüan Dynasties, found no moral fault in such scholars as Hsü Heng (1209-1281) and Wu Ch'eng (1249-1333), who though Chinese had served under the Yüan with high official rank.

The Chinese Republic has similarly compiled an official *History of the Ch'ing Dynasty*, in which this dynasty is treated as the normal successor of the Ming. This history was later banned by the present government, because the treatment of certain events connected with the revolution of 1911 was regarded as unsatisfactory. Hence it is possible that the new official *History of the Ch'ing Dynasty* will eventually be written in

外族（如匈奴）的战争、针对国内叛乱的军事讨伐。因此，似乎很难说目前[1]中国的状况是春秋战国以后中国罕见的局面，尽管今日中国的内忧外患，由于国际因素而加重了。"

布德博士提出的历史事实无疑是确实的。我在上述这一节所关注的不是历史事实本身，而是中国人直到十九世纪末或二十世纪初对历史的看法。把元朝和清朝看作是外族对中国的统治，这是从现代民族主义观点出发的一种看法。从古代起，中国人的确十分强调中国（或华夏）与夷狄之分，但是，所着重的分野，不是种族的不同，而是文化的不同。传统上，中国人把生灵分为三类：中国人、蛮族和禽兽，认为中国人是其中最有文化的，其次是蛮族，兽类则是全无文化的。

蒙古人和满族人征服汉族时，已经在很大程度上接受了中国汉族的文化。他们在政治上居于统治地位，而汉族则在文化上居于统治地位。因此，蒙古人和满族人在中国的统治并未在中国文化或文明上造成断裂或剧变，而这是中国人最关心的一点。因此，中国人历来把元朝和清朝看作如同其他朝代一样的改朝换代，这可以从中国官修史书的朝代排列顺序看出来。例如，明朝推翻元朝，从另一角度说，也可以认为是一次民族革命。但是，明朝修元史时，只把元朝看作是接替宋朝的一个朝代，再如明末清初，被学术界尊崇为有民族气节的学者黄宗羲（公元一六一〇至一六九五年）修《宋元学案》（宋元两代儒家哲学家评传）时，对在元朝政府任高官的汉人许衡（公元一二〇九至一二八一年）、吴澄（公元一二四九至一三三三年）并没有提出道德上的抨击或非议。

中华民国官方在修《清史》时，也把清朝看作只是接替明朝的另一朝代，这部《清史》后来被禁出版，是因为它对一九一一年民国革命叙述不确。新的官修《清史》可能采取一种完全不同的写法，但我在这里

a quite different way. What I am here concerned with, however, is the traditional view. So far as tradition is concerned, the Yüan and Ch'ing were just as "normal" as other dynasties. One may say that the Chinese lack nationalism, but that is precisely my point. They lack nationalism because they have been accustomed to think in terms of *t'ien hsia*, the world.

As to the fact that the Chinese have had to fight such non-Chinese groups as the Hsiung-nu, etc., traditionally what the Chinese have felt is that sometimes it was necessary for them to fight the barbarians, just as sometimes it was necessary to fight the beasts. They did not feel that such people as the Hsiung-nu were in a position to divide the world with China, just as the American people do not feel that the red Indians are in a position to divide America with them.

Because the Chinese did not greatly emphasize racial distinctions, it resulted that during the third and fourth centuries A.D. various non-Chinese peoples were allowed to move freely into China. This movement constituted what is called the "inner colonization," and was a primary cause for the political troubles of the Six Dynasties period. Such "inner colonization" is precisely what Hitler, in his *Mein Kampf,* criticized from a super-nationalistic point of view.

The introduction of Buddhism seems to have given many Chinese the realization that civilized people other than the Chinese existed, but traditionally there have been two kinds of opinion regarding India. Those Chinese who opposed Buddhism believed that the Indians were simply another tribe of barbarians. Those who believed in Buddhism, on the other hand, regarded India as the "pure land of the West." Their praise of India was that of a realm transcending this world. Hence even the introduction of Buddhism, despite its enormous effect upon Chinese life, did not change the belief of the Chinese that they were the only civilized people in the *human* world.

As a result of these concepts, when the Chinese first came in contact with Europeans in the sixteenth and seventeenth centuries, they thought that they were simply barbarians like preceding barbarians, and so they spoke of them as barbarians. As a consequence they did not feel greatly disturbed, even though they suffered many defeats in fighting with them. They began to be disturbed, however, when they found that the Europeans possessed a civilization equal to, though different from, that of the Chinese. What was novel in the situation was not that peoples other than the Chinese existed, but that their civilization was one of

所关心的只是传统中国的看法。就传统来说，元、清两代在中国人心目中和其他汉人执掌政权的朝代一样，完全是"正常"的两个朝代。也许有人会说，中国人缺乏民族意识，我想着重说的正是这一点，中国人不着重民族意识，正是因为习惯于从"天下"来看问题。

至于中国在历史上曾不得不对匈奴等外族进行战争，中国人的传统看法认为，为了抵御蛮族入侵骚扰而进行战争是必要的，就如对兽类入侵，必须抵御一样。中国人并不认为匈奴可以和汉族平分天下，正如美国人并不认可和美洲土著居民平分美洲一样。

中国汉族历来并不特别强调民族之间的分野，因此，在公元三、四世纪间，许多外族移居进入中国。这种民族迁徙可以称之为"内部殖民化"，它成为六朝时期（建都建康〔即今南京〕的吴、东晋、宋、齐、梁、陈六朝，公元二二一至五八九年）中国政治动乱的一个主要原因。而这种"内部殖民化"正是希特勒在他的自传《我的奋斗》中，从超国家主义观点加以批判的地方。

佛教传入中国，使许多中国人认识到，在中国以外，还有其他民族也同样拥有高度文明。但中国人对于印度，历来有两种看法：反对佛教的人士认为，印度无非是另一蛮族；信仰佛教的人士则认为，印度是"西方净土"，把印度看作是超越现实世界的另一个世界。因此，尽管佛教传入中国后，对中国社会产生了巨大的影响，但多数中国人还是认为，中国是现实世界里拥有最高文化的民族。

由于上述的种种观念，当十六、十七世纪，中国人开始与欧洲人接触时，认为欧洲人也无非是新的蛮族，和先前的蛮族一样；因此称欧洲人为"夷人"，尽管在和欧洲人征战中，屡战屡败，并没有对欧洲人十分在意。一直到发现欧洲文明可以和中国文明相颉颃，才开始重视起来。这时所重视的不是在中国人以外还有欧洲人，而是欧洲人的文化

equal power and importance. In Chinese history one can find a parallel for such a situation only in the Ch'un Ch'iu and Chan Kuo periods, when different but equally civilized states existed that fought with one another. That is why the Chinese now feel that there is a repetition in history.

If one reads the writings of the great statesmen of the last century, such as Tseng Kuo-fan (1811-1872) and Li Hung-chang (1823-1901), there is much evidence that they felt about the impact of the West precisely in this way. This note attempts to describe the reasons for their feeling.

所产生的力量和重要性。在中国历史上，能够与此相比的时代只有春秋战国时代，当时，同样拥有高度文明的各国彼此战争。这是何以许多中国人现在觉得历史在重演。

如果翻开十九世纪重要政治家如曾国藩（公元一八一一至一八七二年）、李鸿章（公元一八二三至一九〇一年）的著述，就可以发现，他们正是这样感受西方对中国的影响。这一条注释就是试图解释他们何以有这样的思想和感受。

⑰ THEORIZER OF THE HAN EMPIRE: TUNG CHUNG-SHU

Mencius once said that those who do not delight in killing men would unify the world. (*Mencius*, Ia, 6.) It would seem that he was wrong, because, some hundred years later, it was the state of Ch'in that unified the whole of China. Ch'in was superior to the other states in the arts of both "agriculture and war," that is, it was superior both economically and militarily. It was known at the time as "the state of tigers and wolves". By sheer force of arms, coupled with the ruthless ideology of the Legalists, it succeeded in conquering all its rivals.

● **The Amalgamation of the *Yin-Yang* and Confucianist Schools**

Yet Mencius was not wholly wrong, for the Ch'in dynasty, which was established after the unification of 221 B.C., lasted only about fifteen years. Soon after the death of the First Emperor his empire disintegrated in a series of rebellions against the harsh Ch'in rule, and was succeeded by the Han dynasty (206 B.C.-A.D. 220). The Han inherited the concept of political unity of the Ch'in, and continued its unfinished work, that is, the building up of a new political and social order.

Tung Chung-shu (c. 179-c. 104 B.C.) was the great theorizer in such an attempt. A native of the southern part of the present Hopei province, he was largely instrumental in making Confucianism the orthodox belief of the Han dynasty, at the expense of the other schools of thought. He was also prominent in the creation of the institutional basis for this Confucian orthodoxy: the famed Chinese examination system, which began to take form during his time. Under this system, entry into the ranks of the government officials who ruled the country was not dependent upon noble birth or wealth, but rather upon success in a series of periodic examinations which were conducted by the government simultaneously throughout the country, and were open to all members of society with but trifling exceptions. These examinations, to be sure, were still embryonic in the Han dynasty and did not become really universal until several centuries later. It is to Tung Chung-shu's credit, however, that he was one of the first to propose them, and it is also significant that in so doing he insisted upon the Confucian classics as the ideological basis for their operation.

拾柒 汉帝国的理论家：董仲舒

　　孟子在与梁惠王的对话中曾经说，唯有不嗜杀人的才能统一天下。可是几百年后，秦国靠经济和军事的优势，统一了全中国。当时秦国被称为"虎狼之邦"，它以军事力量以及法家的残忍的统治理论，战胜了对手。这样看来，孟子似乎错了。

● 阴阳家和儒家的合流

　　但是，孟子并没有完全说错。秦朝在公元前二二一年统一中国后，它的统治只维持了约十五年。始皇帝死后不久，秦国内部爆发了一系列反抗秦朝残暴统治的起义，国家陷于分裂，最后被汉朝取而代之。汉王朝（公元前二〇六至公元二二〇年）继承了秦朝中央集权的政治理念，继续从事秦朝未竟的事业，建立起了一个新的政治、社会秩序。

　　汉朝建立中央集权国家的过程中，有一个重要的理论家便是董仲舒（公元前一七九至前一〇四年），他出身于今河北省南部。董仲舒在汉朝废黜百家、独尊儒术，统一全国思想的活动中起了重要的作用。为保证儒术成为统治思想，汉朝废弃过去以贵族门第出身或家族富有作为选拔官员标准，改由政府主持，以儒术为标准，在全国同时举行考试，读书人都可以应试，从中选拔官员，以便从制度上确保儒家思想的统治地位。这是在董仲舒时期创始的，虽然在汉朝还只刚开始，要到几百年后才得以普遍推行，但董仲舒坚持推行这样的制度，并且坚持以儒家经书为正统，对此后历代起了重要作用。

It is said of Tung Chung-shu that he was so devoted to his literary studies that once for three years he did not even look out into his garden. As a result, he wrote a lengthy work known as the *Ch'un ch'iu Fan-lu*, or *Luxuriant Dew from the Spring and Autumn Annals*. It is also said that he used to expound his teachings from behind a curtain, and that these were transmitted by his disciples, one to another, to a remote distance, so that there were some who never had the privilege of seeing his countenance. (See his biography in the *History of the Former Han Dynasty*, ch. 56.)

What Tung Chung-shu tried to do was to give a sort of theoretical justification to the new political and social order of his time. According to him, since man is a part of Heaven, the justification of the behavior of the former must be found in the behavior of the latter. He thought with the *Yin-Yang* school that a close interconnection exists between Heaven and man. Starting with this premise, he combined a metaphysical justification, which derives chiefly from the *Yin-Yang* school, with a political and social philosophy which is chiefly Confucianist.

The word Heaven is a translation of the Chinese word *T'ien*, which is sometimes rendered as "Heaven" and sometimes as "nature." Neither translation is quite adequate, however, especially in Tung Chung-shu's philosophy. My colleague Professor Y. L. Chin has said: "Perhaps if we mean by T'ien both nature and the divinity which presides over nature, with emphasis sometimes on the one and sometimes on the other, we have something approaching the Chinese term." (Unpublished manuscript). This statement is not true in certain cases, for instance, in those of Lao Tzu and Chuang Tzu, but it is certainly so in the case of Tung Chung-shu. In this chapter, when the word Heaven occurs, I ask the reader to recall this statement of Professor Chin as the definition of the word *T'ien* in Tung Chung-shu's philosophy.

In chapter twelve it was pointed out that there were two distinct lines of thought in ancient China, those of the *Yin* and *Yang* and of the Five Elements, each of which provided a positive interpretation for the structure and origin of the universe. Later, however, these two lines became amalgamated, and in Tung Chung-shu this amalgamation is particularly conspicuous. Thus in his philosophy we find both the theory of the *Yin* and *Yang* and that of the Five Elements.

董仲舒青年时代潜心读书，据说他曾在窗上垂帷，三年不曾向窗外眺望，最后终于完成了《春秋繁露》这部巨著。《汉书·董仲舒传》还记载，他"下帷讲诵"，自己在帷中授课，帷外门生，一个对一个口传，以至有些学生，始终未得见他一面。

董仲舒所要做的是：从理论上论证新的政治社会制度的"存在的根据"。他的看法是：既然人是天的一部分，人的所作所为，自然应依据天的所作所为。他和阴阳家持同样的见解，认为天人之间有一种密切的相互作用。从这个前提出发，他把阴阳家的形而上的宇宙观和主要是儒家的政治社会哲学结合起来。

中文里的"天"字在英文里通常译成"上天"（Heaven），也有时译成"自然"（Nature）。这两种译法都有未全尽意的地方，用于翻译董仲舒的哲学思想，更显出这个问题。我的同事金岳霖教授曾在他的一份未定稿中说："在中国哲学里，'天'的含义既包括自然，又包括君临自然的上苍。人们使用这词语时，有时着重在'自然'，有时则着重在'上苍'。这样来理解'天'的含义，可能较为恰当。"这个论断，在某些情况下不一定适用，例如，在理解老庄的哲学时就不能或此或彼，但在读董仲舒的哲学著作时，就需要分辨他在各个特定场合下使用"天"字时的含义。因此，在本章里，当"天"字出现时，请读者用金岳霖教授的这段话来理解董仲舒著作中"天"字的含义。

第十二章里曾经指出，在古代中国，阴阳家和五行家代表两种不同的思想。这两家对宇宙的结构和起源都提出了正面的解释。后来，这两种思想逐渐合流，在董仲舒的思想里，这种合流特别明显，其中既有阴阳的思想，又有五行家的思想。

- **Cosmological Theory**

According to Tung Chung-shu, the universe has ten constituents: Heaven, Earth, the *Yin* and *Yang*, the Five Elements of Wood, Fire, Soil, Metal, and Water, and finally man.[1] His idea of the *Yin* and *Yang* is very concrete. He says: "Within the universe there exist the ethers of the *Yin* and *Yang*. Men are constantly immersed in them, just as fish are constantly immersed in water. The difference between the *Yin* and *Yang* ethers and water is that water is visible, whereas the ethers are invisible." (Ch. 81.)

The order of the Five Elements given by Tung Chung-shu differs from that given by the "Grand Norm." (See ch. 12 of this book.) According to him, the first is Wood, the second, Fire, the third Soil, the fourth Metal, and the fifth Water. These Five Elements "each in turn produces the next and is overcome by the next but one in turn." (Ch. 42.) Thus Wood produces Fire, Fire produces Soil, Soil produces Metal, Metal produces Water, and Water produces Wood. This is the process of their mutual production. But Wood overcomes Soil, Soil overcomes Water, Water overcomes Fire, Fire overcomes Metal, and Metal overcomes Wood. This is the process of their mutual overcoming.

For Tung Chung-shu, as for the *Yin-Yang* school, Wood, Fire, Metal, and Water each presides over one of the four seasons as well as one of the four directions of the compass. Wood presides over the east and spring, Fire over the south and summer, Metal over the west and autumn, and Water over the north and winter. Soil presides over the center and gives assistance to all the other elements. The alternation of the four seasons is explained by the operations of the *Yin* and *Yang*. (Ch. 42.)

The *Yin* and *Yang* wax and wane and follow fixed circuits which take them through all the four directions. When the *Yang* first waxes, it moves to assist Wood in the east, and then there comes spring. As it grows in strength, it moves to the south where it assists Fire, and then there comes summer. But according to the universal law of "reversal" as maintained by the *Lao-tzu* and the *Yi* "Appendices," growth must be followed by decay. Hence the *Yang*, having reached its extreme height, begins to wane, while at the same time the *Yin* begins to wax in turn. The *Yin*, as it does this, moves east to assist Metal,[2] and then there comes autumn. As it gains more strength, it moves north to assist Water, and then there comes winter. But having there reached its climax, it begins to wane, while at the same time the *Yang* starts a new cycle of growth.

Thus the changes of the four seasons result from the waxing and waning movements of the *Yin* and *Yang*, and their succession is really a succession of the *Yin* and *Yang*. Tung Chung-shu says: "The constant

● 对宇宙本体的理论

按照董仲舒在《春秋繁露·天地阴阳》篇的看法，宇宙是由十种成分组成，这十种成分是：天、地、阴、阳、木、火、土、金、水和人。他的阴阳观念很具体。关于阴阳，他说："天地之间，有阴阳之气，常渐人者，若水常渐鱼也。所以异于水者，可见与不可见耳。"

董仲舒所定的五行次序和《书经·洪范》中的次序不同，他以木为第一，火为第二，土为第三，金为第四，水为第五。五行"比相生而间相胜"，这就是说，木生火，火生土，土生金，金生水，水生木，这是"比（邻）相生"；木胜土，土胜水，水胜火，火胜金，金胜木，这是"间相胜"。

董仲舒也和阴阳家一样，认为木、火、金、水，各主一个季节，又各主东西南北之中的一方。木主东方和春季，火主南方和夏季，金主西方和秋季，水主北方和冬季。土居中，助木、火、金、水。四季嬗替则以阴阳运行来解释。

阴阳各有盛衰，有其一定轨道，循四方而运转。阳气初升时，它到东方扶木，从而春天来到。阳气全盛时，它居南方，是为夏季。但是，按照老子和"易传"中"反者道之用"、物极必反的道理，阳气盛极而衰，这时，阴气上升，阴气初盛时，它又到东方（不是西方，因为董仲舒认为天是"任阳不任阴"的，见《春秋繁露·阴阳位》）扶金而秋至；当阴极盛时，它移到北方扶水而冬至。这时阴由盛而衰，阳气重又抬头，开始另一次四季运行。

在董仲舒看来，一年四季的嬗替是阴阳二气运行的结果。

principle of the universe is the succession of the *Yin* and *Yang*. The *Yang* is Heaven's beneficent force, while the *Yin* is its chastising force.... In the course of Heaven, there are three seasons [spring, summer, and autumn] of formation and growth, and one season [winter] of mourning and death." (Ch. 49.)

This shows, according to Tung, that "Heaven has trust in the *Yang* but not in the *Yin*; it likes beneficence but not chastisement." (Ch. 47.) It also shows that "Heaven has its own feelings of joy and anger, and a mind which experiences sadness and pleasure, analogous to those of man. Thus if a grouping is made according to kind, Heaven and man are one." (Ch. 49.)

Man, therefore, both in his physiological and mental aspects, is a replica or duplicate of Heaven. (Ch. 41.) As such, he is far superior to all other things of the world. Man, Heaven, and Earth are "the origins of all things." "Heaven gives them birth, Earth gives them nourishment, and man gives them perfection." (Ch. 19.) As to how man accomplishes this perfection, Tung says that it is done through *li* (ritual) and *yüeh* (music), that is to say, through civilization and culture. If there were no civilization and culture, the world would be like an unfinished work, and the universe itself would suffer imperfection. Thus of Heaven, Earth, and man, he says: "These three are related to each other like the hands and feet; united they give the finished physical form, so that no one of them may be dispensed with." (Ch. 19.)

• Theory of Human Nature

Since Heaven has its *Yin* and *Yang*, and man is a replica of Heaven, the human mind consequently also contains two elements: *hsing* (man's nature) and *ch'ing* (the emotions or feelings). The word *hsing* is used by Tung Chung-shu sometimes in a broader and sometimes a narrower sense. In the narrow sense, it is something that exists separate from and in opposition to *ch'ing*, whereas in the broader sense it embraces *ch'ing*. In this latter meaning, Tung sometimes refers to *hsing* as the "basic stuff."

(Ch. 35.) This basic stuff of man, therefore, consists both of *hsing* (used in the narrow sense) and *ch'ing*. From *hsing* comes the virtue of human-heartedness, whereas from *ch'ing* comes the vice of covetousness. This *hsing*, in the narrow sense, is equivalent to Heaven's *Yang*, and *ch'ing* to its *Yin*. (Ch. 35.)

In this connection Tung Chung-shu takes up the old controversy as to whether human nature, that is, the basic stuff of man, is good or bad. He cannot agree with Mencius that the nature is good, for he says: "Goodness is like a kernel of grain, and the nature is like the growing plant of the

他说："天道之常，一阴一阳。阳者天之德也，阴者天之刑也。……是故，天之道，以三时（春夏秋）成生，以一时（冬）丧死。"（同上）

董仲舒认为，这是"天之任阳不任阴，好德不好刑"。它也表明，"天亦有喜怒之气，哀乐之心，与人相副。以类合之，天人一也"（同上）。

董仲舒由"天人一体"进一步提出：人在身心两方面都是天的复制品（《春秋繁露·为人者天》）。因此，人高于世上万物。在《春秋繁露·立元神》篇中，董仲舒说："天、地、人，万物之本也。天生之，地养之，人成之。"人怎样"成"呢？董仲舒认为，是靠"礼"和"乐"，这就是靠教化和修养，如果没有教化和修养，世界便如同一项未完成的工程，宇宙本身也因之而不完美。因此，董仲舒说：天、地、人"三者相为手足，合以成体，不可一无也"。

● 人性的学说

天地既由阴阳二气而成，人是天地的复制品，人心自然也有两种因素，这就是"性"和"情"。董仲舒在说到"性"时，有时是就广义而言，有时是就狭义而言。就狭义来说，"性"是有别于"情"，又是与"情"相对的。就广义来说，董仲舒认为，"性者，质也。"人的质，就包括"性"（狭义）和"情"，人顺其本性能有仁德，顺其情而有贪欲。董仲舒说到"性"时，就相当于天的"阳"；说到"情"时，就相当于天的"阴"。

董仲舒由此联系到儒家哲学中的老问题：人性究竟是善，抑或恶？他不同意孟子"人性善"的理论，认为："善如米，性如禾。

grain. Though the plant produces the kernel, it cannot itself be called a kernel. [Similarly] though the *hsing* [here used in its broader sense, i.e., the basic stuff] produces goodness, it cannot itself be called goodness. The kernel and goodness are both brought to completion through man's continuation of Heaven's work, and are external [to the latter]. They do not lie within [the scope of] what Heaven itself does. What Heaven does extends to a certain point and then stops. What lies within this stopping point pertains to Heaven. What lies outside of it pertains to the *chiao* [teaching, culture] of the [sage-] kings. The *chiao* of the [sage-] kings lies outside the *hsing* [basic stuff], yet without it the *hsing* cannot be fully developed." (Ch. 36.)

Thus Tung Chung-shu emphasizes the value of culture, which is indeed that which makes man equal to Heaven and Earth. In this respect he approaches Hsün Tzu. He differs from him, however, in that he does not consider the basic stuff of man to be actually evil. Goodness is a continuation of nature, not a reversal of it.

Inasmuch as culture, for Tung, is a continuation of nature, he also approaches Mencius. Thus he writes: "It is said by some that since the nature [of man] contains the beginning of goodness and the mind contains the basic stuff of goodness, how, then, can it be that [the nature itself] is not good? But I reply that this is not so. For the silk cocoon contains silk fibers and yet is not itself silk, and the egg contains the chicken, yet is not itself a chicken. If we follow these analogies, what doubt can there be?" (Ch. 5.) The question raised here represents the view of Mencius. In answering it, Tung Chung-shu makes clear the difference between Mencius and himself.

But the difference between these two philosophers is really not much more than verbal. Tung Chung-shu himself says: "Mencius evaluates [the basic stuff of man] in comparison with the doings of the birds and beasts below, and therefore says that human nature is itself already good. I evaluate it in comparison with the sages above, and therefore say that human nature is not yet good." (Ch. 25.) Thus the difference between

Mencius and Tung Chung-shu is reduced to that between two phrases: "already good" and "not yet good."

- **Social Ethics**

According to Tung Chung-shu, the theory of the *Yin* and *Yang* is also a metaphysical justification of the social order. He writes: "In all things there must be correlates. Thus if there is the upper, there must be the lower. If there is the left, there must be the right…. If there is cold, there

禾虽出米，而禾未可谓米也。性虽出善，而性未可谓善也。米与善，人之继天而成于外也，非在天所为之内也。天所为，有所至止。止之内谓之天，止之外谓之王教。王教在性外，而性不得不遂。"(《春秋繁露·实性》) 这是说，天之所为，有其所止；在这范围内是天的作为，超过这一范围，则要靠圣王的教化；圣王的教化，在人性之外，但若没有圣王的教化，人性便得不到充分的发展。

可以看到，董仲舒十分强调文化的价值，人之能够与天地并列，所靠的是文化。在这方面，他的思想直追荀子而上。他不同于荀子的地方是：他不认为人性恶，而认为善是人性的发展，不是人性的悖逆。

因此，文化是人性的发展，就这一点来说，董仲舒又是继续了孟子的理论。他说："或曰：性有善端，心有善质，尚安非善？应之曰：非也。茧有丝而茧非丝也，卵有雏而卵非雏也。比类率然，有何疑焉？"(《春秋繁露·深察名号》) 这里提问的是孟子的一派，董仲舒在回答时，也阐明了他的思想与孟子不同的地方。

但是，他们之间的不同，其实更多是语言上的不同，董仲舒自己说过："孟子下质于禽兽之所为，故曰性已善；吾上质于圣人之所善，故谓性未善。"(同上) 这样，董仲舒和孟子之间的不同，最后归结为"未善"和"已善"的不同了。

- **社会伦理学说**

董仲舒又以形而上学的阴阳学说作为论证社会秩序的根据。他写道："凡物必有合。合，必有上，必有下，必有左，必有右，必有前，

must be heat. If there is day, there must be night. These are all correlates. The *Yin* is the correlate of the *Yang*, the wife of the husband, the subject of the sovereign. There is nothing that does not have a correlate, and in each correlation there is the *Yin* and *Yang*. Thus the relationships between sovereign and subject, father and son, and husband and wife, are all derived from the principles of the *Yin* and *Yang*. The sovereign is *Yang*, the subject is *Yin*; the father is *Yang*, the son is *Yin*; the husband is *Yang*, the wife is *Yin*.... The three cords [*kang*]of the Way of the [true] King may be sought in Heaven." (Ch. 53.)

According to the Confucianists before this period, there are in society five major human relationships, namely, those between sovereign and subject, father and son, husband and wife, elder and younger brother, and friend and friend. Out of these, Tung selects three and calls them the three *kang*. The literal meaning of *kang* is a major cord in a net, to which all the other strings are attached. Thus the sovereign is the *kang* of his subjects, that is, he is their master. Likewise the husband is the *kang* of the wife, and the father is the *kang* of the son.

Besides the three *kang* there exist the five *ch'ang*, which were upheld by all Confucianists. *Ch'ang* means a norm or constant, and the five *ch'ang* are the five constant virtues of Confucianism, namely, *jen* (human-heartedness), *yi* (righteousness), *li* (propriety, rituals, rules of proper conduct), *chih* (wisdom) and *hsin* (good faith). Although Tung Chung-shu did not especially emphasize this point himself, it was commonly held by all the Han scholars that the five virtues have their correlations in the Five Elements. Thus human-heartedness is correlated with Wood in the east; righteousness with Metal in the west; propriety with Fire in the south; wisdom with Water in the north; and good faith with Soil in the center.[3]

The five *ch'ang* are the virtues of an individual, and the three *kang* are the ethics of society. The compound word *kang-ch'ang* meant, in olden times, morality or moral laws in general. Man must develop his nature in the direction of the moral laws, which are the essentials of culture and civilization.

● Political Philosophy

Not all men, however, can do this by themselves. Hence it is the function of government to help them in their development. Tung Chung-shu writes: "Heaven has produced men with natures that contain the basic stuff of goodness but are not able to be good in themselves.

必有后，必有表，必有里。……有寒必有暑，有昼必有夜，此皆其合也。阴者阳之合，妻者夫之合，子者父之合，臣者君之合。物莫无合，而合各有阴阳。……君臣、父子、夫妇之义，皆与诸阴阳之道。君为阳，臣为阴；父为阳，子为阴；夫为阳，妻为阴。……王道之三纲，可求于天。"（《春秋繁露·基义》）

在此之前，儒家认为，社会是由五种伦常关系组成的：君臣、父子、夫妇、兄弟、朋友。董仲舒从中选出君臣、父子、夫妇三项，称为"三纲"。"纲"的字义本是网上的大绳，网上其他的绳子都连到"纲"上，因此，国君是臣民的纲，即臣民的主宰；同样，夫为妻纲，父为子纲。

"三纲"之外，还有"五常"，这是所有儒家都主张遵奉的道德。"常"的字义是规范、恒常不变；因此，"五常"便用以表达儒家崇奉的五种德行，即：仁、义、礼、智、信。汉代的学者们还把"五常"和"五行"联系起来：仁与木和东方联系起来，义与金和西方联系起来，礼与火和南方联系起来，智与水和北方联系起来，信与土则居中。（见《白虎通义》卷八）董仲舒本人倒并不十分重视"五常"和"五行"的这种联系。

五常是个人的品德，三纲则是社会伦理。在旧时的中国，纲常就用以泛指道德和道德规范。人的自然发展应当依循道德规范的方向，而这是文化和文明的主要内涵。

● 政治哲学

但是，常人靠自己往往不能做到这些要求，因此政府便有责任帮助大众发展品德。董仲舒写道："天生民性有善质，而未能善，

Therefore Heaven has established for them [the institution of] the king to make them good. This is the purpose of Heaven." (Ch. 35.)

The king governs with beneficence, rewards, punishments, and executions. These "four ways of government" are modeled on the four seasons. Tung says: "Beneficence, rewards, punishments, and executions, match spring, summer, autumn, and winter respectively, like the fitting together of [the two parts of] a tally. Therefore I say that the king is co-equal with Heaven, meaning that Heaven has four seasons, while the king has four ways of government. Such are what Heaven and man share in common." (Ch. 55.)

The organization of government is also modeled on the pattern of the four seasons. According to Tung, the fact that government officials are graded into four ranks is modeled on the fact that a year has four seasons. Likewise, the fact that each official in each rank has three assistants under him, is modeled on the fact that each season has three months. The officials are thus graded, because men naturally fall into four grades in regard to their ability and virtue. Hence the government selects all men who deserve to be selected, and employs them according to these natural grades of virtue and ability. "Thus Heaven selects the four seasons, and brings them to completion with the twelve [months]; in this way the transformations of Heaven are completely expressed. And it is only the sage who can similarly give complete expression to the changes of man and harmonize them with those of Heaven." (Ch. 24.)

Since the relation between Heaven and man is so close and intimate, hence, Tung maintains, all wrongdoings in human government must result in the manifestation of abnormal phenomena in the world of nature. As had already been done by the *Yin-Yang* school, he supplies both a teleological and a mechanistic explanation for this theory.

Teleologically speaking, when there is something wrong in human government, this necessarily causes displeasure and anger on the part of Heaven. Such displeasure or anger is expressed through natural visitations or prodigies, such as earthquakes, eclipses of the sun or moon, droughts or floods. These are Heaven's way of warning the ruler to correct his mistakes.

Mechanistically speaking, however, according to Tung Chung-shu, "all things avoid that from which they differ and cleave to that to which they are similar," and "things definitely call to themselves their own kind." Hence abnormalities on the part of man necessarily call forth abnormalities on the part of nature. Tung Chung-shu, contradicting his teleological theory expressed elsewhere, maintains that this is the law of nature and that in it there is nothing supernatural. (Ch. 57.)

于是为之立王以善之，此天意也。"（《春秋繁露·深察名号》）

君王以庆、赏、罚、刑为"四政"，即统治的方法。这四种统治的方法是取法于四季。这便是董仲舒所说："庆赏刑罚与春夏秋冬，以类相应也，如合符。故曰王者配天，谓其道。天有四时，王有四政，四政若四时，通类也，天人所同有也。"（《春秋繁露·四时之副》）政府的组织也以四季为模式，按照一年分为四季，官员也分为四等，各级官员，每人下有三个助手，因每季有三个月。在考核官员时，也分为四等，因为人的能力、品德也天然分为四级。在这样的原则下，政府"选贤"，而后"任能"，根据所选之人的品德、能力，分别任用。这便是董仲舒所说："故天选四时、十二（月），而人变尽矣。尽人之变合之天，唯圣人者能之。"（《春秋繁露·官制象天》）

由于天和人的关系如此密切，因此董仲舒认为，政府的失误必然表现为自然界的异常现象。这个思想早在阴阳家时代便已存在，但董仲舒为它提供了一种既是目的论的又是机械论的解释。

从目的论的角度来看，为政而人事不臧，必定招致天怒。天怒便表现为自然灾害如地震、日食、月食、旱灾、水灾等，这是上天警告君王，要他改正自己的错误。

从机械论的角度来看，董仲舒认为："百物去其所与异，而从其所与同"；"物固以类相召也"（《春秋繁露·同类相动》）。所以人事上的不正常必然引起自然界的不正常。董仲舒认为这是自然规律，并不是什么超自然现象，这个看法和他在其他地方所讲的目的论其实是有矛盾的。

● **Philosophy of History**

In chapter twelve we saw how Tsou Yen maintained the theory that the changes of dynasties in history are influenced by the movements of the Five Powers. A certain dynasty, because it is associated with a certain Power, must conduct its government in a manner appropriate to that Power. Tung Chung-shu modifies this theory by maintaining that the succession of dynasties does not accord with the movement of the Five Powers, but with a sequence of what he calls the "Three Reigns." These are the Black, White, and Red Reigns. Each has its own system of government and each dynasty represents one Reign. (Ch. 23.)

In actual history, according to Tung, the Hsia dynasty (traditionally 2205-1766 B.C.) represented the Black Reign; the Shang dynasty (1766?-1122? B.C.) the White Reign; and the Chou dynasty (1122?-256 B.C.) the Red Reign. This constituted one cycle in the evolution of history. After the Chou dynasty, the new dynasty would again represent the Black Reign, and the same sequence would recur.

It is interesting to note that in modern times, colors have also been used to denote varying systems of social organization, and that they are the same three as those of Tung Chung-shu. Thus, following his theory, we might say that Fascism represents the Black Reign, Capitalism the White Reign, and Communism the Red Reign.

Of course, this is only coincidence. According to Tung Chung-shu, the three Reigns do not differ fundamentally. He maintains that when a new king founds a dynasty, he does so because he has received a special Mandate from Heaven. Hence he must effect certain external changes to make apparent that he has received the new Mandate. These include the shifting of his capital to a new place, assumption of a new title, changing the beginning of the year, and altering the color of clothing worn on official occasions. "As to the great bonds of human relationships," says Tung, "and as to morality, government, moral instruction, customs and the meaning of words, these remain wholly as they were before. For why, indeed, should they be changed? Therefore, the king of a new dynasty has the reputation of changing his institutions, but does not as a matter of fact alter the basic principles." (Ch. 1.)

These basic principles are what Tung calls the *Tao*. His biography in the *History of the Former Han Dynasty* (ch. 56) quotes him as saying: "The great source of *Tao* derives from Heaven; Heaven does not change, nor does the *Tao*."

● 历史哲学

在第十二章里，我们看到邹衍认为，历史中的朝代更替是由于五德运行产生的影响。按照邹衍的学说，每个朝代必须与五德之一相联，因此，这个朝代就应当遵循这五德之一的要求来运转。董仲舒修改了这个理论，认为朝代的更替不是依循五德运行的顺序，而是依循"三统"，即黑统、白统、赤统的顺序。他在《三代改制质文》中说：每个朝代都依循一统，每统又各有其为政的系统。

按董仲舒的说法，夏朝（历来认为时在公元前二二〇五〔二〇七〕至前一七六六〔一六〇〇〕年）代表黑统，商朝（历来认为时在公元前一七六六〔一六〇〇〕至前一一二二〔一〇四六〕年）代表白统，周朝（公元前一一二二〔一〇四六〕至前二五六年）则是赤统。夏、商、周三朝完成了历史循环的一周。继周之后，历史又开始一次新的循环，新的朝代又应当代表黑统。

有趣的是，到了近代，颜色和世界政治又再次联系了起来，并且分为三统：法西斯主义尚黑（统），资本主义尚白（统），而共产主义则尚赤（统）。

这当然只是偶合。在董仲舒的理论中，这三统并没有本质的不同。一个新君建立一个新的朝代，是由于承受天命，因此，他必须采取措施，表明承受天命。这些措施包括迁移国都，改国号，改纪元，改服色。董仲舒说："若夫大纲、人伦、道德、政治、教化、习俗、文义，尽如故，亦何改哉？故王者有改制之名，无改制之实。"（《春秋繁露·楚庄王》）

董仲舒称为政的基本原则为"道"。《汉书·董仲舒传》引述他的话说："道之大原出于天，天不变，道亦不变。"

The theory that the ruler rules through the Mandate of Heaven is not a new one. In the *Book of History* we find sayings implying this theory, and Mencius made it already sufficiently clear. But Tung Chung-shu made it the more articulate by incorporating it into his whole philosophy of nature and man.

In the feudal age, all rulers inherited their authority from their ancestors. Even the First Emperor of the Ch'in dynasty was no exception. But the founder of the Han dynasty was different. Rising from the common people, he succeeded in becoming Emperor of the (to the Chinese) entire civilized world. This needed some justification, and Tung Chung-shu provided that justification.

His theory that a ruler rules through the Mandate of Heaven justified the exercise of imperial authority and at the same time set certain limits on it. The Emperor had to be watchful for manifestations of Heaven's pleasure or displeasure, and to act accordingly. It was the practice of the Han Emperors, and, to a greater or lesser extent, of the Emperors of later dynasties, to examine themselves and the policies of their government, and to try to reform them when abnormal natural phenomena gave them cause to be uneasy.

Tung's theory of the succession of the Reigns also set a certain limit to the tenure of a given dynasty. No matter how good an imperial house may be, the length of its rule is limited. When the end comes, it must give way to another dynasty, the founder of which has received a new Mandate. Such are the measures through which the Confucianists tried to lay restraints upon the power of an absolute monarchy.

● Interpretation of the *Ch'un Ch'iu*

According to Tung Chung-shu, neither the Ch'in nor the Han was the direct successor of the Chou dynasty. In actual fact, he asserted, it was Confucius who received the Mandate of Heaven to succeed the

Chou and to represent the Black Reign. He was not a king *de facto*, but one *de jure*.

This is a strange theory, but it was actually maintained and believed by Tung Chung-shu and his school. The *Ch'un Ch'iu*, or *Spring and Autumn Annals*, which was originally a chronicle of Confucius' native state of Lu, was supposed by them (incorrectly) to be a very important

王者受命于天，并不是一个新理论。在《书经》里，已经有这个思想。孟子把它说得更清楚。董仲舒则更具体地把它纳入了自己的天人一体论。

在封建时代，所有的君王都是从祖先承受君位，甚至秦始皇帝也不例外。只是到了汉朝，情况不同了，汉高祖刘邦出身布衣而君临天下。这需要某种理论的支撑，董仲舒正是提供了这种理论的支撑。

董仲舒的理论认为，一个国君的统治是由于天命，这就为君王行使皇帝的权威提供了合法的根据；同时又对君王的权威施加了某种限制：皇帝必须时刻注意上天的喜怒表现，按照上天的意旨行事。汉朝的皇帝和此后历朝的皇帝，每逢天灾时，都程度不等地要省察自己执政的表现，苛责自身，谋求改进。

董仲舒关于"三统"的理论还有一层作用就是宣告，一个朝代不能企望无限期地统治下去。无论一个皇朝多么好，它的统治仍然是有限期的。在大限来到时，它就必须让位给另一个朝代。新皇朝的创立者将另外承受天命。这是儒家为约束绝对君权而提出的一种限制。

● **对《春秋》的解释**

照董仲舒的看法，继承周朝统治的既不是秦朝，也不是汉朝，而是孔子，他承受天命，创立了黑统。孔子所受天命，不是一种"法统"，而是一种"道统"。

这是一种新颖的理论，但董仲舒和他的学派都追随这个理论。《春秋》本是鲁国的史书。按董仲舒一派的说法，《春秋》乃是孔子

political work of Confucius in which he exercised his right as the new king. He represented the Black Reign and instituted all the changes that go with this Reign. Tung Chung-shu was famous for his interpretation of the *Ch'un Ch'iu*, and could justify all aspects of his philosophy by quotations from it. As a matter of fact, he commonly quoted the *Ch'un Ch'iu* as the main source of his authority. That is why his work is titled the *Ch'un-ch'iu Fan-lu* or *Luxuriant Dew from the Ch'un Ch'iu*.

Tung divides the centuries covered by the *Ch'un Ch'iu* (722-481 B.C.) into three periods, which he calls the "three ages." These are: (1) the age that was personally witnessed by Confucius; (2) that which he heard of through the oral testimony of elder living contemporaries; (3) that which he heard of through transmitted records. According to Tung Chung-shu, Confucius, when writing the *Ch'un Ch'iu*, used differing words or phrases to record the events occurring in these three periods. It is by studying the way in which these words or phrases are used that one may discover the esoteric meaning of the *Ch'un Ch'iu*.

● **Three Stages of Social Progress**

There have been three important commentaries written on the *Ch'un Ch'iu*, and since the Han dynasty these have become classics themselves. They are the Tso Commentary, known as the *Tso Chuan* (which probably was originally not written *in toto* as a commentary on the *Ch'un Ch'iu*, but was later attached to that work), and the Kung Yang and Ku Liang Commentaries. All three are supposedly named after the authors who composed them. Among the three, the Kung Yang Commentary, in particular, interprets the *Ch'un Ch'iu* in agreement with the theories of Tung Chung-shu. Thus in this Commentary we find the same theory of the "three ages." During the latter part of the Han dynasty, Ho Hsiu (129-182) wrote a commentary on the Kung Yang Commentary, in which he still further elaborated this theory.

According to Ho Hsiu, the *Ch'un Ch'iu* is a record of the process through which Confucius ideally transformed the age of decay and disorder into that of "approaching peace," and finally into that of "universal peace." He identifies the earliest of the three ages, "the age of which Confucius heard through transmitted records," as one of "decay and disorder." In this period Confucius devoted his whole attention to his own state of Lu, and took Lu as the center of his reforms. The next period, "the age of which Confucius heard through oral testimony," is identified by Ho

的一部重要著作，在其中，孔子树立了他的道统的统治。孔子代表了黑统，并创建了黑统的各项制度。董仲舒对《春秋》的解释十分著名，他的各项学说都可以从《春秋》中找到根据，换句话说，他的理论权威来自《春秋》，这是他把自己的著作称为《春秋繁露》的缘故。

董仲舒把《春秋》所涵盖的历史时期（公元前七二二至前四八一年）分为三个段落，他称之为"三世"：凡孔子仅从文献记载得知的时期称为"所传闻世"，孔子听说的历史时期称为"所闻世"，孔子在世亲见的历史时期称为"所见世"。董仲舒认为，孔子在叙述这三段历史时，所用的语言和文字是不同的，体会孔子所用的语言不同之处，即所谓"春秋笔法"，人们可以从中找到《春秋》的"微言大义"。

● 社会进步的三个阶段

对《春秋》一书，曾有三部重要的评注，它们自汉朝起，已被列为经书。这三部评注以其传说的作者而命名为：《左（氏）传》、《公羊传》、《穀梁传》。《左传》大概原来不是全为评注《春秋》而作，后来才附加于《春秋》之后。《公羊传》对《春秋》的解释正好符合董仲舒的学说，其中有"三世说"。东汉何休（公元一二九至一八二年）又为《公羊传》作注释，对"三世说"作了进一步的发挥。

按照何休的说法，《春秋》所记述的是孔子以其理想，把"衰乱世"变为"升平世"，再变为"太平世"的过程。他把《春秋》中孔子"所传闻世"，称为"衰乱世"；在这时期，孔子把注意力集中在鲁国，以鲁国作为他的政治改革的中心。第二阶段是孔子由

Hsiu as that of "approaching peace." It was an age in which Confucius, having given good government to his own state, next brought peace and order to all the other Chinese states lying within the "Middle Kingdom." Finally, the last of the three periods, "the age which Confucius personally witnessed," is identified by Ho Hsiu as that of "universal peace." It was an age in which Confucius, having brought all the Chinese states to peace and order, also civilized all the surrounding barbarian tribes. In this period, Ho Hsiu said: "The whole world, far and near, great and small, was like one." [4] Of course Ho Hsiu did not mean that these things were actually accomplished by Confucius. He meant that they were what Confucius would have accomplished if he had actually had the power and authority. Even so, however, the theory remains fantastic, since Confucius himself was alive only during the latter part of the three supposed ages of the *Ch'un Ch'iu*.

Ho Hsiu's account of the way in which Confucius, working out from his own state, ideally brought the entire world to peace and order, is similar to the stages in acquiring world peace that are expounded in the *Great Learning*. In this respect, therefore, the *Ch'un Ch'iu* becomes an exemplification of the *Great Learning*.

This theory of the three stages of social progress is also found in the *Li Yün* or "Evolution of Rites," one of the chapters in the *Li Chi*. According to this treatise, the first stage was a world of disorder, the second was that of "small tranquility," and the third that of "great unity." The *Li Yün* describes this final age as follows: "When the great *Tao* was in practice, the world was common to all; men of talents, virtue and ability were selected; sincerity was emphasized and friendship was cultivated. Therefore, men did not love only their own parents, nor did they treat as children only their own sons. A competent provision was secured for the aged till their death, employment was given to the able-bodied, and a means was provided for the upbringing of the young. Kindness and compassion were shown to widows, orphans, childless men, and those who were disabled by disease, so that they all had the wherewithal for support. Men had their proper work and women had their homes. They hated to see the wealth of natural resources undeveloped, [so they developed it, but this development] was not for their own use. They hated not to exert themselves, [so they worked, but their work] was not for their own profit…. This was called the great unity." (*Li Chi*, ch. 7.)

Though the author of the *Li Yün* put this great unity into a golden age of the past, it certainly represented a current dream of the Han people, who would surely have liked to see something more than simply the political unity of the empire.

前人听说到的历史时期，即"所闻世"，何休称之为"升平世"（接近于太平）。在这时期，孔子已经把鲁国的政治整顿好，并进一步，把他的理想推广到中国境内的华夏族其他国家。第三阶段即孔子亲身经历的历史时期，何休称之为"太平世"，在这时期里，孔子又把他的理想推广到中国以外的蛮荒地区，使周围蛮族地区也得到了教化，这时候"天下远近大小若一"（《公羊传》隐公元年注）。何休并不是说，孔子真的成就了这些工作，而是说，如果孔子掌权的话，他将完成的工作。即使仅仅是荒诞的想象，这种学说也是惊人的，因为事实上，孔子只是生活在所谓春秋三世的后期。

何休描述孔子，从整顿鲁国开始，逐步做到使天下得太平，和《大学》中所说的修身、齐家、治国、平天下的步骤次序很接近，就这一点来说，《春秋》俨然成了《大学》的示范。

这种社会进步三阶段的学说也见之于《礼记》中的《礼运》篇。按《礼运》篇所述，第一阶段时的世界是混乱的，第二阶段达到"小康"，第三阶段则是"大同世界"。

《礼运》篇所描述的"大同世界"是：

"大道之行也，天下为公，选贤与能，讲信修睦。故人不独亲其亲，不独子其子，使老有所终，壮有所用，幼有所长，矜寡孤独废疾者皆有所养，男有分，女有归。货恶其弃于地也，不必藏于己；力恶其不出于身也，不必为己。是故谋闭而不兴，盗窃乱贼而不作，故外户而不闭。是谓大同。"

虽然《礼运》的作者把大同世界说成是过去的黄金时代，但它显然反映了汉代人们的梦想，所向往的已不仅是国家的政治统一，而且还期盼着更多的东西。

⑱ THE ASCENDANCY OF CONFUCIANISM AND REVIVAL OF TAOISM

The Han dynasty was not only the chronological successor of the Ch'in, but in many ways was its continuator as well. It stabilized the unification which the Ch'in had first achieved.

● The Unification of Thought

Among the many policies adopted by Ch'in for this purpose, one of the most important had been that for the unification of thought. After it had conquered all the rival states, Li Ssu, its Prime Minister, submitted a memorial to the Ch'in First Emperor (Ch'in Shih-huang-ti) which said: "Of old, the world was scattered and in confusion.... Men valued what they had themselves privately studied, thus casting into disrepute what their superiors had established. At present, Your Majesty has united the world.... Yet there are those who with their private teachings mutually abet each other, and discredit the institutions of laws and instructions.... If such conditions are not prohibited, the imperial power will decline above and partizanships will form below." (*Historical Records*, ch. 87.)

Then he made a most drastic recommendation: All historical records, save those of Ch'in, all writings of the "hundred schools" of thought, and all other literature, save that kept in custody of the official Erudites, and save works on medicine, pharmacy, divination, agriculture, and arboriculture, should be delivered to the government and burned. As for any individuals who might want to study, they should "take the officials as their teachers." (*Ibid.*, ch. 6.)

The First Emperor approved this recommendation and ordered it carried out in 213 B.C. Actually, sweeping though it was, it was nothing more than the logical application of an idea that had long existed in Legalist circles. Thus Han Fei Tzu had already said: "In the state of the intelligent ruler, there is no literature of books and records, but the laws serve as teachings. There are no sayings of the former kings, but the officials act as teachers." (*Han-fei-tzu*, ch. 49.)

The purpose of Li Ssu's recommendation is apparent. He wanted to be sure that there should be but one world, one government, one history, and one way of thought. Books on medicine and other practical subjects were therefore exempted from the general destruction because, as we should say now, they were technical works and so had nothing to do with "ideology."

The very violence of the Ch'in dynasty, however, led to its speedy downfall, and following the rise of the Han dynasty, a good deal of the

拾捌 儒家兴盛和道家再起

汉朝不仅在时序上是秦朝的后继者，在许多方面，它都继承了秦朝未竟的事业。秦朝完成了中国的统一，汉朝则巩固了统一的中国。

● 思想的统一

秦朝为确保在它统治下中国的统一，采取了许多措施，其中最重要的一项是统一思想的政策。在秦国战胜了其他六国之后，宰相李斯向始皇帝上书说："古者天下散乱，莫能相一……人善其所私学，以非上所建立。今陛下并有天下，别白黑而定一尊；而私学乃相与非法教之制，……如此不禁，则主势降乎上，党与成乎下。"（《史记·李斯列传》）

然后，他提出了极严酷的建议：一切史书，除秦朝史书外，其他"百家"之说和其他文献，除由博士官存档保管者外，并除医书、药书、农牧、卜筮之书以外，都应上交政府，予以焚毁。任何个人若想读书，都应"以吏为师"。（见《史记·秦始皇本纪》）

始皇帝采纳了李斯的建议，并于公元前二一三年付诸实施。这些严酷的措施其实不过是法家一贯思想的合乎逻辑的应用而已。韩非子在他的书中早已说过："明主之国，无书简之文，以法为教；无先王之语，以吏为师。"（《韩非子·五蠹》）

李斯建议的目的十分明显，他一心想确保一个天下（国家），一个政府，一部历史，一种思想。医书和其他实用书籍得免焚毁厄运，因为它们是技术性知识，无关"政治意识形态"。

结果，秦朝正是由于它的严酷统治而迅速灭亡。汉朝兴起后，

ancient literature and the writings of the "hundred schools" came to light again. Yet though they disapproved of the extreme measures of their predecessors, the Han rulers came to feel that a second attempt along different lines should be made to unify the thought of the empire, if political unity were to be long maintained. This new attempt was made by Emperor Wu (140-87 B.C.), who in so doing was following a recommendation made by Tung Chung-shu.

In a memorial presented to the Emperor around the year 136 B.C., Tung wrote: "The principle of Great Unification in the *Ch'un Ch'iu* is a permanent warp passing through the universe, and an expression of what is proper extending from the past to the present. But the teachers of today have diverse Ways, men have diverse doctrines, and each of the philosophic schools has its own particular position and differs in the ideas which it teaches. Hence it is that the rulers possess nothing whereby they may effect general unification." And he concluded his memorial by recommending: "All not within the field of the *Liu Yi* [Six Classics] should be cut short and not allowed to progress further." (*History of the Former Han Dynasty*, ch. 56.)

Emperor Wu approved this recommendation and formally announced that Confucianism, in which these Six Classics held a dominant place, was to be the official state teaching. A considerable time was needed, to be sure, before the Confucianists consolidated their newly gained position, and in the process they adopted many ideas from the other rival schools, thus making of Confucianism something very different from the early Confucianism of the Chou dynasty. We have seen in the last chapter how this process of eclectic amalgamation operated. Nevertheless, from the time of Emperor Wu onward, the Confucianists were given a better chance by the government to expound their teachings than were the other schools.

The principle of Great Unification referred to by Tung Chung-shu is also discussed in the *Kung Yang Commentary* on the *Ch'un Ch'iu*. Thus the opening sentence of the *Ch'un Ch'iu* is: "First year [of Duke Yin], spring, the King's first month." And on this the Commentary remarks: "Why does [the *Ch'un Ch'iu*] speak of 'the King's first month'? It has reference to the Great Unification." According to Tung Chung-shu and the Kung Yang school, this Great Unification was one of the programs that Confucius set up for his ideally established new dynasty when he wrote the *Ch'un Ch'iu*.

The measure carried out by Emperor Wu at Tung Chung-shu's recommendation was more positive and yet more moderate than that suggested by Li Ssu to the First Emperor of Ch'in, even though both

许多古代的文献和"百家"著作又重见天日了。汉朝的皇帝同样想实现全国思想统一，但是看到秦朝严酷到极端的做法不是好办法，打算改而采取另一种做法。这便是董仲舒向汉武帝上书的由来。

公元前一三六年，董仲舒上书汉武帝（公元前一四〇至前八七年在位），其中写道："《春秋》大一统者，天地之常经，古今之通谊也。今师异道，人异论，百家殊方，指意不同，是以上亡以持一统。"他的建议是："诸不在六艺之科、孔子之术者，皆绝其道，勿使并进。"（《汉书·董仲舒传》）

汉武帝采纳了董仲舒的建议，颁令以儒学为国家正统之学，其中"六经"又占有统治地位。但是，儒学要取得"独尊"的地位，不是仅靠一纸法令便能奏效的，还需要一段很长的时间；在这过程中，儒学吸收了不少其他各家的思想，由此树立起来的儒学和东周时孔子自己的思想，两者之间有了很大的差异。在上一章里，我们已经看到这个折中混合的过程是怎样进行的。但自汉武帝以后，儒家由于政府的支持，在宣扬儒家思想上，到底是占据了比其他学派都有利的地位。

董仲舒所鼓吹的"大一统"思想，在《春秋·公羊传》里也曾论及。《春秋》开卷第一句说："元年，春，王正月。"《公羊传》注："何言乎'王正月'？大一统也。"按照董仲舒和公羊学派的看法，"大一统"是孔子作《春秋》时为他理想中的新朝代制定的纲领之一。

汉武帝和秦始皇都致力于从思想上统一中国，但武帝所采纳董仲舒的建议比秦始皇所采纳李斯的建议要温和得多。秦朝对各种哲学

equally aimed at an intellectual unification of the entire empire. Instead of rejecting all schools of philosophy indiscriminately, as did the Ch'in measure, thus leaving a vacuum in the world of thought, the Han measure selected one of them, Confucianism, from among the "hundred schools," and gave it pre-eminence as the state teaching. Another difference is that the Han measure decreed no punishment for the private teaching of the ideas of the other schools. It only provided that persons who wished to be candidates for official positions should study the Six Classics and Confucianism. By thus making Confucianism the basis of government education, it laid the foundation for China's famed examination system used to recruit government officials. In this way the Han measure was in fact a compromise between the Ch'in measure and the previous practice of private teaching, which had become general after the time of Confucius. It is interesting to see that China's first private teacher now became her first state teacher.

● The Position of Confucius in Han Thought

As a result, the position of Confucius became very high by the middle of the first century B.C. About this time, a new type of literature came into existence known as the *wei shu* or apocrypha. *Shu* means book or writing, and *wei* literally means the woof of a fabric, and is used in apposition to *ching*, a word which is usually translated as classic, but literally means warp. It was believed by many people of the Han period that Confucius, after writing the Six Classics, that is, the six warps of his teaching, had still left something unexpressed. Hence, they thought, he then wrote the six woofs, corresponding to the six warps, by way of supplement. Thus the combination of the six warps and six woofs would constitute the entire teaching of Confucius. Actually, of course, the apocrypha are Han forgeries.

In the apocrypha the position of Confucius reached the highest level it has ever had in China. In one of them, for example, the *Ch'un Ch'iu*

Wei: Han Han Tzu, or *Apocryphal Treatise on the Spring and Autumn Annals: Guarded Shoots of the Han Dynasty*, it is written: "Confucius said: 'I have examined the historical records, drawn upon ancient charts, and investigated and collected cases of anomalies, so as to institute laws for the emperors of the Han dynasty.'" And another apocryphal treatise on the *Spring and Autumn Annals*, known as the *Expository Charts on Confucius*, states that Confucius was actually the son of a god, the Black Emperor, and recounts many supposed miracles in his life. Thus in these apocrypha we find Confucius being regarded as a super-human being, a god among men who could foretell the future. If these views had

思想流派的方针是一律禁绝，造成思想界的真空。汉武帝则是在百家中扶植儒家，使它成为正统。汉朝的做法与秦朝不同的另一点是：对私人传授其他各家思想，没有刑罚措施；只是任何人想从政做官，必须学习儒学和六经。官学以儒学为宗，这成为此后中国历代开科取仕的基础。从这里看，汉朝的做法乃是秦朝废黜百家和秦以前孔子开创私人办学的折中。有趣的一点是：中国的第一位私人教师，到这时竟成了中国官方册命的第一位教师。

● 孔子在汉代思想界的地位

由于官方的扶持，因此，到公元前一世纪中叶（西汉末年），孔子的地位已经被推崇得很高。这时候，"纬书"出现了。在织布时，有垂直的经线，有水平的纬线，两者上下交织而成布。汉代尊崇孔子，把《诗》《书》《礼》《乐》《易》《春秋》奉为孔子所作，称为"六经"，也有人认为，孔子在写作"六经"之后，意犹未尽，于是又依"六经"作"纬书"，总共"六纬"，与"六经"相配，认为这是孔子著述思想的全部。事实上，"纬书"乃是汉朝的著作，假托为孔子所作。

在"纬书"中，孔子被抬到他在中国历史上顶峰的地位。例如，春秋纬中《汉含孳》篇写道："孔子曰：丘览史记，援引古图，推集天变，为汉帝制法。"另一篇春秋纬，名为《演孔图》，其中称孔子是黑帝大神的儿子，曾经行了许多神迹。在"纬书"中，孔子被推上了神的地位，认为他可以预知未来。如果这些看法果真得以

prevailed, Confucius would have held in China a position similar to that of Jesus Christ, and Confucianism would have become a religion in the proper sense of the term.

Soon afterwards, however, Confucianists of a more realistic or rationalistic way of thinking protested against these "extraordinary and strange views" about Confucius and Confucianism. According to them, Confucius was neither a god nor a king, but simply a sage. He neither foresaw the coming of the Han Dynasty, nor did he institute laws for any dynasty. He simply inherited the cultural legacy of the great tradition of the past, to which he gave a new spirit and transmitted for all ages.

● The Controversy of the Old and New Text Schools

These Confucianists formed a group known as the Old Text school. This school was so called, because it claimed to possess texts of the Classics which went back before the "fires of Ch'in," that is, the burning of the books of 213 B.C., and hence were written in a form of script that had already become archaic by the time of their recovery. In opposition to this group, Tung Chung-shu and others belonged to the New Text school, so called because its versions of the Classics were written in the form of script that was generally current during the Han dynasty.

The controversy between these two schools has been one of the greatest in the history of Chinese scholarship. It is not necessary here to go into its details. All that need be said is that the Old Text school arose as a reaction or revolution against the New Text school. At the end of the Former Han dynasty, it received backing from Liu Hsin (ca. 46 B.C.- A.D. 23), one of the greatest scholars of the time. Indeed, so great was his enthusiasm that at a much later time he was accused, quite falsely, by followers of the New Text school, of having single-handedly forged all the classics written in the old script.

In recent years it has occurred to me that the origin of these two schools may perhaps go back to the two "wings" of Confucianism that existed before the Ch'in dynasty. The New Text school would thus be a continuation of the idealistic wing in early Confucianism, and the Old Text of the realistic wing. In other words, the one would derive from the group headed by Mencius and the other from that headed by Hsün Tzu.

In the *Hsün-tzu*, there is a chapter titled "Against the Twelve Philosophers," one passage of which says: "There were some who

流行的话，孔子将在中国享有如同耶稣在西方的地位，儒学将成为名副其实的一种宗教了。

但是此后不久，儒家中更现实和讲理性思维的一派起而反对对孔子和儒学的荒诞不经之说。他们认为，孔子既不是神，也不是君王，而纯然是一位圣人。他既未曾预见汉朝的出现，也没有为任何朝代制定法制，他只是继承了古代文化的伟大遗产，赋予它新的精神，使它得以流传后代。

● 汉代经学中古文学派和今文学派之争

这部分儒学家组成所谓"古文学派"，因为他们声称，找到了"秦燹"（燹，音显，指兵火）之前的古籍，是以古文写成，这种文字到西汉末年，已成绝响。与"古文学派"相对立的董仲舒追随者，则尊崇以汉代通行文字写成的经书，被称为"今文学派"。

这两派的争论成为中国学术史上的一场大争论。这里不必详述争论中的各种细节，只要指出一点就够了，即古文派是对今文派的一种抗议性反应，或者也可以看作是一场思想革命。在西汉末年，古文学派得到当时最著名的学者刘歆的支持。他以巨大的热情支持古文学派，以致后来今文学派的追随者指控他一手伪造了古文学派所依据的古文经书。

近年来，我对这两派的争论有一点新的看法，觉得这两派对立可能要追溯到秦以前，儒家内部思想分歧的两翼：今文学派实际是早期儒家中理想主义一翼的继续，而古文学派则是早期儒家中现实主义一翼的继续。换句话说，今文学派可能是源自以孟子为首的一派，而古文学派可能是源自以荀子为首的另一派。

在《荀子》一书中有一篇名为《非十二子》，其中说："略法先王

in a general way followed the former kings but did not know their fundamentals.... Basing themselves on ancient traditions, they developed theories which were called those of the Five Elements. Their views were peculiar, contradictory, and without standards; dark and without illustrations; confined and without explanations. Tzu-ssu [grandson of Confucius] began these and Meng K'o [Mencius] followed." (Ch. 4.)

This passage has long puzzled modern scholars, because both in the *Chung Yung*, supposedly the work of Tzu-ssu, and in the *Mencius*, there is no mention of the Five Elements. Nevertheless, we do find in the *Chung Yung* one passage which reads: "When a nation is about to flourish, there are sure to be happy omens; when it is about to perish, there are sure to be unlucky omens." Likewise the *Mencius* states at one point: "In the course of five hundred years, it is inevitable that a [true] king will arise." (VIIb, 13.) These passages would seem to indicate that both Mencius and the author of the *Chung Yung* (who, if not Tzu-ssu himself, must have been one of his followers) did believe to some extent that an interaction exists between Heaven and man and that history operates in cycles. These doctrines, it will be remembered, were prominent in the *Yin-Yang* or Five Elements school.

If, then, we consider Tung Chung-shu as being in some way connected with Mencius' wing of Confucianism, Hsün Tzu's accusations against this wing assume added significance. For if Tung Chung-shu's views actually go back in embryonic form to those of the followers of Mencius, then the latter, judging from their later development by Tung Chung-shu, could indeed be characterized as "peculiar" and "dark."

This hypothesis is further strengthened by the fact that Mencius, like Tung Chung-shu, attached particular value to the *Ch'un Ch'iu* as the work of Confucius. Thus he said: "Confucius was alarmed [by the disorder of the world] and made the *Ch'un Ch'iu*. The *Ch'un Ch'iu* should be the work of the Son of Heaven. Therefore Confucius said: 'Those who understand me, will do so because of the *Ch'un Ch'iu*, and those who blame me, will do so also because of the *Ch'un Ch'iu*.'" (*Mencius*, IIIb, 9.) Mencius' theory that Confucius, in composing the *Ch'un Ch'iu*, was doing work that pertains to the Son of Heaven, could, if further developed, easily lead to Tung Chung-shu's theory that Confucius had actually received a Mandate from Heaven to become the Son of Heaven.

Tung Chung-shu, furthermore, in expounding his theory of human nature, explicitly compared it with that of Mencius. As we have seen in the last chapter, the differences between the two theories are actually only nominal.

而不知其统，……案往旧造说，谓之五行，甚僻违而无类，幽隐而无说，闭约而无解。……子思唱之，孟轲和之。"

这段话曾令许多现代学者感到困惑不解，因为在《中庸》（历来认为是子思所作）和《孟子》两书中，都未曾提到过"五行"。但是在《中庸》书中有这样一段话："国家将兴，必有祯祥；国家将亡，必有妖孽。"《孟子》书中也曾说过有点类似的话："五百年必有王者兴。"这些话似乎表明，孟子和《中庸》的作者（如果不是子思，也是子思的追随者）都相信，天人之间有某种相互的作用，而且历史的运行是循环性的。这些学说在阴阳家和五行家的思想中都是十分突出的。

如果我们把董仲舒和孟子一派联系起来考虑，荀子对这一派的批判就更有意义。因为，如果把董仲舒的思想溯源到孟子，就会看到从孟子引发到董仲舒一派对它的延伸发展，确实可以说孟子的思想是"僻违""幽隐"了。

这个假说似乎从孟子一方也得到某种印证，因为孟子和董仲舒有共同的见解，认为《春秋》是孔子所作，他说："孔子惧，作《春秋》；《春秋》，天子之事也。是故孔子曰：'知我者其惟《春秋》乎？罪我者其惟《春秋》乎？'"（《孟子·滕文公章句下》）孟子认为，孔子作《春秋》，是做了天子当做的事。循这个思路发展下去，很容易就引导董仲舒得出他的理论，认为孔子的确承受了天命，要他成为天子。

董仲舒在阐述他的人性学说时，还明确地把他的学说和孟子的学说相比较，在上一章里已经指出，他们两人在人性学说上的差别其实不大。

If we accept the hypothesis that the New Text school is the continuation of the idealistic wing of Confucianism headed by Mencius, it is only reasonable to suppose that the Old Text school likewise stems from the realistic wing of Hsün Tzu. Thus it is noticeable that the thinkers of the first century A.D., who were followers of the Old Text school, all took a naturalistic view of the universe similar to that of Hsün Tzu and the Taoists. (Hsün Tzu himself, as we have seen earlier, was influenced by the Taoists in this respect.)

- ● Yang Hsiung and Wang Ch'ung

An example of this point of view is provided by Yang Hsiung (53 B.C-A.D. 18), one of the members of the Old Text school. His *T'ai Hsüan* or *Supreme Mystery* is to a considerable extent permeated with the concept that "reversal is the movement of the *Tao*"—a concept basic both in the *Lao-tzu* and *Book of Changes*.

He also wrote a treatise known as the *Fa Yen* or *Model Speeches*, in which he attacked the *Yin-Yang* school. In this same work, to be sure, he expresses praise for Mencius. This in itself, however, does not invalidate my theory, because even though Mencius may have had some inclination toward the *Yin-Yang* school, he certainly never reached the extremes that characterized the New Text school in the Han Dynasty.

The greatest thinker of the Old Text school is undoubtedly Wang Ch'ung (A.D. 27-ca. 100), an iconoclast with a remarkable spirit of scientific skepticism, whose chief work is the *Lun Heng* or *Critical Essays*. Writing of the spirit which characterizes this work, he says: "Though the *Shih* [*Book of Odes*] numbered three hundred, one phrase can cover them all, namely, 'With undepraved thoughts' [a saying of Confucius in the *Analects*]. And though the chapters of my *Lun Heng* may be numbered in the tens, one phrase covers them all, namely, 'Hatred of fictions and falsehoods.'" (*Lun Heng*, ch. 61.) Again he says: "In things there is nothing more manifest than having results, and in argument there is nothing more decisive than having evidence." (Ch. 67.)

Using this spirit, he vigorously attacks the theories of the *Yin-Yang* school, and especially its doctrine that an interaction exists between Heaven and man, either teleologically or mechanistically. As to its teleological aspect, he writes: "The Way of Heaven is that of spontaneity, which consists of non-activity. But if Heaven were to reprimand men, that would constitute action and would not be spontaneous. The school of Huang [the legendary Yellow Emperor] and Lao [Lao Tzu], in its discussion on the Way of Heaven, has found the truth." (Ch. 42.)

如果接受这种假说，以汉代今文学派为儒家中以孟子为首的理想主义一派的继续，则古文学派源自儒家中以荀子为首的现实主义一派也就顺理成章了。因此，我们可以看到：公元一世纪的古文学派学者在宇宙观方面都与荀子和道家一样，抱有一种自然主义的宇宙观（前已述及，荀子在这方面也受到道家的影响）。

● 扬雄和王充

西汉末到东汉初的古文学派学者扬雄（公元前五三至公元一八年）就是这方面的一个例子。他所著的《太玄》在很大程度上受到《老子》和《易经》中"反者道之用"的思想影响。

他的另一篇著作《法言》表达了他反对阴阳家、称颂孟子的思想。就这一点说，也并没有推翻我的上述观点，因为孟子虽然在某种程度上倾向于阴阳家，但绝没有达到像汉朝今文学派那样极端的程度。

古文学派最大的思想家无疑应推王充（公元二七至约一〇〇年），他的主要著作《论衡》充满对各种偶像的科学怀疑主义精神。在谈到自己这部著作的精神时，王充写道："'《诗》三百，一言以蔽之，曰：'思无邪。'《论衡》篇以十数，亦一言也，曰：'疾虚妄。'"（《论衡·佚文篇》）他又说："事莫明于有效，论莫定于有证。"（《论衡·薄葬篇》）

本着这样的精神，他猛烈攻击阴阳家的学说，特别是阴阳家从目的论或机械论讲天人感应的理论。对天人感应论的目的论方面，王充写道："夫天道，自然也，无为。如谴告人，是有为，非自然也。黄老之家，论说天道，得其实矣。"（《论衡·谴告篇》）

As to the mechanistic aspect of the theory, Wang Ch'ung says: "Man holds a place in the universe like that of a flea or louse under a jacket or robe.... Can the flea or louse, by conducting themselves either properly or improperly, affect the changes or movements in the ether under the jacket?... They are not capable of this, and to suppose that man alone is thus capable is to misconceive of the principle of things and of the ether." (Ch. 43.)

● Taoism and Buddhism

Thus Wang Ch'ung prepared the way for the revival of Taoism that came one century later. In speaking about Taoism, I must emphasize again the distinction between *Tao chia* and *Tao chiao*, that is, between Taoism as a philosophy and Taoism as a religion. By the revival of Taoism, I here mean that of Taoist philosophy. This revived Taoist philosophy I will call Neo-Taoism.

It is interesting to note that Taoism as a religion also had its beginnings toward the end of the Han dynasty, and there are some who refer to this popular form of Taoism as new Taoism. The Old Text school purged Confucianism of its *Yin-Yang* elements, and the latter later mingled with Taoism to form a new kind of eclecticism known as the Taoist religion. In this way, while the position of Confucius was being reduced from that of a divinity to one of a teacher, Lao Tzu was becoming the founder of a religion which ultimately, in imitation of Buddhism, developed temples, a priesthood, and a liturgy. In this way it became an organized religion almost totally unrecognizable to early Taoist philosophy, which is why it is known as the Taoist religion.

In the first century A.D., already before this was happening, Buddhism was introduced into China from India via Central Asia. In the case of Buddhism as of Taoism, I must emphasize the distinction between *Fo chiao* and *Fo hsüeh*, that is, between Buddhism as a religion and Buddhism as a philosophy. As just stated, Buddhism as a religion did much to inspire the institutional organization of religious Taoism. The latter, as an indigenous faith, was greatly stimulated in its development by the nationalistic sentiments of people who watched with resentment the successful invasion of China by the foreign religion of Buddhism. By some, indeed, Buddhism was considered as a religion of the barbarians. Religious Taoism, to some extent, thus grew as an indigenous substitute for Buddhism, and in the process it borrowed a great deal, including institutions, rituals, and even the form of much of its scriptures, from its foreign rival.

对天人感应论的机械论方面，王充写道："人在天地之间，犹蚤虱之在衣裳之内，蝼蚁之在穴隙之中。蚤虱蝼蚁为顺逆横从，能令衣裳穴隙之间气变动乎？蚤虱蝼蚁不能，而独谓人能，不达物气之理也。"（《论衡·变动篇》）

● 道家与佛家

王充以他的思想为一百年后道家的复兴准备了道路。说到道家，需要再一次强调指出"道家"和"道教"的区别。这里所说"道家"的复兴是指"道家"哲学思想的复兴，我称之为"新道家"。

有趣的是，道教也是在汉末兴起，这种道家思想的普及形式也被有些人称为"新道家"。古文学派把阴阳家的思想影响从儒家清除出去，阴阳家此后与道家思想结合而形成了道教。这个过程固然使孔子由神还原为人，却又使老子成为道教的创始人。道教后来模仿佛教，发展出道观（寺庙）、道士（僧人）和道场法事（仪式）。这种有组织的宗教虽以老子为祖师，却与早期的道家哲学毫无相似之处，因此而称为"道教"。

在此之前，公元一世纪时，佛教已经从印度经中亚传入中国。正如道教和道家应当予以区别一样，佛教和佛学也需要予以区别。上面说到，佛教对道教作为一种宗教的兴起，有很大的推动作用。佛教作为一种外来的宗教，在中国竟受到民众的欢迎，一些具有强烈民族情绪的中国人认为，佛教是蛮族的宗教，因而致力于发展中国土生土长的另一种宗教，这便是道教。道教从佛教借来了许多东西，包括宗教体制、仪式，以至其大部分经典的形式。

But besides Buddhism as an institutionalized religion, there also existed Buddhism as a philosophy. And whereas the Taoist religion was almost invariably opposed to the Buddhist religion, Taoist philosophy took Buddhist philosophy as its ally. Taoism, to be sure, is less other-worldly than Buddhism. Nevertheless, some similarity exists between their forms of mysticism. Thus the *Tao* of the Taoists is described as unnamable, and the "real suchness" or ultimate reality of the Buddhists is also described as something that cannot be spoken of. It is neither one, nor is it many; it is neither not-one, nor is it not not-many. Such terminology represents what is called in Chinese "thinking into the not-not."

In the third and fourth centuries A.D., famous scholars, who were usually Taoists, were often intimate friends of famous Buddhist monks. The scholars were usually well-versed in Buddhist *sutras*, and the monks in Taoist texts, especially the *Chuang-tzu*. When they met together, they talked in what was known at that time as *ch'ing t'an*, or "pure conversation." When they reached the subject of the not-not, they stopped talking and just silently understood each other with a smile.

In this kind of situation, one finds the spirit of Ch'an (commonly known in the West under its Japanese name of Zen). The Ch'an school is a branch of Chinese Buddhism which is really a combination of the most subtle and delicate aspects of both the Buddhist and Taoist philosophies. It exercised a great influence later on in Chinese philosophy, poetry and painting, as we shall see in chapter twenty-two, where it will be discussed in detail.

- **Political and Social Background**

For the moment, let us turn back to the political and social background that lay behind the ascendancy of Confucianism in the Han dynasty and the subsequent revival of Taoism. The triumph of the former was not due to mere good luck or the fancy of certain people of the time. There were certain circumstances which made it almost inevitable.

The Ch'in conquered the other states by a spirit of severity and ruthlessness which was shown both in its domestic control and foreign relations, and was based on the Legalist philosophy. After the fall of Ch'in, therefore, everyone blamed the Legalist school for its harshness and complete disregard of the Confucian virtues of human-heartedness and righteousness. It is significant that Emperor Wu, besides issuing his decree making Confucianism the state teaching, also decreed in 141 B.C.

佛教不仅是一种宗教，它还是一种哲学，即佛学。道教尽管在宗教上和佛教针锋相对，但在哲学上，却和佛学结成了同盟。道教没有佛学那样强烈的出世精神，但是它们在宗教神秘主义这一点上却有相似之处。道教称"道无名"，佛家也认为"真如"或终极的真实是"不可说"的，它既不是"一"，又不是"多"；既不是"非一"，又不是"非多"。这种名词术语正如中国汉语所说，是"想入非非"。

公元三、四世纪（两晋时期）时的著名学者在思想上往往是道家，其中不少还和佛教高僧结为至交。这些学者对佛经非常熟悉，而佛教高僧对道家经典，尤其《庄子》也非常熟悉。他们相聚时，往往从事所谓"清谈"。当谈到精妙处，即"非非"处时，往往相视无言而会心微笑，这是一种心领神会的思想交流。

正是在这样的时候，人体会到佛教"禅"的精神。禅宗是中国佛教的一个宗派，它实际是道家哲学和佛学两家精妙之处的汇合，对此后中国的哲学、诗歌、绘画产生了巨大的影响。这一点在后面第二十二章里还会详细论及。

● **政治和社会背景**

汉朝在思想领域里，儒家的高升和其后道家的复兴不能看作仅是由于少数几个思想家的鼓动，更不是儒家、道家交了什么好运，而是在当时情势下几乎可以说是必然的发展。

秦国征服六国，靠的是一种严酷无情的对内政策和纵横捭阖的对外政策，这些政策的理论基础便是法家哲学。到秦朝灭亡后，人人都责怪法家的严酷寡恩和完全无视孔子的仁义之道。汉武帝除颁令以儒家为国学正统外，还颁布了另一道诏令，这便是公元前

that all persons who had become experts in the philosophies of Shen
Pu-hai, Shang Yang and Han Fei (leaders of the Legalist school), as well
as Su Ch'in and Chang Yi (leaders of the Diplomatist school), should be
rejected from government posts.[1]

Thus the Legalist school became the scapegoat for all the blunders of
the Ch'in rulers. And among the various schools, those farthest removed
from the Legalist were the Confucianist and Taoist. Hence it is natural
that there should be a reaction in their favor. During the early part of the
Han dynasty, in fact, Taoism, then known as the "learning of Huang [the
Yellow Emperor] and Lao [Lao Tzu]," became quite influential for some
time. This can be illustrated by the fact that Emperor Wen (179-157 B.C.,
grandfather of Emperor Wu) was a great admirer of the "Huang-Lao
school"; also that, as pointed out in the last chapter, the historian Ssu-ma
T'an, in his "Essay On the Essential Ideas of the Six Schools," gave highest
rank to the Taoist school.

According to the political philosophy of Taoism, a good government
is not one that does many things, but on the contrary that does as little
as possible. Therefore if a sage-king rules, he should try to undo the
bad effects caused by the over-government of his predecessor. This was
precisely what the people of the early part of the Han dynasty needed,
for one of the troubles with the Ch'in had been that it had had too much
government. Hence when the founder of the Han dynasty, Emperor Kao-
tsu, led his victorious revolutionary army toward Ch'ang-an, the Ch'in
capital in present Shensi province, he announced to the people his "three-
item contract": Persons committing homicide were to receive capital
punishment; those injuring or stealing were to be punished accordingly;
but aside from these simple provisions, all other laws and regulations of the
Ch'in government were to be abolished. (*Historical Records*, ch. 8.) In this
way the founder of the Han dynasty was practicing the "learning of Huang
and Lao," even though, no doubt, he was quite unconscious of the fact.

Thus the Taoist philosophy accorded well with the needs of the rulers of the earlier part of the Han dynasty, whose policy was to undo what the Ch'in government had done, and to give the country a chance to recuperate from its long and exhausting wars. When this end had been accomplished, however, the Taoist philosophy became no longer practical, and a more constructive program was called for. This the rulers found in Confucianism.

The social and political philosophy of Confucianism is both conservative yet at the same time revolutionary. It is conservative in that it is essentially a philosophy of aristocracy, yet it is revolutionary in that it

一四一年下令：凡治申不害、商鞅、韩非（法家领袖）以及苏秦、张仪（纵横学领袖）之学的人，一律不准举荐为官。（见《汉书·武帝本纪》）

这样，法家便成了秦朝统治者失败的替罪羊。在诸子百家中，思想距法家最远的是儒家和道家，因此，很自然地，时代思潮便朝着儒家和道家的方向摆动。汉朝初年，道家思想在当时称为"黄老之术"，曾一度盛行，武帝的祖父文帝（公元前一七九至前一五七年在位）便深爱"黄老术"。再如上章指出，历史家司马谈在《论六家要旨》中，对道家的评价也比对其他各家都高。

在道家的政治哲学中，一个好的政府不需要做很多事情，相反地，做事越少越好。因此圣人如果执政，便要把前朝"苛政"的恶果予以消除。这正是汉初大众的要求。汉高祖率领他的革命军向秦国首都咸阳（长安）进发时，向民众宣布"约法三章"：杀人者死，伤人及盗抵罪。除此之外，秦朝一切苛法都予废除。（见《史记·高祖本纪》）汉高祖这样做时，实际是贯彻了"黄老之术"，虽然他并不是自觉的。

因此可以说，道家的政治哲学正迎合了汉初的政治需要，在多年战乱之后，汉帝所想做的正是废除秦朝的苛政，让百姓得以休养生息。及至百姓经过一个时期休养生息之后，君王想的是要有一番作为，这时，道家哲学已经完成了任务，不再适应时代和统治者的需要了，于是，君王又回到了儒家哲学。

儒家的社会政治哲学，可以说既是保守的，同时又是革命的。就其实质说，它的政治主张是维护君主专制统治的；就社会主张看，

gave a new interpretation of this aristocracy. It maintained the distinction between superior man and small man, which had been generally accepted in the feudal China of Confucius' time. But at the same time it insisted that this distinction should not be based, as originally, upon birth, but rather upon individual talent and virtue. Therefore, it considered it quite right that the virtuous and talented among the people should be the ones to occupy noble and high positions in society.

It has been pointed out in chapter two that Confucianism gave a theoretical justification for the family system which has been the backbone of Chinese society. With the disintegration of the feudal system, the common people gained emancipation from their feudal lords, but the old family system remained. Hence Confucianism likewise remained the underlying philosophy of the existing social system.

The main result of the abolition of the feudal system was the formal separation of political power from economic power. It is true that the new landlords retained great influence, even politically, in their local communities. At least, however, they were no longer the actual political rulers of these communities, even though through their wealth and prestige they could often influence the government-appointed officials. This represented a step forward.

The new aristocrats, such as officials and landlords, though many of them were far from being the virtuous and talented persons demanded by Confucianism, nevertheless all had need for something that Confucianism was particularly qualified to supply. This was a knowledge of the complicated ceremonies and rituals needed to maintain the social distinctions. Thus one of the early acts of the founder of the Han dynasty, having conquered all his rivals, was to order Shu-sun Tung, a Confucianist, together with his followers, to draw up a court ceremonial. After the first audience was held at court with the new ceremonies, the founder of the dynasty exclaimed with satisfaction: "Now I realize the nobility of being the Son of Heaven!" (*Historical Records*, ch. 8.)

Shu-sun Tung's action was disapproved of by some of his fellow Confucianists, but its success suggests one reason why the new aristocrats liked Confucianism, even though they might be opposed to or be ignorant of its true spirit.

Most important of all, however, is the fact pointed out by me in chapter three, that what is known in the West as the Confucianist school is really the School of Literati. The Literati were not only thinkers but also scholars versed in the ancient cultural legacy, and this was a combination

它维护当时社会中君子和小人的分野，但同时，它又主张，君子与小人的分野，不按传统的以家庭出身贵贱来划分，而以个人的德才来划分。如果按孔子的主张，有德有才的人方是高贵的，以此作为划分君子和小人的标准，则君子、小人之分，并没有什么不对，倒是社会发展的需要。

在本书第二章里曾经指出，儒家为中国社会以家庭为本位奠定了理论基础。当封建制度瓦解时，民众从封建主的统治下得到解放，但家庭制度并没有改变。因此，社会制度依然是以儒家思想为根本。

废除封建制度的主要结果是政治权力和经济权力的分开。新兴的地主在其本地社会里确实拥有很大的社会势力，甚至还有政治势力；但至少他们已不再当政，只能以他们的财富和社会影响来左右政府官员，这终究是前进了一步。

新的专制统治者，按儒家的德才兼备要求来说，往往达不到理想的标准，因此，往往要寻求儒家的教化，其中首要的是社会的礼制。史书记载，汉初平定天下之后，高祖刘邦诏令儒生叔孙通率领一班人，拟定一套宫廷的礼仪。在首次举行这样的礼仪之后，刘邦踌躇满志地说："吾乃今日知为皇帝之贵也。"(《史记·刘敬叔孙通列传》)

叔孙通的作为也曾遭到其他儒生的抨击，但他的成功表明新的专制统治者欣赏儒家，尽管还不懂得儒家思想是怎么一回事，更不懂得儒家思想的真正精神将会导致对统治者无德无才的不满。

最重要的一点是在本书第三章里我所指出的，西方人所理解的"孔子学派"，实际是中国的"儒家"，他们不仅是思想者，而且谙习古代的文化遗产。这是当时其他各学派所不如儒家的地方。儒生

that the other schools failed to offer. They taught the literature of the past and carried on the great cultural traditions, giving them the best interpretation they could find. In an agrarian country in which people were unusually respectful of the past, these Literati could not fail to become the most influential group.

As for the Legalist school, though it became the scapegoat for the blunders of the Ch'in rulers, it was never wholly discarded. In chapter thirteen, I have pointed out that the Legalists were realistic politicians. They were the ones who could present new methods of government to meet new political conditions. Hence, as the Chinese empire expanded, its rulers could not but rely on the principles and techniques of the Legalists. Consequently, ever since the Han dynasty, orthodox Confucianists have commonly accused the rulers of dynasties of being "Confucianists in appearance but Legalists in reality." As a matter of fact, both Confucianism and Legalism have had their proper sphere of application. The proper sphere for Confucianism is that of social organization, spiritual and moral culture, and learned scholarship. And the proper sphere for Legalism is that of the principles and techniques of practical government.

Taoism, too, has had its opportunities. In Chinese history there have been many periods of political and social confusion and disorder, when people have had little time or interest for classical scholarship, and have been inclined to criticize the existing political and social system. At such times, therefore, Confucianism has naturally tended to weaken and Taoism to become strong. Taoism has then supplied a sharp criticism against the existing political and social system, as well as an escapist system of thought for avoiding harm and danger. These are exactly what meet the desires of a people living in an age of disorder and confusion.

The collapse of the Han dynasty in A.D. 220 was followed by a prolonged period of disunity and confusion which was brought to a close only when the country was finally reunited under the Sui dynasty in A.D. 589. These four centuries were marked by frequent warfare and political cleavage between a series of dynasties that ruled in Central and South China, and another series that had control in the North. It was also marked by the rise to prominence of various nomadic non-Chinese groups, some of whom forcibly broke their way through the Great Wall and settled in North China, and others of whom entered through peaceful colonization. A number of the dynasties of the north were ruled by these alien groups, who, however, failed to extend their power as far south as the Yangtze river. Because of these political characteristics, this

讲解古代的经典，传授古代的文化传统，为此而竭尽所能。在一个农业国家里，人们惯于尊重传统，因此儒生成为最有影响的社会群体，这是很自然的。

至于法家，虽然成为秦朝统治者失败的替罪羊，但也还没有完全被抛弃。在第十三章里，我曾指出，法家是一批讲求现实的政客。在新的政治情势下，怎样采用新的统治方法来应付局势，这是法家之所长。因此，当中华帝国发展时，统治者还是不得不采用法家的思想。自汉以后，正统的儒家往往责备统治者是"外儒内法"。事实上，儒家和法家各有它们被运用的范围。儒家思想占统治地位的范围是社会体制、精神道德教化和学术领域，法家思想占统治地位的则是施政的原则和统治的方法。

道家也有它施展的机会。中国历史中有许多段落陷于政治社会动乱之中，这时候的人民大众倾向于批评现存政治社会制度，既没有时间，也没有兴趣去从事古典学术的探讨。这时，儒家思想自然被削弱；而道家思想则因对现存政治社会制度所抱的尖锐批判态度和为批判者提供了一个超脱现实、逃避政治迫害的思想体系而声势壮大起来，这正迎合了处于社会动乱之中的民众的需要。

公元二二〇年，汉朝灭亡；随之而来的政治分裂和动乱一直拖延到公元五八九年隋朝统一全国，其间四个世纪，中国分裂成南北两部分，南部战乱连绵。另一个特点是在北部一些外族兴起，有的通过战争而在中国北部立国，有的则以和平迁徙的方式移居中国北方。在北方的几个朝代居统治地位的都是汉族之外的

period of four centuries from the Han to the Sui dynasties is commonly known as that of the Six Dynasties, or again, as that of the Northern and Southern Dynasties.

This, then, was politically and socially a dark age, in which pessimism was rife. In some respects it somewhat resembled the roughly contemporary period of the Middle Ages in Europe, and just as in Europe Christianity was the dominant force, so in China the new religion of Buddhism made great strides. It is quite wrong to say, however, as some people do, that it was an age of inferior culture. On the contrary, if we take the word culture in a narrower sense, we may say that it was an age in which, in several respects, we reach one of the peaks of Chinese culture. Painting, calligraphy, poetry, and philosophy were at this time all at their best.

In the next two chapters I shall present the leading indigenous philosophy of the age, a philosophy which I call Neo-Taoism.

外族，但是它们的统治范围始终未曾达到长江流域。这四个世纪在中国历史上称为六朝或南北朝。

这段时期里，政治黑暗，社会动乱，悲观思想弥漫。在某些方面，和大体同时期的中世纪欧洲颇为相似。在欧洲中世纪，基督教成为社会中坚力量；在中国的南北朝时期，佛教迅速发展。有人认为，这时期的中国文化低落，这是完全错误的看法。如果把文化的定义作狭义的理解，可以说，这时期中国文化在绘画、书法、诗歌、哲学等许多方面都是处于发展的高峰时期。

下面两章所要介绍的便是这个时期里居主导地位的哲学，我把这种哲学称作"新道家"。

⑩ NEO-TAOISM: THE RATIONALISTS

Neo-Taoism is a new term for the thought which in the third and fourth centuries A.D. was known as the *hsüan hsüeh*, or literally, "dark learning." The word *hsüan*, meaning dark, abstruse, or mysterious, occurs in the first chapter of the *Lao-tzu*, for example, in which the *Tao* is described as "*hsüan* of the *hsüan*," i.e., "mystery of mysteries." Hence the term *hsüan hsüeh* indicates that this school is a continuation of Taoism.

● The Revival of Interest in the School of Names

In chapters eight, nine, and ten, we have seen how the School of Names contributed to Taoism the idea of "transcending shapes and features." In the third and the fourth centuries, with the Taoist revival, there came a revival of interest in the School of Names. The Neo-Taoists studied Hui Shih and Kung-sun Lung, and linked their *hsüan hsüeh* with what they called *ming-li*, i.e., the "distinguishing of terms [*ming*] and analysis of principles [*li*]." (This phrase is used by Kuo Hsiang in his commentary to the last chapter of the *Chuang-tzu*). As we have seen in chapter eight, this is what Kung-sun Lung also did.

In the *Shih-shuo Hsin-yü*, a book about which we shall read more in the next chapter, it is said: "A visitor asked Yüeh Kuang for the meaning of the statement: 'A *chih* does not reach.' Yüeh Kuang made no comment on the statement, but immediately touched the table with the handle of a fly whisk, saying: 'Does it reach or does it not?' The visitor answered: 'It does.' Yüeh then lifted the fly whisk and asked: 'If it reaches, how can it be taken away?'" (Ch. 4.) This statement that a *chih* does not reach is one of the arguments used by the followers of Kung-sun Lung, as reported in the last chapter of the *Chuang-tzu*. The word *chih* literally means a finger, but in chapter eight I translated it as "universal." Here, however, Yüeh Kuang evidently takes it in its literal sense as finger. The fly whisk cannot reach the table, just as the finger cannot reach the table.

To touch a table with a finger or something else is ordinarily considered as reaching the table. According to Yüeh Kuang, however, if

拾玖 新道家：崇尚理性的玄学

公元三、四世纪盛行的思潮，历来称为"玄学"。"玄"字原出自《老子》第一章，末句形容"道"是"玄之又玄，众妙之门"，意思是指它深远神秘，变化莫测。"玄学"的名字表明它是道家的继续，因此，我称它为"新道家"，这是我起的新名字。

● 名家再次引起人们的兴趣

在前面第八、九、十章里，我们已经看到，名家向道家提供了"超乎形象"这个概念。在公元三、四世纪里，随着道家的再起，对名家的兴趣也再次抬头了。新道家对惠施和公孙龙的理论再次钻研，在"玄学"中提出了"辨名析理"观念。首创这个观念的是郭象，他在《庄子注》的《天下篇注》里，把"玄学"和"辨名析理"结合起来。在本书第八章里，我们看到公孙龙也曾这样做过。

在《世说新语》（下章里，我们还将更多参阅这本书）里，在《文学》篇中说到一个故事："客问乐令'指不至'者，乐亦不复剖析文句，直以麈尾柄触几曰：'至不？'客曰：'至。'乐因又举麈尾曰：'若至者，那得去？'于是客乃悟。"乐令名乐广，是当时一位名士。"指不至"是说战国时名家公孙龙分析：一个名词的内涵就是概念，是不变的；名词的外延与其内涵是两回事，它是可以转化的。人指向一个事物时，不等于就已到达那里，这便是"指不至"所要争论之点，也就是"名"与"实"的道理。至魏晋时，还有人以这一点问乐广，乐广以一个拂麈来说明理论问题，当他用麈尾柄触茶几时问"至不"时，这个"至"是指"至"的共相，它是概念，是不变的，既"到"了就不能"不到"；但拂麈在拂拭几上时又至又去，乐广说："若至者，那得去？"这时，他所用的"至"乃是指具体的"抵达"。名词的概念内涵是不能变的，"至"不能转化为"去"，但名词的外延是能转化的，一个具体的、"至"的东西，又可以转化为"去"。乐广的一系列表示，是辨"至"之名，析"至"之实，这就是"辨名析理"。

用手指指向一张桌子，通常就被认为是已经在概念上到了

the reaching is really reaching, then it cannot be taken away. Since the handle of the fly whisk could be taken away, its apparent reaching was not a real reaching. Thus by examining the term "reaching," Yüeh Kuang analyzed the principle of reaching. This is an illustration of what was known at that time as "conversation on the *ming-li*."

● A Reinterpretation of Confucius

It is to be noticed that the Neo-Taoists, or at least a large part of them, still considered Confucius to be the greatest sage. This was partly because the place of Confucius as the state teacher was by now firmly established, and partly because some of the important Confucian Classics were accepted by the Neo-Taoists, though in the process they were reinterpreted according to the spirit of Lao Tzu and Chuang Tzu.

For instance, the *Analects* contains a saying of Confucius: "Yen Hui was nearly perfect, yet he was often empty." (XI, 18.) By this Confucius probably meant that although Yen Hui, his favorite disciple, was very poor, i.e., "empty," that is, devoid of worldly goods, he was nevertheless very happy, which showed that his virtue was nearly perfect. In the *Chuang-tzu*, however, as we have seen in chapter ten, there is an apocryphal story about Yen Hui's "sitting in forgetfulness," i.e., engaging in mystic meditation. Hence with this story in mind one commentator on the *Analects*, T'ai-shih Shu-ming (474- 546), said:

"Yen Hui disregarded human-heartedness and righteousness, and forgot ceremonies and music. He gave up his body and discarded his knowledge. He forgot everything and became one with the infinite. This is the principle of forgetting things. When all things were forgotten, he was thus empty. And yet, compared with the sages, he was still not perfect. The sages forget that they forget, whereas even the great worthies cannot forget that they forget. If Yen Hui could not forget that he forgot, it would seem that something still remained in his mind. That is why he is said to have been *often* empty." [1]

Another commentator, Ku Huan (died 453), commenting on the same passage, remarks: "The difference between the sages and the worthies is that the latter retain a desire to be without desire, while the former do not have that desire for no desire. Therefore the mind of the sages is perfectly empty, while that of the worthies is only partially so. From the point of

桌子，但是乐广认为，若以概念而论，到了桌子，就不能离开，这才是"至"；但拂尘却又至又去，因此他反问"若至者，那得去"，意思是说，拂尘表面上已到桌子，实际并未到。因此，乐广从"至"之名分析"至"之实，这是"辨名析理"的一个例子。

● 对孔子的重新诠释

新道家中，至少有大部分还以孔子为圣人，究其原因，一部分是因为到魏晋时，以孔子为国家崇奉的先师，这思想已经确立。还有一个原因是，新道家对儒家经书中的重要部分也趋于接受，只是在接受中又按老庄的精神予以重新诠释。

举例来说，《论语·先进》篇里，孔子曾说过："回也其庶乎，屡空。"孔子的意思大概是说，颜回虽然很穷（"空"），但在精神上却是快乐的，由此表明他的道德已接近于完美。在《庄子·大宗师》篇里则衍生出一个颜回"坐忘"——在冥想中与大化合一，以至忘记自我存在——的故事。后来的太史叔明（公元四七四至五四六年）注释《论语》这一段时，心里还想到《庄子·大宗师》里的故事，因此他说："颜子……遗仁义，忘礼乐，隳肢体，黜聪明，坐忘大通，此忘有之义也。忘有顿尽，非空如何？若以圣人验之，圣人忘忘，大贤不能忘忘。不能忘忘，心复为未尽。一未一空，故屡名生也焉。"（皇侃《论语义疏》卷六）这就是说，颜回还是未能全忘自己，因此才意识到自己的"坐忘"，否则，连"坐忘"也应忘记才是。颜回头脑里还未完全虚静，因此他才说自己"常"空。

另一位注释家顾欢（公元四五三年卒）在注释《论语》的同一段时说："夫无欲于无欲者，圣人之常也；有欲于无欲者，贤人之分也。二欲同无，故全空以目圣；一有一无，故每虚以称贤。贤人

view of the world, the worthies lack any desire. But from the point of view of what is not of this world, the worthies do desire to be without desire. The emptiness of Yen Hui's mind was not yet complete. That is why he is said to have been *often* empty." (*Ibid.*)

The Neo-Taoists, despite their Taoism, considered Confucius to be even greater than Lao Tzu and Chuang Tzu. Confucius, they maintained, did not speak about forgetfulness, because he had already forgotten that he had learned to forget. Nor did he speak about absence of desire, because he had already reached the stage of lacking any desire to be without desire. Thus the *Shih-shuo Hsin-yü* records a "pure conversation" between P'ei Hui and Wang Pi. The latter was one of the great figures of the school of "dark learning," whose *Commentaries* on the *Lao-tzu* and *Book of Changes* have become classics in themselves. The conversation reads:

"Wang Pi [226-249], when young, once went to see P'ei Hui. [P'ei] Hui asked him why, since *Wu* [Non-being] is fundamental for all things, Confucius did not speak about it, whereas Lao Tzu expounded this idea without stopping. To this Wang Pi answered: 'The sage [Confucius] identified himself with *Wu* [Non-being] and realized that it could not be made the subject of instruction, with the result that he felt compelled to deal only with *Yu* [Being]. But Lao Tzu and Chuang Tzu had not yet completely left the sphere of *Yu* [Being], with the result that they constantly spoke of their own deficiencies.'" (Ch. 4.) This explanation reflects the idea expressed by Lao Tzu that "he who knows does not speak; he who speaks does not know." (*Lao-tzu*, ch. 56.)

● Hsiang Hsiu and Kuo Hsiang

One of the greatest, if not the greatest, philosophical works of this period is the *Commentary on the Chuang-tzu* by Kuo Hsiang (died ca. 312). There has been a historical problem as to whether this work was really his, for he was accused of being a plagiarist by his contemporaries, who asserted that his *Commentary* was really the work of another slightly earlier scholar, Hsiang Hsiu (ca. 221-ca. 300). It would seem that both men wrote *Commentaries* on the *Chuang-tzu*, and that their ideas were very much the same, so that in the course of time their *Commentaries* probably became combined to form a single work. The *Shih-shuo Hsin-yü* (ch. 4), for example, speaks of a Hsiang-Kuo interpretation (i.e., an interpretation by Hsiang Hsiu and Kuo Hsiang) made on the "Happy Excursion" (the first chapter of the *Chuang-tzu*), as existing in apposition to one by Chih-tun (314-366), a famous Buddhist monk of the time. Hence the present *Commentary on the Chuang-tzu*, though it bears

自'有'观之，则无欲于有欲；自'无'观之，则有欲于无欲。虚而未尽，非屡如何？"

　　新道家尽管是道家，却认为孔子比老子、庄子更高明。他们认为，孔子不讲坐忘，因为他已经忘记了"坐忘"这桩事。孔子也不讲"无欲"，因为他已经修养到这地步，已经没有了"无欲"的欲望。正因此，《世说新语》中记载了裴徽和王弼的一段"清谈"。王弼（公元二二六至二四九年）是玄学大师，他对于《老子》和《易经》的注释都已成为经典著作。王弼和裴徽的对话是这样的：

　　"王辅嗣弱冠诣裴徽，徽问曰：'夫无者，诚万物之所资，圣人莫肯致言，而老子申之无已，何邪？'弼曰：'圣人体无，无又不可以训，故言必及有。老、庄未免于有，恒训其所不足。'"（《世说新语·文学》）这个解释正反映了《老子》第五十六章"知者不言，言者不知"的看法。

● 向秀和郭象

　　在这一时期里，郭象（死于约公元三一二年）所著《庄子注》即便不是其中最重要的哲学著述，也是最重要著作之一。这里有一个史实问题，即：《庄子注》这部书究竟是否郭象所著？郭象的同时代人曾经指控郭象的《庄子注》是剽窃了与他同时而稍早的另一学者向秀（约公元二二一至三〇〇年）的著作。看来，他们两人都著有《庄子注》，思想也十分接近。因此，随时间推移，他们的两部著作渐难分辨，而成为一部著作。《世说新语·文学》篇曾提到对《庄子·逍遥游》篇的向、郭注，以此和僧支遁的释义相对应。因此，现在流传的《庄子注》，虽然署名是郭象注，其实多半是向秀

the name of Kuo Hsiang, seems to represent the joint Hsiang-Kuo interpretation of the *Chuang-tzu*, and probably was the work of both men. The *Chin Shu* or *History of the Chin Dynasty* is probably right, therefore, when in its biography of Hsiang Hsiu it says that he wrote a *Commentary on the Chuang-tzu*, and that then Kuo Hsiang "extended it." (Ch. 49.)

According to this same *History of the Chin Dynasty*, both Hsiang Hsiu and Kuo Hsiang were natives of the present Honan province, and were great figures in the school of "dark learning," as well as being "fine or pure conversationalists." In this chapter I shall take these two philosophers as representative of the exponents of the rationalistic group in Neo-Taoism, and refer to their *Commentary on the Chuang-tzu* as the Hsiang-Kuo interpretation, following the usage of the *Shih-shuo Hsin-yü*.

● **The *Tao* is "Nothing"**

The Hsiang-Kuo interpretation made several most important revisions in the original Taoism of Lao Tzu and Chuang Tzu. The first is that the *Tao* is really *wu*, i.e., "nothing" or "nothingness." Lao Tzu and Chuang Tzu also had maintained that the *Tao* is *Wu*, but by *Wu* they meant having no name. That is, according to them, the *Tao* is not a thing; hence it is unnamable. But according to the Hsiang-Kuo interpretation, the *Tao* is really literally nothing. "The *Tao* is everywhere, but everywhere it is nothing." (*Commentary on the Chuang-tzu*, ch. 6.)

The same text says: "In existence, what is prior to things? We say that the *Yin* and *Yang* are prior to things. But the *Yin* and *Yang* are themselves things; what then, is prior to the *Yin* and *Yang*? We may say that *Tzu Jan* [nature or naturalness] is prior to things. But *Tzu Jan* is simply the naturalness of things. Or we may say that the *Tao* is prior to things. But the *Tao* is nothing. Since it is nothing, how can it be prior to things? We do not know what is prior to things, yet things are continuously produced. This shows that things are spontaneously what they are; there is no Creator of things." (Ch. 22.)

In another passage, it is also stated: "Some people say that the penumbra is produced by the shadow, the shadow by the bodily form, and the bodily form by the Creator. I would like to ask whether the Creator is or is not. If He is not, how can He create things? But if He is, He is simply one of these things, and how can one thing produce another?... Therefore there is no Creator, and everything produces itself. Everything produces itself and is not produced by others. This is the normal way of the universe." (Ch. 2.)

和郭象两人合著。《晋书·向秀传》中称，向秀著《庄子注》，郭象予以"增衍"，这看来较接近于事实。

据《晋书》记载，向秀和郭象都是河南人，都擅玄学，以清谈著称。在本章里，我把这两位哲学家作为新道学中主张理性的流派的代表，在征引《庄子注》一书时，援《世说新语》例，称"向—郭《注》"。

● 道是"无"

向—郭《注》对老庄的早期道家思想作了重要的修订。首先，它把"道"解释为"无"。老子和庄子也主张"道"是"无"，但他们所讲的"无"，意思是说："无以名之。"这是说，他们认为："道"不是一样东西，因此，无从为它命名。而向—郭《注》则以"道"为"无"。道"无所不在，而所在皆无也"。(《大宗师》"在太极之先而不为高……"注）

向—郭《注》中又说："谁得先物者乎哉？吾以阴阳为先物，而阴阳者即所谓物耳。谁又先阴阳者乎？吾以自然为先之，而自然即物之自尔耳。吾以至道为先之矣，而至道乃至无也。既以无矣，又奚为先？然则先物者谁乎哉？而犹有物，无已，明物之自然，非有使然也。"(《知北游》"有先天地生者物耶……"注）

向—郭《注》还说："世或谓罔两待景，景待形，形待造物者。请问：夫造物者，有耶无耶？无也？则胡能造物哉？有也？则不足以物众形。……故造物者无主，而物各自造，物各自造而无所待焉，此天地之正也。"(《齐物论》"恶识所以然……"注）

Lao Tzu and Chuang Tzu denied the existence of a personal Creator by substituting in His place an impersonal *Tao*, which is that by which all things come to be. Hsiang-Kuo went a step further by insisting that the *Tao* is really *nothing*. According to them, the statement of the earlier Taoists that all things come into being from the *Tao* simply means that all things come to be by themselves. Hence they write: "The *Tao* is capable of nothing. To say that anything is derived from the *Tao* means that it comes of itself." (Ch. 6.)

Likewise, the statement of the earlier Taoists that all things come into being from Being, and Being comes into being from Non-being, simply means that Being comes into being by itself. In one passage of the *Commentary* it is said: "Not only is it the case that Non-being cannot become Being, but Being also cannot become Non-being. Though Being may change in thousands of ways, it cannot change itself into Non-being. Therefore there is no time when there is no Being. Being eternally exists." (Ch. 22.)

● The "Self-transformation" of Things

That everything spontaneously produces itself is what Hsiang-Kuo call the theory of *tu hua* or self-transformation. According to this theory, things are not created by any Creator, but these things are nevertheless not lacking in relations, one with another. Relations exist and these relations are necessary. Thus the *Commentary* states: "When a man is born, insignificant though he be, he has the properties that he necessarily has. However trivial his life may be, he needs the whole universe as a condition for his existence. All things in the universe, all that exist, cannot cease to exist without some effect on him. If one factor is lacking, he might not exist. If one principle is violated, he might not be living." (Ch. 6.)

Everything needs every other thing, but everything nevertheless exists for its own sake and not for the sake of any other thing. The *Commentary* says: "In the world, everything considers itself as 'this' and other things as 'other.' The 'this' and the 'other' each works for itself. [They seem to be far away from each other like] the mutual opposition of east and west. Yet the 'this' and the 'other' have a relation to each other like that between the lips and the teeth. The lips do not exist for the teeth, but when the lips are lost, the teeth feel cold. Therefore the work of the 'other' for itself has contributed a great deal to help the 'this.'" (Ch. 17.) According to Hsiang-Kuo, the interrelationship of things is like that between the armies of two

　　老庄否认有一位具有人格的造物主，而代之以没有人格的"道"。它是万物之所由生。向、郭两人更进一步，认为道即"无"。他们还把早期道家主张万物来自"道"解释为万物自然而在。因此，向—郭《注》写道："道，无能也。此言'得之于道'，乃所以明其自得耳。"（《大宗师》"傅说得之，以相武丁……"注）

　　同样，先秦道家说，万物生于有，有生于无，也只是说，有是自在的。向—郭《注》中有一处说："非唯无不得化而为有也，有亦不得化而为无矣。是以夫有之为物，虽千变万化，而不得一为无也。不得一为无，故自古无未有之时而常存也。"（《知北游》"无古无今……"注）

● 万物的"独化"

　　万物自生，这是向—郭《注》里称之为"独化"的理论。按照这个理论，万物不是由一位造物主所造，但万物之间相互关联，这种种关联不仅存在，而且是必要的。向—郭《注》中说："人之生也，形虽七尺而五常必具，故虽区区之身，乃举天地以奉之。故天地万物，凡所有者，不可一日而相无也。一物不具，则生者无由得生；一理不至，则天年无缘得终。"（《大宗师》"知人之所为者……"注）

　　每一物需要每一个"它物"。但每一物仍然是独立自为地存在的。向—郭《注》说："天下莫不相与为彼我，而彼我皆欲自为，斯东西之相反也。然彼我相与为唇齿，唇齿未尝相为，而唇亡则齿寒。故彼之自为，济我之功弘矣，斯相反而不可以相无者也。"（《秋水》"以功观之……"注）照向—郭《注》的说法，事物之间的关联就像两支国际同盟军，每支军队都是为本国而战，但是两支

allied forces. Each army fights for its own country, but each at the same time helps the other, and the defeat or victory of the one cannot but have an effect on the other.

Everything that exists in the universe needs the universe as a whole as a necessary condition for its existence, yet its existence is not directly produced by any other particular thing. When certain conditions or circumstances are present, certain things are necessarily produced. But this does not mean that they are produced by any single Creator or by any individual. In other words, things are produced by conditions in general, and not by any other specific thing in particular. Socialism, for instance, is a product of certain general economic conditions, and was not manufactured by Marx or Engels, still less by the former's *Communist Manifesto*. In this sense, we can say that everything produces itself and is not produced by others.

Hence everything cannot but be what it is. The *Commentary* states: "It is not by accident that we have our life. It is not by chance that our life is what it is. The universe is very extended; things are very numerous. Yet, in it and among them, we are just what we are.... What we are not, we cannot be. What we are, we cannot but be. What we do not do, we cannot do. What we can do, we cannot but do. Let everything be what it is, then there will be peace." (Ch. 5.)

This is also true of social phenomena. The *Commentary* says again: "There is nothing which is not natural.... Peace or disorder, success or failure.... are all the product of nature, not of man." (Ch. 7.) By "the product of nature," Hsiang-Kuo mean that they are the necessary result of certain conditions or circumstances. In chapter 14 of the *Chuang-tzu*, the text states that sages disturb the peace of the world; to which the *Commentary* says: "The current of history, combined with present circumstances, is responsible for the present crisis. It is not due to any certain individuals. It is due to the world at large. The activity of the sages does not disturb the world, but the world itself becomes disorderly."

● **Institutions and Morals**

Hsiang-Kuo consider the universe as being in a continuous state of flux. They write in their *Commentary*: "Change is a force, unobservable yet most strong. It transports heaven and earth toward the new, and carries mountains and hills away from the old. The old does not stop for a moment, but immediately becomes the new. All things ever change...."

军队互相支援；一支军队的胜负，必定对它的同盟军产生影响。

宇宙间存在的每一事物都需要整个宇宙作为它存在的必要条件，而它的存在又并不是由某一个特定事物所产生的。当某些条件具备，在某种情况下，某些事物就必然会发生。这并不意味着，万物是由一位创世主或某个人所创造。换句话说，事物是由一般性条件所产生，而不是由于其他某个特定的事物。举例来说，社会主义是一定经济条件的产物，而不是马克思或恩格斯所制造出来的，更不是马克思的《共产主义宣言》所造出来的。就这一层意义来看，我们可以说，事物是自己生出来，而不是由别的事物产生的的。

正因为如此，每一事物只能是它自己。向—郭《注》中说："故人之生也，非误生也；生之所有，非妄有也。天地虽大，万物虽多，然吾之所遇适在于是，……故凡所不遇，弗能遇也，其所遇，弗能不遇也；凡所不为，弗能为也，其所为，弗能不为也。故付之而自当矣。"（《德充符》"死生存亡……"注）

这个道理也同样适用于社会现象领域。向—郭《注》又说："物无非天也。天也者，自然者也。……治乱成败……非人为也，皆自然耳。"（《大宗师》"庸讵知吾所谓天之非人乎？……"注）这里所说"皆自然耳"是指它们都是一定条件和情况下的产物。《庄子·天运》篇讲到圣人乱天下，向—郭《注》对此评论说："承百代之流而会乎当今之变，其弊至于斯者，非禹也，故曰天下耳。言圣知之迹非乱天下，而天下必有斯乱。"（《天运》"人自为种而天下耳……"注）

● **典制与道德**

向、郭认为，宇宙是在流动不居之中。在向—郭《注》中写道："夫无力之力，莫大于变化者也。故乃揭天地以趋新，负山岳以舍故。故不暂停，忽已涉新，则天地万物无时而不移也。……

All that we meet secretly passes away. We ourselves in the past are not we ourselves now. We still have to go forward with the present. We cannot keep ourselves still." (Ch. 6.)

Society, too, is always in a state of flux. Human needs are constantly changing. Institutions and morals that are good for one time may not be good for another. The *Commentary* says: "The institutions of the former kings served to meet the needs of their own time. But if they continue to exist when time has changed, they become a bogey to the people, and begin to be artificial." (Ch. 14.)

Again: "Those who imitate the sages imitate what they have done. But what they have done has already passed away, and therefore it cannot meet the present situation. It is worthless and should not be imitated. The past is dead while the present is living. If one attempts to handle the living with the dead, one will certainly fail." (Ch. 9.)

Society changes with circumstances. When the circumstances change, institutions and morals should change with them. If they do not, they become artificial and are "a bogey to the people." It is natural that new institutions and new morals should spontaneously produce themselves. The new and the old differ from each other because their times are different. Both of them serve to meet the needs of their time, so neither is superior nor inferior to the other. Hsiang-Kuo do not oppose institutions and morals as such, as did Lao Tzu and Chuang Tzu. They simply oppose those institutions and morals that are out-of-date and therefore unnatural for the present world.

- ● *Yu-wei* and *Wu-wei*

Thus Hsiang-Kuo give a new interpretation to the earlier Taoist ideas about the natural and the artificial and about *yu-wei* or having activity, and *wu-wei* or having no activity (also translated as non-action). When there is a change of social circumstances, new institutions and morals spontaneously produce themselves. To let them go means to follow the natural and be *wu-wei*, i.e., without action. To oppose them and to keep the old ones that are already out-of-date is to be artificial and *yu-wei*, i.e., with action. In one passage of the *Commentary* it is said: "When water runs down from a high to a low place, the current is irresistible. When small things group with what is small, and large things with what is large, their tendency cannot be opposed. When a man is empty and without bias, everyone will contribute his wisdom to him. What does he

今交一臂而失之，皆在冥中去矣。故向者之我，非复今我也。我与今俱往，岂常守故哉！"（《大宗师》"然而夜半有力者负之而走……"注）

社会也是在不断变动之中，人的需要同样是在不断变化之中。典制和道德适应一时，不可能适用于永久。向—郭《注》中说："夫先王典礼，所以适时用也。时过而不弃，即为民妖，所以兴矫效之端也。"（《天运》"围于陈蔡之间……"注）

向—郭《注》中还说："法圣人者，法其迹耳。夫迹者，已去之物，非应变之具也，奚足尚而执之哉！执成迹以御乎无方，无方至而迹滞矣。"（《胠箧》"然而田成子一旦杀齐君而盗其国……"注）

社会随情况而变化，情况变了，典制和道德也应作相应的改变。如果不随之而变，就将扞格不入（"即为民妖"），变成人为的桎梏。新的典制和道德应运而生是自然的事。新的与旧的扞格不入，因为他们所处的时代变了。两者都是应时而生，因此不能说，一个比另一个就一定高明或不如。向、郭并不像老子、庄子那样一般地反对典制和道德，他们所反对的是在现实世界中已经过时、已经背乎自然的典制和道德。

● 有为与无为

向、郭就是这样，对先秦道家思想中的天、人、有为、无为都赋予了新的诠释。在社会情况变动中，新的典制和道德自然应时而生，在这时候，顺应天、顺应自然就要顺应新的典制道德，这就是"天"，就是无为。反对新的典制道德，极力维护旧的典制道德，这便是"人"，便是有为。向—郭《注》中有一段话："夫高下相受，不可逆之流也；小大相群，不得已之势也；旷然无情，群知之府也。

do, who is the leader of men, when facing these currents and tendencies? He simply trusts the wisdom of the time, relies on the necessity of circumstances, and lets the world take care of itself. That is all." (Ch. 6.)

If an individual, in his activities, allows his natural abilities to exercise themselves fully and freely, he is *wu-wei*. Otherwise he is *yu-wei*. In one passage of the *Commentary* it is said: "A good driver must let his horse exercise itself to the full of its ability. The way to do so is to give it freedom.... If he allows his horses to do what they can do, compelling neither the slow ones to run fast nor the fast ones to walk slowly, though he may travel through the whole world with them, they rather enjoy it. Hearing that horses should be set free, some people think that they should be left wild. Hearing the theory of non-action, some people think that lying down is better than walking. These people are far wrong in understanding the ideas of Chuang Tzu." (Ch. 9.) Despite this criticism, it would seem that in their understanding of Chuang Tzu such people were not far wrong. Yet Hsiang-Kuo, in their own interpretation of him, were certainly highly original.

Hsiang-Kuo also give a new interpretation to the ideas of simplicity and primitivity of the earlier Taoists. In their *Commentary* they write: "If by primitivity we mean the undistorted, the man whose character is not distorted is the most primitive, though he may be capable of doing many things. If by simplicity we mean the unmixed, the form of the dragon and the features of the phoenix are the most simple, though their beauty is all surpassing. On the other hand, even the skin of a dog or a goat cannot be primitive and simple, if its natural qualities are distorted by, or mixed with, foreign elements." (Ch.15.)

● **Knowledge and Imitation**

Lao Tzu and Chuang Tzu both opposed sages of the sort ordinarily regarded as such by the world. In the earlier Taoist literature, the word "sage" has two meanings. By it, the Taoists either mean the perfect man (in the Taoist sense) or the man with all sorts of knowledge. Lao Tzu and Chuang Tzu attacked knowledge, and hence the sage of the latter kind, the man who has knowledge. But from the preceding pages we can see that Hsiang-Kuo had no objection to some men's being sages. What they did object to is the attempt of some people to imitate the sages. Plato was born a Plato, and Chuang Tzu a Chuang Tzu. Their genius was as natural as the form of a dragon or the features of a phoenix. They were as "simple" and "primitive" as anything can be. They were not wrong in writing

承百流之会，居师人之极者，奚为哉？任时世之知，委必然之事，付之天下而已。"（《大宗师》"以知为时者……"注）

一个人，在他的活动中让天赋的才能发挥出来，这在他就是无为。反之，就是有为。向—郭《注》中说："夫善御者，将以尽其能也。尽能在于自任，……若乃任驽骥之力，适迟疾之分，虽则足迹接乎八荒之表，而众马之性全矣。而惑者闻任马之性，乃谓放而不乘；闻无为之风，遂云行不如卧；何其往而不返哉！斯失乎庄生之旨远矣。"（《马蹄》"饥之渴之……"注）尽管向、郭作出这样的批评，就这些人对庄子的理解来说，其实错误并不十分严重。而向、郭两人的见解则确是十分有创见的。

向、郭对先秦道家的"纯素之道"思想也作了新的诠释。向—郭《注》中说："苟以不亏为纯，则虽百行同举，万变参备，乃至纯也；苟以不杂为素，则虽龙章凤姿，情乎有非常之观，乃至素也。若不能保其自然之质而杂乎外饰，则虽犬羊之鞸，庸得谓之纯素哉！"（《刻意》"故素也者……"注）

● **知识与模仿**

老、庄都反对通常被社会推崇为圣人的那种人。在先秦道家著述中，"圣人"这个词有两重含义，一重含义是道家推崇的真人，另一重含义是拥有各种知识的饱学之士。老子和庄子都蔑视知识，因此也蔑视那些饱学之士。但是，从下面所述，向、郭并不反对有些人成为圣人，他们所反对的是有些人力图模仿圣人。柏拉图就是柏拉图，庄子就是庄子。他们质朴纯真，他们的天才是龙章凤姿，

their *Republic* and "Happy Excursion," for in so doing they were merely following their own natures.

This view is exemplified in the following passage from the *Commentary*: "By knowledge we mean [the activity that attempts] what is beyond [one's natural ability]. That which is within the proper sphere [of one's natural ability] is not called knowledge. By being within the proper sphere we mean acting according to one's natural ability, attempting nothing that is beyond. If carrying ten thousand *ch'un* [thirty cattles] is in accordance with one's ability, one will not feel the burden as weighty. If discharging ten thousand functions [is in accordance with one's ability], one will not feel the task as taxing." (Ch. 3.) Thus if we understand knowledge in this sense, neither Plato nor Chuang Tzu should be considered as having any knowledge.

It is only the imitators that have knowledge. Hsiang-Kuo seem to have regarded imitation as wrong for three reasons. First, it is useless. They write in the *Commentary*: "Events in ancient times have ceased to exist. Though they may be recorded, it is not possible for them to happen again in the present. The ancient is not the present, and the present is even now changing. Therefore we should give up imitation, act according to our nature, and change with the times. This is the way to perfection." (Ch. 13.) Everything is in a flux. Every day we have new problems, new needs, and meet new situations. We should have new methods to deal with these new situations, problems, and needs. Even at a single given moment, the situations, problems, and needs of different individuals differ from one another. So must their methods. What, then, is the use of imitation?

Second, imitation is fruitless. One passage of the *Commentary* tells us: "With conscious effort, some people have tried to be a Li Chu [a great artisan] or a Shih K'uang [a great musician], but have not succeeded. Yet without knowing how, Li Chu and Shih K'uang were especially talented in their eye and ear. With conscious effort, some people have tried to be sages, but have not succeeded. Yet without knowing how, the sages became sages. Not only is it the sages and Li Chu and Shih K'uang who are difficult to imitate. We cannot even be fools, or dogs, by simply

天质自然。柏拉图写《理想国》，庄子写《逍遥游》，都是一片冰心，直道而行，只是顺乎自己的天性。

这个看法可以举向—郭《注》下列一段话为证："故知之为名，生于失当而灭于冥极。冥极者，任其至分而无毫铢之加。是故虽负万钧，苟当其所能，则忽然不知重之在身。"（《养生主》"而知也无涯……"注）这是说，知识聪明的由来是由于人的欲求超过了人的才智所能。如果人在自己的才智范围之内行事，也就无需知识聪明了。人只要按自己的天生才智行事为人，志无盈求，事毋过用。如果能够力负万钧，他这样负重，也不会觉得力不能胜；一个人如果能日理万机，他这样做时也不会叫苦连天。如果这样来理解知识聪明，则柏拉图和庄子都不算是有任何知识聪明的人了。

照向、郭的看法，唯有东施效颦的人才需要知识聪明。向、郭把模仿看为谬误，大概有三个原因。其一是它无用，在向—郭《注》中他们写道："当古之事，已灭于古矣，虽或传之，岂能使古在今哉！古不在今，今事已变，故绝学任性，与时变化而后至焉。"（《天道》"古之人与其不可传也死矣……"注）在道家看来，"学"就是模仿。这段话的意思是说，古代的事情已经不复存在，虽然载入了史籍，却不能使它们在今日再现。古今不同，今世已变，只能抛弃恋古、仿古的念头，按照人的本性，与时代同变，才能臻于完善。万物都流动，人们每天都遇到新问题、新情况，感到新需要。对付新情况、新问题和新需要，要采取新的方法。即使在同一个时候，不同人的处境、情况和问题也有所不同，解决问题的方法也不可能尽同。一个人如果只知一味模仿，那有什么用？！

其次，模仿是徒劳的。向—郭《注》里有一段说："有情于为离、旷而弗能也，然离、旷以无情而聪明矣；有情于为贤圣而弗能也，然贤圣以无情而贤圣矣。岂直贤圣绝远而离、旷难慕哉？虽下愚聋瞽及鸡鸣狗吠，岂有情于为之，亦终不能也。"（《德充符》"庄子曰：道与之貌……"注）离朱是古代传说中的"明目者"，师旷是春秋晋国的乐师。他们的特殊才能是天生的。其他人想成为离朱、师旷而不能，离朱、师旷并无心成为精工巧匠，却取得了成就。常人想当圣贤而不能，圣贤顺其本性而成为圣贤。如果说，模仿圣贤

wishing or trying to be so." (Ch. 5.) Everything must be what it is. One thing simply cannot be the other.

Third, imitation is harmful. The *Commentary* states again: "There are some people who are not satisfied with their own nature and always attempt what is beyond it. This is to attempt what is impossible, and is like a circle imitating a square, or a fish imitating a bird.... They go ever further, the more remote their goal seems to be. The more knowledge they gain, the more nature they lose." (Ch. 2.)

Again: "The nature of everything has its limit. If one is led on by what is beyond it, one's nature will be lost. One should disregard the inducement, and live according to oneself, not according to others. In this way the integrity of one's nature will be preserved." (Ch. 10.) Not only is there no possibility for one to succeed by imitating others, but by that very act, there is a great probability that one will lose one's self. This is the harm of imitation.

Thus imitation is useless, fruitless, and harmful. The only sensible mode of life is "to live according to oneself," which is also to practice the theory of non-action.

● The Equality of Things

But if one can really live according to oneself, disregarding the inducements offered by others, that means that one is already able to get rid of what Hsiang-Kuo call the "trouble of preferring one thing to another." (Ch. 2.) In other words, one is already able to understand the principle of the equality of things and to see things from a higher point of view. One is already on the royal road to the state of non-distinction of the undifferentiable whole.

In the second chapter of the *Chuang-tzu*, Chuang Tzu emphasized the theory of non-distinction, especially the non-distinction of right and wrong. In their *Commentary*, Hsiang-Kuo expound this theory with more eloquence. Thus to the saying of Chuang Tzu that "the universe is a finger, all things are a horse," the *Commentary* observes: "In order to show that there is no distinction between right and wrong, there is nothing better than illustrating one thing with another. In so doing we see that all things

太远，模仿离、旷太难，常人想成为下愚聋瞽、成为鸡狗，也不可能。每个事物之成为它自己，是身不由己的，它想变为其他事物，是不可能的。

其三，模仿是有害的。向—郭《注》中还说：有些人"不能止乎本性，而求外无已。夫外不可求而求之，譬犹以圆学方，以鱼慕鸟耳。……此愈近彼，愈远实，学弥得而性弥失。"（《齐物论》"五者圆而几向方矣……"注）这是说，有些人不知足于自己的天赋，硬勉强自己做不可能达到的事情，如同一个圆形，要模仿成为方形，鱼要想成为飞鸟。他们的目标定得越高，自己走得越远；知识越多，戕贼本性也愈甚。

不仅如此，"爱生有分，而以所贵引之，则性命丧矣。若乃毁其所贵，弃彼任我，则聪明各全，人含其真也"（《胠箧》"擢乱六律……"注）。事物的本性都有它的局限性。人如果力图超越本性，结果就将丧失本性，只有不顾外面的引诱，顺乎自己的本性，才能保持自己内心的完整。一意模仿别人，不仅不可能成功，还陷入丧失自己的危险。这是刻意模仿带来的危险。

这表明，模仿不仅无用，毫无结果，还将戕贼自己。因此，人的唯一明智的生活方式是"弃彼任我"，这便是在生活中实践"无为"。

● 齐万物

如果一个人能够真正"任我"地生活，不顾外来的压力或引诱，这意味着他已经能够祛除向、郭在《齐物论》注中所说的"偏尚之累"，时刻苦于选此舍彼的烦恼。这也就是说，他已经能够从一个超越的观点，看到万物在本质上并无差别，已经登上"无差别"、"混沌一体"的康庄大道了。

在《齐物论》里，庄子强调事物本质上并无差别的理论观点，其中又特别强调：像儒墨两家那样是己非彼并无意义。向、郭在《庄子注》书中对此也特别着力。对庄子所说"天地一指也，万物一马也"，向—郭《注》说："将明无是无非，莫若反复相喻。反复

agree in that they all consider themselves to be right and others to be wrong. Since they all agree that all others are wrong, hence in the world there can be no right; and since they all agree that they themselves are right, hence in the world there can be no wrong.

"How can it be shown that this is so? If the right is really absolutely right, in the world there should be none that considers it to be wrong. If the wrong is really absolutely wrong, in the world there should be none that considers it to be right. The fact that there are uncertainty between right and wrong, and a confusion in distinctions, shows that the distinctions between right and wrong are due to a partiality of view, and that all things are really in agreement. In our observation, we see this truth everywhere. Therefore, the perfect man, knowing that the universe is a finger and all things are a horse, thus rests in great peace. All things function according to their nature, and enjoy themselves. [Between them] there is no distinction between right and wrong." (Ch. 2.)

● Absolute Freedom and Absolute Happiness

If one can transcend the distinctions between things, one can enjoy the absolute freedom and have the absolute happiness that are described in the first chapter of the *Chuang-tzu*. In the many stories contained in this chapter, Chuang Tzu mentions the great roc bird, the small bird, the cicada, the "small knowledge" of the morning mushroom, whose life extends only to the same evening, the "great knowledge" of the old trees whose experience covers thousands of years, small officers of limited talents, and the philosopher Lieh Tzu who could ride on the wind. Regarding these stories, the Hsiang-Kuo *Commentary* says: "If there is satisfaction for their natures, the roc has nothing to be proud of in comparison with the small bird, and the small bird has no desire for the Celestial Lake [the dwelling place of the roc]. Therefore, though there is a difference between the great and the small, their happiness is the same." (Ch. 1.)

Their happiness, however, is only relative happiness. If things only enjoy themselves in their finite spheres, their enjoyment must also be finite. Thus in his first chapter, Chuang Tzu concludes his stories with

相喻，则彼之与我，既同于自是，又均于相非。均于相非，则天下无是；同于自是，则天下无非。"能够最好地表明事物的是非本无区别，便是把事物拿来比较。这样做时，人们就会发现：所有事物的共同之处就在于都以自己为是，而以别的事物为非。既然它们都确定地认为，一切其他事物都不对，那就是说，天下没有一样东西是对的；既然它们都确定地认为自己是对的，那就表明，世上没有错的东西。

向—郭《注》又说："何以明其然邪？是若果是，则天下不得复有非之者也。非若果非，则天下亦不得复有是之者也。今是非无主，纷然淆乱，明此区区者各信其偏见而同于一致耳。仰视俯察，莫不皆然。是以至人知天地一指也，万物一马也，故浩然大宁，而天地万物各当其分，同于自得，而无是无非也。"这是说，如果自认为"对"的果真绝对正确，则世上便没有"不对"的东西了；如果被指为"错"的东西果真都错，则世上也就没有能自认为"对"的东西了。事实是，在事物的是非上难以确定，分辨是非的界限陷于混乱，这表明，是非之分，无非是一种偏执之见，而在偏执这一点上，万物倒是一致的。仰观俯察，到处都如此。至人有鉴于此，从中知道天地如同一指，万物如同一马，因而得以心平气和。懂得齐万物，万物都顺性"任我"，就都怡然自得了。

● **终极的自由与快乐**

如果人能够超越事物之间的差别，就能够享受像《庄子》第一篇《逍遥游》中提出的绝对自由和绝对快乐。在《逍遥游》里，庄子讲了许多故事，其中提到大鹏、小鸟、蝉等等。朝生暮死的朝菌只有"小知"，千年古树（"大椿"）则有"大知"；小官僚才德有限，而列子则"御风而行"。对此，向—郭《注》说："苟足于其性，则虽大鹏无以自贵于小鸟，小鸟无羡于天池，而荣愿有余矣。故小大虽殊，逍遥一也。"（《逍遥游》"蜩与学鸠笑之曰……"注）

但这种快乐只是相对的快乐。如果万物只是在自身有限的领域中自得其乐，它们的乐也只是极其有限的。针对这一点，庄子在

one about the really independent man who transcends the finite and becomes one with the infinite, so that he enjoys infinite and absolute happiness. Because he transcends the finite and identifies himself with the infinite, he has "no self." Because he follows the nature of things and lets everything enjoy itself, he has "no achievement." And because he is one with the *Tao*, which is unnamable, he has "no name."

This idea is developed by the Hsiang-Kuo *Commentary* with clarity and eloquence: "Everything has its proper nature, and that nature has its proper limitation. The differences between things are like those between small and great knowledge, short and long life.... All believe in their own sphere and none is intrinsically superior to others." After giving different illustrations, Chuang Tzu concludes with the independent man who forgets his own self and its opposite, and who ignores all the differences. "All things enjoy themselves in their own sphere, but the independent man has neither achievement nor name. Therefore, he who unites the great and the small is one who ignores the distinction between the great and the small. If one insists on the distinctions, the roc, the cicada, the small officer, and Lieh Tzu riding on the wind, are all troublesome things. He who equalizes life and death is one who ignores the distinction of life and death. If one insists on the distinction, the *ta ch'un* [an old tree] and the chrysalis, P'eng Tsu [a Chinese Methuselah] and the morning mushroom, all suffer early death. Therefore, he who makes excursion into the realm of non-distinction between great and small has no limitation. He who ignores the distinction of life and death has no terminal. But those whose happiness lies within the finite sphere will certainly suffer limitation. Though they are allowed to make excursions, they are not able to be independent." (Ch. 1.)

In the first chapter, Chuang Tzu describes the independent man as "one who chariots on the normality of the universe, rides upon the transformation of the six elements, and makes excursion into the infinite." On this the Hsiang-Kuo *Commentary* remarks: "The universe is the general name of all things. The universe has all things as its contents, and all things must take *Tzu Jan* [the natural] as their norm. What is spontaneously so, and not made to be so, is the natural. The roc can fly in high places, the quail in low ones. The *ta-ch'un* tree can live for a long time, the mushroom for a short one. All these capacities are natural, and are not caused or learned. They are not caused to be so, but are naturally so; that is the reason why they are normal. Therefore to chariot on the

《逍遥游》的故事里提出了一个独立的人（大鹏），超越有限而融入无限，享受到无限所给予的绝对快乐。他因超越了有限、融入无限而"无我"。他顺乎万物本性，与万物一起得其所哉，因此，在世人眼中，他"一无所成"。他与道成为一体，道无名，依同样的道理，至人也无名。

向、郭在《庄子注》里，把这思想发挥得淋漓尽致："物各有性，性各有极，皆如年知，……历举年知之大小，各信其一方，未有足以相倾者也。"这是说，事物各有其性，事物本性又各有局限。事物之间的差别往往只是数量上的差别，例如大知和小知，长寿和短寿，改变不了人的知识有限、生命有限这个本质。庄子在列举这方面的许多例证之后，举出了他心目中的独立的人，既忘记了自己，又忘记了和自己对立的一方，因此达到了"无差别"境界。因此，万物在各自的范围内自得其乐。独立无待的人既无功，也无名，向—郭《注》中说："是故统小大者，无小无大者也；苟有乎大小，则虽大鹏之与斥鷃，宰官之与御风，同为累物耳。齐死生者，无死无生者也；苟有乎死生，则虽大椿之与蟪蛄，彭祖之与朝菌，均于短折耳。故游于无小无大者，无穷者也；冥乎不死不生者，无极者也。若夫逍遥而系于有方，则虽放之使游而有所穷矣，未能无待也。"（《逍遥游》"小知不及大知，小年不及大年……"注）

庄子在《逍遥游》中描写独立无待的人有如"乘天地之正，而御六气之辩，以游无穷者"。向—郭《注》说："天地者，万物之总名也。天地以万物为体，而万物必以自然为正，自然者，不为而自然者也。故大鹏之能高，斥鷃之能下，椿木之能长，朝菌之能短，凡此皆自然之所能，非为之所能也。不为而自能，所以为正也。

normality of the universe is to follow the nature of things. To ride upon the transformation of the six elements is to make excursion along the road of change and evolution. If one proceeds in this way, where can one reach the end? If one chariots on whatever one meets, what will one be required to depend upon? This is the happiness and freedom of the perfect man who unites his own self with its opposite.

"If one has to depend upon something, one cannot be happy, unless one gets hold of the thing upon which one depends. Although Lieh Tzu could pursue his way in such a fine manner, he still had to depend upon the wind, and the roc was even more dependent. Only he who makes no distinction between himself and other things and follows the great evolution, can really be independent and always free. He not only sets himself free, but also follows the nature of those who have to depend upon something, allowing them to have that something upon which they depend. When they have that upon which they depend, they all enjoy the Great Freedom." (Ch. 1.)

In the Hsiang-Kuo system, the *Tao* is really nothing. In this system, *T'ien* or *T'ien Ti* (literally "Heaven" or "Heaven and Earth," but here translated as the universe) becomes the most important idea. *T'ien* is the general name of things, and is thus the totality of all that is. To see things from the point of view of *T'ien* and to identify oneself with *T'ien*, is to transcend things and their differences, or, as the Neo-Taoists said, "to transcend shapes and features."

Thus the Hsiang-Kuo *Commentary*, besides making important revisions in original Taoism, also expressed more articulately what in the *Chuang-tzu* is only suggestive. Those, however, who prefer suggestiveness to articulateness, would no doubt agree with a certain Ch'an monk who remarked: "People say that it was Kuo Hsiang who wrote a commentary on Chuang Tzu. I would say that it was Chuang Tzu who wrote a commentary on Kuo Hsiang." (See chapter one, page 26.)

故乘天地之正者，即是顺万物之性也；御六气之辩者，即是游变化之涂也；如斯以往，则何往而有穷哉！所遇斯乘，又将恶乎待哉！此乃至德之人玄同彼我者之逍遥也。苟有待焉，则虽列子之轻妙，犹不能以无风而行，故必得其所待，然后逍遥耳，而况大鹏乎！夫唯与物冥而循大变者，为能无待而常通，岂独自通而已哉！又顺有待者，使不失其所待，所待不失，则同于大通矣。”在这里，“通”就是自由。

在向、郭的思想里，“道”即是“无”，“天”或“天地”成为他们最重要的思想。“天”是万物的总称，因此也就是万物的整体，从“天”的观点看万物，把自身融入“天”，就是超越万物和万物的差别性，或如新道家所说：“超乎形象。”

因此，向秀和郭象不仅对先秦道家的思想作了重要的修正，还把庄子在思想上的暗示用具体透彻的语言表达出来。如果有人觉得，任何话语都不宜说得太透，暗示比明确更堪玩味，就会同意从前一个禅宗僧人所说："曾见郭象注庄子，识者云：却是庄子注郭象。"（请参阅本书第一章）

424

⑳ NEO-TAOISM: THE SENTIMENTALISTS

In their *Commentary* to the *Chuang-tzu*, Hsiang Hsiu and Kuo Hsiang gave a theoretical exposition of the man who has a mind or spirit transcending the distinctions of things and who lives "according to himself but not according to others." This quality of such a man is the essence of what the Chinese call *feng liu*.

● *Feng Liu* and the Romantic Spirit

In order to understand *feng liu*, we must turn to the *Shih-shuo Hsin-yü* or *Contemporary Records of New Discourses* (abbreviated as *Shih-shuo*), a work by Liu Yi-ch'ing (403-444), supplemented by a commentary by Liu Hsün (463-521). The Neo-Taoists and their Buddhist friends of the Chin dynasty were famous for what was known at the time as *ch'ing t'an*, that is, pure or fine conversation. The art of such conversation consisted in expressing the best thought, which was usually Taoistic, in the best language and tersest phraseology. Because of its rather precious nature, it could be held only between friends of a comparable and rather high intellectual level, and hence it was regarded as one of the most refined of intellectual activities. The *Shih-shuo* is a record of many such "pure conversations" and their famous participants. Through them, it gives a vivid picture of those people of the third and fourth centuries who were followers of the *feng liu* ideas. Ever since its compilation, therefore, it has been a major source for studying the *feng liu* tradition.

What, then, is the meaning of *feng liu*? It is one of those elusive terms which to the initiated conveys a wealth of ideas, but is most difficult to translate exactly. Literally, the two words that form it mean "wind and stream," which does not seem to help us very much. Nevertheless, they do, perhaps, suggest something of the freedom and ease which are some of the characteristics of the quality of *feng liu*.

I confess that I have not yet understood the full significance of the words romanticism or romantic in English, but I suspect that they are a fairly rough equivalent of *feng liu*. *Feng liu* is chiefly connected with Taoism. This is one of the reasons why I have said in chapter two that the Confucianist and Taoist traditions in Chinese history are in some degree equivalent to the classical and romantic traditions in the West.

贰拾 新道家：豁达率性的风格

向秀和郭象在《庄子注》里从理论上阐述了一个人超越事物差别之后，得以不再依循别人的意旨生活，而率性任情地过自己的生活（"弃彼任我"）。这种思想和生活方式乃是中国古人称为"风流"的实质。

● 风流与浪漫精神

为理解"风流"的含义，需要读《世说新语》（简称《世说》），这是晋朝刘义庆（公元四〇三至四四四年）的著作，刘峻（公元四六三至五二一年）注。晋朝的新道家和他们的佛僧友人以当时所盛称的"清谈"著名，从字面含义说，"清谈"是清新、精妙的谈话。它的艺术性在于运用精妙而又简练的语言，表达（往往是道家的）创意清新的思想。由于它的精微思想和含蓄而富妙趣的语言，因此只能在智力较高又互相熟悉、旗鼓相当的朋友之间进行，而被认为是一种"阳春白雪"式的高水平智力活动。《世说》就是当时名士间清谈的一部辑录，从中可以看到三、四世纪间风流自赏的名士们的生动形象。因此，《世说》一书问世后，便成了探索"风流"传统的一部主要资料书。

究竟"风流"是什么意思？这是一个含义丰富而又难以确切说明的语词。从字面上说，"风流"是荡漾着的"风"和"流水"，和人没有直接的联系，但它似乎暗示了有些人放浪形骸、自由自在的一种生活风格。

我对英语中"浪漫"（romantic）和"浪漫主义"（romanticism）两个词的含义还未能充分领略，但我大致感觉到，这两个词和"风流"的意思颇为接近。在中国思想史上，"风流"主要是和道家思想相连的。这是在本书第二章里，我说中国历史上，儒家和道家的地位与作用有点类似西方历史上的古典主义和浪漫主义的原因之一。

The Han (206 B.C.-A.D. 220) and Chin (265-420) are not only the names of two different dynasties in Chinese history, but also, because of their very different social, political, and cultural characteristics, are designations of two different styles of literature and art, and of two different manners of living. The Han style and manner are ones of dignity and grandeur; those of the Chin are ones of elegance and freedom. Elegance is also one of the characteristics of *feng liu*.

● **"Yang Chu's Garden of Pleasure"**

Something must first be said here about the seventh chapter in the Taoist work known as the *Lieh-tzu*, a chapter titled "Yang Chu" (translated by Anton Forke as *Yang Chu's Garden of Pleasure*). As we have already seen in our chapter six, what is said in this "Yang Chu" chapter cannot represent the view of the genuine Yang Chu of ancient times. The *Lieh-tzu* itself, indeed, is now considered by Chinese scholars as a work of the third century A.D. Hence its "Yang Chu" chapter must also be a production of this period. It accords well with the general trend of thought of that time, and is in fact an expression of one aspect of *feng liu*.

In the "Yang Chu" chapter, a distinction is made between the external and the internal. Thus the spurious "Yang Chu" is reported as saying: "There are four things which do not allow people to have peace. The first is long life, the second is reputation, the third is rank, and the fourth is riches. Those who have these things fear ghosts, fear men, fear power, and fear punishment. They are called fugitives.... Their lives are controlled by externals. But those who follow their destiny do not desire long life. Those who are not fond of honor do not desire reputation. Those who do not want power desire no rank. And those who are not avaricious have no desire for riches. Of this sort of men it may be said that they live in accordance with their nature.... They regulate their lives by internal things."

In another passage an imaginary conversation is recorded between Tzu-ch'an, a famous statesman of the state of Cheng who lived in the sixth century B.C., and his two brothers. Tzu-ch'an governed the state for three years and governed well. But his two brothers were out of his control; one of them was fond of feasting and the other of gallantry.

One day, Tzu-ch'an spoke to his brothers, saying: "Those things in which man is superior to beasts and birds are his mental faculties. Through them he gets righteousness and propriety, and so glory and rank fall to his share. You are only moved by what excites your senses, and indulge only in licentious desires, endangering your lives and natures...."

在中国历史上，汉朝（公元前二〇六至公元二二〇年）和晋朝（公元二六五至四二〇年）不仅是两个不同的朝代，它们的社会、政治、文化都十分不同，以致成为两种文学、艺术和生活方式的代表：汉代的风格是庄严、雄浑，晋代的风格则是俊雅和旷达疏放。俊雅也是"风流"的一个特征。

● **"杨朱的乐园"**

在这里，先要说一下道家著作中《列子》一书（古本已佚失）今本八篇中的第七篇《杨朱》篇（Anton Forke 的英译本把它译作"杨朱的乐园"）。在本书第六章里已经指出，它并不真正代表中国古代哲学家杨朱的思想。现代中国学者考证，今本《列子》（内容多为民间故事、寓言和神话传说）是公元三世纪的一部著述，因此，其中的《杨朱》篇也应是公元三世纪间的著作。它与三世纪的思潮十分吻合，实际上反映了"风流"的一个方面。

在《杨朱》篇里，把"外"和"内"加以区别。这位假托的杨朱说："生民之不得休息，为四事故：一为寿，二为名，三为位，四为货。有此四者，畏鬼畏人，畏威畏刑。此之谓遁人也。可杀可活，制命在外。不逆命，何羡寿？不矜贵，何羡名？不要势，何羡位？不贪富，何羡货？此之谓顺民也，天下无对，制命在内。"

《杨朱》篇里有一段虚构了公元前六世纪郑国著名政治家子产和他的哥哥、弟弟的谈话。子产治国三年，成绩斐然。但是，他的哥哥和弟弟，一个酗酒，一个好色，子产也莫能奈何他们。一天，子产和他的哥哥、弟弟谈话，对他们说："人之所以贵于禽兽者智虑。智虑之所将者礼义，礼义成则名位至矣。若触情而动，耽于嗜欲，则性命危矣。"

To this the brothers answered: "If one tries to set external things in order, these external things do not necessarily become well-ordered, and one's person is already given toil and trouble. But if one tries to set the internal in order, the external things do not necessarily fall into disorder, and one's nature becomes free and at ease. Your system of regulating external things will do temporarily and for a single kingdom, but it is not in harmony with the human heart. Our method of regulating what is internal, on the contrary, can be extended to the whole world, and [when it is extended] there is no need for princes and ministers."

What this chapter calls regulating the internal corresponds to what Hsiang-Kuo call living according to oneself; what it calls regulating external things corresponds to what Hsiang-Kuo call living according to others. One should live according to oneself, and not according to others. That is to say, one should live in accord with one's own reason or impulse, and not according to the customs and morals of the time. To use a common expression of the third and fourth centuries, one should live according to *tzu jan* (the spontaneous, the natural), and not according to *ming chiao* (institutions and morals). All the Neo-Taoists agree on this. But there is still a difference among them between the rationalists and sentimentalists. The former, as represented by Hsiang-Kuo, emphasize living according to reason, while the latter, as represented by the men who will be mentioned below, emphasize living according to impulse.

The idea of living according to impulse is expressed in extreme form in the "Yang Chu" chapter. In one passage we read that Yen P'ing-chung asked Kuan Yi-wu (both famous statesmen of the state of Ch'i in ancient times, though historically they were not contemporaries) about cultivating life. "Kuan Yi-wu replied: 'The only way is to give it its free course, neither checking nor obstructing it.' Yen P'ing-chung asked: 'And as to details?'

"Kuan Yi-wu replied: 'Allow the ear to hear anything that it likes to hear. Allow the eye to see whatever it likes to see. Allow the nose to smell whatever it likes to smell. Allow the mouth to say whatever it likes to say. Allow the body to enjoy whatever it likes to enjoy. Allow the mind to do whatever it likes to do.'

"'What the ear likes to hear is music, and prohibition of the hearing of music is called obstruction to the ear. What the eye likes to see is beauty, and prohibition of the seeing of beauty is called obstruction to sight. What the nose likes to smell is perfume, and prohibition of the smelling of perfume is called obstruction to smell. What the mouth likes to talk about is right and wrong, and prohibition of the talking about right and wrong is called obstruction to understanding. What the body likes to enjoy is rich food and fine clothing, and prohibition of the enjoying of

他的哥哥、弟弟回答说:"夫善治外者,物未必治而身交苦;善治内者,物未必乱而性交逸。以若之治外,其法可暂行于一国,未合于人心;以我之治内,可推之于天下,君臣之道息矣。"

《杨朱》篇所说的"治内"相当于郭象所说的"任我"而活,所说的"治外"相当于郭象所说的"从人"而活。人活着,应当听从自己内心,而不是矫情迎合别人。也就是说,人活着,或循理或顺情,都应当出自纯真的内心,而不是为了迎合时尚。用三、四世纪时通用的语言来说,就是任"自然",而不是循"名教"。这是所有新道家人士都一致的认识,但其间还有区别,以郭象为代表的理性派强调要按理性的要求来生活,而另一批任情派则主张要率性任情地生活,这是下面所要讲的。

《杨朱》篇所代表的就是率性任情一派思想的极端形式。其中有一段是晏平仲(晏婴)问养生于管夷吾(管仲)的故事。(晏婴和管仲都是春秋时代齐国的政治家,但并不同时。)管仲回答说:"肆之而已,勿壅勿阏。"晏婴问:"其目奈何?"("具体内容是什么?")

管仲回答说:"恣耳之所欲听,恣目之所欲视,恣鼻之所欲向,恣口之所欲言,恣体之所欲安,恣意之所欲行。

"夫耳之所欲闻者音声,而不得听,谓之阏聪;目之所欲见者美色,而不得视,谓之阏明;鼻之所欲向者椒兰,而不得嗅,谓之阏膻;口之所欲道者是非,而不得言,谓之阏智;体之所欲安者美厚,

these is called obstruction to the sensations of the body. What the mind likes is to be free, and prohibition of this freedom is called obstruction to the nature.

"'All these obstructions are the main causes of the vexations of life. To get rid of these causes and enjoy oneself until death, for a day, a month, a year, or ten years—this is what I call cultivating life. To cling to these causes and be unable to rid oneself of them, so as thus to have a long but sad life, extending a hundred, a thousand, or even ten thousand years—this is not what I call cultivating life.'

"Kuan Yi-wu then went on: 'Now that I have told you about cultivating life, what about the way of taking care of the dead?' Yen P'ing-chung replied: 'Taking care of the dead is a very simple matter.... For once I am dead, what does it matter to me? They may burn my body, or cast it into deep water, or inter it, or leave it uninterred, or throw it wrapped up in a mat into some ditch, or cover it with princely apparel and embroidered garments and rest it in a stone sarcophagus. All depends on chance.'

"Turning to Pao-shu Huang-tzu, Kuan Yi-wu then said : 'We two have by this made some progress in the way of life and death.'"

● Living According to Impulse

What the "Yang Chu" chapter here describes represents the spirit of the age of Chin, but not the whole or best of that spirit. For in this chapter, as exemplified by the above, what "Yang Chu" seems to be interested in is mostly the search for pleasure of a rather coarse sort. To be sure, the pursuit of such pleasure is not, according to Neo-Taoism, necessarily to be despised. Nevertheless, if this is made our sole aim, without any understanding of what "transcends shapes and features," to use the Neo-Taoist expression, this can hardly be called *feng liu* in the best sense of the term.

In the *Shih-shuo* we have a story about Liu Ling (c. 221-c. 300), one of the Seven Worthies of the Bamboo Grove (seven "famous scholars" who gathered for frequent convivial conversations in a certain bamboo grove). This story tells us that Liu evoked criticism through his habit of remaining completely naked when in his room. To his critics he rejoined: "I take the whole universe as my house and my own room as my clothing. Why, then, do you enter here into my trousers?" (Ch. 23.) Thus Liu Ling, though he sought for pleasure, had a feeling of what lies beyond the

而不得从，谓之阏适；意之所欲为者放逸，而不得行，谓之阏性。

"凡引诸阏，废虐之主。去废虐之主，熙熙然以俟死，一日一月，一年十年：吾所谓养。拘此废虐之主，录而不舍，戚戚然以至久生，百年千年万年：非吾所谓养。"

这是说，凡以上所引乃是人生烦恼的主要原因，把它们除去，以享天年，无论是一天、一月、一年、十年——这便是养生。若死死抓住令人烦恼的事情，在忧戚中生活而不能自拔，纵使长寿，活到百年、千年以至万年，这不是我所说的养生。

接下去，"管夷吾曰：'吾既告子养生矣，送死奈何？'晏平仲曰：'送死略矣。……既死，岂在我哉？焚之亦可，沉之亦可，瘗之亦可，露之亦可，衣薪而弃诸沟壑亦可，衮衣绣裳而纳诸石椁亦可，唯所遇焉。'

"管夷吾顾谓鲍叔、黄子曰：'生死之道，吾二人进之矣。'"（进一步领悟了。）

● 率性的生活

《杨朱》篇这里所描述的可以认为是代表了晋朝的一种精神，但不是全部，也不能说是其中最好的。在这一篇里上面所引述的，《杨朱》所感兴趣的只是一种粗鄙的享乐。在新道家看来，这种享乐也不是必定要予以鄙视，但如果一个人刻意追求这种享乐，那并不是"风流"的真意所在。

《世说》中有一个关于刘伶的故事，刘伶（约公元二二一至约三〇〇年）是竹林七贤之一。故事中说，刘伶在家里喜欢一丝不挂，为此受到别人批评。刘伶回答批评他的人说："我以天地为栋宇，屋室为裈衣（有裆裤），诸君何为入我裈中？"（《世说·任诞》）刘伶在家里一丝不挂，诚然是以此为乐，但他还从中感受到自在于

world, i.e., the universe. This feeling is essential for the quality of *feng liu*.

Those who have this feeling and who cultivate their mind in Taoism, must have a more subtle sensitivity for pleasure and more refined needs than sheerly sensual ones. The *Shih-shuo* records many unconventional activities among the "famous scholars" of the time. They acted according to pure impulse, but not with any thought of sensuous pleasure. Thus one of the stories in the *Shih-shuo* says: "Wang Hui-chih [died c. 388, son of China's greatest calligrapher, Wang Hsi-chih] was living at Shan-yin [near present Hangchow]. One night he was awakened by a heavy snowfall. Opening the window, he saw a gleaming whiteness all about him.... Suddenly he thought of his friend Tai K'uei. Immediately he took a boat and went to see Tai. It required the whole night for him to reach Tai's house, but when he was just about to knock at the door, he stopped and returned home. When asked the reason for this act, he replied: 'I came on the impulse of my pleasure, and now it is ended, so I go back. Why should I see Tai?'" (Ch. 23.)

The *Shih-shuo* records another story which says that Chung Hui (225-264, a statesman, general, and writer) regretted that he had not yet enjoyed the opportunity of meeting Chi K'ang (223-262, a philosopher and writer). Therefore he one day went with several other notables to visit him. Chi K'ang's hobby was that of forging metal, and when Chung Hui arrived there, he found Chi K'ang at his forge under a great tree. Hsiang Hsiu (author of the *Commentary on Chuang-tzu* described in the last chapter) was assisting Chi K'ang to blow the fire with a bellows, and Chi K'ang himself continued his hammering just as if no one else were there. For a while the host and guests did not exchange a single word. But when Chung Hui started to go, Chi K'ang asked him: "What did you hear that caused you to come, and what have you seen that causes you to go?" To this Chung Hui answered: "I heard what I heard, so I came, and I have seen what I have seen, so I go." (Ch. 24.)

The men of the Chin dynasty greatly admired the physical and spiritual beauty of a great personality. Chi K'ang was famous for his personality, which was compared by some people to a jade mountain and by others to a pine tree. (*Shih-shuo*, ch. 14.) Perhaps it was these things that Chung heard of and saw.

Another story in the *Shih-shuo* tells us: "When Wang Hui-chih was traveling by boat, he met Huan Yi traveling by land along the bank. Wang Hui-chih had heard of Huan Yi's fame as a flute player but he was not

天地宇宙之中。这种感觉正是"风流"的实质所在。

有这种超世感觉和追随道家修身养生的人，对"快乐"有一种比对具体物欲享乐更高的需要，也具有更敏锐的感觉。《世说》中记录了当时一些著名学者的脱俗举止。他们率性纯真地行动，却全然无意于物欲的享乐。例如，王羲之的儿子王徽之（字子猷，约公元三八八年卒）住在山阴（离现杭州不远），"夜大雪，眠觉，开室，命酌酒。四望皎然，因起彷徨，咏左思《招隐》诗。忽忆戴安道，时戴在剡，即便夜乘小船就之。经宿方至，造门不前而返。人问其故，王曰：'吾本乘兴而行，兴尽而返，何必见戴？'"（同上）朋友之间有真情，不在于见面亲热一番与否，因此，王徽之去探视戴安道，却又不前而返。

《世说》中另一则说："钟士季（名会，公元二二五至二六四年，是政治家、将军，又是一位文人）精有才理，先不识嵇康（公元二二三至二六二年），钟要于时贤隽之士，俱往寻康。康方大树下锻，向子期（向秀）为佐鼓排。康扬槌不辍，傍若无人，移时不交一言。钟起去，康曰：'何所闻而来？何所见而去？'钟曰：'闻所闻而来，见所见而去。'"（《世说·简傲》）

晋朝人喜欢称颂名人的体态和精神美。嵇康被时人比作"松下风"，称颂他"若孤松"、"若玉山"（《世说·容止》）。大概钟会也听到这些称颂嵇康的话，他约一些显要朋友一起去拜访嵇康，也看到了嵇康令人羡慕的容止。嵇康则并不在意别人的评论，也不以显要来访为意，因此并不理会钟，钟也不需要嵇康的曲意逢迎。两人互相会面，都以孤高自赏，心照可以不宣，因此便有了上面的对话。

《世说》中另一则故事说："王子猷出都，尚在渚下。旧闻桓子野善吹笛，而不相识。遇桓于岸上过，王在船中，客有识之者云：

acquainted with him. When someone told him that the man traveling on the bank was Huan Yi, he sent a messenger to ask him to play the flute. Huan Yi had also heard of the fame of Wang Hui-chih, so he descended from his chariot, sat on a chair, and played the flute three times. After that, he ascended his chariot and went away. The two men did not exchange even a single word." (Ch. 23.)

They did not do this because what they wished to enjoy was only the pure beauty of the music. Wang Hui-chih asked Huan Yi to play the flute for him, because he knew he could play it well, and Huan Yi played for him, because he knew Wang could appreciate his playing. When this had been done, what else was there to talk about?

The *Shih-shuo* contains another story which says that Chih-tun (314-366, famous Buddhist monk) was fond of cranes. Once a friend gave him two young ones. When they grew up, Chih-tun was forced to clip their wings so that they would not fly away. When this was done, the cranes looked despondent, and Chih-tun too was depressed, and said: "Since they have wings that can reach the sky, how can they be content to be a pet of man?" Hence when their feathers had grown again, he let the cranes fly away. (Ch. 2.)

Another story tells us about Juan Chi (210-263, a philosopher and poet), and his nephew Juan Hsien, who were two of the Seven Worthies of the Bamboo Grove. All members of the Juan family were great drinkers, and when they met, they did not bother to drink out of cups, but simply sat around a large wine jar and drank from that. Sometimes the pigs also came, wanting a drink, and then the Juans drank together with the pigs. (Ch. 23.)

The sympathy of Chih-tun for the cranes and the indiscriminate generosity of the Juans to the pigs show that they had a feeling of equality and non-differentiation between themselves and other things of nature. This feeling is essential in order to have the quality of *feng liu* and to be artistic. For a true artist must be able to project his own sentiment to the object he depicts, and then express it through his medium. Chih-tun himself would not have liked to be a pet of man, and he projected this sentiment to the cranes. Though he is not known to have been an artist, he was, in this sense, a very real one.

'是桓子野。'王便令人与相闻，云：'闻君善吹笛，试为我一奏。'桓时已贵显，素闻王名，即便回下车，踞胡床，为作三调。弄毕，便上车去。客主不交一言。"（《世说·任诞》）

两人没有交谈，因为他们共同醉心的是音乐的纯美和心灵在音乐中的交流，王徽之请桓伊为他吹一曲，是为了欣赏音乐。桓伊知道难得遇到知音，而王徽之精于音乐，于是折回来为王吹了三曲，然后登车而去。两人都从对方得到了艺术的满足，这时，彼此还需要说什么呢？

《世说》中还有一段故事记名僧支遁（公元三一四至三六六年）喜欢仙鹤。一次，一位朋友送他一对小鹤。这一对小鹤逐渐长大，支遁怕它们飞走，于是把它们的翅膀剪短。仙鹤展翅想飞时，却飞不起来，垂头丧气地看自己的翅膀。支遁也感到仙鹤懊丧，说道："既有凌霄之志，何肯为人作耳目近玩！"于是等仙鹤翅膀再次长大时，让它们自行飞去了。

《世说》中还有一则故事是讲阮籍（哲学家、诗人，公元二一〇至二六三年）和他的侄子阮咸，两人都名列竹林七贤之中。"诸阮皆能饮酒，仲容至宗人间共集，不复用常杯斟酌，以大瓮盛酒，围坐相向大酌。时有群猪来饮，直接上去，便共饮之。"（同上）

支遁对鹤的同情以及阮氏一家对猪趋近就瓮饮酒不以为意，表明他们看自己和宇宙万物是同等的，没有高下之分，也没有异类之别。这种"同于万物"的感觉正是"风流"的重要思想基础，也是一个人成为艺术家所必须有的品质，因为一个真正的艺术家必须要能够把自己的思想感情注入所要表现的对象，然后通过自身这个中介再表现出来。支遁不愿成为别人的玩物，他把自己的性情注入了仙鹤；虽然人们并不认为他是一个艺术家，其实，就这个意义说，他是一个真正的艺术家。

● The Emotional Factor

As we have seen in chapter ten, the sage, according to Chuang Tzu, has no emotions. He has a high understanding of the nature of things, and so is not affected by their changes and transformations. He "disperses emotion with reason." The *Shih-shuo* records many people who had no emotions. The most famous case is that of Hsieh An (320-385). When he was Prime Minister at the Chin court, the northern state of Ch'in started a large-scale offensive against Chin. Its army was led by the Ch'in Emperor in person, and so great was it that the Emperor boasted that his soldiers, by throwing their whips into the Yangtze River, could block its course. The people of Chin were greatly alarmed, but Hsieh An calmly and quietly appointed one of his nephews, Hsieh Hsün, to lead an army against the invaders. At a battle famous in history as the Battle of the Fei River, in the year 383, Hsieh Hsün won a decisive victory and the men of Ch'in were driven back. When the news of the final victory reached Hsieh An, he was playing chess with a friend. He opened the letter, read it, and then put it aside and continued to play as before. When the friend asked what was the news from the front, Hsieh An, as calmly as ever, replied: "Our boys have decisively defeated the enemy." (Ch. 6.)

The *San Kuo Chih* or *History of the Three Kingdoms*, however, records a discussion between Ho Yen (died 249) and Wang Pi (226-249, greatest commentator on the *Lao-tzu*) on the subject of the emotions. Ho Yen, following the original theory of Chuang Tzu, maintained that "the sage has neither pleasure nor anger, sorrow nor gladness." In this he was seconded by Chung Hui (the man who went to visit Chi K'ang in the story given above). Wang Pi, however, held a different opinion. According to him, "that in which the sage is superior to ordinary people is the spirit. But what the sage has in common with ordinary people are the emotions. The sage has a superior spirit, and therefore is able to be in harmony with the universe and to hold communion with *Wu* [i.e., the *Tao*]. But the sage has ordinary emotions, and therefore cannot respond to things without joy or sorrow. He responds to things, yet is not ensnared by them. It is wrong to say that because the sage has no ensnarement, he therefore has no emotions." (Ch. 28, *Commentary*.)

The theory of Wang Pi can be summarized by the statement that the sage "has emotions but no ensnarement." What this statement exactly means, Wang Pi does not make clear. Its implications were developed much later by Neo-Confucianism, and we shall have a chance to analyze

● 感情

在第十章里我们看到，庄子心目中的圣人能够超脱于常人的感情，他对外物的本性了解得如此透彻，对它们的流动不居和形态变化已经习以为常，而"以理化情"了。《世说》中记载了许多这样的事例，其中十分著名的一个例子是东晋谢安（公元三二〇至三八五年）的故事。他在晋国任丞相时，北方秦国大举攻晋。秦帝亲自率军并吹嘘说，秦军将士，铺天盖地，投鞭长江，可使长江断流。当时晋人十分惊恐，谢安派他的侄儿谢玄率军迎战。公元三八三年，两军在淝水一线决战，谢玄大胜，秦军败退。当战胜的消息报来时，谢安正与友人下棋。他拆信看后，把信放在一旁，继续与客人下棋。客人问，前方有什么消息，谢安悠静地回答说："小儿辈大破贼。"（《世说·雅量》）

《三国志·魏书》中卷二十八《钟会传》引何劭《王弼传》，记载了何晏（公元二四九年卒）与王弼（著名的《老子》注释家，公元二二六至二四九年）两人关于感情的一次谈话。何晏沿袭庄子"以理化情"的看法，"以为'圣人无喜怒哀乐'，其论甚精，钟会等述之。弼与不同，以为'圣人茂于人者，神明也；同于人者，五情也。神明茂，故能体充和以通无；五情同，故不能无哀乐以应物。然则圣人之情，应物而无累于物者也。今以其无累，便谓不复应物，失之多矣'。"

汉代的谶纬经学家以孔子为神，魏晋玄学家认为孔子也是人，但乃是"圣人"，与常人不同之处在于圣人"与无同体"，没有喜、怒、哀、乐等感情。王弼独持己见，认为圣人"有情而无累"。这话究竟是什么意思，王弼没有更多发挥。后来隔了许久，新的儒家——本书第二十四章将加以讨论——对此加以发挥。在这里，我们

them in chapter 24. At present we need merely point out that though many of the Neo-Taoists were very rational, there were also many who were very sentimental.

As stated earlier, the Neo-Taoists stressed subtle sensitivity. Having this sensitivity, coupled with the afore-mentioned theory of self-expression, it is not surprising that many of them gave free vent to their emotions anywhere and at any time these emotions arose.

An example is the *Shih-shuo's* story about Wang Jung (234-305), one of the Seven Worthies of the Bamboo Grove. When Wang lost a child, his friend Shan Chien went to condole him. Wang could not restrain himself from weeping, whereupon Shan said to him: "It was only a baby, so why do you behave like this?" Wang Jung replied: "The sage forgets emotions, and lowly people [who are insensitive] do not reach emotions. It is people like ourselves who have the most emotions." To this Shan Chien agreed and wept also. (Ch. 17.)

This saying of Wang Jung explains very well why many of the Neo-Taoists were sentimentalists. In most cases, however, they were sentimental, not about some personal loss or gain, but about some general aspect of life or of the universe. The *Shih-shuo* says that Wei Chieh (286-312, known as the most beautiful personality of his time), when about to cross the Yangtze River, felt much depressed, and said: "When I see this vast [river], I cannot help but feel that all kinds of sentiments are gathering in my mind. Being not without feeling, how can one endure these emotions?" (Ch. 2.)

The *Shih-shuo* says also that every time Huan Yi, the flute player mentioned earlier, heard people singing, he would exclaim: "What can I do!" Hsieh An heard of this and remarked: "Huan Yi can indeed be said to have deep feelings." (Ch. 23.)

Because of this subtle sensitivity, these men of *feng liu* spirit were often impressed by things that would not ordinarily impress others. They had sentiments about life and the universe as a whole, and also about their own sensitivity and sentiments. The *Shih-shuo* tells us that when Wang Ch'in ascended the Mao Mountain (in present Shantung province), he wept and said: "Wang Po-yu of Lang-ya [i.e., myself] must at last die for his emotions." (Ch. 23.)

只需要指出一点，即：虽然许多新道家注重理性，但也还有许多是重情的。

如前所述，新道家强调含蓄的敏感。由于这种敏感再加上前述重情派的"自我表现"理论，这就无怪乎其中许多人在动情时，不拘时间、地点便宣泄出来。

这方面的一个实例是《世说》引述竹林七贤之一的王戎（公元二三四至三〇五年）的故事。王戎的孩子夭折，"山简往省之，王悲不自胜。简曰：'孩抱中物，何至于此！'王曰：'圣人忘情，最下不及情；情之所钟，正在我辈。'简服其言，更为之恸。"（《世说·伤逝》）

王戎的这番话正好说明，为什么新道家中有许多人如此多情善感。使他们动情的不是个人得失，而是对人生或宇宙的某个方面的领悟和由此而来的感触。《世说》中有一则关于卫玠（公元二八六至三一二年，当时传诵的美男子）的故事说："卫洗马初欲渡江，形神惨悴，语左右云：'见此茫茫，不觉百端交集。苟未免有情，亦复谁能遣此！'"（《世说·言语》）

《世说》中讲到前述工于奏笛的桓伊，还说："桓子野每闻清歌，辄唤'奈何'，谢公闻之，曰：'子野可谓一往有深情。'"（《世说·任诞》）

这些"风流"倜傥的名士，既富于深沉的敏感，胸中块垒自然与常人不同，在别人无动于衷的地方常会怵然于心。他们对人生和宇宙有情，也就包括了对自己有情，以至不能自已。《世说》中记载："王长史登茅山，大恸哭曰：'琅琊王伯舆，终当为情死！'"（同上）琅琊人王伯舆就是指自己。

- **The Factor of Sex**

In the West, romanticism often has in it an element of sex. The Chinese term *feng liu* also has that implication, especially in its later usage. The attitude of the Chin Neo-Taoists towards sex, however, seems to be purely aesthetic rather than sensuous. As illustration, the *Shih-shuo* tells us that the neighbor of Juan Chi had a beautiful wife. The neighbor was a wine merchant, and Juan Chi used to go to his house to drink with the merchant's wife. When Juan became drunk, he would sleep beside her. The husband at first was naturally suspicious, but after paying careful attention, he found that Juan Chi did nothing more than sleep there. (Ch. 23.)

The *Shih-shuo* says again that Shan T'ao (205-283, statesman and general), Chi K'ang, and Juan Chi were great friends. Shan T'ao's wife, Han, noticed the close friendship of the three and asked her husband about it. Shan T'ao said: "At present they are the only men who can be my friends." It was the custom in China then that a lady was not allowed to be introduced to the friends of her husband. Hence Han told her husband that, when next his two friends came, she would like to have a secret peep at them. So on the next visit, she asked her husband to have them stay overnight. She prepared a feast for them, and, during the night, peeped in at the guests through a hole in the wall. So absorbed was she in looking at them that she stood there the whole night. In the morning the husband came to her room and asked: "What do you think of them?" She replied: "In talent you are not equal to them, but with your knowledge, you can make friends with them." To this Shan T'ao said: "They, also, consider my knowledge to be superior." (Ch. 19.)

Thus both Juan Chi and the Lady Han seemed to enjoy the beauty of the opposite sex without any sensuous inclinations. Or, it may be said, they enjoyed the beauty, forgetting the sex element.

Such are the characteristics of the *feng liu* spirit of the Chin Neo-Taoists. According to them, *feng liu* derives from *tzu jan* (spontaneity, naturalness), and *tzu jan* stands in opposition to *ming chiao* (morals and institutions), which form the classical tradition of Confucianism. Even in this period, however, when Confucianism was in eclipse, one famous scholar and writer named Yüeh Kuang (died 304) said: "In the *ming chiao*, too, there is fundamentally room for happiness." (*Shih-shuo*, ch. 1.) As we shall see in chapter twenty-four, Neo-Confucianism was an attempt to find such happiness in *ming-chiao*.

● 情爱

在西方，浪漫主义往往包含有性的因素在其中。在中文里，"风流"的含义也同样有那重意思，特别是到了后来，"风流"这个词在中文里，性的味道显得更多。就晋代新道家来说，他们对性的态度，与其说是注意肉体欲望，不如说是从纯粹审美的角度来对待异性。举例来说，《世说》中有关于阮籍的一则故事。"阮公（籍）邻家妇，有美色，当垆沽酒。阮与王安丰常从妇饮酒，阮醉，便眠其妇侧。夫始殊疑之，伺察，终无他意。"（同上）

《世说》还记载山涛（政治家、将军，公元二〇五至二八三年）、嵇康和阮籍"契若金兰。山妻韩氏，觉公与二人异于常交，问公。公曰：'我当年可以为友者，唯此二生耳。'"当时中国的风俗，妇道人家和丈夫的朋友是不能交往的。因此韩氏对山涛说，下次这两位朋友来时，容她在暗处看看这两位。下次嵇、阮两人来访时，韩氏便置酒肴，要丈夫留两人过夜，她在隔壁墙孔偷窥了一夜。第二天，山涛到夫人房间问道："他们两人如何？"夫人回答："论才华，你不如他们，但你的学识足以与他们相交。"山涛说："他们也认为我的学识在他们之上。"（见《世说·贤媛》）

上面两则故事使我们看到，阮籍和韩氏欣赏异性美，却没有更多的要求；或者可以说，他们对美的欣赏使他们忘记了性的因素。

这些可以说是晋代新道家风格的特点和当时所谓"风流"的实质。在他们的思想里，风流来自"自然"，而自然与儒家倡导的名教（道德规范制度等）则是对立的。这是儒家衰微的时期，而当时的著名学者乐广（公元三〇四年卒）还是说："名教中自有乐地。"（《世说·德行》）本书第二十四章将会讲到，新的儒家便是到"名教"中寻找乐地的一种努力。

㉑ THE FOUNDATION OF CHINESE BUDDHISM

The introduction of Buddhism into China has been one of the greatest events in Chinese history, and since its coming, it has been a major factor in Chinese civilization, exercising particular influence on religion, philosophy, art, and literature.

● Introduction and Development of Buddhism in China

The exact date of the introduction of Buddhism is a disputed problem not yet settled by historians, but it took place probably in the first half of the first century A.D. Traditionally, it is said to have entered during the reign of Emperor Ming (58-75), but there is now evidence that it had already been heard of in China before this time. Its subsequent spread was a long and gradual process. From Chinese literary sources we know that in the first and second centuries A.D., Buddhism was considered as a religion of the occult arts, not greatly differing from the occultism of the *Yin-Yang* school or of the later Taoist religion.

In the second century the theory was actually developed in certain circles that Buddha had been nothing more than a disciple of Lao Tzu. This theory gained its inspiration from a statement in the biography of Lao Tzu in the *Shih Chi* or *Historical Records* (ch. 63), where it is said that Lao Tzu, late in life, disappeared and nobody knew where he went. Elaborating this statement, ardent Taoists created the story that when Lao Tzu went to the West, he finally reached India, where he taught the Buddha and other Indians, and had a total of twenty-nine disciples. The implication was that the teaching of the Buddhist *Sutras* (sacred texts) was simply a foreign variant of that of the *Tao Te Ching*, that is, of the *Lao-tzu*.

In the third and fourth centuries an increasing number of Buddhist texts of a more metaphysical nature was translated, so that Buddhism became better understood. At this time Buddhism was regarded as similar to philosophical Taoism, especially the philosophy of Chuang Tzu, rather than to Taoism as a religion. Often the Buddhist writings were interpreted with ideas taken from philosophical Taoism. This method was called that of *ko yi*, that is, interpretation by analogy.

Such a method naturally led to inaccuracy and distortion. Hence in the fifth century, by which time the flood of translations was rapidly increasing, the use of analogy was definitely abandoned. Yet the fact

贰拾壹 中国佛学的基础

佛教传入中国是中国历史上的一个重大事件。它自传入后，成为中国文明的一个重要因素，对宗教、哲学、艺术和文学都产生了巨大的影响。

● 佛教的传入及其在中国的发展

佛教传入中国，究竟是在什么时候？对这个问题，中国史学界还没有确切的结论，大致可以说是在公元一世纪前半叶。传统的说法是：东汉明帝（公元五八至七五年）时，佛教传入中国。但现在有史料可以证明，在此之前，中原的汉族已经接触到佛教。它此后在中国的传播是一个漫长、缓慢的进程。从中国文献中可以知道，在东汉（公元一、二世纪）时，中国人把佛教看作方术中的一种，与阴阳家及后来的道教方术并没有根本的不同。

公元二世纪时，甚至有一种理论认为，释迦牟尼是老子的一个弟子。这种说法可能渊源于《史记·老子列传》说，老子最后"莫知其所终"。热心的道家由此发展出一个故事说，老子最后西行，到了印度，教了释迦和另二十八位弟子。由此又衍生出佛经源自老子《道德经》的说法。

公元三、四世纪间，佛经译成中文的渐多，人们对佛家的形而上学思想了解较多。这时又出现一种看法，认为佛家的思想和道家，特别是庄子的思想相近，而与道教则不相干。解释佛经的著作往往援引道家思想，这类著作在当时称为"格义"，即从类比中求得它的含义。

这种方法难免带来不准确和曲解的毛病。因此到五世纪，佛经汉译如潮涌现时，"格义"的方法被摈弃了。但是，五世纪时来自

remains that the great Buddhist writers of the fifth century, even including the Indian teacher, Kumarajiva, continued to use Taoist terminology, such as *Yu* (Being, existent), *Wu* (Non-being, non-existent), *yu-wei* (action) and *wu-wei* (non-action), to express Buddhist ideas. The difference between this practice and the method of analogy, however, is that in the latter one sees only the superficial similarity of words, while in the former one sees the inner connections of the ideas expressed by them. Hence, judging from the nature of the works of these writers, this practice, as we shall see later, did not indicate any misunderstanding or distortion of Buddhism, but rather a synthesis of Indian Buddhism with Taoism, leading to the foundation of a Chinese form of Buddhism.

Here it should be pointed out that the terms, "Chinese Buddhism" and "Buddhism in China," are not necessarily synonymous. Thus there were certain schools of Buddhism which confined themselves to the religious and philosophical tradition of India, and made no contact with those of China. An example is the school known by the Chinese as the *Hsiang tsung* or *Wei-shih tsung* (School of Subjective Idealism), which was introduced by the famous Chinese pilgrim to India, Hsüan-tsang (596-664). Schools like this may be called "Buddhism in China." Their influence was confined to restricted groups of people and limited periods. They did not and could not reach the thought of every intellectual, and therefore played little or no part in the development of what may be called the Chinese mind.

On the other hand, "Chinese Buddhism" is the form of Buddhism that has made contact with Chinese thought and thus has developed in conjunction with Chinese philosophical tradition. In later pages we will see that the Middle Path school of Buddhism bears some similarity to philosophical Taoism. Its interaction with the latter resulted in the Ch'an or Zen school, which though Buddhist, is at the same time Chinese. Although a school of Buddhism, its influence on Chinese philosophy, literature, and art has been far reaching.

- **General Concepts of Buddhism**

Following the introduction of Buddhism into China, tremendous efforts were made to translate the Buddhist texts into Chinese. Texts of both the Hinayana (Small Vehicle) and Mahayana (Great Vehicle) divisions of Buddhism were translated, but only the latter gained a permanent place in Chinese Buddhism.

On the whole, the way in which Mahayana Buddhism most influenced the Chinese has been in its concept of the Universal Mind, and in what

印度的佛教著译大师鸠摩罗什（Kumarajiva）还继续使用道家的名词术语如"有"、"无"、"有为"、"无为"等来表达佛家的思想。释义法和"格义"的不同在于："格义"只使读者看到外貌的形似，而释义则令人看到思想的内在联系。它实际是对印度佛教思想和中国道家思想进行一种综合的努力，由此而为中国佛学奠定了基础。

在这里需要指出一点："中国佛学"和"佛学在中国"的含义是不同的。佛教的某些宗派始终坚守印度佛教的宗教和哲学传统，和中国思想不相关联，例如唐代玄奘法师（公元五九六至六六四年）由印度介绍到中国的法相宗（着重一切东西都是"识"所变，亦称"唯识宗"），可以称之为"佛学在中国"。它们在中国的影响仅限于某个圈子里，并仅限于某个时期。它们没有试图去接触中国思想界，因此，对中国人的思想发展也没有产生任何作用。

"中国佛学"则是佛学传入中国后，与中国哲学思想接触后的发展。下面我们将会看到例如"中道宗"，与道家思想便有某些相似之处。中道宗与道家思想的相互作用导致"禅宗"的兴起，它是佛家，而在思想上又是中国的，并形成中国佛教的一个宗派。它虽是佛教的一个宗派，却对中国哲学、文学、艺术产生了深远的影响。

- **佛学的一般概念**

佛教传入中国后，佛经也大量译成中文，其中包括小乘（Hinayana）经典和大乘（Mahayana）经典。在中国佛教中流传的则只限于大乘经典。

总的说来，大乘佛教对中国思想影响最大的有两端：一是它提出

may be called its negative method of metaphysics. Before going into a discussion of these, we must first survey some of the general concepts of Buddhism.

Although there are many schools of Buddhism, each with something different to offer, all generally agree in their belief in the theory of *Karma* (translated in Chinese as *Yeh*). *Karma* or *Yeh* is usually rendered in English as deed or action, but its actual meaning is much wider than that, for what it covers is not merely confined to overt action, but also includes what an individual sentient being speaks and thinks. According to Buddhism, all the phenomena of the universe, or, to be more exact, of the universe of an individual sentient being, are the manifestations of his mind. Whenever he acts, speaks, or even thinks, his mind is doing something, and that something must produce its results, no matter how far in the future. This result is the retribution of the *Karma*. The *Karma* is the cause and its retribution is the effect. The being of an individual is made up of a chain of causes and effects.

The present life of a sentient being is only one aspect in this whole process. Death is not the end of his being, but is only another aspect of the process. What an individual is in this life, comes as a result of what he did in the past, and what he does in the present will determine what he will be in the future. Hence what he does now will bear its fruits in a future life, and what he will do then will again bear its fruits in yet another future life, and so on *ad infinitum.* This chain of causation is what is called *Samsara*, the Wheel of Birth and Death. It is the main source from which come the sufferings of individual sentient beings.

According to Buddhism, all these sufferings arise from the individual's fundamental Ignorance of the nature of things. All things in the universe are the manifestations of the mind and therefore are illusory and impermanent, yet the individual ignorantly craves for and cleaves to them. This fundamental Ignorance is called *Avidya*, which in Chinese is translated as *Wu-ming*, non-enlightenment. From Ignorance come the craving for and cleaving to life, because of which the individual is bound to the eternal Wheel of Birth and Death, from which he can never escape.

The only hope for escape lies in replacing Ignorance with Enlightenment, which in Sanskrit is called *Bodhi*. All the teachings and practices of the various Buddhist schools are attempts to contribute something to the *Bodhi*. From them the individual, in the course of many

的"宇宙为心",另一是它在形而上学中使用的"负的方法"。在对此进行讨论之前,需要先对佛学的一般概念有一个总体的了解。

佛教虽然分为许多宗派,各有自己的思想特色,但各派也有一些共同信奉的基本观念,其中主要是"业"(梵文 karma)的理论。"业"通常解释为人的行动作为,而实际上,它的含义比"行为"要广阔得多,一切有情物(生灵)的思念和言语也都包括在内。按照佛家的看法,宇宙的一切现象,或者更确切地说,任何一个有情物所看出去的世界,都是他内心自造的景象。每当他有所动作,或只是说话,或心里动念,都是心的作为。这个作为必然产生它的后果,不论这后果要等多久才显现出来。这个后果便是"业"的报应。"业"是因,果是"报"。每一个人都是因与果、业与报的连环套。

每一个有情物的今生只是这个无穷锁链中的一环。死并不是生命的终结,而只是这个因果循环的一个中转站。人的今生只是他前生的"业"的果报。他在今生的作为("业")又决定他来世成为什么,他将来的作为又结成更后世的果报,以至于无穷。这个因果的锁链构成"生死轮回"(梵文称 samsara)。一切有情物的"众生皆苦",其主要来源便由于此。

按佛家的看法,所有这些苦难的根源在于人不认识事物的本性。宇宙万物乃是各人自己内心所造的景象,因此它是"幻相",只是昙花一现。但是,人出于自己的无知("无明")而执著地追求("执迷不悟"),这种根本的无知,在梵文里称为 Avidya,中文译为"无明"。由"无明"导致"贪欲",又"执迷不悟",这便把人紧紧缚在生死轮回的巨轮上,无法逃脱。

人从生死轮回中解脱出来的唯一办法便是"觉悟"(梵文作 bodhi)。佛教各派的种种教义和修行都是为启发人对世界和自己的"觉悟"。人觉悟之后,经过多次再世,所积的"业",不再是贪恋

rebirths, may accumulate *Karma* which does not crave for and cleave to things, but avoids craving and cleaving. The result is an emancipation of the individual possessing this *Karma* from the Wheel of Birth and Death. And this emancipation is called *Nirvana*.

What, exactly, does the state of *Nirvana* signify? It may be said to be the identification of the individual with the Universal Mind, or with what is called the Buddha-nature; or it is the realization or self-consciousness of the individual's original identification with the Universal Mind. He *is* the Universal Mind, but formerly he did not realize it, or was not self-conscious of it. The school of Mahayana Buddhism known by the Chinese as the *Hsing tsung* or School of Universal Mind expounded this theory. (For this school, *hsing* or nature and *hsin* or mind are the same.) In expounding it, the school introduced the idea of Universal Mind into Chinese thought.

There were other schools of Mahayana Buddhism, however, such as that known by the Chinese as the *K'ung tsung* or School of Emptiness, also known as the School of the Middle Path, which would not describe *Nirvana* in this way. Their method of approach is what I call the negative method.

- ### The Theory of Double Truth

This School of the Middle Path proposed what it called the theory of double truth: truth in the common sense and truth in the higher sense. Furthermore, it maintained, not only are there these two kinds of truth, but they both exist on varying levels. Thus what, on the lower level, is truth in the higher sense, becomes, on the higher level, merely truth in the common sense. One of the great Chinese Masters of this school, Chi-tsang (549-623), describes this theory as including the three following levels of double truth:

(1) The common people take all things as really *yu* (having being, existent) and know nothing about *wu* (having no being, non-existent).

Therefore the Buddhas have told them that actually all things are *wu* and empty. On this level, to say that all things are *yu* is the common sense truth, and to say that all things are *wu* is the higher sense truth.

(2) To say that all things are *yu* is one-sided, but to say that all things are *wu* is also one-sided. They are both one-sided, because they give people the wrong impression that *wu* or non-existence only results from the absence or removal of *yu* or existence. Yet in actual fact, what is *yu* is simultaneously what is *wu*. For instance, the table standing before us

世界、执迷不悟，而是无贪欲、无执著。这样，人便能从生死轮回之苦中解脱出来，这个解脱便称为"涅槃"（梵文作 Nirvana）。

对"涅槃"这个境界怎样进一步领会呢？可以说，这就是个人和宇宙的心融合为一（宇宙的心又即"佛性"）。个人本来与宇宙本性是一体，他就是宇宙本性的表现，只是人先前不认识这一点，或说，不曾意识到这一点。大乘佛教中的性宗阐发了这个理论（性宗认为，心和性是一回事）。性宗在阐发这个理论时，也就把"宇宙心"（即宇宙本体）的观念带进了中国哲学思想。

大乘佛教还有其他宗派，例如：空宗（也称"中道宗"）。它对"涅槃"有不同的解释。这一派解决问题的方法就是我所称的"负的方法"。

● 二谛义

中道宗（佛学中称三论宗）倡导真谛有两重，把佛教的道理分作供普通人受用的"俗谛"（亦称"世谛"）和更高意义的佛法即"真谛"。由此更进一步，认为在二谛中还各分层次，因此，在俗谛中被认为是真谛的，从真谛看又被认为是俗谛。三论宗的大师吉藏（公元五四九至六二三年）阐述二谛论包括有三个层次的真谛：

第一，普通人看万物为"实有"，而不知"无"。为此，诸佛教导说，万物实际是"无"和"空"。在普通人的层次上，以万物为"有"，就是俗谛；以万物为"无"，就是真谛。

第二，以万物为"有"是偏颇之见；以万物为"无"，也是偏颇之见。这是因为它给人一个错误的印象，以为"无"或"非有"只是由于从存在中把"有"移去，其实，"有"即是"无"。举例来说，

need not be destroyed in order to show that it is ceasing to exist. In actual fact it is ceasing to exist all the time. The reason for this is that when one starts to destroy the table, the table which one thus intends to destroy has already ceased to exist. The table of this actual moment is no longer the table of the preceding moment. It only *looks* like that of the preceding moment. Therefore on the second level of double truth, to say that all things are *yu* and to say that all things are *wu* are both equally common sense truth. What one ought to say is that the "not-one-sided middle path" consists in understanding that things are neither *yu* nor *wu*. This is the higher sense truth.

(3) But to say that the middle truth consists in what is not one-sided (i.e., what is neither *yu* nor *wu*), means to make distinctions. And all distinctions are themselves one-sided. Therefore on the third level, to say that things are neither *yu* nor *wu*, and that herein lies the not-one-sided middle path, is merely common sense truth. The higher truth consists in saying that things are neither *yu* nor *wu*, neither not-*yu* nor not-*wu*, and that the middle path is neither one-sided nor not-one-sided. (*Erh-ti Chang* or *Chapt*er o*n the Double Truth*, sec. 1.)

In this passage I have retained the Chinese words *yu* and *wu*, because in their use the Chinese thinkers of the time saw or felt a similarity between the central problem discussed by Buddhism and that discussed by Taoism, in which the same words are prominent. Though deeper analysis shows that the similarity is in some respects superficial, nevertheless, when the Taoists spoke of *Wu* as transcending shapes and features, and the Buddhists spoke of *Wu* as "not-not," there is a real similarity.

Still another real similarity between the Buddhists of this particular school and the Taoists is their method of approach and the final results achieved by this method. The method is to make use of different levels of discourse. What is said in one level is to be immediately denied by a saying on a higher level. As we have seen in chapter ten, this is also the method used in the *Ch'i Wu Lun* or "Equality of Things" in the *Chuang-tzu*, and it is the method that has just been discussed above.

When all is denied, including the denial of the denial of all, one arrives at the same situation as found in the philosophy of Chuang Tzu, in which all is forgotten, including the fact that one has forgotten all. This state is described by Chuang Tzu as "sitting in forgetfulness," and by the Buddhists as *Nirvana*. One cannot ask this school of Buddhism

我们面前的一张桌子，要表明它不存在时，并不需要把桌子毁掉。事实上，它从来就不存在，因为在人实际拆毁桌子前，他所想拆毁的桌子在他心里已经不存在了。在这刹那间，桌子已不是原来那样子了。它只是"看似"原来那样子。因此，在第二层次上看，说"万物皆有"和说"万物皆无"都是俗谛。只有当人认识到，"事物非有非无"，这才是真谛。

第三，但如果说，中道真谛意味着没有偏颇之见（即非有非无），这就意味着要区别"有"和"无"，而一切区别本身就是偏颇之见。因此，在第三层次上，说事物非有非无，这乃是没有偏颇的看法，又只不过是俗谛；真谛是指：事物非"有"、非"无"，非"非有"、非"非无"；中道既不是"偏颇"，又不是"不偏颇"。（参阅吉藏《二谛章》卷上，载《大藏经》卷四十五）

在这段里，我有意识保留了"有""无"两个字，以显示当时的思想家看到（或感觉到）佛家和道家讨论的中心问题多么相似。更进一步分析便可看出，这种相似在某些方面只是表面性的。尽管如此，当道家以"无"来表达超越的形象时，它与佛家用"无"表达"非非"，两者之间确有相似之处。

在佛家的三论宗和道家之间，还有更深一层的相似之处在于他们的思想方法，他们从哪里入手来探讨问题和所得到的最后结果。这种方法便是运用谈话的不同层次，在一个层次作出的论断，到下一更高的层次又予以否定。在本书前面第二章论到《齐物论》时，可以看到庄子也是使用这个方法。

当一切都被否定，包括否定先前的否定时，人便会发现自己处于庄子哲学中的那种地位：一切都被忘记，包括"忘记一切"这一点也已忘记。这便是庄子所说的"坐忘"，也就是佛家所说的

what, exactly, the state of *Nirvana* is, because, according to it, when one reaches the third level of truth, one cannot affirm anything.

● Philosophy of Seng-chao

One of the great teachers of this same school in China in the fifth century was Kumarajiva, who was an Indian but was born in a state in the present Chinese Turkistan. He came to Ch'ang-an (the present Sian in Shensi province) in 401, and lived there until his death in 413. During these thirteen years, he translated many Buddhist texts into Chinese and taught many disciples, among them some who became very famous and influential. In this chapter I shall mention two of them, Seng-chao and Tao-sheng.

Seng-chao (384-414) came from the vicinity of the above-mentioned city of Ch'ang-an. He first studied Lao Tzu and Chuang Tzu, but later became a disciple of Kumarajiva. He wrote several essays which have been collected as the *Chao Lun* or *Essays of Seng-chao*. One of them, titled "There Is No Real Unreality," says: "All things have that in them which makes them not be *yu* [having being, existent] and also have that in them which makes them not be *wu* [having no being, non-existent]. Because of the former, they are *yu* and yet not *yu*. Because of the latter, they are *wu* and yet not *wu*.... Why is this so? Suppose the *yu* is really *yu*, then it should be *yu* for all time and should not owe its *yu* to the convergence of causes. [According to Buddhism, the existence of anything is due to the convergence of a number of causes.] Suppose the *wu* is really *wu*, then it should be *wu* for all time and should not owe its *wu* to the dissolution of causes. If the *yu* owes its *yu* to causation, then the *yu* is not really *yu*.... But if all things are *wu*, then nothing would come about. If something comes about, it cannot be altogether nothing.... If we want to affirm that things are *yu*, yet there is no real existence of this *yu*. If we want to affirm that they are *wu*, yet they have their shapes and features. To have shapes and features is not the same as *wu*, and to be not really *yu* is not the same as *yu*. This being so, the principle of 'no real unreality' is clear." (*Chao-Lun*, ch. 2.)

In another essay, titled "On the Immutability of Things," Seng-chao says: "Most men's idea of mutability is that things in the past do not come down to the present. They therefore say that there is mutability and no immutability. My idea of immutability is also that things of the past do not come down to the present. Therefore I on the contrary say that there is immutability and no mutability. That there is mutability and

"涅槃"。我们不能问这一派佛家：你所说的"涅槃"究竟是什么意思？因为按照三论宗的理论，人到了第三层真谛时，便什么都无可言说了。

● 僧肇的哲学

五世纪中国佛教三论宗出了一位大师即鸠摩罗什，他本是印度人，但出生于安息国（在今日中国的新疆）。公元四〇一年，他到长安，此后一直住在长安，直到公元四一三年他去世。在这十三年里，他翻译了许多佛教文献，教导了许多弟子。在他的弟子中，有些十分杰出，成为著名的佛教思想家。本章只举其中两位：僧肇和道生。

僧肇（公元三八四至四一四年）出生于长安附近。他本来研读老庄，后来成为鸠摩罗什弟子。他曾撰写了几篇文章，后汇集成《肇论》，意思指僧肇的论著。其中有一篇《不真空论》（意为"空不真"），文中说："然则万物果有其所以不有，有其所以不无。有其所以不有，故虽有而非有；有其所以不无，故虽无而非无。……所以然者，夫有若真有，有自常有，岂待缘而后有哉？譬彼真无，无自常无，岂待缘而后无也？若有不能自有，待缘而后有者，故知有非真有。……万物若无，则不应起，起则非无。……欲言其有，有非真生；欲言其无，事象既形。象形不即无，非真非实有。然则不真空义，显于兹矣。"（《大藏经》卷四十五）

《肇论》的第一论题是《物不迁论》，其中说："夫人之所谓动者，以昔物不至今，故曰动而非静。我之所谓静者，亦以昔物不至今，故曰静而非动。动而非静，以其不来；静而非动，以其不去。……

no immutability is because things of the past do not come down to the present. That there is immutability and no mutability is because things of the past do not vanish away with the past [i.e., though they do not exist today, they did exist in the past].... If we search for past things in the past, they were not *wu* in the past. If we search for these past things in the present, they are not *yu* in the present.... That is to say, past things are in the past, and are not things that have receded from the present. Likewise present things are in the present, and are not something that have come down from the past.... The effect is not the cause, but because of the cause there is the effect. That the effect is not the cause shows that the cause does not come down to the present. And that, there being the cause, there is therefore the effect, shows that causes do not vanish in the past. The cause has neither come down nor has it vanished. Thus the theory of immutability is clear." (*Chao Lun*, ch. 1.)

The idea here is that things undergo constant change at every moment. Anything existing at any given moment is actually a new thing of that moment and not the same as the thing that has existed in the past. In the same essay Seng-chao says: "[There was a man by the name of] Fan-chih who, having become a monk in his early years, returned home when his hair was white. On seeing him the neighbors exclaimed at seeing a man of the past who was still alive. Fan-chih said: 'I look like the man of the past, but I am not he.'" At every moment there has been a Fan-chih. The Fan-chih of this moment is not a Fan-chih who has come down from the past, and the Fan-chih of the past was not a Fan-chih of the present who receded into the past. Juding from the fact that everything changes at every moment, we say that there is change but no permanence. And judging from the fact that everything at every moment remains with that moment, we say that there is permanence but no change.

This is Seng-chao's theory to substantiate the double truth on the second level. On this level, to say that things are *yu* and permanent, and to say that things are *wu* and mutable, are both common sense truth. To say that things are neither *yu* nor *wu*, neither permanent nor mutable, is the higher sense truth.

Seng-chao also gives arguments to substantiate the double truth on the third or highest level. This he does in an essay titled "On *Prajna* [i.e., Wisdom of the Buddha] Not Being Knowledge." *Prajna* is described by Seng-chao as Sage-knowledge, but, he says, this Sage-knowledge is really not knowledge. For knowledge of a thing consists in selecting a quality of that thing and taking that quality as the object of knowledge. But Sage-knowledge consists in knowing about what is called *Wu* (Non-being), and this *Wu* "transcends shapes and features" and has no qualities; hence

求向物于向，于向未尝无；责向物于今，于今未尝有。……是谓昔物自在昔，不从今以至昔；今物自在今，不从昔以至今。……果不俱因，因因而果。因因而果，因不昔灭；果不俱因，因不来今。不灭不来，则不迁之致明矣。"（同上）这是说，人们通常所讲万物变化，意在指出过去之物，已经过去；今日之物，不是过去之物，而是当今的新事物。僧肇在《物不迁论》中又说："梵志出家，白首而归，邻人见之曰：'昔人尚存乎？'梵志曰：'吾犹昔人，非昔人也。'"这是说，每一刹那都有梵志，但现在这一刹那的梵志不是过去来的；过去的梵志也不是从现在倒退回过去的梵志。从事物时刻在变来说，我们只见有变，不见有恒；然而就每一刹那来说，在那一刹那，事物和时间是结合在一起的。因此可以说，有恒常而无变化。

这是僧肇为充分阐述二谛义中的第二层次所提出的理论。在这层次上，说事物是"有而恒常"与说事物是"无而恒变"都是"俗谛"。说事物既非有，又非无，既非恒常又非恒变，则是高一层的真谛。

僧肇还在《般若无知论》里对二谛论的最高层次——第三层次——补充阐述。"般若"（梵文作 Prajna）的含义是"佛的智慧"，"般若无知论"的意思是说：佛的智慧并非知识。般若可以勉强解释为"圣智"，它其实并不是知识。人们通常所说对于事物的知识是举出事物的一项品质，以此作为知识的对象。"圣智"则是指：懂得何谓"无"，而且知道"无"超乎形象，没有任何特性，因此它不可能

it can never be the object of knowledge. To have knowledge of *Wu* is to be one with it. This state of identification with *Wu* is called *Nirvana*. *Nirvana* and *Prajna* are two aspects of one and the same state of affairs. As *Nirvana* is not something to be known, so *Prajna* is knowledge which is not knowledge. (*Chao Lun*, ch. 3.) Hence, on the third level of truth, nothing can be said and one must remain silent.

● Philosophy of Tao-sheng

Seng-chao died when only thirty years old, so that his influence was less than it might otherwise have been. Tao-sheng (died 434), who was a fellow student with Seng-chao under Kumarajiva, was born at P'eng-ch'eng in the northern part of the present Kiangsu province. He became a monk of wide learning, great brilliancy, and eloquence, of whom it is said that when he spoke even the stones beside him nodded their heads in assent. In his later years he taught at Lu-shan in the present Kiangsi province, which was the center of Buddhist learning at that time, and the place where such great monks as Tao-an (died 385) and Hui-yüan (died 416) had lectured. Tao-sheng advanced many theories so new and revolutionary that once he was publicly banished from Nanking by the conservative monks.

Among these is the doctrine that "a good deed entails no retribution." His essay on this subject is now lost. But in the *Hung Ming Chi* or *Collected Essays on Buddhism*, a work compiled by Seng-yu (died 518), there is a treatise by Hui-yüan titled "On the Explanation of Retribution." This essay may represent some aspects of Tao-sheng's concept, though we cannot be sure. Its general idea is to apply the Taoist ideas of *wu-wei* and *wu-hsin* to metaphysics. As we have seen, *wu-wei* literally means non-action, but this non-action does not really signify no action; rather it signifies action that takes place without effort. When one acts spontaneously, without any deliberate discrimination, choice, or effort, one is practicing non-action. *Wu-hsin* also literally means no mind.

When one practices *wu-wei* in the manner described above, one is also practicing *wu-hsin*. If, argues Hui-yüan, one follows the principles of *wu-wei* and *wu-hsin*, one then has no craving for or cleaving to things, even though one may pursue various activities. And since the effect or retribution of one's *Karma* is due to one's craving and cleaving or attachment, one's *Karma* under these circumstances will not entail any

成为知识的对象。要懂得"无",只有与"无"一体,这便是"涅槃"。"涅槃"和"般若"是一而二又二而一的。正如"涅槃"并非知识的对象,"般若"是懂得那并非知识的奥义。因此,进入第三层次的真谛时,人只能缄默,什么也无法说。

● 道生的哲学

僧肇去世时才三十岁,不然,他将会有更大的思想影响。道生和僧肇同为鸠摩罗什的弟子。道生(公元三七四?至四三四年)河北巨鹿人,寓居彭城(今江苏省北部)。他以知识渊博、聪颖过人、能言善辩闻名于时。据说,当他讲经时,甚至顽石也不禁点头。晚年在江西庐山——当时的佛学中心讲学,在他之前的高僧如道安(公元三八五年卒)、慧远(公元四一六年卒)都曾在此讲经。道生在讲学中提出了许多新的理论,这些理论被认为是对佛学传统的"革命",以致他在南京讲经时曾被当地僧人中的守旧派攻击,把他逐出南京。

他所创立的理论包括"善不受报"论,原文现已佚失。在僧佑(公元五一八年卒)编纂的《弘明集》中辑有慧远所著《明报应论》,也是讲善不受报,可能反映了道生的某些思想,但我们对此无法断定。这篇文章的总的意思是从形而上学进一步发挥道家"无为"和"无心"的思想。"无为"的字面含义是"无所作为",但它的真正含义是"无心"而行。一个人顺其自然地行事,不因人、因时、因地而厚此薄彼、先此后彼或有为有不为,这就是无为。按慧远的看法,一个人如果"无为"、"无心",他的人生就无求、无待,而不在于他从事了这项或那项活动。按佛家的看法,人有求就有所执著,于是就有"业",有"业"就有"报应"。因此,人若"无求""无执著",他的"业"就不招致"果报"(参阅《弘明集》卷五,

retribution. (*Chüan* 5.) This theory of Hui-yüan, regardless of whether it is the same as Tao-sheng's original idea or not, is an interesting extension to Buddhist metaphysics of a Taoist theory which originally possessed purely social and ethical significance. As such, it is certainly an important development in Chinese Buddhism, and one that was to be followed later by the Ch'an school.

Another theory of Tao-sheng is that Buddhahood is to be achieved by Sudden Enlightenment. His essay on this subject is also lost, but the theory is preserved in Hsieh Ling-yün's (died 433) *Pien Tsung Lun* or "Discussion of Essentials." It was developed in opposition to another theory, that of gradual attainment, according to which Buddhahood is to be achieved only through the gradual accumulation of learning and practice. Tao-sheng and Hsieh Ling-yün did not deny the importance of such learning and practice, but they maintained that its accumulation, no matter how great, is only a sort of preparatory work, which in itself is insufficient for one ever to achieve Buddhahood. Such achievement is an instantaneous act, like the leaping over of a deep chasm. Either one makes the leap successfully, in which case one reaches the other side and thus achieves Buddhahood in its entirety in a flash, or one fails in one's leap, in which case one remains as one was. There are no intermediate steps between.

The reason advanced for this theory is that to achieve Buddhahood means to be one with *Wu* (Non-being) or, as one might say, with the Universal Mind. The *Wu*, since it transcends shapes and features, is not a "thing" in itself, and so is not something that can be divided into parts. Therefore one cannot gain oneness with a part of it today and oneness with another part of it tomorrow. Oneness means oneness with the whole of it. Anything less than this is no longer oneness.

The *Pien Tsung Lun* records many arguments on this subject between Hsieh Ling-yün and others. One monk named Seng-wei argued that if the student is one with *Wu*, he will no longer speak about it, but if he is to learn about *Wu* in order to get rid of *Yu* (Being), this learning represents a process of gradual enlightenment. To this Hsieh Ling-yün answered that when a student is still in the realm of *Yu*, whatever he does is learning, but not Enlightenment. Enlightenment itself is something beyond *Yu*, though a student must devote himself first to learning, in order to attain Enlightenment.

Seng-wei again asked: If a student devotes himself to learning and hopes thereby for identification with *Wu*, does he in this way make

载《大藏经》卷五十二）。慧远的这个理论，无论是否是道生的原意，它把道家思想中有社会伦理影响的部分，引进了佛家的形而上学中去。这是中国佛学的一个重要发展，后来禅宗又把这个思想接了过去，并继续加以发展。

道生的另一项理论是"顿悟成佛"义。他在这方面的论著也已佚失。但在谢灵运（公元四三三年卒）的《辩宗论》（辨明宗义论）里保存了道生的这个思想。它是在与"渐悟论"的辩论中阐明的。道生和谢灵运并不是反对学佛和修行的重要性，他们的意思是说，学佛和修行只是成佛的预备，仅靠这样的渐进积累远不足以成佛。成佛还要有一个突变的心灵经验，使人跳过深渊，由此岸到达彼岸，在一瞬间完全成佛。人在跳越深渊时，也可能跳不过去，结果还是留在此岸，在此岸和彼岸之间，并无其他中间步骤。

顿悟论的立论依据是：成佛在于与"无"成为一体，或者可以说，和"宇宙心"（Universal mind）成为一体。"无"既超乎形体，便不是"物"；既不是"物"，便不能分割成多少块。因此，人不能今天与这块"无"合一，明天与那块"无"合一。"一体"只能是一个整体，合一只能是与整体合一。凡不是与整体合而为一，便不是一体。

《辩宗论》里记载了谢灵运和别人在这题目上的许多辩论。有一位僧人名叫僧维，他辩论说，如果一个学僧已经与"无"一体，他就再无可说。如果一个人还在学"无"以去"有"，这个"学无以去有"的过程便是渐悟的过程。谢灵运对此回答说，如果一个学僧还处在"有"的领域，则他的努力只是"学"，而不是"悟"。"悟"所指的是超越"有"，一个人学"悟"，并不就是"悟"。

僧维又问，如果一个学僧献身于学，期望与"无"成为一体，

some advancement? If he does not, why does he pursue learning? But if he does, is this not gradual enlightenment? To this Hsieh Ling-yün answered that devotion to learning can have the positive achievement of suppressing the impure element of the mind. Though such suppression seems to be its extinction, in actual fact it is still not without impure attachment. It is only with Sudden Enlightenment that all attachments are gone.

Again Seng-wei asked: If a student devote himself to learning and practice, can he achieve a temporary identification with *Wu*? If he can, this temporary identification is better than no identification at all, and is it not gradual enlightenment? To this Hsieh Ling-yün answered that such temporary identification is a false one. A real identification is by its nature everlasting. Though the temporary identification seems to be a real identification, it is so only in the same sense that the suppression of the impure element of the mind seems to be its extinction.

All these arguments are endorsed by Tao-sheng in a letter also included in the *Pien Tsung Lun.* The latter is now to be found in the *Kuang Hung Ming Chi* or *Further Collections of Essays on Buddhism (chüan* 18*),* a work compiled by Tao-hsüan (596-667).

Another of Tao-sheng's theories is that every sentient being possesses the Buddha-nature or Universal Mind. His essay on this subject is also lost, but its ideas can be gathered from his commentaries on several Buddhist *Sutras.* According to these, every sentient being has the Buddha-nature; only he does not realize that he has it. This Ignorance (*Avidya*) is what binds him to the Wheel of Birth and Death. The necessity, therefore, is for him first to realize that he has the Buddha-nature originally within him, and then, by learning and practice, to "see" his own Buddha-nature. This "seeing" comes as a Sudden Enlightenment, because the Buddha-nature cannot be divided; therefore he either sees it as a whole or does not see it at all. Such "seeing" also means to be one with the Buddha-nature, because the Buddha-nature is not something that can be seen from outside. This is the meaning of Tao-sheng's statement: "By gaining freedom from illusion, one returns to the Ultimate, and by returning to the Ultimate, one attains the Original."[1] The state of attainment of the Original is the state of *Nirvana*.

But *Nirvana* is not something external to and altogether different from the Wheel of Birth and Death, nor is the reality of the

是否能有所进步呢？如果不能进步，则何必学？如果能进步，那岂不就是渐悟？谢灵运对此回答说，献身于学，可以达到排除杂念。但排除杂念不等于消灭杂念，人还是不能免于对杂念的执著，只有经历顿悟，人才消除了杂念。

僧维又问：如果一个学僧学佛修行，能不能与"无"暂成一体？如果能够这样，它比完全不能融入"无"终究稍好一些，这岂不就是"渐悟"？谢灵运回答说，暂时与"无"一体，乃是幻象；真正与"无"一体，必定是持久的，而不是短暂的。这和上面所说，排除杂念不等于消灭杂念的道理是一样的。

谢灵运在和僧维论辩中所持的观点，道生都表示赞同。在《辩宗论》里收录的道生《答王卫军书》，就是一个明证。后来道宣（公元五九六至六六七年）编纂《广弘明集》，其中辑录了《辩宗论》（见《广弘明集》卷十八，载《大藏经》卷五十二）。

道生的另一项理论主张是："一切众生，莫不是佛，亦皆涅槃。"（《法华经疏》）这是说，一切有情都有佛性，或说都有梵心。他关于这个问题的论文也已佚失，但他在这问题上的观点散见于他对几部佛经的注疏中。从中可以看出道生的主张，认为一切有情都有佛性，而不自知。这种"无明"（梵文 Avidya）是人被缚在生死轮回之中的缘由。因此，人首先应当知道自己里面有佛性；然后经过学佛和修行，得"见"自己内有的佛性。这个"见"只能来自一种"顿悟"，因为"佛性"是一个不能分割的整体，人若"见"，所见的必定是那整体，若未见整体，就是未见。佛性又是从外面无法见到的，人若"见"到自己里面的佛性，只能经过与佛性融为一体的体验。这便是道生所说："返迷归极，归极得本。"（《涅槃经集解》卷一）"极"和"本"就是佛性，归极得本所经验的境界便是涅槃。

但是，涅槃并不是全然外在于生死轮回，与生死轮回迥然

Buddha-nature external to and altogether different from the phenomenal world. Once one gains Sudden Enlightenment, the latter is at once the former. Thus Tao-sheng says: "The Enlightenment of Mahayana Buddhism is not to be sought outside the Wheel of Birth and Death. Within it one is enlightened by the affairs of birth and death."[2] The Buddhists use the metaphor of "reaching the other shore" to express the idea of achieving *Nirvana*. Tao-sheng says: "As to reaching the other shore, if one reaches it, one is not reaching the other shore. Both not-reaching and not-not-reaching are really reaching. This shore here means birth and death; the other shore means *Nirvana*." (*Ibid., chüan* 9.) Again he says: "If one sees Buddha, one is not seeing Buddha. When one sees there is no Buddha, one is really seeing Buddha." (*Ibid.*)

This is perhaps also the meaning of another theory of Tao-sheng, that for Buddha there is no "Pure Land" or other world. The world of Buddha is simply here in this present world.

In an essay titled "The Treasure House," which has been traditionally attributed to Seng-chao but seems to be a forgery, it is said: "Suppose there is a man who, in a treasure house of golden utensils, sees the golden utensils, but pays no attention to their shapes and features. Or, even if he does pay attention to their shapes and features, he still recognizes that they are all gold. He is not confused by their varying appearances, and therefore is able to rid himself of their [superficial] distinctions. He always sees that their underlying substance is gold, and does not suffer any illusion. This is an illustration of what a sage is." (Ch. 3.)

This saying may not come from Seng-chao, but its metaphor has been constantly used by later Buddhists. The reality of the Buddha-nature is itself the phenomenal world, just as the golden utensils are themselves the gold. There is no other reality outside the phenomenal world, just as there is no other gold besides the golden utensils. Some people, in their Ignorance, see only the phenomenal world, but not the reality of the Buddha-nature. Other people, in their Enlightenment, see the

Buddha-nature, but this Buddha-nature is still the phenomenal world. What these two kinds of people see is the same, but what one person sees in his Enlightenment has a significance quite different from what the other person sees in his Ignorance. This is the meaning of a common saying of Chinese Buddhism: "When ignorant, one is a common man; when enlightened, one is a sage."

相异；这道理也适用于佛性，它不是完全外在于生死轮回，和现象世界全然相异。人若一旦"顿悟"，现象世界就成了佛的世界。所以道生说："夫大乘之悟，本不近舍生死，远更求之也。斯在生死事中，即用其实为悟矣。"（僧肇《维摩经注》卷七）佛家以"登彼岸"的比喻来表示得涅槃。道生说："言到彼岸：若到彼岸，便是未到。未到，非未到，方是真到。此岸生死，彼岸涅槃。"（同上书，卷九）他还说："若见佛者，未见佛也；不见有佛，乃为见佛耳。"（同上）

这大概也就是道生所主张的另一项理论，即"佛无净土"论，认为佛的世界就在现实世界之中。

《大藏经》卷四十五有一篇《宝藏论》，传说是僧肇所作，实际大概是别人假托之作。其中说："譬如有人于金器藏中，常观于金体，不睹众相。虽睹众相，亦是一金。既不为相所惑，即离分别。常观金体，无有虚谬。喻彼真人，亦复如是。"这是说，如果有一个人常在金器库里，目睹各种金器，而不注意它们的形象，或虽看见它们的形象，但注意的是器物的质地，则他所见乃是器物的真金质地，而不被器物的不同外表所惑。一个圣人所见世界，亦复如此。

这段话虽不一定是来自僧肇，但后来却常被佛家引用。意思是说，除现象世界之外，别无其他实在。因此，佛性的实在性也就在现象世界之中，正如在金器库中，除金器外，别无他物。有的人由于"无明"，在现象世界里，只见世界的诸相，却不见佛性的实在。另有些人，在现象世界中因悟而见到佛性，但所见佛性并未脱出现象世界。这两种人，所看见的现象世界是相同的，但觉悟了的人所见，其意义和未曾觉悟的人（处于"无明"之中）所见却完全不同。这便是在中国佛教里常说的："迷则为凡，悟则为圣。"

Another theory of Tao-sheng is that even the *icchantika* (i.e., the being who opposes Buddhism) is capable of achieving Buddhahood. This is the logical conclusion of the assertion that every sentient being has the Buddha-nature. But it was in direct contradiction to the *Parinirvana Sutra*, as known at that time, and consequently Tao-sheng, because he uttered it, was banished for some time from the capital, Nanking. Many years later, however, when the complete text of the *Parinirvana Sutra* was translated, Tao-sheng's theory was found to be confirmed by one of its passages. His biographer, Hui-chiao (died 554), wrote: "Because his interpretation of the *icchantika* came to be established by Scriptural evidence, his theories of Sudden Enlightenment and that a good deed entails no retribution, also came to be highly honored by the Buddhists of the time." (*Kao-seng Chüan* or *Biographies of Eminent Buddhist Monks, chüan* 7.)

Hui-chiao also reports another saying of Tao-sheng: "The symbol serves to express an idea, and is to be discarded once the idea has been understood. Words serve to explain thought, and ought to be silenced once the thoughts have been absorbed.... It is only those who can grasp the fish and discard the fishing net that are qualified to seek the truth." (*Ibid.*) This figure of speech refers to a saying in the *Chuang-tzu* which says: "The fishing net serves to catch fish. Let us take the fish and forget the net. The snare serves to catch rabbits. Let us take the rabbit and forget the snare." (Ch. 26.) Chinese philosophical tradition makes use of a term called the "net of words." According to this tradition, the best statement is one that does not "fall into the net of words."

We have seen that in Chi-tsang's theory of the three levels of double truth, when one reaches the third level one simply has nothing to say. On that level there is no danger of falling into the net of words. When Tao-sheng speaks of the Buddha-nature, he almost falls into this net, because by speaking of it as the Mind, he gives people the impression that the limitations of definition can be imposed on it. In this respect he is influenced by the *Parinirvana Sutra*, which emphasizes the Buddha-nature, and so he approaches the *Hsing tsung* or School of Universal Mind.

Thus, as we shall see in the next chapter, by the time of Tao-sheng, the theoretical background for Ch'anism had been prepared. The Ch'an Masters themselves, however, were needed to put the theories described in the present chapter into high relief.

In what has been told here we can also find the germ of the Neo-Confucianism of several centuries later. The theory of Tao-sheng that

道生的另一项理论见解是认为，"一阐提人（不信因果报应，断绝善根，极恶之人），皆得成佛。"这是前述"一切有情都有佛性"的自然结论。但是，这和当时所传的《涅槃经》是相悖的。道生因此而被逐出当时的都城，即今南京。一直到多年以后，《涅槃经》的全文译成汉文，人们才发现，道生的主张与《涅槃经》是相合的。慧皎（公元五五四年卒）在为道生写传时说："时人以（道）生推阐提得佛，此语有据；顿悟，不受报等，时亦宪章。"（《高僧传》卷七）

慧皎还辑录了道生所说的另一段话："夫象以尽意，得意则象忘；言以诠理，入理则言息。……若忘荃取鱼，始可与言道矣。"（同上）这个譬喻取自《庄子·外物》篇，原文是："荃者所以在鱼，得鱼而忘荃；蹄者所以在兔，得兔而忘蹄。"在中国哲学传统里，把词语称作"言荃"，依循这个传统，最好的论说是"不落言荃"的论说，就是说，表达的思想不因所用言词而被误导、束缚。

前面已经说到，吉藏把二谛义分为三层，到第三层真谛时，它是"不可言说"的。到第三层真谛时，人不再会"落入言荃"。道生论述佛性时，几乎落入言荃，因为他把佛性几乎说成是"心"。若果真如此，则任何定义的局限性也可应用于佛性了。在这一点上，他受了《涅槃经》强调佛性的影响，因而接近于性宗。

在下一章里，我们将会看到，禅宗的理论基础，到道生的时候已经具备了。禅宗大师们所作的只是把本章所说的内容，予以更加突出。

从本章所述，我们也可以感到若干世纪后新儒家兴起的先声。

every man can become a Buddha reminds us of the theory of Mencius that every man can become a Yao or Shun (two traditional sage-kings). (*Mencius*, VIb, 2.) Mencius also stated that by fully developing our mind, we come to know our nature; and by fully developing our nature, we come to know Heaven. (*Mencius*, VIIa, 1.) But what he called mind and nature are both psychological and not metaphysical. By giving them a metaphysical interpretation along the line suggested by Tao-sheng's theory, one arrives at Neo-Confucianism.

The idea of the Universal Mind is a contribution of India to Chinese philosophy. Before the introduction of Buddhism, there was in Chinese philosophy only the mind, but not the Mind. The *Tao* of the Taoists is the "mystery of mysteries," as Lao Tzu put it, yet it is not Mind. After the period dealt with in this chapter, there is, in Chinese philosophy, not only mind, but also Mind.

道生的"人人皆可以成佛"的理论令人想起孟子"人皆可以为尧舜"的主张。孟子也说:"尽其心者,知其性也。知其性,则知天矣。"(《孟子·尽心章句上》)但是,孟子所说的"心"和"性",都是在心理学范畴之内,而不是在形而上学范畴之内。如果像道生所作的那样,把"心""性"都赋予形而上学的诠释,那便成为新儒家了。

"宇宙心"是印度佛教对中国哲学的一大贡献。在佛教传入中国以前,中国哲学只讲"人心",却没有"宇宙心"。道家所讲的"道",按老子给它的解释,说它"玄而又玄",它还不成为宇宙之心。在佛教传入中国,经历了本章所论述的这个时期以后,中国哲学不仅有了"心"的理论,而且还有了"宇宙心"的理论。

㉒ CH'ANISM: THE PHILOSOPHY OF SILENCE

The Chinese term *Ch'an* (Japanese reading: *Zen*) or *Ch'an-ra* is a phonetic rendering of the Sanskrit *Dhyana*, which is usually translated in English as Meditation. The traditional account of the origin of the Ch'an or Zen school is that the Buddha, in addition to his Scriptures, possessed an esoteric teaching that was transmitted independently of written texts. This teaching he transmitted personally to one of his disciples, who in turn transmitted it to his own disciple. In this way, it was handed down until it reached Bodhidharma, who is supposed to have been the twenty-eighth Patriarch in India, and who came to China some time between 520 and 526, where he became the first *Tsu* (Patriarch, literally, Ancestor) of the Ch'an school in China.

● **Traditional Account of the Origin of Ch'anism**

There Bodhidharma transmitted the esoteric teaching to Hui-k'o (486-593), who was China's second Patriarch. The teaching was thus perpetuated until a major split in the school occurred, caused by the two chief disciples of the fifth Patriarch, Hung-jen (605-675). One of them, Shen-hsiu (died 706), became the founder of the Northern school; the other, Hui-neng (638-713), founded the Southern school. The Southern school soon surpassed the Northern one in popularity, so that Hui-neng came to be recognized as the sixth Patriarch, the true successor of Hung-jen. All the later influential groups in Ch'anism took their rise from the disciples of Hui-neng.[1]

How far we can depend on the earlier part of this traditional account is much questioned, for it is not supported by any documents dated earlier than the eleventh century. It is not our purpose in this chapter to make a scholarly examination of this problem. Suffice it to say that no scholar today takes the tradition very seriously. Indeed, as we have already seen in the last chapter, the theoretical background for Ch'anism had already been created in China by such men as Seng-chao and

Tao-sheng. Given this background, the rise of Ch'anism would seem to have been almost inevitable, without looking to the almost legendary Bodhidharma as its founder.

The split in the Ch'an school caused by Shen-hsiu and Hui-neng is, however, a historical fact. The difference between these founders of the

贰拾贰 禅宗：潜默的哲学

中文的"禅"或"禅那"是梵文 Dhyana 的音译，英文通常把它译为"沉思"或"冥想"（Meditation）。它的起源，按照传统的说法是：释迦所传授的佛法，除见诸佛经的教义之外，还有"以心传心，不立文字；直指人心，见性成佛"的"教外别传"。释迦只传授了一个弟子，这个弟子又传授给一个弟子。这样在印度传了二十八世，到菩提达摩（Bodhidharma）。菩提达摩于南朝宋末（公元五二〇至五二六）年间到中国，成为禅宗在中国的始祖。

● 禅宗起源的旧说

按照传统的说法，菩提达摩来到中国后，把释迦的心法传授给慧可（公元四八六至五九三年），是为中国禅宗的二祖，又经僧璨（？至公元六〇六年）、道信（公元五八〇至六五一年），传到五祖弘忍（公元六〇五至六七五年）。他的弟子神秀（公元七〇六年卒）创北派，弟子慧能（公元六三八至七一三年）创南派。南派在传播中压倒北派，后来禅宗有势力，各派都祖述慧能的弟子，推崇慧能为六祖。（见道原《传灯录》卷一）

这个传统说法中涉及中国禅宗早期历史的部分，可信程度如何曾受到怀疑，因为在十一世纪之前的文献里，找不到支持这种说法的根据。这个历史考证问题也不是本章所要解决的问题。在这里，只要指出，当代学者对此说多半持怀疑态度，已经够了。在上章里，我们看到，禅宗的理论基础在僧肇和道生的时代就已产生。有了这个基础，禅宗的兴起可以说是顺流而下，势所必然，无须再求助于传说中的菩提达摩来充当中国禅宗的创始人。

禅宗由于神秀和慧能而分裂成南、北两派，乃是历史事实。两派

Northern and Southern schools represents the earlier difference between the *Hsing tsung* (Universal Mind school) and *K'ung tsung* (Empty school) that was described in the last chapter. This can be seen in Hui-neng's own autobiography. From this work we learn that Hui-neng was a native of the present Kwangtung province and became a student of Buddhism under Hung-jen. The account continues that one day Hung-jen, realizing that his time was nearly over, summoned his disciples together and told them that a successor must now be appointed; this successor would be the disciple who could write the best poem summarizing the teaching of Ch'anism.

Shen-hsiu then wrote a poem which read:

> The body is like unto the *Bodhi-tree*,
> And the mind to a mirror bright;
> Carefully we cleanse them hour by hour
> Lest dust should fall upon them.

To refute this idea, Hui-neng then wrote the following poem:

> Originally there was no *Bodhi-tree*,
> Nor was there any mirror;
> Since originally there was nothing,
> Whereon can the dust fall?

It is said that Hung-jen approved Hui-neng's poem and appointed him as his successor, the sixth Patriarch.[2]

Shen-hsiu's poem emphasized the Universal Mind or Buddha Nature spoken of by Tao-sheng, while Hui-neng's emphasized the *Wu* (Non-being) of Seng-chao. There are two phrases that often occur in Ch'anism. One is, "The very mind is Buddha"; the other, "not-mind, and not-Buddha." Shen-hsiu's poem is the expression of the first phrase, and Hui-neng's of the second.

• The First Principle Is Inexpressible

In later times the Ch'an school in its major development followed the line set by Hui-neng. In it the combination already begun between the Empty school and Taoism reached its climax. What the Empty school called higher sense truth on the third level, the Ch'anists called the First Principle. As we have seen in the last chapter, on this third level one simply cannot say anything. Hence the First Principle is by its very nature

的分歧可以看为上一章所说性宗与空宗分歧的继续。从慧能的自传《坛经·自序品》中我们知道，慧能是广东人，被弘忍收为弟子。弘忍知道自己大限将到，召集所有弟子各以一首诗偈来概括禅宗信仰要义，体认最好的就继承他的衣钵。神秀的诗偈说：

> 身如菩提树，心如明镜台。
> 时时勤拂拭，莫使染尘埃。

慧能则针对神秀的诗偈，写了以下这首诗偈：

> 菩提本无树，明镜亦非台。
> 本来无一物，何处染尘埃！

据说弘忍赞许慧能的诗偈，把衣钵传给了慧能。（见《六祖坛经》卷一）

神秀的诗偈所强调的是道生所说的宇宙心或佛性，慧能所强调的则是僧肇所说的"无"。在禅宗里，有两句常说的话："即心即佛"，"非心非佛"。神秀的诗偈表达的是前面一句，慧能的诗偈表达的则是后一句。

• 第一义不可说

禅宗后来依循慧能的路线而发展，正是禅宗的发展使空宗和道家思想的结合达到了顶峰。空宗尊为第三层次真谛的道理，禅宗称之为"第一义"。在上一章里，我们已经看到，关于第三层次的真谛，人无可言说。因此，"第一义"的本性便是"不可说"。

inexpressible. The Ch'an Master Wen-yi (died 958) was once asked: "What is the First Principle?" To which he answered: "If I were to tell you, it would become the second principle." (*Wen-yi Ch'an-shih Yii-lu* or *Sayings of the Ch'an Master Wen-yi.*)

It was the principle of the Ch'an Masters to teach their disciples only through personal contact. For the benefit of those who did not have opportunity for such contact, however, written records were made of the sayings of the Masters, which were known as *yü lu* (recorded conversations). This was a practice that was later taken over by the Neo-Confucianists. In these records, we often find that when a student ventured to ask some question about the fundamental principles of Buddhism, he would often be given a beating by his Ch'an Master, or some quite irrelevant answer. He might, for example, be told that the price of a certain vegetable was then three cents. These answers seem very paradoxical to those who are not familiar with the purpose of Ch'anism. But this purpose is simply to let the student know that what he asks about is not answerable. Once he understands that, he understands a great deal.

The First Principle is inexpressible, because what is called the *Wu* is not something about which anything can be said. By calling it "Mind" or any other name, one is at once giving it a definition and thus imposing on it a limitation. As the Ch'anists and Taoists both say, one thereby falls into the "net of words." Ma-tsu or the Patriarch Ma (died 788), a disciple of the disciple of Hui-neng, was once asked: "Why do you say that the very mind is Buddha?" Ma-tsu answered: "I simply want to stop the crying of children." "Suppose they do stop crying?" asked the questioner. "Then not-mind, not-Buddha," was the answer.[3]

Another student asked Ma-tsu: "What kind of man is he who is not linked to *all* things?" The Master answered: "Wait until in one gulp you can drink up all the water in the West River, then I will tell you." (*Ibid.*) Such an act is obviously impossible and by suggesting it Ma-tsu meant to indicate to the student that he would not answer his question. His question, in fact, was really not answerable, because he who is not linked to *all* things is one who transcends *all* things. This being so, how can you ask what kind of man he is?

There were Ch'an Masters who used silence to express the idea of *Wu* or the First Principle. It is said, for example, that when Hui-chung (died 775) was to debate with another monk, he simply mounted his chair and

据《文益禅师语录》记载，有人问文益禅师（公元九五八年卒）："'如何是第一义？'师云：'我向尔道，是第二义。'"

禅师教导弟子的原则是个人接触。为使其他弟子也能受益，禅师的教导被记录下来，成为《语录》（后来新的儒家也采用了这种办法）。从《语录》中可以看到，有的学僧向禅师提出关于禅的根本问题，禅师或者答非所问，如回答说"白菜三分钱一斤"，或甚至把徒弟打一顿。不明个中道理的人，会觉得禅师对徒弟的反应，令人莫名其妙，难以理喻。其实，禅师正是藉此告诉徒弟，这问题是不能回答的（凡对第一义所拟说者作肯定陈述，都是所谓死语，禅宗认为，说死语的人该打），只有靠自己去"悟"，一旦领会，便得彻悟。

第一义不可说，因为"无"不是任何"物"，因此无可说。如果称之为"心"，就是强加给它一个定义，就是对它施加了限制。禅师和道家都称之为落入"言筌"，即掉进了语言的网罗。慧能有一个再传弟子马祖（公元七八八年卒），曾有人问他："和尚为什么说'即心即佛'？"马祖回答："为止小儿啼。"问："啼止时将如何？"曰："非心非佛。"（《古尊宿语录》卷一）

另一个徒弟庞居士问马祖："不与万法为侣者（与万物都无关系者）是什么人？"马祖云："待汝一口吸尽西江水，即向汝道。"一口吸尽西江水，是无人能做的，因此马祖实际是回答说，不回答这个问题。为什么不回答呢？因为这个问题是无法回答的。人若和万物都无联系，他便是超越了万物。既已超越万物，又怎能问，他是什么样的人呢？

还有些禅师以静默来表示"无"或第一义。例如《传灯录》第五卷记载，慧忠国师（公元七七五年卒）"与紫璘供奉论议。既升座，

remained silent. The other monk then said: "Please propose your thesis so I can argue." Hui-chung replied: "I have already proposed my thesis." The monk asked: "What is it?" Hui-chung said: "I know it is beyond your understanding," and with this left his chair. (*Record of the Transmission of the Light, chüan* 5.) The thesis Hui-chung proposed was that of silence. Since the First Principle or *Wu* is not something about which anything can be said, the best way to expound it is to remain silent.

From this point of view no Scriptures or *Sutras* have any real connection with the First Principle. Hence the Ch'an Master Yi-hsüan (died 866), founder of a group in Ch'anism known as the Lin-chi school, said: "If you want to have the right understanding, you must not be deceived by others. You should kill everything that you meet internally or externally. If you meet Buddha, kill Buddha. If you meet the Patriarchs, kill the Patriarchs.... Then you can gain your emancipation." (*Recorded Savings of Ancient Worthies, chüan* 4.)

- **Method of Cultivation**

The knowledge of the First Principle is knowledge that is non-knowledge; hence the method of cultivation is also cultivation that is non-cultivation. It is said that Ma-tsu, before he became a disciple of Huai-jang (died 744), lived on the Heng Mountain (in present Hunan province). There he occupied a solitary hut in which, all alone, he practiced meditation. One day Huai-jang began to grind some bricks in front of the hut. When Ma-tsu saw it, he asked Huai-jang what he was doing. He replied that he was planning to make a mirror. Ma-tsu said: "How can grinding bricks make a mirror?" Huai-jang said: "If grinding bricks cannot make a mirror, how can meditation make a Buddha?" By this saying Ma-tsu was enlightened and thereupon became Huai-jang's disciple. (*Recorded Sayings of Ancient worthies, chüan* 1.)

Thus according to Ch'anism, the best method of cultivation for achieving Buddhahood is not to practice any cultivation. To cultivate oneself in this way is to exercise deliberate effort, which is *yu-wei* (having action). This *yu-wei* will, to be sure, produce some good effect, but it will not be everlasting. The Ch'an Master Hsi-yün (died 847), known as the Master of Huang-po, said: "Supposing that through innumerable lives a man has practiced the six *paramitas* [methods of gaining salvation], done good and attained the Buddha Wisdom, this will still not last forever. The reason lies in causation. When the force of the cause is exhausted, he reverts to the impermanent." (*Recorded Sayings of Ancient Worthies*, *chüan* 3.)

供奉曰：'请师立义，某甲破。'师曰：'立义竟。'供奉曰：'是什么义？'曰：'果然不见，非公境界。'便下座。"慧忠立的义是不可说的第一义，因此他便以缄默来立义，这是紫璘供奉无法破的。

由这一点来看，任何佛经也无法和第一义挂钩。因此，建立临济宗的义玄禅师（公元八六六年卒）曾说："你如欲得如法见解，但莫授人惑。向里向外，逢着便杀。逢佛杀佛，逢祖杀祖，……始得解脱。"（《古尊宿语录》卷四）

● **修禅的方法**

要识得"无"这个第一义的真谛，就是对"无"的意识，这是"识"。因此，修行的方法也只能是"不修之修"。《古尊宿语录》卷一记载，传说马祖在成为怀让（公元七四四年卒）禅师的弟子之前，住在湖南衡山。"独处一庵，惟习坐禅，凡有来访者都不顾"。怀让"一日将砖于庵前磨，马祖亦不顾。时既久，乃问曰：'作什么？'师云：'磨作镜。'马祖云：'磨砖岂能成镜？'师云：'磨砖既不成镜，坐禅岂能成佛？'马祖由此而悟，乃拜怀让为师。"

因此，按禅宗的看法，修禅成佛的最好方法便是"不修之修"。这是什么意思呢？它是说由修禅的人照信佛的人通常理解的那样去修行，这其实是"有为"的修行。这种有为的修行也能产生一些功效，但不能持久。黄檗（希运）禅师（公元八四七年卒）说："设使恒沙劫数，行六度万行，得佛菩提，亦非究竟。何以故？为属因缘造作故。因缘若尽，还归无常。"（《古尊宿语录》卷三）

Again he said: "All deeds are essentially impermanent. All forces have their final day. They are like a dart discharged through the air; when its strength is exhausted, it turns and falls to the ground. They are all connected with the Wheel of Birth and Death. To practice cultivation through them is to misunderstand the Buddha's idea and waste labor." (*Ibid.*)

And yet again: "If you do not understand *wu hsin* [absence of a purposeful mind], then you are attached to objects, and suffer from obstructions.... Actually there is no such thing as *Bodhi* [Wisdom]. That the Buddha talked about it was simply as a means to educate men, just as yellow leaves may be taken as gold coins in order to stop the crying of children.... The only thing to be done is to rid yourself of your old *Karma*, as opportunity offers, and not to create new *Karma* from which will flow new calamities." (*Ibid.*)

Thus the best method of spiritual cultivation is to do one's tasks without deliberate effort or purposeful mind. This is exactly what the Taoists called *wu-wei* (non-action) and *wu-hsin* (no-mind). It is what Hui-yüan's theory signifies, as well as, probably, the statement of Tao-sheng that "a good deed does not entail retribution." This method of cultivation does not aim at doing things in order to obtain resulting good effects, no matter how good these effects may be in themselves. Rather it aims at doing things in such a way as to entail no effects at all. When all one's actions entail no effect, then after the effects of previously accumulated *Karma* have exhausted themselves, one will gain emancipation from the Wheel of Birth and Death and attain *Nirvana*.

To do things without deliberate effort and purposeful mind is to do things naturally and to live naturally. Yi-hsüan said: "To achieve Buddhahood there is no place for deliberate effort. The only method is to carry on one's ordinary and uneventful tasks: relieve one's bowels, pass water, wear one's clothes, eat one's meals, and when tired, lie down. The simple fellow will laugh at you, but the wise will understand." (*Recorded Sayings of Ancient Worthies, chüan* 4.) The reason why those who try to achieve Buddhahood so often fail to follow this course is because they lack self-confidence. Yi-hsüan said: "Nowadays people who engage in spiritual cultivation fail to achieve their ends. Their fault is not having faith in themselves.... Do you wish to know who are the Patriarchs and Buddha? All of you who are before me are the Patriarchs and Buddha." (*Ibid.*)

Thus the way to practice spiritual cultivation is to have adequate confidence in one's self and discard everything else. All one should do is to pursue the ordinary tasks of one's everyday life, and nothing more. This is what the Ch'an Masters call cultivation through non-cultivation.

他又说："诸行尽归无常，势力皆有尽期。犹如箭射于空，力尽还坠。都归生死轮回。如斯修行，不解佛意，虚受辛苦，岂非大错？"（同上）

他还说："若未会无心，著相皆属魔业。……所以菩提等法，本不是有。如来所说，皆是化人。犹如黄叶为金钱，权止小儿啼。……但随缘消旧业，莫更造新殃。"（同上）

因此，最好的修禅便是尽力做眼前当做的事，而无所用心。这正是道家所讲的"无为"和"无心"。这也就是慧远，或者也是道生所说"善不受报"义。实行这样的修持，不是为了达到某种目标，无论这个目标多么崇高。修持不是为了任何目的。这样，当人前世积累的业报已经耗尽，就不会再生出新的业，他便能从生死轮回中解脱出来，达到涅槃。

行事为人，无所用心，就是说，一切顺其自然。义玄禅师曾说："道流佛法，无用功处。只是平常无事，屙屎送尿，着衣吃饭，困来即卧。愚人笑我，智乃知焉。"（《古尊宿语录》卷四）许多一心修持的人，不能照这个样子去做，是因为他们对这种做法没有信心。义玄禅师说："如今学者不得，病在甚处？病在不自信处。你若自信不及，便茫茫地徇一切境转，被它万境回换，不得自由。你若歇得念念驰求心，便与祖佛不别。你欲识得祖佛么？只你面前听法的是。"（同上）

这样说来，修行需要对自己有足够的自信心，而抛弃其他一切得失考虑。人需要去做的是以平常心做平常事，如此而已。这是禅师所说的"不修之修"。

Here a question arises: Granted that this be so, then what is the difference between the man who engages in cultivation of this kind and the man who engages in no cultivation at all? If the latter does precisely what the former does, he too should achieve *Nirvana*, and so there should come a time when there will be no Wheel of Birth and Death at all.

To this question it may be answered that although to wear clothes and eat meals are in themselves common and simple matters, it is still not easy to do them with a completely non-purposeful mind and thus without any attachment. A person likes fine clothes, for example, but dislikes bad ones, and he feels pleased when others admire his clothes. These are all the attachments that result from wearing clothes. What the Ch'an Masters emphasized is that spiritual cultivation does not require special acts, such as the ceremonies and prayers of institutionalized religion. One should simply try to be without a purposeful mind or any attachments in one's daily life; then cultivation results from the mere carrying on of the common and simple affairs of daily life. In the beginning one will need to exert effort in order to be without effort, and to exercise a purposeful mind in order not to have such a mind, just as, in order to forget, one at first needs to remember that one should forget. Later, however, the time comes when one must discard the effort to be without effort, and the mind that purposefully tries to have no purpose, just as one finally forgets to remember that one has to forget.

Thus cultivation through non-cultivation is itself a kind of cultivation, just as knowledge that is not knowledge is nevertheless still a form of knowledge. Such knowledge differs from original ignorance, and cultivation through non-cultivation likewise differs from original naturalness. For original ignorance and naturalness are gifts of nature, whereas knowledge that is not knowledge and cultivation through non-cultivation are both products of the spirit.

• Sudden Enlightenment

The practice of cultivation, no matter for how long, is in itself only a sort of preparatory work. For Buddhahood to be achieved, this cultivation must be climaxed by a Sudden Enlightenment, such as was described in the last chapter as comparable to the leaping over of a precipice. Only after this leaping has taken place can Buddhahood be achieved.

Such Enlightenment is often referred to by the Ch'an Masters as the "vision of the *Tao*." P'u-yüan, known as the Master of Nan-ch'üan (died

由此产生一个问题。如果修行的途径就是如此，那么这样进行修持的人和不从事修持的人还有什么区别？如果没有区别，那么不从事修持的人岂不一样达到涅槃吗？果真如此，大家都能从生死轮回中解脱，岂非就不再有生死轮回了？

对这问题的回答是：尽管吃饭穿衣是寻常事，要在做时无求无心，并不是一件容易事。举例来说，人们通常喜欢漂亮衣着，当衣着受到别人称赞时，心底便不禁顾盼生姿、得意起来。这些都是由穿衣引起的滞着。禅师们所着重的是内心修持，而不需要做任何特殊的事情，诸如宗教组织里的仪式祈祷之类。人只要澄心凝思，一无滞着，这时，以平常心做平常事，自然便是修持。在开始时，或许要用一番心，才能做到无心无待，正如人若要想忘记一件事情，开始时需要提醒自己去忘记。到了后来，渐渐可以"做而无所为"，这时，就需要脱去那一层对自己的勉强，正如人最后忘记了他需要忘记。

因此，不修之修乃是一种修持，正如"不知之知"仍是一种知一样。"不知之知"并非人本来的"无知"，修持得来的自然与人天生的自然也是不同的。人本来的无知和自然是一种天赋，而"不知之知"和"不修之修"则是内心修持的结果。

• 顿悟

按佛家的看法，人的修行，不论多久，就其性质说，都只是心灵的准备。要想成佛，必须经历如上章所说的顿悟，这是一种类似跳过悬崖的内心经验。人只有经过这样的内心经验，才可以成佛。

禅师们往往把这种"悟"称作"见道"。南泉禅师普愿（公元

830), told his disciple: "The *Tao* is not classifiable as either knowledge or non-knowledge. Knowledge is illusory consciousness and non-knowledge is blind unconsciousness. If you really comprehend the indubitable *Tao*, it is like a wide expanse of emptiness, so how can distinctions be forced in it between right and wrong?"(*Recorded Sayings of Ancient Worthies, chüan* 13.) Comprehension of the *Tao* is the same as being one with it. Its wide expanse of emptiness is not a void; it is simply a state in which all distinctions are gone.

This state is described by the Ch'an Masters as one in which "knowledge and truth become undifferentiable, objects and spirit form a single unity, and there ceases to be a distinction between the experiencer and the experienced." (*Ibid., chüan* 32.) "A man who drinks water knows by himself whether it is cold or warm." This last expression first appeared in the *Sutra Spoken by the Sixth Patriarch* (Hui-neng), but it was later widely quoted by the other Ch'an Masters, meaning that only he who experiences the non-distinction of the experiencer and the experienced really knows what it is.

In this state the experiencer has discarded knowledge in the ordinary sense, because this kind of knowledge postulates a distinction between the knower and the known. Nevertheless, he is not without knowledge, because his state differs from that of blind unconsciousness, as Nan-ch'üan calls it. This is what is called the knowledge that is not knowledge.

When the student has reached the verge of Sudden Enlightenment, that is the time when the Master can help him the most. When one is about to make the leap, a certain assistance, no matter how small, is a great help. The Ch'an Masters at this stage used to practice what they called the method of "stick or yell" to help the leap to Enlightenment. Ch'an literature reports many incidents in which a Master, having asked his student to consider some problem, suddenly gave him several blows with a stick or yelled at him. If these acts were done at the right moment, the result would be a Sudden Enlightenment for the student.

The explanation would seem to be that the physical act, thus performed, shocks the student into that psychological awareness of enlightenment for which he has long been preparing.

To describe Sudden Enlightenment, the Ch'an Masters use the metaphor of "the bottom of a tub falling out." When this happens, all its contents are suddenly gone. In the same way, when one is suddenly

八三〇年卒）曾对弟子说："道不属知不知，知是妄觉，不知是无记。若真达不疑之道，犹如太虚廓然，岂可强是非也！"（《古尊宿语录》卷十三）人悟道也就是与道合而为一。这时，广漠无垠的"道"不再是"无"，而是一种"无差别境界"。

这种境界按禅师的经验乃是"智与理冥，境与神会，如人饮水，冷暖自知"（《古尊宿语录》卷三十二）。"如人饮水，冷暖自知"，最初见于《六祖坛经》，后来的禅师往往援引这两句话，以示人与外部世界的"无差别境界"不是言语所能表达，只有靠人自己经验才能体会。

在这种境界里，人已经抛弃了通常意义的知识，因为这种知识首先就把"人"这个认识主体和"世界"这个认识客体分开了。但正如南泉禅师上述前两句话所示，"不知之知"把禅僧带入一种知识与真理不分、人的心灵与它的对象合为一体的状态，以至认识的主体和认识的客体不再有任何区别。这不是没有知识，它与盲目的无知是全然不同的。这是"不知之知"，是南泉禅师所要表达的意思。

当禅僧处在顿悟前夕时，他特别需要师父的帮助。当学僧要在心灵中跳过那道悬崖时，师父给予的些许帮助，就意味着极大的帮助。在这时候，禅师采用的方法往往是"一声棒喝"。禅宗在文献里记载了许多这样的例子。师父向徒弟提出许多问题后，会突然用棒或竹篦打他几下。如果时间正好，徒弟往往因此而得到顿悟。怎样解释这一点呢？看来，师父打徒弟，正是藉这样的行动，把徒弟推入在悬崖上向前一跃的那种心理状态，而这是徒弟在精神上早已等待着的一刻。

为形容"顿悟"，禅师们用一个比喻说："如桶底子脱。"当桶底忽然脱落时，桶里的东西，在刹那间都掉出去了。人在修禅的过程中，到一个时候，心里的种种负担，会像是忽然没有了，各种问题

enlightened, he finds all his problems suddenly solved. They are solved not in the sense that he gains some positive solution for them, but in the sense that all the problems have ceased any longer to be problems. That is why the *Tao* is called "the indubitable *Tao.*"

- ## The Attainment of Non-attainment

The attainment of Sudden Enlightenment does not entail the attainment of anything further. The Ch'an Master Ch'ing-yüan, known as the Master of Shu-chou (died 1120), said: "If you now comprehend it, where is that which you did not comprehend before? What you were deluded about before is what you are now enlightened about, and what you are now enlightened about is what you were deluded about before." (*Recorded Sayings of Ancient Worthies, chüan* 32.) As we have seen in the last chapter, the real is the phenomenal, according to Seng-chao and Tao-sheng. In Ch'anism there is the common expression that "the mountain is the mountain, the river is the river." In one's state of delusion, one sees the mountain as the mountain and the river as the river. But after Enlightenment one still sees the mountain as the mountain and the river as the river.

The Ch'an Masters also use another common expression: "Riding an ass to search for the ass." By this they mean a search for reality outside of the phenomenal, in other words, to search for *Nirvana* outside of the Wheel of Birth and Death. Shu-chou said: "There are only two diseases: one is riding an ass to search for the ass; the other is riding an ass and being unwilling to dismount. You say that riding an ass to search for the ass is silly and that he who does it should be punished. This is a very serious disease. But I tell you, do not search for the ass at all. The intelligent man, understanding my meaning, stops to search for the ass, and thus the deluded state of his mind ceases to exist.

"But if, having found the ass, one is unwilling to dismount, this disease is most difficult to cure. I say to you, do not ride the ass at all.

You yourself are the ass. Everything is the ass. Why do you ride on it? If you ride, you cannot cure your disease. But if you do not ride, the universe is as a great expanse open to your view. With these two diseases expelled, nothing remains to affect your mind. This is spiritual cultivation. You need do nothing more." (*Ibid*.) If one insists that after attaining Enlightenment one will still attain something else, this is to ride an ass and be unwilling to dismount.

都自行解决了。这不是通常人们理解的解决了思想问题，而是所有原来的问题，都不再成其为问题了。这就是何以称"道"为"不疑之道"的缘故。

● **无成之功**

人经历"顿悟"之后，并不是由此得到了另一样东西。舒州禅师清远（公元一一二二年卒）曾说："如今明得了，向前明不得的，在什么处？所以道，向前迷的，便是即今悟的；即今悟的，便是向前迷的。"（同上）这是说，人在"悟"了之后，先前的"迷"岂还在吗？先前的"迷"已被今日的"悟"所替代。今日的"悟"便是先前的"迷"。在上一章里，我们看到，僧肇和道生指出：真实只是一个现象。禅宗有一句惯用语："山是山，水是水。"当人在迷雾中时，看山是山，看水是水；在人顿悟之后，山还是山，水还是水。

禅师还有另一句常用的话："骑驴觅驴。"它被用来指人想在现象之外找真实，或人想在生死轮回之外找涅槃。舒州禅师说："只有两种病：一是骑驴觅驴，一是骑驴不肯下。你道骑却驴了，更觅驴，可杀，是大病；山僧向你道，不要觅。灵利人当下识得，除却觅驴病，狂心遂息。

"既识得驴了，骑了不肯下，此一病最难医。山僧向你道：不要骑。你便是驴，尽山河大地是个驴，你作么生骑？你若骑，管取病不去。若不骑，十方世界廓落地。此二病一时去，心下无一事，名为道人，复有什么事？"（同上）人在顿悟之后，如还坚持要得到别的什么东西，就如同骑驴觅驴和骑驴不肯下一样。

Huang-po said: "[If there be Enlightenment], speech or silence, activity or inactivity, and every sight and sound, all pertain to Buddha. Where should you go to find the Buddha? Do not place a head on top of a head or a mouth beside a mouth." (*Recorded Sayings of Ancient Worthies, chüan* 3.) If there be Enlightenment, everything pertains to Buddha and everywhere there is Buddha. It is said that one Ch'an monk went into a temple and spat on the statue of the Buddha. When he was criticized, he said: "Please show me a place where there is no Buddha." (*Record of the Transmission of the Light, chüan* 27.)

Thus the Ch'an sage lives just as everyone else lives, and does what everyone else does. In passing from delusion to Enlightenment, he has left his mortal humanity behind and has entered sagehood. But after that he still has to leave sagehood behind and to enter once more into mortal humanity. This is described by the Ch'an Masters as "rising yet another step over the top of the hundred-foot bamboo." The top of the bamboo symbolizes the climax of the achievement of Enlightenment. "Rising yet another step" means that after Enlightenment has come, the sage still has other things to do. What he has to do, however, is no more than the ordinary things of daily life. As Nan-ch'uan said: "After coming to understand the other side, you come back and live on this side." (*Recorded Sayings of Ancient Worthies, chüan* 12.)

Although the sage continues living on this side, his understanding of the other side is not in vain. Although what he does is just what everyone else does, yet it has a different significance to him. As Hui-hai, known as the Master of Pai-ch'ang (died 814), said: "That which before Enlightenment is called lustful anger, is after Enlightenment called the Buddha Wisdom. The man is no different from what he was before; it is only that what he does is different." (*Recorded Sayings of Ancient Worthies, chüan* 1.) It would seem that there must be some textual error in this last sentence. What Pai-ch'ang apparently intended to say was: "What the man does is no different from what he did before; it is only that the man himself is not the same as he was."

The man is not the same, because although what he does is what everyone else does, he has no attachment to anything. This is the meaning of the common Ch'an saying: "To eat all day and yet not swallow a single grain; to wear clothes all day and yet not touch a single thread." (*Recorded Sayings of Ancient Worthies, chüan* 3 and 16.)

There is yet another common saying: "In carrying water and chopping firewood: therein lies the wonderful *Tao.*" (*Record of the Transmission of the Light, chüan* 8.) One may ask: If this is so, does not the wonderful *Tao*

黄檗禅师说: "语默动静，一切声色，尽是佛事。何处觅佛？不可更头上安头，嘴上安嘴。"(《古尊宿语录》卷三) 如果达到顿悟，这时候一切都是佛事，处处都见佛陀。据说，有一个禅僧进入庙里，向佛像身上吐痰。庙里人批评他，他说: "请告我，何处无菩萨？"(《传灯录》卷二十七)

因此，禅师像寻常人那样生活，做寻常人所做的事情；经过从迷到悟的过程，他已把肉体的性情放下，而进入了禅定的境界。而在此之后，他还要离开禅定的境界，重返世俗人间。这便是禅师所说的"百尺竿头，更进一步"。到了百尺竿头，便是象征着顿悟，"更进一步"是表明到了顿悟，已经到了悟的顶峰，但前面还有事情要做。还要做的无非还是寻常生活中的寻常事情。正如南泉禅师所说: "直向那边会了，却来这里行履。"(《古尊宿语录》卷十二)

圣人虽然仍旧生活在此岸世界之中，但他对彼岸世界的领悟并不是白费了工夫。他所做的事情虽然还和普通人一样，但这些事情对圣人却有不同的意义。百丈禅师怀海（公元八一四年卒）曾说: "未悟未解时名贪嗔，悟了唤作佛慧。故云: '不异旧时人，异旧时行履处。'"(《古尊宿语录》卷一) 此处末句文字可能有误，怀海法师想说的显然是"不异旧时行履处，只异旧时人"。

人和旧时不同了，因为他的所作所为虽然和别人一样，但他对任何事物都没有滞着。这就是禅语常说的: "终日吃饭，未曾咬着一粒米；终日着衣，未曾挂着一缕丝。"(《古尊宿语录》卷三，卷十六)

禅僧还有另一句常说的话: "担水砍柴，无非妙道。"(《传灯录》卷八) 人们或许会问: 如果担水砍柴皆是妙道，那么，"事父事君"

also lie in serving one's family and the state? If we were to draw the logical conclusion from the Ch'an doctrines that have been analyzed above, we should be forced to answer yes. The Ch'an Masters themselves, however, did not give this logical answer. It was reserved for the Neo-Confucianists, who are the subject of our next several chapters, to do so.

难道就没有妙道在其中吗？如果从禅宗教义里寻找这个问题的逻辑结论，回答只能是肯定的。但是，禅师们并没有正面回答这个问题。这个问题只有留待新的儒家去回答。这是在下面几章里将要讨论的问题。

⑳ NEO-CONFUCIANISM: THE COSMOLOGISTS

In 589, after centuries of division, China was again unified by the Sui dynasty (589-617). The Sui, however, soon gave way to the powerful and highly centralized dynasty of T'ang (618-906). Both culturally and politically the T'ang was a golden age in China, which equalled and in some ways surpassed that of Han.

The examination system for the selection of officials, in which the Confucian Classics held a pre-eminent position, was reestablished in 622. In 628 Emperor T'ai-tsung (627-649) ordered that a Confucian temple be established in the Imperial University, and in 630 he again ordered scholars to prepare an official edition of the Confucian Classics. As part of this work, standard commentaries on the Classics were selected from among the numerous commentaries that had been written before that time, and official subcommentaries were written to elucidate these standard commentaries. The resulting Classical texts, with their official commentaries and subcommentaries, were then commanded by the Emperor to be taught in the Imperial University. In this way Confucianism was reaffirmed as the official teaching of the state.

But Confucianism had by this time already lost the vitality which it had once manifested in the form of such men as Mencius, Hsün Tzu, and Tung Chung-shu. The original texts were there, and their commentaries and subcommentaries were even more numerous than before, yet they failed to meet the spiritual interest and needs of the age. After the revival of Taoism and the introduction of Buddhism, people had become more interested in metaphysical problems and in what I call super-moral values, or, as they were then phrased, the problems of the nature and Destiny (of man). As we have seen in chapters four, seven, and fifteen, discussions on such problems are not lacking in such Confucian works as the *Confucian Analects*, the *Mencius*, the *Doctrine of the Mean*, and especially the *Book of Changes*. These, however, needed a genuinely new interpretation and elucidation in order to meet the problems of the new age, and this type of interpretation was as yet lacking despite the efforts of the Emperor's scholars.

● **Han Yü and Li Ao**

It was not until the latter part of the T'ang dynasty that there arose two men, Han Yü (768-824) and Li Ao (died c. 844), who really tried to

---

贰拾叁 更新的儒家：宇宙论者

　　公元五八九年，中国在经历几世纪分裂之后，又统一在隋朝（公元五八九〔五八一〕至六一七〔六一八〕年）统治之下。但是不久之后，隋朝又被比它更强大、更加中央集权化的唐朝（公元六一八至九〇七年）所取代。从文化和政治上看，唐朝是中国漫长历史中的黄金时代，可以与汉代相媲美，甚至在某些方面还超过了汉朝。

　　公元六二二年，以儒家经典为主要标准开科取仕的制度，开始建立。公元六二八年，唐太宗（公元六二七至六四九年在位）下令，太庙中修建孔庙。公元六三〇年又下诏，命硕学大儒审定儒家经典标准文本，然后从当时流行的各种注释文本中选出标准文本，再据以作出官方审定的注疏。经过这样的程序，选出的经书标准文本和注释文本与新编写的注疏，都由皇帝颁布，在太学中讲授。这样，儒家思想再次成为国家确认的官学，通行全国。

　　但是这时的儒学已经丧失了过去在孟子、荀子、董仲舒时代所拥有的活力，虽然经书文献都照旧存在，注释之类比过去更多，但它们既不能满足时代的需要，也引不起人们的兴趣。在道家思想再起和佛教传入中国之后，人们对形而上学的问题和我称之为"超道德"的价值，在当时人称为"性命之学"，实际是人的本性和命运的问题，感到更大的兴趣。本书前面第四章、第七章和第十五章里都曾指出，在《论语》《孟子》《中庸》里，尤其是在《易经》里，并不乏对这些问题的探讨。但是，新的时代，新的问题，使人们感到，旧的思想传统已不足以应付时代的挑战，尽管皇帝手下的官方学者已经做了巨大的努力。

● **韩愈和李翱**

　　一直到唐中叶以后，韩愈（公元七六八至八二四年）和李翱（公元

reinterpret such works as the *Ta Hsüeh* or *Great Learning* and *Chung
Yung* or *Doctrine of the Mean*, in such a way as would answer the
problems of their time. In his essay titled *Yüan Tao* or "On the Origin
and Nature of the Truth," Han Yü wrote: "What I call the *Tao* is not
what has hitherto been called the *Tao* by the Taoists and the Buddhists.
Yao [a traditional sage-king of antiquity] transmitted the *Tao* to Shun
[another traditional sage-king supposed to be the successor of Yao]. Shun
transmitted it to Yü [successor of Shun and founder of the Hsia dynasty].
Yü transmitted it to [Kings] Wen and Wu and the Duke of Chou [the
three founders of the Chou dynasty]. Wen and Wu and the Duke of Chou
transmitted it to Confucius, and Confucius transmitted it to Mencius.
After Mencius, it was no longer transmitted. Hsün [Tzu] and Yang
[Hsiung] selected from it, but without reaching the essential portion; they
discussed it, but without sufficient clarity." (*Ch'ang-li Hsien-sheng Chi*, or
Collected Works of Han Yü, chüan 11.)

And Li Ao, in an essay titled "On the Restoration of the Nature,"
writes very similarly: "The ancient Sages transmitted this teaching to
Yen Tzu [i.e., Yen Hui, the favored disciple of Confucius]. Tzu-ssu, the
grandson of Confucius, received the teaching of his grandfather and
composed the *Doctrine of the Mean* in forty-seven sections which he
transmitted to Mencius.... Alas, though writings dealing with the nature
and Destiny are still preserved, none of the scholars understand them,
and therefore they all plunge into Taoism and Buddhism. Ignorant people
say that the followers of the Master [i.e., of Confucius] are incapable
of investigating the theories on the nature and Destiny, and everybody
believes them. When some one asked me about this, I transmitted to
him what I knew.... My hope is that this long obstructed and abandoned
Truth may be transmitted in the world." (*Li Wen-kung Chi* or *Collected
Works of Li Ao, chüan* 2.)

The theory of the transmission of the Truth from Yao and Shun
downward, though already roughly suggested by Mencius (*Mencius*

VIIb, 38), was evidently reinspired in Han Yü and Li Ao by the Ch'an theory that the esoteric teaching of the Buddha had been transmitted through a line of Patriarchs to Hung-jen and Hui-neng. At a later time one of the Ch'eng brothers (see chapter 24) even stated unequivocally that the *Chung Yung* or *Doctrine of the Mean* was the esoteric teaching of Confucius. (Quoted by Chu Hsi in his introduction to his *Commentary on the Chung Yung*.) It was widely believed that the transmission of the Truth had become interrupted after Mencius. Li Ao, however, apparently felt that he himself possessed a certain understanding of it, and that through his teaching he could thus act as a continuator of Mencius. To do this became the ambition of all Neo-Confucianists after Li Ao's time. All

八四四年卒）才对《大学》和《中庸》作出新的解释来回应时代提出的新问题。韩愈在所著《原道》篇里说："斯吾所谓道也，非向所谓老与佛之道也。尧以是传之舜，舜以是传之禹，禹以是传之汤，汤以是传之文、武、周公，文、武、周公传之孔子，孔子传之孟轲，轲之死，不得其传焉。荀与扬也，择焉而不精，语焉而不详。"（《昌黎先生文集》卷十一）

李翱在《复性书》中也发表了类似的见解说："昔者，圣人以之传于颜子。……子思，仲尼之孙，得其祖之道，述《中庸》四十七篇，以传于孟轲。……呜呼！性命之书虽存，学者莫能明，是故皆入于庄、列、老、释。不知者谓夫子之徒不足以穷性命之道，信之者皆是也。有问于我，我以吾之所知而传焉，……而缺绝废弃不扬之道几可以传于时。"（《李文公集》卷二）

关于"道"即世代相传的"道统说"，孟子已大略提及（见《孟子·尽心章句下》），到了韩愈和李翱又再次兴起。这显然是由于佛教禅宗提出：它的师承关系来自释迦以教外别传的心法传授弟子，经过列祖，直到弘忍和慧能。后来，程氏兄弟中有一位（参阅本书第二十四章）更明确说，《中庸》或中庸之道"乃孔门传授心法"（朱熹在《中庸章句》前言中引）。后世许多人认为，道统的传承到孟轲而中断。只是李翱显然认为自己对于道统有所了解，并相信自己的教化活动是继承了孟子的统绪。自此以后，经过更新的

of them accepted Han Yü's theory of the orthodox line of transmission of the *Tao* or Truth, and maintained that they were themselves links in that transmission. Their claim is not without justification, because, as we shall see in this and the following chapters, Neo-Confucianism is indeed the continuation of the idealistic wing of ancient Confucianism, and especially of the mystic tendency of Mencius. That is the reason why these men have been known as the *Tao hsüeh chia* and their philosophy as the *Tao hsüeh*, i.e., the Study of the *Tao* or Truth. The term Neo-Confucianism is a newly coined western equivalent for *Tao hsüeh*.

There are three lines of thought that can be traced as the main sources of Neo-Confucianism. The first, of course, is Confucianism itself. The second is Buddhism, together with Taoism via the medium of Ch'anism, for of all the schools of Buddhism, Ch'anism was the most influential at the time of the formation of Neo-Confucianism. To the Neo-Confucianists, Ch'anism and Buddhism are synonymous terms, and, as stated in the last chapter, in one sense Neo-Confucianism may be said to be the logical development of Ch'anism. Finally, the third is the Taoist religion, of which the cosmological views of the *Yin-Yang* School formed an important element. The cosmology of the Neo-Confucianists is chiefly connected with this line of thought.

These three lines of thought were heterogeneous and even in many respects contradictory. Hence it took time for philosophers to make a unity out of them, especially since this unity was not simply an eclecticism, but a genuine system forming a homogeneous whole. Therefore although the beginning of Neo-Confucianism may be traced back to Han Yü and Li Ao, its system of thought did not become clearly formed until the eleventh century. This was the time when the Sung dynasty (960-1279), which reunited China after a period of confusion following the collapse of the T'ang, was at the height of its splendor and prosperity. The earliest of the Neo-Confucianists were chiefly interested in cosmology.

● Cosmology of Chou Tun-yi

The first cosmological philosopher is Chou Tun-yi, better known as the Master of Lien-hsi (1017-73). He was a native of Tao-chou in the present Hunan province, and in his late years lived on the famous mountain, Lu-shan, the same place where Hui-yüan and Tao-sheng had

儒家都接受韩愈的"道统说",并以继承了道统自诩。他们这样说也并非没有理由,因为在本章后文和以下各章里可以看到:更新了的儒家确实是继承了孔子学派中的理想主义支派,特别是孟子的神秘主义倾向。因此,这些人被称为"道学家",他们的哲学被称为"道学",即研究"道"亦即"真理"的学问。西方曾把宋、明"道学"(亦称为"宋明理学")这种经过更新的儒学称作"新儒学"。(现在,国内外有些学者则称二十世纪的儒学为"新儒学",这是容易混淆的地方。)

宋代经过更新的儒学有三个思想来源。第一个思想来源当然是儒家本身的思想。第二个思想来源是佛家思想、连同经由禅宗的中介而来的道家思想。在更新的儒学形成的时期,佛教各宗派以禅宗为最盛,以致新的儒家认为,禅宗和佛教是同义词。如前所述,就某种意义说,更新的儒学可以认作是禅宗思想合乎逻辑的发展。更新的儒学还有第三个思想来源便是道教,阴阳学家的宇宙论观点在其中占有重要地位。新的儒家所持的宇宙论观点,主要便是由来于此。

这三种思想成分混杂在一起,有不少地方还互相矛盾。当时的哲学家要把这些思想结合,构成一个统一的思想体系,自然需要相当时间。因此,虽然新的儒家,其思想可以上溯到唐代的韩愈和李翱,但它的思想体系明晰形成则要等到十一世纪的宋朝(公元九六〇至一二七九年)。唐代经过鼎盛时期之后,自九世纪后期,经过半个多世纪由混乱走向崩溃,于公元九〇七年灭亡。直到十世纪后半叶,中国才在宋初恢复统一。更新的儒学形成初期,它所关注的主要是宇宙论问题。

● 周敦颐的宇宙论

第一个讲宇宙论的哲学家是周敦颐(公元一〇一七至一〇七三年),以他的别号濂溪先生更为人所知。他是道州(在今湖南省)人,晚年居庐山,也就是本书第二十一章述及慧远和道生讲授佛学

taught Buddhism, as described in chapter twenty-one. Long before his time, some of the religious Taoists had prepared a number of mystic diagrams as graphic portrayals of the esoteric principles by which they believed a properly initiated individual could attain to immortality. Chou Tun-yi is said to have come into possession of one of these diagrams, which he thereupon reinterpreted and modified into a diagram of his own designed to illustrate the process of cosmic evolution. Or rather, he studied and developed the ideas found in certain passages in the "Appendices" of the *Book of Changes*, and used the Taoist diagram by way of illustration. His resulting diagram is called the *T'ai-chi T'u* or *Diagram of the Supreme Ultimate*, and his interpretation of it is called the *T'ai-chi T'u Shuo* or *Explanation of the Diagram of the Supreme Ultimate*. The *Shuo* or *Explanation* can be read quite intelligibly without referring to the diagram itself.

The text of the Explanation reads as follows: "The Ultimateless [*Wu Chi*]! And yet the Supreme Ultimate [*T'ai Chi*]! The Supreme Ultimate through Movement produces the *Yang*. This Movement, having reached its limit, is followed by Quiescence, and by this Quiescence, it produces the *Yin*. When Quiescence has reached its limit, there is a return to Movement. Thus Movement and Quiescence, in alternation, become each the source of the other. The distinction between the *Yin* and *Yang* is determined and the Two Forms [i.e., the *Yin* and *Yang*] stand revealed.

"By the transformations of the *Yang* and the union there with of the *Yin*, Water, Fire, Wood, Metal and Soil are produced. These Five Ethers [*ch'i*, i.e., Elements] become diffused in harmonious order, and the four seasons proceed in their course.

"The Five Elements are the one *Yin* and *Yang*; the *Yin* and *Yang* are the one Supreme Ultimate; and the Supreme Ultimate is fundamentally the Ultimateless. The Five Elements come into being each having its own particular nature.

"The true substance of the Ultimateless and the essence of the Two [Forms] and Five [Elements] unite in mysterious union, so that consolidation ensues. The principle of *Ch'ien* [the trigram symbolizing the *Yang*] becomes the male element, and the principle of *K'un* [the trigram symbolizing the *Yin*] becomes the female element. The Two Ethers [the *Yin* and *Yang*] by their interaction operate to produce all things, and these in their turn produce and reproduce, so that transformation and change continue without end.

"It is man alone, however, who receives these in their highest excellence and hence is the most intelligent [of all beings]. His bodily form thereupon is produced and his spirit develops intelligence and consciousness. The five principles of his nature [the five constant virtues corresponding to the Five Elements] react [to external phenomena],

的地方。早在周敦颐之前，一些道教僧人便已用图像来解说他们秘传的、令人可以长生不老的道术。据说，周敦颐得到了一张这样的图像，他把这张图像改画，用以说明宇宙演进的过程。也可以说，周敦颐从《易大传》的一些段落中得到启发，把其中思想加以发展，而用道教的图录来阐述他的思想。他用以说明自己思想的图像名为"太极图"，他对太极图的说明则被称为《太极图说》，仅读《太极图说》，便足以说明周敦颐的宇宙论思想。

《太极图说》的内容如下：

"无极而太极，太极动而生阳，动极而静，静而生阴，静极复动。一动一静，互为其根；分阴分阳，两仪立焉。

"阳变阴合，而生水、火、木、金、土；五气顺布，四时行焉。

"五行，一阴阳也；阴阳，一太极也。太极，本无极也。五行之生也，各一其性。

"无极之真，二五之精，妙合而凝。'乾道成男，坤道成女。'二气交感，化生万物。万物生生而变化无穷焉。

"唯人也，得其秀而最灵。形既生矣，神发知矣，五性感动

so that the distinction between good and evil emerges and the myriad phenomena of conduct appear. The sage regulates himself by means of the mean, correctness, human-heartedness, and righteousness, and takes Quiescence as the essential. [Chou Tun-yi himself commentes on this: 'Having no desire, he is therefore in the state of Quiescence.'] Thus he establishes himself as the highest standard for mankind...."(*Chou Lien-hsi Chi* or *Collected Works of Chou Tun-yi, chüan* 1.)

In the *Book of Changes*, "Appendix III," it is said: "In the *Yi* there is the Supreme Ultimate, which produces the Two Forms." Chou Tun-yi's *Explanation* is a development of the idea of this passage. Brief though it is, it provides the basic outline for the cosmology of Chu Hsi (1130-1200), one of the greatest, if not the greatest, of the Neo-Confucians, about whom I shall have more to say in chapter twenty-five.

- ● **Method of Spiritual Cultivation**

The ultimate purpose of Buddhism is to teach men how to achieve Buddhahood—a problem that was one of the most vital to the people of that time. Likewise, the ultimate purpose of Neo-confucianism is to teach men how to achieve Confucian Sagehood. The difference between the Buddha of Buddhism and the Sage of Neo-Confucianism is that while the Buddha must promote his spiritual cultivation outside of society and the human world, the Sage must do so within these human bonds. The most important development in Chinese Buddhism was its attempt to depreciate the other-worldliness of original Buddhism. This attempt came close to success when the Ch'an Masters stated that "in carrying water and chopping firewood, therein lies the wonderful *Tao*." But, as I said in the last chapter, they did not push this idea to its logical conclusion by saying that in serving one's family and the state therein also lies the wonderful *Tao*. The reason, of course, is that, once they had said this, their teaching would have ceased to be Buddhism.

For the Neo-Confucianists, too, how to achieve Sagehood is one of the main problems, and Chou Tun-yi's answer is that one should "be quiescent," which he further defines as a state of *wu-yü* or "having no desires." In his second major treatise, the *T'ung Shu* or *General Principles of the Book of Changes*, we find that by *wu-yü* he means much the same as the *wu-wei* (having no effort) and *wu-hsin* (having no mind) of Taoism and Ch'anism. The fact that he uses *wu-yü*, however, instead of these other two terms, shows how he attempts to move away from the other-worldliness of Buddhism. So far as the terms are concerned, the *wu* in *wu-yü* is not so all inclusive as that in *wu-hsin*.

而善恶分，万事出矣。圣人定之以中正仁义而主静（自注：无欲故静），立人极焉。……"（《周濂溪集》卷一）

"易传"的《系辞上》说："易有太极，是生两仪。"周敦颐的《太极图说》便是这个思想的发展。它的文字虽然简短，却已经为后来朱熹的宇宙论提供了基本的轮廓。在更新的儒学大师中，朱熹是最重要的一位，在后面第二十五章里，将对他进一步加以讨论。

● **精神修养的方法**

佛教的最终目的是引人成佛，这是当时人们最关切的一个问题。更新的儒学也有一个最终目的，便是引人成圣。成佛和成圣的区别在于：佛所提倡的修行是在社会之外，而修养成圣则需要在人海之中。与印度佛教相比较，中国佛教最重要的发展便是把原始佛教的出世性质大大减少。禅宗主张"担水砍柴，无非妙道"，正说明这种努力已接近于成功。可是，正如我在上一章末尾所指出的，禅师们并未把他们的思想推到逻辑的极致，而宣告"事父事君，亦是妙道"，其原因是，如果走到这一步，他们的教化便不再是佛教了。

对新的儒家来说，如何成圣同样是他们的一个主要问题。周敦颐对这个问题的回答是"主静"，"主静"的含义就是"无欲"。继《太极图说》之后，周敦颐的第二篇重要著作是《通书》（内容是"《易经》原理"）。在其中，周敦颐解释的"无欲"，和道家所讲的"无为"，以及禅宗对"无心"的解释是差不多的。他不用"无为""无心"的提法，而用"无欲"的提法，正表明他力求区别于佛教的出世性质，因为"无欲"的内涵比较明确，不像"无心"那样无所不包。

In the *T'ung Shu* Chou Tun-yi writes: "*Wu-yü* results in vacuity when in quiescence, and straightforwardness when in movement. Vacuity in quiescence leads to enlightenment, and enlightenment leads to comprehension. [Likewise] straightforwardness in movement leads to impartiality, and impartiality leads to universality. One is almost [a sage when one has] such enlightenment, comprehension, impartiality, and universality." (*Collected Works, chüan* 5.)

The word *yü* used by the Neo-Confucians always means selfish desire or simply selfishness. Sometimes they prefix it by the word *ssu* (selfish), in order to make their meaning clearer. Chou Tun-yi's idea in this passage may be illustrated by a passage from the *Mencius*, often quoted by the Neo-Confucians: "If today men suddenly see a child about to fall into a well, they will without exception experience a feeling of alarm and distress. This will not be as a way whereby to gain the favor of the child's parents, nor whereby they may seek the praise of their neighbors and friends, nor are they so because they dislike the reputation [of being unvirtuous]." (*Mencius*, IIa, 6.)

According to the Neo-Confucians, what Mencius here describes is the natural and spontaneous response of any man when placed in such a situation. Man is by nature fundamentally good. Therefore his innate state is one in which he has no selfish desires in his mind, or as Chou expresses it, one of "vacuity in quiescence." As applied to conduct, it will lead to an immediate impulse to try to save the child, and this sort of intuitive conduct is what Chou calls "straightforwardness in movement." If, however, the man does not act on his first impulse, but pauses instead to think the matter over, he may then consider that the child in distress is a son of his enemy, and therefore he should not save it, or that it is the son of his friend and therefore he should save it. In either case, he is motivated by secondary selfish thoughts and thereby loses both his original state of vacuity in quiescence and the corollary state of straightforwardness in movement.

When the mind lacks all selfish desires it becomes, according to the Neo-Confucianists, like a brilliant mirror, which is always ready to reflect objectively any object that comes before it. The brilliancy of the mirror is compared with the mind's "enlightenment," and its readiness to reflect with the mind's "comprehension." When the mind lacks any selfish desires, its natural response to external stimuli results in actions that are straightforward. Being straightforward, they are impartial, and

在《通书》中，周敦颐写道："无欲则静虚动直。静虚则明，明则通（通达、贯通，"易传"《系辞上》：'一阖一辟谓之变，往来不穷谓之通。'）。动直则公，公则溥（音朴，义广大）。明通公溥，庶矣乎！"（《周濂溪集》卷五）

新的儒家所用的"欲"字，往往指自私的欲望，或直指自私，有时前面冠以"私"字，使意思更加明确。周敦颐这段话的意思可以用新的儒家常常援引的《孟子·公孙丑章句上》一段话来说明，这段话是："今人乍见孺子将入于井，皆有怵惕恻隐之心。非所以内交于孺子之父母也，非所以要誉于乡党朋友也，非恶其声而然也。"

照新的儒家的解释，孟子在这里所说的是任何人处在这情况下的自然反应。人的本性基本上是善的。因此，就人的内心状态来说，他的脑子里本来没有自私的欲望。用周敦颐的话来说，就是"静虚"。从"静虚"状态出发，人处于上述状况下，他的自然冲动便是要立刻抢救这个孩子。这种直觉的行动便是周敦颐所说的"动直"。但是，如果人不是凭自己的本能冲动去行事，而是停下来左右思量，他也许会想，这个孩子的父亲是我的仇人，所以不必理睬这事；或者想，这是我的朋友的孩子，所以我一定要去搭救。无论出于哪一种考虑，他是受自私的再思考所驱使。这样，他便失去了原来的"静虚之心"，也不会有"动直之心"。

照新的儒家的说法，如果人没有私欲，他的内心便如同一面明镜，能够时刻反照镜前的事物。这时，镜子的明亮就如同人内心的清明，时刻准备反照心里洞察的眼前局面。当人心里没有自私的欲望时，它对外界刺激的自然反应是直截了当的，就是所谓"动直"。人在"动直"时，内心是正而又直的，由于大公无私，因此，不会

being impartial, they are carried out without discrimination. Such is their nature of universality.

This is Chou Tun-yi's method of achieving Sagehood, and consists, like that of the Ch'an monks, of living naturally and acting naturally.

- **Cosmology of Shao Yung**

Another cosmological philosopher to be mentioned in this chapter is Shao Yung, known as the Master of Pai-ch'üan (1011-77). He was a native of the present Honan province. Though in a way somewhat different from that of Chou Tun-yi, he too developed his cosmological theory from the *Book of Changes*, and, like Chou, made use of diagrams to illustrate his theory.

In chapter eighteen we have seen that the Han dynasty saw the appearance of a number of *wei shu* or apocrypha, which were supposed to complement the original Six Classics. In the *Yi Wei*, or *Apocryphal Treatise on the Book of Changes*, the theory is developed of the "influence" of each of the sixty-four hexagrams upon a certain period of the year. According to this theory, each of the twelve months is under the jurisdiction of several of the hexagrams, one of which plays a leading role in the affairs of that month and is hence known as its "sovereign hexagram." These sovereign hexagrams are *Fu* ䷗, *Lin* ䷒, *T'ai* ䷊, *Ta Chuang* ䷡, *Chüeh* ䷪, *Ch'ien* ䷀, *Kou* ䷫, *Tun* ䷠, *P'i* ䷋, *Kuan* ䷓, *Po* ䷖, *and K'un* ䷁. The reason for their importance is that they graphically represent the waxing and waning of the *Yang* and *Yin* principles throughout the year.

In these hexagrams, as we have seen in chapter twelve, the unbroken lines represent the *Yang*, which is associated with heat, while the broken lines represent the *Yin*, which is associated with cold. The hexagram *Fu* ䷗, with five broken lines above and one unbroken line below, is the "sovereign hexagram" of that month in which the *Yin* (cold) has reached its apogee and the *Yang* (heat) then begins to reappear. That is the eleventh month of the traditional Chinese calendar, the month in which the winter solstice occurs. The hexagram *Ch'ien* ☰, with its six unbroken lines, is the "sovereign hexagram" of the fourth month, in which the *Yang* is at its apogee. The hexagram *Kou* ☰, with five unbroken lines above and one broken line below, is the "sovereign hexagram" of the fifth month, in which the summer solstice is followed by the rebirth of the *Yin*. And the hexagram *K'un* ☷, with its six broken lines, is the "sovereign hexagram" of the tenth month, in which the *Yin* is at its apogee, just before the rebirth of the *Yang* which follows the winter solstice. The other

畸轻畸重，厚此薄彼。这便是人天生的"公"性，就是所谓"溥"。

这便是周敦颐提出的成圣之方，它接近禅僧所倡导的"率性而活，率性而行"。

● 邵雍的宇宙论

在这里还应提到另一位讲宇宙论的哲学家邵雍（公元一○一一至一○七七年），号康节先生，出生河南。他也从《易经》发展出宇宙论，并且也用图解来说明他的原理。

在本书第十八章里，我们看到汉朝出现一批纬书，假托是六经注疏。在《易纬》里，提出"卦气说"，主张六十四卦中每一卦，都影响每年的一段时候。按照"卦气说"，一年十二个月，每个月都处于几个卦象的统治之下，其中有一卦是当月的"主卦"，因此，全年有十二"主卦"，它们是：复䷗，临䷒，泰䷊，大壮䷡，夬䷪，乾䷀，姤䷫，遁䷠，否䷋，观䷓，剥䷖，坤䷁。它们之所以重要是因为从中反映了一年里阴阳二气的消长。

在前面第十二章里曾经讲过，在卦象中，直线贯底代表阳，与热相联；直线中断代表阴，与寒冷相联。在复卦䷗中，一爻为阳，随后五爻都是阴，表明寒气已到极盛，阴极而阳生，这是中国阴历十一月的主卦，冬至就在此月。再看乾卦，六爻都是阳☰，阳极而阴生，是阴历四月的主卦。继它之后的姤卦☴，一爻为阴，以上五爻为阳，表明夏至以后阴气再来，这是阴历五月的主卦。再看坤卦☷，六爻都是阴，表明阴气盛极，下个月就冬至而阳生。其他各卦

hexagrams indicate the intermediate stages in the waxing and waning of the *Yin* and *Yang*.

The twelve hexagrams in *toto* constitute a cycle. After the influence of the *Yin* has reached its apogee, that of the *Yang* appears at the very bottom of the following hexagram. Rising upward, it becomes steadily greater month by month and hexagram by hexagram, until it reaches its apogee. Then the *Yin* again appears at the bottom of the following hexagram, and grows in its turn until it too reigns supreme. It is followed in turn by the reborn *Yang*, and thus the cycle of the year and of the hexagrams begins again. Such is the inevitable course of nature.

It is to be noticed that Shao Yung's theory of the universe gives further illumination to the theory of the twelve sovereign hexagrams. As in the case of Chou Tun-yi, he deduces his system from a statement in "Appendix III" of the *Book of Changes* which reads: "In the *Yi* there is the Supreme Ultimate. The Supreme Ultimate produces the Two Forms. The Two Forms produce the Four Emblems, and the Four Emblems produce the eight trigrams." To illustrate this process, Shao Yung made a diagram as follows:

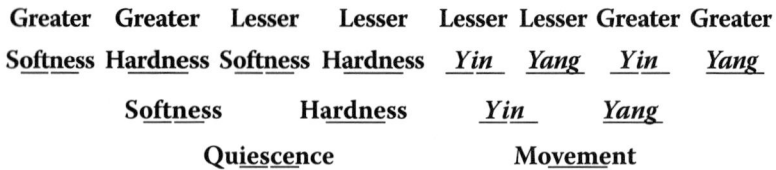

Greater	Greater	Lesser	Lesser	Lesser	Lesser	Greater	Greater
Softness	Hardness	Softness	Hardness	*Yin*	*Yang*	*Yin*	*Yang*
	Softness		Hardness		*Yin*		*Yang*
		Quiescence			Movement		

The first or lower tier of this diagram shows the Two Forms, which, in Shao Yung's system, are not the *Yin* and *Yang* but Movement and Quiescence. The second tier, looked at in conjunction with the first, shows the Four Emblems. For instance, by combining the unbroken line beneath *Yang* in the middle tier, with the unbroken line beneath Movement below, we obtain two unbroken lines which are the emblem of the *Yang*. That is to say, the *Yang* is not, for Shao Yung, represented by a single unbroken line —, but by two unbroken lines ⚌. Likewise, by combining the broken line beneath *Yin* in the central tier with the unbroken line beneath Movement below, we obtain one broken line above and one unbroken line below, which are the emblem of *Yin*. That is to say, the emblem of the *Yin* is not - - but ⚏.

In the same way, the third or highest tier looked at in conjunction with both the central and lower tier, represents the eight trigrams. For instance, by combining the unbroken line beneath Greater *Yang* above with the unbroken line beneath *Yang* in the middle and the unbroken line beneath Movement below, we obtain a combination of three unbroken

则是表示阴阳消长的中间阶段。

这十二卦合在一起，表明阴阳消长，周而复始。阴极则阳生，此后阳气逐月上升，以至于极盛；这时，阴气再现，继以阴气逐月上升。阴气升到极点，阳气再现。于是，新的阴阳消长的循环又再开始，这是自然界不可避免的往复进程。

这里需要注意的一点是，邵雍的宇宙论使得十二个主卦象的理论更加清楚了。邵雍也如同周敦颐那样，从"易传"的《系辞上》的一段话开始，这段话说："易有太极，是生两仪，两仪生四象，四象生八卦，八卦定吉凶，吉凶生大业。"为阐明这个过程，邵雍画出下图：

太柔	太刚	少柔	少刚	少阴	少阳	太阴	太阳
	柔		刚		阴		阳
		静			动		

这个图的最下面第一层是两仪，在邵雍的体系中，它们不是阴阳，而是动静。上到第二层与第一层相联而得四象。如果把第二层的"阳"和第一层的"动"结合，乃是两根横贯到底的直线，象征"阳"。这就是说，在邵雍看来，四象中，"阳"不是以一根直线 — 来代表，而是以两根直线 ⚌ 来代表。依同例，如果把第二层的"阴"和第一层的"动"结合，所得到的是四象中的"阴"，它的符号不是一根中断的线 - -，而是两根线 ⚏。

依同例，把第三层和第一、二层联结起来看，也构成八卦。例中，把太阳下的乾爻与第二层的"阳"和第一层的"动"联起来，

lines, which is the trigram for *Ch'ien*, ☰. Likewise, by combining the broken line beneath Greater *Yin* above with the unbroken line beneath *Yang* in the middle and the unbroken line beneath Movement below, we obtain the combination of one broken line above and two unbroken lines below, which is the trigram for *Tui*, ☱. And still again, by combining the unbroken line beneath Lesser *Yang* above with the broken line beneath *Yin* in the middle and the unbroken line beneath Movement below, we obtain the trigram for *Li*, ☲. By following the same process through the other combinations, we obtain the entire eight trigrams in the following sequence: *Ch'ien* ☰, *Tui* ☱, *Li* ☲, *Chen* ☳, *Sun* ☴, *K'an* ☵, *Ken* ☶, and *K'un* ☷. Each of these trigrams represents a certain principle or influence.

The materialization of these principles results in Heaven, Earth, and all things of the universe. As Shao Yung says: "Heaven is produced from Movement and Earth from Quiescence. The alternating interplay of Movement and Quiescence gives utmost development to the course of Heaven and Earth. At the first appearance of Movement, the *Yang* is produced, and this Movement having reached its apogee, the *Yin* is then produced. The alternating interplay of the *Yang* and *Yin* gives utmost development to the functioning aspect of Heaven. With the first appearance of Quiescence, Softness is produced, and this Quiescence having reached its apogee, Hardness is then produced. The alternating interplay of Hardness and Softness gives utmost development to the functioning aspect of Earth."[1] The terms Hardness and Softness are, like the others, borrowed by Shao Yung from "Appendix III" of the *Book of Changes*, which says: "The Way of Heaven is established with the *Yin* and *Yang*. The Way of Earth is established with Softness and Hardness. The Way of Man is established with human-heartedness and righteousness."

Shao Yung writes further: "The Greater *Yang* constitutes the sun, the Greater *Yin* the moon, the Lesser *Yang* the stars, the Lesser *Yin* the zodiacal spaces. The interplay of the sun, moon, stars, and zodiacal spaces gives utmost development to the substance of Heaven. The Greater

Softness constitutes water, the Greater Hardness fire, the Lesser Softness soil, and the Lesser Hardness stone. The interplay of water, fire, soil, and stone gives utmost development to the substance of Earth." (*Ibid*.)

This is Shao Yung's theory of the origin of the universe, deduced strictly from his diagram. In this diagram, the Supreme Ultimate itself is not actually shown, but it is understood as being symbolized by the empty space beneath the first tier of the diagram. Shao Yung writes: "The Supreme Ultimate is a Unity which does not move. It produces a Duality, and this Duality is spirituality.... Spirituality produces numbers, the numbers produce emblems, and the emblems produce implements [i.e., individual things]." (*Ibid*., ch. 12b.) These numbers and emblems are illustrated in the diagram.

便构成乾卦☰。如果把第三层的"太阴"与第二层的"阳"和第一层的"动"联结起来，便得到兑卦☱。把第三层的"少阳"与第二层的"阴"和第一层的"动"联结起来，这就是离卦☲。按同样的方法可以得到全部八卦，其顺序是：乾☰，兑☱，离☲，震☳，巽☴，坎☵，艮☶，坤☷。八个卦象各代表一定的原则和影响力。

这些原则便具体化为天地和宇宙万物。邵雍说："天生于动者也，地生于静者也，一动一静交而天地之道尽之矣；动之始则阳生焉，动之极则阴生焉，一阴一阳交而天之用尽之矣；静之始则柔生焉，静之极则刚生焉，一刚一柔交而地之用尽之矣。"（《皇极经世·观物内篇》）邵雍所用的"刚"和"柔"，也像他用的其他术语一样，是来自"易传"，其上是这样说的："立天之道，曰阴与阳；立地之道，曰柔与刚；立人之道，曰仁与义。"（《说卦传》）

邵雍继续写道："太阳为日，太阴为月；少阳为星，少阴为辰，日月星辰交而天之体尽之矣。……太柔为水，太刚为火；少柔为土，少刚为石，水火土石交而地之体尽之矣。"（《皇极经世·观物内篇》）

这是邵雍关于宇宙来源的理论，完全是从他的图中演化出来的。在他的图里，并没有把太极画出来，但是看的人可以领会到，太极是在第一层以下的空白之中。对此，邵雍写道："太极一也，不动；生二，二则神也。神生数，数生象，象生器。"（《皇极经世·观物外篇》）这些数和象都在图中表现出来。

● **Law of the Evolution of Things**

By adding a fourth, fifth, and sixth tier to the above diagram, and following the same procedure of combination that was used there, we arrive at a diagram in which all the sixty-four hexagrams (derived from combination of the eight primary trigrams) are shown. If this diagram is then cut into two equal halves, each of which is bent into a half circle, and if the two half circles are then joined together, we have another of Shao's diagrams, known as "the circular diagram of the sixty-four hexagrams."

Upon examining this diagram (here, for the sake of simplicity, reduced from sixty-four to the twelve "sovereign hexagrams"), we see that these twelve appear in it in their proper sequence as follows (looking from the center, and progressing clockwise from above):

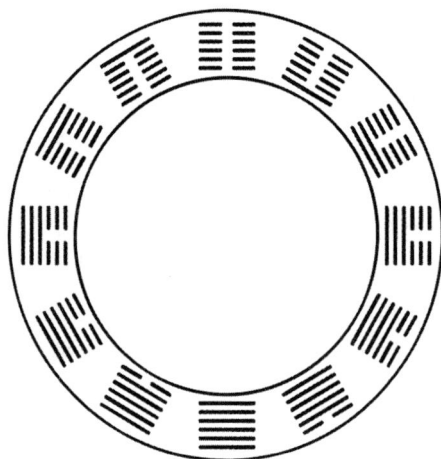

This sequence is automatically arrived at by what is called "the method of doubling," because, as we have seen, the number of emblems in each tier in the diagram is always double that of the tier immediately below, so that combination of all six tiers results in the sixty-four hexagrams at the top. This simple progression makes the diagram appear as both something natural and at the same time mysterious. As a result, it was hailed by most of the Neo-Confucianists as one of the greatest discoveries of Shao Yung, in which could be found the universal law governing the evolution of all things, and the key to the mystery of the universe.

This law not only applies to the alternation of the seasons throughout the year, but also to the alternation of day and night every twenty-four hours. According to Shao Yung and the other Neo-Confucianists, the

● 事物演化的规律

在上图的基础上，再加上第四、第五、第六层，还是采用上述的联结办法，就可以从最初的八卦互相联结中演化出全部六十四卦。如果把包括六十四卦的图切为两半，每半弯成半圆；再把两个半圆合在一起，就构成邵雍的另一幅圆图，名为《六十四卦圆图方位图》。

如果我们考察这个圆图（为简化起见，把六十四卦象简化为十二主卦象），就会看到这十二个主卦象的顺序如下（处在中心，按顺时针方向看）：

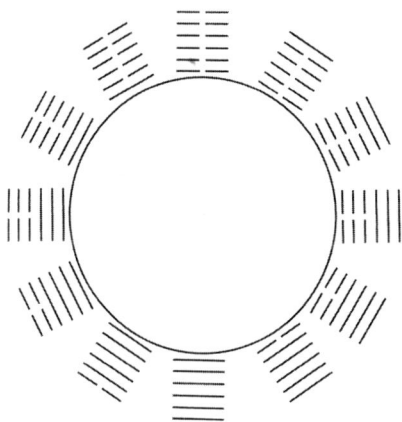

这个顺序可用所谓"加一倍法"自动显现出来。因为在圆图里，每一层符号的数目比在它之下的一层，数目要多一倍。因此，最上层、即第六层的符号数目刚好是六十四，六层就组成六十四卦。这个简单的级数既十分自然，又显得十分奥秘。在更新的儒家中间，绝大多数都认为这是邵雍的一大发现，从中可以找到万物演化的普遍规律和揭示宇宙奥秘的钥匙。

这个规律不仅能够说明一年四季的变化，还能够说明一天十二时辰的昼夜交替。按照邵雍和其他新的儒家的理论，阴可以解释为

Yin can be interpreted as merely the negation of the *Yang*. Hence, if the *Yang* is the constructive force of the universe, the *Yin* is its destructive principle. Interpreting the *Yin* and *Yang* in this sense, the law represented by the diagram indicates the way in which all things of the universe go through phases of construction and destruction. Thus, the first or lowest line of the hexagram *Fu* ䷗ shows the beginning of the phase of construction, and in hexagram *Ch'ien* ䷀ we find the completion of this phase. The first line of the hexagram *Kou* ䷫ shows the beginning of the phase of destruction, and in hexagram *K'un* ䷁ this phase is completed. In this way the diagram graphically illustrates the universal law that everything involves its own negation, a principle that was stressed both by Lao Tzu and the "Appendices" of the *Book of Changes*.

The world as a whole is no exception to this universal law. Thus Shao Yung maintains that with the first line of the hexagram *Fu*, the world comes into existence. With the hexagram *T'ai*, the individual things that belong to it begin to be produced. Mankind then appears, and with the hexagram *Ch'ien* the golden age of civilization is reached. There follows a process of continuous decay, until with the hexagram *Po* all individual things disintegrate, and with the hexagram *K'un* the whole world ceases to be. Thereupon another world begins with the first line of the recurring hexagram *Fu*, and the whole process is repeated. Each world which is thus created and destroyed has a duration of 129, 600 years.

Shao Yung's major work is the *Huang-chi Ching-shih*, which is an elaborate chronological diagram of our existing world. According to its chronology, the golden age of our world has already passed away. It was the age of Yao, the traditional philosopher king of China who reputedly ruled in the twenty-fourth century B.C. We today are now in an age corresponding to the hexagram *Po*, the time of the beginning of decline of all things. As we have seen in chapter fourteen, most Chinese philosophers have considered the process of history to be one of continuous degeneration, in which everything of the present falls short of the ideal past. Shao Yung's theory gives this view a metaphysical justification.

The theory that everything involves its own negation sounds Hegelian. But according to Hegel, when a thing is negated, a new thing commences on a higher level, whereas according to Lao Tzu and the "Appendices" of the *Book of Changes*, when a thing is negated, the new thing simply repeats the old. This is a philosophy characteristic of an agrarian people, as I pointed out in chapter two.

仅是阳的否定。因此，如果阳是宇宙中的积极建设性力量，阴便是宇宙中的消极破坏性力量。从这样的角度来看阴阳原理，圆图显示的演化规律便可用以说明宇宙万物的生灭过程。这样来看复卦䷗，它的第一爻表明生的开端，到乾卦䷀，表明生的完成，然后，姤卦䷫，表明处于灭的开始；到坤卦䷁，表明灭的完成。这个圆图形象地表明了"一切事物都包含有对它自身的否定"这样一个普遍定律。这是老子和"易传"都强调的一个原理。

整个世界也逃不脱这个普遍法则。邵雍由此认为，复卦的初爻表明世界的出现；演进到泰卦，表明个体事物在世界上出现；发展到乾卦，人类文明到达了顶峰。此后则是不断地没落，到剥卦，表明一切个体事物的分崩离析；到坤卦，表明世界不复存在。在此之后，另一个世界，如同复卦的初爻那样开始出现，世界的生灭过程又再重演一遍。世界由生到灭的过程所经历的时间是十二万九千六百年。

在邵雍的主要著作《皇极经世》中有我们这个世界的详细年表。按照这个年表，现存世界的黄金时代——尧的时代——已经过去。在人们的憧憬里，尧是柏拉图描绘的哲学家—国王，他生活于公元前二十四世纪。至于现今的世界，相当于剥卦，这是万物没落的开始。在第十四章里我们曾谈到，中国的许多哲学家都持有一种历史退化论思想，认为理想世界在过去，现实世界里样样不如过去。邵雍的理论正好为这种历史退化思想提供了形而上学的根据。

认为一切事物都包含有对它自身的否定，这个看法很有点黑格尔的味道。但是按照黑格尔的理论，当一个事物被否定时，另一个新生的事物在更高的层面上开始了。按照老子和"易传"的思想，当一个事物被否定时，另一个事物又重复过去的旧事物。这是农业社会的思想，在本书第二章里，已经对它谈过了。

● Cosmology of Chang Tsai

The third cosmological philosopher to be mentioned in this chapter is Chang Tsai, known as the Master of Heng-ch'ü (1020-77). He was a native of the present Shensi province. He too, though from yet another point of view, developed a cosmological theory based on the "Appendices" of the *Book of Changes*. In this he especially emphasized the idea of *Ch'i*, a concept which became more and more important in the cosmological and metaphysical theories of the later Neo-Confucianists. The word *ch'i* literally means gas or ether. In Neo-Confucianism its meaning is sometimes more abstract and sometimes more concrete, according to the different systems of the particular philosophers. When its meaning is more abstract, it approaches the concept of matter, as found in the philosophy of Plato and Aristotle, in contrast to the Platonic Idea or the Aristotelian Form. In this sense, it means the primary undifferentiated material out of which all individual things are formed. When, however, its meaning is concrete, it means the physical matter that makes up all existing individual things. It is in this concrete sense that Chang Tsai speaks of *Ch'i*.

Chang Tsai, like his predecessors, bases his cosmological theory on the passage in "Appendix III" of the *Book of Changes* that states: "In the *Yi* there is the Supreme Ultimate which produces the Two Forms [i.e., the *Yin* and *Yang*]." For him, however, the Supreme Ultimate is nothing other than the *Ch'i*. In his main work, the *Cheng Meng* or *Correct Discipline for Beginners*, he writes: "The Great Harmony is known as the *Tao* [by which he here means the Supreme Ultimate]. Because in it there are interacting qualities of floating and sinking, rising and falling, movement and quiescence, therefore there appear in it the beginnings of the emanating forces which agitate one another, overcome or are overcome by one another, and contract or expand, one with regard to the other." (*Chang-tzu Ch'üan-shu* or *Collected Works of the Master Chang, chüan* 2.)

The Great Harmony is a name for the *Ch'i* in its entirety, which Chang Tsai also describes as "wandering air." (*Ibid.*) The qualities of floating, rising, and movement are those of the *Yang*, while those of sinking, falling, and quiescence are those of the *Yin*. The *Ch'i*, when influenced by the *Yang* qualities, floats and rises, while when influenced by the *Yin* qualities, it sinks and falls. As a result the *Ch'i* is constantly either

● 张载的宇宙论

这一章里要提到的第三位宇宙论哲学家是陕西的张载（公元一○二○至一○七七年），别号横渠先生。他同样是从"易传"里发展出宇宙论，但所持的却是另一种观点。他特别强调"气"，这个"气"的观念在后来的更新的儒家们的宇宙论和形而上学思想里，越来越居于重要的地位。"气"的字义本来是指和固体、液体相对应的一种物质状态，而更新的儒学家们，由于各自的理论体系不同，使用这个字时，有时比此更抽象，有时又比此更具体。在用以表示更抽象的含义时，它的含义接近于柏拉图和亚里士多德哲学中的"质料"（Matter），柏拉图用以和他所说的"理念"（Idea）相区别，亚里士多德则用以和他所说的"形式"（Form）相区别。在这个意义上，"气"是一种原始混沌的质料，各种个体的事物都是由它而出。当"气"被用以表达更具体的含义时，它所指的是构成个体事物的物质性质料。张载使用"气"这个概念，便是就它的具体含义来说的。

张载也像上述的前人一样，以"易传"的《系辞上》中一段话作为他的宇宙论的根据，这段话是："易有太极，是生两仪（"两仪"即阴阳）。"但是，他认为，太极就是"气"。在他的主要著作《正蒙》开头，张载写道："太和所谓道（指太极），中涵浮沉、升降，动静相感之性，是生氤氲、相荡、胜负、屈伸之始。"（《正蒙太和篇》，《张子全书》卷二）道是指宇宙这个无始无终、不息不休的流行过程。这个过程，照张载说，就是"气"。"气"是动的，意味矛盾和矛盾的统一，就是"太和"，因此，"太和"是"气"的全体之名。张载又用"游气"来称"气"，以表明"气"内部阴阳两端循环不已，其中的"浮"、"升"、"动"是阳性的，"沉"、"降"、"静"是阴性的。气受到阳性的影响时，便浮、升、动，受到阴性的影响时，

condensing or dispersing. Its condensation results in the formation of concrete things; its dispersion results in the dissolution of these same things.

In the *Cheng Meng,* Chang Tsai writes: "When the *Ch'i* condenses, its visibility becomes apparent so that there are then the shapes [of individual things]. When it disperses, its visibility is no longer apparent and there are no shapes. At the time of its condensation, can one say otherwise than that this is but temporary? But at the time of its dispersing, can one hastily say that it is then non-existent?" (*Ibid.*) Thus Chang Tsai tries to get away from the Taoist and Buddhist idea of *Wu* (Non-being). He says: "If one knows the Void is the *Ch'i,* one knows that there is no *Wu.*" The Void is not really an absolute vacuum; it is simply the *Ch'i* in its state of dispersion in which it is no longer visible.

One particularly famous passage of the *Cheng Meng* has become known as the *Hsi Ming* or "Western Inscription," because it was separately inscribed on the western wall of Chang Tsai's study. In this passage Chang maintains that since all things in the universe are constituted of one and the same *Ch'i,* therefore men and all other things are but part of one great body. We should serve *Ch'ien* and *K'un* (by which Chang means Heaven and Earth) as we do our own parents, and regard all men as we do our brothers. We should extend the virtue of filial piety and practice it through service to the universal parents. Yet, no extraordinary acts are needed for this service. Every moral activity, if one can understand it, is an activity that serves the universal parents. If, for instance, one loves other men simply because they are members of the same society as one's own, then one is doing his social duty and is serving society. But if one loves them not merely because they are members of the same society, but also because they are children of the universal parents, then by loving them one not only serves society, but at the same time serves the parents of the universe as a whole. The passage concludes with the saying: "In life I follow and serve [the universal parents], and when death comes, I rest." (*Ibid.*)

This essay has been greatly admired by later Neo Confucianists, because it clearly distinguished the Confucian attitude towards life from that of Buddhism and of Taoist philosophy and religion. Chang Tsai writes elsewhere: "The Great Void [i.e., the Great Harmony, the *Tao*] cannot but consist of *Ch'i*; this *Ch'i* cannot but condense to form all things; and these things cannot but become dispersed so as to form [once more] the Great Void. The perpetuation of these movements in a cycle is inevitable and thus spontaneous." (*Ibid. chüan* 2.)

便沉、降、静。因此，气不断或聚或散，气聚的时候，便从中生成具体的个别事物；气散的时候，这些事物便分崩离析而朽坏。

在《正蒙太和篇》中，张载写道："气聚，则离明得施而有形；不聚，则离明不得施而无形。方其聚也，安得不谓之客；方其散也，安得遽谓之无？！"（同上）张载正是这样，力拒道家和佛家以有为"无"的思想。他说："知太虚即气，即无无。"（"太虚"是指"气"的本体，是宇宙结构，"太和"是指宇宙的精神面貌。）太虚不是绝对真空，它只是宇宙处于气散的状况，而人凭肉眼看不见而已。

《正蒙》中有一篇《西铭》，特别著名，因为这是张载贴在书斋西墙的一篇座右铭。在《西铭》里，张载认为，宇宙万物都来自同一个"气"，因此，世人和万物都是一体，人应当服侍乾坤（张载所说的"乾坤"，含义就是"天地"）就如同服侍父母一样，应当看待世人就如同自己的兄弟一样。人对父母应当尽孝道，对宇宙这个扩大的父母，同样应当尽孝道。在观念上扩大，但并不需要为此做什么额外、特殊的事情，人为社会大众所做的事情（也就是"立德"），都同时是为宇宙父母所做的事情。例如，当一个人出自对别人的同胞之心而爱人，这时他所做的就是服务社会，尽一己对社会的义务。而如果一个人爱别人，不仅因为别人是社会同胞，还因为都是宇宙父母的儿女，这时，人所做的就不仅是服务社会，而是服侍宇宙父母了。《西铭》末尾说：只要活着，我就追随、服侍宇宙父母，到死亡来临，我就安息。

后来的新儒家对张载的《西铭》都十分赞赏，因为它把儒家对人生的态度和佛教、道家对人生的态度区分开来。张载在《正蒙太和篇》中还写道："太虚不能无气，气不能不聚而为万物，万物不能不散而为太虚。循是出入，是皆不得已而然也。"（《张子全书》卷二）

The sage is one who fully understands this course. Therefore, he neither tries to be outside it, as do the Buddhists, who seek to break the chain of causation and thus bring life to an end; nor does he try to prolong his life, as do the religious Taoists, who seek to nurture their body and thus remain as long as possible within the human sphere. The sage, because he understands the nature of the universe, therefore knows that "life entails no gain nor death any loss." (*Ibid.*) Hence he simply tries to live a normal life. In life he does what his duty as a member of society and as a member of the universe requires him to do, and when death comes, he "rests."

He does what every man should do, but because of his understanding, what he does acquires new significance. The Neo-Confucianists developed a point of view from which all the moral activities valued by the Confucianists acquire a further value that is super-moral. They all have in them that quality that the Ch'anists called the wonderful *Tao*. It is in this sense that Neo-Confucianism is actually a further development of Ch'anism.

圣人就是对万事万物的过程充分理解的人。因此，他不像佛教徒那样，自外于万事万物的流程，企图藉此打断因果锁链，结束生命的自然流程。他也不像道教徒那样，企图以"养生"来延长生命，久留于人世。圣人既洞察宇宙的动的本性，因此，知道"生无所得"，"死无所丧"（《正蒙诚明篇》，《张子全书》卷三）；因此，安然地过一个寻常人的生活，"存，吾顺事；没，吾宁也"。（活着，便尽一个社会成员、一个宇宙成员应尽的责任；死亡来临，便安息了。）

圣人所做的，无非是每个人应该做的事。但是因为他理解宇宙万事万物的流程，因此他所做的具有一种新的意义。新的儒家对先秦儒家所重视的"立德"，又赋予它一层新的、超越道德的价值。这些新的儒家都具有禅僧所说的"妙道"。就这一点说，这种更新的儒学实际上成为禅学的进一步发展。

㉔ NEO-CONFUCIANISM: THE BEGINNING OF THE TWO SCHOOLS

Neo-confucianism came to be divided into two main schools, which, by happy coincidence, were initiated by two brothers, known as the two Ch'eng Masters. Ch'eng Yi (1033-1108), the younger brother, initiated a school which was completed by Chu Hsi (1130-1200) and was known as the Ch'eng-Chu school or *Li hsüeh* (School of Laws or Principles). Ch'eng Hao (1032-1085), the elder brother, initiated another school which was continued by Lu Chiu-yüan(1139-1193) and completed by Wang Shou-jen (1472-1528), and was known as the Lu-Wang school or *Hsin hsüeh*(School of Mind). The full significance of the difference between the two schools was not recognized at the time of the two Ch'eng Masters themselves, but Chu Hsi and Lu Chiu-yüan began a great controversy which has been carried on until the present day.

As we shall see in the following chapters, the main issue between the two groups was really one of fundamental philosophical importance. In terms of Western philosophy, it was one as to whether the laws of nature are or are not legislated by the mind or Mind. That has been the issue between Platonic realism and Kantian idealism, and may be said to be *the* issue in metaphysics. If it were solved, there would not be much other controversy left. In this chapter I am not going to discuss this issue in detail, but only to suggest its beginnings in the history of Chinese philosophy.

• Ch'eng Hao's Idea of *Jen*

The Ch'eng brothers were natives of the present Honan province. The elder of them, Ch'eng Hao, was known as Master Ming-tao, and the younger, Ch'eng Yi, as the Master of Yi-ch'uan. Their father was a friend of Chou Tun-yi and the cousin of Chang Tsai. Hence in their youth the

Ch'eng brothers received some teaching from Chou Tun-yi, and later they constantly held discussions with Chang Tsai. Furthermore, they lived not far from Shao Yung, with whom they often met. The close contact between these five philosophers was certainly a very happy incident in the history of Chinese philosophy.

贰拾肆 更新的儒家：两个学派的开端

进入北宋到公元十一世纪下半叶，更新的儒家分成两个不同的学派，分别以周敦颐的两个学生，程颢、程颐两兄弟为创始人，他们被称为"二程"。这真是一种历史的可喜巧合。弟弟程颐（公元一〇三三至一一〇八年）创立了自己的学派，由朱熹（公元一一三〇至一二〇〇年）集大成，史称"程朱学派"或"理学"。哥哥程颢（公元一〇三二至一〇八五年）创立了另一个学派，由陆象山（公元一一三九至一一九三年）和王守仁（号阳明，公元一四七二至一五二八年）完成，史称"陆王学派"或"心学"。程氏兄弟并未意识到他们创立的两个不同学派具有何等重要的意义，但是由朱熹和陆象山开始的学术争论，直到今天也仍然在进行着。

在以下各章里，我们将会看到，这两个学派所争论的主要问题乃是哲学的根本问题。用西方哲学的语言来说，他们所争论的问题是：自然中的规律，是否人头脑中的臆造，或宇宙的心的创作？这是柏拉图学派的实在论和康德学派的观念论历来争论的中心问题，可以说，也是形而上学的中心问题。这个问题如果解决了，剩下的争论就不多了。在这一章里，我不准备对这个问题进行详尽的讨论，只是指出中国哲学史上对它进行探讨的开端。

● 程颢对"仁"的认识

程氏兄弟是河南人。年长的程颢，号明道，世称"明道先生"；他的弟弟程颐，号伊川，世称"伊川先生"。他们的父亲和周敦颐是朋友，和张载是表兄弟。因此，程氏兄弟在年轻时曾受到周敦颐的教诲，后来又常和张载进行学术探讨。还有，他们和邵雍住处相隔不远，可以经常相聚。这五位哲学家之间的密切往还，成为中国哲学史上的一段美谈。

Ch'eng Hao greatly admired Chang Tsai's *Hsi Ming* or "Western Inscription," because its central theme of the oneness of all things is also the main idea in his philosophy. According to him, oneness with all things is the main characteristic of the virtue of *jen* (human-heartedness). He says: "The learner needs first to comprehend *jen*. The man of *jen* is undifferentiably one with all things. Righteousness, propriety, wisdom, and good faith, all these are *jen*. Get to comprehend this truth and cultivate it with sincerity and attentiveness, that is all that is required.... The *Tao* has nothing that stands in contrast to it; even the word great is inadequate to express it. The function of Heaven and Earth is our function. Mencius said that all things are complete within us. We must reflect and realize that this is really so. Then it is a source of immense joy. If we reflect and do not realize that it is really so, then there are still two things [the self and not-self] that stand in contrast with each other. Even if we try to unite the self and not-self, we still do not form a unity, and so how can there then be joy? In the 'Correcting of the Ignorant' [another name for Chang Tsai's *Hsi Ming*] there is a perfect statement of this unity. If we cultivate ourselves with this idea, there is nothing further required to be done. We must do something, and never stop and never forget, yet never help to grow, doing it without the slightest effort. This is the way of spiritual cultivation." (*Erh Ch'eng Yi-shu* or *Literary Remains of the Two Ch'engs, chüan* 24.)

In chapter seven I have fully discussed the statement of Mencius referred to by Ch'eng Hao in the above quotation. One must do something, but "never help to grow"; this is Mencius' method for cultivating the Great Morale, a method which was greatly admired by the Neo-Confucianists. According to Ch'eng Hao, one must first understand the principle that one is originally one with all things. Then all one needs to do is to keep this in mind and act in accordance with it sincerely and attentively. Through the accumulation of such practices, one will really come to feel that one is one with all things. The statement that one must act in accordance with this principle sincerely and attentively means that there is something one must do. There must, however, be no artificial striving to achieve the unity. In this sense, one must be "without the slightest effort."

The difference between Ch'eng Hao and Mencius is that the former gives to *jen* a much more metaphysical interpretation than does the latter. "Appendix III" of the *Book of Changes* contains the statement: "The supreme virtue of Heaven and Earth is *sheng*." The word *sheng* here may mean simply production or to produce; it may also mean life or to give

程颢十分称许张载的《西铭》，因为它所揭示的"万物一体"这个主题也是程颢哲学的中心。程颢认为，人达到视自己与万物一体正是"仁"的主要特征。他说："学者须先识仁。仁者，浑然与物同体。义、礼、知、信皆仁也。识得此理，以诚敬存之而已，不须防检，不须穷索。……此道与物无对，大不足以名之，天地之用皆我之用。孟子言'万物皆备于我'，须反身而诚，乃为大乐。若反身未诚，则犹是二物有对，以己合彼，终未有之，又安得乐？《订顽》（即《西铭》。——引者注）意思乃备言此体。以此意存之，更有何事？'必有事焉而勿正，心勿忘，勿助长'，未尝致纤毫之力，此其存之之道。"（《河南程氏遗书》卷二上）

在本书第七章里，我曾就程颢所引孟子说的一段话加以讨论。人应当有所为（"必有事焉"），但不要"揠苗助长"。这是孟子养其浩然之气的方法。新的儒家十分推崇这段话。程颢更认为，做人的第一要务就是要懂得万物一体的道理；然后，牢记这一点，并且真诚用心去做，这就够了。人若日积月累地这样下工夫，就会真正感觉到自己和万物融为一体。程颢所讲的"真诚用心去做"，是提醒人要下工夫，但又不是矫揉造作。这便是程颢所说的"心勿忘，勿助长。未尝致纤毫之力，此其存之之道"。

程颢和孟子的区别在于：程颢对"仁"的诠释带有更多形而上学的意味。"易传"《系辞下》有这样一句话："天地之大德曰生。"这里的"生"字，可以理解为"产生"，也可以理解为"赋予生命"。

birth to life. In chapter fifteen I translated *sheng* as to produce, because that seems to be the meaning that best harmonizes with the ideas of the "Appendices." But according to Ch'eng Hao and other Neo-Confucianists, *sheng* really means life or to give birth to life. According to them there is a tendency toward life in all things, and this tendency constitutes the *jen* of Heaven and Earth.

It so happens that the expression "not-*jen*" is a technical term for paralysis in Chinese medicine. Ch'eng Hao says: "The doctor describes the paralysis of a man's arms or legs as not-*jen*; this is a very good description [of the disease]. The man of *jen* takes Heaven and Earth as being one with himself. To him there is nothing that is not himself. Having recognized them as himself, what cannot he do for them? If there is no such relationship with the self, it follows that there is no connection between the self and others. If the hand or foot are not-*jen*, it means that the *ch'i* [vital force] is not circulating freely and the parts [of the body] are not connected with each other."(*Ibid., chüan* 2a.)

Thus, according to Ch'eng Hao, metaphysically there is an inner connection between all things. What Mencius called the "feeling of commiseration" or the "unbearing mind" is simply an expression of this connection between ourselves and other things. It often happens, however, that our "unbearing mind" is obscured by selfishness, or, to use the Neo-Confucian term, by selfish desires or simply desires. Hence the original unity is lost. What is necessary is simply to remember that originally there is a oneness between oneself and all things, and to act accordingly with sincerity and attentiveness. In this way the original unity will be restored in due course. Such is the general idea of the philosophy of Ch'eng Hao, which Lu Chiu-yüan and Wang Shou-jen later developed in detail.

● Origin of the Ch'eng-Chu Idea of *Li*

In chapter eight we have seen that already in early times Kung-sun Lung made clear the distinction between universals and things. He insisted that whiteness is whiteness even though nothing is in itself white in the world. It would seem that he had some idea of the Platonic distinction of the two worlds, the eternal and the temporal, the intelligible and the visible. This idea was not developed by later philosophers, however, and the philosophy of the School of Names did not become a main current in Chinese thought. On the contrary, this thought moved in another direction, and it took more than one thousand years for Chinese

在本书第十五章里，我把"生"解释为"产生"，因为那样解释和"易传"的全部思想可以更加和谐。但是在程颢和其他新的儒家的思想里，"生"的含义主要是"生命"或"赋予生命"。他们认为，万物本性天然是向着生命，这便是天地之仁。

在中国传统医学里，把人身体麻痹称为"不仁"。程颢说："医书言手足痿痹为不仁，此言最善名状。仁者，以天地万物为一体，莫非己也。认得为己，何所不至？若不有诸己，自不与己相干，如手足不仁，气已不贯，皆不属己。"（《遗书》卷二上）

因此，在程颢看来，万物之间有一种形而上的内在联系。孟子所称的"恻隐之心"、"不忍人之心"，正是表现出人和万物之间的这种内在联系。然而，人们的"不忍人之心"往往被私心或欲望（或称"私欲"）所蔽，使人丢失了原有的与万物一体的意识。人所需要的是记起自己与万物原是一体，真诚用心地照着去做。这将使人逐渐恢复与万物一体的意识。这便是程颢的哲学主张。后来陆象山和王守仁又把这思想更细致地予以发挥。

● **程朱的"理"的观念的来源**

在前面第八章里，我们看到，早在先秦时，公孙龙已经明确区别共相和事物本身，指出它们不是一回事。他提出，即便世上没有任何白的东西，白的共相仍然存在着。公孙龙似乎看到了柏拉图所分辨的"两个世界"——永恒的世界和在时间流程中的世界、可认知的世界和可见的世界。但是，后来的中国哲学家没有对这个思想继续发挥，名家在中国哲学中也不占主要地位。结果是这种思想朝

philosophers to turn their attention once more to the problem of eternal ideas. The two main thinkers to do so are Ch'eng Yi and Chu Hsi.

The philosophy of Ch'eng Yi and Chu Hsi, however, is not a continuation of the School of Names. They paid no attention to Kung-sun Lung or to the *ming-li* (principles based on the analysis of names) discussed by the Neo-Taoists whom we have treated in chapter nineteen. They developed their idea of *Li* (abstract Principles or Laws) directly from the "Appendices" of the *Book of Changes*. I have pointed out in chapter fifteen that a distinction exists between the *Tao* of Taoism and the *tao* of the "Appendices." The *Tao* of Taoism is the unitary first "that" from which all things in the universe come to be. The *tao* of the "Appendices," on the contrary, are multiple, and are the principles which govern each separate category of things in the universe. It is from this concept that Ch'eng Yi and Chu Hsi derived the idea of *Li*.

The immediate stimulus for Ch'eng Yi and Chu Hsi, however, seems to be the thought of Chang Tsai and Shao Yung. In the last chapter we have seen that Chang Tsai explained the appearance and disappearance of concrete particulars in terms of the condensation and dispersion of the *Ch'i*. The condensation of the *Ch'i* results in the formation and appearance of things. But this theory fails to explain the reason for the different categories of things. Granted that a flower and a leaf are both condensations of the *Ch'i*, we are still at a loss as to why a flower is a flower and a leaf a leaf. It is here that Ch'eng Yi's and Chu Hsi's idea of *Li* comes in. According to them, the universe as we see it is a result not only of the *Ch'i* but also of the *Li*. Different categories of things exist, because the condensation of the *Ch'i* takes place in different ways in accordance with different *Li*. A flower is a flower, because it is the condensation of the *Ch'i* taking place in accordance with the *Li* of the flower; and a leaf is a leaf, because it is the condensation of the *Ch'i* taking place in accordance with the *Li* of the leaf.

Shao Yung's diagrams also helped to suggest the idea of *Li*. According to Shao, what the diagrams represent is the law that governs the transformations of individual things. This law is antecedent not only to the diagrams, but also to the existence of individual things. Shao maintained that before the trigrams were first drawn by their discoverer, the *Book of Changes* already ideally existed. One of the Ch'eng Masters says: "[In one of his poems], Yao-fu [i.e., Shao Yung] writes: 'Before the drawing [of the trigrams by Fu Hsi, a traditional sage supposed to have lived in the twenty-ninth century B.C.], there was already the *Book of*

另一个方向发展。直到一千多年之后，中国哲学家才又再次注意到永恒观念这个问题。再次提出这问题的两位哲学家便是程颐和朱熹。

程颐和朱熹的哲学并不是先秦名家的继续。他们对公孙龙和新道家所讨论的"名理"并未在意，本书第十九章里已经讨论了这个问题。他们的"理"的观念直接来自"易传"。在本书第十五章里，我曾经指出，道家所讲的"道"和"易传"所讲的"道"有所不同。道家所讲的"道"是宇宙万物所由出的"太一"，"易传"所讲的"道"则是宇宙万物中每一类事物内含的原理。程颐和朱熹正是从"易传"所讲的"道"，发展出他们所讲的"理"。

程颐和朱熹所受的直接启发可能是来自张载和邵雍。在上一章里，我们看到张载用"气"的聚散来解释万物的生成和消灭。张载的这个理论有一个缺陷，就是无法解释万物为什么分成不同的门类，即便我们接受花和叶都是由"气"聚而生，还是无法解释为什么有的成为花，而有的成为叶。程颐和朱熹的"理"的观念便是针对这一点而提出的。他们认为，我们所见的宇宙，不仅是"气"聚而生，还因为其中有它各自的"理"，万物各从其类，因为"气"的聚结，各依不同的"理"。花之所以成为花，是因为它的"气"按照花的"理"而聚结，于是便生成为花；叶所以成为叶，是因为它的"气"是按照叶的"理"聚结，因此便生成为叶了。

邵雍的图解也推进了"理"的概念的形成。按照邵雍的说法，他的图解正是为了说明事物演化的规律。这个事物演化的规律不仅早在有图解之前便已存在，并且在各类事物出现之前，便已经存在了。邵雍认为，在六十四卦产生以前，《易经》的思想早已存在了。程氏兄弟中有一位引邵雍诗说："尧夫诗：'……须信画前原有易，

Changes.'... This idea has never been said before." (*Literary Remains of the Two Ch'engs, chüan* 2a.) This theory is the same as that of the new realists, who maintain that there is a Mathematics before there is mathematics.

- ### Ch'eng Yi's Concept of *Li*

The combination of the philosophy of Chang Tsai and Shao Yung suggests the distinction between what the Greek philosophers called the form and the matter of things. This distinction Ch'eng Yi and Chu Hsi made very clear. For them, just as for Plato and Aristotle, all things in the world, if they are to exist at all, must be the embodiment of some principle in some material. If a certain thing exists, there must be for it a certain principle. If there be a certain principle, however, there may or may not exist a corresponding thing. The principle is what they call *Li*, and the material is what they call *Ch'i*. The latter, for Chu Hsi, is much more abstract than is the *Ch'i* in Chang Tsai's system.

Ch'eng Yi also distinguishes between what is "within shapes" and what is "above shapes." The origin of these two terms is traceable to "Appendix III" of the *Book of Changes*: "What is above shapes is called the *Tao*; what is within shapes is called the implements." In the system of Ch'eng Yi and Chu Hsi, this distinction corresponds to that between the abstract and concrete in Western philosophy. The *Li* are the *Tao* which is "above shapes," or, as we would say, abstract; while the "implements," by which Ch'eng Yi and Chu Hsi mean particular things, are "within shapes," or, as we would say, concrete.

According to Ch'eng Yi, the *Li* are eternal, and can neither be added to nor reduced. As he says: "Existence or non-existence, addition or reduction, cannot be postulated about *Li*. All *Li* are complete in themselves; in them there can never be deficiency." (*Literary Remains of the Two Ch'engs, chüan* 2a.) Again he says: "All the *Li* are pervasively present. We cannot say that the *tao* of kingship was more when Yao [a traditional sage-king] exemplified it as a king, nor can we say that the *tao* of sonship was more when Shun [the successor of Yao, known for his

filial piety] exemplified it as a son. These [the *Li*] remain what they are."
(*Ibid.*) Ch'eng Yi also describes the world "above shapes" as "void, with
nothing in it, yet filled with all." (*Ibid.*) It is void because in it there are no
concrete things; yet it is filled with all the *Li*. All the *Li* are there eternally,
no matter whether or not instances of them occur in the actual world,
nor does it matter whether we human beings know of them or not.

自从删后更无诗.'……此意古原无人道来."(《遗书》卷二上）这个
理论和新实在论者的理论相同，后者认为，在数学诞生之前，已经有
了数学的全部道理。

● 程颐的"理"的观念

如果把张载和邵雍的哲学结合起来，就相当于希腊哲学家们所讲
的事物形式和质料的区别。程颐和朱熹对这个区别说得非常清楚。他
们——也如同柏拉图和亚里士多德一样——认为世上的事物，其所以
能存在，必须有一个"理"，而且居于某个"物"之中。如果有一物，
就必有一理。但如有一理，可能有，也可能没有与它相应的物。这个
道理，程朱称之为"理"；与"理"相应的"质料"，程朱称之为"气"。
如果把朱熹的理论体系和张载的理论体系相较，则朱熹所讲的"气"，
比张载所讲的"气"要抽象得多。

程颐还区别"形而上"和"形而下"。这两个概念的来源也是出自
"易传"，《系辞上》说："形而上者谓之道，形而下者谓之器。"在程朱
的思想体系中，这个区别相当于西方哲学中的"抽象"与"具体"。"理"
乃是"道"，是"形而上"，或如西方哲学所说的"抽象"。至于"器"，
程颐和朱熹用以指个别事物，或如西方哲学所说，是"具体"的。

按程颐的说法，"理"是外在的，人对"理"，既不能增一分，也
不能减一分。他说："这上头来，更怎生说得存亡加减？是佗元无少
欠，百理具备。"(《遗书》卷二上）又说："百理俱在，平铺放着。几
时道尧尽君道，添得些君道多；舜尽子道，添得些孝道多？元来依
旧。"（同上）程颐还描绘形而上世界是"冲漠无朕，万象森然"（同
上）。意思是说，在形而上世界里，虚无一物，却又万物具陈。虚无
一物，因为其中没有具体事物；万物俱陈，因为万物的"理"都在
其中。"理"是客观存在着的，无论现实世界中有没有它的具体实例，
也不在于人是否知道它们。

Ch'eng Yi's method of spiritual cultivation is expressed in his famous statement: "In cultivation one needs attentiveness; in the advancement of learning, one needs the extension of knowledge." (*Literary Remains of the Two Ch'engs, chüan* 18.) The word "attentiveness" is a translation of the Chinese word *ching*, which may also be translated as seriousness or earnestness. We have seen that Ch'eng Hao also said that the "learner" must first understand that all things are originally one, and then cultivate this understanding with sincerity and attentiveness. Attentiveness is the key word used by Neo-Confucianists after this time to describe their method of spiritual cultivation. It replaces the word used by Chou Tun-Yi for this process, which was a different word also pronounced *ching* but meaning quiescence. The replacement of "quiescence" by "attentiveness" in the methodology of spiritual cultivation marks further the departure of Neo-Confucianism from Ch'anism.

As pointed out in chapter twenty-two, effort is needed for the process of cultivation. Even if one's ultimate aim is to be effortless, it requires an initial effort to attain the effortless state. This, however, the Ch'anists do not state, nor is it expressed by Chou Tun-yi's quiescence. Use of the word attentiveness, however, brings this idea of effort into the foreground.

In cultivation one must be attentive, but attentive to what? This is a controversial question between the two schools of Neo-Confucianism, which I will return to in the next two chapters.

● Method of Dealing with the Emotions

In chapter twenty I said that Wang Pi maintained the theory that the sage "has emotions but is without ensnarement." It is also said in the *Chuang-tzu*: "The mind of the perfect man is like a mirror. It does not move with things, nor does it anticipate them. It responds to things, but does not retain them. Therefore the perfect man is able to deal successfully with things but is not affected by them."(Ch. 7.) Wang Pi's theory of the emotions seems to be an extension of this statement of Chuang Tzu.

The Neo-Confucian method of dealing with the emotions follows the same line as Wang Pi's. Its essential is the disconnecting of the emotions from the self. Ch'eng Hao says: "The normality of Heaven and Earth is that their mind is in all things, yet of themselves they have no

程颐的精神修养方法见于他所说的一段名言:"涵养须用敬,进学则在致知。"(《遗书》卷十八)在中文里,"敬"的意思是严肃、真诚,心不分散。上文已经提到,程颢也说,学者必须首先认识万物本是一体,"识得此理,以诚敬存之"。此后新的儒家都十分看重一个"敬"字,以此作为精神修养的关键。周敦颐强调的是"静",程朱强调的是"敬",以"敬"字取代"静"字,正表明更新的儒学在精神修养方法上和禅学的进一步分道扬镳。

在第二十二章里曾经指出,新的儒家强调修养下工夫。虽说人的最终目标是无所用心,但为达到无所用心,还是要用很大气力的。对这一点,禅师们不大提及,周敦颐主"静",也不着重讲修养须用的工夫。程朱强调一个"敬"字,就把修养须用工夫这一点凸显出来了。

修养须要"敬",那么,"敬"什么呢?这是更新的儒学两派之间争论的一个问题。在下面的两章里,还会回到这个问题上来。

● 陶冶感情的方法

在第二十章里,我说到王弼的理论,认为圣人"有情而无累"。《庄子》也说:"至人之用心若镜,不将不迎,应而不藏,故能胜物而不伤。"(《应帝王》)这是说,一个接近于完美的人,心如明镜,不为物所移,对外物无求无待;物来而对应,但不存之于心。因此,接近完美的人能在对应中战胜外物,而不为外物所伤累。王弼的看法,似乎是从庄子的思想中引申出来的。

新的儒家所讲陶冶感情的方法和王弼的主张是一脉相承的。它的要旨是把感情和私己分开。程颢在《答横渠先生定性书》(论"定性",实际是"定心",即孟子所说"不动心")中说:"夫天地之常,

mind. The normality of the sage is that his emotion follows the nature of things, yet of himself he has no emotion. Therefore, for the superior man nothing is better than being impersonal and impartial, and responding to things spontaneously as they come. The general trouble with man is that he is selfish and rationalistic. Being selfish, he cannot take action as a spontaneous response. Being rationalistic, he cannot take intuition as his natural guide. When the sage is pleased, it is because the thing is there which is rightly the object of pleasure. When the sage is angry, it is because the thing is there which is rightly the object of anger. Therefore the pleasure and anger of the sage are not connected with his mind, but with things." (*Ming-tao Wen-chi* or *Collected Writings of Ch'eng Hao, chüan* 2.)

This is a part of Ch'eng Hao's "Letter on the Calmness of the Nature," which was written to Chang Tsai. The impersonalness, impartiality, and action with spontaneity and without self-rationalization, of which Ch'eng Hao speaks, are the same as the vacuity and straightforwardness spoken of by Chou Tun-yi. The same illustration from Mencius that was used in connection with Chou Tun-yi can be applied here.

According to Ch'eng Hao's view, it is natural that even the sage should sometimes experience pleasure or anger. But since his mind has an impersonal, objective, and impartial attitude, when these feelings come, they are simply objective phenomena in the universe, and are not especially connected with his self. When he is pleased or angry, it is simply the external things, deserving of either pleasure or anger, that produce corresponding feelings in his mind. His mind is like a mirror on which anything may be reflected. As a result of this attitude, when the object has gone, the emotion it produced goes with it. In this way the sage, though he has emotions, is without ensnarement. Let us return to the illustration mentioned earlier. Suppose a man sees a child about to fall into a well. If he follows his natural impulse, he will immediately rush forward to save the child. His success will certainly give him pleasure and his failure will equally certainly cause him sorrow. But since his action is impersonal and impartial, once the affair is finished, his emotion is also gone. Thus he has emotions, but is without ensnarement.

Another illustration commonly used by the Neo-Confucianists is that of Yen Hui, the favorite disciple of Confucius, of whom the latter said: "Hui did not transfer his anger." (*Analects*, VI, 2.) When a man is angry, he often abuses other people and destroys things that apparently have nothing to

以其心普万物而无心；圣人之常，以其情顺万物而无情。故君子之学，莫若廓然而大公，物来而顺应。……人之情各有所蔽，故不能适道，大率患在于自私而用智。自私则不能以有为为应迹，用智则不能以明觉为自然。……圣人之喜，以物之当喜；圣人之怒，以物之当怒。是圣人之喜怒，不系于心而系于物也。"（《明道文集》卷二）

在答张载的这封信里，程颢讲，圣人有喜有怒，情顺万物；有情无私，廓然大公；对应自然，一无智巧。这和周敦颐所说的"静虚动直"是一个意思。前面第二十三章论到周敦颐时，从《孟子·公孙丑章句上》中所引"见孺子将落井"时人的自然心情，这个例证为程颢在这里所说，圣人喜怒，不系于心而系于物，也一样适用。

按照程颢的看法，圣人也有快乐，有愤怒。但由于圣人心怀天下、客观公正，因此圣人的各种感情乃是宇宙中客观的现象，并不特别与个人联结在一起。圣人的快乐和愤怒是因为外界的事物值得引起快乐或愤怒，于是在圣人心里引起相应的感情。又由于圣人的心如同明镜一样反照外界事物，当外物移去时，它引起的感情反应也就消逝。因此，圣人虽有感情，却不会陷入感情的网罗。让我们再回到前面援引过的"见孺子将落井"的故事，如果一个人处于这样的时刻，他的自然反应就是冲过去抢救孩子。如果救回了孩子，他自然感到高兴；如果孩子已抢救不及，他自然是哀伤。但由于他的行动不是出于私己，事过以后，感情又会趋于平静，因此，不会陷入感情的网罗。

新的儒家常用的另一个例子是颜回的故事。《论语·雍也》章记载，孔子称许颜回"不迁怒"。通常人们在发怒的时候，往往会把怒气转移发泄在与他发怒这件事无关的人或物件上头，这便是

do with his emotion at all. This is called "transferring anger." He transfers his anger from something that is the object of his anger to something that is not. The Neo-Confucianists took this statement of Confucius very seriously, and considered this quality of Yen Hui as the most significant in the great Confucian disciple, whom they considered next to Confucius himself in spiritual perfection. Thus Ch'eng Yi comments: "We must understand why it is that Yen Hui did not transfer his anger. In a bright mirror, a beautiful object produces a beautiful reflection, while an ugly object produces an ugly one. But the mirror itself has no likes or dislikes. There are some people who, being offended in their home, discharge their anger in the street. But the anger of the sage operates only in accordance with the nature of things; it is never he himself who possesses the anger. The superior man is the master of things; the small man is their slave." (*Literary Remains of the Two Ch'engs, chüan* 18.)

Thus according to the Neo-Confucianists, the reason why Yen Hui did not transfer his anger is because his emotion was not connected with the self. A thing might act to produce some emotion in his mind, just as an object may appear in a mirror, but his self was not connected with the emotion. Therefore there was nothing to be transferred to other objects. He responded to the thing that produced the emotion in his mind, but he himself was not ensnared by it. He was considered to be a happy man, and for that, was greatly admired by the Neo-Confucianists.

• The Search for Happiness

In chapter twenty I have said that Neo-Confucianism attempted to find happiness in *ming chiao* (morals, institutions). The search for happiness, indeed, is one of the professed aims of the Neo-Confucianists. Ch'eng Hao says, for example: "When we studied under Chou [Tun-yi], he always asked us to find out wherein lay the happiness of K'ung [Confucius] and Yen [Hui], and what they found enjoyable." (*Literary Remains of the Two Ch'engs, chüan* 2a.) There are, in fact, many passages in the *Analects* recording the happiness of Confucius and his disciple. Those commonly quoted by the Neo-Confucianists include the following:

"Confucius said: 'With coarse rice to eat, with only water to drink, and my bended arm for a pillow, I am happy in the midst of these things. Riches and honor acquired by means that I know to be wrong are to me as a floating cloud.'" (*Analects*, VII, 15.)

About Yen Hui, Confucius said: "Incomparable indeed was Hui. A handful of rice to eat, a gourdful of water to drink, and living in a mean street: these, others would have found unbearably depressing, but for

"迁怒"。新的儒家对孔子的这句话十分认真，认为在颜回这个完美仅次于孔子的人身上，"不迁怒"是他的一个极重要的品质。对此，程颐评论说："须是理会得因何不迁怒。……譬如明镜，好物来时，便见是好；恶物来时，便见是恶。镜何尝有好恶也？世之人固有怒于室而色于市。……若圣人因物而未尝有怒。……君子役物，小人役于物。"（《遗书》卷十八）

因此，在新的儒家看来，颜回不迁怒是因为他的感情并不和私己联结在一起。一事来临，可能在他心里引起某些感情，但这种感情都是由于外物与自我无关，因此，在转向其他的人或事物时，无怒可迁。人心里对外界的反应包括了感情上的反应，但却不应让自己成为感情的掳物。颜回以"不改其乐"被孔子称许，新的儒家对这种"乐"也推崇备至。

● 寻孔颜乐处

在第二十章里，我曾说，新的儒家试图从名教（道德、礼制）中寻求快乐，这是指生命的快乐，而不是指寻求一点生活的乐趣。寻求快乐，对新的儒家来说是一件大事。例如，程颢说："昔受学于周茂叔（即周敦颐——引者注），每令寻仲尼、颜子乐处，所乐何事。"（《遗书》卷二上）在《论语》里，有很多段落记载孔子和弟子们的"乐"。新的儒家经常援引的有如：

"子曰：饭疏食饮水，曲肱而枕之，乐亦在其中矣。不义而富且贵，于我如浮云。"（《论语·述而》）

"子曰：贤哉，回也！一箪食，一瓢饮，在陋巷，人不堪其忧，

Hui's happiness they made no difference at all. Incomparable indeed was Hui." (*Ibid.*, VI, 9.)

Another passage says that once when Confucius was sitting with several of his disciples, he asked each of them to express his desires. One replied that he would like to be minister of war in a certain state, another to be minister of finance, and still another to be master of ceremonies. But the fourth, Tseng Tien, paid no attention to what others were saying, but continued to strum his lute. When the others had finished, Confucius asked him to speak. He replied: "[My desire would be], in the last month of spring, with the dress of the season all complete, along with five or six young men, and six or seven boys, to go to wash in the river Yi, enjoy the breezes among the rain altars, and return home singing." Whereupon Confucius said: "I am with Tien." (XI, 25.)

Commenting on the first two passages, Ch'eng Yi says that there is nothing to be enjoyed in eating coarse rice and drinking water *per se.* What the passages mean is simply that Confucius and Yen Hui remained happy, despite the fact that they had only this meager fare. (See *Ch'eng-shih Ching-shuo* or *Notes on the Classics by the Ch'engs, chüan* 6.) This comment is correct in itself, but the question remains what it was that did constitute their happiness.

A certain man once asked Ch'eng Yi: "Why is it that the happiness of Yen Hui remained unaffected [by external hardships]?" Ch'eng Yi answered: "[Do you know] what it was that Yen Hui enjoyed?" The man replied: "He enjoyed the *Tao.*" To which Ch'eng Yi said: "If Yen Hui enjoyed the *Tao*, he was not Yen Hui." (*Erh-Ch'eng Wai-shu* or *External Collection of Sayings of the Two Ch'engs, chüan* 7.) This statement is very much like that of the Ch'an Masters, which is why Chu Hsi, editor of the *Literary Remains of the Two Ch'engs*, did not include it there but placed it instead into the subsidiary work known as the *External Collection.* Nevertheless, the saying contains some truth. The happiness of the sage is a natural outcome of his state of mind, described by Chou Tun-yi as "vacuous in quiescence and straightforward in movement," and by Ch'eng Hao as "impersonal, impartial, and responding to things spontaneously." He does not enjoy the *Tao*; he simply enjoys what he himself is.

This view of the Neo-Confucianists can be seen by their interpretation of the third passage from the *Analects* quoted above. Chu Hsi's comment on this passage reads: "The learning of Tseng Tien would seem to have attained to the complete elimination of selfish desires, and to the

回也不改其乐。贤哉，回也！"(《论语·雍也》)

《论语·先进》里还记载，有一次，孔子和四个弟子在一起谈话，孔子让弟子们各抒其志。一个说，希望成为一国的军事统帅。另一个说，希望在一个小国负责经济发展，三年经济起飞。还有一个，希望充当国家典礼局长。问到第四个弟子曾点，他一直自己弹琴，没有在意别人谈什么。孔子问到他时，他回答说："'暮春者，春服既成，冠者五六人，童子六七人，浴乎沂，风乎舞雩（音雨，古代祭天祈雨的羽舞），咏而归。'夫子喟然叹曰：'吾与点也！'"

对上述第一段，程颐分析说，吃糙米，饮凉水，并不给人什么乐趣，这两章的意思是说，尽管生活如此清苦，孔子仍然不改其乐。对第二段，程颐解释说："箪、瓢、陋巷，非可乐也，盖自有其乐耳。'其'字当玩味，自有深意。"(《遗书》卷十二）程颐这样分析是对的，但孔、颜究竟乐在何处？问题还没有得到解答。

曾有一位鲜于侁（音伸）问程颐说："'颜子何以能不改其乐？'正叔（程颐别号）曰：'颜子所乐者何事？'侁曰：'乐道而已。'伊川曰：'使颜子而乐道，不为颜子矣。'"(《二程遗书·外书》)程颐的这个回答很像禅师们的回答，这是朱熹编纂《二程遗书》时，不把这段收入正文，而把它列入《外书》的缘故。但是，这段话确有一定的道理。圣人的快乐是他内心状况的自然反照，即周敦颐所说的"静虚动直"，也可以用程颢所说"廓然而大公，物来而顺应"来描述。圣人如果停留于"乐道"，则他和道、主观和客观还是分离的；圣人以己为乐，是因为他已经和道合为一体，乐的主体和乐的客体已经结合，圣人所乐的正是存在的这种状态。

新的儒家的这种看法也反映于对上面第三段《论语·先进》引文的解释。朱熹对这段话解释说："曾点之学，盖有以见夫人欲尽处，

Heavenly Laws in their pervasiveness, which are to be found everywhere without the slightest deficiency. This is why, both in activity and at rest, he was so simple and at ease. Speaking about his intention, he simply based himself on his existing station [in society and the universe] and enjoyed the ordinary state of affairs. He did not have the slightest idea of living according to [the views of] others, but lived according to himself. His mind was so vast that it lay in a single stream with Heaven and Earth, in which all things enjoy themselves. This mysterious sense is behind his words and can be dimly seen [by us]. The other three disciples only paid attention to the lesser branches of affairs, so that they could beat no comparison with the mood of Tseng Tien. That is why the Master [Confucius] deeply approved of him." (*Lun-yü Chi-chu* or *Collected Comments on the Analects, chüan* 6.)

In chapter twenty I have said that the essential quality of *feng liu* is to have a mind that transcends the distinctions of things and lives in accord with itself, rather than with others. According to Chu Hsi's interpretation, Tseng Tien was precisely a person of this kind. He was happy, because he was *feng liu*. In this statement of Chu Hsi we also see the romantic element in Neo-Confucianism. The Neo-Confucianists, as I have said, tried to seek happiness in *ming chiao*, but at the same time, according to them, *ming chiao* is not the opposite of *tzu jan* (nature, natural), but rather its development. This, the Neo-Confucianists maintained, was the main thesis of Confucius and Mencius.

Did the Neo-Confucianists themselves succeed in carrying out this idea? They did, and their success can be seen in the following translation of two poems, one by Shao Yung and the other by Ch'eng Hao. Shao Yung was a very happy man and was referred to by Ch'eng Hao as a *feng liu* hero. He named his house the *An Lo Wo* or Happy Nest, and called himself the Master of Happiness. His poem, titled "Song on Happiness," reads:

The name of the Master of Happiness is not known.

For thirty years he has lived on the bank of the Lo river.

His feelings are those of the wind and moon;

His spirit is on the river and lake.

(To him there is no distinction)

Between low position and high rank,

Between poverty and riches.

天理流行，随处充满，无少欠阙。故其动静之际，从容如此。而其言志，则又不过即其所居之位，乐其日用之常，初无舍己为人之意。而其胸次悠然，直与天地万物上下同流，各得其所之妙，隐然自见于言外。视三子之规规于事为之末者，其气象不侔矣。故夫子叹息而深许之。"（《论语集注》卷六）

在第二十章里我曾谈到，风流的主要特性在于心超脱于万物的畛别之上，率性而行，自事其心，不求取悦于人。在朱熹看来，曾点正是这样的一个人。他快乐，因为他实践了风流的真精神。从朱熹的这番话里，我们也能体会到新的儒家有一种浪漫主义的气息。前面我曾说过，新的儒家从名教中寻求快乐。同时，还要看到，新的儒家并不把名教和自然对立起来，而是把名教看作自然的发展。在新的儒家看来，这乃是孔孟思想的真谛。

新的儒家是否成功地实践了他们自己的思想主张呢？是的，他们确实这样实践，并且获得了成功。下面的两首诗，第一首的作者是邵雍，第二首的作者是程颢。从诗中可以看出，邵雍是一个快乐的人。程颢称他为"风流人豪"。他把自己的住所命名为"安乐窝"，自号"安乐先生"。下面这首诗的题目是《安乐吟》：

安乐先生，不显姓氏。

垂三十年，居洛之涘。

风月情怀，江湖性气。

色斯其举，翔而后至。

无贱无贫，无富无贵。

He does not move with things nor anticipate them.

He has no restraints and no taboos.

He is poor but has no sorrow,

He drinks, but never to intoxication.

He gathers the springtime of the world into his mind.

He has a small pond on which to read poems,

He has a small window under which to sleep;

He has a small carriage with which to divert his mind,

He has a great pen with which to enjoy his will.

He sometimes wears a sun hat;

He sometimes wears a sleeveless shirt;

He sometimes sits in the forests;

He sometimes walks on the river bank.

He enjoys seeing good men;

He enjoys hearing about good conduct;

He enjoys speaking good words;

He enjoys carrying out a good will.

He does not flatter the Ch'an Masters;

He does not praise the man of occult arts.

He does not leave his home,

Yet he is one with Heaven and Earth.

He cannot be conquered by a great army;

He cannot be induced by a great salary.

Thus he has been a happy man,

For sixty-five years.[1]

Ch'eng Hao's poem, titled "Autumn Days," reads:

In these late years there is nothing that comes

That is not easy and simple;

Each morning through my window shines the sun,

    As I awake.

All creatures run their course in true content,

    As I calmly observe.

The pleasure of each season through the year,

    I enjoy with others.

无将无迎，无拘无束。

窘未尝忧，饮不至醉。

收天下春，归之肝肺。

盆池资吟，瓮牖荐睡。

小车赏心，大笔快志。

或戴接篱，或著半臂。

或坐林间，或行水际。

乐见善人，乐闻善事。

乐道善言，乐行善意。

闻人之恶，若负芒刺。

闻人之善，如佩兰蕙。

不佞禅伯，不谀方士。

不出户庭，直际天地。

三军莫凌，万钟莫致。

为快活人，六十五岁。

（《伊川击壤集》卷十四）

程颢的诗，题为《秋日偶成》：

闲来无事不从容，睡觉东窗日已红。

万物静观皆自得，四时佳兴与人同。

> Beyond Heaven and Earth and all that has shape,
>> The *Tao* is there.
> The winds and clouds about me shift and change,
>> My thought is there.
> By riches and high estate, I am not to be polluted;
> Neither poverty nor low rank can affect my happiness.
>> A man like this is a hero indeed![2]

Men such as these are heroes in the sense that they cannot be conquered. Yet they are not such in the ordinary sense. They are what is known as the *feng liu* hero.

Among the Neo-Confucianists there were some who criticized Shao Yung to the effect that he made too much display of his happiness. But no such criticism is ever made about Ch'eng Hao. In any case we find here a combination of Chinese romanticism (*feng liu*) and classicism (*ming chiao*) at its best.

道通天地有形外，思入风云变态中。

富贵不淫贫贱乐，男儿到此是豪雄。

（《明道文集》卷一）

达到这种精神境界的人堪称是英雄，因为他们是不可征服的。但他们不是通常的所谓"英雄"，而是"风流人豪"。

也有些新的儒家批评邵雍过分夸张了自己的快乐，但对于程颢，则没有这样的批评。我们总算找到了中国式浪漫主义（风流）和古典主义（名教）结合的最美好的实例。

㉕ NEO-CONFUCIANISM: THE SCHOOL OF PLATONIC IDEAS

Only twenty-two years after the death of Ch'eng Yi (1033-1108), Chu Hsi (1130-1200) was born in the present Fukien province. The political change that took place during these twenty years is tremendous. The Sung dynasty, although culturally outstanding, was militarily never as strong as the Han and T'ang dynasties, and was under constant threat from outside tribes in the north and northwest. Its greatest catastrophe came when it lost its capital, the present city of Kaifeng, to the Jurchen, a Tungusic tribe from the northeast, and was compelled to reestablish itself south of the Yangtze River in 1127. This event marked the division of the Sung dynasty into two lesser parts: the Northern Sung (960-1126) and the Southern Sung (1127-1279).

● **Position of Chu Hsi in Chinese History**

Chu Hsi, better known simply as Chu Tzu or the Master Chu, was a philosopher of subtle argument, clear thinking, wide knowledge and voluminous literary output. His *Recorded Sayings* alone amount to 140 *chüan* or books. With him, the philosophic system of the Ch'eng-Chu school, also known as the *Li hsüeh* or School of *Li*, reached its culmination. Though the supremacy of this school was several times to be disputed, notably by the Lu-Wang school and by certain scholars of the Ch'ing dynasty, it remained the most influential single system of philosophy until the introduction of Western philosophy in China in recent decades.

In chapter seventeen I have said that the dynastic governments of China ensured the supremacy of their official ideology through the examination system. Persons who took the state examinations were required to write essays based on the official versions and commentaries of the Confucian Classics. In chapter twenty-three I also said that one of the major acts of Emperor T'ai-tsung of the T'ang dynasty was to determine the official version and "correct meaning" of the Classics. During the Sung dynasty, the great statesman and reformer, Wang An-shih (1021-1086), prepared "new interpretations" to some of these Classics, and in 1075 Emperor Shen-tsung ordered that Wang's interpretations should be made official. This order, however, was soon cancelled when the political rivals of Wang An-shih gained control of the government.

贰拾伍 更新的儒学：主张柏拉图式理念的理学

程颐逝世（公元一一○八年）相隔仅二十二年，朱熹（公元一一三○）出生于今福建。在这二十二年里，中国政局发生了巨大的变化，宋朝虽然孕育了灿烂的文化，但在军事实力上，远远不及汉朝和唐朝，因此，经常处于北方和西北方少数民族的军事威胁之下。公元一一二七年，北宋京城开封为来自中国东北的女真族金国（属通古斯系统）所攻陷，宋朝被迫迁都到长江以南的杭州。以这场灾难为标志，宋朝分为北宋（公元九六○至一一二七年）和南宋（公元一一二七至一二七九年）两个阶段。

● **朱熹在中国历史上的地位**

朱熹在中国学术史上，常被称为朱子。他不仅学问渊博、深思明辨，而且留下了大量著作，仅语录就有一百四十卷之多。程颐开创的理学到朱熹而完成。这个哲学体系的领袖地位虽然曾遭到陆王"心学"和清朝一些学者的挑战，但直到十九世纪末、二十世纪初，西方学术传入中国之前，程朱的理学始终是中国最有影响的哲学学派。

在第十七章里，我说到中国历代朝廷用科举制度来树立官方意识形态的优势地位。参加科举考试的读书人必须按照官方审定的儒家经书及其注释、注疏，撰写文章为巩固该朝统治献策。在第二十三章里，我还提到，唐太宗亲自审定儒家经书的"正义"（正确含义）。到了宋朝，以推行改革著名的政治家王安石（公元一○二一至一○八六年）亲自为一些儒家经书制定"新义"。公元一○七五年，宋神宗诏令，以王安石制定的经书"新义"为朝廷认可的"正义"。但是这项诏令不久便撤回，因为反对王安石的一派官僚取代王安石派而掌权，王安石所制定的一切便都被否定了。

It is to be remembered that the Neo-Confucianists considered the *Confucian Analects*, the *Mencius*, the *Chung Yung* or *Doctrine of the Mean*, and the *Ta Hsüeh* or *Great Learning*, as the most important texts, which they grouped together, giving to them the collective title of the "Four Books." For these Chu Hsi wrote a *Commentary*, which he considered to be the most important of his writings. It is said that even on the day before his death, he was still working on a revision of this *Commentary*. He also wrote *Commentaries* on the *Book of Changes* and the *Shih Ching* or *Book of Odes*. In 1313 Emperor Jen-tsung of the Yüan, the Mongol dynasty that succeeded the Sung, ordered that the "Four Books" should be the main texts used in the state examinations, and that their official interpretation should follow Chu Hsi's commentaries. The same governmental indorsement was given to Chu Hsi's commentaries on the other Classics; persons hoping for success in the examinations had to interpret these works in accordance with Chu's commentaries. This practice was continued throughout the Ming and Ch'ing dynasties, until the abolition of the state examination system in 1905, when the government tried to introduce a modern educational system.

As pointed out in chapter eighteen, one of the main reasons why Confucianism gained supremacy in the Han dynasty was its success in combining speculative thought with scholarship. In Chu Hsi himself these two aspects of Confucianism are outstandingly exemplified. His wide knowledge and learning made him a notable scholar, and his deep insight and clear thinking made him a philosopher of the first rank. It is no accident that he has been the dominant figure in Chinese thought during the last several centuries.

● *Li* or Principle

In the last chapter we have examined Ch'eng Yi's theory of *Li*, i.e., Principles or Laws. By Chu Hsi this theory was made still clearer. He says: "What are *hsing shang* or above shapes, so that they lack shapes or even shadows, are *Li*. What are *hsing hsia* or within shapes, so that they have shapes and body, are things." (*Chu-tzu Yü-lei* or *Classified Recorded Sayings of the Master Chu, chüan* 95.) A thing is a concrete instance of its *Li*. Unless there be such-and-such a *Li*, there cannot be such-and-such a thing. Chu Hsi says: "When a certain affair is done, that shows there is a certain *Li*." (*Ibid., chüan* 101.)

For everything, whether it be natural or artificial, there is its *Li*. In the *Recorded Sayings*, one passage reads: "(Question:) 'How can dried

新的儒家认为《论语》、《孟子》、《大学》和《中庸》是儒家最重要的经书，这四部书被称为"四书"。朱熹作《四书集注》，认为这是他的最重要著作。据说他直到临去世前一天还在修改这部注疏。他还写了《周易本义》和《诗集传》。公元一二七九年，元朝取代宋朝统治中国。公元一三一三年，元仁宗发布诏令，以"四书"为开科取士的标准，并以朱熹所作《四书集注》为解释"四书"的依据。凡指望中举的读书人都必须熟读朱熹的经书注疏，不能离开朱熹的集注，另行解释"四书"。明、清两朝沿袭元制，直到一九〇五年，清朝政府废科举，办学校，才废除了这套做法。

在第十八章里，我曾指出，儒家思想在汉朝取得学术界的优势地位，有一个重要原因是由于儒家成功地把思辨哲学与学问结合起来。儒家思想的这两方面特点在朱熹身上充分显示出来。他学问渊博，是当时著名的学者；他又深思明辨，是一位第一流的哲学家。几世纪来，朱熹成为中国思想界的主要人物，不是偶然的。

● **"理"或原理**

在上一章里，我们考察了程颐关于"理"的理论。到朱熹手里，这个理被阐述得更加明晰。他说："形而上者，无形无影是此理；形而下者，有情有状是此器。"（《朱子语类》卷九十五）一物是它的理的实例，若没有某个理，便不可能有某个物。朱熹说："做出那事，便是这里有那理。"（《语类》卷一百一）

一切事物，无论是自然的，或人为的，都自有其理。《朱子

and withered things also possess the nature?' (Answer:) 'They all possess *Li* from the first moment of their existence. Therefore it is said: In the universe there is not a single thing that is without its nature.' Walking on the steps, the Master [Chu Hsi] continued: 'For the bricks of these steps there is the *Li* of bricks.' And sitting down, he said: 'For the bamboo chair, there is the *Li* of the bamboo chair. You may say that dried and withered things have no life or vitality, yet among them, too, there are none that do not have *Li*.'"(*chüan* 4.)

Another passage reads: "(Question:) 'Do things without feeling also possess *Li*?' (Answer:) 'Most certainly they possess *Li*. For example, a ship can go only on water, while a cart can go only on land.'" (*Ibid.*) And still another passage reads: "(Question:) 'Is there *Li* in dried and withered things?' (Answer:) 'As soon as a thing exists, the *Li* is inherent in it. Even in the case of a writing brush—though it is not produced by nature but by man, who takes the long and soft hairs of the hare to make it—as soon as that brush exists, *Li* is inherent in it." (*Ibid.*) The *Li* that is inherent in the writing brush is the nature of that brush. The same is true of all other kinds of things in the universe: each kind has its own *Li*, so that whenever the members of a certain kind of thing exist, the *Li* of that kind is inherent in them and constitutes their nature. It is this *Li* that makes them what they are. Thus according to the Ch'eng-Chu school, not all categories of objects possess mind, i.e., are sentient; nevertheless, all of them do possess their own particular nature, i.e., *Li*.

For this reason, there are the *Li* for things already before the concrete things themselves exist. In a letter answering Liu Shu-wen, Chu Hsi writes: "There are *Li*, even if there are no things. In that case there are only such-and-such *Li*, but not such-and-such things." (*Chu Wen-kung Wen-chi* or *Collected Literary Writings of Chu Hsi*, *chüan* 46.) For instance, even prior to the human invention of ships and carts, the *Li* of ships and carts are already present. What is called the invention of ships and carts, therefore, is nothing more than the discovery by mankind of the *Li* of ships and carts, and the construction of these objects accordingly. All *Li* are present even before the formation of the physical universe. In the *Recorded Sayings* one passage reads: "(Question:) 'Before heaven and earth had yet come into existence, were all the things of later times already there?' (Answer:) 'Only the *Li* were there.'" (*Chüan* 1.) The *Li* are always there; that is to say, they are eternal.

- ## *T'ai Chi* or the Supreme Ultimate

For every kind of thing there is the *Li*, which makes it what it ought

语类》中有一段："问：枯槁之物亦有性，是如何？曰：是它合下有此理。故曰：天下无性外之物。因行阶云：阶砖便有砖之理。因坐云：竹椅便有竹椅之理。"（《语类》卷四）

《语类》中还有另一段话："问：理是人、物同得于天者，如物之无情者，亦有理否？曰：固是有理。如舟只可行之于水，车只可行之于陆。"（同上）还有一段话说："问：枯槁有理否？曰：才有物，便有理。天不曾生个笔，人把兔毫来做笔，才有笔，便有理。"（同上）这是说，毛笔之性便成为毛笔之理。宇宙万物莫不如此。一类事物便有一类事物之理，在这类事物中，任何一件开始存在，这一类事物的理便进入该物之中，成为该物之性。一个事物之所以成为该事物，乃是由于其中之理。因此，按照程朱学派的看法，事物分门别类，并非每一类都有"心"，即有"情"，但各类事物都有其特性，就是它们的"理"。

因此，在具体事物存在之前，这些事物的理便已存在。朱熹在一封《答刘叔文书》中说："若在理上看，则虽未有物而已有物之理。然亦但有其理而已，未尝实有其物也。"（《朱文公文集》卷四十六）举例来说，在人未曾发明舟车之前，舟车的"理"已经存在。所谓"发明"舟车，无非是人发现了舟车之理，于是按照它去制成舟车而已。在宇宙未生成之前，一切"理"便都已存在了。《朱子语类》卷一有一段话说："徐问：天地未判时，下面许多都已有否？曰：只是都有此理。"又说："未有天地之先，毕竟也只有理。"理是早已存在的。这就是说，理是永恒的。

- ## 太极

每类事物都有它的"理"，这"理"便是事物之所以然。这"理"

to be. The *Li* is the *chi* of that thing, i.e., it is its ultimate standard. (The word *chi* originally was a name for the ridge pole at the peak of the roof of a building. As used in Neo-Confucianism, it means the highest ideal prototype of things.) For the universe as a whole, there must also be an ultimate standard, which is supreme and all embracing. It embraces the multitude of *Li* for all things and is the highest summation of all of them. Therefore it is called the Supreme Ultimate or *T'ai Chi*. As Chu Hsi says: "Everything has an ultimate, which is the ultimate *Li*. That which unites and embraces the *Li* of heaven, earth, and all things is the Supreme Ultimate." (*Recorded Sayings, chüan* 94.)

· He also says: "The Supreme Ultimate is simply what is highest of all, beyond which nothing can be. It is the most high, most mystical, and most abstruse, surpassing everything. Lest anyone should imagine that the Supreme Ultimate has bodily form, Lien-hsi [i.e., Chou Tun-yi] has said of it: 'The Ultimateless, and yet also the Supreme Ultimate.' That is, it is in the realm of no things that there is to be found the highest *Li*." (*Chu-tzu Ch'üan-shu*, or *Complete Works of the Master Chu, chüan* 49.) From these statements we see that the position of the Supreme Ultimate in Chu Hsi's system corresponds to the Idea of the Good or to God in the systems of Plato and Aristotle respectively.

There is one point in Chu Hsi's system, however, that makes his Supreme Ultimate more mystical than Plato's Idea of the Good or Aristotle's God. This is the fact that, according to Chu Hsi, the Supreme Ultimate is not only the summation of the *Li* of the universe as a whole, but is at the same time immanent in the individual examples of each category of things. Every particular thing has inherent in it the *Li* of its particular category of things, but at the same time the Supreme Ultimate in its entirety is inherent in it too. Chu Hsi says: "With regard to heaven and earth in general, the Supreme Ultimate is in heaven and earth. And with regard to the myriad things in particular, the Supreme Ultimate is in every one of them too." (*Recorded Sayings, chüan* 94.)

But if this is so, does not the Supreme Ultimate lose its unity? Chu

Hsi's answer is no. In the *Recorded Sayings* he says: "There is but one Supreme Ultimate, which is received by the individuals of all things. This one Supreme Ultimate is received by each individual in its entirety and undivided. It is like the moon shining in the heavens, of which, though it is reflected in rivers and lakes and thus is everywhere visible, we would not therefore say that it is divided." (*Ibid.*)

We know that in Plato's philosophy there is a difficulty in explaining the relation between the intellectual and sensible worlds, and between the one and the many. Chu Hsi, too, has this difficulty, which he meets with

便是该事物的"气"，这就是说，"理"是事物的终极标准（"极"字原意是屋脊的大梁，新的儒家用以表示事物的最高原型）。整个宇宙也必定有一个终极标准，它是至高的，又是无所不包的。它包括了万有的万般之"理"，又是一切"理"的概括，因此称为"太极"。朱熹说："事事物物，皆有个极，是道理极致。总天地万物之理，便是太极。"（《语类》卷九十四）

他还说："无极，只是极至，更无去处了。至高至妙，至精至神，是没去处。濂溪（周敦颐——引者注）恐人道太极有形，故曰无极而太极。是无之中有个至极之理。"（同上）由这些话中，可见太极在朱熹的思想体系中的地位，相当于柏拉图思想体系中的"善"的观念，或亚里士多德思想体系中的"神"的观念。

但是，在朱熹的思想体系中，有一点使得他的思想体系中的"太极"，比柏拉图的"善"的观念或亚里士多德的"神"的观念，更具有神秘性。这一点便是在朱熹的思想体系里，太极不仅是宇宙万有之理，同时还内在于每类事物的每个个体之中。每个事物继承了它这类事物的理，在这个个别的理之中，又有太极整体之理。朱熹说："在天地言，则天地中有太极；在万物言，则万物中各有太极。"（《语类》卷一）

但如果这样，太极是否失去了它的统一性呢？朱熹回答说，否。在《语类》中，朱熹说："本只是一太极，而万物各有禀受，又自各全具一太极尔。如月在天，只一而已；及散在江湖，则随处可见，不可谓月已分也。"（《语类》卷九十四）

我们知道，在柏拉图哲学中，理念世界和感觉世界的关系，以及"一"和"多"的关系，怎样解释清楚，是一个难题。朱熹也同样

an illustration which is really a metaphor of constant use in Buddhism. The question as to how the *Li* of a whole class of things is related to the individual things within that class, and as to whether this relationship may also involve a division of the *Li*, is not raised. If it were, I think Chu Hsi would meet it with the same illustration.

- ### *Ch'i* or Matter

If there were nothing but *Li*, there could be nothing more than a world that is "above shapes." Our own concrete physical world, however, is made possible by the presence of *Ch'i* upon which is imposed the pattern of the *Li*. "In the universe," says Chu Hsi, "there are *Li* and *Ch'i*. The *Li* is the *Tao* that pertains to 'what is above shapes', and is the source from which all things are produced. The *Ch'i* is the material [literally, instrument] that pertains to 'what is within shapes', and is the means whereby things are produced. Hence men or things, at the moment of their production, must receive this *Li* in order that they may have a nature of their own. They must receive this *Ch'i* in order that they may have their bodily form." ("Reply to Huang Tao-fu," *Collected Literary Writings, chüan* 58.)

Again he says: "It seems to me that the *Ch'i* depends upon the *Li* for its operation. Thus when there is an agglomeration of *Ch'i*, the *Li* is also present within it. It is so, because the *Ch'i* has the capacity to condense and thus form things; but the *Li* lacks volition or plan, and has no creative power.... The *Li* constitutes only a pure, empty, and vast world, without shapes or traces, and so incapable of producing anything. But the *Ch'i* has the capacity to undergo fermentation and condensation, and thus bring things into existence. And yet, whenever the *Ch'i* exists, the *Li* is present within it." (*Recorded Sayings, chüan* 1.) Here we see how Chu Hsi says what Chang Tsai should have said but did not. Any individual thing is a condensation of *Ch'i*, but it is not only an individual thing; it is at the same time a member of some category of objects. As such, it is not merely a condensation of the *Ch'i*, but is a condensation that takes place in accordance with the *Li* for that category of objects as a whole. That is why, whenever there is a condensation of the *Ch'i*, *Li* must always necessarily be present within it.

The question as to the relative priority of *Li* and *Ch'i* is one much discussed by Chu Hsi and his disciples. On one occasion he says: "Before the instances of it exist, there is the *Li*. For example, before there exist any sovereign and subject, there is the *Li* of the relationship between

遇到这个难题。朱熹用月亮这个实例来解释，这本是佛家常用的比喻。至于一类事物之理和个别事物之理，它们之间的关系是否涉及"理"被分裂的问题，这未被提出。如果有人提出的话，估计朱熹会用同样的月亮比喻来打发这问题。

- **"气"**

  如果存在于外界的只是"理"，那么世界只是一个"形而上"的世界。但是，我们的外部世界还有物质世界，这是由于在"气"之上还加上有"理"的模式。朱熹曾说："天地之间，有理有气。理也者，形而上之道也，生物之本也；气也者，形而下之器也，生物之具也。是以人、物之生，必禀此理，然后有性；必禀此气，然后有形。"（《答黄道夫书》，《文集》卷五十八）

  他又说："疑此气是依傍这理行。及此气之聚，则理亦在焉。盖气则能凝结造作；理却无情意，无计度，无造作。……若理则只是个净洁空阔的世界，无形迹，它却不会造作。气则能酝酿凝聚生物也。但有此气，则理便在其中。"（《语类》卷一）从中我们可以看到，这本是张载可以讲的话，但是张载没有讲，这话由朱熹讲了出来。任何个别事物乃是气的凝聚，但这个别事物不是独立自存的，它还是一类事物中的一分子。作为一类事物中的一分子，它不仅是气的一般性的凝聚，而是按照这类事物的理的模式而凝聚的。这就是何以任何时候气的凝聚总有理在其中。

  关于理和气孰先孰后，这是朱熹和他的门生讨论很久的问题。朱熹有一次说："未有这事，先有这理。如未有君臣，已先有君臣

sovereign and subject. Before there exist any father and son, there is the *Li* of the relationship between father and son." (*Recorded Sayings, chüan* 95.) That there is a *Li* prior to the instances of it in our physical universe, is certainly clear from Chu Hsi's statement. But is *Li* in general also prior to *Ch'i* in general? Chu Hsi says: "*Li* is never separable from *Ch'i*. Nevertheless, *Li* pertains to 'what is above shapes,' whereas *Ch'i* pertains to 'what is within shapes.' Hence if we speak of 'what is above shapes' and 'what is within shapes,' how can there not be priority and posteriority?" (*Ibid., chüan* 1.)

Elsewhere there is a passage: "(Question:) 'When there is *Li*, there is then *Ch'i*. It seems that we cannot say that either one is prior to the other.' (Answer:) 'In reality, *Li* is prior. We cannot say, however, that there is *Li* today and *Ch'i* tomorrow. Yet there must be a priority of the one to the other.'" (*Complete Works, chüan* 49.) From these passages we can see that what Chu Hsi has in mind is that as a matter of fact "there is no *Li* without *Ch'i* and no *Ch'i* without *Li*." (*Recorded Sayings, chüan* 1.) There is no time when there is no *Ch'i*. And since *Li* is eternal, it is absurd to speak about it as having a beginning. Hence the question as to whether it is *Li* or *Ch'i* that comes into being first is really nonsensical. Nevertheless, to speak about the beginning of *Ch'i* is only a *factual* absurdity, while to speak about the beginning of *Li* is a *logical* one. In this sense it is not incorrect, as between *Li* and *Ch'i*, to say that there is priority and posteriority.

Another question is this: As between *Li* and *Ch'i*, which is it that Plato and Aristotle would have called the "First Mover"? *Li* cannot be so, because it "lacks volition or plan, and has no creative power." But though *Li* itself does not move, yet in the "pure, empty, and wide world" of *Li* there are the *Li* of movement and the *Li* of quiescence. The *Li* of movement does not itself move, nor does the *Li* of quiescence itself rest, but as soon as the *Ch'i* "receives" them, the latter begins to move or rest. The *Ch'i* that moves is called the *Yang*; the *Ch'i* that rests is called the *Yin*. Thus, according to Chu Hsi, the dualistic elements that are the fundamentals of the universe in Chinese cosmology are produced. He says: "Whereas the *Yang* is in movement and the *Yin* in quiescence, the Supreme Ultimate is neither in movement nor in quiescence. But there are the *Li* of movement and of quiescence. These *Li* are invisible, and

之理；未有父子，已先有父子之理。"（《语类》卷九十五）朱熹显然认为，在物质世界里，有事物之前，已经先有一事物之理。但是，一般说来，理是否在气之先？朱熹说："理未尝离乎气。然理形而上者，气形而下者，自形而上下言，岂无先后？"（《语类》卷一）

《语类》中还有一段话说："问：有是理便有是气，似不可分先后。曰：要之也先有理。只不可说，今日有是理，明日却有是气。也须有先后。"（同上）这些段落使我们看到，朱熹的中心思想是认为："天下未有无理之气，亦未有无气之理。"（同上）但是，他认为，"不可说今日有是理，明日却有是气"。为什么？因为时间和气是同时存在的，若没有气，便没有时间，因此不能说"'明日'有是气"。另一方面，理是永恒的，永恒进入时间，又超越时间，因此，把理说成在气（时间）之后"开始存在"乃是荒谬的，因此提出"理和气孰先孰后"的问题，在宇宙本体论上是没有意义的。尽管如此，说"气的开始"意味着以为先有时间，而后有气，可以说是事实上的谬误，而说"（永恒的）理的开始"则是一个逻辑上的谬误。就这个意义，也就是从宇宙本体论联系到宇宙发生论来说，问"理和气孰先孰后"的问题，也不能认为就是不正确。但宇宙发生论的问题，只有回到宇宙本体论去，以求得解决。

另一个问题是：如果用柏拉图和亚里士多德的哲学思维来说，理和气之间，哪一个是"第一推动力"？理不能成为"第一推动力"。因为理自身"缺少意志和设计，从而没有创造力"。但理的自身虽然不动，在它的"纯净、虚空又广阔的世界"里，有"动静之理"，它们是理，动之理本身并不动，正如静之理本身并不静。气一旦"禀受"了动静之理，它就开始"动"或"静"，气之动者称为"阳"，气之静者称为"阴"。按照朱熹的解释，中国宇宙论的二元因素就是这样来的。他说："阳动阴静，非太极动静，只是理有动静。

become manifest to us only when there are the movement of the *Yang* and the quiescence of the *Yin*. The *Li* rests upon the *Yin* and *Yang* just as a man rides on a horse." (*Complete Works, chüan* 49.) Thus the Supreme Ultimate, like God in the philosophy of Aristotle, is not moved, yet at the same time is the mover of all.

The interaction of the *Yin* and *Yang* results in the production of the Five Elements, and from these the physical universe as we know it is produced. In his cosmological theory, Chu Hsi endorses most of the theories of Chou Tun-yi and Shao Yung.

● **Nature and Mind**

From the above we see that, according to Chu Hsi, when an individual thing comes into existence, a certain *Li* is inherent in it, which makes it what it is and constitutes its nature. And a man, like other things, is a concrete particular produced in the concrete world. Hence what we call human nature is simply the *Li* of humanity that is inherent in the individual. The saying of Ch'eng Yi that "the nature is *Li*" is endorsed and commented on by Chu Hsi in many places. The *Li* here spoken of is not *Li* in its universal form; it is simply the *Li* that is inherent in the individual. This explains the rather paradoxical saying of Ch'eng Hao: "When something is said about the nature, it is then already not the nature." By this he simply means that it is then the individualized *Li*, and not *Li* in its universal form.

A man, in order to have concrete existence, must be the embodiment of *Ch'i*. The *Li* for all men is the same, and it is the *Ch'i* that makes them different. Chu Hsi says: "Whenever there is *Li*, then there is *Ch'i*. Whenever there is *Ch'i* there must be *Li*. Those who receive a *Ch'i* that is clear, are the sages in whom the nature is like a pearl lying in clear cold water. But those who receive a *Ch'i* that is turbid, are the foolish and degenerate in whom the nature is like a pearl lying in muddy water." (*Recorded Sayings, chüan* 4.) Thus any individual, besides what he receives from *Li*, also has what he receives from *Ch'i*, and this is what Chu Hsi calls the physical endowment.

Such is Chu Hsi's theory of the origin of evil. As pointed out by Plato long ago, every individual, in order to have concreteness, must be an embodiment of matter, by which, consequently, he is implicated, so that he necessarily falls short of the ideal. A concrete circle, for example, can only be relatively and not absolutely round. That is the irony of the

理不可见，因阴阳而后知。理搭在阴阳上，如人跨马相似。"（《语类》卷九十四）因此，太极如同亚里士多德哲学中的神，他虽不动，却是万物的推动者。

阴阳相交，生出五行，由此而生成万物。朱熹的宇宙论对周敦颐和邵雍的理论的一大部分都是赞同的。

● 性和心

从上所述可以看出，朱熹认为，每一事物从生成时便有一个理居于其中，这个理使事物得以生成，并构成事物的本性。人和其他万物一样，是在具体世界中的一个具体事物。因此，人性就是人类得以生成之理居于个别人之中。朱熹赞同程颐所说的"性即是理"，并多次加以引述。这里所说的"理"不是宇宙之"理"，而是个体所禀受的"理"。程颐曾经说过一句看似矛盾的话："才说性，便已不是性。"从朱熹的理论可以懂得程颐这话的意思是说，人说到物性时，是指个体之中的理，而不是理的普遍形式。

一个人必须禀气而后生。人类之理是共同的，但人各有不同，是因为所禀受的气不同。朱熹说："有是理而后有是气，有是气则必有是理。但禀气之清者，为圣为贤，如宝珠在清冷水中；禀气之浊者，为愚为不肖，如珠在浊水中。"（《语类》卷四）因此任何人，除所禀受之理外，还有禀受之气，这是朱熹所说的"气禀"。

这也就是朱熹关于恶的来源的学说。柏拉图早就指出，人形成个体，必须有质料的具体化，这个具体化的人必然不及人的原型理念那样完美。举例来说，任何具体的圆形必定不像"圆"的理念那样绝对的圆。这是现实世界无可避免的厄运，现实世界

concrete world, in which man is no exception. Chu Hsi says: "Everything depends on its physical endowment. *Li*, on the other hand, is nothing but good, for since it is *Li*, how can it be evil? What is evil lies in the physical endowment. Mencius' doctrine asserts absolutely that the nature is good. In this he apparently takes account only of the nature *per se* but not of the *Ch'i*, and thus in this respect his statement is incomplete. The Ch'eng school, however, supplements this with the doctrine of the physical nature, and so in it we get a complete and all-round view of the problem." (*Complete Works, chüan* 43.)

The term "physical nature" here means the nature as it is found actually inherent in the physical endowment of an individual. As thus found, it always strives for the ideal, as Plato would say, but always falls short of it and cannot attain it. *Li* in its originally universal form, however, Chu Hsi calls "the nature of Heaven and Earth," by way of distinction. This distinction was already made by Chang Tsai and is followed by Ch'eng Yi and Chu Hsi. According to them, the use of this distinction completely solves the old controversy as to whether human nature is good and bad.

In Chu Hsi's system, nature is different from mind. In the *Recorded Sayings*, one passage reads: "(Question:) 'Is the mental faculty in man the mind or the nature?' (Answer:) 'The mental faculty is the mind but not the nature. The nature is nothing but *Li*.'" (*Chüan* 5.) Another passage reads: "(Question:) 'With regard to consciousness: is it the mental faculty of the mind that is thus conscious, or is it the action of the *Ch'i*?' (Answer:) 'It is not wholly *Ch'i*. There is first the *Li* of consciousness; but by itself it cannot exercise consciousness. There can be consciousness only when the *Ch'i* has agglomerated to form physical shapes, and the *Li* has united with the *Ch'i*. The case is similar to that of the flame of this candle. It is because the latter receives this rich fat that we have so much light.'" (*Ibid.*)

Thus the mind, just as all other individual things, is the embodiment of *Li* with *Ch'i*. The distinction between mind and nature is that mind is concrete and nature is abstract. Mind can have activities, such as thinking and feeling, but nature cannot. But whenever such an activity takes place in our mind, we can deduce that there is a corresponding *Li* in our nature. Chu Hsi says: "In discussing the nature, it is important first of all to know what kind of entity the nature is. Master Ch'eng put it well when he said: 'Nature is *Li*.' Now if we regard it as *Li*, then surely it is without shapes and features. It is nothing but principle. In man the principles of human-heartedness, righteousness, propriety, and wisdom belong to the nature. They are principles only. It is because of them that we are capable

中的人也不例外。朱熹说: "却看你禀得气如何。然此理却只是善。既是此理,如何得恶? 所谓恶者,却是气也。孟子之论,尽是说性善,至有不善,说是陷溺。是说其补(本)无不善,后来方有不善耳。若如此,却似论性不论气,有些不备。却得程氏说出气质来接一接,便接得有首尾,一齐圆备了。"(《朱子全书》卷四十三)

这里所说"气质之性"是指一个人禀受的天性。柏拉图说,人的天性总是向着他的理念原型,却总是不及那理念原型,总是达不到那理念原型。朱熹把理原来的普遍形式称为"天地之性",以和人所禀受之性相区别。张载早已对此加以区别,程颐和朱熹继承了这个思想。他们认为,这种区别便得以解决关于人性善和人心恶的争论。

在朱熹的理论体系中,人性和人心是两回事。在《朱子语类》中有一段话说: "问: 灵处是心抑是性? 曰: 灵处只是心,不是性。性只是理。"(《语类》卷五) 又说: "问: 知觉是心之灵,固如此,抑气之为耶? 曰: 不专是气,是先有知觉之理。理未知觉,气聚成形,理与气合,便成知觉。譬如这烛火,是因得这脂膏,便有许多光焰。"(同上)

因此,心和其他的个别事物一样,是理加上气之后的体现。心和性的区别在于心是具体的,性是抽象的。心可以活动,例如思想、感觉,性却不能有这些活动。但是,当人心里这样活动时,可以由此推论出,在人性中有相应的理。朱熹说: "论性,要须先识得性是个什么样物事。程子'性即理也',此说最好。今且以理言之,毕竟却无形影,只是这一个道理。在人,仁、义、礼、智,性也,然四者有何形状? 亦只是有如此道理。有如此道理,便做得许多事

of having commiseration, that we can be ashamed of wrongdoing, that we can be courteous, and that we can distinguish between what is right and wrong. Take as an illustration the nature of drugs: some have cooling and some heating properties. But in the drugs themselves you cannot see the shapes of these properties. It is only by the result that follows upon taking the drug that we know what its property is; and this constitutes its nature." (*Complete Works, chüan* 42.)

In chapter seven we have seen how Mencius maintained that in human nature there are four constant virtues which manifest themselves as the "four beginnings." In the above quotation Chu Hsi gives a metaphysical justification to this theory of Mencius, which is primarily psychological. According to Chu, the four constant virtues pertain to *Li* and belong to the nature, while the four beginnings are the operations of the mind. We cannot know the abstract except through the concrete. We cannot know our nature except through our mind. As we shall see in the next chapter, the Lu-Wang school maintained that the mind is the nature. This is one of the main issues between the two schools.

● **Political Philosophy**

If every kind of thing in this world has its own *Li*, then for the state, as an organization having concrete existence, there must also be the *Li* of statehood or government. If the state is organized and governed in accordance with this *Li*, it will be stable and prosperous; if not, it will become disorganized and fall into disorder. According to Chu Hsi, this *Li* is the principle of government as taught and practiced by the former sage-kings. But it is not something subjective. It is eternally there, no matter whether or not it is taught or practiced. Regarding this point, Chu had some warm debates with his friend Ch'en Liang (1143-1194), who held a different point of view. Arguing with him, he wrote: "During a period of fifteen hundred years, the *Tao* [the principle of government], as handed down by Yao and Shun [two traditional sage-kings].... and

Confucius, has never been put into practice for even a single day in the world. But beyond human intervention, it is eternally there. It is simply what it is, and is eternal and immortal. It cannot perish, even though men have done violence to it during the last fifteen hundred years." ("Reply to Ch'en Liang," *Collected Literary Writings, chüan* 36.) "The *Tao*," he said again, "does not cease to be. What ceases to be is man's practice of it." (*Ibid.*)

出来，所以能恻隐、羞恶、辞让、是非也。譬如论药性，性寒、性热之类，药上亦无讨这形状处，只是服了后，却做得冷、做得热的，便是性。"（《语类》卷四）

在第七章里，我们看到，孟子认为，人性有四种德性，是为常性，构成"德之四端"。孟子的分析主要是心理学的分析，而在上面这段引文中，朱熹为孟子的学说提供了形而上学的根据。按照朱熹的说法，这四种恒德属于理的范围，因此，它们是性，而"德之四端"则是心的活动。我们只能通过具体，才能认识抽象。同样，我们只有通过心的活动，才能认识人性。在下一章里，我们将会看到，陆王学派认为，心即是性。这是程朱和陆王两派理学思想分歧的一个主要问题。

● **政治哲学**

如果世上每一样事物都有它的理，那么，国家作为一个具体存在的事物，也必定有国家和政府的理。如果国家和政府都是按理组织、按理行事，它就安定兴旺；否则，它就瓦解而陷于混乱。按照朱熹的看法，这个政治上的原理就是先前圣王教导和推行的为政之道。这不是由人主观制定的，其中的理是永恒的，无论是否有人教导或推行，它是永恒存在着的。关于这一点，朱熹和他的友人陈亮（公元一一四三至一一九四年）持有不同的见解，为此曾进行过热烈的争论。在和陈亮的辩论中，朱熹写道："千五百年之间，……尧、舜、三王、周公、孔子所传之道，未尝一日得行于天地之间也。若论道之常存，却又初非人所能预。只是此个，自是亘古亘今常在不灭之物。虽千五百年被人作坏，终殄灭它不得耳。"（《答陈同甫书》，《文集》卷三十六）他又说："盖道未尝息，而人自息之。"（同上）

As a matter of fact, not only have the sage-kings governed their states in accordance with the *Tao*, but all persons who have achieved something in politics must, to a certain degree, have followed the same *Tao*, even though sometimes unconsciously or incompletely. Chu Hsi writes: "I always think that this *Li* [principle of government] is one and the same both in times past and present. Those who follow it, succeed; those who violate it, fail. Not only did the sages of antiquity practice it, but even among the heroes of modern times, none can have any achievement without following this *Li*. Herein, however, is a difference. The ancient sages, being cultivated in the wisest way in what is fundamental, could hold the golden mean, and therefore what they did was all entirely good from the beginning to the end. The so-called heroes of modern times, however, have never undergone such cultivation, and have only moved in the world of selfish desires. Those of them who were talented have succeeded in coming into a seeming agreement [with the *Li*], each making accomplishment to the extent that he followed this *Li*. There is one aspect in which all the so-called heroes are the same; that is, what they do can never be completely in accordance with the *Li*, and therefore is not perfectly good." (*Ibid.*)

To illustrate Chu Hsi's theory, let us take as an example the building of a house. A house must be built in accordance with the principles of architecture. These principles eternally remain, even if in the physical world itself no house is actually built. A great architect is a man who fully understands these principles and makes his plans in accordance with them. For example, the house he builds must be strong and durable. Not only great architects, however, but all who want to build a house, must follow the same principles, if their houses are to be built at all. Such non-professional architects, however, may simply follow these principles through intuition or practical experience, without understanding or even knowing about them. As a result, the houses they build cannot completely accord with the principles of architecture and therefore cannot be of the best. Such is the difference between the government of the sage-kings and that of the lesser so-called heroes.

As we have seen in chapter seven, Mencius maintained that there are two kinds of government: that of the *wang* or king and that of the *pa* or military lord. Chu Hsi's argument with Ch'en Liang is a continuation of the same controversy. Chu Hsi and other Neo-Confucianists maintain that all governments from the Han and T'ang dynasties downward have been those of *pa*, because their rulers have all governed in their own

事实上，不仅先前的圣王按照为政之理来治理国家，任何在政治上有所成就的人，都是由于在不同程度上，遵行了为政之道（理），即便他们不自知，或实行得并不完善。朱熹写道："常窃以为，亘古亘今，只是一理，顺之者成，逆之者败。固非古之圣贤所能独然，而后世之所谓英雄豪杰者，亦未有能舍此理而得有所建立成就者也。但古之圣贤，从本根上便有惟精惟一功夫，所以能执其中，彻头彻尾，无不尽善。后来所谓英雄，则未尝有此功夫，但在利欲场中，头出头没。其资美者，乃能有所暗合，而随其分数之多少以有所立；然其中或否，不能尽善，则一而已。"（同上）

为阐明朱熹的学说，让我们以建造房屋为例。一幢房屋要想建成，必须按照建筑学的原理来建造。这些原理是永恒存在的，甚至即便世上没有一座房屋，建筑学的原理还是存在着。任何人要想成为一个伟大的建筑师，必须充分懂得建筑学的原理，按照建筑学的原理来设计、施工，这样，他设计建造的房屋才能牢固持久。不仅大建筑师，任何人要想建造牢固持久的房屋，都必须遵守这些原理。那些没有受过专门训练的外行建筑工头，在建造房屋时，或许是靠本能，或许是靠一点实际的经验，他们对建筑学的原理或者不懂得其中道理，或甚至根本不知道。结果他们所造的房屋，由于不符合或不完全符合建筑学原理，因而不能牢固耐久。先前的圣王和后代的所谓英雄，他们执政的结果不同，道理是一样的。

在前面第七章里，我们看到孟子把治国之道分为两种：王道和霸道，后者就是靠暴力统治。朱熹和陈亮的争论乃是奉行王道与实行霸道之争的继续。朱熹和其他新的儒家认为，汉唐以降的历代政权，执政者都是谋私利，而不是为大众；他们的统治不是王道，

interests and not in the interests of the people. Here again, therefore, Chu Hsi follows Mencius, but, as before, gives a metaphysical justification to the latter's theory, which is primarily political.

- **Method of Spiritual Cultivation**

The Platonic idea that we cannot have a perfect state "until the philosopher becomes king or the king philosopher," is shared by most Chinese thinkers. In the *Republic*, Plato dwells at great length upon the education of the philosopher who is to become king. And Chu Hsi too, as we have seen, says that the sage-kings of antiquity were cultivated in the wisest way in what is fundamental. What is this method of cultivation? Chu Hsi has already told us that in every man, and indeed in everything, there is the Supreme Ultimate in its entirety. Since the Supreme Ultimate is the totality of the *Li* of all things, hence these *Li* are all within us, but, because of our physical endowment, they are not properly manifested. The Supreme Ultimate that is within us is like a pearl in turbid water. What we have to do is to make this pearl become visible. The method for so doing is, for Chu Hsi, the same as that taught by Ch'eng Yi, which, as we have seen in the last chapter, is twofold: "The extension of knowledge through the investigation of things," and "the attentiveness of the mind."

This method has its basis in the *Ta Hsüeh* or *Great Learning*, which was considered by the Neo-Confucianists as "the beginner's door for entering the life of virtue." As we have seen in chapter sixteen, the method of self-cultivation as taught by the *Great Learning* begins with the "extension of knowledge" and "investigation of things." According to the Ch'eng-Chu school, the purpose of the "investigation of things" is to extend our knowledge of the eternal *Li*.

Why does not this method start with the investigation of *Li* instead of things? Chu Hsi says: "The *Great Learning* speaks of the investigation of things but not of the investigation of *Li*. The reason is that to investigate

Li is like clutching at emptiness in which there is nothing to catch hold. When it simply speaks of 'the investigation of things,' it means that we should seek for 'what is above shapes' through 'what is within shapes.'" (*Complete Works, chüan* 46.) In other words, *Li* are abstract and things are concrete. We investigate the abstract through the concrete. What we as a result come to see lies both within the eternal world and within

而是霸道。在这里，朱熹是孟子的追随者，但也和先前一样，朱熹对孟子的政治理论，也提供了形而上学的论证。

● **修心养性的方法**

　　柏拉图曾经认为，除非哲学家执政，或执政者成为哲学家，否则不可能指望有完美的国家。中国哲学家中的多数也持这种看法。柏拉图在《理想国》里，用了很多篇幅讨论哲学家执政应先受什么样的教育。朱熹在《答陈亮书》中也说，古代圣王"从本根上便有惟精惟一功夫"，圣王对王道之本曾受到最明智的教育。究竟其具体内容是什么，修养的方法是什么？朱熹认为，在每个人里面，甚至在每一事物里面，都有太极，太极便是万物之理的总体。因此，万物之理，俱备于我。但是人由于禀受有不足或缺陷，因此未将万物之理充分表现出来，如同珍珠湮没在浊水里一样。人所当做的就是把珍珠再现出来。所用的方法便是程颐已经说过（见上章）的两方面："格物致知"，即对外界事物调查研究，扩大自己的知识，以及"用敬"，即专心致志，心不旁骛。

　　这个方法最初见于《大学》，新的儒家把《大学》看作是"初学入德之门"。在前面第十六章里，我们已经看到，《大学》所教导的自我修养方法，第一步便是"格物致知"。按程朱派的看法，了解外部世界的目的便是扩大我们对永恒之理的认识。

　　这个方法为什么不从"穷理"，而要从"格物"入手？朱熹说："《大学》说'格物'，却不说'穷理'。盖说穷理，则似悬空无捉摸处。只说'格物'，则只就那形而下之器上，便寻那形而上之道。"（《全书》卷四十六）"格物"是为了从有形之物中体认超越物体的"理"，也就是"道"。换句话说，理是抽象的，物是具体的，我们要做的是："格物"以"穷理"。我们所得的结果是：既领悟了理念

our own nature. The more we know *Li,* the more our nature, ordinarily concealed by our physical endowment, becomes visible to us.

As Chu Hsi says: "There is no human intelligence [utterly] lacking knowledge, and no single thing in the world without *Li.* But because the investigation of *Li* is not exhaustive, this knowledge is in some ways not complete. This is why the first instruction of the *Great Learning* is that the student must, for all the separate things in the world, by means of the *Li* which he already understands, proceed further to gain exhaustive knowledge of those [with which he is not yet familiar], thus striving to extend [his knowledge] to the farthest point. When one has exerted oneself for a long time, finally one morning a complete understanding will open before one. Thereupon there will be a thorough comprehension of all the multitude of things, external or internal, fine or coarse, and every exercise of the mind will be marked by complete enlightenment." (*Commentary* on the *Great Learning,* ch. 5.) Here we have again the theory of Sudden Enlightenment.

This seems to be enough in itself, so why should it be supplemented by the "attentiveness of the mind"? The answer is that without such attentiveness, the investigation of things is likely to be simply a kind of intellectual exercise and thus will not lead to the desired goal of Sudden Enlightenment. In investigating things we must keep in mind that what we are doing is to make visible our nature, to cleanse the pearl so that it can shine forth. In order to be enlightened, we must always think about Enlightenment. This is the function of the attentiveness of mind.

Chu Hsi's method of spiritual cultivation is very like that of Plato. His theory that in our nature there are the *Li* of all things, is very like Plato's theory of a previous knowledge. According to Plato, "We acquire knowledge before birth of all the essences." (*Phaedo* 75.) Because there is this previous knowledge, therefore he who "has learned to see the beautiful in due course and succession," can "suddenly perceive a nature of wondrous beauty." (*Symposium* 211.) This, too, is a form of Sudden Enlightenment.

的永恒世界，又领悟了自己内心之性。我们越多领悟"理"，也就越多地领悟"心性"，它通常往往被人的禀受所蔽，人通过"格物穷理"，使"理"这个珍珠再现出来。

有如朱熹所说："盖人心之灵莫不有知，而天下之物莫不有理，惟于理有未穷，故其知有不尽也。是以《大学》始教，必使学者即凡天下之物，莫不因其已知之理而益穷之，以求至乎其极。至于用力之久，而一旦豁然贯通焉，则众物之表里精粗无不到，而吾心之全体大用无不明矣。"（《大学章句·补格物传》）这里，我们再次看见了"顿悟"的学说。

朱熹说到这里，似乎已经说清楚了他的思想，为什么还要再加上"用敬"呢？回答是：若不"用敬"，"格物"很容易成为一种单纯的智力活动，而达不到"顿悟"的目标。在"格物"的过程中，人实际在做的乃是再现自己的本性，使沉溺在浊水中的珍珠重现光辉。为达到"悟"，人就当时时刻刻以"悟"为念，"用敬"的真意就在于此。

朱熹的精神修养方法和柏拉图的精神修养方法十分相像。他认为，人性中原有万物之理，和柏拉图讲人有"与生俱来"的宿慧也十分相像。柏拉图曾说："我们在出生之前，已经有了对各种价值和事物本质的悟性知识。"（《斐多篇》第七十五段）由于有"宿慧"，因此，"人如学会按适当的次序［参阅《宴饮篇》第二百一十一段：'由鉴赏外界的美的形式到（自身）对美的实践，由对美的实践到对美的思想领悟，由对美的思想领悟而最后达到绝对的美。'］领略各种各样美的事物"，最后，会"突然领悟到奇妙无比的美的世界的本质"（《宴饮篇》第二百一十一段）。这其实也是"顿悟"的一种形式。

㉖ NEO-CONFUCIANISM: THE SCHOOL OF UNIVERSAL MIND

As we have seen in chapter twenty-four, the Lu-Wang school, also known as the *Hsin hsüeh* or Mind school, was initiated by Ch'eng Hao and completed by Lu Chiu-yüan and Wang Shou-jen. Lu Chiu-yüan (1139-1193), popularly known as the Master of Hsiang-shan, was a native of the present Kiangsi province. He and Chu Hsi were friends, despite their widely divergent philosophic views. Their verbal and written debates on major philosophical problems evoked great interest in their day.

- **Lu Chiu-yüan's Conception of the Mind**

Both Lu Chiu-yüan and Wang Shou-jen are said to have become convinced of the truth of their ideas as a result of experiencing Sudden Enlightenment. One day, it is said, Lu was reading an ancient book in which he came upon the two words *yü* and *chou*. An expositor remarked: "What comprises the four points of the compass together with what is above and below: this is called *yü*. What comprises past, present, and future: this is called *chou*." Thereupon Lu Chiu-yüan experienced an instantaneous enlightenment and said: "All affairs within the universe come within the scope of my duty; the scope of my duty includes all affairs within the universe." (*Lu Hsiang-shan Ch'üan-chi* or *Collected Works of Lu Hsiang-shan, chüan* 33.) And on another occasion he said: "The universe is my mind; my mind is the universe." (*Ibid., chüan* 36.)

Whereas Chu Hsi endorses Ch'eng Yi's saying that "the nature is *Li*," Lu Chiu-yüan replies that "the mind is *Li*." (*Collected Works, chüan* 12.) The two sayings differ only by one word, yet in them lies the fundamental division between the two schools. As we have seen in the last chapter, the mind, in Chu Hsi's system, is conceived of as the concrete embodiment of *Li* as found in *Ch'i*; hence it is not the same as the abstract *Li* itself. Chu Hsi, consequently, can only say that the nature is *Li*, but not that the mind is *Li*. But in Lu Chiu-yüan's system, on the contrary, the mind itself is the nature, and he considers the presumed distinction between nature and mind as nothing more than a verbal one. Regarding such verbal distinctions, he says: "Scholars of today devote most of their time to the explanation of words. For instance, such words as feeling, nature, mind, and ability all mean one and the same thing. It is only accidental that a single entity is denoted by different terms." (*Collected Works, chüan* 35.)

Yet as we have seen in the last chapter, Chu Hsi's distinction between nature and mind is certainly far from a verbal one, for from his point

贰拾陆 更新的儒学中的另一派：宇宙心学

在第二十四章里我们看到，陆王学派，或称心学，肇始于程颢，经陆象山和王守仁而完成。陆九渊，人称象山先生，是今江西人。他和朱熹是朋友，而在哲学见解上则有巨大的分歧，为此两人在重大的哲学问题上，以口头和文字进行辩论，在当时已经引起人们的很大兴趣。

● 陆九渊论心

据说陆九渊和王守仁都经历了"顿悟"而确信他们的思想乃是真理。陆九渊有一天"读古书至'宇宙'两字，解者曰：'四方上下曰宇，往古来今曰宙。'忽大省曰：'宇宙内事，乃己分内事；己分内事，乃宇宙内事。'"（《象山全集》卷三十三）另外，他还说："宇宙便是吾心，吾心便是宇宙。"（《全集》卷三十六）

朱熹支持程颐的说法，认为"性即是理"，而陆九渊却说："心即是理。"这两句话相差只一个字，却是两个学派基本分歧之所在。在上一章里我们看到，在朱熹的思想体系中，心被理解为"理在气中"的具体表现，据此，心与抽象的理不能等同。因此，朱熹只能说：性即是理，而不能说心即是理。但是陆九渊的思想体系却正相反，他认为心即是性。这两者只是文字上的不同。关于这种文字上的不同，陆九渊说："今之学者读书，只是解字，更不求血脉。且如情、性、心、才，都是一般物事，言偶不同耳。"（《全集》卷三十五）

在上一章里，我们可以看到，朱熹所说"心"和"性"的区别，

of view, there actually exists such a distinction in reality. This reality as seen by him, however, is not the same as that seen by Lu Chiu-yüan. For the former, reality consists of two worlds, the one abstract, the other concrete. For the latter, however, it consists of only one world, which is the mind or Mind.

But the sayings of Lu Chiu-yüan give us only a sketchy indication of what the world system of the Mind school is. For a more complete exposition, we must turn to the sayings and writings of Wang Shou-jen.

- ## Wang Shou-Jen's Conception of the Universe

Wang Shou-jen (1472-1528) was a native of the present Chekiang province, and is generally known as the Master of Yang-ming. He was not only an outstanding philosopher, but was also notable as a practical statesman of high capacity and moral integrity. In his early years he was an ardent follower of the Ch'eng-Chu school; and, determined to carry out Chu Hsi's teaching, once started to investigate the principle or *Li* of bamboo. He concentrated his mind upon the bamboo day and night for seven consecutive days, yet failed to discover anything. Finally he was forced to give up the attempt in great despair. Afterward, however, while living amid primitive surroundings in the mountains of southwest China, to which he had been temporarily exiled because of political intrigue at court, enlightenment came to him suddenly one night. As a result, he gained a new understanding of the central idea of the *Great Learning*, and from this viewpoint reinterpreted this work. In this way he completed and systematized the teaching of the Mind school.

In the *Ch'uan Hsi Lu* or *Record of Instructions*, which is a selection of Wang Shou-jen's recorded sayings made by one of his disciples, one passage reads: "While the Master was taking recreation at Nan-chen, one of our friends, pointing at the flowers and trees on a cliff, said: 'You say there is nothing under heaven that is external to the mind. What relation, then, do these high mountain flowers and trees, which blossom and drop of themselves, have to my mind?' The Master replied: 'When you do not see these flowers, they and your mind both become quiescent. When you see them, their color at once becomes clear. From this fact you know that these flowers are not external to your mind.'" (Pt. 3.)

Another passage reads: "The Master asked: 'According to you, what is the mind of Heaven and Earth?' The disciple answered: 'I have often heard that man is the mind of Heaven and Earth.' 'And what is it in man that is called his mind?' 'It is simply the spirituality or consciousness.' 'From this we know that in Heaven and Earth there is one spirituality or

远不止于文字上的不同，在他看来，心和性在实际里是不同的。朱熹所见的实际和陆象山所见的实际不同：朱熹认为现实包含有两个世界，一个是抽象的，另一个是具体的；而在陆九渊看来，现实只包含心的世界。

陆九渊关于心学的言论著作只是勾勒了一个轮廓，为全面了解心学，我们还须读王守仁的言论和著作。

● 王守仁的宇宙观

王守仁（公元一四七二至一五二八年）生于明代，浙江人，人称"阳明先生"。他不仅是一位杰出的哲学家，还是一位有能力、有道德操守的政治家。他早年曾追随程朱理学，并决心依照朱熹的思想，从"格竹子之理"开始。为此，他七天七夜专心致志地求竹子之理，结果并无所悟。他被迫放弃"格物"这条路。后来，由于朝廷政争，被贬贵州，在山区落后原始的生活环境里，有一晚他得到顿悟，对《大学》的主旨有了新的认识。由此而对《大学》有了全新的诠释，完成了心学的思想体系。他的思想言论由门人辑录为《传习录》，其中有一段说："先生游南镇，一友指岩中花树问曰：'天下无心外之物，如此花树，在深山中，自开自落，于我心亦何相干？'先生云：'尔未看此花时，此花与尔心同归于寂，尔来看此花时，则此花颜色，一时明白起来。便知此花，不在尔的心外。'"（《传习录》下，《王文成公全书》卷三）

另一段说："先生云：'尔看这个天地中间，什么是天地的心？'对曰：'尝闻人是天地的心。'曰：'人又什么叫作心？'对曰：'只是一个灵明。''可知，充天塞地，中间只有这个灵明。人只为形体

consciousness. But because of his bodily form, man has separated himself from the whole. My spirituality or consciousness is the ruler of Heaven and Earth, spirits and things.... If Heaven, Earth, spirits, and things are separated from my spirituality or consciousness, they cease to be. And if my spirituality or consciousness is separated from them, it ceases to be also. Thus they are all actually one body, so how can they be separated?'" (Pt. 3.)

From these sayings we gain an idea of Wang Shou-jen's conception of the universe. In this conception, the universe is a spiritual whole, in which there is only one world, the concrete actual world that we ourselves experience. Thus there is no place for that other world of abstract *Li*, which Chu Hsi so much emphasized.

Wang Shou-jen also maintains that mind is *Li*: "Mind is *Li*. How can there be affairs and *Li* outside the mind?" (*Record of Instructions*, pt. 1.) Again: "The substance of the mind is the nature and the nature is *Li*. Therefore, since there is the mind of filial love, hence there is the *Li* of filial piety. If there were no such a mind, there would be no such a *Li*. And since there is the mind of loyalty to the sovereign, hence there is the *Li* of loyalty. If there were no such a mind, there would be no such a *Li*. How can *Li* be outside our mind?" (*Ibid.*, pt. 2.) From these sayings we can see still more clearly the difference between Chu Hsi and Wang Shou-jen and between the two schools they represent. According to Chu Hsi's system, we can only say that since there is the *Li* of filial piety, therefore there is the mind of loving one's parents; and since there is the *Li* of loyalty, therefore there is the mind of loyalty to one's sovereign. We cannot, however, say the converse. But what Wang Shou-jen said is precisely this converse. According to Chu Hsi's system, all the *Li* are eternally there, no matter whether there is mind or not. But according to Wang Shou-jen's system, if there is no mind, there will be no *Li*. Thus the mind is the legislator of the universe and is that by which the *Li* are legislated.

● "The Illustrious Virtue"

With this conception of the universe, Wang Shou-jen gives a metaphysical justification to the *Great Learning*. As we have seen in chapter sixteen, this work speaks of what are later called the "three major cords" and eight "minor wires." The three "cords" are "to manifest the illustrious virtue, love people, and rest in the highest good." Wang Shou-jen defines great learning as the learning of the great man. Regarding the

自间隔了。我的灵明，便是天地鬼神的主宰。……天地鬼神万物，离却我的灵明，便没有天地鬼神万物了。我的灵明，离却天地鬼神万物，亦没有我的灵明。如此便是一气流通的，如何与它间隔得？'"（《全书》卷三）

从这些段落中，我们可以知道王守仁对宇宙的概念，认为宇宙是一个自身完整的精神实体，这个精神实体便构成了我们经验中的世界。此外，并没有另一个朱熹所强调的抽象的"理的世界"。

王守仁还主张心即是理。在《传习录》（《全书》卷一）有一段说："心即理也。天下又有心外之事、心外之理乎？"在《全书》卷二《答顾东桥书》中又说："心之体，性也。性即理也。故有孝亲之心，即有孝之理；无孝亲之心，即无孝之理矣。有忠君之心，即有忠之理；无忠君之心，即无忠之理矣。理岂外于吾心耶？"由这些话里，我们可以更清楚地看到朱熹和王守仁以及理学、心学两派思想的分歧。照朱熹的说法，我们先懂得孝之理，然后有孝亲之心；先有忠之理，而后有忠君之心。我们不能把这话倒过来说，而王守仁恰恰是把这话颠倒过来。按照朱熹的思想，理是客观外在的实在，无论心存在与否。而按照王守仁的思想，若没有心，便没有理。心为宇宙立法，理是由心立的。

● "明德"

在这样的宇宙概念之上，王守仁对《大学》赋予一种形而上学的意义。在前面第十六章里，曾经说到《大学》抒发了后来对它所称的"三纲领"："大学之道，在明明德，在亲民，在止于至善。"王守仁解释《大学》就是学作大人之学。关于"在明明德"，他写道：

"manifestation of the illustrious virtue," he writes: "The great man is an all-pervading unity, which is one with Heaven, Earth, and all things. He considers the world as one family, and the Middle Kingdom as one man. Those who emphasize the distinction of bodily forms and thus make cleavage between the self and others are the small men. The reason that the great man is able to be one with Heaven, Earth, and all things, is not that he is thus for some purpose, but because the human-heartedness of his mind is naturally so. The mind of the small man is exactly the same, only he himself makes it small. When the small man sees a child about to fall into a well, he will certainly experience a feeling of alarm and distress. This shows that in his love he is one with the child. And when he hears the pitiful cry or sees the frightened appearance of a bird or beast, he will certainly find it unbearable to witness them. This shows that in his love he is one with birds and beasts.... From all this it may be seen that the original unity lies in the small man [as well as the great man]. Even the small man has his heavenly nature, the light of which cannot be obscured. Therefore it is called the illustrious virtue.... Thus when there is no obscuring caused by selfish desires, even the small man has the love for the whole, just as does the great man. But when there is this obscuring, even the mind of the great man is divided and hampered, just as is the small man. The learning of the great man serves simply to clear away the obscuring and thus to manifest the illustrious virtue, so as thus to restore the original unity of Heaven, Earth, and all things. It is not possible to add anything to this original state." [1]

Regarding the second of the "three cords" in the *Great Learning*, that of "loving people," Wang Shou-jen writes: "To manifest the illustrious virtue is to establish the nature of the unity of Heaven, Earth, and all things; to love people is to exercise the function of that unity. Therefore the manifestation of the illustrious virtue consists in loving people, and to love people is to manifest the illustrious virtue. If I love my own father, the fathers of some other men, and the fathers of all men, my love will be truly extended with my love of these fathers…. Beginning with all these human relationships, and reaching to mountains, rivers, spirits and gods, birds and beasts, grasses and trees, all should be loved in order to extend our love. In this way there is nothing that is not manifested in our illustrious virtue; and then we are really one with Heaven, Earth and all things." (*Ibid.*)

Regarding the third "cord," that of "resting in the highest good," he writes: "The highest good is the highest standard for the manifesting of the illustrious virtue and loving people. Our original nature is purely

"大人者，以天地万物为一体者也。其视天下犹一家，中国犹一人焉。若夫间形骸而分尔我者，小人矣。大人之能以天地万物为一体也，非意之也，其心之仁，本若是其与天地万物而为一也。岂惟大人，虽小人之心，亦莫不然。彼顾自小之耳。是故见孺子之入井，而必有怵惕恻隐之心焉，是其仁与孺子而为一体也。孺子犹同类者也，见鸟兽之哀鸣觳觫而必有不忍之心焉，是其仁之与鸟兽而为一体也。……是其一体之仁也，虽小人之心，亦必有之。是乃根于天命之性，而自然灵昭不昧者也。是故谓之明德。……是故苟无私欲之蔽，则虽小人之心，而其一体之仁，犹大人也。一有私欲之蔽，则虽大人之心，而其分隔隘陋，犹小人矣。故夫为大人之学者，亦惟去其私欲之蔽，以自明其明德，复其天地万物一体之本然而已耳；非能于本体之外，而有所增益之也。"（《大学问》，《全书》卷二十六）

关于"三纲领"中的第二条"在亲民"，王守仁说："明明德者，立其天地万物一体之体也；亲民者，达其天地万物一体之用也。故明明德必在于亲民，而亲民乃所以明其明德也。亲吾之父以及人之父，以及天下人之父，而后吾之仁实与吾之父、人之父、与天下人之父而为一体矣，实与之为一体而后孝之明德始明矣。……君臣也，夫妇也，朋友也，以至于山川神鬼鸟兽草木也，莫不实有以亲之，以达吾一体之仁。然后吾之明德始无不明，而真能以天地万物为一体矣。"（同上）

关于"止于至善"，王守仁写道："至善者，明德、亲民之极则也。

good. What cannot be obscured in it is the manifestation of the highest good and of the nature of the illustrious virtue, and is also what I call intuitive knowledge. When things come to it, right is right, wrong is wrong, important is important, and inferior is inferior. It responds to things and changes with circumstances, yet it always attains the natural mean. This is the highest standard for the actions of man and of things, to which nothing can be added, and from which nothing can be reduced. If there is any addition or reduction, that is selfishness and a petty kind of rationalization, and is not the highest good." (*Ibid.*)

- **Intuitive Knowledge**

Thus the three "main cords" are reduced to a single "cord," that of the manifestation of the illustrious virtue, which is simply the original nature of our mind. All of us, whether good or bad, fundamentally have the same mind, which can never be wholly obscured by our selfishness, and always manifests itself in our immediate intuitive reaction to things. A case in point is the feeling of alarm which we all automatically experience upon suddenly seeing a child about to fall into a well. In our first reaction to things, we know naturally and spontaneously that the right is right and the wrong is wrong. This knowing is the manifestation of our original nature, and for it Wang uses the term "intuitive knowledge" (literally, "good knowledge"). All we need to do is simply to follow the dictates of this knowledge and go unhesitatingly forward. For if we try to find excuses for not immediately following these dictates, we are then adding something to, or reducing something from, the intuitive knowledge, and are thus losing the highest good. The act of looking for excuses is a rationalization which is due to selfishness. As we have seen in chapters twenty-three and twenty-four, Chou Tun-yi and Ch'eng Hao expressed the same theory, but Wang Shou-jen here gives it a more metaphysical basis.

It is said that when Yang Chien (died 1226) first met Lu Chiu-yüan, he asked the latter what our original mind is. It may be noted in passing that this term, "original mind," was originally a Ch'anist one, but it also came to be used by the Neo-Confucianists of the Lu-Wang school. Answering the question, Lu Chiu-yüan recited the passage in the *Mencius* about the "four beginnings." Yang Chien said that he had read this passage since boyhood, but still did not know of what the original mind consists. He was then an official, and during the conversation was called upon to attend to some official business, in the course of which he had to pass a

天命之性，粹然至善，其灵昭不昧者，此其至善之发见，是乃明德之本体，而即所谓良知者也。至善之发见，是而是焉，非而非焉，轻重厚薄，随感随应，变动不居，而亦莫不有天然之中。是乃民彝物则之极，而不容少有拟议增损于其间也。少有拟议增损于其间，则是私意小智，而非至善之谓矣。"（同上）

● 良知——来自直觉的认识

这样，"三纲领"实际上被归结为一条，即：在明明德，这就是心的本性。一切人，无论善恶，从基本上，都同有此心。人的自私也不能把本性完全泯灭，往往在人对外界事物的本能反应中表现出来。人突然发现一个幼儿即将落入井中的本能反应便足以说明这一点。人对事物的第一个反应表明，人内心里，知道什么是对的，什么是错的。这种非意识是人的本性的表现，王阳明称之为"良知"（按字面的意思就是"对良善的知识"）。人所当做的便是服从良知的命令，毫不迟疑地去做。如果人不立即遵照良知的命令去做，而寻找不做的理由，便是在良知上加以增益或减损，这便失去了至善。其实人寻找借口不去遵行良知的命令，乃是出于私欲。在前面第二十三、二十四章里，我们看到周敦颐和程颢也持同样的主张，王守仁则对这个理论赋予了一个形而上学的基础。

据说，杨简（一二二六年卒，南宋哲学家，陆九渊弟子）初见陆九渊时问，人的本心如何？在这里值得提一下，"本心"原是禅学的用语，但陆王学派也沿用了这个词语。陆九渊在回答杨简的问题时，援引了《孟子》中论到善之四端的一段。杨简说，他从孩提时代便已学过这一段，却始终不明白人的本心何所指。杨简时任富阳主簿，在谈话中间出去处理了一桩诉讼案，然后回来与陆九渊继续

verdict on a certain lawsuit. When the business was concluded, he turned to Lu Chiu-yüan again with the same question. Lu then said: "Just now in announcing your verdict, the right you knew to be right, and the wrong you knew to be wrong. That is your original mind." Yang said: "Is there anything else?" To which Lu in a very loud voice answered: "What else do you want?" Thereupon Yang was suddenly enlightened and thus became the disciple of Lu. (*Tz'u-hu Yi-shu* or *Literary Remains of Yang Chien, chüan* 18.)

Another story says that a follower of Wang Shou-jen once caught a thief in his house at night, whereupon he gave him a lecture about intuitive knowledge. The thief laughed and asked: "Tell me, please, where is my intuitive knowledge?" At that time the weather was hot, so the thief's captor invited him first to take off his jacket, then his shirt, and then continued: "It is still too hot. Why not take off your trousers too?" At this the thief hesitated and replied: "That does not seem to be quite right." Thereupon his captor shouted at him: "There is your intuitive knowledge!"

The story does not say whether the thief gained enlightenment as a result of this conversation, but it and the preceding story certainly are typical of the Ch'an technique of initiating a student to Enlightenment. They show that every man possesses that intuitive knowledge which is the manifestation of his original mind, and through which he immediately knows that right is right and wrong is wrong. Everyone, in his original nature, is a sage. That is why the followers of Wang Shou-jen were in the habit of saying that "the streets are full of sages."

What they meant by this is that every man is potentially a sage. He can become an actual sage if he but follow the dictates of his intuitive knowledge and act accordingly. What he needs to do, in other words, is to carry his intuitive knowledge into practice, or, in Wang Shou-jen's terminology, to extend his intuitive knowledge. Thus the "extension of intuitive knowledge" became the key term in Wang's philosophy, and in his later years he mentioned only these words.

- **"The Rectification of Affairs"**

It will be remembered that the *Great Learning* also speaks of "eight minor wires," which are the eight steps to be followed in the spiritual cultivation of the self. The first two of them are the "extension of knowledge" and "investigation of things." According to Wang Shou-jen, the extension of knowledge means the extension of the intuitive knowledge. Cultivation of the self is nothing more than the following of one's intuitive knowledge and putting it into practice.

谈话。陆九渊说：刚才你断案，知道怎样判断是非，这便是你的本心。杨简问：仅止于此吗？陆九渊大声回答说："你还要什么？"杨简就此顿悟，由此成为陆九渊的弟子。（见《慈湖遗书》卷十八）

还有另一个关于王守仁弟子的故事。这位弟子有一次半夜里捉到一个小偷，便对小偷讲说"良知"的道理。那小偷笑着问道："请问，我的良知在哪里？"当时天气很热，王守仁的这个弟子请小偷脱掉外衣，随后又请他脱掉内衣，小偷都照办了。接下去请小偷脱掉裤子时，小偷犹豫说，这恐怕不妥吧。王守仁的弟子便对小偷说："这便是你的良知！"

这个故事没有说，小偷是否在这次谈话里得到顿悟。但是，这个故事和前一个故事都使用了禅师启发禅僧顿悟的方法。它们的用意都在于表明，每个人都有良知，这良知便是人的本心。人凭着良知，懂得什么是对的，什么是错的。人人按本性说，都是圣人。这便是何以王守仁的学生惯于说"满街都是圣人"。

他们这样说的意思是：人人都可以成圣。人只要秉着良知去分辨是非，遵行良知的命令，就真的成为圣人了。换句话说，人所当做的是遵行良知的命令；用王守仁的话来说，就是"致良知"：这是王守仁哲学的中心思想，他在晚年时反复讲的就是这三个字。

- **"正事"**

《大学》里还讲"八条目"，它的内容是个人精神修养的八个步骤，第一、二步便讲"致知"与"格物"。按照王守仁的思想，"致知"便是"致良知"。个人精神修养无他，就是顺自己的良知去生活，把来自直觉的知识付诸实行。

The Chinese term for the "investigation of things" is *ko wu*, and it is Ch'eng Yi and Chu Hsi who interpret it as having this meaning. According to Wang Shou-jen, however, *ko* means to rectify and *wu* means affairs. *Ko wu*, therefore, does not mean "investigation of things," but "rectification of affairs." The intuitive knowledge, he maintains, cannot be extended through the techniques of contemplation and meditation taught by the Buddhists. It must be extended through our daily experience in dealing with ordinary affairs. Thus he says: "The activity of the mind is called *yi* [will, thought], and the objects toward which *yi* is directed are called *wu* [things, affairs]. For instance, when the object of one's *yi* is the serving of one's parents, then this serving of one's parents is the *wu*. And when the object of one's *yi* is the serving of the sovereign, then this serving of the sovereign is the *wu*." (*Record of Instructions*, pt. 1.) The *wu* may be right or wrong, but as soon as this can be determined, our intuitive knowledge will immediately know it. When our intuitive knowledge knows a thing to be right, we must sincerely do it, and when our intuitive knowledge knows it to be wrong, we must sincerely stop doing it. In this manner we rectify our affairs and at the same time extend our intuitive knowledge. There is no other means of extending our intuitive knowledge except through the rectification of our affairs. That is why the *Great Learning* says: "The extension of knowledge consists in the rectification of affairs."

The next two steps of the "eight wires" are "sincerity of thought [*yi*] and rectification of the mind." According to Wang Shou-jen, sincerity of thought is nothing more than the rectification of affairs and the extension of intuitive knowledge, both being carried out with the utmost sincerity. When we try to find excuses for not following the dictates of our intuitive knowledge, we are insincere in thought, and this insincerity is the same as what Ch'eng Hao and Wang Shou-jen call selfishness and rationalization. When our thought is sincere, our mind is rectified; the rectification of the mind is no other than sincerity in thought.

The next four steps of the "eight wires" are the cultivation of the self, regulation of the family, setting in order of the state and bringing of peace to the world. According to Wang Shou-jen, the cultivation of the self is the same as the extension of the intuitive knowledge. For how can we cultivate ourselves without extending our intuitive knowledge? And in cultivating ourselves what should we do besides extending our intuitive knowledge? In extending our intuitive knowledge, we must love people, and in loving people, how can we do otherwise than regulate our family, and contribute our best to creating order in our state, and bringing peace to the world? Thus all the "eight wires" may after all be reduced to a single "wire," which is the extension of the intuitive knowledge.

在中文里，"格物"按程颐和朱熹的解释就是剖析事物，王守仁的解释不同，他认为"格者，正也"，"物者，事也"（《大学问》，《全书》卷二十六）。这样，"格物"便不再是"剖析事物"，而成为"匡正事物"了。他认为，人的直觉知识不可能按佛家教导的冥思默想方法而得到延展，它只有通过人们处理日常事务的经验而得到延展。王守仁说："心之所发便是意（意志、思想）。……意之所在便是物。如意在于事亲，即事亲便是一物；意在于事君，即事君便是一物。"（《传习录》上，《全书》卷一）物有是非之别，人可以本着良知（直觉知识）来作出判断。当人从良知认识到一件事是对的，就应当真诚去做；当人的良知告诉人，某件事是错的，他就应当真诚地不去做。这样，便匡正了他的事务，同时延展了良知（致良知）。人的良知只有通过匡正自己事务的行动实践而得到延展，除此之外，没有别的办法。《大学》说"致知在格物"，含义就在此。

八条目的下两步是"诚意"和"正心"。王守仁以为，诚意无非是"正事"和"致知"，因为实践这两点都需要真诚。人对自己的良知的命令，寻找借口不去执行时，便是没有诚意，这个不真诚和程颢、王守仁所说的自私和自我辩解并没有区别。人在意诚时，他的心是正的。正心就要诚意。

八条目的后四步是修身、齐家、治国、平天下。王守仁认为，修身就是致良知。若不在"致良知"上用工夫，怎能修身呢？修身的含义，除去"致良知"外，还能再有什么呢？人努力"致良知"时，自然爱大众；人在爱大众时，自然努力治家，尽力谋求国家井然有序和天下太平。因此，八条目也归结到一条，就是"致良知"。

What is the intuitive knowledge? It is simply the inner light of our mind, the original unity of the universe, or, as the *Great Learning* calls it, the illustrious virtue. Hence the extension of the intuitive knowledge is nothing else than the manifestation of the illustrious virtue. Thus all the ideas of the *Great Learning* are reduced to the one idea expressed in the key words, the extension of the intuitive knowledge.

To quote Wang Shou-jen again: "The mind of man is Heaven. There is nothing that is not included in the mind of man. All of us are this single Heaven, but because of the obscurings caused by selfishness, the original state of Heaven is not made manifest. Every time we extend our intuitive knowledge, we clear away the obscurings, and when all of them are cleared away, our original nature is restored, and we again become part of this Heaven. The intuitive knowledge of the part is the intuitive knowledge of the whole. The intuitive knowledge of the whole is the intuitive knowledge of the part. Everything is the single whole." (*Record of Instructions*, pt. 1.)

- **Attentiveness of the Mind**

Thus Wang Shou-jen's system follows the same lines as those of Chou Tun-yi, Ch'eng Hao and Lu Chiu-yüan, but he expresses it in more systematic and precise terms. The fact that the "cords" and "wires" of the *Great Learning* fit so well into his system brings both conviction to himself and authority to others.

The system and its method of spiritual cultivation are simple and direct—qualities which themselves give it a powerful appeal. What we need is first of all the understanding that each and every one of us possesses the original mind, which is one with the universe. This understanding is referred to by Lu Chiu-yüan as "first establishing the most important," a phrase he borrows from Mencius. On one occasion he said: "Recently there have been people who have criticized me by saying that apart from the single statement in which I lay emphasis upon first establishing the most important, I have no other tricks to offer. When I heard this, I exclaimed: 'Quite so!'" (*Collected Works, chüan* 34.)

In chapter twenty-four it was pointed out that, according to the Neo-Confucianists, spiritual cultivation requires that one should be attentive; but attentive to what? According to the Lu-Wang school, one must "first establish the most important," and then be attentive to it. And it is the criticism of this school that the Ch'eng-Chu school, without "first establishing the most important," starts immediately and haphazardly with the task of investigating things. Under these conditions, even

什么是"良知"？它就是人内心的亮光，或如《大学》称之为"明德"。因此，"致良知"也就是"明明德"。这样，《大学》的全部思想就归结为"致良知"了。

再次用王守仁的话来说："人心是天渊，无所不赅。原是一个天，只为私欲障碍，则天之本体失了。……如今念念致良知，将此障碍窒塞，一齐去尽，则本体已复，便是天渊了。……一节之知，即全体之知；全体之知，即一节之知。总是一个本体。"（《传习录》下，《全书》卷三）

● **"用敬"**

由此可见，王守仁的思想体系和宋代周敦颐、程颢、陆九渊是一脉相承的，只是王守仁用词更明确、表达更为系统。《大学》的三纲领、八条目如此恰当地被纳入他的体系，使他的话更有自信，也更足以服人。

王守仁的思想体系和他的精神修养方法如此简单明了，这个特点使他的主张具有极大的吸引力。人只需要首先懂得，人人都有本来的一颗心，这颗心与天地是一体。这就是陆九渊所说的"先立乎其大者"，这句话原是来自《孟子》。陆九渊曾说："近有议吾者云：除了'先立乎其大者'一句，全无伎俩。吾闻之曰：'诚然。'"（《象山全集》卷三十四）

在第二十四章里说到，新的儒家认为，精神修养的关键在于一个"敬"字。但是，"敬"什么呢？按照陆王心学的看法，人应当"先立乎其大者"，然后"用敬"存之。陆王学派批评程朱学派，还未"先立乎其大者"，便迫不及待地去"格物"。这样，即便

attentiveness of mind cannot lead to any results in spiritual cultivation. This procedure is compared by the Lu-Wang school to starting a fire for cooking, without having any rice in the pot.

To this, however, the Ch'eng-Chu school would reply that unless one begins with the investigation of things, how can anything be definitely established? If one excludes this investigation of things, the only way left of "establishing the most important" is through instantaneous Enlightenment. And this the Ch'eng-Chu school regarded as more Ch'anist than Confucianist.

In chapter twenty-four, we have seen that Ch'eng Hao also says that the student must first understand *jen* (human-heartedness), which is the unity of all things, and then cultivate it with sincerity and attentiveness. Nothing else requires to be done. We merely need have confidence in ourselves and go straight forward. Lu Chiu-yüan remarks in similar strain: "Be courageous, be zealous, break open the net, burn the thorns in your path, and wash away the mire." (*Ibid.*) When so doing, even the authority of Confucius need no longer necessarily be respected. As Lu states again: "If in learning one gains a comprehension of what is fundamental, then the Six Classics become but one's footnotes." (*Ibid.*) In this respect we see clearly that the Lu-Wang school is a continuation of Ch'anism.

• Criticism of Buddhism

Yet both the Lu-Wang and Ch'eng-Chu schools strongly criticize Buddhism. In this criticism, the difference between the two is again revealed. Thus Chu Hsi says: "When the Buddhists speak of 'emptiness', this does not mean that they are [entirely] incorrect. But they must know that in this emptiness there are the *Li*. For if we are merely to say that we are 'empty', without understanding that there are still the real *Li*, what is the use [of such a doctrine]? The case is like that of a pool of clear water, the cold clearness of which extends to the very bottom. When it is first seen, it will appear to have no water in it at all, and a person will then say that this pool is only 'empty.' If this person does not put in his hand to feel whether there is coldness or warmth, he will not know that there is water within. And such, precisely, is the view of the Buddhists." (*Recorded Sayings, chüan* 126.) Again he says: "The Confucianists consider *Li* as without birth and indestructible. The Buddhists consider spirituality and consciousness as without birth and indestructible." (*Ibid*.) According to Chu Hsi, the Buddhists are not without justification in saying that the concrete world is empty, because things in the concrete world do change

"用敬"，也全无功效。陆王学派把程朱的做法比作烧火做饭，但锅内却无米。

程朱学派对此的回答是：若不从"格物"做起，怎能知道要"立"的是什么呢？如果排除了"格物"，就讲"先立乎其大者"，那就只能靠"顿悟"。按程朱学派的意见，这种主张的禅学成分多于儒学成分。

在二十四章里我们看到，程颢也说，"学者须先识仁"，与万物同为一体；然后以诚敬存之。除此以外，不须再做他事。人所需要的是确信自己、勇往直前。陆象山的主张也很相近，他说："激励奋迅，决破罗网，焚烧荆棘，荡夷污泽。"（同上）照这样做去，连孔子的权威也可不再需要了。如陆象山所说："学苟知本，六经皆我注脚。"（同上）在这方面，我们可以清楚看出，陆王心学乃是禅学思想的继续。

● 对佛学的批评

但是，陆王心学和程朱理学对佛学都持尖锐批评的态度，而在对佛学的思想批判中，程朱理学和陆王心学的分歧又再次显现出来。朱熹曾说："释氏说空，不是便不是，但空里面须有道理始得。若只说道我是个空，而不知有个实的道理，却做甚用。譬如一渊清水，清泠彻底，看来一如无水相似，他便道此渊只是空的。不曾将手去探是冷温，不知道有水在里面，释氏之见正如此。"（《朱子语类》卷一百二十六）在这里，朱熹指出，在佛家所见的"空"之中，其实有个"理"在。他又说："儒者以理为不生不灭，释氏以神、识为不生不灭。"（同上）按朱熹的意见，佛家以具体的世界为空，并不无道理，因为具体世界的一切都流动不居，因此都只是暂时的。

and are impermanent. But there are also the *Li*, which are eternal and not subject to change. In this sense, then, the universe is not empty. The Buddhists do not know that the *Li* are real, because they are abstract, just as some men do not see the water in the pool, because it is colorless.

Wang Shou-jen also criticizes Buddhism, but from quite a different point of view: "When the Taoists [i. e., the religious Taoists] speak of *hsü* [vacuity, unrealness], can the Confucian sage add to it a hair of *shih* [actualness, realness]? And when the Buddhists speak of *wu* [non-being, non-existence], can the Confucian sage add to it a hair of *yu* [being, existence]? But when the Taoists speak of *hsü*, their motive is to preserve life, whereas when the Buddhists speak of *wu*, their motive is to escape the suffering of life and death. When they add these ideas to the original nature of the mind, their original meaning of *hsü* and *wu* is somewhat lost, and thereby the original nature of the mind is not free from obstruction. The Confucian sage simply restores the original condition of the intuitive knowledge and adds to it no idea whatsoever.... Heaven, Earth, and all things all lie within the function and activity of our intuitive knowledge. How, then, can there be anything outside it to hinder or obstruct it?" (*Record of Instructions*, pt. 3.)

Again he says: "The claim of the Buddhists that they have no attachment to phenomena shows that they do have attachment to them. And the fact that we Confucianists do not claim to have no attachment to phenomena, shows that we do not have attachment to them.... The Buddhists are afraid of the troubles involved in human relationships, and therefore escape from them. They are forced to escape because they are already attached to them. But we Confucianists are different. There being the relationship between father and son, we respond to it with love. There being the relationship between sovereign and subject, we respond to it with righteousness. And there being the relationship between husband and wife, we respond to it with mutual respect. We have no attachment to phenomena." (*Ibid.*)

If we follow this argument, we can say that the Neo-Confucianists more consistently adhere to the fundamental ideas of Taoism and Buddhism than do the Taoists and Buddhists themselves. They are more Taoistic than the Taoists, and more Buddhistic than the Buddhists.

但世界还有理，它是永恒不变的。就这一点看，世界不是空。佛家不识得理的真实性，只因理是抽象的；犹如有些人看不见池中的水，只因为水没有颜色。

王守仁也批评佛教，但批评的出发点不同。在《传习录》下卷里，王守仁说："仙家说到'虚'，圣人岂能'虚'上加得一毫'实'？佛家说到'无'，圣人岂能'无'上加得一毫'有'？但仙家说虚，从养生上来；佛家说无，从出离生死苦海上来。却于本体上加却这些子意思在，便不是它虚无的本色了，便于本体有障碍。圣人只是还它良知的本色，更不著些子意思在。……天地万物，俱在我良知的发用流行中，何尝又有一物超于良知之外，能作得障碍？"（《全书》卷三）

他又说："佛氏不著相，其实著了相（著相，意为"执著"）；吾儒著相，其实不著相。……（佛）都是为了君臣父子夫妇著相，便须逃避。如吾儒，有个父子，还它以仁；有个君臣，还它以义；有个夫妇，还它以别。何尝著父子君臣夫妇的相？"（同上）

如果依循这种辩论的思路，可以认为，新的儒家在坚持道家和佛家的基本思想上，比道家和佛家自己更加一贯和彻底，他们是比道家更道地的道家，也是比佛家更道地的佛家。

㉗ THE INTRODUCTION OF WESTERN PHILOSOPHY

Every system of philosophy is likely to be misunderstood and misused, and so it was with the two schools of Neo-Confucianism. According to Chu Hsi, one must in principle start with the investigation of things in order to understand the eternal *Li* or Laws, but this principle Chu Hsi himself did not strictly carry out. In the record of his sayings, we see that he did make certain observations on natural and social phenomena, but most of his time was devoted to the study of, and comment on, the Classics. He not only believed that there are eternal *Li*, but also that the utterances of the ancient sages are these eternal *Li*. So in his system there is an element of authoritarianism and conservatism, which became more and more apparent as the tradition of the Ch'eng-Chu school went on. And the fact that this school became the official state teaching did much to increase this tendency.

● **Reaction Against Neo-Confucianism**

The Lu-Wang school is a revolution against this conservatism, and in the time of Wang Shou-jen, the revolutionary movement was at its highest. In a very simple way, it appealed directly to the intuitive knowledge of every man, which is the inner light of his "original mind." Though never recognized by the government, as was the Ch'eng-Chu school, the Lu-Wang school became as influential as the former.

But the philosophy of Wang Shou-jen was also misunderstood and misused. According to Wang, what the intuitive knowledge immediately knows is the ethical aspect of our will or thought. It can only tell us what we ought to do, but not *how* to do it. It lacks what Americans would now call "know-how." In order to know how to do what we ought to do in certain situations, Wang said that we have to study practical methods of action in relation to the existing state of affairs. Later on, however, his followers seemed to come to the belief that the intuitive knowledge can itself tell us everything, including the "know-how." This is absurd, and the followers of the Lu-Wang school have certainly suffered the consequences of this absurdity.

At the end of the last chapter we have seen that Wang Shou-jen used the Ch'an method of argument to criticize Buddhism. This is precisely the sort of argument that is most likely to be misused. A satiric story tells

贰拾柒 西方哲学的传入

任何哲学思想体系都往往被人误解和误用。更新的儒学的两派也难免这样的厄运。朱熹的主张是：从原则上说，人应当由"格物"入手，从中求得永恒之理，即法则。但是朱熹自己便没有严格遵行这个原则。在《朱子语类》中，可以看到，他对自然现象和社会现象的确进行了一些观察，但是他的主要精力和时间是用在对经书的研究和评论上。他不仅深信有永恒之理，而且认为古圣先贤的言论便是这种永恒之理。因此在他的思想中，有一种权威主义和保守主义的成分，在程朱学派后来的发展中，这种倾向更加明显。这个学派的思想被后来的统治者树立为官方的正统思想，更加重了它的权威主义和保守主义色彩。

● 反对更新的儒学的思潮

陆王便是对哲学保守主义的一种革命，到王守仁的时代，这种革命运动达到了最高潮。它简捷了当地诉诸每一个人的直觉，这直觉便是每个人"本心"的内在亮光。陆王学派虽然从未像程朱学派那样得到官方的确认，却像程朱学派同样地有影响。

但是，王守仁的哲学也同样受到误解和误用。本来，王守仁所主张的是：人凭直觉会立刻知道自己的意志或思想是对，或是错。它能告诉人的是应当做的事，却不能告诉人怎样去做，它缺少的是现在美国人所称的"知道怎样干"（Know how）。王守仁认为，在具体情况下，要想知道怎么做，需要结合具体情况，研究行动的具体办法。但是，后来王守仁的追随者们似乎相信，直觉可以把样样事情都告诉人，包括"知道怎么干"。这便走到了荒谬的地步，陆王学派的追随者们也因此而吃了苦头。

在上一章末尾我们看到，王守仁用禅宗辩论的办法来批评

us that when a scholar once paid a visit to a certain Buddhist temple, he was treated with only scant respect by the monk in charge. While he was there, however, the temple was also visited by a prominent official, to whom the monk showed the greatest respect. After the official had gone, the scholar asked the monk the reason for this difference. The monk answered: "To respect is not to respect, and not to respect is to respect." The scholar immediately gave him a hearty blow on the face. The monk protested angrily: "Why do you beat me?" To which the scholar replied: "To beat is not to beat, and not to beat is to beat." This story became current after the time of Wang Shou-jen, and no doubt was intended to criticize him and the Ch'anists.

The Ming dynasty (1368-1643), under which Wang Shou-jen lived and had his influence, was a native Chinese dynasty which replaced the Yüan or Mongol dynasty (1280-1367). In due course it in turn was overthrown as a result of internal revolts coupled with invasion from the outside, and was replaced by the Ch'ing dynasty (1644-1911), under which, for the second time in Chinese history, all of China was ruled by an alien group, this time the Manchus. The Manchus, however, were far more sympathetic to Chinese culture than the Mongols had been, and the first two-thirds of their dynasty was, on the whole, a period of internal peace and prosperity for China, during which, in certain respects, Chinese culture made important advances, though in other respects it was a period of growing cultural and social conservatism. Officially, the Ch'eng-Chu school was even more firmly entrenched than before. Unofficially, however, the Ch'ing dynasty witnessed an important reaction against both this school and the Lu-Wang school. The leaders of this reaction accused both schools of having, under the influence of Ch'anism and Taoism, misinterpreted the ideas of Confucius, and of thus having lost the practical aspect of original Confucianism. One of the attackers said: "Chu Hsi was a Taoist monk, and Lu Chiu-yüan was a Buddhist monk." This accusation, in a sense, is not entirely unjustified, as we have seen in the last two chapters.

From the point of view of philosophy, however, it is entirely irrelevant. As was pointed out in chapter twenty-three, Neo-Confucianism is a synthesis of Confucianism, Buddhism, philosophical Taoism (through Ch'anism), and religious Taoism. From the point of view of the history of Chinese philosophy, such a synthesis represents a development, and therefore is a virtue rather than a vice.

佛教。正是这种论辩方法最容易被歪曲误用。后来流传一个带讥刺意味的故事说，曾有一个书生到一座寺庙游览，遭到寺僧的冷遇。他在庙里时，看见寺僧对前来游览的大官毕恭毕敬。大官走了之后，这个书生质问寺僧，见达官贵人就趋炎附势，对布衣书生就不爱理睬，是何道理？僧人回答："敬乃不敬，不敬却正是敬。"书生听寺僧这样回答，抡起巴掌，打了和尚一个耳光。和尚气愤地质问书生，为什么打人？书生回答："打乃是不打，不打却是打。"在王守仁后流传这样的故事，无疑是对心学和禅学的一种讥讽。

王守仁生活于明朝（公元一三六八至一六四四年），心学的盛行也是在明朝。明朝取代元朝（公元一二八○〔一二○六〕至一三六八年），历时二百七十五年，最后，在内部农民起义和外族入侵的双重打击下覆灭，为清朝（公元一六四四〔一六一六〕至一九一一年）所取代。清朝的统治者满族比在元朝居统治地位的蒙古族对中国汉族的传统文化抱着远为同情的态度。清朝统治中国二百六十七年，前面的三分之二时间，可以说大体上为中国带来了和平与繁荣。在这段时间里，中国文化在一些方面有了重要的发展，而在其他一些方面则又日益严重地趋向文化和社会的保守主义。就官方态度来看，程朱学派的思想更加牢固地被官方树立起来。然而在非官方控制的领域里，程朱学派的理学和陆王学派的心学都遭到知识界的抵制。领导这种抵制运动的学人批判更新的儒学在禅宗和道教的影响下，都曲解了孔子的思想，把儒家思想原有的实践方面丢失殆尽。曾有对更新的儒学持批判态度的书生说："朱子道，陆子禅。"这种指责在一定意义上不无道理，在前面两章里已经说过，这里不再赘述。

从哲学本身说，这种指责并无意义。在本书第二十四章里已经指出，更新的儒学是儒学、佛学和道家思想（经过禅学）、道教思想的融合。从中国哲学史的观点看，这种思想融合是一种发展，因此是得而不是失。

In the Ch'ing dynasty, however, when the orthodox position of Confucianism was stronger than ever before, to assert that Neo-Confucianism was not the same as pure Confucianism was equal to asserting that Neo-Confucianism was false and wrong. According to its opponents, indeed, the harmful effects of Neo-Confucianism were even greater than those of Buddhism and Taoism, because its seeming agreement with original Confucianism could more easily deceive people and so lead them astray.

For this reason the scholars of the Ch'ing dynasty started a "back-to-the-Han" movement, meaning by this a return to the commentaries that the scholars of the Han dynasty had written on the early Classics. They believed that because these Han scholars lived nearer in time to Confucius and before the introduction of Buddhism into China, their interpretations of the Classics must therefore be purer and closer to the genuine ideas of Confucius. Consequently, they studied numerous writings of the Han scholars which the Neo-Confucianists had discarded, and termed this study the *Han hsüeh* or learning of the Han dynasty. It was so called in contrast to that of the Neo-Confucianists, which they termed the *Sung hsüeh* or learning of the Sung dynasty, because the major schools of Neo-Confucianism had flourished in this dynasty. Through the eighteenth century until the beginning of the present century, the controversy between the Ch'ing adherents of the *Han hsüeh* and *Sung hsüeh* has been one of the greatest in the history of Chinese thought. From our present point of view, it was really one as between the philosophical and scholarly interpretation of the ancient texts. The scholarly interpretation emphasized what it believed was their actual meaning; the philosophical interpretation emphasized what it believed they *ought* to have meant.

Because of the emphasis of the *Han hsüeh* scholars on the scholarly interpretation of ancient texts, they made marked developments in such fields as textual criticism, higher criticism, and philology. Indeed, their historical, philological, and other studies became the greatest single cultural achievement of the Ch'ing dynasty.

Philosophically, the contribution of the *Han hsüeh* scholars was less important, but culturally, they did much to open the minds of their time to the wider reaches of Chinese literary achievement. During the Ming dynasty, most educated people, under the influence of Neo-Confucianism, a knowledge of which was required for success in the state examinations, devoted their whole attention to the "Four Books" (the *Confucian Analects, Mencius, Great Learning,* and *Doctrine of the Mean*). As a result, they knew but little about other literature. Once the Ch'ing scholars became interested in the scholarly reevaluation of the

就清朝说，儒家思想的正统地位胜过以往历代，而更新的儒学被指责为背离原来的儒家思想，无异说它是假的，因而是错谬的。在反对更新的儒学的人看来，更新的儒学比佛教、道教的思想更为有害，因为它貌似原来的儒学，从而更容易把人引入歧途。

为此，清朝的学者提倡"汉学"，就是以汉代的经书注疏为论学依据。他们认为，西汉离孔子的时代较近，而且当时佛学还未传入中国，因此汉代注释的儒家经典，自然更符合孔子的原意。这样一来，清代学者对遭到宋明两代新的儒家忽视的汉代学者著述十分重视，把这种研究称为"汉学"；而把更新的儒学称为"宋学"，因为更新的儒学及其主要流派都兴起于宋朝。贯穿整个十八世纪，直到十九世纪末、二十世纪初，清代"汉学"和"宋学"之争成为这一时期中国哲学史上的大事，其实所论的无非是对古代文献的看法，其中涉及对古代著作的哲学内容和经书文字的考订，从文字考订引出对经书本意的阐述，进而论证它们的哲学含义应当是什么。

由于汉学家重视古代文献的研究，清代学者在古书校勘、古文字学、历史语言学等方面，做出了成绩。这是清代文化史上的巨大成就。

就哲学来说，清代汉学家的思想成就比较逊色，但是在文化上，清儒使人们看到古代文化的广阔视野，起了打开人们眼界的作用。明朝的书生为应付科举，其中以朱熹的《四书集注》为判卷标准，因此读书人的注意力都集中于"四书"，对"四书"以外的其他典籍所知甚少。"汉学"的本意虽然希望儒生集中注意先秦两汉

ancient texts, however, they could not confine themselves simply to the Confucian Classics. These, to be sure, engaged their first attention, but when the work in this field had been done, they began to study all the other ancient texts of the schools other than orthodox Confucianism, including such writings as the *Mo-tzu, Hsün-tzu* and *Han-fei-tzu*, which had long been neglected. They worked to correct the many corruptions that had crept into the texts, and to explain the ancient usage of words and phrases. It is owing to their labors that these texts are today so much more readable than they were, for example, in the Ming dynasty. Their work did much to help the revival of interest in the philosophical study of these philosophers that has taken place in recent decades under the stimulus of the introduction of Western philosophy. This is a topic to which we shall now turn.

- ### Movement for a Confucian Religion

It is not necessary to examine here precisely the manner in which the Chinese first came in contact with Western culture. Suffice it to say that already toward the end of the Ming dynasty, i.e., in the latter part of the sixteenth century and early part of the seventeenth, many Chinese scholars became impressed by the mathematics and astronomy that were introduced to China at that time by Jesuit missionary scholars. If Europeans call China and surrounding areas the Far East, the Chinese in the period of early Sino-European contacts referred to Europe as the Far West or *T'ai Hsi.* In earlier centuries they had spoken of India as "the West"; hence they could only refer to countries to the west of India as the "Far West." This term has now been discarded, but it was in common usage as late as the end of the last century.

In chapter sixteen I said that the distinction which the Chinese have traditionally made between themselves and foreigners or "barbarians" has been more cultural than racial. Their sense of nationalism has been more developed in regard to culture than to politics. Being the inheritors of an ancient civilization, and one geographically far removed from any other of comparable importance, it has been difficult for them to conceive how any other people could be cultured and yet live in a manner different from themselves. Hence whenever they have come into contact with an alien culture, they have been inclined to despise and resist it—not so much as something alien, but simply because they have thought it to be inferior or wrong. As we have seen in chapter eighteen, the introduction

的儒家，但读书人一旦打开了眼界，便很难一心只读圣贤书。除了正统儒家之外，读书人也去读《墨子》、《荀子》、《韩非子》等长期被弃置在旁的典籍。因年代久远而湮没的古文字学重受重视，古代文献经后世传抄而出现的错讹别字，现在得到订正。由于清朝汉学家的辛劳，现在我们读古代典籍，比明朝时容易得多。清代"朴学"的成就，使学人对古代思想的研究兴趣又重新兴起。中国人在近几十年接触西方思想时，自然要反问中国传统思想，以求两相比较。这样，我们就转到西方哲学传入中国带来的各种影响这个主题上来了。

● 孔教运动

在这里不需要仔细考察中国人开始接触西方文化时的态度，只指出一点就够了，那就是明朝末年，十六世纪末、十七世纪初西欧天主教耶稣会士来华，把当时欧洲的天文、数学成就介绍到中国，给许多中国儒生以深刻的印象。当时的欧洲人称中国和东亚是"远东"，中国人则称欧洲是"泰西"。在先前的一千多年里，中国人称印度为"西天"，对印度以西便笼统称为"泰西"。这个名词现在已经弃置不用，但直到上世纪末，"泰西"这个词还是十分流行的。

在第十六章里曾经说到，中国人历来是以文化差异，而不是以民族差异来区分自身与外族（"化外"、"夷狄"）。中国人的民族意识更多来自文化，而不是来自政治。中国的地理位置远离其他重要国家，又拥有古老的文明，在这种地理、文化环境里，中国人很难设想，居然还有其他民族也拥有发达的文明，而在生活方式上却与中国人全然不同。因此，中国人接触外来文化时，往往倾向于蔑视并且加以抵制，主要不是排斥外来的东西，而是认为外来文化是低级的，甚至是错误的。在第十八章里我们看到，佛教传入中国，激起了

of Buddhism stimulated the foundation of religious Taoism, which came as a sort of nationalistic reaction to the alien faith. In the same way, the introduction of Western culture, in which Christian missionaries played a leading part, created a very similar reaction.

In the sixteenth and seventeenth centuries, as just noted, the missionary scholars impressed the Chinese not so much by their religion as by their attainments in mathematics and astronomy. But later, especially during the nineteenth century, with the growing military, industrial, and commercial predominance of Europe, and the coincident decline of China's political strength under the Manchus, the impetus of Christianity became increasingly felt by the Chinese. After several major controversies had broken out in the nineteenth century between missionaries and Chinese, a movement for a native Confucian religion to counteract the growing impact of the West started at the very end of that century by the famous statesman and reformer, K'ang Yu-wei (1858-1927). This event was no mere accident—even from the point of view of the inner development of Chinese thought—because the scholars of the *Han hsüeh* had already paved the way.

In chapters seventeen and eighteen, we saw that the Han dynasty was dominated by two schools of Confucianism: one the Old Text and the other the New Text school. With the revival during the Ch'ing dynasty of the study of the works of the Han scholars, the old controversy between these two schools was also revived. We have also seen that the New Text school, headed by Tung Chung-shu, believed Confucius to have been the founder of an ideal new dynasty, and later even went so far as to consider him as a supernatural being having a mission to perform on this earth, a veritable god among men. K'ang Yu-wei was a leader of the Ch'ing adherents of the New Text school in the *Han hsüeh*, and found in this school plenty of material for establishing Confucianism as an organized religion in the proper sense of the word.

In studying Tung Chung-shu, we have already read Tung's fantastic theory about Confucius. The theory of K'ang Yu-wei is even more so. As we have seen, in the *Ch'un Ch'iu* or *Spring and Autumn Annals*, or rather in the theory of its Han commentators, as well as in the *Li Chi* or *Book of Rites*, there is the concept that the world passes through three ages or stages of progress. K'ang Yu-wei now revived this theory, interpreting it to mean that the age of Confucius had been the first age of decay and disorder. In our own times, he maintained, the growing communications between East and West, and the political and social reforms in Europe

中国道教的兴起，这是一种以中国本民族宗教抵制外来宗教信仰的努力。当西方文化传入中国，而基督教传教士在这种文化传播中起了主导作用，它所引起的反应也十分相似。

十六、十七世纪，欧洲基督教传教士学者给中国人深刻印象的，不是他们的宗教信仰方面，而是他们在数学和天文学方面的成就。但是后来，特别是十九世纪，欧洲大国在军事、工业、商业上居于优势地位，向外扩张；而与此同时，中国的政治力量在满族统治下正趋于衰落。这时，中国人感到基督教对于文化的推动力量。十九世纪下半叶，外国传教士和中国人之间爆发了几次大规模冲突，十九世纪末，中国著名的政治改革家康有为（公元一八五八至一九二七年）发起孔教运动，以对抗日益增长的西方影响。这一事件并非偶然的——甚至从中国思想发展角度看，也不是偶然的，因为汉学家们已经为此铺平了道路。

在第十七、十八章里我们看到，汉代经学分古文学派和今文学派。汉学在清朝的再起，使古文学派和今文学派的争论也再次抬头了。汉代以董仲舒为首的今文学家深信孔子创立了一个理想的新朝代，这一派后来甚至把孔子奉为超人，认为他降世是为了完成在人间的使命。康有为是清代今文学派的领袖，他从古代文献里找出许多材料，力图把儒家建立为一种宗教，并且建立起相应的孔教组织。

在介绍董仲舒时我们已经读到董仲舒关于孔子的怪诞理论，康有为比董仲舒有过之无不及。汉代的注疏家们从《春秋》和《礼记》中引申出社会进化有三个世代（衰乱世、升平世、太平世）的理论，康有为把这个理论加以发展，他在一九○二年著《论语注》时说："孔子生当据乱之世。今者，大地既通，欧美大变，盖进至升平之世矣。

and America, show that men are progressing from the stage of disorder to the second higher stage, that of approaching peace. And this in turn will be followed by the unity of the whole world, which will be the realization of the last stage of human progress, that of great peace. Writing in 1902, he said: "Confucius knew all these things beforehand."(*Lun-yü Chu* or *Commentary to the Analects, chüan* 2.)

K'ang Yu-wei was the leader of the notable political reforms of 1898, which, however, lasted only a few months, and were followed by his own flight abroad, the execution of several of his followers, and renewed political reaction on the part of the Manchu government. In his opinion, what he was advocating was not the adoption of the new civilization of the West, but rather the realization of the ancient and genuine teachings of Confucius. He wrote many commentaries on the Confucian Classics and read his new ideas into them. Besides these, he also in 1884 wrote a book titled the *Ta T'ung Shu* or *Book of the Great Unity*, in which he gave a concrete picture of the utopia that will be realized in the third stage of human progress, according to the Confucian scheme. Although this book is so bold and revolutionary that it will startle even most utopian writers, K'ang Yu-wei himself was far from being a utopian. He insisted that his program could not be put into practice except in the highest and last stage of human civilization. For his immediate practical political program he insisted on merely instituting a constitutional monarchy. Thus throughout his life he was hated first by the conservatives because he was too radical, and later by the radicals because he was too conservative.

But the twentieth century is not one of religion, and together with, or in addition to, the introduction of Christianity into China, there also came modern science, which is the opposite of religion. Thus the influence of Christianity *per se* has been limited in China, and the movement for a Confucian religion suffered an early death. Nevertheless, with the overthrow of the Ch'ing dynasty and its replacement by the Republic in 1912, there was a demand by K'ang Yu-wei's followers, when the first Constitution of the Republic was drafted in 1915, that it state that the Republic adopt Confucianism as the state religion. A vigorous controversy developed over this point, until a compromise was reached, the Constitution asserting that the Chinese Republic would adopt Confucianism, not as a state religion, but as the fundamental principle for ethical discipline. This Constitution was never put into practice, and no more has since been heard about Confucianism as a religion in the sense intended by K'ang Yu-wei.

It is to be noted that up to 1898, K'ang Yu-wei and his comrades knew very little, if anything, about Western philosophy. His friend T'an Ssu-t'ung

异日大地大小远近如一，国土既尽，种类不分，风化齐同，则如一而太平矣。孔子已预知之。"（《论语注》卷二）

康有为是一八九八年戊戌维新的领袖人物。这场改革只进行了几个月，便遭到镇压，康有为的一些追随者被杀，康有为自己逃亡日本，清朝当局重又加强镇压。其实，康有为认为自己并不是鼓吹西方文化，而是为了实现中国古代孔子的理想。他为儒家经书撰写了不少注疏，把他的思想写入这些注疏之中。除这些书之外，一八八四年，他还写了一本《大同书》，其中描绘孔子学说预见到的人类进化第三阶段"太平世"时的世界。这部书如此大胆，如此革命化，以致最大胆的未来社会空想家都为之吃惊，而康有为自己并不是一个乌托邦主义者。他坚持认为，他的理想只有到人类社会发展到最高阶段时，才能实施。而目前阶段，他所主张的只是君主立宪制。康有为在世时，保守派首先憎恨他，因为他太激进。后来，激进派憎恨他，因为他太保守。

但是，二十世纪并不是一个热衷于宗教的世纪。在基督教传入中国的同时，或者说，凌驾于基督教之上的是传来了科学，它和宗教正好背道而驰。因此，基督教本身在中国的影响是有限的，孔教运动也早已夭折了。一九一一年辛亥革命推翻了清朝统治，一九一二年中华民国临时政府成立，取代了清朝政府。一九一五年起草中华民国宪法时，康有为的追随者曾要求中华民国以孔教为国教。这一点引起了激烈的争论，最后达成了一个妥协方案，在宪法草案中写入"中华民国以儒家思想为伦理道德的基本准则"。这个宪法从未付诸实行。此后，康有为所倡导的以儒学为基础而建立的儒教，也无声无息了。

应当提到的是，直到一八九八年，康有为和他的同志们对西方哲学

(1865-1898), who died a martyr's death when the political reform movement failed, was a much more subtle thinker than K'ang himself. He wrote a book titled *Jen Hsüeh* or *Science of Jen* (human-heartedness), which introduces into Neo-Confucianism some ideas taken from modern chemistry and physics. In the beginning of his work, he lists certain books to be read before one studies his *Science of Jen.* In that list, among books on Western thought, he mentions only the *New Testament* and "some treatises on mathematics, physics, chemistry, and sociology." It is plain that men of his time knew very little about Western philosophy, and that their knowledge of Western culture, in addition to machines and warships, was confined primarily to science and Christianity.

● Introduction of Western Thought

The greatest authority on Western thought at the beginning of the present century was Yen Fu (1853-1920). In his early years he was sent to England by the government to study naval science, and while there read some of the works on the humanities current at the time. After returning to China, he translated into Chinese the following works: Thomas Huxley, *Evolution and Ethics*; Adam Smith, *An Inquiry into the Nature and Causes of the Wealth of Nations*; Herbert Spencer, *The Study of Sociology*; John Stuart Mill, *On Liberty*, and half of his *A System of Logic*; E. Jenks, *A History of Politics*; Montesquieu, *Esprit des Lois*; and an adapted translation of Jevons, *Lessons in Logic*. Yen Fu began to translate these works after the first Sino-Japanese war of 1894-95. After that he became very famous and his translations were widely read.

There are three reasons to account for this popularity. The first is that China's defeat in the Sino-Japanese war, following a series of earlier humiliations at the hands of the West, shook the confidence of the Chinese people in the superiority of their own ancient civilization, and therefore gave them a desire to know something about Western thought. Before that time they fancied that Westerners were only superior in

science, machines, guns, and warships, but had nothing spiritual to offer.
The second reason is that Yen Fu wrote comments on many passages of

所知极少。康有为的朋友谭嗣同（公元一八六五至一八九八年）在维新运动失败后以身殉难，被清政府处决。就思想说，谭嗣同比康有为更敏锐。他曾著有《仁学》一书，其中吸收了近代化学和物理学的一些思想。在《仁学》书首，作者举出了读者在读《仁学》之前应当阅读的一些书籍，其中涉及西方思想的只是《新约圣经》和"有关数学、物理、化学和社会学方面的著作"。显然当时人们对西方哲学的知识十分有限，他们所知道的西方文化，除坚船利炮外，只限于科学和基督教。

● 西方思想的传入

二十世纪初的中国，关于西方思想的最大权威应推严复（公元一八五三至一九二〇年），他年轻时被清政府派往英国学习海军，在英国读到当时英国流行的一些人文学著作。回国后，他翻译了赫胥黎的《天演论》（Thomas Huxley: *Evolution and Ethics*）、亚当·斯密的《原富》（Adam Smith: *An Inquiry into the Nature and Causes of the Wealth of Nations*）、斯宾塞的《群学肄言》（Herbert Spenser: *The Study of Sociology*）、约翰·穆勒的《群己权界论》（John Stuart Mill: *On Liberty*）和他的《名学》（John Stuart Mill: *A System of Logic*）前半部、甄克斯的《社会通诠》（E. Jenks: *A History of Politics*）、孟德斯鸠的《法意》（Montesquieu: *De L'esprit des Lois*）以及编译的耶方斯《名学浅说》（Jevons: *Elementary Lessons on Logic*）。严复从事这些著作的翻译工作是在一八九四至一八九五年中日战争之后。他由此而著名，他的译作也广泛流传。

这些译作的广泛流传可以归因于三点。首先是中国在鸦片战争、英法联军入侵中败于西方国家，随后，又在甲午战争中败于日本。在此之前，中国人认为西方国家所恃的只是洋枪大炮和战舰，这都是科学技术，至于精神方面，西方国家并无长处。日本由明治维新，全面学习西方而战败中国，这极大地动摇了中国人对自己古老文明优越性的自信，由此而想对西方有所了解。第二个原因是，严复在他的译作中插进许多评论，比较这些西方作者的思想和中国

his translations, in which he compared certain ideas of his author with ideas in Chinese philosophy, in order to give a better understanding to his readers. This practice is something like the *ko yi* or interpretation by analogy, which was mentioned in chapter twenty in connection with the translation of Buddhist texts. And the third reason is that in Yen Fu's translations, the modern English of Spencer, Mill, and others was converted into Chinese of the most classical style. In reading these authors in his translation, one has the same impression as that of reading such ancient Chinese works as the *Mo-tzu* or *Hsün-tzu*. Because of their traditional respect for literary accomplishment, the Chinese of Yen Fu's time still had the superstition that any thought that can be expressed in the classical style is *ipso facto* as valuable as are the Chinese classical works themselves.

But the list of his translations shows that Yen Fu introduced very little Western philosophy. Among them, the ones really concerned with the subject are Jevons' *Lessons in Logic* and Mill's *System of Logic*, of which the former was an abridged summary, and the latter was left unfinished. Yen Fu recommended Spencer as the greatest Western philosopher of all time, thus showing that his knowledge of Western philosophy was rather limited.

There was another scholar of Yen Fu's time who in this respect had a better understanding and deeper insight, but who did not become known to the public until after he gave up the study of philosophy. He was Wang Kuo-wei (1877-1927), a scholar renowned as one of the greatest historians, archaeologists, and literary writers of recent times. Before he was thirty, he had already studied Schopenhauer and Kant, in this respect differing from Yen Fu, who studied almost none but English thinkers. But after he became thirty, Wang Kuo-wei gave up the study of philosophy, for a reason mentioned in one of his writings titled "A Self-Account at the Age of Thirty." In this he says:

"I have been tired of philosophy for a considerable time. Among philosophical theories, it is a general rule that those that can be loved cannot be believed, and those that can be believed cannot be loved. I know truth, and yet I love absurd yet great metaphysics, sublime ethics, and pure aesthetics. These are what I love most. Yet in searching for what is believable, I am inclined to believe in the positivistic theory of truth, the hedonistic theory of ethics, and the empiricist theory of aesthetics. I know these are believable, but I cannot love them, and I feel the other theories are lovable, but I cannot believe in them. This is the great vexation that I have experienced during the past two or three years.

哲学思想的异同，以便于读者理解。这个做法类似本书第二十章所述，先前佛经被译为中文时所用的"格义"法，也就是类比法。第三个原因是，严复以他的中国古典文学修养翻译斯宾塞、穆勒等人的当代英语，使中国读者阅读这些外国著作，如同阅读中国古代经书典籍。中国人历来尊敬学术，以为凡能用中国古典文字表达的思想，就值得尊敬，一如尊敬中国古典经书一样。

但是，从上列严复的译作目录中可以看出，严复介绍西方哲学著作很少，只有耶方斯的《名学浅说》和穆勒的《名学》，而前者只是节译与综述，后者只译了一半。严复推崇斯宾塞，说"欧洲自有生民以来无此作也"（《天演论》导言一，按语），这就说明他的哲学知识十分有限。

与严复同时还有另一位学者，对西方哲学有更深的理解，并且有真知灼见，这就是王国维（公元一八七七至一九二七年），但是他直到放弃哲学研究之后才以历史学、考古学和文学的成就驰名中国学术界。他在三十岁之前已经研究了叔本华（Arthur Schopenhauer）和康德（Immanuel Kant）的著作。严复所读的西方学术著作都是英国学者的著作，王国维却和严复不同。可惜他在三十岁时放弃了对西方哲学的研究，王国维在他的《三十自述》中陈述了其中原因。他说：

"余疲于哲学有日矣。哲学上之说，大都可爱者不可信，可信者不可爱。余爱真理，而余又爱其谬误伟大之形而上学、高严之伦理学与纯粹之美学，此吾人所酷嗜也。然求其可信者，则宁在知识论上之实证论、伦理学上之快乐论与美学上之经验论。知其可信而不能爱，觉其可爱而不能信，此近二三年中最大之烦闷，而近日之

Recently my interest has gradually transferred itself from philosophy to literature, because I wish to find in the latter direct consolation." [1]

He says again that such men as Spencer in England and Wundt in Germany are but second-rate philosophers, their philosophies being but a syncretism of science or of earlier systems. Other philosophers known to him at that time were only historians of philosophy. He said that he himself could become a competent historian of philosophy, if he continued to study it. "But," said he, "I cannot be a pure philosopher, and yet I do not like to be an historian of philosophy. This is another reason why I am tired of philosophy." (*Ibid.*)

I have quoted Wang Kuo-wei at length, because judging from these quotations, I think he had some insight into Western philosophy. He knew, as a Chinese expression says, "what is sweet and what is bitter in it." But on the whole, at the beginning of this century, there were very few Chinese who knew anything about Western philosophy. When I myself was an undergraduate student in Shanghai, we had a course on elementary logic, but there was no one in Shanghai at the time capable of teaching such a course. At last a teacher was found who asked us to buy a copy of Jevons' *Lessons in Logic* and to use it as a textbook. He asked us to read it in the way a teacher of English expects his pupils to go through an English reader. When we came to the lesson on judgment, he called on me to spell the word "judgment," in order to make sure that I would not insert an "e" between the "g" and "m"!

Before long we were at the mercy of another teacher who conscientiously tried to make the course a real one on logic. There are many exercises at the end of Jevons' book which this teacher did not ask us to do, but I nonetheless prepared them on my own account. It so happened that there was one exercise that was beyond my understanding, which I requested the teacher to expound after class. After discussing it with me for half an hour without being able to solve it, he finally said: "Let me think it over and I shall do it for you the next time I come." He never came again, and for this I felt rather sorry, for I had no desire to embarrass him.

The University of Peking was then the only national university in China which was supposed to have three departments of philosophy: Chinese, Western, and Indian. But as the University was then

嗜好，所以渐由哲学而移于文学，而欲于其中求直接之慰藉者也。"（《静安文集续编·自序二》）这里王国维说，他是因为在西方哲学中找不到能够沁人心灵的安慰，才由哲学转向文学的。

王国维又说：英国的斯宾塞和德国的冯特（Wilhelm Max Wundt）都只是二流的哲学家，他们的哲学不过是与科学的调和，或是前人哲学的调和；而他所知的其他哲学家不过是哲学史家。他认为自己如果继续读哲学，可以成为一个胜任的哲学史家。"然为哲学家则不能，为哲学史（家）则又不喜，此亦疲于哲学之一原因也"。

这里大段引述王国维的话，是因为我以为，从这些引述的话中可以看出他对西方哲学有一些具洞察力的见解。正如中国成语所说，他知道哲学中的"甘苦"。但总的说来，在二十世纪初，懂得西方哲学的中国人很少。我自己在上海中国公学读大学本科时，课程中有"逻辑学初步"，但当时在上海，没有人能够担任这门课的教席。最后找到一位教师，他要求学生买耶方斯的《名学浅说》编译本作为教科书，而把这本书作为学习英语的课本来读。当读到"逻辑判断"一节时，他要我背诵"判断"这个字的英语（judgment）拼法，想看我是否知道，在"g"和"m"中间不应加进英文字母"e"。

不久以后，我们又换了另一位教师。他是真心实意地把这门课作为逻辑来教。在耶方斯的《名学浅说》一书课文后面有许多练习题，教师并没有要求学生做这些练习题。我不管教师怎么说，自己按照这些习题，逐一去做，碰到一个习题，是我所不懂得的，我便在课后请老师给我讲解。他费了半小时，还未能讲解清楚，最后说："让我再想想，下次给你讲。"此后，他便不再来上课了。为这件事，我对老师深抱歉意，因为我并不是故意和他为难。

当时北京大学是全国国立大学之中，唯一计划开设中国哲学、西方哲学、印度哲学三门（门相当于后来的系）的学校。但是，按照

constituted, there was only the one department of Chinese philosophy. In 1915 it was stated that a department of Western philosophy would be established, since a professor had been engaged who had studied philosophy in Germany and presumably could teach courses in that subject. I accordingly went to Peking in that year and was admitted as an undergraduate, but to my disappointment the professor who was to have taught us had just died, and I had therefore to study in the department of Chinese philosophy.

In this department we had professors who were scholars representing the Old Text, New Text, Ch'eng-Chu, and Lu-Wang schools. One of them, a follower of the Lu-Wang school, taught us a course on the history of Chinese philosophy, a two-year course meeting four hours a week. He began with the traditional sage-kings, Yao and Shun, and by the end of the first semester had gone only as far as the Duke of Chou—that is to say, about five centuries before Confucius. We asked him how long, if he continued at this rate, it would take to finish the course. "Well," he replied, "in the study of philosophy there is no such thing as finishing or not finishing. If you want this course to be finished, I can finish it in one word; if you do not want it to be finished, it can never be finished."

- **Introduction of Western Philosophy**

John Dewey and Bertrand Russell were invited in 1919-20 to lecture at the University of Peking and other places. They were the first Western philosophers to come to China, and from them the Chinese for the first time received an authentic account of Western philosophy. But what they lectured about was mostly their own philosophy. This gave their hearers the impression that the traditional philosophical systems had all been superseded and discarded. With but little knowledge of the history of Western philosophy, the great majority of the audience failed to see the significance of their theories. One cannot understand a philosophy unless one at the same time understands the earlier traditions which it either approves or refutes. So these two philosophers, though well received by many, were understood by few. Their visit to China, nevertheless, opened new intellectual horizons for most of the students at that time. In this respect, their stay had great cultural and educational value.

In chapter twenty-one I have said that there is a distinction between Chinese Buddhism and Buddhism in China, and that the contribution

大学当时的科系设置，只有一个"中国哲学门"。一九一五年，据说即将成立"西方哲学门"，已经请到一位曾到德国学习哲学的教授前来授课。于是，当年我便到北京，进入北大作为本科生，但是遗憾的是，这位预定要来授课的教授不幸逝世，因此我只好转入中国哲学门学习。

在中国哲学门里，我们的教授之中，有的标榜古文经学，有的标榜今文经学，有的标榜程朱理学，有的标榜陆王心学。其中一位主张心学的教授开设"中国哲学史"课，每周四课时，讲两年。他按传统的讲法，从尧舜讲起，到第一学期结束时，刚讲到周公——就是说，离孔子的时代还有五百年。学生请教他，需要多少时间讲完这门课。他回答说："学哲学，无所谓学完或没有学完。如果你们要求我结束这门课，我可以一句话就讲完这门课，如果你们不愿结束，这门课可以一直讲下去。"

● **西方哲学的传入**

一九一九年到一九二〇年间，美国的约翰·杜威和英国的伯特兰·罗素两位哲学家应邀到中国，在北京大学和其他地方讲学。这是第一次有西方哲学家来中国讲学，也是中国人第一次听到有关西方哲学的第一手介绍。但是他们所讲的，主要是他们自己的哲学，使得听众以为西方的传统哲学思想已经过时而被弃置一旁了。大部分听众对于西方哲学史知识太少，因此对杜威、罗素两位的哲学的意义，也就弄不清楚。为要懂得一种哲学思想，首先要知道在它之前的哲学传统思想，然后才能理解，当前的哲学思想对过去的思想，在哪些地方是赞成的，在哪些地方是否定的。因此，这两位哲学家，在中国虽然受到热烈的欢迎，他们的思想，却很少人懂得。无论如何，他们对中国的访问，为当时的中国青年学生终究是展开了新的思想文化地平线。就这一点来说，他们在中国的讲学具有巨大的文化和教育价值。

在本书第二十一章里，我曾说到"中国佛教"和"佛教在中国"

of Buddhism to Chinese philosophy is the idea of Universal Mind. In the introduction of Western philosophy there have been similar cases. Following the visit of Dewey and Russell, for example, there have been many other philosophical systems that, at one time or another, have become popular in China. So far, however, almost all of them have simply represented Western philosophy in China. None has yet become an integral part of the development of the Chinese mind, as did Ch'an Buddhism.

So far as I can see, the permanent contribution of Western philosophy to Chinese philosophy is the method of logical analysis. In chapter twenty-one I have said that Buddhism and Taoism both use the negative method. The analytic method is just the opposite of this, and hence may be called the positive method. The negative method attempts to eliminate distinctions and to tell what its object is not, whereas the positive method attempts to make distinctions and tell what its object is. It is not very important for the Chinese that the negative method of Buddhism was introduced, because they had it already in Taoism, though Buddhism did serve to reinforce it. The introduction of the positive method, however, is really a matter of the greatest importance. It gives the Chinese a new way of thinking, and a change in their whole mentality. But as we shall see in the next chapter, it will not replace the other method; it will merely supplement it.

It is the method, not the ready-made conclusions of Western philosophy, that is important. A Chinese story relates that once a man met an immortal who asked him what he wanted. The man said that he wanted gold. The immortal touched several pieces of stone with his finger and they immediately turned to gold. The immortal asked the man to take them but he refused. "What else do you want?" the immortal asked. "I want your finger," the man replied. The analytic method is the finger of the Western philosophers, and the Chinese want the finger.

That is the reason why among the different branches of philosophical study in the West, the first to attract the attention of the Chinese was logic. Even before Yen Fu's translation of J. S. Mill's *System of Logic*, Li Chih-tsao (died 1630) had already translated with the Jesuit Fathers a mediaeval textbook on Aristotelean logic. His translation was titled *Ming-li T'an* or *An Investigation of Ming-li.* We have seen in chapter nineteen that *ming-li* means the analysis of principles through the analysis of names. Yen Fu translated logic as *ming hsüeh* or the Science of

有不同的含义，我也说到，佛教对中国哲学的贡献是"宇宙心"的概念。西方哲学传入中国也有类似的情况。举例来说，继杜威和罗素访华讲学之后，曾有许多不同的哲学思想体系在中国流行过一时。但是，迄今为止，几乎所有这些学说都只是代表了"西方哲学在中国"，还没有一种哲学能像禅学那样，融入中国人的思想，成为其中的一部分。

就我认识之所及，西方哲学对中国哲学的持久贡献在于它的逻辑分析方法。在第二十一章里，我曾说过，佛家和道家都使用"负的方法"。西方哲学的"分析方法"正好是"负的方法"的反面；因此，也许可以称之为"正的方法"。负的方法致力于消泯差别，告诉人：它的对象不是什么，而正的方法则致力于突出区别，使人知道它的对象是什么。对中国人来说，佛学带来的负的方法并不十分重要，因为中国人在道家思想里已经有了负的方法，佛家思想只是加强了它。而从西方引进了正的方法却有十分重大的意义，它不仅使中国人有一种新的思维方法，还改变了中国人的心态。但是在下一章里，我们将会看到，它不能取代"负的方法"，而只是加以补充。

西方哲学对中国人的重要性，不在于它已达到的现成结论，而在于它使用的方法。中国有一个故事说，有个人遇到一位神仙，神仙问他想要什么。这人回答说，想要金子。神仙便伸出手指点石成金，把几块金子给这个人。但他不要。问他还要什么，他回答说，我要你的手指。分析方法就是西方哲学的手指，中国人要的就是这个手指。

这就是何以在西方众多哲学流派之中，首先吸引中国人的是逻辑。甚至在严复翻译穆勒的《名学》之前，十七世纪的明末中国学者李之藻（死于公元一六三〇年）便曾和一位耶稣会士合作，翻译了一本中世纪欧洲的亚里士多德逻辑教科书，这部书的名称是《名理探》。在本书第十九章里，我们看到，"名理"的含义就是通过分析名字来辨明原理。严复把"逻辑"译作"名学"。在本书第八章

Names. As we have seen in chapter eight, the essence of the philosophy of the School of Names as represented by Kung-sun Lung is precisely the analysis of principles through the analysis of names. But in that chapter I also pointed out that this philosophy is not exactly the same as logic. There is a similarity, however, and when the Chinese first heard something about Western logic, they immediately noticed the similarity, and so connected it with their own School of Names.

Up to recent times the most fruitful result of the introduction of Western philosophy has been the revival of the study of Chinese philosophy, including Buddhism. There is nothing paradoxical in this statement. When one encounters new ideas that are unfamiliar, it is only natural that one should turn to familiar ones for illustration, comparison, and mutual confirmation. And when one turns to these ideas, armed with the analytic method, it is only natural that one should make an analysis of them. We have already seen at the beginning of this chapter that for the study of the ancient schools of thought other than Confucianist, the scholars of the *Han hsüeh* paved the way. Their interpretation of the ancient texts was primarily textual and philological, rather than philosophical. But that is exactly what is needed before one applies the analytic method to analyze the philosophical ideas of the various ancient Chinese schools of thought.

Because logic was the first aspect of Western philosophy that attracted the attention of the Chinese, it is natural that among the ancient Chinese schools, the School of Names was also the first to receive detailed study in recent years. Dr. Hu Shih's book, *The Development of the Logical Method in Ancient China*, since its first publication in 1922 has been one of the important contributions to this study. Scholars like Liang Ch'i-chao (1873-1930) have also contributed much to the study of the School of Names and of the other schools.

The interpretation and analysis of the old ideas through use of the analytic method characterized the spirit of the age up to the outbreak of the Sino-Japanese war in 1937. Even Christian missionaries could not escape from the influence of this spirit. This may be why many missionaries in China have translated Chinese philosophical works and written books on Chinese philosophy in Western languages, whereas few have translated Western philosophical works and written books on Western philosophy in Chinese. Thus in the philosophical field they seem to have conducted what might be called a reverse form of missionary work. It is possible to have reverse missionary work, just as it is possible to have reverse lend-lease.

里我们看到，以公孙龙为代表的中国名家哲学的实质正是通过分析名字来辨析原理。但是，在那一章里我还指出，名家的哲学思想还不就等于逻辑学，它们之间有相似之处，使中国人初听西方逻辑学时，会立刻注意到它与中国古代名家的相似之处，而把两者联系起来。

直到如今，西方哲学传入中国的最丰硕成果是振兴了对中国哲学——包括佛学——的研究。这句话并不难理解。人们在接触到不熟悉的新思想时，很自然地，便会找自己熟悉的思想去加以比较，求得互相印证。而当人把它们对照比较时，自然便要对它加以分析。正如在本章开始时我们看到，清儒研究儒家以外的先秦各家思想，得力于汉学（朴学）为它们铺平了研究道路。汉学所从事的是文本考订和古文字学的校勘注释，而不是哲学思想研究。这恰好是运用分析方法分析先秦各家哲学必要的先行工作。

由于逻辑是西方哲学吸引中国人的首要方面，当代中国哲学家重新考察先秦哲学思想时，也很自然首先是对名家进行研究。一九二二年，胡适博士所著《先秦名学史》问世，成为这种研究的一项重要成果。其他学者如梁启超（公元一八七三至一九三〇年）也对名家和其他学派的研究做出许多贡献。

一直到一九三七年中日战争之前，中国学术的时代精神可以说就是用分析方法对中国古代思想重新加以解释。甚至西方的基督教传教士也同样受到这种思潮的影响。这或者可以解释，何以有相当一批在华的西方传教士，用西方语言翻译中国哲学典籍，或著书介绍中国古典哲学，而很少有传教士把西方哲学典籍译为中文，或撰写关于西方哲学的中文著述，介绍给中国人。结果，就哲学方面看，可以说西方传教士所做的，乃是中国思想向西方的倒流。本来是向中国传播西方思想，很可能倒造成相反的结果，就如同"租借"关系里的租借双方也可能倒转过来一样。

㉘ CHINESE PHILOSOPHY IN THE MODERN WORLD

After all that has been said about the evolution and development of Chinese philosophy, readers may be inclined to ask such questions as: What is contemporary Chinese philosophy like, especially that of the war period? What will Chinese philosophy contribute to the future philosophy of the world? As a matter of fact, I have often been asked these questions, and have been somewhat embarrassed by them, because it is difficult to explain what a certain philosophy is to someone who is unfamiliar with the traditions that it either represents or opposes. However, now that the reader has gained some acquaintance with the traditions of Chinese philosophy, I am going to try to answer these questions by continuing the story of the last chapter.

● The Philosopher and the Historian of Philosophy

In so doing, I propose to confine myself to my own story, not at all because I think this is the only story worth telling, but because it is the story I know best and it can, perhaps, serve as a sort of illustration. This, I think, is better than merely giving a list of names and "isms," without any fuller exposition of any of them, a procedure which results in no kind of picture at all. By simply saying that a philosopher is a certain "ist," and nothing more, one usually creates misunderstanding instead of understanding.

My own larger *History of Chinese Philosophy*, the second and last volume of which was published in 1934, three years before the outbreak of the Sino-Japanese war, and the first volume of which was translated into English by Dr. Bodde and published in Peiping in 1937, three months after the war began, is an expression of that spirit of the age mentioned by me at the end of the last chapter. In that work I utilized the results of the studies of the *Han hsüeh* scholars on the texts of the ancient philosophers, and at the same time applied the analytic method to clarify the ideas of these philosophers. From the point of view of the historian, the use of this method has its limits, because the ideas of the ancient philosophers, in their original form, may not be as clear as in the presentation of their modern expositor. The function of a history of philosophy is to tell us what the words of the philosophers of the past actually meant to these men themselves, and not what we think they

贰拾捌 厕身现代世界的中国哲学

在介绍了中国哲学的演变和发展后，读者可能会问：当前中国哲学，特别是抗日战争以来的中国哲学是什么样？中国哲学对未来世界的哲学能做出什么贡献？事实上，常常有人向我提出这样的问题，而且使我感到很窘，因为要把一种哲学介绍给对这种哲学传统并不熟悉的人，无论介绍者赞成或反对这种哲学，都不是一件容易的事。现在，本书的读者对中国哲学传统已经有所认识，我就接着上一章的故事讲下去，试着回答这些问题。

● 哲学家和哲学史家

接着讲上一章的故事，我所谈将限于自身经历的范围之内，并不是除此以外都不值得谈，而是因为这是我最清楚的故事，用它来做一个实例，比列举一大串名字、开一个"主义"名单，而对其中任何一个题目都不能详加说明，要有意义得多。对一个哲学家，仅仅说他是个什么"主义者"、什么"论者"，所造成对他的误解，会比对他增添的了解还更多。

我曾写了两卷本的《中国哲学史》，第二卷于一九三四年出版，那是中国抗日战争爆发前三年。第一卷已由布德教授译成英文，于一九三七年在北平出版，那是抗日战争已经爆发三个月之后。那部书就是我在上一章末所讲的当代中国哲学精神的表现，在其中我运用清代儒家对中国古代哲学典籍校勘考订的成果，并运用分析方法来澄清这些古代哲学家的思想。从历史家的眼光来看，这种方法有它的局限性。这是因为古代哲学家的思想本来或者并不像现代诠释者所看到的那么清楚。哲学史的作用是告诉我们：过去的哲学家们说了些什么，他们说这些话时是什么意思，而不是我们认为这些话

ought to mean. In my *History* I have tried my best to keep my use of the analytic method within its proper limits.

From the point of view of the pure philosopher, however, to clarify the ideas of the philosophers of the past, and push their theories to their logical conclusions in order to show their validity or absurdity, is certainly more interesting and important than merely to find out what they themselves thought about these ideas and theories. In so doing there is a process of development from the old to the new, and this development is another phase of the spirit of the age mentioned above. Such a work, however, is no longer the scholarly one of an historian, but the creative one of a philosopher. I share the feeling of Wang Kuo-wei, that is to say, I do not like to be simply an historian of philosophy. Therefore after I had finished the writing of my *History*, I immediately prepared for new work. But at this juncture the war broke out in the summer of 1937.

● **Philosophical Production in Wartime**

Before the war, the philosophy departments of the University of Peking, from which I graduated, and of Tsing Hua University, where I am now teaching, were considered to be the strongest in China. Each of them has had its own tradition and emphasis. Those of the University of Peking have been toward historical studies and scholarship, with an idealistic philosophical trend, which, in terms of Western philosophy, is Kantian and Hegelian, and, in terms of Chinese philosophy, is Lu-Wang. The tradition and emphasis of Tsing Hua, on the contrary, have been toward the use of logical analysis for the study of philosophical problems, with a realistic philosophical trend, which, in terms of Western philosophy, is Platonic in the sense that the philosophy of neo-realism is Platonic, and in terms of Chinese philosophy, is Ch'eng-Chu.

These two universities are both situated in Peiping (formerly known as Peking), and on the outbreak of the war they both moved to the southwest, where they combined with a third, the Nankai University of Tientsin, to form the Southwest Associated University throughout the entire war period. Together, their two Philosophy Departments formed a rare and wonderful combination, comprising nine professors representing all the important schools both of Chinese and Western philosophy. At first, the Associated University as a whole was situated in Changsha in Hunan province, but our Philosophy Department, together with the other Departments of the humanities, was separately located in Hengshan, known as the South Holy Mountain.

应当意味着什么。在我的哲学史里，我尽力使用分析方法来说清楚作者的原意，也就是说，把分析方法的作用，限制在适当的范围之内。

但是，从纯哲学家的角度看，把过去哲学家的思想予以澄清，并把这些思想引申到它们的逻辑结论，从中表明它们是正确或是谬误，比仅仅弄清楚他们的原意当然要有趣得多，也重要得多。这样做包含着"从旧到新"、从传统到现代的思想发展过程。这种发展乃是上述时代精神的又一阶段。这样做已经超出了一个历史家的学术工作范围，而进入一个哲学家的创作范围了。王国维先生对哲学的思想评论，我也有同感。这就是说，我不满足于自己仅仅成为一个哲学史家。因此，在完成了这部《中国哲学史》之后，我立即着手准备新的工作。但这时正是一九三七年夏，抗日战争爆发了。

● 抗日战争时期的哲学耕耘

抗战前，北京大学的哲学系（我是从那里毕业的）和清华大学的哲学系（这是现在我任教的大学）被认为是全中国大学哲学系中最强的。这两所大学各有自己的传统和重点。北京大学以历史研究和它的学术水平著称，哲学上倾向于观念论，用西方哲学的术语来说，是康德和黑格尔派；用中国哲学的术语来说，则是陆王学派。清华的传统和重点则相反，倾向于使用逻辑分析来研究哲学问题，反映了实在论哲学的趋势，如果用西方哲学的术语来说，它是柏拉图派（因为新实在论学是柏拉图式的）；如用中国哲学的术语来说，它属于程朱学派。

这两所大学都坐落在北平（从前称北京）。战争爆发后，两所大学都迁往西南，再加上南开大学，共同组成西南联合大学，度过整个抗日战争时期。北大和清华的两个哲学系结合成一个罕见的奇妙联合体，其中九位教授代表了中国和西方哲学的各重要派别。起初，联合大学设在湖南长沙，哲学系和其他人文各系则在南岳衡山。

We stayed there only about four months before moving again to Kunming, farther southwest, in the spring of 1938. These few months, however, were spiritually very stimulating. We were then in a national crisis which was the greatest in our history, and we were in the same place where Huai-jang had tried to grind a brick into a mirror, as mentioned in chapter twenty-two, and where Chu Hsi had also once lived. We were sufferers of the same fate met by the Southern Sung dynasty, that of being driven southward by a foreign army. Yet we lived in a wonderful society of philosophers, writers, and scholars, all in one building. It was this combination of the historical moment, the geographical location, and the human gathering, that made the occasion so exceptionally stimulating and inspiring.

During these few months, myself and my colleagues, Professors T'ang Yung-t'ung and Y. L. Chin, finished books on which we had been working. T'ang's book is the first part of his *History of Chinese Buddhism*. Chin's book is titled *On the Tao*, and mine the *Hsin Li-hsüeh* or *New Li-hsüeh*. Chin and myself have many ideas in common, but my work is a development of the Ch'eng-Chu school, as the title indicates, while his is the result of an independent study of metaphysical problems. Later in Kunming I wrote a series of other books: the *Hsin Shih-lun*, also titled *China's Road to Freedom*; the *Hsin Yüan-jen* or *New Treatise on the Nature of Man*; the *Hsin Yüan-tao*, also titled *The Spirit of Chinese Philosophy*, which has been translated from the manuscript by Mr. E. R. Hughes of Oxford University and is published in London; and the *Hsin Chih-yen* or *New Treatise on the Methodology of Metaphysics*. (All these, in their original Chinese editions, have been published by the Commercial Press, Shanghai.) In the following, I shall try to summarize some of their results, as an illustration of one trend in contemporary Chinese philosophy, and in so doing we may perhaps get a partial glimpse of what Chinese philosophy can contribute to future philosophy.

Philosophical, or rather metaphysical, reasoning starts with the experience that something exists. This something may be a sensation, an emotion, or anything else. From the statement: "Something exists," I have in my *Hsin Li-hsüeh* deduced all the metaphysical ideas or concepts not only of the Ch'eng-Chu school but also of the Taoists. They are all considered in such a way that they are simply the logical implications of the statement that something exists. It is not difficult to see how the ideas

我们在湖南为时仅四个月。一九三八年春，又继续向西南后方迁移，最后到达昆明。在湖南的几个月，正是中华民族历史上最危急的时期，然而这段时期在国民精神上却是最昂扬向上的时期。我们所困处的衡山，在历史上，曾是怀让磨砖作镜的地方（见本书第二十二章），朱熹也曾在那里住过。我们与南宋时代被外来敌人追逐南迁的民众经历着同样的苦难命运。但是，当时聚在一起的有哲学家、作家、学者，大家住在一座楼里，形成一个奇妙的社会。其时、其地、其人，结合在一起，这是一个非常激励人心、激发人们灵感的时期。

在这几个月里，我以及我的同事们，包括汤用彤教授、金岳霖教授，相继完成自己的著作。汤用彤教授写完了《中国佛教史》的第一部分；金岳霖教授完成了他的《原道》；我完成了《新理学》。金岳霖教授和我有许多共同的想法，但是我的工作如我的书名所表明的，乃是试图对程朱理学加以发展；金岳霖教授的《原道》则是对中国传统形而上学问题进行独创性的研究。后来在昆明，我继续写了几本书：《新事论》（又名《中国走向自由之路》）、《新世训》、《新原人》（人性新论）、《新原道》（又名《中国哲学之精神》，牛津大学的休士先生〔E. R. Hughes〕曾把它译成英文，在伦敦出版），还有《新知言》（形而上学方法新论），这些书都曾由上海商务印书馆出版。下面我将综述它们取得的成果，作为当代中国哲学趋势之一的实例，从中或许可以部分看出中国哲学对未来哲学可能做出的贡献。

哲学，或说形而上学的思考，是由于人经验到某种存在而引起的。这个某种存在可能是感觉，或是感情，或是其他的什么。在《新理学》中我说："某个事物存在着。"程朱学派，以至道家，都从这句话演绎出他们的全部形而上学思想和概念。从"某个事物存在着"

of *Li* and *Ch'i* are deducible from this statement, and other ideas are also treated in the same way. For instance, the idea of Movement is treated by me not as a cosmological idea for some actual initial movement of the world, but as a metaphysical idea implied in the idea of existence itself. To exist is an activity, a movement. If we think about the world in its static aspect, we will say with the Taoists that before anything comes into being there must first be the being of Being. And if we think about the world in its dynamic aspect, we will say with the Confucianists that before anything comes to exist, there must first be Movement, which is simply another way of speaking of the activity of existing. In what I call men's pictorial form of thinking, which is really imagination, men imagine Being or Movement as God, the Father of all things. In imaginative thought of this kind, one has religion or cosmology, but not philosophy or metaphysics.

Following the same line of argument, I have been able in my *Hsin Li-hsüeh* to deduce all the metaphysical ideas of Chinese philosophy and to integrate them into a clear and systematic whole. The book was favorably received because in it critics seemed to feel that the structure of Chinese philosophy was more clearly stated than hitherto. It was considered as representing a revival of Chinese philosophy, which was taken as the symbol of a revival of the Chinese nation.

In the Ch'eng-Chu school, as we have seen in the last chapter, there is a certain element of authoritarianism and conservatism, but this is avoided in my *Hsin Li-hsüeh*. In my opinion, metaphysics can know only that there are the *Li*, but not the content of each *Li*. It is the business of science to find out the content of the individual *Li*, using the scientific and pragmatic method. The *Li* in themselves are absolute and eternal, but as they are known to us, that is, in the laws and theories of science, they are relative and changeable.

The realization of the *Li* requires a material basis. The various types of society are the realization of the various *Li* of social structure, and the material basis each *Li* requires for its realization is the economic foundation of a given type of society. In the sphere of history, therefore, I believe in an economic interpretation, and in my book, *China's Road to Freedom*, I apply this interpretation to Chinese civilization and history, as I also have in chapter two of the present book.

推演出"理"和"气"的观念并不困难；其他观念也可以用同样的方法演绎出来。例如，"动"的观念，我不需要有一个"第一推动力"来开始世界的原始运动；而是把它作为一个形而上学的观念，是"存在"这个观念自身就蕴涵着的。存在就是一种活动，一种运动。如果把世界看作一种静止的存在，我们便是接受了道家的说法，认为在任何事物进入世界之前，首先存在着"有"。如果从动的角度来观察世界，我们便是接受了儒家的说法，认为在任何事物存在之前，必先有"动"；这无异说，事物开始存在，乃是一种活动。在我称之为"人的图像式思考"——亦即想象——之中，人把存在或运动想象为神，为万物之父。在这样的想象式思考之中，人得到的是宗教或宇宙论，而不是哲学或形而上学。

从这样的思想线索发展下去，在《新理学》里，我演绎出中国哲学的全部形而上学观念，并把它们结合为一个清楚的思想体系。这部书得到很好的反映，认为它对中国哲学结构的阐述比过去任何一部书都更清楚；并且认为它代表着中国哲学的复兴，而这乃是中华民族复兴的象征。

在上一章里我们看到，程朱学派含有一种权威主义和保守主义的因素，而《新理学》避免了这个缺陷。我认为，形而上学能够使人知道"理"的存在，但不能使人从中知道每一事物的具体的理。为发现每一具体事物的理，有待人们运用科学的、实践的方法去逐一发现。各种事物的理是绝对的、永恒的，但人们对它们的认识——即人们对科学法则和理论的认识——则是相对和可变的。

理的具体化需要一个物质基础。各种类型的社会便是社会结构中包含的各方面理的体现。每一种理的实现都需要一定的物质作为基础，这个物质基础便是任何一种社会的经济基础。因此我相信，人类历史要用经济来加以解释。在《新事论》（中国走向自由之路）里，我便是运用这个原理来解释中国文明和中国历史。在本书第二章里，也是这样做的。

I think Wang Kuo-wei's trouble in philosophy has been due to his failure to realize that each branch of knowledge has its own sphere of application. One does not need to believe in any theory of metaphysics, if that theory does not make much assertion about matters of fact. If it does make such assertions, however, it is bad metaphysics, which is the same as bad science. This does not mean that a good metaphysical theory is unbelievable, but only that it is so evident that one does not need to say that he believes in it, just as one need not say that one believes in mathematics. The difference between metaphysics and mathematics and logic is that in the latter two one does not need to start with the statement that something exists, which is an assertion about matters of fact, and is the only one that metaphysics need make.

● **The Nature of Philosophy**

The method I use in the *Hsin Li-hsüeh* is wholly analytic. After writing that book, however, I began to realize the importance of the negative method which has been mentioned in chapter twenty-one. At present, if someone were to ask me for a definition of philosophy, I would reply paradoxically that philosophy, especially metaphysics, is that branch of knowledge which, in its development, will ultimately become "the knowledge that is not knowledge." If this be so, then the negative method needs to be used. Philosophy, especially metaphysics, is useless for the increase of our knowledge regarding matters of fact, but is indispensable for the elevation of our mind. These few points are not merely my own opinion, but, as we have previously seen, represent certain aspects of the Chinese philosophical tradition. It is these aspects that I think can contribute something to future world philosophy. In the following I shall try to develop them a little further.

Philosophy, as well as other branches of knowledge, must start with experience. But philosophy, especially metaphysics, differs from these other branches in that its development will lead it ultimately to that "something" which transcends experience. In this "something" there is that which cannot logically be sensed, but can only be thought. For instance, one can sense a square table, but cannot sense squareness. This

我想，王国维在哲学上的苦闷是由于他未曾理解，知识的每一分支都有它自己应用的领域。任何形而上学的理论，如果不能对事实加以肯定，就没有值得人相信的理由。而另一方面，如果它对事实作出许多肯定，则它就是一种坏的形而上学，其中道理，和我们评价一种坏的科学的根据是一样的。这不是说，好的形而上学理论是不可信的，而是说，它如此明显，以致人们不需要声明说自己相信它，就像人们不需要声明自己相信数学一样。形而上学和数学以及逻辑不同，数学和逻辑不需要以"某个事物存在着"作为它的工作前提。形而上学则需要从这句话开始，这是对事实的肯定，是形而上学唯一需要肯定的一点。

- **哲学的性质**

在《新理学》一书中，我使用的方法完全是分析方法。在写完那本书之后，我开始感到负的方法（见本书第二十一章）的重要性。现在如果有人问我哲学的定义是什么，我将会辩证地（哲学术语称之为"悖论"）回答：哲学，特别是形而上学，乃是知识的一个分支，在它的发展过程中，最终成为"对于什么不是知识的知识"，即"不知之知"。如果这个看法不错的话，为达到这样的认识就需要使用负的方法。哲学，特别是形而上学，为我们增进对事实的知识并无用处，但是，它为我们提高自己的心智（心灵和智性）则是必不可少的。这里所讲的几点，并不仅仅是我个人的看法，而是如前面所述，代表了中国哲学的某些方面。正是这些方面，我以为可能对未来的世界哲学做出一些贡献。下面，我将对此稍加展开，来予以陈述。

哲学和知识的其他分支一样，必须从经验开始。但是哲学，尤其是形而上学，与知识的其他分支不同之处，在于它的发展将最终引导它到超越经验的"某个事物"。在那"某个事物"里，有某个可以体会却无法凭逻辑来感知的东西。举例来说，人可以通过感性来感到一张方桌子，但人无法感觉到"方"。这并不是因为人的

is not because one's sense organ is insufficiently developed, but because squareness is a *Li*, which logically can only be thought but not sensed.

In the "something" there is also that which not only cannot be sensed, but strictly speaking, cannot even be thought. In chapter one I said that philosophy is systematic reflective thinking on life. Because of its reflective nature, it ultimately has to think on "something" that logically cannot be the object of thought. For instance, the universe, because it is the totality of all that is, cannot logically be the object of thought. As we have seen in chapter nineteen, the Chinese word *T'ien* or Heaven is sometimes used in this sense of totality, as when Kuo Hsiang says: "Heaven is the name of all things." Since the universe is the totality of all that is, therefore when one thinks about it, one is thinking reflectively, because the thinking and the thinker must also be included in the totality. But when one thinks about that totality, the totality that lies in one's thought does not include the thought itself. For it is the object of the thought and so stands in contrast to it. Hence the totality that one is thinking about is not actually the totality of all that is. Yet one must first think about totality in order to realize that it is unthinkable. One needs thought in order to be conscious of the unthinkable, just as sometimes one needs a sound in order to be conscious of silence. One must think about the unthinkable, yet as soon as one tries to do so, it immediately slips away. This is the most fascinating and also most troublesome aspect of philosophy.

What logically cannot be sensed transcends experience; what can neither be sensed nor thought of transcends intellect. Concerning what transcends experience and intellect, one cannot say very much. Hence philosophy, or at least metaphysics, must be simple in its nature. Otherwise it again becomes simply bad science. And with its simple ideas, it suffices for its function.

- ## The Spheres of Living

What is the function of philosophy? In chapter one I suggested that, according to Chinese philosophical tradition, its function is not the increase of positive knowledge of matters of fact, but the elevation of the mind. Here it would seem well to explain more clearly what I mean by this statement.

感官不够发达，而是因为"方"乃是一个"理"；逻辑上已经决定：它只能存在于人的思维里，却不可能感觉到。

在那"某个事物"里，还有严格说来，不仅是人无法感觉，甚至是人无法思想的东西。在第一章里，我说，哲学是人对于人生的系统反思。由于这种反思的性质，哲学最终不得不思索在逻辑上不可能成为人思考的对象。在本书第十九章里，我举出"天"这个词，有时也被用以指总体；例如郭象说："天者，万物之总名也。"宇宙既是一切存在的总体，当人思考这一点时，人只能是进行反思，因为这种思考连同思考者自身都必定要包括在"万物"之内。但是，当人对万物进行思考时，万物处于人的思考之中，便不可能包括它处在其中的这个思想。"万物"既成为人思考的对象，它便必须处于思考着的人的对面。因此，人认为自己在思考"万物"时，实际上所思考的不可能包含"万有的总体"。但是，人必须先思考"总体"这个概念，然后才能体会，思考万有是做不到的。人需要思考，才能体会到事物之中有些是"不可思议"的，正如有时人需要有一点声音，才意识到周围多么安静。人需要想那"不可思议"的，但是当人开始这样去想时，它就立刻溜得无影无踪了。这是哲学最迷人又最恼人的地方。

从逻辑上说，不可能被感知的东西，自然超越于经验之上。既不可能被感知，又不可能成为思考对象的东西，自然超越于智性之上。对那既超越于经验，又超越于智性的，人不可能说多少话。因此哲学，或至少形而上学是如此，它的本性决定它必然是非常简单。否则，它将成为另一种坏科学。正由于靠它的单纯的思想，哲学得以充分地完成它的任务。

- ### 人生的境界
  哲学的任务是什么？在第一章里我说，按照中国哲学的传统，哲学的任务不是为了人对客观实际增加正面的知识，而是为了提高人的心智。这里正是对这句话加以说明的一个好机会。

In my book, *The New Treatise on the Nature of Man*, I have observed that man differs from other animals in that when he does something, he understands what he is doing, and is conscious that he is doing it. It is this understanding and self-consciousness that give significance for him to what he is doing. The various significances that thus attach to his various acts, in their totality, constitute what I call his sphere of living. Different men may do the same things, but according to their different degrees of understanding and self-consciousness, these things may have varying significance to them. Every individual has his own sphere of living, which is not quite the same as that of any other individual. Yet in spite of these individual differences, we can classify the various spheres of living into four general grades. Beginning with the lowest, they are: the innocent sphere, the utilitarian sphere, the moral sphere, and the transcendent sphere.

A man may simply do what his instinct or the custom of his society leads him to do. Like children and primitive people, he does what he does without being self-conscious or greatly understanding what he is doing. Thus what he does has little significance, if any, for him. His sphere of living is what I call the innocent sphere.

Or man may be aware of himself, and be doing everything for himself. That does not mean that he is necessarily an immoral man. He may do something, the consequences of which are beneficial to others, but his motivation for so doing is self-benefit. Thus everything he does has the significance of utility for himself. His sphere of living is what I call the utilitarian sphere.

Yet again a man may come to understand that a society exists, of which he is a member. This society constitutes a whole and he is a part of that whole. Having this understanding, he does everything for the benefit of the society, or as the Confucianists say, he does everything "for the sake of righteousness, and not for the sake of personal profit." He is the truly moral man and what he does is moral action in the strict sense of the word. Everything he does has a moral significance. Hence his sphere of living is what I call the moral sphere.

And finally, a man may come to understand that over and above society as a whole, there is the great whole which is the universe. He is not only a member of society, but at the same time a member of the

在我所著《新原人》(人性新论)里，我说过自己的看法：人与其他动物不同，在于当他做什么事时，他知道自己在做的是什么事，并且自己意识到，是在做这件事。正是这种理解和自我意识使人感到他正在做的事情的意义。人的各种行动带来了人生的各种意义；这些意义的总体构成了我所称的"人生境界"。不同的人们可能做同样的事情，但是他们对这些事情的认识和自我意识不同，因此，这些事情对他们来说，意义也不同。每个人有他的生命活动的范围，与其他任何人都不完全一样。尽管人和人之间有种种差别，我们仍可以把各种生命活动范围归结为四等。由最低的说起，这四等是：一本天然的"自然境界"，讲求实际利害的"功利境界"，"正其义，不谋其利"的"道德境界"，超越世俗、自同于大全的"天地境界"。

一个人可以按照他的本能或社会习俗而生活。这样的人好像儿童或原始社会中的人，他们做各种事情，而对自己所做的事缺乏自觉，或并不真正意识到它的意义。因此，他所做的对自己并没有什么意义，这种人生是"自然境界"的人生。

还有一种人，他有私，时刻意识到自己，所做的事情都是为了自己。这不一定表明他就是全然不讲道德。他也可以做一些于别人有益的事情，但他这样做的动机是为了自己的好处。因此，他所做的每一件事，对他自己来说，都是"有用"的。他的人生境界可以称作"功利境界"。

还可能有些人，懂得世上并不是只有自己，还存在着一个社会，它是一个整体，自己是社会的一个组成部分。本着这样的理解，他做任何事情，都是为了整个社会的好处；或者用儒家的话来说，他行事为人是为义，而不是为利（"正其义而不谋其利"），他是真正有道德的人，所做的都合乎道德，都具有道德的意义。他的人生境界可以称之为"道德境界"。

最后，人也可以达到一种认识：知道在社会整体之上，还有一个大全的整体，就是宇宙。他不仅是社会的一个成员，还是宇宙的

universe. He is a citizen of the social organization, but at the same time a citizen of Heaven, as Mencius says. Having this understanding, he does everything for the benefit of the universe. He understands the significance of what he does and is self-conscious of the fact that he is doing what he does. This understanding and self-consciousness constitute for him a higher sphere of living which I call the transcendent sphere.

Of the four spheres of living, the innocent and the utilitarian are the products of man as he is, while the moral and the transcendent are those of man as he ought to be. The former two are the gifts of nature, while the latter two are the creations of the spirit. The innocent sphere is the lowest, the utilitarian comes next, then the moral, and finally the transcendent. They are so because the innocent sphere requires almost no understanding and self-consciousness, whereas the utilitarian and the moral require more, and the transcendent requires most. The moral sphere is that of moral values, and the transcendent is that of super-moral values.

According to the tradition of Chinese philosophy, the function of philosophy is to help man to achieve the two higher spheres of living, and especially the highest. The transcendent sphere may also be called the sphere of philosophy, because it cannot be achieved unless through philosophy one gains some understanding of the universe. But the moral sphere, too, is a product of philosophy. Moral actions are not simply actions that accord with the moral rule, nor is moral man one who simply cultivates certain moral habits. He must act and live with an understanding of the moral principles involved, and it is the business of philosophy to give him this understanding.

To live in the moral sphere of living is to be a *hsien* or morally perfect man, and to live in the transcendent sphere is to be a *sheng* or sage. Philosophy teaches the way of how to be a sage. As I pointed out in chapter one, to be a sage is to reach the highest perfection of man as man. This is the noble function of philosophy.

In the *Republic*, Plato said that the philosopher must be elevated from the "cave" of the sensory world to the world of intellect. If the philosopher is in the world of intellect, he is also in the transcendent sphere of living. Yet the highest achievement of the man living in this sphere is the identification of himself with the universe, and in this identification, he also transcends the intellect.

一个成员。就社会组织来说，他是一个公民，但他同时还是一个"天民"，或称"宇宙公民"。这是孟子早已指出的。一个人具有这样的意义，在做每一件事时，都意识到，这是为宇宙的好处。他懂得自己所做的事情的意义，并且自觉地这样做。这种理解和自觉使他处于一个更高的人生境界，我称之为在精神上超越人间世的"天地境界"。

在这四种人生的境界中，前两种都是人的自然状态，后两种是人应有的生命状态。前两个境界可以说是来自天然，后两种境界则是人自己的心灵所创造的。自然境界是最低级的存在，功利境界比自然境界稍高一点，更高是道德境界，最高是天地境界。这样排列是因为，自然境界的人生不需要对人生有任何理解和自我意识；功利境界和道德境界需要有一点对人生的理解和自我意识；天地境界需要的人生理解和自我意识则最高。道德境界所讲求的是道德价值，天地境界所讲求的则是超越道德的价值。

按照中国哲学的传统，哲学的任务是为了帮助人达到后两种人生境界，特别是天地境界。天地境界也可以称之为"哲学境界"，因为唯有经验哲学给人的宇宙情怀，人方始可能达到天地境界。道德境界其实也是一种哲学境界，因为道德行动并不仅仅是符合道德规范的行动，或由于人养成某些符合道德的习惯，它还要求人懂得自己行为中涉及的种种道德问题，而这正是哲学所要给予他的。

人在道德境界中生活的衡量标准是"贤"，它的含义是"道德完美"。人在天地境界里生活，则是追求"成圣"。哲学就是启发人追求"成圣"。在本书第一章里我曾说，成圣是人所能达到的生命最高点。这便是哲学的崇高任务。

柏拉图在《理想国》一书中曾说，哲学家必须从感觉世界的"洞穴"里上升到"智性的世界"。哲学家如果是在智性世界中生活，他也就是超越于人间世。在这样的境界里，最高的成就是和宇宙合一。在这种和宇宙的融合中，他也超越了智性。

Previous chapters have already shown us that Chinese philosophy has always tended to stress that the sage need do nothing extraordinary in order to be a sage. He cannot perform miracles, nor need he try to do so. He does nothing more than most people do, but, having high understanding, what he does has a different significance to him. In other words, he does what he does in a state of enlightenment, while other people do what they do in a state of ignorance. As the Ch'an monks say: "Understanding—this one word is the source of all mysteries." It is the significance which results from this understanding that constitutes his highest sphere of living.

Thus the Chinese sage is both of this world and the other world, and Chinese philosophy is both this-worldly and other-worldly. With the scientific advancement of the future, I believe that religion with its dogmas and superstitions will give way to science; man's craving for the world beyond, however, will be met by the philosophy of the future—a philosophy which is therefore likely to be both this-worldly and other-worldly. In this respect Chinese philosophy may have something to contribute.

- ● The Methodology of Metaphysics

In my work, *A New Treatise on the Methodology of Metaphysics*, I maintain that there are two methods, the positive and the negative. The essence of the positive method is to talk about the object of metaphysics which is the subject of its inquiry; the essence of the negative method is not to talk about it. By so doing, the negative method reveals certain aspects of the nature of that something, namely those aspects that are not susceptible to positive description and analysis.

In chapter two I have indicated my agreement with Professor Northrop that philosophy in the West started with what he calls the concept by postulation, whereas Chinese philosophy started with what he calls concept by intuition. As a result, Western philosophy has naturally been dominated by the positive method, and Chinese philosophy by the negative one. This is especially true of Taoism, which started and ended with the undifferentiable whole. In the *Lao-tzu* and *Chuang-tzu*, one does not learn what the *Tao* actually is, but only what it is not. But if one knows what it is not, one does get some idea of what it is.

在前面我们已经看到，中国哲学强调一点：圣人并不需要为当圣人而做什么特别的事情。他不可能施行神迹，也不需要去那样做。圣人所做的事无非就是寻常人所做的事，但是他对所做的事有高度的理解，这些事对他有一种不同的意义。换句话说，寻常人在蒙昧状态（佛家称之为"无明"）中做事，圣人则是在完全自觉（觉而又悟）的状态中做事。禅僧常说："觉字乃万妙之源。"由厕身宇宙之中的"觉"而直觉地"悟"到和宇宙融为一体，这便是天地境界。

因此，中国人所说的圣人，既在世界里生活，又不属于世界；中国哲学既是现世的，又是彼岸世界的。随着未来的科学进步，我相信宗教的教条和迷信将让位给科学，人对于彼岸世界的追求将在未来的哲学中得到满足。这个未来哲学既是现世的，又是彼岸的。在这方面，中国哲学可能有所贡献。

● **形而上学中的方法论**

在《新知言》一书中，我提出，有两种方法，即：正的方法和负的方法。正的方法的实质是讨论形而上学的对象，这成为哲学研究的主题。负的方法的实质是对要探讨的形而上学对象不直接讨论，只说它不是什么，在这样做的时候，负的方法得以显示那"某物"的无从正面描述和分析的某些本性。

在本书第二章里，我已经表示，同意诺斯洛普教授所说，西方哲学从不证自明的"公设的概念"开始，而中国哲学则从"直觉的概念"开始。由于这个缘故，西方哲学的方法论是理所当然地由正的方法占统治地位，而中国哲学的方法论则理所当然地是负的方法占统治地位。中国哲学的这个方法论特点在道家思想中尤其明显，它始于混沌的大全，又终于混沌的大全。在《老子》和《庄子》两书中，始终没有说"道"到底是什么，只说了"道"不是什么。而一个人如果懂得了"道"不是什么，也就对"道"有所领悟了。

This negative method of Taoism was reinforced by Buddhism, as we have seen. The combination of Taoism and Buddhism resulted in Ch'anism, which I should like to call a philosophy of silence. If one understands and realizes the meaning and significance of silence, one gains something of the object of metaphysics.

In the West, Kant may be said to have used the negative method of metaphysics. In his *Critique of Pure Reason*, he found the unknowable, the noumenon. To Kant and other Western philosophers, because the unknowable is unknowable, one can therefore say nothing about it, and so it is better to abandon metaphysics entirely and stop at epistemology. But to those who are accustomed to the negative method, it is taken for granted that, since the unknowable is unknowable, we should say nothing about it. The business of metaphysics is not to say something about the unknowable, but only to say something about the fact that the unknowable is unknowable. When one knows that the unknowable is unknowable, one does know, after all, something about it. On this point, Kant did a great deal.

The great metaphysical systems of all philosophy, whether negative or positive in their methodology, have crowned themselves with mysticism. The negative method is essentially that of mysticism. But even in the cases of Plato, Aristotle, and Spinoza, who used the positive method at its best, the climaxes of their systems are all of a mystical nature. When the philosopher in the *Republic* beholds and identifies himself with the Idea of the Good, or the philosopher in the *Metaphysics* with God "thinking on thinking," or the philosopher in the *Ethics* finds himself "seeing things from the point of view of eternity" and enjoying the "intellectual love of God," what can they do but be silent? Is their state not better described by such phrases as "not one," "not many," "not not-one," "not not-many"?

Thus the two methods do not contradict but rather complement each other. A perfect metaphysical system should start with the positive method and end with the negative one. If it does not end with the negative method, it fails to reach the final climax of philosophy. But if it does not start with the positive method, it lacks the clear thinking that is essential for philosophy. Mysticism is not the opposite of clear thinking, nor is it below it. Rather, it is beyond it. It is not anti-rational; it is super-rational.

　　道家的这种负的方法，如我们先前所述，在佛教思想中又加强了。道家和佛家思想的结合，形成了禅学：我更倾向于把它称作"潜默的哲学"。如果一个人领悟到潜默的含义和它的意味深长，他便对形而上学的对象有所领悟了。

　　在西方，康德可以说是在形而上学中运用了负的方法。他在《纯粹理性批判》一书中探索到"不可知"的"物本体"（the noumenon, thing-in-itself）。对康德和其他西方哲学家来说，由于"不可知"的不可知，因此，人对它无话可说。既然如此，最明智的态度便是对形而上学止步不前，而以探究认识论领域为限。但是对那些惯于以负的方法来思考的人，"不可知"的不可知，乃是理所当然，从而应当对它缄默。形而上学不是要对"不可知"说出一番话来，而是应当说"不可知"是不可知的。人如果懂得"不可知"是不可知的，对它就是有所领悟了。在这一点上，康德已经做出了巨大的贡献。

　　在各种哲学的形而上学体系里，无论它们采取的方法是负的方法或正的方法，最后都往往戴上了神秘主义的皇冠。负的方法便是神秘主义的方法。但即便是运用正的方法的哲学大师如柏拉图、亚里士多德、斯宾诺莎，他们的哲学体系的高峰都是含有神秘主义色彩的。在柏拉图的《理想国》里，哲学家见到了"至善"，并与之融为一体；在亚里士多德的《形而上学》里，哲学家面对着"正在对思想进行思索"（thinking on thinking）的上帝；在斯宾诺莎的《伦理学》中，哲学家发现自己"从永恒的观点来看眼前的事物"从而享受到"神的智性之爱"：在这样的时候，他们除了静默之外，还有什么是可以用语言来表达的呢？用"非一"、"非多"、"非非一"、"非非多"来形容他们这时的心态，岂不更好吗？

　　因此，正的方法和负的方法不是互相矛盾而是互相补充的。一个完整的形而上学体系应当从正的方法开始，而以负的方法告终。它若不以负的方法告终，便不可能登上哲学的高峰。但如果它不从正的方法开始，便缺少了对哲学来说最重要的明晰思考。神秘主义不是和明晰思考对立的，也不是低于明晰思考，毋宁说，它是超越于明晰思考的。它不是反理性，而是超理性的。

In the history of Chinese philosophy, the positive method was never fully developed; in fact, it was much neglected. Therefore, Chinese philosophy has lacked clear thinking, which is one of the reasons why it is marked by simplicity. Lacking clear thinking, its simplicity has been quite naive. Its simplicity as such is commendable, but its naiveté must be removed through the exercise of clear thinking. Clear thinking is not the end of philosophy, but it is the indispensable discipline that every philosopher needs. Certainly it is what Chinese philosophers need. On the other hand, the history of Western philosophy has not seen a full development of the negative method. It is the combination of the two that will produce the philosophy of the future.

A Ch'an story describes how a certain teacher used to stick out his thumb when he was asked to explain the Buddhist *Tao*. On such occasions, he would simply remain silent, but would display his thumb. Noticing this, his boy attendant began to imitate him. One day the teacher saw him in this act, and quick as lightning chopped off the boy's thumb. The boy ran away crying. The teacher called him to come back, and just as the boy turned his head, the teacher again stuck out his own thumb. Thereupon the boy received Sudden Enlightenment.

Whether this story is true or not, it suggests the truth that before the negative method is used, the philosopher or student of philosophy must pass through the positive method, and before the simplicity of philosophy is reached, he must pass through its complexity.

One must speak very much before one keeps silent.

在中国哲学的历史上，正的方法始终未曾得到充分的发展，或者应当说，它被过分地忽略了。因此，中国哲学里缺少明晰的思考，这是中国哲学往往被视为简单的原因之一。由于缺乏明晰的思考，哲学容易幼稚，然而"简明"本身又是一个优点。中国哲学所需要的是：除去幼稚气息，代以明晰思考。有了明晰思考，并不就是哲学的终结，它不过是任何哲学家都应有的思维训练，中国的哲学家们当然需要这样的思维训练。另一方面，人们在西方哲学的历史上也看不见负的方法的充分发展。未来的哲学将在这两者的结合中发展出来。

禅宗里有一个故事说，有一位禅师，每当被问到佛教的"道"如何解释时，他便竖起大拇指，一句话不说，只是让人看他的大拇指。服侍他的小和尚也学会了这样做。一天，禅师看到小和尚也这样做，他飞快地拿刀砍掉了小和尚的拇指。小和尚哭着跑开去。这时，禅师喊他，他刚回头，禅师又竖起了自己的大拇指。据说，小和尚就此得到了"顿悟"。

不管这个故事是真是假，它告诉人，在学会使用负的方法之前，哲学家或学哲学的人，都必须经过使用正的方法这个阶段。在达到哲学的单纯之前，需先穿过复杂的哲学思辨丛林。

人往往需要说很多话，然后才能归入潜默。

EDITOR'S INTRODUCTION

In spite of the innumerable books that have been written about China in recent years, it is remarkable how little really authentic knowledge we in the West have about the philosophy of that country. Even most well-educated Americans, if asked to list some of China's major philosophers, will, unless they are China specialists, be unable to name more than Confucius and possibly Lao Tzu. This statement, I suspect, applies almost as strongly to the average professional teacher of philosophy as it does to the layman.

Books and articles in English on the subject are not lacking, to be sure, but with few exceptions they are either too specialized to be popular or too popular to have much value. The present volume, indeed, is the first in English that attempts to give a really comprehensive and systematic account of Chinese thought as a whole, from its beginnings with Confucius to the present day. The fact that it is the work of a Chinese scholar who is generally acknowledged by his countrymen to be supremely well qualified for the task, makes its appearance all the more significant.

As we read this book, we see that Chinese philosophy is far wider in scope than either Confucius or Lao Tzu, or even the Confucian and Taoist schools with which they are linked. In the course of some twenty-five centuries, Chinese thinkers have touched upon well-nigh all the major subjects that have engaged the attention of philosophers in the West, and though the schools to which they have belonged have often borne the same name through many centuries, their actual ideological content has changed greatly from one age to another. Could Confucius, for example, have been reincarnated through a Buddhist process of metempsychosis so as to meet his great twelfth century follower, Chu Hsi, he would probably hardly have guessed that the ideas preached by the latter were the orthodox "Confucianism" of that time.

Beneath this diversity, however, we find certain themes occurring and reoccurring; one of them is what Dr. Fung describes in his first chapter as that of "sageliness within and kingliness without." How to acquire the *Tao* or Way to become an inner sage and outer king? This, understood in a somewhat figurative rather than strictly literal sense, has been a central problem of Chinese philosophy, and gives it, as Dr. Fung points out, its dual quality of being both this-worldly and other-worldly. It is this point that Dr. Fung took as the main thesis of his recent book *The Spirit*

英文版编者引言

近年来，有关中国的各种著作不可胜数，但是需要承认，我们西方人对中国哲学的真实知识实在少得可怜。即便是受过良好教育的美国人，如果请他们列举中国的主要哲学家，除非是汉学专家，大概能举出的中国哲学家只有孔子，或可能再加一个老子。这个看法，甚至对一般哲学教师来说，恐怕也不为过。

有关中国哲学的英文书籍和文章为数并不少，但通常不是太专业，就是通俗到了乏味、没有价值的地步。读者现在手持的这卷书堪称是第一本对中国哲学，从古代的孔子直到今日，进行全面介绍的英文书籍。这样一本书出自中国知识界公认的最优秀学者之一的笔下，它的问世，就有了更大的意义。

读这本书的时候，我们会发现，中国哲学的内涵远远超过孔子和老子，或儒道两家著述所涵盖的范围。在漫长的二十五个世纪里，凡西方哲学家所曾涉及的主要问题，中国的思想家们无不思考过。还应看到的是：在多少世纪里，哲学家们所属的学派，尽管还继承了自古以来的名称，其思想内容却随时代的变迁而十分不同了。举例来说，如果孔子像佛家轮回理论所说那样，转世到十二世纪朱熹的同一时代，他大概很难想到，朱熹的思想竟成为当时正统的儒家思想。

在这种多样性的后面，我们也会发现，有些主题反复出现，其中之一是冯博士在本书第一章里所描述的"内圣外王"之道。怎样能够得道，从而得以做到内圣外王？如果就精义而不是从字面看，这可以说是中国哲学的中心问题，并且如冯博士所指出的，它使中国哲学具有现世和超越的两重性。这一点是冯博士最近新著

of Chinese Philosophy. I shall not spoil his story at this point except to suggest that this same quality, half-consciously perceived by the West, has perhaps helped to create that common impression of China as a land peopled both by mystic sages, who sit in eternal meditation on mountain peaks below pine trees, and by exceedingly practical and somewhat matter-of-fact men of affairs.

During the 1930's, when I began my study of Chinese philosophy and other aspects of Chinese culture in Peiping, one of my happiest contacts came in 1934-35 when I attended Dr. Fung's class on Chinese philosophy at Tsing Hua University. He had then just published the second volume of his monumental *History of Chinese Philosophy*, which speedily became the standard work in its field. One day when I came to class, Dr. Fung asked me whether I knew of anyone who would be willing to translate his book into English. As a result, I agreed to undertake the task, and my translation of the first volume was published in the summer of 1937, just after the outbreak of the Sino-Japanese war. At the time, I hoped to translate the second volume within two or three years.

Meanwhile, however, my work took me from China, the long years of war followed, and many other tasks intervened. Aside from a few sporadic efforts, therefore, it was only with the coming of Dr. Fung from China to the University of Pennsylvania in the autumn of 1946 as Visiting Professor of Chinese that I was able to begin anew. Since then I have translated a series of individual chapters from volume two which have already appeared, or will probably appear, in the *Harvard Journal of Asiatic Studies*, a publication of the Harvard-Yenching Institute in Cambridge, Mass. A list of them will be found in the bibliography at the back of this book, and when completed they will be published as a single volume. Under a grant recently awarded to me under the terms of the Fulbright Act, providing for the sending of American scholars and teachers to China and other countries, I expect to leave shortly for a year in Peiping, where I hope to complete the translation of the entire second volume by the autumn of 1949.

Last year, however, while I was beginning this work in Philadelphia, Dr. Fung decided that he would himself like to write in English a shorter version of his original *History*. For this he enlisted my aid as editor, and the present book is the result.

《新原道》一书的主题。笔者不敢在此妄论冯博士此书的全部精义，而只想指出：西方仅仅一知半解的这种哲学精神，使中国人在西方人眼中成为既有高居峰巅、在松树下沉思默想的圣人，又有十分实际、只问眼前的俗人。

回想二十世纪三十年代我在北平学习中国哲学与文化其他方面的时候，令我最感愉快的是：一九三四至一九三五年间，到清华大学随冯博士读中国哲学。当时，冯博士刚完成他的两卷本巨著《中国哲学史》的第二卷。这部书很快便在中国的同类著作中居于数一数二的地位。有一天，冯博士问我，是否知道有什么人愿意从事把此书译成英文的工作。结果是，我承担起这项工作。一九三七年夏，日本刚发动侵华战争之际，我所翻译的冯博士《中国哲学史》第一卷出版。当时，我期望在两三年内，可以完成此书第二卷的翻译工作。

此后，我因工作关系离开了中国，接着是漫长的战争，还有其他的任务打断了我的原定计划。直到一九四六年秋冯博士应聘到宾夕法尼亚大学担任客座教授，我才得以重新开始原先的计划。自此以后，我选择了冯博士的《中国哲学史》第二卷中的若干章，有的已在哈佛燕京学社出版的《哈佛亚洲研究》杂志发表，有的即将在该刊发表，其目录已收入本书参考书目。由于得到富布赖特法案资助，美国学者可以到中国和其他国家进行研究，我将于近期赴北平，计划逗留一年，希望到一九四九年秋能够完成《中国哲学史》第二卷的翻译工作。

去年，我在宾州大学开始了这项工作。这时，冯博士决心自己动手，把他先前的著作《中国哲学史》缩写为英文的一卷本，并要我予以协助。结果就是现在的这本书。

In subject matter this book for the most part follows the original Chinese work fairly closely. Its first sixteen chapters correspond roughly to the latter's volume one, and its remaining chapters to volume two. It is, however, considerably shorter, as is evident from the fact that my translation of the first volume of the original *History* covers 454 rather large pages, and the Chinese edition is in turn 50 pages shorter than volume two. This shortening has been achieved for the present book by omitting entirely some of the lesser thinkers dealt with in the original *History* and reducing the space allotted to the remainder. Footnotes have also been largely avoided, and such matters as detailed bibliographical references, discussions on the dating and authenticity of various texts, and much biographical data have been eliminated. Yet the resulting volume is a product of solid scholarship, which may be relied on as a remarkably accurate and well-rounded account of its subject.

There are other features, too, which distinguish it from the usual abridgement. In the first place, it has been written with the Western reader specifically in mind, which means that its treatment and subject matter are not always the same as they would be in a book intended solely for a Chinese public. Such is the case with its first two chapters, for example, which do not occur in the original *History* at all, and the same is true of a good part of its chapter twenty-seven.

In the second place, it embodies a number of conclusions and points of emphasis which were arrived at by Dr. Fung only after the publication of his original *History* in 1934. The third chapter, for example, summarizes a theory that was first published by Dr. Fung in Chinese only in 1936, in a separate *Supplement* to his original *History*. The final chapter, devoted to Dr. Fung's own philosophical ideas, is also necessarily new, since these ideas were first expressed in a series of creative philosophical books which he wrote during the war years. Likewise, the treatment of Neo-Taoism and Buddhism in chapters nineteen to twenty-two has been considerably changed from that in the *History*. (The corresponding chapters in the latter work, however, are to be revised by Dr. Fung along similar lines before I translate them into English.)

The choice of subject matter, treatment, and actual writing of the present book are, of course, almost entirely the work of Dr. Fung himself. My own contribution has been primarily that of editing his manuscript with the needs of the Western reader in mind, so as to make its English correct and readable. Many of the quotations from original texts have

这本书的内容主题与中文的《中国哲学史》两卷本并无出入，本书第一章到第十六章大致相当于两卷本的第一卷，第十七章到书末相当于第二卷。但本书的篇幅却明显地缩短了。举例来说，我所译的两卷本中的第一卷有四百五十四页，而本书比第一卷还减少了五十页。其所以能做到这一点，是由于本书删除了原两卷本中一些次要的思想家，对主要思想家所用的篇幅也减少了。本书对两卷本中思想家的生平、著作时间的真伪的考证、参考书目和注释也压缩了篇幅。尽管有这些不同，学术水平并未因此减色，它的资料和诠释都十分准确，立论也平实全面。

本书与一般的缩写本相较，还有其他一些特色。首先，本书是作者为西方读者而写的，因此，它的内容和论述角度和为中国读者写时有所不同。本书的首两章是中文两卷本所没有的，便是一例；第二十七章的大部分也是新写的。

其次，本书里有些结论性的见解和重点，是冯博士自一九三四年完成两卷本之后的新见解。例如，第三章所概括的理论是冯博士于一九三六年两卷本所作的一个附录中提出的。在本书末章，冯博士论述他自己的哲学见解，这些见解原来散见于冯博士在抗日战争年间所发表的各部著作，收入本书时，又经作者重新写过。第十九章至第二十二章论述新道学和佛学各章，与两卷本相比，有明显的改动。（冯博士准备对两卷本的有关部分根据本书加以修改，然后再交我翻译。）

本书的内容主题、处理方式和具体写作，不消说，都是冯博士亲自动手的。我的工作主要是考虑西方读者的需要，就语言和易读性做一些编辑加工。本书中的许多引文都是按我所译两卷本的译文，

been borrowed, with occasional trifling changes, from my translations of the same passages in the longer *History*, when available, but in other cases Dr. Fung has prepared renditions of his own for key terms or passages, or has used those contained in E. R. Hughes' translation, *The Spirit of Chinese Philosophy*. Many other quotations, of course, are entirely new. The Bibliography and Index have been compiled by me.

The general reader may find it helpful to be given a brief résumé of the course of Chinese history, before concluding this introduction. Traditionally, the history begins with a series of sage-kings, said to have reigned in the latter part of the third millennium B.C. It is the uncritical acceptance, both by Chinese and Westerners alike, of the stories about these men, that has created the erroneous widespread impression regarding the excessive antiquity of Chinese civilization. Today, however, scholars are generally agreed that these sage-kings are little more than mythical figures, and that the stories about them are the idealized inventions of a much later period. The historical existence of China's first dynasty, the *Hsia* (trad. 2205-1766 B.C.), is likewise uncertain, though it may some day be confirmed by future archaeology.

With the *Shang* dynasty (trad. 1766-1123 B.C.), however, we reach firmer historical ground. Its capital, which has been partially excavated, has yielded an abundance of inscriptions carved on bone and tortoise shell. It is these inscriptions that were prepared in conjunction with the method of divination described in chapter twelve.

Coming to the *Chou* dynasty (1122?-256 B.C.), we have abundant historical records, and the Chou is also the golden age of Chinese philosophy. During its early centuries, a large number of small states, most of them grouped around the valley of the Yellow River in North China, were linked together through common ties of allegiance to the Chou royal house in a feudal system roughly analogous to that of medieval Europe. As time wore on, however, this feudal system gradually disintegrated, resulting in the eclipse of the Chou royal power, the steady increase of bitter warfare between the now independent states, and other violent political, social, and economic upheavals. It was men's efforts to find answers to the resulting pressing problems that confronted them, that caused the appearance of the first Chinese organized philosophical thought, which constitutes the cultural glory of the age. Confucius (551-479 B.C.) was the earliest of these philosophers, and was followed by a

原封不动地搬过来，只做了微小的变动。涉及中国哲学专有名词的翻译，冯博士往往自己已有成竹在胸，或是借用 E. R. Hughes 在《中国哲学之精神》（ *The Spirit of Chinese Philosophy* ）中的英文译名。其他许多引文的英译都是新的。参考书目和索引则是我编的。

为一般读者着想，在这里简单回顾一下中国历史的发展，在阅读本书时可能略微省一点力。中国古史传说历来由约公元前三千年以前的圣王尧舜禹等开始。长期以来，中外知识界对这类传说都没有质疑，由此造成中国历史异常悠久的印象。今日，中国史学界已经取得一致的见解：有关古代圣王的传说，是后人编造出来的故事，那些圣王充其量也只是神话中的人物。中国历史中的第一个朝代——夏朝（历来认为其起讫年代是约公元前二二〇五〔二〇七〇〕至前一七六六〔一六〇〇〕年）也难以确定，只有等待将来考古学的发现来予以认证。

历来认为继夏朝之后的商朝（起讫年代是公元前一七六六〔一六〇〇〕至前一一二二〔一〇四六〕年），其历史证据较为充分。商都的一部分已经发掘出来，出土了一大批刻在甲骨上的文字。这批甲骨文就是本书第十二章谈到的卜辞。

继商以后的周朝（公元前一一二二〔一〇四六〕至前二五六年）留下了丰富的史料。周朝也是中国哲学史上的黄金时代。在它的最初几个世纪里，黄河中下游谷地的一大批小国都臣服周王室，这种君臣关系大体上和欧洲中世纪的情况相仿。随着时间的迁移，这种封建体制逐渐瓦解，出现一批独立的国家。它们彼此之间进行战争，再加上政治、社会、经济的动乱，严重削弱了周朝的统治。面临种种紧迫的社会政治问题，人们要寻求解答，于是中国出现了第一次有组织的哲学思想运动，它构成中国古代的灿烂文化。孔子（公元前五五一至前四七九年）是这批哲学家中间最早的一个。

host of others belonging to widely differing schools of thought. Most of the subject matter in chapters three to sixteen of the present book is concerned with these schools. Politically, the same centuries following Confucius are appropriately known as the Period of the Warring States.

The state of Ch'in, from which the name China is probably derived, brought this age to an end in the year 221 B.C. by annihilating the last of the other opposing states, thus for the first time creating a really unified Chinese empire. The resulting *Ch'in* dynasty replaced the old feudal aristocracy by a centrally appointed nonhereditary bureaucracy, thus instituting a form of government that has since set a pattern for all later dynasties. With the sole exception of the creation of the Chinese Republic in 1912, these events marked the greatest single change in China's political history.

The very harshness exercised by the Ch'in to achieve this end led to its speedy overthrow. Its work of unification was continued, however, by the politically powerful *Han* dynasty (206 B.C.-A.D. 220), under which the empire was expanded to include most of present day China proper, together with much of present Chinese Turkistan. This political unification was accompanied by a corresponding unification in the field of thought. Most of the Chou philosophic schools disappeared as separate schools, though many of their ideas were absorbed into Confucianism and Taoism, which now became dominant. These developments are described in chapters seventeen to eighteen.

Following the four hundred years of Han rule, there came another four centuries which may be termed the Period of Disunity (A.D. 221-589), during much of which China was usually divided between a series of short-lived dynasties in the south, and another series of equally short dynasties in the north. Several of the latter were ruled by non-Chinese nomadic groups, who during this period succeeded in forcing their way past the Great Wall. For the Chinese people as a whole these centuries, sometimes referred to as China's dark ages, were ones of frequent suffering. Culturally, nevertheless, they were outstanding in many ways, and philosophically they were marked by the temporary eclipse of Confucianism, and the dominance of Neo-Taoism and Buddhism. These two latter philosophies are the subjects of chapters nineteen to twenty-one.

The *Sui* (589-617) and especially *T'ang* (618-906) dynasties, however, brought renewed unity and political strength to China, and in many ways

继他之后，兴起了一批哲学家，他们各抱不同的思想主张。本书的第三章到第十六章的内容就是讨论这些思想家的不同主张。在政治史上，孔子以后的几个世纪（公元前四八〇至前二二二年）通称为战国时期。

秦国并吞六国后，于公元前二二一年建立秦朝，第一次建立了真正统一的中华帝国。秦朝以中央集权、由中央政府委派地方官僚代替了过去各地区贵族割据、政权世袭的制度，由此开创了中国自此以后历朝的政治体制。这是中国政治史上，除一九一一年推翻帝制、建立民国之外，最重大的历史变革。

秦朝为达到它的政治目标，采取了严酷的手段，由此激起的反抗使秦朝很快便被推翻。它进行的统一中国的工作在继起的强大的汉帝国（公元前二〇六至公元二二〇年）统治下继续进行。在汉帝国统治时期，中国的疆界扩张到今日中国本土的大部分，包括新疆的大部分。与政治统一伴随而来的是思想的统一。周朝的诸子百家，作为单独的学派不再存在，但它们的思想往往融入了儒家或道家。儒道两家这时成为两大主要的思想流派。本书第十七、十八两章便是叙述这个发展。

两汉四百年统治之后，继之而来的四百年也许可以称之为分裂时期（公元二二一至五八九年）。在这四个世纪的大部分时间里，中国南方分裂为许多统治时间不长的小国，北方也同样分裂成这样的一批小国。有些北朝的小国由非汉族的游牧民族组成，却跨越长城，在长城以南建立了国家。过去中国历史上，把这一时期看作"五胡乱华"，看作"黑暗时期"，因为民众遭受了许多苦难。但在文化上，这是非常杰出的时期。在哲学上，儒家思想暂时消沉，代之而起的是新道家和佛家思想。这两个流派的思想介绍便构成了本书第十九章到第二十一章的内容。

隋朝（公元五八九〔五八一〕至六一七〔六一八〕年）唐朝（公元六一八至九〇七年）在政治上重建了中国的统一，不仅国力得到

marked a high-water mark in cultural achievement. Under the T'ang, Buddhism reached its peak, and one of its schools, Ch'anism, is treated in chapter twenty-two. Afterwards, however, Buddhism entered the gradual decline which it has ever since followed; Confucianism, on the contrary, began once more a rise which brought it to eventual supremacy. The early steps in this revival are described in the beginning of chapter twenty-three.

The collapse of the T'ang was followed by an uneasy interlude of fifty odd years. Then came the *Sung* dynasty (960-1279), which though politically weaker than the T'ang, was culturally equally brilliant. In the field of thought, it was marked by the greatest recrudescence of Confucianism which had been seen since the Han dynasty. This movement, known to the West as Neo-Confucianism, is described in chapters twenty-three to twenty-five.

The *Yüan* dynasty (1280-1367), which replaced the Sung, is notable as the first under which all of China was ruled by an alien group, the Mongols. Culturally, however, it was comparatively unimportant. The *Ming* dynasty (1368-1643) which followed restored the country to Chinese rule, but though it was a pleasant period in which to live, it contributed little to culture that was radically new. In philosophy, however, it was notable as the dynasty under which the school in Neo-Confucianism known as that of Universal Mind reached its culmination. This development is described in chapter twenty-six.

Under the following *Ch'ing* dynasty (1644-1911), all of China again fell under non-Chinese rule, this time that of the Manchus. Yet until the beginning of the nineteenth century it was one of the most prosperous periods of Chinese history, and also one which saw definite advances in certain cultural fields, though declines in others. Politically, the empire was extended even beyond the frontiers which it had achieved under the Han and T'ang. Beginning in the early nineteenth century, however, Manchu power steadily decayed, and China's resulting internal weakness unfortunately coincided with the growing political and economic pressure of the industrialized West. The ways in which these various developments influenced the field of thought are described in chapter twenty-seven.

The overthrow of the Manchus in 1911, resulting in the abolition of the oldest monarchical system in the world, marks a turning point in Chinese history. During the decades following the establishment of the *Republic* in 1912, China has been faced with the need of simultaneously

发展，文化也登上发展的高峰。在唐代，佛教也获得空前的发展。其中的禅宗是本书第二十二章的内容。自此之后，佛家在中国渐趋没落。另一方面，儒家却再度兴起，并在思想界建立起主导的地位。本书第二十三章开始的地方描述了儒家复兴的初期情况。

唐朝覆灭后，有五十年动荡不定。然后宋朝（公元九六〇至一二七九年）兴起。它虽在政治上不如唐朝强大，但在文化上却创造出同样辉煌的成就。从思想史看，这一时期里，儒家思想重新兴起，其繁荣为汉朝以来所未有。这场哲学运动在西方称为"新儒家"。本书第二十三章到第二十五章，对这段历史作了介绍。

取代宋朝的是元朝（公元一二八〇〔一二〇六〕至一三六七〔一三六八〕年）。它是全中国第一次被一个非汉民族——蒙古族——所统治，这一点在文化上的影响倒并不很大。明朝（公元一三六八至一六四四年）使中国回到汉族统治之下。从社会生活来说，明朝比元朝愉快些，但社会经过一番剧烈变化，文化却没有相应的新鲜气息。在哲学思想方面，值得一提的是：心学发展到了高峰。本书第二十六章叙述了这个发展。

在清朝（公元一六四四〔一六一六〕至一九一一年）统治下，中国再度由非汉民族的满族统治。直到十九世纪之前，清朝统治的中国繁荣昌盛，版图甚至超过了汉唐；在文化方面，有的领域有所前进，有的领域则出现衰退。十九世纪以后，清朝统治走下坡路，内部衰弱和西方工业国家的政治、经济压力接踵而来。这些发展对思想领域的影响，请看本书第二十七章。

一九一一年的民国革命，推翻清朝统治，也推翻了世界最古老的王权体制，成为中国历史的一个转折点。一九一二年，中华民国成立。此后几十年间，中国在社会、政治、经济各方面都亟待

making sweeping changes in her social, political, and economic fabric alike. We in the West have required some three centuries to pass through similar changes. It is scarcely surprising, therefore, that long years of political and intellectual disorder in China—disorder greatly aggravated by fierce aggression from the outside—have been the result. Indeed, as we look around us at the Western nations today, it is obvious that among them, too, gigantic changes are still in the making, the outcome of which no man can predict. Little wonder, then, that in China the future looks dark and uncertain. Yet Chinese history shows us that repeatedly in the past, though often at untold cost in human suffering, the Chinese have succeeded in surmounting and recuperating from the crises that have faced them. They can do so again, but only provided that the world as a whole learns quickly to accept the same cosmopolitanism that has been prominent in much of Chinese political thinking. (See chapters sixteen and twenty-one.) In the changes that China is yet to make, a good deal of her past ideology must inevitably be discarded. Some of it, however, will survive as a permanent contribution to future world philosophy. Possible ways in which this contribution may be made are suggested by Dr. Fung in his final chapter.

Derk Bodde
May, 1948
Philadelphia, Pa.

改革，这些改革，在西方国家用了约三个世纪，中国只能迎头赶上。改革在短时间内纷至沓来，势必造成内部在政治和思想上的动荡，外国又乘机进行侵略压迫。我们环顾西方各国，同样可以看到：这一时期发生着巨大的变革，它的后果，现在还难以预料。中国的未来难以预料，也是不足为奇的。但中国过去的历史不止一次地告诉人们，中国人常常能够战胜种种困难向前进，尽管需要为此付出巨大的代价。现在中国人同样能够做到这一点，重要的是：世界各国能够迅速吸收中国政治思想中的天下为公思想（见本书第十六章到第二十一章）。中国在它未来的变革中，势必要抛弃许多过去的意识形态，但是，其中也将有一些会保留在世界的哲学遗产之中。中国哲学在哪些方面能对世界有所贡献，冯博士在本书末章对此进行了探讨。

德克·布德[1]

NOTES 注释

AUTHOR'S PREFACE

¹ 本书英文原本出版时，中文名为《中国哲学小史》，但一九三三年商务印书馆曾出版著者另一本《中国哲学小史》，作为万有文库百科小丛书之一。因此，著者将本书定名为《中国哲学简史》。

² 《中国哲学史》上卷，布德译，书名 *A History of Chinese Philosophy*, Vol. 1: *The Period of Philosophers* (from the Beginnings to Circa 100 B.C.), 由 Henry Vetch, Peiping: Allen and Unwin, London 于一九三七年出版。布德继续译出下卷后，上、下两卷均由 Princeton University Press 于一九五二年出版。

³ 《新原道》，一名《中国哲学之精神》，休士译，书名 *The Spirit of Chinese Philosophy*, 由 London: Routledge & Kegan Paul 于一九四七年出版。

❶

¹ *Journal of American Oriental Society*, Vol. 62, No. 4, pp. 293-9. Reprinted in *China*, pp. 18-28 (H. F. MacNair, ed.), University of California Press, 1946.

❷

¹ Translated by Arthur Waley.

² Filmer S. C. Northrop, "The Complementary Emphases of Eastern Intuition Philosophy and Western Scientific Philosophy," in *Philosophy: East and West*, C. A. Moore, ed., p. 187, Princeton University Press, 1946.

❸

¹ 中括号内年代以国家公布的《我国历代纪元表》为准，下同。——译者注

❹

¹ The word "Tzu" or "Master" is a polite suffix added to names of most philosophers of the Chou dynasty, such as Chuang Tzu, Hsün Tzu, etc., and meaning "Master Chuang," "Master Hsün," etc.

❻

¹ See Anton Forke, *Yang Chu's Garden of Pleasure*, and James Legge, *The Chinese Classics*, Vol. 3: *Prolegomena*, pp. 92-9.

⑫

[1] See Cheng Hsüan's (A.D. 127-200) commentary to the "Monthly Commands" in the *Book of Rites*, ch. 4.

[2] See *Lives and Opinions of Eminent Philosophers*, Book VIII, ch. 19.

⑮

[1] See Cheng Hsüan (A.D. 127-200), *Discussion of the Yi*, quoted by K'ung Ying-ta (574-648), in the Preface to his sub-commentary on Wang Pi's (226-49) *Commentary on the Yi*.

[2] See the *Tso Chuan*, twentieth year of Duke Chao, 522 B.C.

⑯

[1] 公元一九四七至一九四八年。——译者注

⑰

[1] See the *Ch'un-ch'iu Fan-lu*, ch. 81. All quotations in the present chapter, unless otherwise stated, are from this work.

[2] Not west, though west is the direction for autumn. The reason for this is, according to Tung, that "Heaven has trust in the *Yang*, but not in the *Yin*."

[3] See the *Pai Hu T'ung Yi* or *General Principles from the White Tiger* [*Lodge*], a work compiled in A.D. 79, *chüan* 8.

[4] See Ho Hsiu's *Commentary on the Kung Yang Commentary to the Ch'un Ch'iu*, 1st year of Duke Yin, 722 B.C.

⑱

[1] See the *History of the Former Han Dynasty*, ch. 6.

⑲

[1] Quoted by Huang Kan (488-545), in his *Sub-Commentary on the Analects*, *chüan* 6.

㉑

[1] Quoted in the *Nieh-pan-ching Chi-chieh* or *Collected Commentaries to the Parinirvana Sutra*, *chüan* 1.

[2] Quoted in Seng-chao's *Wei-mou-ching Chu* or *Commentary to the Vimalakirti Sutra*, *chüan* 7.

㉒

1 For the traditional account, see Yang Yi (974-1020), *Ch'uan Teng Lu* or *Record of the Transmission of the Light*, *chüan* 1.

2 See the *Liu-tsu T'an-ching* or *Sutra Spoken by the Sixth Patriarch*, *chüan* 1.

3 Yi-tsang (of the Sung dynasty), *Ku-tsun-hsü Yü-lu* or *Recorded Sayings of Ancient Worthies*, *chüan* 1.

㉓

1 *Kuan-wu P'ien* or "Observation of Things," Inner Chapter, in the *Huang-chi Ching-shih* or *Cosmological Chronology*, ch. 11a.

㉔

1 *Yi-ch'uan Chi-jang Chi*, *chüan* 14.

2 *Collected Writings of Ch'eng Hao*, *chüan* 1.

㉖

1 *Ta Hsüeh Wen* or *Questions on the Great Learning* in the *Wang Wen-ch'eng-kung Ch'üan-shu* or *Complete Works of Wang Shou-jen*, *chüan* 26.

㉗

1 *Ching-an Wen-chi* or *Collected Literary Writings of Wang Kuo-wei, Second Collection*.

EDITOR'S INTRODUCTION

1 德克·布德（Derk Bodde，一九〇九至二〇〇三年），美国宾夕法尼亚大学汉语研究中心教授，一生致力于向西方世界介绍中国历史及文化，曾用二十年时间，将冯友兰先生两卷本《中国哲学史》译为英文。一九四六至一九四七年冯友兰先生在宾夕法尼亚大学用英文讲授中国哲学史，此英文讲稿后由布德整理成书，就是这本《中国哲学简史》。

BIBLIOGRAPHY COMPILED BY THE EDITOR

GENERAL

This bibliography is intended to be suggestive rather than exhaustive, and is wholly confined to books and articles in English. For a much more comprehensive bibliography, see Wing-tsit Chan, *An Outline and an Annotated Bibliography of Chinese Philosophy* (Yale University, Far Eastern Publications, 1959). The University of Hawaii Press publishes a quarterly journal, *Philosophy East and West* (Vol. 1, 1951, onward), which contains many articles and book reviews on Chinese philosophy.

By far the most comprehensive and authoritative survey of Chinese philosophy is Fung Yu-lan's *A History of Chinese Philosophy,* translated from the Chinese by Derk Bodde (2 vols.; Princeton University Press, 1952-53; 2d printing, 1959-60). A brief but stimulating summary is by H. G. Creel, *Chinese Thought: From Confucius to Mao Tse-tung* (University of Chicago Press, 1953; paperback ed., a Mentor book, New York: New American Library, 1960). For an extremely original and thought-provoking, though sometimes controversial, analysis from the point of view of science, see Joseph Needham's monumental *Science and Civilisation in China,* Vol. 2, *History of Scientific Thought* (Cambridge University Press, 1956).

Anthologies—only the first of which is devoted wholly to philosophy—include E. R. Hughes, *Chinese Philosophy in Classical Times* (Everyman's Library, London: Dent, and New York: Dutton, 1942); Wm. Theodore De Bary, Wing-tsit Chan, and Burton Watson, *Sources of Chinese Tradition* (Columbia University Press, 1960); and Lin Yutang, *The Wisdom of China and India* (New York: Random House, 1942). Wing-tsit Chan's *A Source Book in Chinese Philosophy* is promised for publication—probably in 1961—by Princeton University Press.

Four symposia—all save the first centered more on the interplay between thought and institutions than on philosophy *per se*—are Arthur F. Wright, ed., *Studies in Chinese Thought* (University of Chicago Press, 1953); John K. Fairbank, ed., *Chinese Thought and Institutions* (same, 1957); David S. Nivison and Arthur F. Wright, eds., *Confucianism in Action* (Stanford University Press, 1959); and Arthur F. Wright, ed., *The Confucian Persuasion* (same, 1960). An interesting study of early Confucianism,

Taoism, and Legalism is Arthur Waley's *Three Ways of Thought in Ancient China* (London: Allen & Unwin, 1939; paperback ed., an Anchor Book, New York: Doubleday, 1956). Hu Shih's *The Development of the Logical Method in Ancient China* (Shanghai: Oriental Book Co., 3d ed., 1928) was epoch-making at the time of its appearance in 1922, but has now been largely superseded.

CHAPTER 1: THE SPIRIT OF CHINESE PHILOSOPHY

For a more extended summary of salient features in Chinese philosophy, see Derk Bodde, "Harmony and Conflict in Chinese Philosophy," in the above-cited *Studies in Chinese Thought*, pp. 19-80.

CHAPTER 2: THE BACKGROUND OF CHINESE PHILOSOPHY

For theories concerning the environmental and social background of Chinese civilization, see Wolfram Eberhard, *Conquerors and Rulers: Social Forces in Medieval China* (Leiden: E. J. Brill, 1952) and Owen Lattimore, *Inner Asian Frontiers of China* (New York: American Geographical Society, 2d ed., 1951).

CHAPTER 3: THE ORIGIN OF THE SCHOOLS

This is the summary of a theory expounded by Fung Yu-lan in a Chinese-language *Supplement* to the Chinese edition of his *History of Chinese Philosophy*, Vol. 1.

CHAPTER 4: CONFUCIUS, THE FIRST TEACHER

The standard English translation of the *Confucian Analects* is still that in James Legge, *The Chinese Classics*, Vol. 1 (Hong Kong: 1861; 2d ed., Oxford: Clarendon Press, 1893). A more recent and very interesting version is by Arthur Waley, *The Analects of Confucius* (London: Allen & Unwin, 1938). For a brilliant, though sometimes controversial, study of Confucius and of the development of Confucianism after his time, see H. G. Creel, *Confucius: The Man and the Myth* (New York: John Day, 1949).

CHAPTER 5: MO TZU, THE FIRST OPPONENT OF CONFUCIUS

On Mo Tzu, see Y. P. Mei, transl., *The Ethical and Political Works of Motse*

(London: Probsthain, 1929), and Y. P. Mei, *Mo-tse, the Neglected Rival of Confucius* (London: Probsthain, 1934).

CHAPTER 6: THE FIRST PHASE OF TAOISM: YANG CHU

For the "Yang Chu" chapter in the *Lieh-tzu*, see below under ch. 20.

CHAPTER 7: THE IDEALISTIC WING OF CONFUCIANISM: MENCIUS

The standard translation of the *Mencius* is in James Legge, *The Chinese Classics*, Vol. 2 (Hong Kong: 1861; 2d ed., Oxford: Clarendon Press, 1895).

CHAPTER 8: THE SCHOOL OF NAMES

Attempts to translate the corrupt and exceedingly difficult *Kung-sun Lung-tzu* have been made by Alfred Forke, "The Chinese Sophists," *Journal of the North China Branch of the Royal Asiatic Society*, Vol. 34 (1901-02), pp. 1-85; Max Perleberg, *The Works of Kung-sun Lung-tzu* (Hong Kong, 1952); Y. P. Mei, "The *Kung-sun Lung-tzu*," *Harvard Journal of Asiatic Studies*, Vol. 16 (1953), pp. 404-37; A. C. Graham, "Kung-sun Lung's Essay on Meanings and Things," *Journal of Oriental Studies*, Vol. 2 (1955), pp. 282-301. See also Graham, "The Composition of the Gongsuen Long Tzyy," *Asia Major*, n.s. Vol. 5 (1956), pp. 147-83.

CHAPTER 9: THE SECOND PHASE OF TAOISM: LAO TZU

Of the innumerable translations of the *Lao-tzu* (also known as the *Tao Te Ching*), two of the best are Arthur Waley, *The Way and Its Power: A Study of the Tao Te Ching and Its Place in Chinese Thought* (New York and Boston: Houghton Mifflin, 1935; paperback ed., an Evergreen book, New York: Grove Press, 1958), and J. J. L. Duyvendak, *Tao Te Ching: The Book of the Way and Its Virtue* (London: John Murray, 1954). For an extremely interesting analysis of Lao Tzu's ideas, followed by an account of the historical evolution of Taoism, see Holmes Welch, *The Parting of the Way: Lao Tzu and the Taoist Movement* (Boston: Beacon Press, 1957).

CHAPTER 10: THE THIRD PHASE OF TAOISM: CHUANG TZU

The best translation, but covering only the first seven chapters, is Fung Yu-lan, *Chuang Tzu: A New Selected Translation with an Exposition of the Philosophy of Kuo Hsiang* (Shanghai: Commercial Press, 1933). A complete but unsatisfactory translation is that of Herbert A. Giles, *Chuang Tzu, Mystic, Moralist, and Social Reformer* (Shanghai: Kelly & Walsh, 2d revised ed., 1926).

CHAPTER 11: THE LATER MOHISTS

No complete translation of the writings of the later Mohists has yet been attempted in English.

CHAPTER 12: THE YIN-YANG SCHOOL AND EARLY CHINESE COSMOGONY

For translations of the *Book of Changes,* see below under ch. 15. For the *Yüeh Ling* or "Monthly Commands," see translation of James Legge in *Sacred Books of the East* (Oxford: Clarendon Press, 1885), Vol. 27, pp. 249-310, and for the *Hung Fan* or "Grand Norm," see Legge's translation in *ibid.* (2d ed., 1899), Vol. 3, pp. 139-48.

CHAPTER 13: THE REALISTIC WING OF CONFUCIANISM: HSÜN TZU

On Hsün Tzu, see H. H. Dubs, transl., *The Works of Hsüntze* (London: Probsthain, 1928), and H. H. Dubs, *Hsüntze, The Moulder of Ancient Confucianism* (London: Probsthain, 1927). For the *Li Chi* or *Book of Rites,* see translation of James Legge in *Sacred Books of the East* (Oxford: Clarendon Press, 1885), Vols. 27-28.

CHAPTER 14: HAN FEI TZU AND THE LEGALIST SCHOOL

See J. J. L. Duyvendak, transl., *The Book of Lord Shang: A Classic of the Chinese School of Law* (London: Probsthain, 1928); W. K. Liao, transl., *The Complete Works of Han Fei Tzu: A Classic of Chinese Legalism* (2 vols.; London: Probsthain, 1939, 1959); D. Bodde, *China's First Unifier: A Study of the Ch'in Dynasty as Seen in the Life of Li Ssu* (280?-208 B.C.) (Leiden: E. J. Brill, 1938).

CHAPTER 15: CONFUCIANIST METAPHYSICS

The *Book of Changes* has been translated by James Legge in *Sacred Books of the East*, Vol. 16 (Oxford: Clarendon Press, 2d ed., 1899); also by Richard Wilhelm into German and from this by Cary F. Baynes into English, as *The I Ching or Book of Changes* (2 vols.; New York: Pantheon Books, 1950). Legge's translation of the *Doctrine of the Mean* appears in *The Chinese Classics*, Vol. 1 (cited above under ch. 4); also in his *Li Ki*, in *Sacred Books of the East*, Vol. 28 (Oxford: Clarendon Press, 1885), pp. 301-29. Another translation is that of E. R. Hughes, *The Great Learning and the Mean-in-Action* (New York: Dutton, 1943).

CHAPTER 16: WORLD POLITICS AND WORLD PHILOSOPHY

On the *Great Learning*, see translation of James Legge in *The Chinese Classics*, Vol. 1, and in *Sacred Books of the East* (both cited above under ch. 15), Vol. 28, pp. 411-24; also that of E. R. Hughes (cited above under ch. 15). Some of the ideas and events treated in this chapter are also discussed in D. Bodde, *China's First Unifier* (cited above under ch. 14). See, as well, items in L. C. Porter, compiler, with translations by Porter and Fung Yu-lan, *Aids to the Study of Chinese Philosophy* (Peiping: Yenching University, 1934).

CHAPTER 17: THEORIZER OF THE HAN EMPIRE: TUNG CHUNG-SHU

On Tung Chung-shu, see also Yao Shan-yu, "The Cosmological and Anthropological Philosophy of Tung Chung-shu," *Journal of the North China Branch of the Royal Asiatic Society*, Vol. 73 (1948), pp. 40-68. On the *Li Yün* or "Evolution of Rites," see translation of James Legge in *Sacred Books of the East* (Oxford: Clarendon Press, 1885), Vol. 27, pp. 364-93.

CHAPTER 18: THE ASCENDANCY OF CONFUCIANISM AND REVIVAL OF TAOISM

On the Burning of the Books, see D. Bodde, *China's First Unifier* (cited above under ch. 14). On the apocrypha, see Tjan Tjoe Som, *Po Hu T'Ung: The Comprehensive Discussions in the White Tiger Hall*, Vol. 1 (Leiden: E. J. Brill, 1949), pp. 100-20. On the ascendancy of Confucianism, see H. H. Dubs, "The Victory of Han Confucianism," in Dubs, transl., *History of the Former Han Dynasty*, Vol. 2 (Baltimore: Waverly Press, 1944), pp. 341-53. On Wang Ch'ung, see Alfred Forke, transl., *Lun-Heng* (2 vols.; London: Luzac, 1907, 1911).

CHAPTER 19: NEO-TAOISM: THE RATIONALISTS

See also the account of Kuo Hsiang in Fung Yu-lan, *Chuang Tzu* (cited above under ch. 10), pp. 145-57.

CHAPTER 20: NEO-TAOISM: THE SENTIMENTALISTS

The material in this chapter is almost entirely new. For the "Yang Chu" chapter in the *Lieh-tzu*, see Anton Forke, transl., *Yang Chu's Garden of Pleasure* (London: John Murray, 1912).

CHAPTER 21: THE FOUNDATION OF CHINESE BUDDHISM

A brief but excellent survey of the impact of Buddhism on Chinese civilization is by Arthur F. Wright, *Buddhism in Chinese History* (Stanford University Press, 1959). For a short summary of the philosophical aspects of Chinese (and Japanese) Buddhism, see J. Takakusu, *The Essentials of Buddhist Philosophy* (University of Hawaii Press, 1947). On Seng-chao, see Walter Liebenthal, transl., *The Book of Chao* (Peiping: Catholic University of Peking, 1948). See also many other articles by Liebenthal on early Chinese Buddhism, including, on Tao-sheng, "The World Conception of Chu Tao-sheng," *Monumenta Nipponica*, Vol. 12, Nos. 1-2 (1956), pp. 65-103; Nos. 3-4 (1956), pp. 73-100.

CHAPTER 22: CH'ANISM: THE PHILOSOPHY OF SILENCE

Of the enormous modern flow of literature—good, bad and indifferent—stimulated by Ch'an (Zen) Buddhism, mention should be made of the prolific writings of D. T. Suzuki, including his *Manual of Zen Buddhism* (Kyoto: Eastern Buddhist Society, 1935), and *Essays in Zen Buddhism* (London: Luzac, 1st series, 1927, 2d series, 1933, 3d series, 1934). See also Hu Shih, "Development of Zen Buddhism in China," *The Chinese Social and Political Science Review*, Vol. 15 (1931), pp. 475-505.

CHAPTER 23: NEO-CONFUCIANISM: THE COSMOLOGISTS

On this and the next two chapters, see also the account—lively but marred by factual inaccuracies—by Carsun Chang, *The Development of Neo-Confucian Thought* (New York: Bookman Associates, 1957).

CHAPTER 24: NEO-CONFUCIANISM: THE BEGINNING OF THE TWO SCHOOLS

On the Ch'eng brothers, see the excellent study by A. C. Graham, *Two Chinese Philosophers: Ch'eng Ming-tao and Ch'eng Yi-ch'uan* (London: Lund Humphries, 1958).

CHAPTER 25: NEO-CONFUCIANISM: THE SCHOOL OF PLATONIC IDEAS

On Chu Hsi, see J. Percy Bruce, transl., *The Philosophy of Human Nature*, by *Chu Hsi* (London: Probsthain, 1922), and J. Percy Bruce, *Chu Hsi and His Masters: An Introduction to Chu Hsi and the Sung School of Chinese Philosophy* (London: Probsthain, 1923).

CHAPTER 26: NEO-CONFUCIANISM: THE SCHOOL OF UNIVERSAL MIND

On Lu Chiu-yüan, see Hsiu-chi Huang, *Lu Hsiang-shan: A Twelfth Century Chinese Idealist Philosopher* (New Haven: American Oriental Society, 1944). On Wang Shou-jen, see Frederick Goodrich Henke, transl., *The Philosophy of Wang Yang-ming* (London and Chicago: Open Court Publishing Co., 1916).

CHAPTER 27: THE INTRODUCTION OF WESTERN PHILOSOPHY

For a general survey of thought during the Ch'ing dynasty (1644-1911), see Liang Ch'i-ch'ao, *Intellectual Trends in the Ch'ing Period*, translated from the Chinese by Immanuel C. Y. Hsü (Harvard University Press, 1959). On the "Han Learning" and some of its major philosophical exponents, see articles by Mansfield Freeman in *Journal of the North China Branch of the Royal Asiatic Society*, Vol. 57 (1926), pp. 70-91; Vol. 59 (1928), pp. 78-110; Vol. 64 (1933), pp. 50-71. On K'ang Yu-wei, see Laurence G. Thompson, transl., *Ta T'ung Shu: The One-World Philosophy of K'ang Yu-wei* (London: Allen & Unwin, 1958). On the ideological impact of the West on

China, see, *inter alia*, Joseph R. Levenson, *Confucian China and Its Modern Fate: The Problem of Intellectual Continuity* (University of California Press, 1958).

CHAPTER 28: CHINESE PHILOSOPHY IN THE MODERN WORLD

Fung Yu-lan's *Hsin Yüan-tao* has been translated by E. R. Hughes as *The Spirit of Chinese Philosophy* (London: Routledge & Kegan Paul, 1947). For surveys of Chinese philosophical (and religious) developments in recent years, see Wing-tsit Chan, "Trends in Contemporary Philosophy," in H. F. MacNair, ed., *China* (University of California Press, 1946), pp. 312-30, and Chan, *Religious Trends in Modern China* (Columbia University Press, 1953); also O. Brière, *Fifty Years of Chinese Philosophy, 1898-1950,* translated from the French by Laurence G. Thompson (London: Allen & Unwin, 1956).

译后记

　　冯友兰先生的《中国哲学简史》英文版由美国麦克米伦公司于一九四八年出版，迄今已经半个多世纪了。在这半个多世纪里，世界和中国都经历了巨大的变化，冯先生也已经仙逝多年。但是，细心的读者读冯先生的这部著作，会觉得如同是新著一样。为什么会是这样？我想，原因之一是因为，冯先生治中国哲学史六十余年，他不仅是迄今无出其右的中国哲学史家，而且是"贞元六书"的作者，自己就是一位哲学家。《简史》问世之时，是在冯先生两卷本《中国哲学史》出版十几年，又在"贞元六书"完成之后；资料是古代的，眼光却是现代的；运用史料时是史家，探讨问题时却是哲学家。就篇幅说，此书远少于《中国哲学史新编》；就内容说，却正好最鲜明地表现了冯先生自己的特色。原因之二是，冯先生轻松驾驭着中国哲学史和西方哲学史这两部历史，来写作这部《简史》，思想资料是中国的，考虑哲学问题的眼光却是世界的，这是迄今在国际学术界还未见有第二位能做到的。这本书引人入胜，就由于它的这些特色。

　　翻译本书，如同探险，个中乐趣，其味无穷。念自严几道先生悬"信、达、雅"为译事三难之后，三字已成翻译通则。朱光潜先生认为，三字中，"信"字最为重要，这不难理解，但要做到，并非易事。翻译外文书刊，大概诗歌、哲学两类著作最费斟酌。这两类著作如果依循原著，逐字逐词按字义翻译，应不是十分困难；难的是在翻译这两类著作时，不能只满足于"形似"，还要求其"传神"。这本是中国文化传统中对艺术的要求；仔细想一下便能发现，无论是诗人、艺术家、哲学家，都往往是社会里受过一定教育、有一定生活经历而十分敏感的人，在物质和精神两方面生活的磨难中对历史、时代、社会、人生进行反思。社会变动越急剧，这种反思也越像大海波涛一样无法自已。人的生活感受往往超过自己用语言文字表达的能力，为此而"言不尽意"。在中国，还有时是由于两千年专制统治形成的社会环境限制，而不能畅所欲言，于是只好运用比喻和暗示而"意在言外"。诗人、艺术家、哲学家除了在自己作品已说的之外，常"言有尽而意无穷"。视听艺术诉诸人的形象思维，语言艺术则离不开语言，因此，中国的诗人和哲学家都同样强调"言外之意"。艺术家的手法和哲学表达自己思想的方式，在这一点上十分相似，这成为中国艺术的特色，也成为中国哲学的特色。为此，诗歌和哲学著作的翻译，往往需要迈过"形似"，而要求"传神"。如果低于这样的要求，译者便难免会感到内疚。这是我在翻译本书时，常常深夜扪心、惴惴不安的地方。举例来说，魏晋以后十章，在书中篇幅虽较先秦、两汉部分为少，而涵盖历史事件和时间则远超过前半，牵涉的问题也远超过前半。

第十九、二十两章

第十九章标题："Neo-Taoism: The Rationalists"，布德教授的英文标题在逻辑上似略有毛病，"ism"是学说，后面"ist"则通常是指人，前后不够一致。但英文原文在中间使用的冒号":"也可以使它有另一种理解，作者是说："新道家是一种理性主义者。"中文旧译"新道家：主理派"，是可以这样理解的。但接下去，第二十章标题是"新道家：主情派"。读者在这里不免要问：冯先生的意思是说，新道家既是"主理"的又是"主情"的，抑或新道家中既有一个"主理派"，又另有一个"主情派"呢？中文旧译本对十九、二十两章的标题分为"主理派"和"主情派"，很容易使读者体会成他们是两派，这究竟是否冯先生的原意？如果冯先生认为，新道家中有两派，则第二十章的内容和第十九章的内容应该针锋相对，表明是两派；而现在冯著第二十章的内容在于该章末尾结束语所说"晋代新道家风格的特点和当时所谓'风流'的实质"，"重理"和"任情"在第二十章里，都从属于解释"风流"。这样，第二十章的主人公和第十九章的主人公就不是两批人，而是同一批人了。既是同一批人，处于同一个时代，为什么在本书里又分写为两章呢？我的体会是为了着重说明"晋代新道家风格的特点和当时所谓'风流'的实质"。这个问题为什么值得中国哲学史家特别关注呢？我体会，这与冯先生对哲学的认识——"哲学是对于人生的有系统的反思"——有内在的关系。中国历史上，先秦、魏晋、晚唐、南宋等，都是社会剧烈动荡的时代。在这样的时代里，旧的社会秩序被打乱，社会结构被破坏，思想界、知识界为自己，也为社会寻找出路时，首先遇到的是与王权的关系。如战国时期屈原和楚怀王的关系；西汉初，刘邦踌躇满志当上皇帝后，张良与刘邦的关系；东汉末诸葛亮《诫子书》中说"淡泊以明志，宁静以致远"的人生哲学。但在"士"来说，仅仅超脱了眼前政治的激流漩涡，却还未曾超脱历史。个人既无法左右历史，只有在精神上努力超脱，这正是魏晋文士面临的人生处境。"风流"便是魏晋文士的生活态度和生活风度，这对外界现实，无论是物质或非物质，都毫不粘着，不为物役；"风流"是指事物本质所具的神韵，可以不需要文字语言，却自然在人的生活中表现出来。因此后来司空图在《诗品》中可以说："不着一字，尽得风流。"鲁迅曾有文，论不少魏晋文士服用药酒，引起全身燥热，为此衣带必须宽松，动作自然从容。这项考证似并未体现出魏晋文士的真正精神面貌。古代思想史著作中，像冯先生此书对魏晋文士思想和风格提出一个完整的认识，在中国哲学史上实属首创。冯先生不仅介绍魏晋文士特有的精神面貌，在介绍北宋五子时，同样把周濂溪教二程"寻孔颜乐处"、把张载《西铭》重点介绍出来，刻画出中国古代思想家的风貌。鲁迅曾认为，中国文人若不做官，便隐居山林，隐居其实只是为做官提高身价。这是讲受儒家思想影响的文人。冯先生在这里指出：中国除浸透儒家思想的"儒生"外，还有另一种读书人，身上另有一种超越世俗的气质，这不仅是由于"学"，由于道家和佛家思想的蕴积，还由于乱世给人的锤炼。"道"既无在无不在，在求道之人的身上，也无时不在，在战乱之世就更突出。这是中国哲学的精神，它不仅是时代精神，也是中国文化、中国哲学一贯的精神，这也是中国传统文化教人领会的"美"，也是中国哲学所讲人之所以为人的精神所在。冯先生的哲学挚友金岳霖先生在他的名著《原道》一书全循逻辑阐明中国哲学之后，最后说，只讲理性之人并不可爱。王国维先生曾叹息读哲学时，自己所信的不可爱，认为可爱的却又不可信，因此而苦恼，以致不得不放弃哲学。王国维、金岳霖两位所苦恼的，正是西方哲学的窘境。冯先生在本书末说到中国哲学可能对西方哲学有所贡献的是在精神境界方面，也正在此。因此我觉得，十九、二十两章是冯先生此书精义，垂范后世之处。而旧译在此处给读者的印象，似乎突出了两派，却贬低了原文要讲的时代风格（"风流"实质）。从英文看，"sentimentalists"通常译作"感伤主义者"，也可作"多情善感的人"，勉强译作"重情"是可以的，但如果把"主情"和"主理"对立起来，则恐不是原著本意。细读第二十章，着重讲的是魏晋名士的"风流"的实质，明确提到两派的是一句话："在这里，我们只需要指出一点，即：虽然许多新道家注重理性，但也还有许多是重情的。"这里指出，"虽然许多"新道家注重理性，同时，"许多"也重情。我的理解，这话的含义，重点在于讲新的道家虽然崇尚理性，同时却又是重情的，是充满人性的。这是新的道家的两重性，也是特性。原书在此因是标题，只能简略，故而比较含糊。旧译循英文本标题，而把它延伸到新道家分"主理""主情"两派，对读者似易误导。现把第十九章标题译作"新道家：崇尚理性的玄学"，把第二十章标题译作"新道家：豁达率性的风格"。与布德教授的文本略有出入（旧译也有类似做法，如把英文本"杨朱的乐园"改译为《列子》的《杨朱》篇），但对原著内容是否较为忠实一点？

第二十三章

本书原文用"新儒家"。现在学术界用"新儒家"一词来指二十世纪的儒学和这一派学者，现已流行成俗。为此，拙译中，对第二十三至第二十六章，凡"新儒学"译作"更新的儒学"，"新儒家"译作"新的儒家"，以区别于二十世纪的"新儒学"，便利当今读者。

旧译第二十三章标题"新儒家：宇宙发生论者"。按布德教授英文本是"Neo-Confucianism: The Cosmologists"。在西方，Cosmology是"宇宙论"；"宇宙发生论"则另有英文专用术语是"Cosmogony"。西方从事哲学工作的人都对宇宙的本体论和发生论加以区别。在中国，阴阳五行学说是宇宙发生论，讲"宇宙心"，"宇宙之理"则更多是属本体论范围，因此，还是回到布德教授用词"cosmology"，译作"宇宙论"。

第二十四章

末一节标题"寻求快乐"，旧中译本循布德教授英文本用词，本无缺失。但这是西方哲学的概念，西方哲学所说的"寻求快乐"与新的儒家所讲的生命之"乐"，只是"形似"，在实质上是不同的。冯先生讲中国哲学史，从智性的探索开始，以智性的"生命之乐"为终结。无论前面所说的"风流"实质和此处讲"快乐"都是中国哲学思想精华，为以前易遭冷落处，这是以哲学为工具和以哲学供自己（亦即人人）受用的根本不同之处。冯先生此书的引人入胜之处、净化人心之处、精彩之处，窃以为要从这些地方去找。现根据原著内容，将小标题改译为"寻孔颜乐处"，行文和旧译也略有不同。翻译工作按译者的体会，似乎有两个过程：第一步是循词探意，理解原著的文字；然后，第二步所要求的是循意探词。翻译本书时，译者常常设想的是：如果冯先生这时是在讲课，他会怎样讲呢？这可能是一种冒险的设想，但翻译本来就是冒险。翻译本书，只能循中国哲学之意、循冯先生之意，来探求译文如何达意，因此总是设想几种方案，经过比较，才敢论定。

第二十八章

第二十八章是全书结束，也是全书高潮。末后，作者说："在各种哲学的形而上学体系里，无论它们采取的方法是负的方法或正的方法，最后都往往戴上了神秘主义的皇冠。"原文作"The great metaphysical systems of all philosophy, ...have crowned themselves with mysticism"，旧译作"哲学上一切伟大的形而上学系统，……无一不把自己戴上'神秘主义'的大帽子"。译者体会，冯先生这话是十分严肃、十分深刻的话。哲学通常分"宇宙论（本体论）"、"人生论（包括伦理学）"、"认识论"三部分。西方哲学自前苏格拉底时期，探索的是宇宙本质，即本体论，即形而上学。中国哲学史上，最初也是探索对外部世界的总体认识，然后探索人世、人事变化及其所由来。人从已知出发，去探索未知，这是对无限的探索，最后总要到达人的认识的边际极限，所谓"神秘主义"，其实无非是指到达认识边际极限后，人向前眺望自己不懂得、无法加以解释的东西，只有称之为"奥秘"。

说到"这是奥秘",意思是说,在言语所能及的范围里,这是最后的一句话了。这可以说是为前面所说自己的理论"戴上冠冕"。任何严肃、实事求是而谦虚的哲学家都会承认自己认识能力"有限",已说的话已经说到了头,再向前就无法多说,只能称之为"神秘"了。也就是冯先生在本书最后所说,已经说了许许多多话,然后应该进入潜默,也就是神游于无限了。英语行文可以称为"戴上神秘主义的冠冕",但这不是"戴大帽子"!此书旧译把"戴上皇冠"(crown)译成"戴大帽子",恐不免"以词害意"。所以,此处按"冠冕"本意行文,译作"戴上皇冠"。

冯先生在本书第一章末后对翻译讲了十分精辟的见解,认为一种翻译,终究不过是一种解释;实际上,除了译者传达的这个意思,原文还可能含有许多别的意思。原文是富于暗示的,而译文则不是,也不可能是。所以译文把原文固有的丰富内容丢掉了许多。翻译此书时,常常吃惊,冯先生此书写作于五十多年前,怎么竟像是对着当前的时代,为新的一代而写的新著一样?从书中读到冯先生的思想风采,心向神往,希望不要轻忽辱没一分一毫。同时又觉得能做的十分有限,为此战战兢兢,如履薄冰,自知缺点错误在所难免,敬请读者随时指正。在惴惴小心之中,又因为窥见了一座大花园而有一种喜乐。这是翻译本书特有的一种经验,一种受用。

赵复三

二〇〇四年七月十五日